ADULPHE DELEGORGUE'S

TRAVELS
IN SOUTHERN AFRICA

VOLUME II

Killie Campbell Africana Library Publications

Number 1. PAULINA DLAMINI: SERVANT OF TWO KINGS
Compiled by H. Filter; edited and translated by S. Borquin

Number 2. 'NOT EITHER AN EXPERIMENTAL DOLL'
The separate worlds of three South African Women
Introduced and annotated by Shula Marks

Number 3. THE PRAISES OF DINGANA (Izibongo ZikaDingana)
Edited by D.K. Rycroft and A.B. Ngcobo

Number 4. AFRICAN POEMS OF THOMAS PRINGLE
Edited by Ernest Pereira and Michael Chapman

Number 5. ADULPHE DELEGORGUE'S
TRAVELS IN SOUTHERN AFRICA Volume I
*Translated by Fleur Webb; introduced and annotated
by Stephanie Alexander and Colin Webb*

Number 6. THE HUNTING JOURNAL
OF ROBERT BRIGGS STRUTHERS, 1852–56
In the Zulu Kingdom and the Tsonga Regions
Edited by Patricia Merrett and Ronald Butcher

Number 7. THE NATAL PAPERS OF 'JOHN ROSS'
By Charles Rawden Maclean
Edited by Stephen Gray

Number 8. ALONE AMONG THE ZULUS
By Catherine Barter
Edited by Patricia Merrett

Number 9. ADULPHE DELEGORGUE'S
TRAVELS IN SOUTHERN AFRICA Volume II
*Translated by Fleur Webb; introduced and annotated
by Stephanie Alexander and Bill Guest*

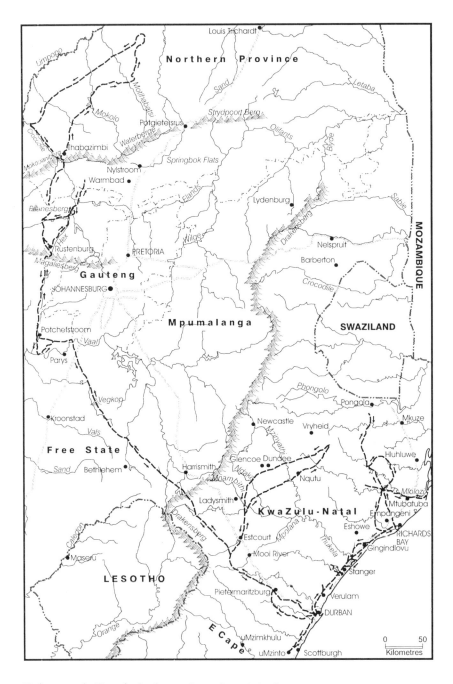

Delegorgue's Travels (redrawn from the original)

ADULPHE DELEGORGUE'S

TRAVELS
IN SOUTHERN AFRICA

VOLUME II

Translated by

FLEUR WEBB

Introduced and annotated by

STEPHANIE J. ALEXANDER

and

BILL GUEST

Killie Campbell Africana Library
Durban
University of Natal Press
Pietermaritzburg
1997

ISBN 0 86980 727 7 (Volume One)
ISBN 0 86980 926 9 (Volume Two)
ISBN 0 86980 529 0 (Set)

The Publisher regrets that the paper used for Vol. I could not be matched for Vol. II.

Typeset in the University of Natal Press
Pietermaritzburg
Printed by Kohler Carton and Print
Box 955, Pinetown, 3600 South Africa

DEDICATION

This second volume of Adulphe Delegorgue's *Travels in Southern Africa* is dedicated to the memory of Colin Webb. It was he who initiated and inspired the translation and publication in English of Delegorgue's work, and who introduced and compiled the general index to Volume I. He did not live to see the completion of Volume II.

CONTENTS

List of Illustrations   x
General Introduction . . . . *Bill Guest*   xi
Adulphe Delegorgue – Scientist . . . . . . *Stephanie Alexander*   xxi
Translator's Note . . . . *Fleur Webb*   xxxi
Summary of Volume I, Chapter XX   xxxii

Travels in Southern Africa

Chapter		*Page*
XXI	More elephants . . .	1
XXII	Souzouana . . .	10
XXIII	I am the victim of theft . . .	28
XXIV	The Touguela in flood . . .	35
XXV	Arrival of the frigate *Southampton* . . .	45
XXVI	My embarrassing position during the hostilities . . .	78
XXVII	Customs of the Amazoulous . . .	112
XXVIII	Hunting in the territory of Natal . . .	133
XXIX	Journey to the land of Massilicatzi . . .	154
XXX	Mooi-Rivier . . .	171
XXXI	Aquisition of the *Catoblepas gorgon* . . .	181
XXXII	We find ourselves in Waayen-Poort . . .	192
XXXIII	Departure from Waayen-Poort . . .	206
XXXIV	We stay for a month . . .	224
XXXV	Reasons for an excursion into the north . . .	236
XXXVI	The customs of the Makatisses . . .	277

Vocabulary of the Zulu Language   285
Taxonomic section
   Note on lists of species . . . . *Stephanie Alexander*   297
   Entomology   300
      Catalogue of the Lepidoptera   301
      Catalogue of Coleoptera   317
      Diptera   328
   Ornithology   329
Annotated Natural History Index . . . . . . *Stephanie Alexander*   332
Annotated General Index . . . . *Bill Guest*   378

ISBN 0 86980 926 9 (Volume Two) *should be* 0 86980 936 0

ERRATUM

ILLUSTRATIONS

Delegorgue's travels, on a modern map   iv

A herd of elephants   xxxiv

The engagement on Sunday 16 December 1838   69

A buffalo charge   139

An impala   183

Hunting map showing various species of animals   331

Delegorgue's travels, redrawn from
    the original map   Inside back cover

The illustrations are all reproduced from Volume II of the 1847 edition of *Voyage dans l'Afrique Australe*. The cover picture is from *Portraits of the Game and Wild Animals of Southern Africa* by W. Cornwallis Harris (1840) and shows the Sable Antelope.

The Cartographic Unit of the University of Natal, Pietermaritzburg, is warmly thanked for its skillful redrawing of the original maps, and for the modern map on p. iv.

GENERAL INTRODUCTION

The second volume of Adulphe Delegorgue's *Travels in Southern Africa* relates the latter part of his adventures in Natal and Zululand, and the extension of his odyssey of observation and despoliation beyond the Drakensberg into 'the land of Massilicatzi'. His interest continues to focus, as before, not only on the flora and fauna of the region but also on its human inhabitants, concerning whom he offers firm and sometimes entertaining opinions.

As the earlier chapters of his *Travels* have already reflected, Delegorgue's explorations coincided with a series of historically formative events in southern Africa. The second volume recounts at first hand the Boer–British struggle for control of Natal, the earlier ill-fated land negotiations between the Boer leader Piet Retief and King Dingane ka Senzangakona, and the subsequent violent course of events that led to the latter's overthrow and the installation of his half-brother Mpande as Zulu King. Delegorgue's personal encounters with some of the leading participants in this unfolding drama, and his own participation in the Boer commando that drove Dingane northwards to his death, lend an authenticity to his account which he is at pains to sustain to its end.

Delegorgue's venture across the mountains deep into the interior of the subcontinent was prompted in part by his fall from favour with Mpande, but also by the expedition already undertaken in that direction by the Swedish naturalist J.G. Wahlberg, in whose company he had arrived at Port Natal in June 1839. In the Orange Free State ruined indigenous homesteads and skeletal remains at the Vegkop battlesite, where the Boers had repulsed Mzilikazi's Ndebele in October 1836, confronted Delegorgue with evidence of the population migrations and violent displacements that had also been taking place on the highveld of southern Africa. Beyond the Vaal River a visit to the recently established town of Potchefstroom and then to the Magaliesberg farm of A.H. Potgieter, victorious Boer general over the Ndebele at Vegkop and Mosega, confirmed the expanding success of the Trekker advance from the Cape colony into the huge regions beyond the Orange and Vaal Rivers. North of the Magaliesberg range another battlesite, scene of the Ndebele massacre of a Griqua commando, and further on more abandoned homesteads as well as cowering survivors who fled at the sight of strangers, bore additional testimony to the nature of recent events. Any possibility of a confrontation with Mzilikazi himself was denied Delegorgue by the unwillingness of his servants to continue towards the northern reaches of the Limpopo River, though even he did not relish the prospect of such a meeting.

Delegorgue was obviously aware of the misfortunes which had befallen many of the indigenous inhabitants of the land beyond the Vaal River. Yet he had barely crossed to its northern bank before indulging in unfavourable comparisons between these 'wretched sort of people' and the Zulu whom he so admired. His impressions were doubtless coloured by the early realization that the conversational Zulu which he had acquired on the eastern seaboard was of little value in the interior of the subcontinent when confronted with Tswana and 'Sissoutou'. With regard to the latter, he admitted to 'an aversion to this harsh tongue in which R's abounded, pronounced like the roll of a drum; it seemed to reflect the rigorous climate and the poverty of the people'. This reluctance to extend his linguistic repertoire is reflected in his written versions of the names of persons and places north of the Vaal river, some of which it has been impossible to identify with the precision that he, and the reader, would wish.

While Delegorgue's willing grasp of Zulu was not extended to other indigenous languages neither was his enthusiasm for those, with individual exceptions, who spoke them. The Zulu, in his view, were the 'French of south-east Africa' while all the black communities of the interior highveld, or 'Makatisses' (Mantatees) as he loosely called them, were akin to the German-speaking world 'with their harsh language, and their divisions into a hundred different principalities'. Even the history of the Zulu, under Shaka, 'resembled that of the French in Europe under Napoleon'. In Delegorgue's estimation the Zulu were the finest physical specimens to be found among the indigenous peoples of southern Africa, with proportions 'more graceful' than those of the French. They were a justifiably proud people with a strong sense of nationhood, good humoured, hospitable, polite and as courageous and disciplined as the legendary Spartans of classical Greece.

By contrast, the 'Makatisses' of the subcontinents's central plateau were described as being physically repulsive, cowardly, dishonest, greedy, dirty and generally disobliging. Delegorgue did concede to some similarities between them and the Zulu, notably with regard to notions of justice and laws of inheritance. He even admitted that their huts were better constructed than those of the Zulu but they remained physically and morally inferior, and 'bourgeois in the extreme'. By way of example, they performed 'only the most sedate of dances' in contrast to the vigorous efforts of the Zulu.

In common with his admiration for the Zulu, Delegorgue did not modify his initial disdain for the emigrant Boers, the people of the

Great Trek into the interior. He shared their love of hunting and dislike for the English, sympathized with their efforts to achieve political independence and considered them to be 'the bravest wagon drivers in the world'. He appreciated the hospitality of individuals like Servaas Van Breda of Congella and the 'enterprising' Vermaes who lived north of Potchefstroom but he disliked the officiousness of the celebrated Commandant-general A.W.J. Pretorius and the stiff formality of the similarly well-known leader A.H. Potgieter. Isak van Niekerk (Niewkerk), to whom he entrusted a wagon-load of his precious scientific specimens, proved to be downright dishonest and in general he continued to regard the Boers as 'uncouth' and 'ignorant', their 'churlishness' contrasting unfavourably with the urbane politeness of the Zulu. One can only speculate as to what extent Delegorgue's sometimes jaundiced opinions of the people he encountered were influenced by a growing sense of lassitude which he misdiagnosed as the consequence of prolonged celibacy before realising that he was playing host to a large intestinal parasite.

Other views expressed by Delegorgue were too deep-rooted to have been formed by temporary indisposition. His implacable hostility towards England, whose philanthropy he regarded as merely a cloak for ruthless commercial ambition, was not unique in the post-Napoleonic era of his youth. He was barely seven years old in 1821 when his revered Bonaparte died in exile on the British-held island of Saint Helena, under circumstances which many Frenchmen considered highly suspicious. His contempt for philanthropists in general and missionaries in particular expressed an underlying rejection of religion. He insisted that there was 'nothing more stupid in this world than a people which allows itself to be ruled by a superstition'. He pitied black converts to Christianity who encouraged their womenfolk to pray instead of cultivating their fields and he admired the beautiful simplicity of traditional Zulu weddings conducted in the complete absence of any priests.

The missionaries whom Delegorgue met, like the Revd Francis Owen and the Revd Aldin Grout, along with some like Dr Philip who he only heard about, were all accused of meddling interference which served only to sow 'strife and division' among those whom they sought to convert. In his opinion the 'civilization' which they so proudly purveyed was of dubious value to those who had previously managed without it, imposing upon their simple lifestyles unnecessary comforts at the price of numerous avoidable complications. The impact on the natural environment was similarly disastrous. The weapons of 'civilized man' quickly decimated the *fauna*, obliging the once-proud lion to prey off domesticated livestock and attack the trek-oxen of unwary travellers.

Delegorgue felt deep affection for his own span of oxen, 'good companions with many excellent qualities', but this did not extend to other creatures. His personal despoliation of a wide range of species was extensive. Many were added to his accumulation of specimens, for his commercial instinct was strong. His own grandfather had possessed an impressive natural history collection and he was well aware that in Europe there was a ready market of wealthy amateur naturalists and public museums. He frankly conceded that hunters often spared lion because they were a dangerous quarry and their skins did not fetch a good price; further, that 'no man is as covetous as a naturalist; he would, if he could, put a whole country into a few narrow boxes.' He did have occasional misgivings. When a gazelle had the misfortune to cross his path he commented that it was

> such a pity to kill these timid, charming creatures only to have them later displayed in an imperfect imitation of life. But what alternative is there for the naturalist without the considerable resources necessary to make a collection of living animals? What else can he do but observe them in the state of nature and then accept that their skins will provide the evidence which he owes to science and to public curiosity. And so he is obliged to be ruthless and destroy the things he most admires in nature's collection of masterpieces.

Yet Delegorgue also shot for the pot, and for the sheer pleasure of 'the hunting by which, and for which, we lived'. He recognized 'the mischief' he was doing but insisted that he was 'a hunter first and foremost' who trembled with excitement at the mention of elephant and felt 'an inexpressible sense of joy' in the midst of a dangerous encounter with an injured rhinoceros. The sight of wounded elephants falling in a heap on top of one another was a source of intense amusement to him and his companions, while a rhinoceros that he mistook at distance for a tented wagon was dispatched as punishment for the disappointment it caused.

The second volume of Delegorgue's *Travels* should nevertheless not be dismissed as the repetitive hunting tales of a dyspeptic and physically exhausted explorer who consoled himself by criticizing the human inhabitants of the region and despoiling it of its fauna. Apart from his services to the sciences, which are considered elsewhere in this volume, Delegorgue produced an insightful and historically valuable account of his experiences in southern Africa at a time of transforming significance for the future. It reflects the wide-ranging scientific and non-scientific interests of its author and includes a Zulu vocabulary which is not comprehensive but pre-dates the better-known Zulu dictionaries produced by J.L. Döhne and Bishop J.W. Colenso by a decade and more.

Delegorgue's personal opinions, often prejudiced and sometimes amusing, were always brutally honest. He was highly critical of his eighteenth century compatriot François Le Vaillant for his inaccuracies and fanciful embellishments, taking justifiable pride in his own 'love of the truth'. He conceded that he might be guilty of error but never of 'calculated mistakes'. What appear to be his more outrageous flights of fancy can be substantiated. For example, the reports of other nineteenth century travellers corroborate the enormous pit traps which he claimed to have discovered in the vicinity of the Crocodile River. These were apparently constructed in several parts of the southern African interior and the dimensions which he described were by no means exaggerated. It inclines one to accept his claim that he saw no need for fabrication in the presence of 'an abundance of interesting fact'.

In addition to its scientific and historical dimensions Delegorgue's book can also be enjoyed as a rollicking adventure story in which his forceful personality pervades every page. Enormously self-assured, occasionally arrogant, he displayed admirable courage in facing known and unknown dangers, amply demonstrating his contention that while fear induces paralysis confidence is one's only salvation in crisis situations. Above all, Delegorgue's writings are infused with an infectious enthusiasm for the business of exploration and discovery. The prospect of venturing far beyond the Magaliesberg and Pilansberg mountains into a part of Africa which seemingly no white man other than J.G. Wahlberg had seen before was, in his view, a 'great privilege . . . reserved for us for centuries'. Readers will hopefully share in that sense of excitement as they explore these later chapters of Adulphe Delegorgue's *Travels in Southern Africa*.

*　　*　　*　　*　　*

The production of this volume would not have been possible without the contributions made by several people. Special thanks are due to the late Colin Webb for initiating this project, and to Fleur Webb for her loving and eminently readable translation. As a former student of both of them it is an honour for me to have been involved in this endeavour, though it is the poorer for Colin Webb's untimely death before its completion.

I am indebted to Stephanie Alexander for the scientific expertise which she has applied to the analysis of Delegorgue's text, and to Margery Moberly of the University of Natal Press for her encouragement and persistence in bringing the work to fruition. What is placed before the reader bears testimony to her professionalism in the planning, direction and technical production of this book. I also wish to express my gratitude to Helena Margeot and her able team for the maps emanating from the Cartographic Unit of the Geography Department at the University of Natal in Pietermaritzburg, and to several colleagues at this and other institutions who willingly responded to appeals for editorial assistance. Neil Parsons, Andrew Manson, John Wright, Adrian Koopman, Wilfred Jonckheere, John Laband and Juliet Leeb-du Toit all rose to the occasion when requested to do so. Jane and Vincent Carruthers were generous with their knowledge and hospitality in familiarizing me with that part of the Magaliesberg range which Delegorgue traversed more than a hundred and fifty years ago.

Last but not least I thank my wife Denise for her great interest in yet another of my historical enthusiasms.

BILL GUEST

Pietermaritzburg, March 1997

WORKS CONSULTED

BIBLIOGRAPHIES, GUIDES AND WORKS OF REFERENCE

Botha, T.J.R. *Watername in Natal*. Pretoria, 1977.

Breutz, P.-L. *The tribes of Rustenburg and Pilansberg districts*. Pretoria, 1953.

Bryant, A.T. comp. *Zulu-English dictionary*. Pietermaritzburg, 1905.

Cope, A.T. *A Select bibliography relating to the Zulu people of Natal and Zululand*. Durban, 1974.

Dictionary of South African biography. Cape Town, Durban 1968–81. 4v.

Doke, C.M. and Vilakazi, B.W., comps. *Zulu-English dictionary*. Johannesburg, 1972.

Lugg, H.C. *Zulu place names in Natal*, revised by A.T. Cope, Durban, 1968.

Merrett, C.E. *Index to the 1:50000 map series. Part I, Natal*. Pietermaritzburg, 1977.

Merrett, C.E. *A Selected bibliography of Natal maps, 1800–1977*. Boston, 1979.

Müller, C.F.J., ed. *South African history and historians: a bibliography*, ed. by C.F.J. Müller and others. Pretoria, 1979.

Pettman, C. *South African place names*. Rivonia, 1985.

Raper, P.E. *Dictionary of South African place names*. Rivonia, 1987.

Stayt, D. *Where on earth? A guide to the place names of Natal and Zululand.* Durban, 1971.

Standard Encyclopaedia of Southern Africa. Cape Town, 1970–76. 12v.

Webb's guide to the official records of the Colony of Natal: an expanded and revised edition together with indexes, comp. by J. Verbeek, M. Nathanson and E. Peel. Pietermaritzburg, 1984.

PUBLISHED SOURCES

Axelson, E. *Portuguese in south-east Africa, 1600–1700.* Johannesburg, 1960.

Becker, P. *Path of blood.* Harmondsworth, 1962.

Becker, P. *Rule of fear: The life and times of Dingane King of the Zulu.* London, 1964.

Bird, J. *The Annals of Natal.* Pietermaritzburg, 1888. 2v.

Bonner, P. *Kings, commoners and concessionaires: the evolution and dissolution of the nineteenth century Swazi state.* Cambridge and Johannesburg, 1983.

Brookes, E.H. and Webb, C. de B. *A History of Natal.* Pietermaritzburg, 1965.

Bryant, A.T. *Olden times in Zululand and Natal.* London, 1929.

Bryant, A.T. *A History of the Zulu and neighbouring tribes.* Cape Town, 1964.

Carruthers, V. *The Magaliesberg.* Johannesburg, 1990.

Chase, J.C. *The Natal papers: a reprint of all notices and public documents, 1488–1843.* 2 pts. Grahamstown, 1843.

Cory, Sir G.E., Preller, G. and Blommaert, W. *Die Retief–Dingaan ooreenkoms.* In *Annale van die Universiteit van Stellenbosch,* Serie B, No 1. Cape Town, 1924.

Davenport, T.R.H. *South Africa: A modern history.* Basingstoke, 1991.

Delegorgue, A. *Travels in Southern Africa.* Translated by Fleur Webb. Introduced and indexed by Stephanie J. Alexander and Colin de B. Webb. Pietermaritzburg, 1990. vol I.

Denoon, D. and Nyeko, B. *Southern Africa since 1800.* London, 1972.

Duminy, A.H. and Guest, B., eds., *Natal and Zululand from earliest times to 1910: a new history.* Pietermaritzburg, 1989.

Du Plessis, A.J. *Die Republiek Natalia.* Archives Year Book for South African History, 1942, Part I. Cape Town, 1943.

Edgecombe, D.R., Laband, J.P.C. and Thompson, P.S. comps. *The debate on Zulu origins: a selection of papers on the Zulu kingdom and early colonial Natal.* Pietermaritzburg, 1992.

Fage, J.D. and Oliver, R., eds., *Cambridge history of Africa.* Cambridge, 1975–76. 8v.

Gardiner, A.F. *Narrative of a journey to the Zoolu country in South Africa, undertaken in 1835.* Facsimile reprint, Cape Town, 1966.

Gibson, J.Y. *The story of the Zulus.* Pietermaritzburg, 1903.

Hall, M. *The changing past: farmers, kings and traders in South Africa 200–1860.* Cape Town, 1987.

Hamilton, C., ed., *The 'mfecane' aftermath.* Johannesburg and Pietermaritzburg, 1995.

Hammond-Tooke, W.D., ed. *The Bantu-speaking peoples of Southern Africa.* 2nd ed. London, 1974.

Harris, W.C. *The wild sports of southern Africa.* London, 1852.

Holden, W.C. *History of the colony of Natal.* London, 1855.

Howarth, T.E.B. *Citizen-king: the life of Louis-Philippe king of the French.* London, 1961.

Hugo, M. *Piet Retief.* Johannesburg, 1961.

Jansen, E.G. *Die Voortrekkers in Natal.* Cape Town, 1938.

Krauss, F. *Travel Journal/Cape to Zululand: observations by a collector and naturalist,* ed. by O.H. Spohr. Cape Town, 1973.

Krige, E.J. *The social system of the Zulus.* Pietermaritzburg, 1950.

Lugg, H.C. *Historic Natal and Zululand.* Pietermaritzburg, 1948.

Lye, W.F. and Murray, C. *Transformations on the highveld: the Tswana and Southern Sotho.* Cape Town, 1980.

Mackeurtan, G. *The cradle days of Natal, 1497–1845.* London, 1931.

Maylam, P.R. *A history of the African people of South Africa: from the early iron age to the 1970s.* Cape Town and Johannesburg, 1986.

Notule Natalse Volksraad (met bylae), 1838–1845. South African Archival Records, Natal No. 1. Cape Town, 1953.

Parsons, N. *A new history of Southern Africa.* London, 1993. 2nd. ed.

Preller, G.S. *Andries Pretorius: lewensbeskrywing van die Voortrekker kommandant-generaal.* Johannesburg, 1973.

Preller, G.S. *Piet Retief en ander trekleiers.* Pretoria, 1908.

Preller, G.S. *Voortrekkermense.* Cape Town, 1918–38.

Rasmussen, R.K. *Migrant kingdom: Mzilikazi's Ndebele in South Africa.* London and Cape Town, 1978.

Samuelson, R.C.A. *Long, long ago.* Durban, 1929.

Shooter, J. *The Kafirs of Natal and the Zulu country.* London, 1857.

Smail, J.L. *Monuments and trails of the Voortrekkers.* Cape Town, 1968.

Smith, A. *Andrew Smith and Natal: documents relating to the early history of the province,* ed. by P.R. Kirby. Van Riebeeck Society, No 36. Cape Town, 1955.

Smith, A. *Andrew Smith's journal of his expedition into the interior of South Africa 1834–6.* Cape Town, 1975.

Smith, E. *The life and times of Daniel Lindley (1801–1880): missionary to the Zulus, pastor of the Voortrekkers . . .* London, 1949.

Stow, G.W. *The native races of South Africa.* London, 1905.

Tabler, E.C. *Pioneers of Natal and south-eastern Africa, 1552–1878.* Cape Town, 1977.

Theal, G.McC. *History of the Boers in South Africa.* London, 1887.

Thompson, L.M. (ed). *African societies in Southern Africa.* London, 1969.

Wahlberg, J.A. *Travel journals (and some letters): South Africa and Namibia/Botswana, 1838–1856.* ed. by A. Craig and C. Hummel with O. West and M. Roberts. Second Series No 23, Van Riebeeck Society, Cape Town, 1994.

Walker, N. 'Game traps: their importance in Southern Africa'. *Botswana notes and records,* 23, 1991, pp 235–42.

Watt, E.P. *Febana: the true story of Farewell.* London, 1962.

Webb, C. deB. and Wright, J.B., eds. *The James Stuart archive of recorded oral evidence relating to the history of the Zulu and neighbouring peoples.* Pietermaritzburg, 1976, 1979, 1982, 1986. 4v.

Wilson, M. and Thompson, L.M. eds. *The Oxford history of South Africa. VI: South Africa to 1870.* Oxford, 1969.

Wood, W. *Statements respecting Dingaan, king of the Zoolahs, with some particulars relative to the massacres of Messrs Retief and Biggars, and their parties.* Cape Town, 1840.

UNPUBLISHED SOURCES

Cubbin, A.E. 'A study in objectivity: the death of Piet Retief'. MA, University of the Orange Free State, 1980.

Cubbin, A.E. 'Origins of the British settlement at Port Natal, May 1824–July 1842'. D.Phil, University of the Orange Free State, 1983.

Okihiro, G.Y. 'Hunters, herders, cultivators and traders: interaction and change in the Kgalagadi, nineteenth century'. Ph.D., University of California, L.A., 1976.

Wright, J.B. 'The dynamics of power and conflict in the Thukela-Mzimkhulu region in the late eighteenth and early nineteenth centuries: a critical reconstruction'. Ph.D., University of the Witwatersrand, 1990.

ADULPHE DELEGORGUE – SCIENTIST

SOME FURTHER REFLECTIONS

Adulphe Delegorgue's *Travels* was written as a continuous narrative: had he intended the two-volume format, he would certainly have chosen a more felicitous point at which to interrupt the flow, and would have ended the first volume with a flourish, and started the second with some ceremony. No. The subdivision was doubtless a technicality, probably decided on at the printer's, without particular regard for internal symmetry or cadence.

Is there, in view of this, any real need for further commentary on Delegorgue's scientific endeavours and scientific thinking? These are after all generously covered in the essay 'Adulphe Delegorgue – Scientist' which forms part of the editorial introduction to Volume I, and which examines his background and training, as well as the unusual aspects of his intellect and temperament that made his approach to natural history uniquely interesting. If Volumes I and II are artificial entities, it would surely be as artificial to treat what is essentially a continuous theme again, and separately, here?

Indeed, there would be little point in writing merely to reiterate or amplify what has already been said, and a swift first reading of Volume II suggests that only a few very broad comments need be made, partly because natural history often yields place to other material, partly because much of the biology seems to be the mixture as before. Thus, Delegorgue continues to report the sighting of the large, the noisy, the spectacular, the edible, the troublesome. He continues to ignore, or to brush aside with only a passing reference, hosts of smaller, less colourful creatures (though he included many in his collections) and to write as if, apart from a few parasites, pests and the insects he collected from time to time, there are no invertebrates in South Africa at all. He continues to hunt, but with a vigour and intensity that begin to look worryingly like bloodlust, tinged at times rather horridly with a childish destructiveness. The conservation-conscious reader will be repelled, even sickened, by accounts of the killings of elephant, rhino, buffalo, antelope, (and on, and on) that in their wantonness exceed those recounted in Volume I. It is no comfort to reason, in these depleted times when so many species and their environment are endangered, that in the 17th, 18th and 19th centuries the supply of game seemed limitless, and that Delegorgue's contribution to the generalised slaughter was probably relatively modest. It is no comfort, either, that he himself, unless the animals have been killed for the pot, usually follows particularly bloody hunting stories with almost maudlin reflections on the nobility and beauty and innocence of living things, on the reprehensibility of his own role in their destruction, and on the 'fact' that the hunting instinct and the scientist's commitment to truth must nevertheless override all scruples.

In short, it would be easy to dismiss this, and therefore most of Delegorgue's scientific pretensions, as so much hypocritical eyewash, and to see Delegorgue himself as having become just another European opportunist, greedy and exploitative, his real aim to return to France laden with exotic spoils and to achieve glory – and monetary reward – through publication of his memoir. Of this later Delegorgue, therefore, it would seem that the less said, the better.

A slower and more thoughtful reading will, however, show that although there may be an element of truth in the unattractive picture just presented, it is but a detail in the larger and more complex canvas that was Delegorgue, and that some further analysis is desirable. It should be remembered that he edited the 36 chapters of the *Travels* from the notes he had made during the whole of his more than five years in South Africa. These notes had probably been kept sporadically, rather than religiously day-by-day, and were therefore at once both less complete and more readable than, say, the terse daily entries of the more rigorously trained J.A. Wahlberg, his Swedish contemporary and friend. Because of this, and because, also, he probably excised what he deemed boring or repetitive (though some repeated material does occur in the text), and certainly made later additions, the time-scale is not always clear. Events that loom large in the narrative compel the telescoping of other events or of uneventful periods, while a few skips back and forth in time confuse things even further.

What we do know from the book as a whole is that the man who returned home in 1844 was no longer the eager boy who, at 23, had come to the Cape, full of book learning, romantic ideals and ambitions, replete with energy, optimism and self-confidence, technically well-equipped, self-reliant and ready for anything. For in the intervening years Delegorgue had endured much. He had lived and travelled rough, often for months at a time, in inhospitable country and among not always friendly people. He had faced all kinds of dangers, and had had many a brush with death. He had more than once been seriously ill, and, probably through a combination of poor nutrition and the stress induced by intellectual and spiritual, if not physical, isolation (and perhaps a certain hypochondria), had experienced severe reactions to pests and parasites that would normally have little effect. In the light of this, it is hardly surprising that there was a hardening, a growing callousness and a blunting of sensibilities.

Which makes it all the more remarkable that so many of the positive aspects of his character, and of his approach to living things and the world at large, were so little affected.

Thus, although his hunting stories are repugnant to the modern reader, he never sinks to the same depths as did Wahlberg, that meticulous scientist whose contribution to the study of the southern African flora and fauna is widely acknowledged. Wahlberg, frustrated by the dearth of new plants and animals in south-west Africa, lost control and took his feelings out on the animals, slaughtering them 'almost as a man possessed' in ghastly shooting sprees. Also, though Delegorgue's quasi-philosophical, quasi-scientific excuses for killing and maiming may be false, this very falseness speaks of an inner disquiet, even of remorse – whether he felt this at the time, or later, during the editing process. Further, Volume II contains a number of well-written and beautifully observed descriptions of the appearance, biology and behaviour of several big game animals. The style is instructive but conversational and the tone is one of unselfconscious affection and respect for the subjects. These were certainly penned on the spot, but are so different from the main body of the text that they may not have been part of his routine notes. Instead, they may have been specially written for a particular audience: possibly they were sections of letters to family or friends, retrieved for interpolation later.

Clearly, it is even more difficult here than it was in Volume I for the modern reader to reconcile Delegorgue the killer with Delegorgue the naturalist. Wahlberg's story tells us that a far more prolific killer can also be a superb naturalist producing work of enduring quality. We must accept that, at a time when hunters were regarded as gentlemen and heroes, the pursuit of game would have been considered an appropriate way for a young man deprived for so long of the company of confrères, and of the society of women, to relieve his frustrations. We must accept too, that killing was a necessary part of the work of the naturalist, as indeed it still is to a far more limited extent today. What can be said in Delegorgue's favour is that although the killer from time to time eclipses the naturalist, it is the curiosity, the delight in discovery, of the naturalist that enlivens and sustains him during the whole of his South African sojourn.

It is Delegorgue the naturalist who builds a special laboratory hut in the bush to protect himself and his specimens – the cured skins, the cleaned skeletons – from the elements, and who works there day and night. It is Delegorgue the naturalist who carefully rolls skins for packing, and pads skulls and horns before enclosing them in specially made bags. It is Delegorgue the naturalist – and competent entomologist, a hitherto hidden talent – who pauses for a fortnight at a time to collect, preserve and mount pinned insects in what must have been dozens of specially pest-proofed insect boxes, despite the derision occasioned by the exchanging of his elephant gun for nets and pins. It is Delegorgue the naturalist who turns his glass on horn borers and botfly larvae, and who indignantly inspects and identifies the tiny larvae damaging his beetle specimens.

Finally, it is Delegorgue the naturalist, insatiably curious, always with an opinion, who enquires into the lives of the peoples he encounters. Relying on his easy sociability across barriers of race and language, he asks questions, notes answers and, with customary irony, comments and evaluates. The anthropological material in Volume II may not be unique, but it is presented from an unusual viewpoint, so that, along with run-of-the-mill facts about crops, food preparation and dress, there are interesting glimpses into matters more intimate. Even his probing, clinical approach, however, disappointingly fails to elicit a definite answer on the matter of female circumcision among the 'Makatisses'.

For the general reader the historical and anthropological chapters will be the high points of Volume II. The biologist, however, will be disappointed, not for want of action or of colourful encounters with animals, but because of a detectable intellectual stagnation in this sphere. Delegorgue had had no access to a library for years, and only minimal contact with other naturalists. The spark of wit and originality has not gone out, but is much dimmed, to be replaced at times by an obsessiveness (as with the pursuit of the sable antelope) which is much less attractive. His attempts to be scholarly here are no more than rehashes of ideas covered in Volume I, and his repeated emphasis on his own scientific integrity grows tedious. Also, his thinking is increasingly tainted with anthropomorphism, a fashionable conceit of some 18th-century natural history writers, such as the great Buffon, into whose 44-volume *Histoire Naturelle* Delegorgue had dipped as a boy. It is depressing to see a man of his intelligence some 60 years later equating the appearance and behaviour of animals with those of degenerate human beings, with the implication that what in his opinion is cowardly, stupid, cunning or just ugly, deserves to be killed. This is unworthy in a man who had earlier vowed to question established authority and push beyond the frontiers of accepted thought and knowledge, a man, who, had he lived long enough, should surely have rejoiced at the publication of *The Origin of Species* in 1859.

Even more than does Volume I, Volume II of the *Travels* omits much that the modern reader would wish to know. We discover that Delegorgue's skill as a laboratory, museum and field technician, and as an entomologist, was more extensive than Volume I had led us to believe, but we still do not know how or where he had acquired it. We know from footnotes and a few comments in the text that he had consulted recent scientific and taxonomic literature before publication, but we have no idea which library or other resources he used. And from both the text and the species lists we gain a tantalizing glimpse of what must have been a network of French travellers, collectors and natural history specialists, some often on the move, some stationed in foreign parts, some in French laboratories studying collections brought or sent in by others. Somehow, although his background set him apart from almost all of them in one way or another, Delegorgue was a member of this group. How had he developed and maintained these valuable contacts? Had he, for example, been corresponding with Alexis Verreaux, whose welcome when Delegorgue stayed with him at the Cape before embarking for home was so warm? Had he been in regular touch with the entomologists who so readily worked on his insect collections? Only Macquart of Lille Museum (Diptera) is formally acknowledged, but a glance down the long list of beetles will show that several different authorities had named new species after Delegorgue or had created species names which were obviously of Delegorgueian origin, e.g., *amazoulousiana, massilicatziana.* It is difficult to guess who compiled the beetle list (one very tentative suggestion might be F.E. Guérin-Méneville), but, as is discussed in the introduction to this appended material (p298), it is clear that J.B.A.D. de Boisduval not only prepared the list of butterflies and moths, but also wrote the descriptions. For Boisduval to have allowed Delegorgue to include this material as his own speaks either of a complaisance most unusual in a taxonomist, or else of a considerable friendship and the understanding that there would be future collaboration.

Like many another naturalist before and after him, Adulphe Delegorgue came to the Cape to find the 'something new' that Pliny the Elder had promised (in his 1st-century *Natural History*) would always come 'out of Africa'. He found it, of course, in great measure. There were two main results of his findings. The first was that a new Delegorgue, older, wiser and probably more cynical, had been superimposed upon the bright young man of five years before; a Delegorgue who, ever restless and unable to settle, would be furiously working towards future travels and who would, sadly, perish en route to his next destination, in 1850. The second was this book, chronicle of the travels of an extraordinary adventurer, scientist and observer, a man whose approach to life and to discovery was bold and buoyantly openhearted, and yet who left behind him an air of mystery. Both this book and its author were and still are, 'something new out of Africa'.

* * * * *

The annotated Natural History Index to Volume II of Delegorgue's *Travels*, and the species lists in the Taxonomic Section with my commentary upon them, would have been much the poorer without specialist help. Warm thanks are due, first, to the three people who generously contributed to the elucidation of Delegorgue's insects. Jason Londt of the Natal Museum, Pietermaritzburg, responded with good humour and time-consuming thoroughness to a range of entomological queries, and kindly approached his colleague, Rolf Oberprieler of the Plant Protection Research Institute, Agricultural Research Council, Pretoria, on my behalf. He, in turn, swiftly supplied much information about 18th- and 19th- century lepidopterists, of which I have made liberal use. Dr D.W. (Jakes) Ewer again participated, and this time, in addition to tracking down several obscure facts, undertook the very considerable task of translating the descriptions of butterflies and moths in the Catalogue of Lepidoptera. These thus appear here in English for the first time – a graceful, 19th-century taxonomic English, as far as possible in keeping with the French original, yet entomologically authoritative and bearing Jakes' unmistakable stamp. His contribution is a great asset to this volume, and I am as ever much indebted to him.

Two of Delegorgue's birds eluded my own best efforts. David Johnson of the Natal Parks Board kindly suggested several lines of enquiry. After a few false starts I discovered Peter Ryan of the University of Cape Town's Percy FitzPatrick Institute of African Ornithology, who suggested a very credible identity for Delegorgue's mysterious '*manches des velours*' (velvet sleeves). Adrian Craig of Rhodes University tackled the problem of the equally mysterious 'blac', and obtained the identification from his colleague Michel Louette of the Royal Museum for Central Africa, Tervuren, Belgium. I am most grateful to them all, not only for unhesitatingly sharing their expertise, but for doing so in such an open and friendly way.

Several friends, associates and former colleagues were forthcoming on a range of subjects. I thank in particular Brett Hendey of the Durban Natural History Museum (fossil bovids), Neal Young of the Natal Museum (taxidermy), Jay Malherbe (diseases of cattle) and Michelle Hamer (phyllopod Crustacea). I thank also the Natal Society Library which, through the good offices of Pat McKenzie, permitted me to retain certain vital literature on (very) extended loan.

Once again, L.R. Alexander unstintingly provided support, encouragement and invaluable practical help, without which the completion of this project would have been very difficult indeed. I wish to remember here also, and with love, L.D. and F.W. Warren: the *Travels* would have meant a great deal to them.

STEPHANIE ALEXANDER

Pietermaritzburg, April 1997

WORKS CONSULTED

Annecke, D.P. and Moran, V.C. (1982). *Insects and mites of cultivated plants in South Africa*. Durban, Pretoria: Butterworth.

Arthur, D.R. (1962). *Ticks and disease*. London: Pergamon Press.

Attwater, D. (1965). *The Penguin dictionary of saints*. Harmondsworth: Penguin.

Bartholomew, J. (1936). *The Oxford advanced atlas* (5th ed.). London: O.U.P.

Branch, B. (1994). *Field guide to snakes and other reptiles of southern Africa* (2nd ed.). Cape Town: Struik.

Burton, M. and Burton, R. (eds) (1968). *Purnell's encyclopaedia of animal life* Vols 1–6. London: Purnell.

Cassell's French-English, English-French dictionary (E.A. Baker ed.) (1920). London: Cassell.

Cassell's German & English dictionary (H.T. Betteridge, ed.) (1968). London: Cassell.

Chambers Encyclopaedia (New ed.) (1950). Vols 1–15. London: Newnes.

Coates Palgrave, K. and Drummond, R.B. (1983). *Trees of southern Africa* (2nd ed.) (E.J. Moll, ed.). Cape Town: Struik.

Collins' Afrikaans-English, English-Afrikaans dictionary (A. Coetzee, ed.) (1969, repr. 1994). Glasgow: Harper Collins.

Dictionary of South African biography Vol II (1972), pp. 811–12: P.J. Verreaux; Vol III (1977), pp. 204–5: P.-A. Delalande.

Ellerman, J.R., Morrison-Scott, T.C.S. and Hayman, R.W. (1953). *Southern African mammals 1758 to 1951: a reclassification*. London: British Museum (Nat. Hist.).

Encyclopaedia Britannica (1926). 13th Standard Edition, Vols 1–32. London & New York: Encyclopaedia Britannica Co., Ltd.

FitzSimons, V.F.M. (1970). *A field guide to the snakes of southern Africa*. London: Collins.

Fox, F.W. and Norwood Young, M.E. (1982). *Food from the veld: edible wild plants of southern Africa*. Johannesburg: Delta Books.

Grove, D.I. (1990). *A history of human helminthology*. Wallingford, Oxon: C.A.B. International.

Harrap's shorter French and English dictionary (1940). London: Harrap.

Harris, W.C. (1840, repr. 1986). *Portraits of the game and wild animals of southern Africa, delineated from life in their native haunts*. Alberton: Galago.

Harrison, L.J.S. and Sewell, M.M.H. (1991). *The zoonotic Taeniae of Africa* In *Parasitic helminths and zoonoses in Africa*. London: Unwin Hyman.

Hill, R.W. and Wyse, G.A. (1989). *Animal physiology* (2nd ed.). New York: Harper & Row.

Hutchings, A., Scott, A., Lewis, G. and Cunningham, A. (1996). *Zulu medicinal plants: an inventory.* Pietermaritzburg: University of Natal Press (in association with the University of Zululand, and the National Botanical Institute, Cape Town).

Imms, A.D. (1946). *A general textbook of entomology* (6th ed.). London: Methuen.

International dictionary of medicine and biology (3 vols) (1996). New York: John Wiley & Sons.

Jaeger, E.C. (1955). *A source-book of biological names and terms* (3rd ed.). Springfield, Illinois: Thomas.

Langenscheidt's standard dictionary of the French and English languages (K. Urwin, ed.) (1968). London: Hodder & Stoughton.

Ledger, J. (ed.) (1979). *S.H. Skaife: African insect life* (2nd ed.). Cape Town: Struik.

Maclean, G.L. (1993). *Roberts' birds of southern Africa* (6th ed.). Cape Town: John Voelcker Bird Book Fund.

Mahoney, R. (1966). *Laboratory techniques in zoology.* London: Butterworth.

Meglitsch, P.A. and Schram, F.R. (1991). *Invertebrate zoology* (3rd ed.). New York: O.U.P.

Merck Index (1996) (12th ed., S. Budavari, ed.). Whitehouse Station, N.J.: Merck & Co. Inc.

Oxford English Dictionary (1971) (complete: Compact ed., 2 vols). Oxford: O.U.P.

Partington, J.R. (1937). *A text-book of inorganic chemistry* (5th ed.). London: Macmillan.

Pinhey, E.C.G. (1975). *Moths of southern Africa.* Cape Town: Tafelberg.

Pooley, E. (1993). *The complete field guide to trees of Natal, Zululand and Transkei.* Durban: Natal Flora Publications Trust.

Rankin, J.C. and Davenport, J.A. (1981). *Animal osmoregulation.* Glasgow, London: Blackie & Son.

Rattray Taylor, G. (1963). *The science of life: a picture history of biology.* London: Thames & Hudson.

Scholtz, C.H. and Holm, E. (1985). *Insects of southern Africa.* Durban: Butterworth.

Schram, F.R. (1986). *Crustacea.* New York: O.U.P.

Shorter Oxford English dictionary on historical principles (1944). (3rd ed., C.T. Onions, ed., 2 vols). Oxford: Clarendon Press.

Sinclair, I. (1993). *Sasol birds of southern Africa.* Cape Town: Struik.

Skinner, J.D. and Smithers, R.H.N. (1990). *The mammals of the southern*

African subregion (2nd ed.). Pretoria: University of Pretoria.

Smith, A. (1836).* *Report of the expedition for exploring central Africa, from the Cape of Good Hope ... 1834 ...* Cape Town: Government Gazette Office.

Smith, A. (1836).* *Illustrations of the zoology of South Africa – Mammalia,* Part 12. London: Smith and Elder.

Smith, C.A. (1966). *Common names of South African plants* (E.P. Phillips and E. van Hoepen, eds). Pretoria: Government Printer.

Stanek, V.J. (1962). *Pictorial encyclopaedia of the animal kingdom* (G. Theiner, trans.). London: Paul Hamlyn.

Stark, A.C. and Sclater, W.L. (1900–1906). *The birds of South Africa* Vols. I - IV. *(The fauna of South Africa,* W.L. Sclater, gen. ed.). London: R.H. Porter.

Victoria Regina Atlas (2nd ed.) (1902). Edinburgh & London: W.& A.K. Johnston, Ltd.

Wahlberg, J.A. (1994). *Johan August Wahlberg: travel journals (and some letters), South Africa and Namibia/Botswana, 1838 - 1856* (M. Roberts, trans., A. Craig and H.C. Hummel, eds). V.R.S. 2nd Series: 23. Cape Town: Van Riebeeck Society.

Wigglesworth, V.B. (1964). *The life of insects.* London: Weidenfeld & Nicolson.

Wingate, P. and Wingate, R. (1988). *The Penguin medical encyclopaedia* (3rd ed.). Harmondsworth: Penguin.

Wooldridge, W.R. (1960). *Farm animals in health and disease* (2nd ed.). London: Crosby Lockwood.

*Not seen in the original.

TRANSLATOR'S NOTE

Once again, in translating Delegorgue's mid-nineteenth century French, my object has been to try to preserve the spirit of another age while making the text readily accessible to the late twentieth-century English reader. This has required some simplification of language, and occasionally some interpretation rather than exact translation, but no sacrifice of essential information. As in Volume I, the author's unique, and often inconsistent, spellings of personal and place names have been retained. This is not affectation, but an attempt to preserve some of the Gallic flavour.

I would like to thank gunsmiths Clint Rafferty and Vere Bresler for their patience and interest in answering my questions about firearms and ammunition. I would also like to thank Dr. Tim Maggs for information on iron smelting and assegai making, Dr. Clive Spinage for help in understanding pit traps and Prof. Adrian Koopman for his introductory note to the Zulu vocabulary. I am particularly grateful to our publisher and friend Margery Moberly for happy hours spent in discussion and for useful advice.

In addition to the dictionaries and reference books listed in Volume I, I have made use of Bird's *Annals of Natal*. Pietermaritzburg, 1882.

FLEUR WEBB

Pietermaritzburg, April 1997

TRAVELS IN SOUTHERN AFRICA

SUMMARY OF CHAPTER XX

The last chapter of Volume I opens in the middle of a hunting expedition in the land of the Amazoulous in January 1842. Delegorgue describes encounters with a huge herd of elephants, with a honey-guide and with an *iphesy* (spitting snake), and gives a day-by-day account of a protracted search for further elephants. After relating the events of 7 February he interrupts his narrative with a long account of the habits of elephants and methods of hunting them. Here he draws together everything he has learned from his reading, his observations, from his own hunting experiences and from those of other travellers.

Delegorgue resumes the narrative of the hunt at the beginning of Chapter XXI and the reader rejoins the author as he and his party continue their relentless search for ivory and museum specimens.

VOYAGE

DANS

L'AFRIQUE AUSTRALE

NOTAMMENT

**dans le territoire de Natal
dans celui des Cafres Amazoulous et Makatisses
et jusqu'au tropique du Capricorne**

Durant les années 1838, 1839, 1840, 1841, 1842, 1843 & 1844

Avec Dessins et Cartes

PAR

M. Adulphe DELEGORGUE

(DE DOUAI)

TOME SECOND.

PARIS

AU DEPOT DE LIBRAIRIE, RUE DES MOULINS, 8.

PRÈS LA RUE THÉRÈSE.

Adresser les demandes et mandats à Mme CROISSANT.

A HERD OF ELEPHANTS

TRAVELS

IN

SOUTHERN AFRICA

(CONTINUED)

CHAPTER XXI

More elephants — Om-Ghet-Janne and his 600 trackers — A wonderful hunt —
A lion — Behaviour of Om-Ghet-Janne — My regrets — Return to camp — I
dispatch a wagon-load of specimens back to Natal

Up until 19 January little happened to distinguish one day from
the next. The heat was growing so intense, and decay was setting in
so rapidly, that preparation of the larger specimens was becoming
impossible. Henning got back at last, after some first-rate hunting.
Within a couple of days he had killed an elephant, although not one
of much consequence. On the third day, after twice wounding a
female which was standing near some makanos trees, he had gone
after her in a furious chase during the course of which he had
narrowly escaped being trampled underfoot. On the tenth day, just as
he was making ready for the return journey, fortune favoured him
when he came upon several male elephants. As he had at his disposal
a great number of beaters, Henning set them to work driving the
animals back and forth within firing range. Before the hour was up,
five of the elephants had fallen, while the remaining two were still
within his sights. But the incessant battering of the gun's recoil had
so bruised his shoulder, that Henning was unable to sustain his fire

1

and had been obliged to abandon the hunt. On the journey back he had killed yet again, making a total of seven elephants in only twelve days! This was success beyond our wildest dreams.

My intention was to pursue our good fortune and to neglect nothing which might contribute to its continuation. To tell the truth, I had not anticipated such remarkable success when I was making preparations to leave Natal; my ammunition was almost spent and I lacked guns of sufficient calibre; besides, the numerous specimens which I had already collected made it necessary that I should send my wagon back to the bay. But in order to do this without too much inconvenience, I would require three additional Cafres. I remembered the obliging offers of Om-Ghet-Janne and I resolved to seek his assistance.

On the last day of February I arrived at the chief's house. Along the way we wounded one elephant and found another, of average size, lying dead. Om-Ghet-Janne was unable to grant my request. He was subject to a superior chief by the name of Souquaba who would certainly have disapproved of any arrangement being made without his consent, and Souquaba was away from home.

On 1 March I was confined to the *mouzi* with a raging headache. On the 2nd, as the headache was still severe, I attempted to get rid of it by means of exercise. I set out with my men and we were already busy looking for elephants when we came across Om-Ghet-Janne. 'Wait until tomorrow,' he said. 'Tomorrow you will have several hundred men to help you; tomorrow you are sure to succeed. You are alone today and can do nothing worthwhile. It will be as much as you can do to kill one or two elephants, and that means goodbye to the rest of the troop. Just listen to me and come back to the *mouzi*. I will take care of everything; I dare even promise you success.'

As I was quite incapable of serious hunting that day, I allowed myself to be persuaded by Om-Ghet-Janne, requesting only that upon his return, he would summon all the available men for the next day and dispatch trackers in every direction.

Five or six hundred men responded to this call and came to meet us at Om-Ghet-Janne's place. There was an air of joyful anticipation. Each man carried a hunting shield, several assegais and an axe. After walking for two hours, we spotted some elephants down below and made our way towards them. The guides up in front, so as not to alarm the animals, began issuing their instructions in whispers. A sharp whistle was the signal to beware. In spite of all our caution, we were unable to overtake the troop; it simply moved out of range. We followed after, crossing the Om-Philos-Mouniama at least ten times. As a diversion, we had an encounter with a ratel, or stinking badger, which I stabbed to death with an assegai.

2

It was past midday and the heat was suffocating; we were weary and longing to rest, when some Cafre scouts arrived to tell us that they had seen a large number of elephants standing on a peninsula formed by a bend in the Om-Philos, about five miles away. The situation was splendid but there was not a moment to be lost. We quickened our steps and soon arrived near the place, having twice again been obliged to cross the river of a thousand coils. Before us lay an isthmus 300 feet wide, while the peninsula itself measured 1200; to the right rose a mountain 300 feet high which several of the Cafres climbed to position themselves on look-out. We were upwind from the elephants, but still a considerable distance away. I posted men wherever I judged it to be necessary. We advanced towards the battleground, crossing the Om-Philos twice more before we reached it.

We approached the peninsula from the side opposite the isthmus and directly downwind from our quarry. We had not proceeded more than 200 paces when we encountered part of the herd. Three shots were fired and all simultaneously struck the largest of the elephants, causing riotous confusion. There was a clashing of tusks, drowned by shrill squeals and trumpeting, and then the 'long noses' retreated in disorder under cover of thick dust. The ground shook for 100 paces all around as they tried to escape towards the open country via the isthmus. Then suddenly, blocking their way, my Zoulous rose up in a great surge, beating their shields with the shafts of their assegais and creating a tremendous din. Becoming aware of the presence of men who were cutting off their retreat, the animals halted, hesitated and then turned back.

Hardly had we had time to reload than they were grouping themselves into a wide and formidable battlefront which, like a great solid rampart, began advancing towards us at a trot, threatening to destroy everything in its path. Fortunately, the terrain was open and offered visibility of up to sixty paces.

'Stand by and shoot to kill.' Three shots rang out; although none reached its target the leaders stopped short, turned aside and followed a group which had broken away to the right. A good number made for the escape routes, but at each gap in the rushes on the banks, a man had been positioned, beating on his shield. The animals, whose only desire was to escape, found themselves bedevilled at every point and forced to run the risk of open combat. This place, which fortune had provided, was in fact an amphitheatre, a stage fit for the battle of the pygmies and the giants, a battleground where mere children would confront their elders and the foolish would challenge the wise. Had we all been trampled underfoot, the just rewards of our foolhardiness would have merited applause.

What paltry reason can justify the death and destruction of such

3

beautiful, strong and excellent animals? What are a couple of hundred pounds of ivory compared with the long service which such animals might render to man for generations?

I was perfectly conscious of the mischief I was doing but I was a hunter first and foremost. The elephant is reckoned the *nec plus ultra* where *ignamazane* (game) is concerned. I desired no other; all the animals of creation, whatsoever they may be, are as nothing compared with the elephant. South African hunters are also of this opinion; I have often heard them say so. I began to think as they did and I still do to this day. These men, who, whether from necessity or for pleasure, spend half their lives hunting in the bush, know what they are talking about.

Kotje Dafel, Henning's father, was the most famous lion hunter in all Natal. This man, who had killed so many lions that he had lost count of them, had never, manly as he was, succeeded in killing a single elephant. He frankly admitted that his heart beat too wildly to take accurate aim when he approached one of these commanding giants, while a lion meant nothing to him. I understood perfectly; the mere mention of the word *uncklove* made me tremble with excitement. It is for this reason that anything resembling an elephant had only to pass my way to be greeted by a shot; there are many still alive and walking about today who bear testimony to our encounters.

Our scouts had no difficulty in following the movements of the animals, while remaining in contact with us. One of these Cafres, who was gifted with a powerful voice, called out the direction the animals were taking; he informed us whenever they stopped and so accurately described their position in relation to ours, that we were guided surely and directly towards our objective. Accompanying us was a man who was intelligent and alert as well as brave and swift of foot. Appearing to receive his orders from on high, he led us unfailingly to within thirty paces of our quarry. Thus served, how could we not succeed? It was by these means that we were guided to a place where we saw seven elephants. The approach was easy; I brought mine down at fifty paces as he faced me three-quarters on.

Kotchobana, Boulandje and I fanned out and began firing at everything within range. My guide then led me to where there were seven more elephants, standing together in a group. They were quite quiet and peaceful and so I was able to crouch down only thirty paces away and to observe them with impunity. Two or three minutes passed and no animal big enough to tempt my fire had yet emerged, when I noticed a young elephant about six feet high with the most peculiar countenance. His face was so comical that I wanted to burst out laughing, for, protruding beyond his lips were tusks only ten inches long. I had a sudden desire to shoot him so that I could inspect him at leisure when he was dead, but I hesitated too long in pulling the trigger and he turned his head away just as I fired so that the shot missed him and hit a neighbouring elephant in the groin.

The sound of the shot going off did not appear to disturb the animals. I backed away on all fours, reloaded and returned to take up my former position. I had been waiting for some while for a favourable opportunity, when I noticed that the animals were beginning to cluster into a group with their heads together at the centre and their hindquarters, which were impervious to our bullets, turned outwards. A loud but ineffectual shot rang out; it was Kotchobana firing at the same group from the other side. At last, one of the heads moved sufficiently for me to see the temple; my bullet struck home and the elephant fell.

I gave an involuntary shout of joy, '*fyle*' (he is dead) and the elephants, which until then had been peaceful, grew restive and moved off. Added to this I had a further disappointment, that of seeing the one I thought I had killed stagger to his feet and set off after the others. So as not to waste any time, I reloaded where I stood and darted off in pursuit. I fired a second shot into his ear, convinced that it would finish him off and indeed we found him shortly afterwards lying dead only two paces away from another elephant which I had struck with an earlier bullet and killed without realising it at the time.

A few minutes later we came upon a great number of elephants which took fright and fled, sweeping up and carrying along with them isolated groups standing in their way. Together they formed an impressive force which headed noisily towards the isthmus where the shield-rattlers were positioned on both sides. These latter were so intimidated by the sight of the mighty squadron advancing and uprooting trees in its path that, expecting to be crushed underfoot, they turned and fled, allowing the gigantic herd to pass by.

Although the number of elephants which remained on the peninsula was reduced by half, we were still faced with a heavy task. In our favour was the fact that the largest troop numbered no more than twenty-eight, while others comprised ten, seven or even five. We kept up a continuous fire, pausing only to retreat and reload. But, as every hunter knows, guns may fail and aim become less accurate; so it was with us; we fired a great number of shots without notable success.

Kotchobana on his side, and I on mine, kept up a continuous barrage of fire; it was every man for himself. A troop of females was hard by. I decided to close in on them and crawled to within thirty paces. One of them saw me and raised her trunk. She began to advance towards me, slowly at first and then she quickened speed. At twenty paces, I took aim and missed. She was gaining ground. It was time to turn and run, but I stood firm, reloaded and aimed for the chest. At fifteen paces I fired a shot which stopped her in her tracks and forced her to retreat. Half an hour later the same sequence of events occurred all over again: the elephant advanced, I fired and missed, the elephant retreated. There was a slight difference however. Stepping back as soon as I had fired, I found myself almost under the feet of four other elephants heading in the opposite direction. It was like falling between Scylla and Charybdis.

So much running and leaping about in the intense heat, enveloped by clouds of dust, had left us feeling parched. We needed to drink and, for the third time, we went down to the river. Here I met up with Kotchobana. We agreed on the number of elephants we had killed; we were certain that four must be lying dead. By this time, quite exhausted, we called a halt to the hunt. The men on look-out could now leave their posts and come to join us. The sun was sinking and we had a long way to go before reaching the *mouzi*. We were tramping along with our guns on our shoulders when more elephants appeared. Kotchobana, who was very sharp, brought one down and, not to be outdone, I immediately set off in pursuit of the others, panting as I ran. I had already covered 300 paces when I stopped short in front of a black bush. I had noticed the rays of the sun shining through it on to an object which was tawny and rounded in shape. My first thought was that a young elephant had fallen dead and was lying under the bush. I went up closer to look and when I was only ten paces off, I noticed two eyes like burning coals watching me. Next I became aware of a white nose and a broad forehead. It was an enormous lion; I could make out the outline of his golden body. His eyes stared unblinking into mine as he gathered himself together ready to leap. Boulandje was five paces closer to him than I was, but more to one side. The lion seemed to be unaware of Boulandje, and Boulandje had not seen the lion. With apparent unconcern, I cocked my firearm, taking care that the catch on the trigger would not make too loud a click.

'Boulandje, *hyza lapa*, come here.' Conditioned to passive obedience, he came towards me without question.

'*Nannzy ebobiss*, there is a lion.'

'*Upi na?* Where is he?'

'*Nannzy, bona lapa*, there he is; look over there.'

'*Mena tanta boulala yena*, I want to kill him.'

Hardly had his eyes encountered the lion's gaze, than an alarming nervous tremor took hold of his body; he began swaying, his teeth chattered and his hands shook as though he were suffering from intense cold. He had the greatest difficulty in articulating: '*Nee baas*, no master.'

I changed my mind. Boulandje was certainly not the man I needed to second me. I glanced towards the lion which had become a virtual

6

Medusa's head in the eyes of my trembling companion, who was standing rooted to the spot.

'*Amba*, go away,' I said to him and began walking backwards. As for danger there was none at all; the lion was more surprised than I was.

When I had retreated about thirty-five paces, I met up with all the Cafres who had come to join the fray. There were about eighty of them, all armed with *om-kondos* (assegais) and I loudly offered them this proposition: 'If you want a dead lion, follow me and be ready to stab him if I miss and he leaps at me.' My suggestion was greeted with a complete lack of enthusiasm. As some of the more curious came closer to try to get a glimpse of the lion, I repeated my offer and took aim. 'I need only ten of you. Come and stand five paces behind me. I'll answer for the success of my shot if the gun does not misfire.'

No one seemed interested. I alone wanted the thing; they did not. I looked around for a tree; everywhere else there were trees, but here there were none, nothing but tangled bushes from which there arose, as if in defiance, stunted, rickety stems, worm-eaten and red with the earth of ant-heaps, standing no more than ten feet high. In short, I was wasting my time looking for what did not exist and in appealing for help to those who responded like women. I called for Kotchobana and told him that I had a sufficiently good opinion of his courage to request him to second me. Although armed with a powerful gun, he too gave a blank refusal.

I had no one to count on but myself and to ensure that my hand would not tremble when I took aim at the redoubtable head, I set about cutting a forked stick. But while I was thus engaged, the chief, Om-Ghet-Janne, guessing my intention, seized my gun by the barrel upon which I was resting my right hand and, arming himself with authority, said to me, 'No you must not shoot; you would cause the death or the mutilation of many of my men.'

This argument was much more persuasive than physical force would have been, for that would not have deterred me. In persisting, I would have violated the authority of this man. I did not pull the trigger, but the memory of that lion still rankles to this day.

The elephants had disappeared; my men and I, wishing to establish our possession of the dead, went off in search of them, in order to cut off their tails. Instead of the five we had expected, within a quarter of an hour we had found six, five of whom were lying within a radius of one hundred paces. The operation completed, we set off in the direction of the *mouzi* which lay three or four leagues distant.

The sun was dipping beneath the horizon when suddenly two eland (*canna*) shot off at a gallop only 200 paces in front of us. I hit the second one which somersaulted into the air, its heart pierced by the bullet which I had intended for the lion. Night soon enveloped us; elephants were moving about in the bush nearby and in spite of my prohibition, Kotchobana, his imagination still seething with the day's impressions, was quite unable to resist firing off his last shot. This foolish act reaped its just reward. The troop moved off but, coming across our tracks, it turned back and followed them and then charged; rending the air with noisy trumpeting. There was a sudden retreat on our part during which the bearers of the eland meat hastily disposed of their burden in order to be able to run faster. By the time we had all found each other again it was very dark; the mimosa branches drew blood as they scratched our hands and faces; soon we were obliged to clutch on to each other so that we would not get lost among the tortuous paths where even our guides had difficulty finding the way.

In the distance, as usual, the local lions were roaring and though I was not much afraid during daylight hours, I confess that when night came, I felt quite weak and faint-hearted. We arrived back at the huts at about half past ten; we chatted, we supped and when it was time to go to sleep, I was the last to do so, and even then my sleep was troubled by the most persistent and strange dream. My lion appeared before me, his enormous head on a level with the ground and his immense hindquarters rising above it; his eyes were aflame and his nose was white; he did not move but remained fixed there like an enormous Barye bronze; and there was I, unable to move, unable to pull the trigger. It was cruel. I was reminded of the torture of Tantalus.

But did I not deserve to suffer remorse? If I had fired in the first place I would have killed him on the spot, for my gun was well primed and my arm and my eye were in fine fettle from all the exercise they had had that day and would not have betrayed me – remember the eland which fell at 200 paces at a full gallop – could I possibly have failed to hit that great head from only ten paces away? Oh no! It would have been impossible. Each succeeding night I experienced the same torment and each morning when I awoke I swore that if ever another such opportunity came my way, I would not waste time in looking for assistance, for the Cafres had not manhood enough to back me.

O Amazoulous! Are you the same people who captured a living wild elephant and dragged it before Dingaan, the despot? You yourselves tell the story, I have heard it many times. I know that the matter is beyond doubt, but I find it hard to believe. Of course it is true that you had no choice; on both sides death awaited you. It was preferable to be killed by the elephant than by order of the despot. Such being the case, I understood how the impossible became possible. You did the impossible to avoid running into even greater danger. As for me, my case was quite different. I had no wish to play the despot, nor could I have done so, and because I did not do so, sleep deserted my eyelids for many a day.

On 5 March we returned to camp having exhausted all our ammunition. Between the 7th and 14th Henning killed two elephants and captured a little one which was soon following him about like a dog. Kotchobana killed a young animal which stood only about three feet high. He was more fortunate on the 19th when two enormous animals fell beneath his fire; one of them had tusks six feet long, measured along the curve.

The 21st saw the return of Souzouana whom I had commissioned to bear gifts to Panda with the object of obtaining the services of three men to accompany my wagon back to the bay. Well, Souzouana returned with an unfavourable answer. Panda had not consented to receive him. He had refused to see him or to hear him personally; an intermediary had been employed to convey messages between the two. The presents had given pleasure; they had even been enthusiastically received. Panda thanked me for them, but yet I realised that once again I had failed to honour Cafre custom. I had transgressed the rules of civility by not dispatching one of my own people. Panda was offended that Souzouana had been charged with the message; he had shown his displeasure; this augured ill, said Souzouana. 'Panda is trying to pick a quarrel with me. His heart is not white towards me. He wishes to have me killed; he will kill me.'

When I tried to persuade him otherwise, and assure him that he must be wrong in attributing such intentions to Panda, he replied, wrinkling up his face, 'You will see, you will see; before two moons have died, Souzouana will have been pierced by an *omkondo* and this body which you see here will have been devoured by the hyaenas.'

Souzouana was obviously a prey to sinister thoughts which had upset his reason. Gently I told him that he must be out of his mind, for I did not understand what Panda's motives might be in wanting to be rid of an old warrior as brave and good as Souzouana.

Convinced that I had failed completely in my negotiations, and aware that the departure of my wagon could no longer be delayed, because of the possible flooding of the rivers,[1] I gave Henning three men, a sufficient number to make his task manageable. He set off on 22 March at eight o'clock in the morning. I accompanied him as far as Om-Landelle's place where I spent the night. The next morning we bade each other farewell and wished each other success.

---

1   It is worth noting that the great rains up-country were late that year for generally, towards the middle of March, the rivers are full – November, December, January and February being the months when torrential rains fall.

CHAPTER XXII

Souzouana — His uneasiness — Another visit to Om-Ghet-Janne — Dearth of elephants compels us to proceed northwards — the Mona — Maputa — Zimpy — Om-Kouzi — Omkouzana — A profitable hunt — Makaza — More hunting — My gun breaks — Return

I made my way towards Om-Schlaty-Om-Koulu for the sole purpose of going to see the big dead elephant whose head might well be of use to me. On the way I learnt that elephants had been seen in that vicinity the day before. This information determined me immediately to return to camp to fetch the heavy gun and suitable ammunition. As I passed the fields cultivated by Souzouana, I killed with a single shot, a bustard of the largest kind to be found in Africa. On top of its head a collection of longish feathers forms a kind of flat crest; its neck, covered in tapering feathers, looks blueish from a distance; the back is tawny brown, the stomach dirty white. The bird is nothing but a ball of fat, generally believed to weigh as much as a man; the flesh is delicious. The colonists call it *groote-kuyf-pauw*; to the naturalist it is *otis-kori*. My first concern was to preserve this fine specimen.

On the 26th I travelled along the high ground that looks over Om-Schlaty-Om-Koulou from the east; we then crossed Om-Philos-Om-Schlopu to reach the forests where we hoped to discover something of interest. Unfortunately, we found only spoor that was five or six days old. At about two o'clock we reached the place where the enormous body was lying. The skull, which was still intact, was of colossal proportions. When the back of the head rested flat on the ground, the distance to the tip of the tusks was eight feet. I fell in love with it at first sight and I was already planning to have it hauled from the infected site so that I could clean it, when the Zoulous who were watching me pointed out that nobody was prepared to carry it. In vain I promised gifts of all the knives in the world, axes, iron, woollen blankets, glass beads; nothing could persuade them. I began to think of how I could hang the two sections from trees to keep them out of the reach of hyaenas, as I had done on a previous occasion; but the mimosas would not do because the bark broke off into small brittle pieces and there were no trees to suit my purpose in the vicinity.

What was to be done? Burial was not possible, the ground was too hard and, anyhow, the grave would be bound to be raided by hyaenas the very first night. All I could do was to cover the body with a pile

10

of thorny branches which should prevent any approach to within six paces. One would have thought that this precaution should have been sufficient, but the hyaena can be very persistent. When I passed that way a few days later, I noticed with regret that these animals had made their way through the branches and, at their leisure, had crunched the bones of my elephant head.

Not only had the Amazoulous, who were following me in the hope of some treat, refused to carry the cranium and the lower jaw, but they claimed exemption from carrying the tusks as well. I was wrong to give way to them on the first point; next they wanted concessions on others, for such is their manner of proceeding, until eventually their demands amount to insolence. As they had already had the fat, I was within my rights to insist that they carry the tusks back to my camp. This had been the tacit understanding which these people claimed to be exempt from now that they had enjoyed the benefits. I forcibly impressed my wishes upon them and the tusks, although they were very heavy, duly arrived that same evening at the *Mouzi* of Bayé-Bank. I must admit that the task was a hard one for these men as the heat continued very intense, without a breath of air, and the way was relentlessly uphill. It became necessary to replace the original bearers and to force others to take their place.

I returned to my camp on the 27th, having spent an hour with Souzouana who would not consent to let me go without regaling me on Cafre beer. I found him busy with a bull which he had just had slaughtered although, only two days previously, there had been plenty of meat from one of his cows which had been killed by a lion.

'Good Heavens, Souzouana,' I said to him, 'the way you're going, you'll soon have nothing left. If you needed meat, why did you not ask me? We would have killed you a buffalo.'

'A buffalo? Oh, a buffalo would not have done; it is *inkounzi* which my dead brother desires.'

'What? Your dead brother?'

'Oh yes, my dead brother.'

'You have lost a brother, then? Was it a long time ago?'

'Child, has not everyone without exception a dead brother? Leave off your questioning.'

I was very curious to know more about this dead brother of the Amazoulous. Souzouana, who was feeling the need to unburden his heart, described to me, without actually defining him, what a dead brother might be.

'For some time now, a series of misfortunes has befallen me and mine; within the last three days, a lion has killed three of my cows; a young man has died in my *mouzi*; I have incurred the wrath of Panda; the hunt has brought no return; my crops are drying up in the fields; my children are sick and. most recently, a panther found his way into my *mouzi* in spite of the fifteen foot hedge of thorns. It is my dead brother who has done all this because he wishes for the heart and the blood of a bull. Now that I have satisfied his desire, I hope that he will leave me in peace.'

'How do you know that such was his wish?'

'Ah, the *inianga* said so; the *inianga* knows that it is so.'

'Do you feel easier now?'

'Yes, by Dingaan!'

'But what if your dead brother asks for further sacrifices?'

'I shall make them until he no longer asks.'

'And if he is unreasonable in his demands?'

'That does not often happen.'

Calamities, according to these people, are a certain sign that the dead brother requires the blood of a cow, an ox or a bull. If a boa python happens to make his way through a *mouzi*, this is seen as an indication of the requirements of the dead brother; the boa is even seen as a manifestation of the brother. The Amazoulous do not kill the snake; they respect it although they do not worship it, for they worship nothing, believe in nothing, except the power of their dead brother whom they cannot describe any better than I can.[1] I dare to hope that no one will be so absurd as to attempt to elevate this superstition to the status of a religion. However, there are men so obsessed by stereotypes that, to confirm their own beliefs they will endeavour to prove that all the peoples of the earth have a religion of some sort, based on the assumption of there being one god – or even several – whom they visualise according to their own perceptions.

On the 29th I set out, leaving my camp unguarded in the belief that I could trust to the honesty of the Amazoulous. My way lay north-north east. I spent the night at a *mouzi* not far from the place where I had once killed one of the biggest elands I had ever seen, which I later exchanged for a pot of beer. I was so thirsty that day that I would have sold my birthright for a drink, if I had come across somebody who wanted to buy it.

The next day torrential rain prevented me from leaving the *mouzi*. The day after that, although the rain was not over, boredom, and the

---

1 Ethnologists might well profit by these observations which I am happy to pass on. Certain negroes of the west coast of the Congo and of Guinea, worship a snake which they call 'divine boa' and which may well be no different from the boa python of Natal, believed by the Cafres, from what I have seen, to be their dead brother or his messenger. Is it not remarkable that, although separated by so great a distance, peoples of different races and customs should attach a similar idea to the same creature which, unlike the sun and the moon, possesses no qualities that might be expected to stir the imagination, but which is venerated nevertheless? Might one not conclude from this that the Cafres belong to a race of men which originated in the north and spread into the eastern parts of southern Africa only a few centuries ago?

12

smoke which made my eyes water, drove me from the *mouzi* at daybreak and I reached Om-Ghet-Janne's place about midday. It was a bad time of the year; the last of the summer heat, which showed no signs of abating, offered only the relief of intermittent cloudbursts. These extremes of climate contributed to our discomfort.

On 1 April we could do nothing. On the 2nd we scoured the country for five leagues around; we found neither elephant nor spoor. On the way back I killed a buffalo which we shared with our hosts. The 3rd was once again a day of enforced inactivity. On the 4th we had no more success than on the 2nd; my men and I, wearied by our unprofitable endeavours, returned to Om-Ghet-Janne's, planning an excursion further north beyond Om-Kouzi. To his great regret, we took our leave of Om-Ghet-Janne on the 5th, as soon as it was day. One or two of his men accompanied us. Before long we crossed the Mona.[1]

As we progressed, we came upon cultivated fields; *mouzis*, poised like crowns on hilltops. were growing more numerous; the population seemed denser, which indicated that the Mona valley was much sought after for its fertility and its agreeable location. This piece of land, seven leagues long by a half, or sometimes only a quarter, of a league wide, supported 25 000 souls.

I mused upon the happiness of these simple people. Here I would build my thatched cottage with bare white walls and bid farewell to the civilized world, taking with me only gun, powder and shot. The water of the Mona, and sometimes the innocent *tchouala*, would be sufficient for my needs for a hundred years. At home, I would have peace; further off, but not too far away, there would be activity – elephants, buffaloes, rhinoceros, all there for the taking. Nothing could be simpler than to realise this dream. To obtain Panda's consent would present no problems. Just as my dreams were growing more substantial, we passed by a *mouzi* which had been overturned and partially burned.

This was the work of Panda. The sad evidence of this deed was there before my eyes and quickly changed my ideas. My country house crumbled, my future happiness was dashed before it could materialise; this was not the place where I could live free from oppression. Six weeks previously, a band of loyal Amazoulous had fallen upon the *mouzi* at daybreak, killing all who tried to escape. They set fire to the earth where thirty families were living; the chiefs and the headmen lay dead upon the ground. The anger of Panda must be appeased. This bloody deed was the means to an end; the

---

1 The little river of Mona arises beyond the *mouzi* of Maputa and flows from north to south into the Om-Philos-Mouniama after passing in front of Om-Ghet-Janne's *mouzi*. It fertilises a rich valley seven leagues long.

anger was but a pretext; the real reason was that Panda coveted the cattle belonging to this chief, who was too rich for his own good. And no one denied Panda the right of inheritance from all those convicted of political crimes.[1]

By about three o'clock, we had climbed to the upper reaches of the valley. Here we crossed the Mona at the place where it flows over enormous grey-blue stones and we began the ascent of the steep rounded hill which was crowned by the *mouzi* of Maputa.

This chief, a man of the first importance among the Amazoulous, was away at the time visiting another of his *mouzis*, which lay three leagues off in a place that was denuded of forest, but rich in kaffircorn. Wishing to meet him as soon as possible, I set off in the direction which had been indicated to us. Two successive waterfalls on the Mona, each forty feet high, held us up for a while. We crossed beneath them to discover a country of pastures which had nothing in common with the country of mimosas.

That evening, shortly before nightfall, I was shaking the hand of Maputa who welcomed me with every appearance of pleasure. He offered us an abundance of good things, while apologising for not presenting me with a cow for supper. His cattle, he said, were too far off, apart from which, he was obliged to keep them available for Panda in case he should ask for them.

I was well aware that the manners of the white men in their dealings with the Cafres were never graced with this sort of delicacy and generosity and so I hastened to thank him, assuring him that I would have refused the cow even had he offered it to me because, if such a practice were to become known to the Boers, they would soon come streaming across the Amazoulou country, spending each night at the home of some great chief, with the sole intention of collecting a nice little herd of cattle.

The huts we slept in differed in their construction from the ordinary Amazoulou huts. They were thicker, warmer, and the door which was made of basketwork, closed hermetically and was protected by an overhanging roof. These huts seemed well suited to the climate in higher altitudes. As there was almost no wood in these parts, we were obliged to endure the smoke from fires made of dried cowdung which was used for heating as well as for cooking.

On the 6th, when we took leave of Maputa, he delegated one of his headmen to accompany me to see to all my needs, and most

---

1 I talk of men convicted of political crimes, yet there is no act of indictment and no trial either, I would have done better to have said 'victim' – victim of the despot's caprice. However, as the king always justifies these murders on the grounds that such and such a person has conspired against his life, or intends to desert his native land, the implication is that he is guilty of treason, a crime which in our society would be described as political.

particularly to raise a body of men to assist me in the hunt at Om-Kouzi. After we had journeyed for an hour, we came upon a great *mouzi* where there were many warriors.[1] As we entered the *mouzi* we saw groups of men and women standing about chattering excitedly. I was about to enquire what the matter was when I saw, stretched out on the ground, and tied to a stout pole, a long slender panther, its head covered with an *om-gobo*. It was dead, although blood was still flowing from several wounds. This is the story they told me.

The previous night, between eleven o'clock and midnight, the whole *mouzi* was asleep. In one of the huts, where a half extinguished fire was smouldering, lay three living creatures; a woman and her child occupied the upper end of one side of the hut, while a dog slept at the lower end on the other side; the door was ajar. A panther, which was prowling near the approaches to the hut, picked up the dog's scent and, lying flat on its stomach, crawled up to the door and put its nose inside. All was still; for a moment it hesitated; its prey was so close! It pushed open the door, the dog barked and the panther immediately fell upon it, tearing it to pieces.

On hearing the cries of the woman, who could not escape through the door except by climbing over the dog and the panther, which was all teeth and claws, armed men came running. This is the strange manner in which they dealt with the situation: The basket-work door was drawn shut and firmly secured; four men thrust their spears through it in such a way that the points, intersecting like bayonets, would prevent the animal from attempting to remove or open it; the men remained outside, each holding another assegaai in his right hand in case of need. At the same time, an opening of ten or twelve inches in diameter was made at ground level on the left side of the upper part of the hut and, to illuminate the work, fires were lit all around. The mother and child were soon pulled out half dead with fright, and the rescue-hole blocked up by means of straw mats and sticks. Now the panther was alone inside the hut with the dead dog; it could be heard throwing itself against the walls in an attempt to tear them down and escape.

The Amazoulous turned the animal's despairing rage to their own advantage. A hundred, two hundred, *omkondos* were thrust between the slats of the framework of the hut, their sharp converging points confronting the furious creature. Some of them it pushed aside with its paws, some it succeeded in breaking, but a good number wounded it and when, enraged and howling, it rushed at the door where the

---

1 The *mouzis* which are situated near the northern borders of the country are larger and more densely populated to enable them to resist attack from the enemy tribes of the Amasouazis or the Makazanes.

light beckoned, the four men waiting there ran their spears through its forequarters. It had already received a hundred wounds, not to mention the fact that its eyes had been put out, when, with a terrible leap, it impaled itself through the heart.

I did not simply invent this tale as a diversion. I saw with my own eyes the woman, the child, the panther and the weapons used to kill it. I even inspected the bloody site. What is more, I brought back the skin and the head of the intrepid beast as a memento of the resourcefulness of Maputo's people.

When I had heard the story, I approached the group and asked why the panther's head was covered with an *om-gobo* and why they had taken the trouble to tie the animal so firmly to a stick with its legs crossed.

'It is so that we can carry him to Panda,' they replied.

'But why should you do that? Can this really be of interest to Panda?'

'Yes, to be sure. Whenever a panther, a cheetah or a lion is killed, the animal is always carried before Panda who is well pleased to be assured that his people are courageous and know how to use their weapons.'

'But from here to Panda's place takes more than three days, maybe four. The heát is great, putrefaction is rapid; the animal will arrive quite rotten. Take my advice; remove the skin, it will be easier to carry and Panda will be able to make use of it.'

'Yes, that is true. But such is not the way of the black man. How would Panda be able to judge the proportions of the animal from simply seeing the skin?'

'Well, by appearances of course, it is easy.'

'He does not wish it thus.'

'But what will he say when you lay a stinking carcass at his feet?'

'Panda? Panda will say . . . well, he'll say . . . he'll say: "It is good, I have seen. Now throw it far away, it smells bad." Then he will ask to be told the story, and he will give a cow to the one who killed the animal . . . or maybe he will not, if such is his pleasure.'

'So, you are going to exhaust yourselves, and all for nothing perhaps?'

'We do not know.'

Then I asked Maputa once more if I could take the skin, with the firm promise of recompense. While he was making up his mind, I had already set to work. Afterwards, we pushed on to Zimpy, which we reached the same evening. Zimpy means iron in the Zoulou language. Here we found the blast furnaces, the forges, the workshops where the metal is wrought from the local ore which is sufficiently rich and abundant to prove attractive one day to European manufacturers.

The inhabitants of Zimpy and the surrounding territory had

resisted Djaka at the time of his conquests. In spite of their courage they had been obliged to give way before a people who were both numerous and disciplined. Many of them fell beneath the onslaught; the rest, who had taken refuge in the bush, remained hidden for as long as the prince's anger prevailed, and when they returned to reconstruct their *mouzis*, having submitted to the rule of the victorious king and intermingled with his subjects, these people found that their cattle had been taken. Furthermore, Djaka forbade them to own cattle, with the intention of compelling them to live by the manufacture of iron for which they were to be paid in cereals only and not in reproductive kind, which required labour.

Djaka had a continual need for quantities of iron for his frequent wars and by these means he was assured of an ample supply, forged by his own subjects. The inhabitants of Zimpy and the surrounding territory were therefore obliged to support themselves by this industry which was as yet still in its infancy, as they had never aspired to progress beyond the achievements of their forefathers. At the time that I was there the yield was very low, but they had patience and many hands and so they produced more even than was required.

This is what I saw: In a special enclosure, twenty-five paces long by twelve paces wide, were three parallel pits, not far apart. They were oval in shape, six feet long, three feet wide and three feet deep. At the extremity of each, and passing underground, two tubes of sun-dried clay could be seen, which converged into one about a foot from the walls of the pit, creating the effect of forcing the compressed air towards the centre of the fireplace. Squatting on his heels between these two tubes was a man, pressing alternately with his left and right hands on two bags across whose upper aperture were attached two sticks, rather in the manner of certain crochet purses, while the lower orifice, where the air was expelled, was fixed on to a horn, so held as to conduct the air directly into the enlarged opening of the clay tube. When the fingers were spread wide, the bag, on being raised, filled with air which was expelled again when the man's fist was pressed down, forcing the air out from below. Such then were their bellows, imperfect certainly, and not sparing of labour, but sufficient to their needs. Four relays of six men each were constantly employed in manning the bellows. The work lasted from eight o'clock in the evening until its final completion at midnight.

The following day I enquired as to the result of the work and was informed by one of the smiths that they expected to obtain no more than ten pounds of iron, for the ore had been ill chosen; they had simply found it lying about on a hillslope and had not excavated for it underground.

Reckoned at the rate of a day's work in Europe, and taking into

17

account the preparations of one sort or another, not to mention the quantity of beer drunk by the workers, these ten pounds would have cost 150 francs to produce.

Patiently I watched them cleaning out the furnaces which were still hot. I saw each particle of iron, many of them in the form of droplets varying in size, being gathered up and set aside. The harder pieces were placed on a stone which served as an anvil and were flattened by blows from another stone. The softer pieces were placed on top, in order of size, and the insignificant bits were put in the centre. From all these pieces, balls were made which were then heated and beaten to form a solid lump; then they were amalgamated so as to present some resemblance to a rough ingot from which were to come picks, axes and *om-kondos*.

To judge by our standards, all this is not particularly ingenious at first sight, but for my part I, who had no idea at all of metallurgy, must confess that I received my first lesson from these people. Their skill in working the iron is worthy of note; their methods, however imperfect and crude they may seem, nevertheless enable them to produce some fine pieces. Their weapons are elegant; sometimes they will twist the four-sided shaft of an *om-kondo*; sometimes they will add as an adornment, a spiral of barbs which wound the flesh cruelly.

Several times I found myself admiring the superb workmanship of weapons which had simply been filed with sharp edged stones, but which looked as though they had been turned on a lathe, particularly when they had undergone polishing by means of sand and a thong made of leather or bark.

These sharp stones which I mention come from a green sandstone and are exceedingly hard. The Cafre artists, for want of a vice, hold the stone firm with their feet and rub the iron against the sharp edge, turning it all the while. They are so skilful and deft in performing this work that I found it impossible to conceal my amazement.

The headman who was accompanying us had, without my knowledge, sent out advance scouts, instructing them to wait for us at the ford on the Om-Kouzi. After walking for some hours, we came to the banks of the Om-Kouzane[1] which we soon left behind us.

We pushed on again and when we were within sight of the Om-Kouzi, some of the scouts arrived with the information that there were four elephants standing on the edge of a large open space near the river. We approached with the greatest caution to within eighty paces where it became possible to distinguish more clearly, and then

---

1 Diminutive of Om-Kouzi meaning the little Om-Kouzi. The Cafres believe that there is a kind of kinship between two rivers which run close together and which share a confluence.

18

we discovered, to our disappointment, that our guides had been completely mistaken, for it turned out that the elephants were nothing but four rhinoceroses which are similar in shape and gait. They were lying down when we saw them. When we were within sixty paces of them, they got up, extending their nostrils and flapping their ears in an effort to smell and hear. As we had not come looking for them, we passed them by, without firing a shot. Their worshipful masters[1] settled themselves down again. They were of the *rhinoceros simus* species.

A quarter of an hour later we had crossed to the opposite bank of the Om-Kouzi, where a large number of elephants had been seen, backed up against high sloping ground which was lightly wooded and dissected here and there by ravines. Unfortunately, while we were still 1 000 paces away from them, the animals fled in panic. However, the disbanding of the troop was favourable to us, offering us almost certain advantages, and it was after all not surprising that the mass had been excited to panic. Many of the females had their young beside them and in this condition their anxiety is extreme.

Owing to the lie of the land, one of the groups which had broken away was obliged to pass to within 200 paces of us. The animals were making for the river and, as the slope was in their favour, they went down it so rapidly that when we arrived on the scene we were too late; they must already have crossed the Om-Kouzi. We climbed back up the slope again to scour the ravines. Emerging into the open to get a clearer view of the surrounding countryside, we heard a heavy thudding sound, accompanied by thick clouds of dust. Unaware of our proximity, a body of elephants was bearing down upon us. The three in front were abreast and there were eleven in all.

I was the first to see them 'Elephants! Kotchobana! Boulandje! Look out! Get out of the way! They're on top of us! Fire point blank; don't be afraid.'

There were some bushes at hand and in no time we had taken cover. Thank Heavens! the elephants were quite unaware of our presence. But eventually, diabolical temptation got the better of us, and we succumbed to the irresistible desire to thrust our heads out from the bushes. It was only natural that we should want to establish our position in relation to the elephants before we fired; not only that, but we had the uneasy feeling that they were making directly towards us. Even if they did not trample us, these animals were quite capable of thrashing us with their trunks, and what a beating that could be! They saw us at last, when only twenty-five paces separated us, but by then, the impetus was too great, and all they could do to avoid us was to swerve away ten paces to the right. I laid claim to

---

1 A.D. uses a masonic title; he was a Free Mason. *Translator's note*

the first one and fired; he fell, collapsing on his knees. Kotchobana took on the second, which fell in a kneeling position on top of the first one. Boulandje fired; his elephant fell in a heap on top of the other two. And then, one by one, all the others were brought to their knees. My God, what wouldn't we have done with twenty, or better still, forty loaded guns?

'Stand by to reload boys; jump to it.'

But all we could do, was to collapse in helpless laughter at the ludicrous scene before us. What a time the elephants took to extricate themselves from the disordered and confused heap. I had ample leisure to fire a parting shot at the back-side of one of the last to leave.

One alone remained, standing upright, and apparently defying us. We saw immediately that he had been struck in the humerus; it was Kotchobana's elephant. I made four or five attempts to get him to face me three-quarters on, but each time, as if he realised what I was trying to do, he charged at me, and then appeared to change his mind for fear of falling. In order to succeed, I had to send Boulandje to create a diversion on the other side; then my bullet lodged in his brain and he collapsed like an edifice when the foundations are removed.

I can say in all truthfulness that, never in all my experience as a hunter, had I seen the sort of thing which I have just described. However I believe that animals which live together in herds tend to imitate their leaders.

Half an hour after this strange encounter, the memory of which gave rise to merriment for a long time to come, some Cafres positioned on a hilltop signalled to us that there were seven elephants whose proximity we had not even suspected.

'They are right here, close by. Can't you hear them moving about? Come on Kotchobana.'

He and Boulandje were on my left, while on my right there was a line of bushes which obscured my view; my men could see the elephants but I saw nothing. Without making a sound, we got to within twenty-five paces of them; I saw the rump of a large female turned towards me.

Disturbed, the animal began to turn her head around. I had anticipated the movement and, shouldering my gun, I was about to put a ball into the base of her outstretched ear. But I found that this would be impossible; the movement had been too sudden. By now the elephant had turned completely about and, confronting me with lowered head, prepared to charge.

'*Hahy om pondo*, no teeth!' shouted Kotchobana who, at the sight of imminent danger, had decamped at full speed, followed by Boulandje, both making extraordinary efforts to burn up the ground.

20

Completely absorbed by my elephant, I neither saw nor heard anything. I held my ground, took careful aim, and 'bang', I turned tail and ran.

'Did you not see, master? It was an elephant without teeth which you have just shot. Those are the ones which are wild and terrible,' Kotchobana said to me.

'No teeth, is it possible? I noticed nothing.'

'What, master?'

'I swear it is true. All I was looking for was the best place for my bullet.'

'And where did you hit it?'

'Right in the middle of the forehead, just above the root of the trunk.'

The next moment I was retracing the eighteen paces from where I was standing, to the place where the elephant lay stone dead. It was an enormous female and indeed toothless, known to the Hollanders as *poeskop*, which Levaillant translates as 'snubnosed', perhaps because it is impossible to find an acceptable word in French for this expression, although one encounters it in the common parlance of the people of Provence.

I went back alone to savour the pleasure of gazing upon my victim, counting myself fortunate not to have been hers, and I would have prolonged for some time still this hunter's delight had not a sudden shot rung out, only forty paces away, followed by a cry of anguish. Perhaps there were still more? In twenty leaps and bounds, I had caught up with my men who were calmly reloading, only two paces away from a fallen elephant which they had wounded in the shoulder. It was disgorging blood through its trunk which it was still waving about in the air, as if to grasp at something. Another one down to Kotchobana!

'What about the others?'

'Gone.'

'Far?'

'We don't know.'

'Let's follow.'

We followed for a long time. Tracks intersected each other all over the place. We were all growing weary.

'Where shall we sleep tonight?'

'At Zimpy, if you like, or else at Makaza's place, up there to the north.'

'That's it; Makaza's place. I prefer to see something new.'

We started on our way and soon came to a plain which we crossed. On our right was a wooded ravine; under one of the biggest trees, we could just make out something black which was moving about. The proportions were those of an elephant; that is in fact what it was, and

21

there were others nearby. Kotchobana begged me to let him go on alone; he said that he was quite sure that the animals were enormous and would need bullets of a sixth of a pound. I let him go, and from the fork of a tree I followed him with my eyes. Twenty minutes later: 'Bang!' – the biggest elephant fell. Kotchobana recharged; the animal got up and walked away. A moment later another one fell, got up again, and walked away as the first one had done.

I had noticed the animals separating and taking different directions. Without delay I went after them. I wounded five of them in succession without bringing a single one down. A female, followed by her young, unexpectedly charged me and I was obliged to take to my heels without firing. There were only ten paces between us when a branch, which tore at my face and my shoulder, almost put me at her mercy; only my legs saved me.

Finally, I withdrew from the chase while my men set off in pursuit of a large elephant which they had wounded and which was heading off towards the distant ferruginous mountains. As we were leaving the woods, my guide said, 'Master, there is an elephant behind us, going in the same direction.'

He was 300 paces away walking slowly along. Ahead of us was a ravine which must bar his way. The ground was bare of cover. I slithered down into the ravine and, crossing it, clambered up the other side, all the while observing the progress of the elephant which was making straight for the place where I was standing. Blood was streaming down the sides of his head from the wounds my bullets had made. He was an old growler, who looked as though he should have been wearing a kerchief tied around his temples, which would have suited him to perfection.

I let him come closer, and when I supposed that he was going to see me, I dropped down into the ravine, crossed the sandy bed and moved to exactly beneath the spot on the bank where he was going to stop; I was in fact only fifteen feet beneath the piece of earth which was about to support the animal. When he appeared above my head there were barely three paces between us. I had expected that his position would favour me, but in fact I was reduced to shooting him in the forehead; I had hoped to see his throat but, at that moment, it was protected by his trunk, and the best I could do was to put a bullet through the sunken bones at the top of his head. The elephant turned away in a wretched state, and walked off like a drunkard. Unfortunately, his pace was too rapid; he soon disappeared into the bush where the failing light of the declining day did not permit of pursuit. Perhaps, after all, it was fortunate for me that I had not killed him while he stood fifteen feet above me on the perpendicular side of the ravine; he might well have crushed me as he fell.

The five gunshots which were repeated by the mountain echoes,

22

led me to believe that Kotchobana must have some work in hand. And so it proved to be when he returned some time later with his inseparable Boulandje at his side. They had killed only one elephant, but it was a colossal one, more than twelve feet high, and the tusks each weighed sixty-five pounds.

After walking for two hours, we made a kind of triumphal entry into Makaza's *mouzi*, preceded by our four tails which had been cut from elephants freshly killed that same day. Anticipation of the fat that was to come, put smiles on the faces of these black people; it was already known that *our* elephants were of the finest quality. However, in spite of all the good will, Makaza and his people could offer me nothing more than sugar cane for supper. Although I found it delicious, it did not in any way satisfy the needs of my stomach.

The next day there was beer, maize and a great number of Cafre stews, and so much sugar cane that ten elephants could have satiated themselves without depriving me of my share. Each *mouzi* which had taken part in the cutting up of the elephants, felt duty bound to feed me, and so twice a day, each of them dispatched a long line of women, bearing on their heads dishes destined for the white man. My hosts were not displeased, as it meant that for some time there was no need to prepare any food at the *mouzi*.

The most obvious inconvenience resulting from this abundance, was the invasion of hundreds of millions of ants, attracted by the sticky remains of the sugar cane which we scattered about all over the place. It became impossible to lie for any length of time on the floor of a hut, because of the activity of these little creatures.

Hunting was resumed on the 10th. Six hundred men were to assist us as scouts and trackers, but their duties were not onerous for, within two hours, we saw, coming down the mountainside and spreading out into the bush, two separate herds of elephants numbering sixty to eighty each. It took us only a quarter of an hour to surround them and, finding themselves trapped between the walls of the valley on one side, and the hedges of men on the other, the animals soon began to grow restive. Then for two hours we set about them, like gladiators in the arena, retreating in the path of this one, attacking that one, leaving evidence of deep wounds on many. We had four hundred of our men drawn up in rows on the steep slopes, like Romans watching the Games, and each time that a troop attempted to find a breach, it was driven back by the *koluma* of the Cafre spectators. Buffeted about from one side to the other, the animals met with the same welcome wherever they turned. Foiled at every attempt, they grew impatient, and finally settled on a last resort, that of occupying the centre and staying there.

Panting and exhausted by these fruitless manoeuvres, the poor animals raised their trunks breathlessly in search of air. From time to time, jets of water spurted up from their midst, and fell in a fine rain on their heads, their ears and their backs, for the elephant, like the camel, keeps in reserve a certain amount of water for this purpose, as well as for the needs of his stomach.

We wounded many of them; out of twenty shots which I fired I must have hit at least six. Of the six, which I hit in the head from ten paces, three fell immediately, but got up again later. Kotchobana should have been rewarded with equal success but, with the greatest difficulty, he managed to get only one. Our powder was tainted; I did not hesitate to double my charge, which was already much too strong, measured by European standards, but no good came of it, for the next moment the chamber blew.

Let us picture for a moment, the partridge hunter who has inadvertently just shot away his ramrod, or else has forgotten his percussion caps, or some other indispensable thing. Obviously, it is a great disappointment to him but one which is easily remedied for, in civilized countries, percussion caps and ramrods are everywhere to be found. But in my case, it was very different; elephants are not partridges; an iron part is not as easily replaced as a wooden one and in addition to all that, I was forty leagues from my camp, which was itself seventy leagues distant from Natal, the only place where I could find some sort of blacksmith. Unable to repair my weapon, I turned away crestfallen.

A prey to gloomy thoughts, I went off and sat down on a rock from where I could see droves of elephants moving about on all sides. I watched without seeing, without wanting to see, as fifteen elephants came trotting towards us. A bank, eighteen feet high, virtually assured our safety, but I was, in any case, quite unmoved at the sight. A young Zoulou was by my side. Honest and brave and true, he had stuck to my heels all the morning.

'Master, do you see what I see?'

'My God, how provoking! Come on, Imphana, let's find lots of stones and pelt them.'

In a childlike act of desperation, we picked up lumps of heavy ore.

The elephants were filing past beneath us, only eight paces away, and we rained down our missiles on their heads, their ears and their backs, inflicting many a bump and bruise. If, at that moment, a stone had dislodged itself from the moon and gone clean through one of them, I would certainly have taken all the credit for myself; it would have seemed quite possible, considering the force I was using. I hit one near the eye and he frowned, which made me think that he must have felt it.

When the troop had passed by, our mood changed to one of wild hilarity; it was the best thing we could have done, to play wars like little boys, with the most sedate and serious of animals as the enemy.

It was just what I needed to divert me from the reality of my misfortune. I would have given ten elephant's teeth for a new chamber and some good powder. The episode may not in itself seem very important, but it is none the less the reason why more than one elephant is still alive and walking about today in the bush at Om-Kouzi.

Heavy rain came up, dampening the spirits of my men and making more difficult their pursuit of their prey. We met up with them at the Om-Kouzi and waded across the river up to the armpits in the fast flowing red-brown water. An hour later we were back at Makaza's place.

On the 11th, the day passed in fruitless pursuit of elephants. All we saw were buffaloes, cannas and herds of quaggas numbering four to five hundred. I watched a widow-shrike[1] with a long tail, which lives in noisy communities of seven or eight. I mention it because, when one travels from south to north, one's first encounter with the bird is on the banks of the Om-Kouzi. It is remarkable for its size, its long tail and its family life. This bird has a total length of eighteen to twenty inches, one third of which is accounted for by the body, while the tail makes up the other two-thirds; in the main it is black; the little coverts on the wings are white, as is the lower part of the back, down to the rump; a touch of white marks the big wing feathers, halfway along their length; the small feathers are white-tipped; the tail, made up of twelve feathers, is layered.

I decided, after all, not to visit the Om-Pongola river; the journey there would have meant walking for six hours and I had heard that there wouldn't be many elephants anyway. So on the 12th I took the road to Zimpy and got my men to beat the bush along the way. Three hours walking brought us to some forests, quite isolated from the plain, where rhinoceros abounded. Soon we came upon fresh elephant spoor and shortly afterwards we saw the animals themselves. Kotchobana and Boulandje set off immediately.

---

1   Further to my mentioning the long-tailed shrike, (*Melanoleucus*) I find it useful to associate the places which I visited with certain species which are still to be found there today; they are reliable indicators that will serve those who come after me - more constant and easier to remember than the names of mountains or rivers which disappear with the local population in the wake of some disastrous war. A traveller who explores new lands should, or so it seems to me, always proceed in this way; the route which he followed will be more recognisable to those who come after, and the distance which he travelled will not be contested. Personally I never neglected this attention. As a proof of the latitudes which I reached, I collected specimens indigenous to the area. I preserved them when I judged it to be necessary. I describe them and, with proof of this kind, I do not fear the expressions of doubt which have been richly deserved by more than one traveller: 'But did the gentleman really make the journey he has described?' - a remark which is quite in order these days when one knows of famous travellers who have written about things they have seen only in their dreams.

The sound of repeated gunshots made me regret bitterly the condition of my own weapon; but the compensation for the torment I endured was the unexpected opportunity for observations which I believe worth mentioning here and which I hope will contribute to the history of elephant behaviour. It is so difficult to establish details of the life of these animals in their wild state, that I consider it my good fortune to have been able to make these observations.

When the first shots were fired, a female, separated from the rest of the herd, found herself isolated and tried to rejoin the others. She could tell from the scent that men had recently passed that way or were still in the vicinity. For 500 paces before her, as she stood at the edge of the bush, stretched an open space. She set off to cross it with swaying gait, and we all said,

'An elephant. Here comes an elephant.' A Cafre standing beside me, the very one who was carrying my broken gun, said,

'Master, two elephants'.

'Where?'

'There', he said, pointing an index finger at the animal which was approaching.

'That's only one. Where is the other?'

'Underneath; open your eyes.'

Indeed, a young animal was walking along underneath its mother, between her four legs and she, to help her nurseling, had threaded her trunk beneath her body and attached it to that of her infant. Does this not bring to mind the picture of a woman holding her child by the hand? Of all animals, is not the elephant the only one able to behave in this manner? And nature has given her one excellent arm, furnished with only one hand but one with incomparable sensitivity of touch.

Kotchobana killed two elephants. Some of the men came to tell me, and I set off at once to confirm the news. The Zoulous said that they would go ahead of me to protect me from rhinoceros which might suddenly loom up in front of us. These men walked with raised spears, ready to strike any animal which approached too close. Having completed our expedition, we decided to return to Makaza's where we spent the night.

On the 13th we reached Zimpy. We had not bothered to look for elephants on the way because our ammunition was coming to an end. On the 14th we saw Maputa, whom I thanked sincerely for the efficient protection afforded us. On the 15th, we recounted to Om-Ghet-Janne the story of our success at Om-Kouzi. Our account seemed to displease him, for it appeared to him that we preferred these parts to Om-Philos-Mouniama. Om-Ghet-Janne feared that we would come traipsing across his *mouzi* each time that we wanted to hunt beyond it.

I must confess that I was already promising myself a return visit to the banks of the Om-Kouzi; but man proposes and God disposes; this present occasion turned out to be the last. Two of my men, Houahouaho and Nanana, sent by Henning, were waiting for me at Om-Ghet-Janne's to tell me that the Touguela was in flood and my wagon, which was on its way back to Natal; was unable to cross. This news was all the more disagreeable to me for I was already planning my next trip. Certainly, my presence at the scene could not hasten events, but the anxiety of knowing that my collection was in a tented wagon explosed to the inclemency of the season, determined me to set off as quickly as possible.

CHAPTER XXIII

I am the victim of theft — I lodge a complaint with Panda — Methods of investigation — Judges and justice among the Amazoulous — Panda's duplicity

By about five o'clock in the afternoon of the 16th, I had already covered eighteen leagues and had reached the high ground from where I could look down on to my camp. My anxious eye sought my tent and my storehouse, in short all the components of the dwelling which I had innocently entrusted to the loyalty of the Amazoulous. My tent had been overturned; it was possible that the wind had loosened the ropes. We hurried down to the campsite and found that the door of my *pondock* was open. It was soon apparent that all kinds of damage had been done during my absence. Everything pointed to the hyaenas as the culprits, and I was planning to take my revenge on them, when one of my servants brought me the leather thong to which the padlock was attached. It was made of strong buffalo hide and had been slashed in such a way that no hyaena could have been responsible. Everyone inspected it and all were of the same opinion, '*Knema py omkondo* – cut by an assegai'. I was in complete agreement.

Men of evil intent had come to rob me, or to do me some other harm. They had selected for their attack the things which mattered most to me – my collection of specimens; the skulls, the skeletons, the great birds which were still drying, even my big bustard, which I had left lying in a corner of the tent, had been pitilessly ripped apart. I could find only one of its wings, caught up in a thorn bush. There was more of malice in this act than the desire to acquire ill-gotten gains.

Having established the motive, I resolved to obtain satisfaction and retribution. But where to find the culprit? There lay the difficulty. 'No matter,' I thought. As I was Panda's guest, this was his affair. I must go to him with my complaint. However, I procrastinated for two whole days. Finally, the fear of another attack goaded me into action. I set off, and spent the first night on the far side of Om-grooty.

I arrived at Panda's *mouzi* of Sképèle on the 20th, and had the good fortune to be granted an immediate audience. I came straight to the point and informed Panda of the reason for my visit. He showed evidence of much astonishment and an even greater degree of disapproval at what had happened. Finally his indignation was such that, accompanying his words with a blood-thirsty gesture, he pronounced the brief and terrible sentence: '*Om-tagaty boulala*! Let the sorcerer be put to death.' It only remained to find him.

28

On the 21st I had another short audience with the king, during the course of which I observed that he was as much vexed by the fact that my camp had been rifled, as he was by my approaching him with demands that justice should be done. In addition, he was troubled to hear that I intended to leave soon for Natal; this information caused him particularly to frown, for he now found himself disturbed by more than one serious matter. He had recently received representations from Captain Smith, commander of the English observation corps at Hamgazy.[1] As my arrival in his country had been under the patronage of the Boers, he imagined that something had transpired in connection with which I was going off to inform the farmers. At the time I was unaware of this. Had I known, my conduct would have been more prudent and I would not have opposed Panda in any way.

'Go', he said to me at last; 'two of my headmen will go with you to Souzouana; they will find the culprit and justice will be done . . . but Souzouana has done wrong; he has failed in his duty and it is for this reason that I wish him ill. It was from his mouth, and not from yours, that I should have learnt of this misdeed.' Obviously Panda was taking advantage of every excuse to pick a quarrel with Souzouana, for Souzouana was guilty of a serious offence – that of being too rich.

I went away feeling vaguely dissatisfied, turning over thoughts in my mind as to where events were leading. Was it not obvious that Panda, for his own ends, intended laying all the blame on Souzouana? Souzouana had in fact predicted something of the sort. 'If you go and lay a charge with Panda,' he had said to me, 'it is I who will bear the brunt of his anger.'

To which I had replied, 'You are the chief, Souzouana; make some enquiries; find me the perpetrator of this deed, then go yourself and denounce him to the king; I will allow you time to do this.'

But the poor wretched man was convinced that Panda wished to destroy him. What use could he see in doing anything other than the one thing which would save him from death. And that one thing was to send all his cattle, down to the very last one, as a gift to the despot. Unfortunately, Souzouana was a Cafre, and never has any Cafre had the strength of mind willingly to make so great a sacrifice.

I was accompanied back to Souzouana's kraal by the two headmen appointed by Panda to perform the combined office of examining magistrate, prosecutor and presiding judge, I noticed immediately that they differed from other men in their bearing and manner. There was something in the general impression they made which struck me

1   Little river situated near the Om-Zimvobo on the Ama-Pondo frontier.

particularly, and I tried to analyse what it was. Gradually I realised that men of law among the Amazoulous are not very different from our own.

A high forehead, lightly lined by the habit of profound thought; strongly pronounced features which suggested weakness of body, along with strength of will, these were the characteristics which impressed me most at first sight. The eye was searching but inscrutable, the nose, flattened at the sides, flared out into highly sensitive nostrils which twitched delicately from time to time; the wide mouth rarely spoke, but when it did, the words were wonderfully well enunciated. But it was not the sort of eloquence which stirs the blood as do the passionate words of the warrior; it was a simple delivery, sober, calm, cold and doubtless very sound. The ears were large and set close to the head. One noticed that the muscles of the neck looked weak, and there was something spindly about the back of the head. The body, which was so thin that one could count the ribs, tapered off into two long, clumsy, weak arms on which the swollen veins were prominent, and terminated in two ugly withered legs which appeared to have no calves and which stood upon two big flat feet.

You will notice that this description is diametrically opposed to the generally accepted one of the Amazoulou Cafre, that great hunter and warrior – a fact which added further interest to my study of the judges. When they needed to squat down by the wayside to rest, they did so gravely, stiffly, after having taken a thousand fastidious precautions. When they rose again it was with difficulty; their movements were strained, their faces were contorted by the effort, while the other men moved from the crouching to the standing position as rapidly as a spring which is released.

And that is not all; these judges appeared to expect that every respect and attention should constantly be paid them; their bearing appeared to demand it. In these surroundings, where physical force is held in such high esteem, I was astonished to see that these men who, though still young, looked decrepit and broken-down, expected to have more honour paid them than was paid to seasoned warriors. It was as if they had said, 'Black men, in order to serve, we have sacrificed the strength of our limbs so that we might acquire a greater strength of mind. Let therefore our path be made easy for us. Make way.' And although one was tempted to laugh at their gaunt bodies and affected manner, everyone stood aside to let the Cafre judges pass.

I declare that the conclusions I reached at the time pleased me greatly; these were that in whatever country one may find oneself and among whatever people, the occupations men follow give rise to the same virtues and vices, engender the same habits, develop or destroy the body in the same way, with the result that one may easily recognise the herdsman, the soldier, the doctor, whether he be European, Chinese, Eskimo or Cafre.

When they arrived at Souzouana's, their first concern was to ensure that they were offered a cow and a great deal of *tchouala*. Souzouana neglected nothing to win the goodwill of these agents of Panda. Good weather was essential in order that the investigation should proceed for, under the despotic government of the Amazoulous, justice is not carried to private persons; on the contrary, it is the private persons who gather at the scene of the trial, which is chosen by the officials in charge.

The 26th, a day of fine weather, witnessed the gathering within the enclosure of the *mouzi* of all the men, both young and old, from three leagues around. Two thousand persons were present, all of them men, because it was deemed impossible that a woman could commit a crime.

The men of justice began by asking whether anybody was absent, but no one was missing. The entrance to the enclosure was shut. In a few brief words, the purpose of the gathering was officially announced and after the matter had been explained, a question was asked to which each man without exception was expected to reply. 'Do you know of anything which has a bearing on the present matter? If you know anything at all relating to it, you will answer "*vouma*". If you do not, you will say "*naba*".' Do not forget that, by his silence, he who knows something renders himself as guilty as the perpetrator of the crime'.

A great number of '*nabas*' had already been returned, when it came to the turn of one of the sons of Souzouana. '*Vouma*', he said. All eyes were immediately fixed upon him, and more than one mouth was agape. The young man pointed his finger at Phétéganne, the son of Om- Kamtinganne, chief of a neighbouring *mouzi*. Phétéganne, prior to the date of the crime, had held a conversation with him during which he had enquired about the period of my absence. He had remarked on the ease with which one could gain access to my storeroom and take what one pleased, and gave an indication of his intention to do so. Further investigation established that, on the day the deed was done, Phétéganne had left his hunting companions without explanation, that on his return he had not been able to give good reason for his absence, and that articles which belonged to me had been seen in his possession.

Phétéganne's relatives and neighbours who were present, indicated to him by their reproaches how his unworthy conduct angered them. He was seized, pinioned and taken into one of the huts, where his limbs were bound. A messenger was immediately despatched to Panda to inform him that the man responsible for the crime had been discovered. '*Om-tagaty boulala,*' said the judges, and everybody went home.

The 17th was a rainy day; nothing happens among the Amazoulous on those days, not even executions. But on the 28th, as the sun was shining brightly, ten of Om-Landelle's warriors took hold of Phétéganne and led him to a narrow valley close to their *mouzi*. Once there, they did not delay in performing their task. Phétéganne had already admitted that he alone was responsible for the plunder. He reiterated his confession while being tied to a tree and, with no sign of emotion, he watched the warriors step back fifteen paces to form a terrible semi-circle in front of him.

Then three times were the *om-kondos* with their quivering shafts raised in the air and three times were they hurled at the body of Phétéganne, piercing it through. Phétéganne was dead, put to death for housebreaking, a terrible punishment for so slight an offence, but in Panda's domain, there is no prison, no bastinado, nothing but death, whatever the degree of the crime. And I can assure you that there is no other country in the world where thieves are so few.

Panda had said to me when initially I approached him, that he did not believe in the truth of my accusation, because he did not understand how any thief could exist in his kingdom. Subsequently, he said that he only believed it because I was white and because I could produce proof and witnesses. While continuing to insist on my rights, I nevertheless tried to persuade Panda to employ other means of doing justice. I pointed out that his system of capital punishment exceeded reasonable limits, and that each execution deprived him of a warrior capable of rendering him good service. 'As for that,' he said, 'the white men have often told me the same thing. They wish to change the ways of black men, but they cannot offer an effective alternative. A man is bad, so I put him to death, not only for himself but to prevent the contagion spreading. Would you like me to have a big hole dug and put him into it? He would have to be fed, and that would impose a burden on others. The painful life that he would lead down in the hole would make him even more bitter towards his fellow men and, if he managed to escape, he would be ten times more wicked and he would do ten times more harm. When a criminal is put to death, everyone is reassured. As for depriving me of a warrior, as you say,' and here Panda began to laugh pityingly, 'my men, my warriors, as everybody knows, are more numerous than the locusts; and when a locust falls to the ground, does anyone notice his absence from the swarm?'

I admit that I could find nothing to say in reply because, in order to alter customs of this sort, it would be necessary first of all to remodel the whole system and consequently to heap upon these people the same burdens as civilized nations must bear. And so, in order to avoid one simple evil, however great, one would probably end up producing a thousand complicated ones. For it is a debatable question whether civilisation brings advantages to peoples who have previously contrived to manage with few virtues but who have proportionately few vices either. What profit would there be in increasing the proportions? None at all surely. Consider the physical aspect: everyone knows that the simplest life is the one which suits man best. Well, will not civilisation destroy this simplicity? Civilization introduces these people to a thousand comforts, a thousand delights of which they have no need, since they do not even suspect their existence. This is the luxury which beguiles, the cup of honey offered to the fly. Civilization will also bring a thousand maladies in its train, that dreary procession which follows on after the advantages. Weigh up the pros and cons and consider them well, then tell me whether it would not be better that our proffered moral and intellectual gifts should be refused. Would not we Europeans readily give up the luxuries which had their origins in the two Americas, in order to be free of the ills which accompany them? Why then spread the corruption? Seemingly reasonable excuses are made, I know. England, above all other nations, wishes to appear philanthropic; she likes to call herself so, but believe me, philanthropy is no more that a cloak she wraps herself in, the better to conceal her ambition. Her commercial interests, continually seeking outlets, are the only real motive. And if England could find any clear advantage in wiping a million savages off the face of the earth, she would probably do so. She expands abroad simply in order to reap the profits; it matters little to her whether she has a right to the gold or whether she spills the blood of the people. Her only consideration is profit.

Justice having been done as Panda understood it, I put my collection of bones and my hunting equipment in order, and left my camp in the care of Kotchobana, Boulandje and Djantje, hoping to be back in as short a time as possible. Souzouana, whom I saw as I passed through his *mouzi*, indicated to me in wild gestures and astonishingly rapid speech how much my departure affected him. This man, who was as a rule so sensible, seemed to be suffering from a kind of delirium. I attributed it to the excessive consumption of *tchouala* and I begged him to go and lie down until he felt better.

'Not at all,' he said, 'you are mistaken. Panda has explained his intentions towards me in such a manner that there can be no doubt. These are his very words: "My heart tells me that Phétéganne was not the true culprit, but Souzouana." You see then that Panda wants to have me killed; he will kill me and he only awaits your departure to do so. You are leaving; well, go then and when you return Souzouana will be no more.'

The atmosphere at the *mouzi* was one of general consternation, but still I remained persuaded that the *tchouala* alone was responsible for inflaming all those heads. My belief was further confirmed when Baye-Bank, one of Souzouana's sons, approached me, This young man, who was drunk with despair, was holding an assegai in his right hand, and in his left hand, four assegais covered by a shield. He began addressing me from some way off, for he had much to tell me. He hastened towards me, foaming at the lips as he spoke; he gesticulated a great deal and reinforced his words by thrusting the point of his weapon against my chest.

'Come young man – you too have drunk too much *tchouala* this morning. I will listen to you no longer, because you are talking nonsense.'

At this point the assegai was thrust at me, but I pushed it aside with a *tonga* which I was using as a walking stick. Several men then took hold of Baye-Bank from behind and relieved him of his *onkondos*.

'Come on – Nanana, Houahouaho, all these people are mad; let's go – Goodbye Souzouana, *Sani-Gouschleg* – keep well.'

'Keep well – ah yes, keep well,' he said with a look of despair.

'Today you may well say "Keep well" to Souzouana, who will be killed by Panda tomorrow.'

These were the last words that I heard from good, brave, hapless Souzouana, words which echoed with so melancholy a sound for many a day in my heart. Even today, I cannot recall them without pain. Shortly before Souzouana repeated that Panda would have him put to death as soon as I was gone, I had said to him, 'If you are so sure of it, come with me and take refuge in Natal.'

To which the brave old man had replied, 'What? Me? Take flight? You want Souzouana to run away? Do you think you speak to a woman? Souzouana has never turned his back on danger and, certain as he is of the fate which awaits him, Souzouana will remain here. It is here that he will be run through with an *omkondo*, right here in front, in the chest. Souzouana run away? Never!'

So I left Om-Philos on 30 April and on 2 May, after a hard journey, I reached the *mouzi* of Nonglas where my wagon was waiting. But from that time until 25 August 1842, when I returned to my camp, there was to be a series of events which belong to the history of Natal and which had a great bearing on the fate of that country. Although these historical events are not my principal concern. I believe it will be of some use to tell of what I learnt, sometimes unfortunately, at great cost to myself for my dwelling was situated almost half-way between the two camps, right under the pathway of the English cannon balls flying overhead.

CHAPTER XXIV

The Touguela in flood — My wagon held up on the bank — My return to Natal on foot — On the way I learn that the English have taken possession once more — Claims and rights of both parties — War breaks out — The Conguela affair — Defeat of the English troops — Capture of the point by the Boers — The camp besieged

After I had inspected my collections and spent two days at Nonglas's *mouzi*, I decided to try and cross the swollen Touguela whose waters were running twenty to fifty feet deep as they flowed rapidly down to the sea. I made up my mind to do this in spite of urgent representations from Panda, who despatched more than twenty headmen to beg me, and finally to command me, not to return immediately to Natal. Having made up my mind to cross the river, I built a raft of dead wood and, at the risk of drowning myself as well as Houahouaho, who could not swim, or of being snapped at by crocodiles, I launched the frail and spongy craft. Houahouaho was clinging to it like a monkey, for he had never been upon the water and did not realise that it was possible to float. When the worm-eaten wood became waterlogged and started to submerge, he cried out in fear, 'We are sinking; we are drowning,' which put me quite out of countenance. It is true that the water had risen up to our waists, and that the twenty-foot poles, which I had intended we should use to punt across, had turned out to be too short. We were drifting rapidly with the current and drowning or crocodiles might well have proved to be our fate.

But never have I been able to tolerate howling, particularly when it is inspired by fear; weeping and wailing dishearten even the bravest. I felt that I had need of all my strength, my composure and my resolution. I don't know how it happened, but Houahouaho, the howler, was whacked on the head with a stick. I assured him that it was quite unintentional, but this accident, whatever the cause, might well have saved us both, for Houahouaho stifled his wails and I was able to concentrate on paddling. Before long, I felt my pole touch bottom and we were soon able to set foot on the shore, even though we were at least 1 500 paces downstream from the spot where I had originally intended to land.

We had been lucky. When we disembarked, Houahouaho stamped three times on the earth, just to make sure that it was real, swearing that I would never catch him at that game again.

'Why were you so miserable just now, Houahouaho?'

35

'Ah, master, it was the water and the crocodiles. However manly you may be, it is possible that you may drown and be eaten up by crocodiles, or else you are eaten up before being drowned. What can you do about drowning and crocodiles, hey, tell me that?'

'Well, as for drowning, you can learn to swim, and there is a way of dealing with crocodiles.'

'What way is that?'

'You make them let go by poking your finger in their eye.'

'Master, I have seen you in the water; you are not afraid of it; you swim like a fish; but if you were swimming and some crocodile came along and caught you by the leg, I would like to see you poking your finger in its eye.'

In fact, the lesson I gave Houahouaho was only what I had read in some book or other, where it was claimed that a certain tribe of people practise this method of escaping from the jaws of the crocodile but, like my friend Houahouaho, I have always doubted the possibility of attempting it in the water. As soon as he has snapped closed his jaws, the crocodile, in order to submerge his prey, delivers a blow with his tail which is so quick and powerful that it would be impossible to attempt such a manoeuvre, even supposing that one were able to preserve one's composure.

In the course of subsequent conversation about our famous crossing, Houahouaho said that he wouldn't much mind being killed on land, but that he shuddered at the idea of dying in the water. In fact, the Amazoulous are rather hydrophobic; very few of them can swim and not one of them will touch food from the rivers or the sea.

An hour later, we came to the *mouzi* of Koudou, who welcomed me like an old friend. His first words were to inform me of the arrival at Natal of the English from Hamgazy, under the command of Captain Smith. There were 250 troopers and 60 wagons, drawn by 600 oxen, driven or accompanied by 250 servants who were mostly settlers from the Albany district, or frontier Cafres.

This news pleased me rather at first because I hoped that the English would enforce respect for the law at Natal, but once again, as on a thousand other occasions, I was to be proved wrong. Koudou also told me that his people were waiting to see the English and the Boers come to blows, so that they would know who was to be master of the land at Natal.

I, too, found a certain excitement in anticipation of the encounter. Having just waged war against animals, I was now about to see men doing battle; perhaps I would even take part in the events which would flare up within a matter of days. Without having thought much as to which side I should give my allegiance, I nevertheless welcomed the idea of playing my part.

Two days of rapid travel brought me from Touguela to Port Natal.

There I found everything in an uproar; the Boer women were inciting their husbands to fight and these cold men, suddenly stung into action, had begun to feel the stirrings of enthusiasm. Already there had been a few skirmishes. Captain Smith had set up camp on an open plain 800 metres from the bay, near some little marshes, and when he began building some makeshift shelters for his soldiers, Pretorius, the Boer commander, thought fit to call upon him to cease doing so.

Captain Smith, who styled himself commandant of Natal by the grace of Her Majesty Queen Victoria, would not recognise Pretorius, let alone comply with his demands. Pretorius, whose full complement of reinforcements had not yet arrived, protracted the ensuing negotiations to great lengths for he was not in a position to enforce his demands. During one of these parleys, Captain Smith complained of the affected manner in which the Boer horsemen came prancing and caracoling around his camp, and stated firmly that he might find himself in the position of having to drive them off with gunfire if Pretorius did not maintain order.

Pretorius agreed to this demand and having once shown compliance, he found himself expected to make further concessions. Captain Smith asked that the village of Conguela be evacuated, but this Pretorius refused to do. Notwithstanding the agreement, the Boer horsemen, in defiance of the *rooye-baatjes*, continued their visits to the English camp which they encircled, prancing and capering as before. Provoked by this insolent challenge, Captain Smith set off from his camp with 100 armed men and two pieces of artillery to march on Conguela and dislodge the Boers. It was three o'clock in the afternoon.

Long before the English emerged from the bush through which the first third of their route led, the Boers had had word of their advance. They despatched forty of their number to the scene to confront the English detachment, whose red coats contrasted vividly with the green background of the vegetation The English called a halt, and battle lines were drawn. All was in readiness to form a square, protected on either flank by one of the six-pounders. The Boers also halted, but in a disorderly manner. A man bearing a flag of truce was dispatched to Captain Smith, who sent him back immediately, demanding to see Pretorius in person.

Such was the state of affairs when I reached Port Natal. During the days that followed, Pretorius, emboldened by the arrival of reinforcements, increased his demands; not only did he forbid the English to build their huts, but he requested that they decamp forthwith and march away from the territory of Port Natal, leaving their arms and ammunition behind them. This proposal was accorded the reception it deserved.

The next day, in revenge, Pretorius refused to read a letter from Captain Smith because it was directed simply to 'M.H. Pretorius', without the title 'Commandant'. Captain Smith, forseeing that confrontation was inevitable, resorted to the methods of the press-gang to obtain the provisions he needed from the local traders; rice, flour, sugar, coffee, all were commandeered without permission. Many people were displeased by the brutal manner in which this was done.

I was at home one fine morning (23 May 1842) when 150 Boers, who had turned my house into their guardhouse, made off with 600 draught oxen belonging to the English in reprisal. Cannon shots were fired after the raiders, but without success. Later more cannon balls whistled over my cottage and the noise struck terror into the Boers who had never before been exposed to such fire. The show of force on the part of the Boers was a serious insult to the English flag and could have been interpreted as a signal to begin hostilities.

In reply to the demonstration, Captain Smith brought out the greater part of his force but then, fearing that they would be drawn into an ambush, he changed his mind and ordered them back.

'That's all right,' said the Boers who were watching unobserved, 'the redcoats are only showing off'. When night came the Boers, wary as schoolboys after a prank, took care to post look-outs and to send out scouts. At the time I was a mile from my house visiting some Germans. Our conversation turned on the events of the day; we all predicted that before long the English would try to take their revenge and we all began to think about protecting our property. I wondered whether I should be out visiting when I ought to be at home where I had a thousand things to look after. Half an hour later I arrived back at my house to find a number of horses tied up all around the verandah. My rooms were full of people; the floor was strewn with sleeping men and there were stacks of guns in the corners. My first reaction was one of extreme irritation. I had the strange impression that my home no longer belonged to me. If they had only asked, I would have consented without hesitation, and perhaps even with pleasure. The sleepers had helped themselves to fifty cotton blankets which had arrived that very day and which I intended for the Amazoulous. Another reason for my displeasure was that my bed was occupied by two men who were certainly sleeping there more comfortably than they would have done in their own.

As defensive of my rights as I had been when I was a sailor and someone was occupying my hammock, I would happily have seen them all keel-hauled. Unfortunately, all that I could do was to haul off the blankets they had wrapped themselves in and bundle them out. There were eighteen of them, but the job was quickly done and without further ceremony I showed them the door.

Every man is master in his own home and I intended to be the only master in mine, but to make sure that I would be obeyed, I took up an excellent double-barrelled gun which I intended to use if I encountered any violent opposition. Confronted with such eloquent persuasion, no one said a word and they all went out. As the horses which were tied to the verandah posts were stamping restlessly, I cut them loose without any concern for the anger of their masters.

Baart Pretorius, a brother of the commandant-general, who was in command of the guard-house, angry that I had turned him out of my bed at the double, had the audacity to come to me and make reproaches concerning my improper behaviour towards my guests. My only reply was to forbid him to approach my house if he did not want to risk being shot, and I added that I had already noticed that a number of my things had disappeared. 'Just wait until tomorrow Baart,' I said to him, 'when we will know who the real master of Natal is going to be; whether it is Pretorius or Smith, justice must be done. You in your capacity as commander of the outpost will be answerable for the theft.' And I went to bed, alone in my house except for my Cafre Houahouaho who had been very much disturbed by all the cannon fire that day.

For the first time, he found himself in a country inhabited by many white men, all of them armed and all of whom talked only of war. 'Strange people,' he said, 'when they open their mouths it is to utter the name of their enemy; it is to say "strike, shoot, kill, destroy everything". Their horses stamp with impatience, and blow through their nostrils. When the cannon fires everything trembles and the big cannon ball, which no one can see, roars through the air and falls so far away that no Zoulou would believe it. Master, will we soon return to Om-Philos?'

In the eyes of my savage, these white men were much more barbarous than the Amazoulous appear to the eyes of the European. About midnight, I heard the crackle of gunfire, drowned by the rumble of a cannon and I thought I was dreaming of the events of the previous day. Three times I told myself that it was only a dream but the noise grew louder. I sat up and listened; it was anything but a dream; there could no longer be a doubt; they were fighting; it must be at Conguela.

Unconcerned, as usual, by business that had nothing to do with me, I turned over; but half an hour later I was awakened once more by another volley of gunfire which was even louder than the first. This time it came from the English camp. The noise went on until four o'clock in the morning when, tired out by the incessant firing, I at last fell asleep and slept until seven.

In the morning, the first men I encountered were some Boers, the very ones I had evicted from my house the previous night. Their greeting was far from amiable, in fact they showed signs of being about to shoot me. 'We are in times of war,' said one of them; 'in war it is permitted to kill; let us get rid of this Frenchman;' and he checked the priming of his gun.

'Careful, Oud-Keerl!' I said to him; 'you go too fast! In war one kills, it is true, but only when there is a risk of being killed oneself, by an armed man. Wait a moment while I fetch my gun. That is the only way acceptable to God.'[1]

For him and his comrades there was little advantage in the sort of combat I proposed, which was the equivalent of a duel. Equal opportunity in combat means nothing to the Boers. Anyhow, they were convinced that I was in the wrong, and my proposition was considered an outrageous defiance. One of them seized me by the collar, another by the arm. I could have overcome these two adversaries had not four gun butts been raised above my head to persuade me that resistance might not be profitable.

'You would not dare,' I said, looking them straight in the eye; 'you would not dare! It is possible that we might meet again.'

'Bah' said one. 'Tonight we have killed enough Englishmen to be able to boast that we can handle guns. Just keep on the way you are going if you want to join their ranks.'

I was sufficiently in possession of my wits to seize this opportunity. Beginning with an oath which was familiar to the Boers, I asked: 'Do you compare me to an Englishman? Have you so poor an opinion of a Frenchman that you would make a traitor of him? Do not presume to insult my nation; a bullet in the head would be as nothing to me compared to that insult, and either you or I would surely end up with a bullet in the head. Let go of me.'

Their hands had grown tired of holding me; I freed myself with a jerk and, as I remained standing where I was, no one thought of taking hold of me again. 'What was this business of yours with the English last night?' I asked with sudden interest. Eager to tell of their exploits, two or three of them started talking at once and this is what I learnt.

Secretly leaving his camp at about a quarter past eleven, with a detachment of 110 fusiliers and the two six pounders, Captain Smith set off for the bay by the shortest route. Intending to make his way along the shore near the margin of mangroves, he hoped to fetch up opposite Conguela or perhaps even to make his way around the settlement and cut off the Boer retreat. He believed that he would succeed because he acted under cover of darkness, and because

---

1 This was the turn of phrase which I was obliged to use; to speak of honour would be to use language which they do not understand, for their whole education is drawn from the Bible.

Conguela sheltered a number of women and children, he counted on the menfolk accepting any conditions that he chose to impose.

The Boers would never have suspected that he would march along the strand; Captain Smith and his troops would surely have passed unnoticed had it not been for the sharp sound of the hastily stocked ammunition wagon running into the cannon. A lone scout left his outpost to investigate the sound, discovered the English and galloped off at full tilt to Conguela where he gave the alarm.

The women and children were led off to a nearby clearing in the forest and twenty-five Boer marksmen were posted along the shore behind some isolated mangroves where they waited like hunters stalking a leopard. The English detachment was due to come by at a distance of 110 paces. There was a moment of expectation and then they appeared alongside. The silence of the night was shattered by a gunshot which was immediately followed by four others. One ox from each gun team, two soldiers and an officer fell beneath the fire; each shot had found its mark and had killed a man or a draught animal. As the teams of oxen had become involved in the action the cannons could not be moved and were levelled and loaded, after a fashion. The confusion was compounded; there was firing from both sides; but the first shots fired at the English had broken their morale. Their heavy return fire was ineffectual while the sporadic fire of the Boers found its mark without fail. A small boat carrying a mortar attempted to find a navigable channel in a bid to come inshore and support the English force, but its efforts were in vain.

Hardly had three minutes elapsed after the first volley was fired when the retreat was sounded. Realising that his company had been put to rout, Captain Smith availed himself of the services of his horse and was the first to arrive back in camp, leaving his men to extricate themselves as best they could and abandoning the two cannon without spiking them.

From then on it was every man for himself; floundering about in the sand and the mud, the redcoats soon found themselves threatened by the rising waters of the incoming tide. Almost all of them jettisoned their cartridge pouches and many of them their muskets as well; some of them, fearful of finding their way through the mangroves, made for the open water and were drowned.

As far as the Boers were concerned, the opportunity was superb, but if the truth must be told. their commandant was foolish and cowardly and inept. He could easily have cut off the fugitives' retreat without striking a blow and taken them all prisoner. By these means he would have obtained his objective without delay but this he failed to do. With the arrival of reinforcements, one might have expected this kind of success and who could say whether England, mortified by constant set-backs, would not have abandoned her unjust action against the emigrants who, after all had only come there to avoid making revolution in the Cape Colony.

Thirty or forty minutes after the débâcle, the Boers formed a semi-circle around the English camp, fired some shots, but did not attempt to take it by storm. The firing continued without interruption until four o'clock in the morning but it was largely ineffectual. A few more of the English were killed and one of the Boers fell – their only loss that night. This is an exact account of the events as told to me at the time.

On 25 May, the Boers, tired after the activities of the night, called a halt to their harassment of the English in their camp. Captain Smith was able to write his report to the governor, Sir George Napier, in which he stated that of the 138 men, including officers, under his command at Conguela, thirty-four had been killed, sixty-three wounded and six were missing or drowned.

For a first attempt, the Boers must have considered themselves to have been successful beyond reasonable expectation; accordingly they were forever thanking God for his part in it, and calling themselves his chosen people; had he not performed the same miracle for them as he had for the Hebrews? Had not the waters closed upon their enemies? If I had dared to tell them that the tide always came in twice every twenty-four hours, they would have blown my brains out. This only goes to show that there is nothing more stupid in this world than a people which allows itself to be ruled by superstition.

At that time there was a ship in the bay: it was the *Mazeppa* with a cargo of supplies and arms for the troops. Nothing had occurred to disrupt the unloading which had gone on since the ship's arrival. Communication between the camp and the Point remained open, watched over by twenty-five men under the command of an officer. Half the cargo had already reached its destination when the Boers began to realise that what was indispensable to their enemy might well be of use to them.

During the night of 25 to 26 May, 100 Boers left Conguela and made their way stealthily to the mouth of the Om-Guinée thence to proceed along the shore to the Point, having given the camp a wide berth to avoid detection. When they were still two kilometres from the sentry post at the Point they entered the bush which lined the shore. Here they were obliged to crawl slowly along on their stomachs and, one behind the other like a long snake, they slithered towards their objective. For more than half an hour they lay within reach of the first sentries, holding their breath and taking care not to rustle the smallest twig until daylight came,

At first light they shot the sentries. The alarm was given; the Boers burst out into the open and fired at the first of the enemy troops who appeared. The cannon returned their fire at point blank range but it was badly aimed and the grapeshot rattled into the upper branches of the trees and was lost. Resistance was impossible and the English soldiers, along with several townsmen of the same nationality, took refuge in a large stone battlemented building where they intended to make a stand and sell their lives dearly. The Boers had already taken some prisoners; those who subsequently tried to escape were shot down in full view of the refugees within the stronghold whose resolution crumbled at the sight. Called upon to surrender, they opened their doors and thirty-five men gave themselves up to the mercy of the Boers.

That same day, these men were dispatched to Pieters-Mauritz-Burg where the soldiers were well treated while the civilians were not. As it was important to the Boers that the *Mazeppa* should not be allowed to leave, they dragged her anchors ashore. This was a miscalculation. The Boers know nothing of ships; they did not think of removing the rudder and, when the *Mazeppa* was ready to go, it got under way without the slightest difficulty.

This was the signal to surround the camp; the cannons captured from the English were turned against them; the transport of supplies continued, but this time it was the Boers who benefited at England's expense, while the besieged troops were reduced to living off dead horses.

This state of affairs could well in time have given rise to very serious consequences had not an Englishman called Richard King, who had lain hidden on board the *Mazeppa*, risked his life carrying the news of the disaster to Graham's Town.

Up until 25 June, 651 cannon balls had been fired on the camp by the Boers; they struck a number of wagons which would always be repaired by the next morning. A single sortie took place; the English succeeded in dislodging some sleeping rustics from a trench, but in the end their losses exceeded those of the Boers. In spite of this they described their action as victorious.

By now the Boers were growing weary of making attacks which never seemed to produce any results. This was because they had too little military science to attempt more effective methods and too little resolution to act more forcefully. Consequently, an ignoble, cowardly and base request was addressed to me by one of their number after an agreement had been reached with the majority of their council. This man was under orders to request, but not to insist, to be prudent and discreet so that if needs be the matter could be denied. To fulfil this charge, he thought fit to have recourse to a third person, and chose to this end a German called Krockmann, who then approached me in the performance of an unpleasant duty.

I was to hand over to the Boers certain poisons which I used in preparing my specimens: arsenic and corrosive sublimate which they knew I kept in considerable quantities. The plan was to throw ten or fifteen pounds of these dangerous substances into the spring near the camp which provided more than half the water consumed by the besieged troops. Even if they did not succeed in poisoning them they would at least have the advantage of having brought about such a shortage of water that the enemy would be forced to surrender.

I need hardly say how repelled I was by such a proposition. I had, however, sufficient self-control to hide my true feelings.

'It is a capital idea,' I said to the go-between. 'I bitterly regret not having by me a sufficient quantity to have the required effect. My poisons are at Om-Philos where I shall be needing my whole supply for the large amount of work which I have on hand.'

It was a lie which I told to help me out of a difficult situation. In fact I had at home a store of seven pounds of arsenic and two pounds of corrosive sublimate which, early next morning, I hurried off to throw into the reeds. I scattered to the wind the white powder whose action, had it been used, could not have failed to produce the most disastrous results.

CHAPTER XXV

Arrival of the frigate *Southampton* and the schooner *Congh* — The Boers are demoralised — Plunder of Conguela — Appeal to the Cafres by the English — The treaty signed — Act of submission — Amnesty with exception — Retrospective glance — Cause of the Boer emigration from the colony to Port Natal — Their leader Retief — Their dealings with Massilicatzi — Authentic documents — Dingaan treacherously murders the men of the deputation — Massacre of Boschjesmans Rivier — Revenge taken by the Boers on the Amazoulous — Steps taken by the English government — The *punishment bill* proves the English had no right to these territories

During the night of 25 to 26 June, after many attempted attacks by the Boers and a fair amount of patience on the part of the English, a signal of salvation appeared in the sky; a rocket filled with sparks of hope rose up into the air, huge and majestic, at the very moment that the sound of a powerful cannon shot rang out; it was the English frigate *Southampton* which was approaching the anchorage in the roads, laden with men burning with the desire to liberate their compatriots.

The faces of the Boers dropped; they were going to have to deal with these men who were not only fresh but numerous, a very different proposition from the skeletons in the camp. They were dumbfounded, for confronting them was the prospect of having to abandon their dream of an independence which they were already abusing. At the English camp, on the other hand, the joy must have been great; to escape from their prison of sand and the incessant whine of bullets; to see food and water again in abundance and not be obliged to eat the flesh of crows, this was surely a prospect to keep more than one Englishman awake.

When daylight came, two ships were in the roads: the frigate *Southampton* and the schooner *Congh*.[1] Up until two o'clock in the afternoon there was no sign of anything happening. The tide was rising, although there was still not much water, when a sail appeared coming in over the bar and making for the port channel. Thirty Boers were guarding the Point and many more should have joined them but due to fear and the lack of discipline, everyone did as he pleased and it did not please them to be there.

Two cannon were trained on the *Congh* whose decks were crowded with men, but in spite of the balls that rained down on the boats being towed along behind, the schooner continued on its way,

1 This was, of course, H.M.S. *Conch*. *Translator's note*

unperturbed, answering the fire with its two guns. Meanwhile the *Southampton* with its formidable battery, launched a number of missiles, the effect of which was to produce more terror than destruction. The entry into port, the anchoring, and the disembarkation took no longer than twenty minutes. More than one Englishman was killed, while not a single Boer was even wounded. When the danger became imminent, the latter, satisfied with their show of force, packed up and went back to Conguela.

It was now possible for the forces under Lieutenant-Colonel Cloete to join up with those under the command of Captain Smith. That same evening, the Boers took the wise decision to clear out of Conguela. Darkness covered their retreat, which they carried out in a disheartened manner, a strong contrast to their mood of the previous fortnight. Six hundred of them withdrew to a position six leagues distant from Port Natal from where they opened negotiations with Lieutenant-Colonel Cloete.

The most ardent wish of Captain Smith and his men was to wreak revenge. This was opposed with all the authority at his command by the colonel in charge, thus dividing opinion among the English troops. The fact was, that to lead the English forces twenty leagues inland from the coast would have been to expose them to the dangers of a sometimes rough and hazardous terrain. And there was no doubt that Pieters-mauritz-burg would be vigorously defended, for it was virtually a den of Boers; their families, their fortunes, all were there. Even before they reached their destination the British could be cut to pieces.

Whatever resolution would later be taken, the English needed to provide themselves with draught animals to haul the cannon and the ammunition wagons, should a move have to be made. With the peace not yet signed, this is the strange contrivance to which Lieutenant-Colonel Cloete resorted: a proclamation addressed to the Cafres was sent to the missionary Adams to be read by him to the natives on the banks of the Om-laas, the Lofa, the Om-Komas and at other places. As one of the three original documents came into my hands, I am able to give you an authentic copy.

All Cafres are requested to seize, wherever they may find them, horses and oxen belonging to the Boers and to bring them to the English camp where a recompense will be paid. This service will also merit the protection of the English forces. It is particularly requested of the Cafres that they do not use arms against the Boers except in cases where the latter resort to the use of guns to repossess their property.

This done at the Point of Natal. July 1842

Signed: A. J. Cloete Lieutenant-Colonel.
Dep. Quarter Master Gen, Commanding.

It would be reasonable to suppose that no Boer could calmly sit by and watch his herds, which constitute his whole fortune, being driven off, without resorting to the use of arms. Should this happen, the Cafre, who would be the real aggressor, would aquire the right to defend himself. This measure would be bound to have the effect of setting hitherto neutral natives against the Boers. Mighty England was reduced to this miserable expedient. In the pursuit of her own interests she put at risk the naked bodies of those who were not her own subjects; she incited to uprising the mass of black vultures whose eyes had long coveted the Boer cattle. But if it was an easy matter to unleash them, to restrain them again afterwards was impossible. And how laughable was this promised protection; the English military force was barely sufficient to ensure that the wishes of the British government were respected. What she was unable to do for herself, she promised to do for others.

To begin with, the excited Cafres spread out all along the approaches to Natal and whenever they found herds, they rushed at them as fiercely as wild dogs. The first they came across were undefended; their owners were friends of the English. Barely a quarter of these were driven back to the camp. The operation proved much more difficult with some of the other herds; bullets were fired and marauders were killed. Growing by experience more prudent, the natives turned to attacking at night; white families were murdered in fearful fashion and their herds were driven off. When the Boers recovered from their initial shock, they set out to find the large *mouzi* from which many of the attacks originated. During the night, forty of them surrounded this *mouzi* and when day broke and the black bodies began to emerge, one after another they were targeted and shot down. Sixty Cafres paid with their lives for the theft they had committed at the instigation of Lieutenant-Colonel Cloete.

Complaints were lodged by the Cafres. English protection was requested and the reply was that nothing could be done. Surely this was conduct unworthy. For my part, I judged it ignoble, and many Cafres today know what sort of trust they can place in British promises.

Lieutenant-Colonel Cloete succeeded in obtaining more than the number of teams he required for his purposes, but he took care not to march on Pieters-Mauritz-Burg immediately. By these delaying tactics he gained time, for the Boers, divided among themselves, and realising that resistance was impossible, finally agreed to accept the articles imposed by the English government.

As far as I know, no one has yet written down concisely and coherently an account of these events in the history of Port Natal, where for the first time, white newcomers were tearing each other apart against a background of virgin nature. I thought therefore that

I might perform a useful service by telling impartially what I saw with my own eyes and heard with my own ears. Believing also that the principal documents could be of historical interest, I present here the exact translation of two of them.[1]

Act of Submission

Pietermaritzburg, 15 July 1842

We, the undersigned, duly authorised by the emigrant farmers of Pietermaritzburg, Natal and the adjacent country, do hereby tender, for them and ourselves, our solemn declaration of submission to the authority of Her Majesty the Queen of England. And we do further accept and subscribe to the following terms that have been required.

1. The immediate release of all prisoners, whether soldiers or civilians.
2. The giving up of all cannon in our possession, those taken as well as others, with the munitions and stores belonging to them.
3. The restitution of all public and private property which had been confiscated.

Signed: J. Boshoff, P. Bester, P.A.R. Otto, C.J. van Heerden,
M.H. Marais, J. du Plessis, E.F. Potgieter,
W.J. Pretorius, J. Bodenstein, L.S. Botma,
H.P. Lombardt, J.H. Bruwer

President and members of the council

Acceptance of the act of submission, granting of pardon to the Boers; promises and non-disclosures of Lieutenant-Colonel Cloete.

Ratification of Treaty with Boers

Pietermaritzburg, 15 July 1842

The emigrant farmers of Pieters-Mauritz-Burg, Natal and adjacent country having by their duly authorised Commissioners this day complied with and fulfilled the several conditions required of them, namely:

1st   Entered a solemn declaration of submission to Her Majesty's authority.
2nd   The immediate release of all prisoners, whether soldiers or civilians.
3rd   The giving up of all cannon in their possession.
4th   The restitution of all public or private property.

---

1   The English originals of Delegorgue's translatation into French are reproduced here from Bird's *Annals of Natal* Vol. II p.64. *Translator's note*

I do hereby, acting under the authority of his excellency the Governor and Commander-in-Chief of the Cape of Good Hope, grant and ratify to the said emigrant farmers the following articles as agreed upon this day at Pieters-Mauritz-Burg.

1. A general amnesty or free pardon to all persons who have been engaged in resistance to Her Majesty's troops and authority with the exception of:

   Joachim Prinsloo, A.W. Pretorius, J.J. Burgher, Michiel van Breda, Servaas van Breda

   whose fate will be determined by the special consideration of His Excellency the Governor.[1]

2. All private property, whether of houses, goods or chattels shall be respected.
3. The emigrant farmers shall be permitted to return to their farms, with their guns and horses, unmolested.
4. The farmers shall be taken under protection against any attacks of the Zoulous or other native tribes.
5. The tenure of their lands shall not be interfered with but must be left for the final determination and settlement of Her Majesty's government.
6. The existing administration and civil institutions under acknowledgement of Her Majesty's supremacy shall not be interfered with till the pleasure of Her Majesty shall be made known. But those are not to extend any jurisdiction to Port Natal, which is placed for the present under the exclusive control of the Military Commandant of Her Majesty's troops, the limits of Port Natal being defined by the Umlazi to the west, the Umgeni to the east and a line along the ridges and crests of the Berea Hills joining those two rivers to the north.
7. The Kafirs shall for the present remain in the unmolested occupation of the grounds upon which they were on the arrival of Her Majesty's troops, subject to such future arrangements the Government may find necessary to make for general security.
8. All port and custom dues belong to Her Majesty and must be left at the disposal of Her Majesty's Government.

Signed: A.J. Cloete
Lieut-Colonel Dep. Qr-Mr-General Commanding

By command
Signed: W.J. D'Urban
Major 25th Regiment.

---

1   From Delegorgue's own addition and does not appear in Bird. *Translator's note*

Additional Article

In consideration of Mr. A.W. Pretorius having co-operated in the final adjustment of these articles, and of his personal humane conduct to the prisoners and his general moderation the amnesty granted in the first article is hereby fully extended to him.

Signed: A.J. Cloete
Lieutenant-Colonel Dep Qr-Mr-General Commanding.

By command

Signed: W.J. D'Urban
Major 25th Regiment.

And so there remained four men excluded from the amnesty and abandoned to the mercy of the Governor of the Cape. Lieutenant-Colonel Cloete did not choose to lay a hand on them, probably because an incident of that kind would have jeopardised the acceptance of the conditions. The four excluded persons were at liberty to escape at their leisure.

Sir George Napier thought that this was a serious mistake; an example should have been made to frighten the Boers. Apart from which, did not the shades of the soldiers killed in the war claim a bloody revenge? When the news reached the Cape, the English population demonstrated their fury in the streets. They loudly proclaimed that Lieutenant-Colonel Cloete was a frightened man who had been unable to take advantage of the victory; the conditions he had laid down were too lenient. News of a dozen men hanged would have brought a smile to English lips. When so much philanthropy has emanated from the heart, it may sometimes run dry! The governor, Sir George Napier, a fierce, blunt, weak-minded man, who still suffered from the loss of an arm at Toulouse, would passionately have wished to assuage his own ills with the comfort of knowing that the four outlaws were to feel the rope around their necks. The satisfaction which he would derive from the suffering of other men might perhaps, for a quarter of an hour, enable him to forget his wounds.

It was then that he conceived the amazing idea of putting a price on each of the four heads! To think that this sort of thing can still happen in our day! Our journalists could have known nothing of it at the time, or they would not have failed to publish it. I am performing a duty today by making public a textual translation of the astonishing proclamation of the governor, Sir George Napier. Have we French not had the whole of the English press on our backs because Colonel Pelissier resorted, at last, to the only possible means of overcoming the Bedouins who had taken refuge in the caves of Dakra. Is it not right and proper to draw attention to an act which is the more blameworthy for being unnecessary, particularly as he who dictated it was, at the

50

time, comfortably seated in an armchair, far from any danger and consequently in a state of perfect composure? This is the document:

Proclamation

By His Excellency Major-General Sir George Thomas Napier, K.C.B. Governor and Commander-in-Chief of Her Majesty's Castle, Town and Settlement of the Cape of Good Hope, in South Africa, and of the Territories and Dependencies thereof, and Ordinary and Vice-Admiral of the same, Commanding the Forces etc. etc.

Whereas certain subjects of Her Majesty resident in Port Natal and certain territories adjacent or appertaining thereto, did lately, contrary to their duty and allegiance, levy and make rebellion and war against Her Majesty and did thereby expose themselves to the pains and penalties of high treason:

And whereas for various reasons moving me thereunto, I did authorise and empower Lieutenant-Colonel Cloete, the officer commanding the expedition recently dispatched from this colony for the suppression of the said rebellion, to offer a free pardon to such of Her Majesty's subjects as should return to their allegiance, with the exception of such person or persons as he should find, from information to be acquired on the spot, had forfeited by their marked and conspicuous criminality all claims to share in Her Majesty's clemency:

And whereas Lieutenant-Colonel Cloete, acting under such power and authority, did upon the Fifteenth day of July 1842, grant a general amnesty or free pardon to all persons who might have been engaged in resistance to Her Majesty's troops and authority, with the exception of Joachim Prinsloo, Jacobus Johannes Burger, Michiel van Breda, and Servaas van Breda, whose cases were left for my special consideration:

And whereas, after maturely considering the character and circumstances of the said resistance, as well as the cases of the said persons last mentioned, I have come to the conclusion that the said persons shall, if possible, be made amenable to justice and dealt with according to law:

I do hereby proclaim and offer a reward of One Thousand Pounds to any person or persons who shall apprehend and lodge in any of Her Majesty's prisons or with the officer commanding Her Majesty's forces at Port Natal, the said Joachim Prinsloo, Jacobus Johannes Burger, Michiel van Breda, and Servaas van Breda; or Two Hundred and Fifty pounds for each of the said persons, who shall be apprehended and lodged in manner aforesaid.

GOD SAVE THE QUEEN

Given under my hand and the public seal of the Settlement, at Cape Town this 11th day of August, 1842.

Signed: George Napier
           By command of His Excellency the Governor.

Signed: J. More Graig,
           Acting Secretary to Government.

In order that no one should remain ignorant of it, this proclamation was posted up in all the public places at Natal in addition to being peddled about among the families of the outlaws who lost no time in sending copies to those whom it directly concerned.

These proceedings did not frighten them in the least; they knew that, even if a traitor could be found, they would be in no danger for a traitor would not have the courage to come forward. One of them used the proclamation to teach his young son to read. He gave him a lesson in patriotism at the same time, inculcating in him the first feelings of independence and emphasising particularly a horror of the English. Another had the proclamation framed and showed it to all his visitors; to some he said it was the finest chapter of his life; to others, who could not read, he said it was a most honourable letter from his friend Governor Napier. The remaining two outlaws, who were not of a witty disposition, simply lit their pipes with it. As for Sir George Napier, he got off with paying no more than the cost of the paper.

When the uselessness of this measure was recognised, another proclamation took its place, completely superseding it. Of course, the unavoidable granting of pardon was attributed to the gracious clemency of Her Majesty, who probably has not the least idea of where her country of Natal is to be found, although it was long ago baptized Victoria in her name. She would know even less about what sort of men live there.

We have seen how the Boers were treated as rebels, capable of high treason; now should we not examine the injustice of this designation? Let us go back to the beginning.

After the English occupation of the Cape Colony, the Dutch settlers did not take long to complain loudly of the prejudiced manner in which they were treated and the attitude of the new government towards them. The charge was well-founded but ineffectual. English protection was a meaningless word; the government even went so far as to forbid the colonists the right to protect themselves, refusing to hear their grievances, and often siding with the native tribes which had played the part of the aggressor, while condemning the plundered Boers whose burnt-out houses and murdered families cried out for vengeance.

In the exercise of this sort of philanthropy, the Boer was no longer considered a man. The situation was becoming untenable; people began drawing nearer to the towns to escape the plundering of the Cafres, with the result that, by about 1820, the eastern part of the colony, which was divided from the Cafre country by the Groote- Vish-Rivier, was denuded of inhabitants. This resulted in a depletion of the treasury, to remedy which a number of settlers were brought out from England. These people were scattered about in family groups, wherever there were springs of fresh water. As their numbers grew, towns sprang up; Port Elizabeth and Graham's Town date their origins to this time.

Some of the Boers now began returning to their former dwellings where they hoped to live in peace, finding security now in numbers. But the Cafres, who cannot resist the temptation to steal cattle when they see them in abundance, began making daily raids which continued for a long time unpunished. Eventually complaints were pouring in from both English and Dutch settlers to the governor, Sir Benjamin d'Urban, whose first duty it was to respond to them. The year 1835 saw 8 000 well-organised men, almost all of them mounted, pouring over the borders into Cafrerie and bringing back 50 000 head of cattle. Of this number a third bore the brand of owners who had taken part in the expedition.

These men reclaimed their property, but in spite of the benevolent attitude of Sir Benjamin d'Urban, the government took the lion's share which it sold for its own profit, without granting the least indemnity to the settlers who were thus twice dispossessed. This glaring injustice which could hardly be expected to reconcile the Boers to the English government, irritated them to the highest degree. But it was only later that their anger reached its peak and then it was concentrated upon a cause which was in itself praiseworthy.

When the liberation of the slaves became an issue, things started going very badly. The sum to be paid for the slaves was assessed at more than fifty percent below their real value. Recompense being payable only in London, agents extorted an enormous commission for their services, but not a penny left England. Instead of the money, the colonists were obliged to accept goods to the value of the recompense due to them.

In short, while English commerce was happy to make enormous profits, the colonist's share was no more than eight per cent. In addition he found himself obliged to pay dearly for the smallest task performed by the newly-freed men, who had grown arrogant to the point of insult. The land was no longer being cultivated and the Boers were forced to start thinking where they could go to escape persecution. I say persecution, for so it was; not only were the freemen, who were unused to liberty, placed on an equal footing with their former masters, but in each case that came before the courts on a charge of lack of respect or ill-treatment, the magistrate gave hardly a hearing to the witness for the defence, with the result that more than one white man was imprisoned solely on the evidence, whether true or false, of the black plaintiff.

To these charges were added others, too many to mention, which finally brought the exasperation of the Boers to a head. A revolution must inevitably have ensued but the Boers, religious in the sense that they read the Bible once a week, tried to find the answer to the question of whether it was permissible to rise up against an oppressive force.

Up spoke Retief, the descendant of an old French family which had emigrated after the revocation of the Edict of Nantes. Retief, who was distinguished among his peers for his fine judgement and his unaffected manners, weighed up the question on his own personal scale of values.

According to him, there was no choice; rebellion would give rise to a river of blood, after which the tranquillity sought by the patriarchs would be more elusive than ever. Had he so wished, Graham's Town, Colesberg, Port Elizabeth were his to command; within a fortnight their storehouses and their arsenals full of gunpowder, guns and cannon would be at his disposal. The Boers would have had arms to last ten years, which meant that they could have sustained ten years of war if the English did not withdraw their claims. And in the event of a reversal of fortune, beyond them lay the deserts of the interior. Retief was endowed with a great soul, a great heart and a good head; but too much delicacy made him incapable of turning against the power of the oppressor. This noble spirit saw the opening up of vast uninhabited lands, where the richest of vegetation grew tall and green. That was where their future lay; there at least, the Boers would spill only the blood of lions, while the blood of men would be spared.

Retief pointed towards those vast green lands and, trusting in this man of destiny, 17 000 souls, men, women and children, followed him. How powerful the influence of one man may be. He went, leaving behind many who grieved at his going, for Retief was loved as much by the English as by the Boers. There was great sympathy for his cause; prayers were offered up for him and his companions. Many English people shared these sentiments for it did not take much good sense to be aware of the increasing oppression to which the Boers were being subjected. These poor devils, sacrificing forever the sweet contentment of life in the land of their birth, ventured into the unknown, conveying their families and all their worldly goods on four wagon wheels, and driving before them their horned fortune. Their native earth was sprinkled with more than a few tears for she, the foster mother, was still beloved, although her breast had rejected them; other nurslings, ill-natured and foreign, had taken their place, elbowing aside the first-comers who were poor and simple.

They drew strength from their unity for they were all family and friends together. Together they read the Bible and their strength was reinforced, for they believed that they were God's chosen people, before whom lay the promised land far beyond the deserts, its gateway marked out by great columns placed there by the hand of the Creator.

This was in 1836. The Triechard expedition, which had set out in advance, sent back favourable accounts of the virgin land ahead, until then, innocent of the knowledge of white men. Retief, after crossing the great river (Oranje Rivier), followed in the tracks of the advance party towards Vaal Rivier, the yellow river. Not far from Zuyker-Bosch-Rand, mountain of the sugar bushes, he made a halt, dividing up his people into a number of parties, so that all might find pastures for the numerous herds which they had brought with them from the colony.

Those to whom the leadership of the various parties now fell were

Retief, Gert Maritz, Pieter Huys, Henderick Potgieter, W. Pretorius. Because of the season, they stayed on to allow their herds to replenish themselves. The country to the south of the Vaal Rivier was dotted with wagons and tents which one noticed only after first seeing the great herds of varying colours grazing on the wide carpet of green.

Massilicatzi, living on the banks of the Morikoe, not far from the springs of Malappo, far away in the north, Massilicatzi heard something of all this from his spies, and he looked with distrust on this influx of people. As he had no intention of accepting any settlement of this kind, even a hundred leagues away from where he lived, and as the opportunity seemed favourable to make off with many beautiful herds, and as Massilicatzi had taken a fancy to the idea of white women and white houses (tents), he decided to send ten thousand of his warriors against the Boers and to take them unawares.

Thirty-six Boers, with their wives and children, camped beneath the mountain now called Gevecht-Kop, had a few hours advance warning of the approach of a great body of armed men. They were not sure whether to believe this, but prudence suggested that precautions should be taken. Their wagons were drawn into a circle and chained together, and the spaces between were filled with thorny mimosa branches; guns were checked and munitions made ready. This was done in the dark and all night long the watch dogs barked their warning with unusual persistence.

When day came, every gully spewed forth black men of diabolic aspect; green Gevecht-Kop turned black. Everywhere along the rocky outcrop warriors were perched like crows. Below them lay the enemy, silently breathing, but for how long? Two flanks swept down from the mountain like two strong black arms, stretching out to seize their prey, and in an instant the camp was surrounded; the massacre was about to begin.

Fortunately for the Boers, only one regiment came in to the attack. With terrifying yells and wild gesticulation they advanced like a wave crashing on the shore, until the front line was broken by the first volley of gunfire, and they withdrew leaving behind a barrier of 100 corpses. Astonishment spread among the ranks that followed; there was a moment of hesitation and wonderment that a single bullet was able to pierce five or six or even seven heads. A second volley was rewarded with the same success, then the firing became more sporadic, for to defend several fronts, all at the same time, the Boers had had to divide up into small groups. Sometimes the Cafres came close enough to touch the wagons, in spite of the gunfire which continued unrelenting; while the Boers fired, the women loaded and the children passed the ammunition.

The attack went on for an hour and a half, with all those inside the camp exerting every reserve of strength and skill. All around, the earth was strewn with dead bodies. When the ardour of the Amadebelés had been quenched by their losses, they withdrew on to the mountain from which vantage point they could watch what was happening down below. The Boers were taking stock; the guns were washed, and the camp cleared of eleven hundred assegais which had fallen inside. The Boer losses were two dead and two wounded; several women had distinguished themselves by breaking the heads of warriors who had attempted to crawl into the camp under the wagons. More than six hundred Cafres lay where they had fallen. The bulk of the army, after having spent the whole day watching and rounding up the herds, left their vantage point after sunset to return to Massilicatzi, in fear of his wrath for they had failed to fulfil his command to bring back ten white women and ten white houses.

Other Boer parties had been less fortunate; families had been taken unawares and massacred. The survivors joined forces and went south to find reinforcements and to prepare for revenge.

A hundred and twenty leagues away to the south-east, lived another Cafre chief, a cruel and powerful despot; his name was Dingaan, king of the Amazoulous. Dingaan learnt of the bounty won by Massilicatzi and proceeded to pick a trumped-up quarrel with him, relating to the stolen cattle. Dingaan was angry that Massilicatzi had not shared the booty and, in spite of the severe winter which was setting in over the high country, Dingaan mobilised 25 000 men and dispatched them towards the Mountains of Quathlambène and beyond to Kuruichane and Mosega, to where Massilicatzi, his enemy, lived.

The Amadebelés, although they faced an adversary whose feet were cracked by the frost and whose naked bodies were shrivelled by the cold of the night, were unable to withstand the onslaught of the Amazoulou attack. They were defeated and lost many cattle. A few days previously, it had been the Boers who had come to avenge the atrocities and the plunder committed by order of Massilicatzi. The Amadebelés were overrun and 6 000 head of cattle were driven off by the Boers. Massilicatzi, gripped by fear in the wake of the Amazoulou expedition, hastily gathered together the remnants of his people and led them away to settle at the bend of the Oury or Lympopo River (Manice River) between 21° and 22° south latitude.

When this business was done, Retief struck camp at Zand-Rivier and went on his way towards the land of Natal, the promised land, which, after travelling seven scoften,[1] he glimpsed for the first time from the rocky summits of the Draak-Berg.

It took some time to find a practicable way down but, by dint of much effort, Retief was eventually successful. He watched over the descent of the long train of a thousand wagons as they slithered their

---

1   The schofte of the South African Dutch is the distance travelled in a day by an ordinary wagon drawn by oxen.

way two thousand feet down the escarpment, laden with families who were overjoyed that they had come at last to a land that was not only rich, but protected from their oppressors by two natural barriers.

They soon crossed a river of pure limpid water: it was the Touguela, and Retief made his camp not far from the source. From here, he pushed on as far as Huys-Doorn and finally went down himself to the bay of Port Natal to gather all the information relevant to his plans. Upon his arrival there for the first time on 19 October 1837, he met with Mr A. Biggar who had been entrusted, by the handful of English settlers living at Natal, with the management of their general affairs and of their private interests.

Retief was well received, and announced his plan of seeking an interview with Dingaan to discover the chief's intentions towards the immigrants, as well as to explain away any unfavourable impression that he might have received touching the Boer character. For Retief had got wind of the intrigues of the missionaries who had ready access to the ear of the despot. His letter to Dingaan gave some indication of his suspicions, which I subsequently saw confirmed by the Amazoulous themselves.

I have in my possession the whole of this curious correspondence, with all the principal documents concerning the events of the time; should the necessity arise, I would be able to provide proof of my submissions. Indeed, I would publish them all if I did not fear tiring those of my readers who have no interest in discovering the early history of Natal. I will therefore confine myself to the most important.

First letter from Retief to Dingaan

Port Natal
19th October 1837

To the chief of the Amazoulou

I seize the opportunity of the return of your messengers to inform you that my greatest desire is to have a personal interview with you in order to explain certain rumours, which might have reached your ears, touching the intentions of the party from the colony which desires to settle in the uninhabited country adjacent to the Amazoulou territory.

Our fervent wish is to live in peace with the Amazoulou nation. You will have doubtless learnt of the latest breach of our relations with Massilicatzi following frequent and disastrous raids carried out by his tribe in consequence of which, and after having made every attempt to settle our differences, it became absolutely necessary to declare war on him.

I shall set out in a few days for the Amazoulou country with the object of discussing our future relations. The hope of living in peace and mutual understanding with the Amazoulou nation is the sincere wish of your true friend.

Signed: Retief, governor, etc.

This letter was despatched to Dingaan after it had been read to Mr Biggar and a gathering of Natal settlers. These latter, with the intention of creating ties of friendship with Retief, and demonstrating to him their support, dedicated the following address to him in which, surprisingly, not a single missionary's name appears, although these people, as a rule, meddle in whatever is going on and try to exert their influence over public matters, with the intention of turning everything to their own advantage.

Address to Mr Pieter Retief by the English residents of Port Natal

We, the undersigned inhabitants of Port Natal (original settlers), welcome with sincere pleasure the arrival of a deputation from the emigrant farmers under Pieter Retief Esquire, their governor. We beg him kindly to present our good wishes to his constituents and to assure them of our desire to receive them as friends and, perhaps eventually, as neighbours and, above all, of our wish that a good mutual understanding should always exist between us.

Signed: Alex Biggar, John Kemble, J-D. Steller, W. Bottomley, Thos. Holstead, C. Pickman, H. Ogle, Thos. Carden, George Biggar, R. King, John Cane, Char. Adams, D.C. Toohey, F. Fynn

Retief, delighted to find the local residents so well disposed, replied to them as follows:

Port Natal
23rd October 1837

Gentlemen, after so flattering a reception as I have received upon my arrival at Port-Natal, there remains no reason for me to regret my arduous journey of forty-eight[1] hours in the saddle. With my hand on my heart, I declare that the sentiments expressed by you are those which I cherish also. I do not doubt that the Almighty, in disposing of events, will ordain that we should be united for our mutual happiness. If it pleases God, I hope, upon my return from seeing Dingaan, to enter into further communications with you. I remain, gentlemen your obedient servant and faithful friend.

Signed: P. Retief

To Biggar Esq. and other Signatories.

These documents will suffice to confirm that relations were harmonious between the Boers and the English settlers of Port-Natal.

---

1 Bird says 'ninety hours'. *Translator's note*

They will also illustrate how regrettable was the interference of the missionaries and what the effect was of their underhand dealings with Dingaan who, they hoped, would use the force of the Amazoulou nation to thrust back into the interior the Boers whose unexpected presence cast a shadow over their own machinations.

Without further ado, Retief went off to Ungunkuncklove (the great elephant) where Dingaan lived. Five days in the saddle brought him to this place. Retief was pressed for time, but Dingaan showed no inclination to discuss any serious subject on the first or the second day. Instead, the despot put on a display of national and war dances, performed by several thousand men. Only on the third day, did Dingaan agree to hear Retief; but no sooner had the leader of the emigrants expressed the hope of settling his people south of the Touguela, than Dingaan said to him: 'Retief, you must know that a great number of cattle has just been stolen from me. It has not yet been possible to find out who has done this. You and your people are strangers to me. Until now, I have known you only by your words which, I grant, reveal a pure heart. But what shall I reply to your expressed desire to settle close by my country when I know for certain that the tracks of my stolen cattle lead to the places whence you have come. Is it not right that I should delay my decision until further light should be cast on the matter?'

Retief and his men, who were perfectly guiltless of the theft, tried their best to prove their innocence and, when a description of Dingaan's cattle was given, the Boers recalled having seen some of them at the kraal of Synkoyala who lived at the top of Quathlambène. Retief, deeply concerned to absolve himself and to give Dingaan a proof of his sincerity, promised that he would not only bring back the cattle, but the thief as well, so that there could be no further doubt of the blamelessness of the Boers' intentions.

This promise was greeted by Dingaan with such joy that he offered to cede to Retief all the territory conquered by Djacka from Touguela to Omzim-Vobu, if he were fortunate enough to succeed in his difficult undertaking.

Before very long Retief was back, bringing Dingaan not only his stolen cattle, but Synkoyala himself, clapped in irons. This time, he was accompanied by seventy Boers, some thirty servants and 200 horses; it was 3 February 1838.

As there had previously been a correspondence between Retief and Dingaan whose scribe and interpreter was the English missionary F. Owen, and as these letters are in my possession, I believe it to be fitting that I should translate them here for the information of those who might be interested.

To Mr. P. Retief

Sir, the king desires me to inform you that he took from Massilicatzi the sheep which accompany the bearers of the present letter; that these sheep belong to the Dutch and that he is desirous of returning them to their proper owners; that his army took many others, apart from those that you see, but that they died by the hundred on the journey; that many more have died since they arrived here and that he sends you the skins. According to what he has been able to learn from a woman brought from Massilicatzi's country, there were only nine head of cattle belonging to the Dutch, which his army seized, and these have all died since they arrived here, otherwise he would have sent them to you. Om-Schlala, the *om-douna* who commanded the army, said that Massilicatzi fled with numerous herds, and he supposes that the greater part must belong to the Dutch. The king was much grieved by Massilicatzi's attack on the Boers. He says he does not expect all the sheep he is sending will arrive at Port Natal, because many of them will certainly die on the way. He says that he is very pleased with the letter which you sent him.

I am, sir, etc
  Signed: J. Owen. English missionary.

  + The chief's mark.

P.S. The sheep leaving here today number 110. The king is sending the skins, which he mentioned, as far as Touguela and he says, 'You can send a wagon there to collect them if you like.'

It is hardly worth mentioning that the missionary Owen was probably some wretched artisan from England who could find nothing better to do than to enlist in the legions of those who preceded the advance of civilisation. His awkward manner speaks plainly of the sort of man he is; at all events, I thought I should mention it, so that people might know the sort of sorry creature England sometimes chooses to propagate her ideas.

Here is another letter addressed to Mr. P. Retief, written for Dingaan by the same Owen.

Ungunklove 8 November 1837

Sir, In reply to yours of 24th October, this sets down the conversation which has just taken place. I am sorry to hear that you have suffered such great losses at the hand of Massilicatzi. I have taken from Massilicatzi a great number of your sheep etc. etc. (the contents of the first letter are repeated).

Now, as to the request which you have addressed to me concerning the territory, I am almost inclined to grant it you, but first of all, I wish to inform you that a great number of cattle have been stolen from me by men wearing clothes, riding horses and carrying guns. The Amazoulous assure me that these men were Boers, and that the raiding party proceeded to Port Natal; they now wish to know (the Zoulous) what they can expect.

Now, my greatest wish is that you should let it be seen that you are not guilty of the charges brought against you, because for the present, I believe you are. My request is that you should recover my cattle and bring them back to me and, if it is possible, you will also bring me the thief. If you do this, you will allay my suspicions and you will be given reason to believe that I am your friend, for I shall grant your request. I shall let you have sufficient men to drive the herds which you will recover for me, and this will remove all suspicion that the stolen cattle are in Dutch hands, and I wish also to give you men whom you could send back to me with reports. If any herds were taken that are not mine, I pray you to send them to me.

Witness: F. Owen

+ Chief's mark

To Pieter Retief Esquire, governor of the Dutch emigrants.

On reading these two letters, one is persuaded of the fairness of the Boer claims. Dingaan was master of the territory; having no need of it for his own people, he could dispose of it as he wished. One sees that he was brought of his own free will to surrender the land on condition only that the terms imposed on Retief should be fulfilled.

The following letter is the last communication from P. Retief to the king of the Amazoulous.

To Dingaan, king of the Amazoulous

Port Natal
8th November 1837

It is with pleasure that I acknowledge your friendship and your justness touching the flocks which you retrieved from Massilicatzi. I thank you for the skins which you have so kindly offered to return to me, but I wish you to keep them for your own use and profit. I have no difficulty in believing that so small a number of my cattle should have been retrieved by your army from the clutches of Massilicatzi for, having seen numbers of yours in various villages, I noticed none of mine among them.

Massilicatzi, I do not doubt, has fled far away, for he must believe that I shall punish him for his improper conduct. Have I not already grounds for complaint in that I have been constrained to kill so many of his nation simply because they executed his cruel orders.

That which has just befallen Massilicatzi leads me to believe that the Almighty, the all-knowing God, will not permit him to live much longer. God's great book teaches us that kings who behave as Massilicatzi has done, are severely punished and that it is not granted to them to live and reign for long; and if you wish to learn more about how God deals with evil kings like these, you can find out from the missionaries who live in your country. You may believe all that these preachers tell you concerning God and his government of the world.

Regarding such matters, I advise you to speak frequently with these gentlemen, whose wish it is to preach to you God's work, for they will teach you of how justly God has ruled, and still rules, over all the kings of the earth.

I assure you that it is an excellent thing that you have permitted preachers to settle in your country; what is more, I vouch for it that preachers have come to you because God put it into their hearts to do so, and they can show you from the Bible that what I tell you here is the truth.

As a friend, I must tell you this great truth, that all men, whether black or white, who will not hear and believe the word of God, will be wretched. These gentlemen did not come to ask you for land or cattle, even less did they come to cause you any sort of vexation, but only to preach to you and your people the word of God.

Now I cordially thank the king for his kind and favourable response to my request, and I hope that the king will recall his word and his promise when I return. You may be assured that I shall do the same. I believe it possible that, before I return, you will be made uneasy by warnings touching the request which I addressed to you and the promise which you gave me; and I believe it possible that further reports will reach the king's ears respecting me and my people, accounts which might have the appearance of truth. If you should hear such talk, I beg that you will tell me on my return who has spoken these things. I do not fear to meet, in your presence, any man who may have spoken ill of me and my people. My request is that you will not grant a hearing, before my return, to whomsoever tries to stir up trouble concerning the land where I wish to live.

As for the thieves who took your cattle, and what they have said, namely that they were Boers, it was a clever device to induce you to believe that I was a thief, so that they might escape with impunity. I am confident that I shall prove to the king that my people and I are innocent of this crime; knowing my innocence, I feel that you have imposed upon me a severe obligation which I must fulfil in order to prove that I am not guilty. As for this deed which you require me to perform, accompanied as it is by expense, difficulty and risk to life, I must be answerable to you, to the world and to God, who knows all.

I go now, placing my trust in God, who gives me hope that I shall be able to execute this enterprise in such a manner as to be able to give a satisfactory answer to all. That said, I shall await convincing proof that I am dealing with a king who keeps his word.

I hope that some of your men, particularly those belonging to the kraals from which cattle were stolen, will be instructed to follow me as agreed, and that they will obey all my orders promptly.

I thank you for the kind reception you have given me, in return for which I shall always endeavour to give proof of equal good will.

Yours truly

Signed: P. Retief.

62

P.S. I enclose, for the information of the king, an account of the people assassinated and the herds plundered by Massilicatzi: 20 white persons and 26 persons of colour massacred, among whom were 9 women and 5 children; livestock stolen from 27 persons: saddle horses, 51; breeding horses, 45; draught oxen, 945; breeding cattle, 3 726; sheep and goats, 50,745, and 9 guns and 4 wagons.

Signed: P. Retief.

Thus is was that, after having accomplished his difficult mission, Retief presented himself once more before Dingaan, whose promises he believed he could trust; so great was his trust that he had even prepared in advance the deed of cession which Dingaan had only to sign.

But although he knew that secret plots had been hatched against him and his people,[1] although he had, by all possible means, tried to deal tactfully with the sensibilities of the missionaries whom he knew to be capable of standing in his way, doing him great harm,[2] Retief was not sufficiently on his guard. This is a brief account of all that came to pass during that final visit.

It was the morning of Saturday 3 February 1838, when P. Retief and his party reached Ungunklove, Dingaan's capital. Before they entered, they enacted for the king's pleasure, a mock battle on horseback. This display appeared to afford Dingaan much pleasure and he was quick to express the wish to hear a volley of a hundred gunshots. Retief declined discreetly and Dingaan, appearing not to give the matter another thought, made a signal for the dancing to begin. This was a singular honour paid to the visitors and it continued unabated throughout Saturday and Sunday.

On Monday 5th, in the morning, Dingaan dismissed most of his regiments, keeping beside him only those made up of young recruits, the *abafanas*, and two élite regiments called Om-Schlanga-Om-Schlopu, the white shields, and Om-Schlanga-Mouniama, the black shields. The previous day, on being pressed by Retief, he had signed, before witnesses, the treaty by which he surrendered to the Boers all the land from north to south between the Touguela and Om-Zimvobo rivers and from east to west between the sea and the mountains of Quathlambène. The business seemed to trouble him keenly; sometimes he wore an unaccustomed glowering look which was observed by a young English settler who was living at the time at Mr Owen's house. This young man came to the Boers and expressed fears which had their origin in veiled

---

1 When Dingaan made enquiries about the Boers, Owen and Gardiner told him, 'These men have removed themselves from the authority of their king. They would not behave in this way if they were good subjects. They are tramps who would make dangerous neighbours. They will repay the good you do them with evil.'
2 This is apparent in his last letter to Dingaan.

and sinister words he had heard exchanged in the intimacy of the Owen household.

The Boers did not heed his words and William Wood, for that was the name of the young settler, withdrew into Owen's house. Owen took care not to appear but was a witness to the following scene from within.

Dingaan, on leaving his hut, went to the upper part of the *mouzi* and seated himself in his great armchair, carved all of a piece. His two principal regiments were ranged to left and right of him, with the captain of each standing on the side nearest the royal throne the better to receive and transmit the orders of the king.

A circle was drawn up and a message was sent to Retief, begging him to enter the enclosure and to bring all his party with him in order to receive Dingaan's messages of farewell. Upon receiving this request, Retief and his men, as well as his servants, entered the enclosure, all except for two men, who went off to find the horses. The guns were left unguarded under the two milk trees (*kooker-boom*) which stood outside the *mouzi*. As Retief drew near, the king said to him that, he must often speak the name of Dingaan, when he arrived back among the farmers of Natal and that he must tell them that Dingaan's greatest desire was to see them go out and take possession of the land which he had just given them. Then he wished Retief's party a pleasant journey back and without further ado, he begged them to be seated and to drink *tchouala*, an invitation which the Boers unfortunately accepted.

Retief was standing beside the king while the farmers and their servants were a little way off. Dingaan ordered his troops to sing and dance for the entertainment of the Boers. The air rang with warlike chanting and the earth shook beneath the stamping of feet.

The dancing had been in progress for barely a quarter of an hour, when Dingaan rose and began to intone a chant which was familiar to the Amazoulous but with improvised words which were completely incomprehensible to the Boers. Then came the last verse:

'Drink, oh drink down the beer; your burning gullets crave it;

Drink all you can; for tomorrow you will drink no more!

Come my warriors! Leap up, seize, hold fast! And kill, kill all these sorcerers!'

The terrible death sentence, *'Om-tagaty boulala'*, had been pronounced. Order gave way to scenes of unparalleled confusion. Ten Cafres pounced upon each Boer, quickly overpowering their victims who, in despair, whipped out knives and slashed about wildly. Twenty of the assailants were cut down in this manner but, at last, all the Boers were overpowered, by the weight of numbers. In their helpless rage, they bit into the naked bodies wherever they could find a place to sink their teeth.

Above the uproar of the sudden attack and the desperate resistance there rose a single voice, that of the tyrant. 'Take out the heart and liver of their king and lay them on the road by which the farmers came.'

The Boers were pinioned and dragged to a hillside 300 paces away where, in obedience to Dingaan's repeated order, the Amazoulous set about killing their victims, striking some of them on the head with tongas and breaking the necks of others by forcefully twisting their heads backwards. Only the body of Retief was cut open and the heart and liver, wrapped in a piece of cloth, carried before Dingaan. The corpses remained where they had fallen, with no one venturing to touch even their clothing.

When the killing was over, Dingaan's two favourite captains approached the king and talked to him at length; they were Schlala and Tomboussa. The outcome of the discussion was that a powerful contingent was dispatched to the wagon encampment at Boschjesmans Rivier, where Retief had left the women and children of his unfortunate companions. The order was given to kill everybody without exception, men, women and children, whether white or black.

The hideous pack, without taking time even to wash away the blood of the Boers they had just killed, stretched like a fearful black snake over the green carpet of the surrounding hills, uttering piercing yells, terrifying warcries, in anticipation of a repetition of the deeds they had done that day. But from Ungunkuncklove to Boschjesmans Rivier the distance is great and the rivers were swollen, so that the horrible black company was unable to reach its destination before the evening of the 16th.

On 17 February 1838, dawn was just beginning to break and all were still asleep in the camp when it was surrounded and invaded by 10 000 Amazoulous. More than one of the inhabitants, never to awake again, passed from sleep to death. The alarm was given; the victims' despairing cries, the piercing screams of the women and children, were mingled with the ferocious yells of their attackers. There was no mercy; the iron blade was wrenched out from the husband's chest, only to be plunged into the wife's bosom and then thrust through the bodies of the children. An immense tide of blood was flowing everywhere; black feet waded up to the ankles in the crimson pool, so that they seemed to be shod in red boots. Once assured that they were dealing now only with women and children, the savages took a cruel pleasure in running their victims through, slashing open the bellies of pregnant women while they still lived, wrenching out the fruit of the womb which they seized by the feet and swung against the iron wagon wheels to crack open the head. The mothers entreated their torturers to dispatch them with a single blow but no, this mercy was not granted them; it was only when the plundering was over and the cruel Zoulous about to depart, that they raised their bloody *tongas* once more for the final thrust.

All were pitilessly slaughtered at that spot where there now stands a new town, all that is, except for a young girl whom I later saw at Draakensberg. She had fallen beneath the dead bodies of her family and survived nineteen assegai wounds. Apart from a handful of men, 317 women and children perished in this massacre, and brought to 616 the total number of individuals of both sexes murdered by the Cafres.

The Amazoulous, covered in blood, but not satiated with carnage, then divided up into several detachments, the strongest of which set off to attack the camp at Blaw-Kranz-Rivier. But there, already resolutely waiting to meet them, were H. Potgieter, Jacobus Huys and G. Maritz. The welcome they received forced them to abandon all hope of victory and to retreat, leaving behind in the field 5 000 or 6 000 dead.

While all this was happening, 3 000 Amazoulous were trying to cross the ford on the Boschjesmans Rivier in order to reach a little camp and murder the inhabitants, who had only thirty-four armed men to protect them. All who attempted to cross the river singly were carried away by the strong current, which made the Amazoulous wonder whether perhaps it would be better to form a living chain. They noticed that the Boers did not fire at them while they were attempting to do this.

There sat the Boers on the southern shore, with their long guns carelessly lying across their knees, while from the northern shore a human chain groped its way through the water towards the southern bank where it would soon make contact, and thus have a firmly established link on both shores. This was the moment the Boers had been waiting for. Two shots went off, the two links were broken and the thirty or forty men in the middle, now cut adrift, were carried away by the current, sucked into a vortex, disappeared, and surfaced again before being finally engulfed. A few castaways climbed on to some rocks and counted themselves fortunate, but only for a moment, for they were soon shot by the Boer children. Two or three attempts were made by the Amazoulous to re-form the chain but, each time, those who made the link to the bank were picked off, resulting in the same disintegration as before and the same drowning.

Boschjesmans Rivier swallowed up beneath its fast flowing waters the bodies of more than 200 Cafres, and saved the 34 sharp-shooters from being torn apart by 3 000 Amazoulous.

No sooner had the news of the treachery of Dingaan and the ensuing disastrous events spread through the various Boer camps and among the English settlers at Port Natal, than indignation rose to fever pitch. The settlers of Natal gathered together some 1 000 men, Hottentot and Cafre as well as white, 250 of whom were armed with muskets, the rest with shields and assegais. This body of men was intended to invade the Amazoulou country by crossing the Touguela a league inland from the mouth. Meanwhile, the Boers had gathered together 340 men, all well mounted and well armed, who were to cross the Touguela in the upper reaches, twelve or fifteen leagues from the source.

Having of necessity to divide his forces, Dingaan could not but suffer a decisive setback, while the settlers and the Boers were confident of success. On 6 April 1838, the Boer commando set out under the command of Pieter Uys and J. Potgieter. When they crossed into Dingaan's territory, the Boers noticed that the country round about had been abandoned. It was only when they approached Ungunkuncklove that they encountered opposition.

There they came upon the Amazoulou army, 7 000 strong and divided into three divisions, which were posted at vantage points among rocks forming a semi-circle. The approach to the royal residence passed through a narrow gorge running through this semi-circle so that enemy warriors were on every side, ready to counter-attack. The third division was lying in ambush with the apparent object of closing in on the Boers if they entered the circle, and cutting off their retreat.

In spite of the huge discrepancy in numbers, the Boers resolved to attack without delay. They divided up into two, more or less equal, contingents which enabled them to confront two of the Zoulou divisions. At the first encounter, one of the Zoulou divisions was put to flight, but it seems that the rattling of assegais on shields frightened the Boer horses to such a degree that they could no longer be controlled.

This meant that the party under P. Uys was left to face the full impact of the Zoulou army alone. To their credit they stood their ground and, with their sustained and perfectly accurate fire, they sowed confusion among the ranks of the enemy; but then the Amazoulous, summoning up all their resources of courage, returned boldly to the attack and the gallant little company found itself suddenly surrounded on all sides.

Each Boer fought like a madman, while the tenacity of the Amazoulous appeared to increase in proportion to their losses. Attack rivalled counter-attack in their fury until, an hour and a half later, the Boers, realising that the danger was growing ever more pressing, decided to concentrate their fire on one point in the circle.

It was the matter of a moment; a breach was opened up through the wall of warriors and, urged to a full gallop, the horses swept through to the other side, with their riders firing from the saddle, as the boldest of their assailants continued to rain assegais upon them.

According to the lowest and most probable estimates, the Amazoulous lost about 600 men in this encounter, the bravest and most fiery of all, who, obeying the call of their hot blood, had been in the forefront of the attack. When the Amazoulous gave way before the irresistible thrust and the destructive fire of the Boer attack, Pieter Uys, accompanied by some twenty men, followed after them in hot pursuit, until he suddenly found himself in a gorge, surrounded by a great number of the enemy. By this time, only nine of his companions remained. Uys defended himself in the most heroic manner possible, with his young son aged twelve at his side, until the boy fell and he himself was nailed to his horse by an assegai which had pierced his thigh. After falling to the ground, exhausted from loss of blood, his last words were: 'Fight on my brave friends, until you force your way through the ranks of the enemy. As for me, I am dying.'

The Boers left ten dead on the field. As they retreated, they killed a number of the Amazoulous who were pursuing them. The Amazoulous, forced to abandon the possibility of further action that day, sent out seven spies with instructions to reconnoitre the position the Boers would occupy that night. Unfortunately for these spies, they were seen by some Boers from their position in a mielie field. Their retreat was cut off, not one was able to fulfil the mission on which he had been sent, for all fell beneath the Boers' bullets.

On the same day as this bloody business took place, the English settlers set off from the bay of Natal to support the Boers, albeit at some distance. On 16 April, they crossed the Touguela and seized many herds of cattle after defeating their owners. This party numbered between 800 and 1 000 which included 250 musketeers who were, in the main, Cafres. On the 17th, at daybreak, they found themselves surrounded by a large contingent of Amazoulous commanded by Panda. They had only just heard of the defeat of the Boers and the costly advantage won by the Amazoulous, which doubtless contributed not a little to dampening their courage.

The encounter was a bloody one and became even more desperate when Ogle's Cafres gave way and fled. For two hours, the gunfire reverberated from the distant hills. Then, after the collapse of the party from Natal, there was silence. Of those who had continued to resist, only 15 men escaped by casting themselves without hesitation into the Touguela, in spite of the crocodiles.

Thirteen Europeans, 10 Hottentots and 600 or 700 Cafres from Port Natal were killed that day by the Amazoulous, who themselves lost three entire regiments, each comprising 1 000 men.

Soon after this incident, 25 000 Amazoulou warriors set out for Port Natal where they spread through the countryside, plundering cattle and all movable property, and inflicting on their prisoners the cruellest acts of revenge.

Having been warned in time, the inhabitants were able to seek refuge on a ship which had recently entered the harbour, but the Cafres of Om-Guinée were less fortunate: hiding in the woods with their women and children, they were soon discovered. The men were simply run through with assegais, while the women were reserved for a cruel amusement; covered in dry grass, their arms tied to their backs, they were shut up in a kraal while the spectators outside threw burning coals at them. Driven to frenzied despair by the flames, their bodies

THE ENGAGEMENT ON SUNDAY 16 DECEMBER 1838

performed terrible contortions which the Zoulous called 'dancing' and which they regarded as amusing recreation, providing their hearts, which remained cruel and inhuman while the war lasted, with all the joy they were capable of feeling.

A few days after these disastrous events, there arrived at Port Natal two Boers, J. Uys and L. Badenhorst, who had been delegated to make arrangements with the settlers about combining forces, and to promise that two hundred of their men would be provided to protect the town. Five months later, the Boers and the Amazoulous, having licked their wounds, began to think again of getting to grips with each other and wanted only an opportunity to present itself. Then, moved by the dictates of noble philanthropy, as he always was, Governor Napier published a proclamation forbidding the export of powder, lead and firearms. He wished, he said, to stop the blood-letting, affecting not to believe in the possibility that the Boers were slaughtered by the Cafres for the want of sufficient arms. At the same time, he made shameful propositions to these very Boers, such as that they should return to live in the colony, where he promised them advantages they had never previously enjoyed. On 20 November 1839, as a further act of philanthropy, he sent Major Charter with 100 troops of the line, to prevent the Boers from taking their revenge on the Cafres. But, in reality, it was an attempt to take possession, a fact that was admitted to later by the commanders themselves, for, with their complete lack of means of locomotion, it was impossible for the English infantry to prevent the Boers from making war against the Cafres, if they wished to do so. Nor was it any easier for them to protect the Boers against a Cafre invasion. They were hardly capable of defending themselves in this sort of warfare, which was unfamiliar to them.

In spite of the protests of the governor, Sir George Napier, which were conveyed by Major Charter to the Boers, the latter did not remain inactive during the months of November and December 1838, and January 1839. Under the command of Pretorius, they entered Dingaan's country to wreak a glorious revenge and to make good their losses. After various encounters and a few skirmishes in which patrols shot a number of straggling Cafres who were real or supposed spies, the Boers arrived on 15 December at the foot of an isolated mountain near the Om-Siniaty (river of buffaloes). Nearby, meandering through the fields of tall grass, was a little river, known since as Bloed Rivier (river of blood). It was from here that they were to watch the famous sunrise on Sunday 16 December 1838, the greatest day in their history. They were ready to defend themselves for, since the day before, they had known of the approach of a Cafre army numbering 30 000 to 36 000 men. The atmosphere in the camp was not one of trepidation, for never before had the Boers been so united; there were 900 men, well-armed and resolute, trusting in the power of their guns and in the might of the cannons with which, this time, they had taken care to arm themselves. The countryside stretched clear away into the distance, without obstruction of rock or tree; the sky was blue, the air was pure, it was that last moment of the day before the twilight came. An advance party of scouts, thinking they heard a rustling in the grass, discovered that the Amazoulous were advancing in battle order, with a great captain at the head of each regiment.

The alarm was given just as the enemy moved swiftly into position to encircle the camp. The daylight was still sufficient to illuminate the attackers. The cannon opened fire, spewing out a hail of grapeshot which flattened in its path numbers of black bodies, sometimes as many as forty at a time. Then came the ringing report of the Boer guns, lodging their bullets with such deadly accuracy that the Cafres were disheartened.

This was the first encounter in which the Amazoulous had retaliated with firearms. They had taken the guns off the settlers killed at Touguela, but their ill-aimed shots produced no visible effect. The thousands of assegais streaking through the air would have inflicted much damage had a closer approach been possible; but the Boers had the advantage, whenever the attack grew particularly menacing in any sector, of being able to rake the vanguard with grapeshot.

When the battle had been raging for two hours, to the disadvantage of the Cafres whose dead littered the ground, the Boer commander, fearing that he could not sustain his attack for lack of ammunition, ordered a sortie, and a fight to the death, for their assailants must, at all costs, be routed before a cease-fire became inevitable.

This offensive was not without danger; it would have been infinitely safer for the Boers to remain entrenched, even were their fire to slacken off. However that may be, the attack, by its very boldness, was met with stunned disbelief by the Cafres; terror spread through the ranks, resulting in rapid retreat. Such was the relentless fury of the Boers that several lone horsemen, riding out after fugitives, pursued them as far as two leagues before shooting them down.

These fugitives, disbanded and wandering about at random, took advantage of holes, stones, a field of long grass, a river or a bank of reeds to attempt to conceal themselves and thus escape from their pursuers. The Boer children were the first to discover these hiding places. Some hundreds of Cafres tried to emulate crocodiles, or at least hippopotamuses, by submerging their bodies in the water up to their noses; hidden by a bank of reeds they hoped to lie concealed until nightfall when darkness would cover their escape. The discovery of this subterfuge was a matter of pride to the children. They wanted to be allowed to deal with the situation themselves but some of the men joined forces with them in cutting off the retreat of this new species of amphibian. The 'amphibians' dived at the sight of a gun aimed at their heads, but the want of air, that element so indispensable to the lungs, obliged them to raise their noses above the water. When the noses appeared, the heads got a bullet through them and sank, never to rise again. This is how several hundred Amazoulous died in the River of Blood which took its name from what happened there.

This method of dealing with the situation will probably appear inhumane to Europeans, but what were the Boers to do, considering that it was practically impossible to keep prisoners. Certainly, any European would have done the same in the circumstances. The count of the dead on the battle field was in excess of 3 200; the number of the wounded was unknown but must have been even higher. Such was the outcome of a few hours discharge of musketry on the part of 900 South Africans who owed their salvation to the shape of their guns, the charge they used, the nature of their bullets and to their undisputed skill in marksmanship.

After having crossed the Om-Schlatousse on the 19th, the Boers arrived on the 20th within sight of Dingaan's capital, which was still smouldering, having been set alight the day before on the orders of the despot as he fled. The *mouzi* was oval-shaped, 600 or 800 paces long, empty in the middle with, on the periphery, 1 800 huts arranged in rows, each of which was capable of housing twenty warriors.

On the 21st, the Boers set up their camp on the hilltop where, the year before, Pieter Retief and his unfortunate companions had been murdered. This sight filled each man with deep anguish; on that spot, the hatred which they bore the Cafres was revived, providing them with a powerful excuse for their ruthlessness. One of them wrote: 'The sight of the scene of torture, irrefutable proof of which lay in the bones of our dead relatives and friends, inspired the deepest horror in those of us who remembered them. We continually averted our gaze, for our hearts were full, and tears flowed from our eyes. It was all there before us, down to the straps of mildewed leather which had been used to bind them and which could still be seen attached to the bones. The splintered sticks and clubs which had been used to batter them we found by the thousand beside the pathway along which they had been dragged. These sticks were, for the most part, of the kind that the Amazoulous use in their dancing; others were of the sort they use in building their houses, or fencing their kraals. Among all the other skeletons and remains which were lying there, one could recognise those of the Boers by the battered skulls, as well as by the position in which they lay among heaps of the stones which the Cafres had used to put a final end to their suffering.'

The skeleton of P. Retief was recognisable by the tattered remains of clothing which still clung to it and, as if God had wanted to proclaim the right of the Boers to the land granted by Dingaan, one single object lay by him; preserved from corruption was his wallet of tanned leather in which various documents were enclosed. Opened in the presence of all, a paper written in English excited much curiosity. Edward Parker, whom chance had led to be part of the expedition, translated it, and revealed by this simple memorial the right of the Boers to the country of Natal. This clear and concise document has about it something so sacred that I reproduce it here in English as I copied it from the original.

Unkunkinglove
4th February 1838

Know all men by this:

That whereas Pieter Retief, governor of the Dutch emigrant farmers has retaken my cattle which Sinkonyella had stolen from me, which cattle he, the said Retief, delivered unto me; I, Dingaan, king of the Zoolas, do hereby certify and declare that I thought fit to resign unto him, Retief and his countrymen, the place called Port Natal, together with all the land annexed, that is to say, from the Togela to the Om-Sovoobo rivers westward, and from the sea to the north, as far as the land may be useful and in my possession.

Which I did by this and give unto them for their everlasting property.

+ Mark of king Dingaan
+ Marao Great Counsellor
+ Juliavius Great Counsellor
+ Manondo Great Counsellor

Witnesses
M. Oosthuisen
A.C. Greyling
B.J. Liebenberg

The fact of the granting of the territory was known to all; only the title deed was missing and it was upon this solemn occasion that it was found. There is no doubt that, if the Boer case were to be taken before a tribunal of nations, these men would be awarded a just decision; they would be granted free possession of the land that was duly ceded to them in the first instance, and then later repossessed at the cost of much bloodshed. But the law of the jungle, it appears, governs nations; cannon, with their hearts of iron, are today the only judges recognised as competent. It is sad to reflect that it should be thus. For what recourse is available to the weak and oppressed nations? A day will come perhaps, not so far off as one may think, when liberty will flower for the Boers, whose roots in the Cape will put forth shoots that will reach up to the Equator.

In January 1840, an expedition left Pieters-Mauritz-Burg, invaded the country of the Amazoulous and drove Dingaan beyond the borders, where the despot was killed by the Ama-Souazis, his natural enemies. The expedition, after establishing Panda in the place of the fallen tyrant, brought back 40 000 head of cattle. I have already given details of this expedition in which I took part.

It was just after this that the intentions of the British government became apparent; their claims were based on the fact that Holland had relinquished, in favour of Britain, all her possessions in South Africa. But it is well known that never had any corner of the territory of Natal been colonised by Holland.

In order to prove its credibility, the English government, or those who defended its cause before the tribunal of public opinion, published a document in which it is claimed that England reserved to herself alone the superintendance of all the land as far as 25° south latitude. But this document, completely useless in doing what it set out to do, is nevertheless most useful in illustrating the stupidity of those who believe they have exclusive rights to philanthropy, and in proving irrefutably that, impelled by blind fanaticism, they were treading the paths of injustice, and finally, in testifying to the fact that England has no rights over these lands. This curious document merits inclusion here. It appears under the following title:

The Cape of Good Hope Punishment Bill. Anno sexto et septimo Gulielmi IV, regis; cap LVII. Act to prevent and punish crimes committed by the subjects of His Majesty within the circumference of certain territories adjacent to the colony of the Cape of Good Hope. (13th August 1836)

In as much as the inhabitants of the territories adjacent to the colony of the Cape of Good Hope, and situated to the south of the 25th degree, are still in an uncivilised state; that offences against the property and the person of these inhabitants are frequently committed with impunity within this territory by the subjects of His Majesty; with intent to remedy this situation it has been determined by the king's excellent majesty, and with the counsel and consent of the lords spiritual and temporal, as well as of the commons, in the present assembly of parliament, and by authority of the same, that the laws, which are presently and will be henceforth, in force in the colony of the Cape of Good Hope, for the punishment of crime, will be and are extended and declared applicable to all His Majesty's subjects in all territories adjacent to the aforesaid colony, namely those to the south of 25° south latitude, and that all crimes or offences committed by any of His Majesty's subjects in these territories, in contravention of all such laws, will be brought before the courts and will be subject to examination, trial and prosecution, and upon conviction, punished in such a manner as if the crime had been committed within the confines of the aforesaid colony.

In as much as it is necessary to prevent, as far as is possible, that crimes be committed by His Majesty's subjects within the radius of the territories mentioned, and to take measures to arrest, detain and bring to justice those of His Majesty's subjects who have committed such crimes, it has been resolved that the governor of the aforesaid colony should be empowered to call upon any individual or individuals among

His Majesty's subjects, residing in or on the borders of the above mentioned territories, to form one or several commissions which he would authorise to perform in these territories the office of a magistrate in order to prevent the perpetration of all crimes and offences by His Majesty's subjects and, in order to arrest, place under guard and bring to judgment before the courts above mentioned, any subject of His Majesty accused with sufficient evidence before the aforesaid commission, of crimes or offences perpetrated in the aforesaid territories. Furthermore it will be incumbent on the governor of the aforesaid colony to require the aforesaid commission to define, with all possible precision, the limits within which the jurisdiction of such magistrates will be exercised and that, within these defined limits, as has just been stated, each magistrate will exercise and have use of all power and authority over His Majesty's subjects residing or passing through these places as he will have been especially invested by such commissions, provided always that the commissions only confer such power and authority when these measures have been recognised as urgently necessary for the accomplishment, with promptitude and effectiveness, of the proposed objectives mentioned above.

Further, it has been decreed that all such commissions will be constituted to act solely upon His Majesty's pleasure and, during this time, the governor of the aforementioned colony is charged and required to transmit to His Majesty a copy of the proceedings of these commissions after having previously addressed this to one of His Majesty's principal secretaries of state for the purpose of receiving his approbation or his prohibition and, moreover, it has been decreed that nothing in this or in any commission or commissions whatever intends, nor is it appropriate that it should intend, to invest His Majesty, his heirs or successors, with any claim or title whatsoever, to the possession or sovereignty over any of the territories mentioned, or to derogate the rights of the tribes or peoples inhabiting these territories, or of the chiefs or governors, or to claim such sovereignty or possession.

And moreover, it has been decreed that, in the implementation of this act any person legally administering the government of the aforesaid colony will be judged and deemed to represent the views of the government.

A reading of these documents will suffice to prove that under William IV, England did not wish to take possession of these countries; at the time she admitted not having any right to them. And since then, although her views have changed, she has not been able to acquire such rights. It would thus be impossible for her to produce valid title if she were required to give an account of her actions which no nation would presume to censure in matters relating to South Africa.

One is struck by the singularity of the idea which inspired this document when one notices that all of the guarantees are given to the Cafres against the whites, while the whites are given none in return. Thus, traders or travellers could be murdered by the Cafres without the latter being liable to receive the punishment which would have awaited whites on their return had they committed comparable crimes. Rigorous justice was enforced against one side which did not apply to the other; surely one of the strangest arrangements thought up by the philanthropists, who were so much preoccupied in procuring the happiness of the natives that they were quite unaware of the rights of anybody else.

Fortunately, the stupidity of such a measure rendered impossible the idea of putting it into practice, and so there was never any need to complain about its complete lack of justice. To define the parallel of 25° south latitude would have presented the first difficulty, and would have required the expenditure of a great deal of time, money and perhaps even of men, because the philanthropists, in spite of their excessive love of the black population, are often no better treated by them than if their sentiments, whether true or false, had been the opposite. In these sorts of matters impartial justice is usually done.

How could witnesses be induced to uproot themselves to go and testify before a recognised court? Was it not a mockery to have these peasant magistrates examining cases among the Cafres? To delegate the office of dispenser of justice to whoever came along, someone who was often quite incompetent, to grant him unlimited power over his neighbours for the duration of the period of His Majesty's good pleasure; this could all be likened to a weighty British dream, emanating from a philanthropic brain while the stomach was still busy digesting.

It is only too true to say that the majority of men who are required by their position in society to govern colonies have no deep knowledge of the different races whom favour, and sometimes disfavour, have placed beneath their guardianship. Often these men are too hasty in their choice of a system, or at the worst, they adopt a policy they are pushed into by powerful forces from whom they have much to fear if they refuse or if they oppose. This is why it is inevitable that things will go wrong; it could not be otherwise.

Sir Benjamin d'Urban, openly and wholeheartedly pursued a policy which put colonial interests first, while paying little heed to those with vested interests; Sir Benjamin d'Urban, because he earned popularity by right and proper means, saw his achievements undervalued by his government and his post awarded to another.

It was only natural that his successor, Sir George Napier, who intended to remain in government, did not choose to follow in his footsteps. He had no need to make much of an effort because he was the sort of man whose character was most suited to serve the views of any association which called itself philanthropic. So, Sir George Napier took his cue from Dr Philip; he protected the missionaries, sided with the bastaards and the Cafres, insulted the Boers, disregarded even the English settlers and greeted only the merchants, in that stiff and unbending manner which distinguishes the English aristocrat.

Sir George Napier maintained his position without much trouble during the five years of his governorship, simply for the reason that he made himself loathed by the great majority of the inhabitants of the Cape colony. Furthermore, he was extolled in England as a worthy and able governor; and Lord Stanley himself, although he did not exactly share the ideas of Sir George Napier and had given evidence of a difference of opinion on several occasions, even Lord Stanley was obliged to associate himself with the sentiments of the capital, and compliment the ex-governor of the Cape on his fine, prudent and philanthropic administration.

In all this, I who have not made a profound study of political economy, have been astounded that the most complete disapproval here in this country, could be translated into overwhelming approbation over there. Alone, I should never have solved the problem, but I subsequently learnt that the English government is not its own master; that it is dependent on a vast association whose branches extend throughout the world; an order which poisons, by civilisation; the order in fact which has poisoned China; a deleterious society which is everywhere obeyed and has as its counterpart in Rome the only too well-known sect of Loyola. The most undisguised egoism drives this powerful society and if it achieves an harmonious relationship with those who govern, this is because the latter are its dependents. If this society finds acceptance in England among the aristocracy it is because the interests of the English aristocracy are closely linked to its own; if the English adopt without hesitation the aims of this society, it is because they themselves participate in the benefits.

But the metropolitan power alone reaps the harvest of such a system; the colonies bring endless tribute to the great mother, who swallows it all up. And so, although certainly rich in resources, the colonies must make enormous sacrifices while they receive nothing in return. They grow tired and anxious and, when they cast a glance in other directions, the most devastating despair overcomes them; for there is no salvation; no hope of success.

This is why the English colonies do not contemplate separating their interests from those of the metropolitan power by means of revolution. Nothing holds them in this position of subservience but the necessity to which they are reduced. This situation will not change until the day when England is preoccupied with important wars and can no longer operate this system of trade with her colonies. Then the whole edifice will crumble and, of all the world powers, America is the only one whose situation will allow her to salvage the rich spoils of the great shipwreck.

CHAPTER XXVI

My embarrassing position during the hostilities — Encounter with a lion — Kotje Dafel the great lion hunter — Behaviour of the lion — The advantages and the disadvantages of hunting — Tenacity of the lion — Taken advantage of by the Kaal-Kaffers — Usefulness of the horse in this sort of hunt – Rage and despair of the lion; his courage — Faint-heartedness of the cornered lion — Strange method of putting him to flight — His behaviour at night — His lying in wait — Generous humour of this animal — His peaceful behaviour towards man — His undeniable usefulness — Services which he renders to the Makaschla Cafres — His size and strength — His method of hunting — His fights — Among the Amazoulous once more — Panda's attitude towards me changed — I am requested to stop hunting — My last fruitless endeavours — Final departure for Port Natal — Cafre deserters — Nocturnal flight — Ununongo — The trouble he causes me — Major Smith's justice.

During the period of the hostilities, my position had been an embarrassing one because, on one hand, I found it impossible to side with the English while, on the other, I could not bring myself to swell the ranks of the Boers, who were uncouth, and ignorant enough to boast that they would make mighty England tremble. I cared for neither and, rather than take sides, I kept to myself. I would have inclined towards the Boers, if the commandant-general had been more sympathetic. His brother, Baart Pretorius, and the eighteen scouts, whom I had evicted from my house, had laid a charge against me, requesting that I should be made an example of, and punished.

Commandant Pretorius sent for me to impress upon me, as he put it, the seriousness of my misdemeanour, in spite of the fact that I had suffered the loss of about twenty pounds sterling, which was the value of my possessions that had been stolen. Taking the circumstances into consideration, there might have been some excuse for his attitude up until that point. Growing more and more heated, while I was obliged to listen, he ended his harangue by saying something which made a very unpleasant impression on me. 'We have,' he said, 'thirty men in chains, Monsieur Delegorgue, and we can always find room for another.'

These threatening words were still very much in my mind when this same Pretorius sent for me again, this time with a request that I would be kind enough to take charge of two six-pounders captured from the English. It was a question of positioning them ready to fire, setting up outworks and directing the fire at the English camp. I had been in charge of a gun in the royal navy. I remembered the excitement I used to feel at the sound of cannon fire. No invitation could have been more acceptable to me; the prospect of firing 110 cannon shots every day was very much to my taste. But the iron chains Pretorius had threatened me with still rattled in my memory and I had no wish to oblige him. I remembered the man's former arrogance as he uttered the threat, a strange contrast to his present entreaties. 'Come,' he said, 'by accepting, you do us a great service, for none of my people understand how to perform such work.'

'Mr. Pretorius,' I replied, 'you know that it is my intention to return to the Cape in a few months time. If I should fire a single cannon shot at the English, those chains, which you so lightly promised me three days ago, would be waiting for me when I arrived there. My situation prohibits my doing anything at all for you. I would like to have been able to help you, because your cause seems to me to be just, but you will understand that threats do not dispose a man favourably, and my position as a foreigner obliges me to remain neutral. I dare to hope that this neutrality will be respected.'

Whereupon we turned our backs on each other. Of the two, I believe it was I who was the more satisfied.

The following day, in an attempt to impress upon me his displeasure by a show of power, Pretorius issued instructions that I should leave my dwelling and take up residence at Conguela. 'You are too isolated over there,' he said to me. 'Your conduct cannot be watched and what is more, the balls fired from the English camp pass right over your house. For these reasons you will come to live at Conguela and you will remain here.'

In spite of the cannon balls whistling overhead, I would have preferred to remain at home; I had grown used to the rumble of gunfire. However I had no choice but to submit and bid farewell to my beloved cottage.

Mr Van Breda of Conguela received me very properly into his agreeable family circle, offering me generous hospitality, the cost of which, it must be admitted, was largely borne by the British government, for the supplies we consumed had been captured from the English soldiers and, as meat was provided from the common herd, it was a time of plenty. However, we soon grew weary of the enormous quantities of beef which were distributed every day; some antelope or other would have made a pleasant change. No sooner had the ladies of the house expressed this wish at dinner one day, than I took up my double-barrelled gun and went off into the bush behind the settlement

There is a little marshy valley quite nearby, a little valley only 110 paces long. A narrow pathway of red sand winds its way upward from the far end and one must climb this pathway to reach the forest. I groped my way along, straining ears and eyes in the hope of hearing or seeing some *Cephalopus natalensis*. I had just reached the top of the pathway when, three paces to my left, an animal which I had taken by surprise darted away. It was a panther and too quick for me. Hardly had I had time to raise my gun, than it disappeared into the bush. I was sorry. Such opportunities are rare, although these animals are fairly plentiful.

I had not gone fifteen paces when an offensive smell led me to a dead cow. In itself, this circumstance was not of much interest, but I became aware of a troop of monkeys perched in some nearby trees. The unusual sound they were making inclined me to believe that they were of the species which the Cafres call *izi-mango*[1] and I held my breath in the hope of discovering more about these rare creatures.

I was soon to be disillusioned, for they were nothing but the common species called *om-kaho*, chattering in an unaccustomed manner. Certainly this was not an expression of their usual feelings; it was not the language they would normally use; what could have brought about this change, I wondered. I intended to find out, while at the same time not neglecting any opportunity of killing one of the big ones if he got within my sights. They allowed me to come up close and I crouched down, looking upwards at them, more and more surprised by the strangeness of this chatter and by the clumsy way they were leaping from branch to branch.

This breed of supremely bold jumpers, unequalled in their agility and their insolence, who understood very well how far a bullet could travel, were now behaving quite unlike themselves. They gave the impression of having grown old and decrepit; like timid uncertain chameleons, they crept along the branches, trembling; the shortest leap seemed beyond them; there was hesitation in their every movement, there was fear in their eyes; they would have liked to move away from the branches under which I was crouching, but they dared not.

I waited and waited, but not a single monkey of the size I was looking for came within my sights. With a hunter's patience, I did not take my eyes off them. There was a bush nearby, twelve paces away, that was larger and more luxuriant than its neighbours. It was growing right under the trees in which the frightened troop of monkeys was huddling. Something moved across my line of vision and I became aware of a tawny shape and then a long body, crouching low, which moved in behind the bush. My eyes followed the movement and I caught a glimpse of a rump, three feet high, from which was hanging a thin tufted tail. 'That's all right,' I thought, 'this is the calf belonging to that dead cow which was probably killed last night by hyaenas.' I felt that this was a likely explanation since Mr Van Breda's house was only 200 paces away.

1   This species of monkey is new, if it is not the *Simia monoides* unique to the Paris museum, whose country of origin is unknown.

After waiting another six minutes or so, I stood up, hoping that, as a result of my movement, I would notice some change in the monkeys' behaviour, but there was no change; they were quite unaffected by my presence and their staccato cries continued as before. I had just made up my mind to shoot the best specimen I could get, when the tawny body behind the bush stretched itself out noiselessly and revealed itself completely to my gaze.

It was a great lioness of unusual size. As she raised her head and watched the monkeys, without suspecting the presence of a man, she offered me the target of her exposed right flank.

My first instinct was to take aim, but then I realised the futility of it, for I had only a double-barrelled gun loaded to kill delicate antelope, with buckshot in one barrel and in the other, a bullet of pure lead resting on a charge which was a third of the usual hunting strength; only enough to bring down small game at forty paces; hardly more than a pistol shot. I felt as deeply as any man could feel at the prospect of having to forego so rare an opportunity. I suffered vexation and resentment the more keenly in the absence of any other emotion to divert me. From the very beginning, encounters of this nature produced no terror in me. However, knowing how ineffectual my weapon was, I might have lost my nerve had I not concentrated all my attention on seeking out the animal's weakest point. I decided to hit her between the eyes. Shouldering my gun, I waited for her to turn her head in my direction, knowing that my white shirt could not fail to attract her attention as light colours are known to do.

I had not long to wait. Slowly, the lioness turned her head towards me; her eyes which were completely closed looked like two black slits. She had had the time to become physically aware of my presence, but not to understand what I was about. My bullet struck her above the right eye and she dropped to the ground, falling on her left side. Greatly pleased with my shot which, in spite of its lack of force, was a good one, I scampered off smartly down wind, jumping over the smaller bushes and ducking under branches, intent on reaching the bottom of the valley as soon as I could.

Only when I was within reach of the walls of the settlement, did I stop to draw breath; I was gasping so much I could not get a word out. Not only was it the headlong dash, but also the feeling of exaltation, which so dilated my respiratory organs as to prevent speech. The Van Breda ladies burst out laughing because I had not breath enough to answer their question: 'Where is the little buck, then?'

'Oh, little buck did you say? Instead of the little buck you wanted, first I met a panther and then a lioness.'

'And you shot it?'

'Of course; at fifteen paces. You see, when I'd shot her and she fell,

I set off smartly and now here I am. I need a man to come with me to look for the animal; I know that the shot was a good one but I don't think the bullet was strong enough. Looking for a wounded animal is much more dangerous than just meeting one, so I want a man who knows what he is doing.'

'At the *leager,*' the ladies said, 'you will find Kotje-Dafel. He is the best man to help you. He will be very pleased to go with you.'

And so it turned out. Kotje-Dafel, who was the father of Henning, accepted my request eagerly. 'If it is a matter of lions,' he said to me, 'I will certainly give you the assistance you ask, on condition that you lend me your services when it comes to elephants, because, you see, Kotje-Dafel knows lions as you know elephants. You need him now and one day he will need you.'

As he said this, he was buckling on his bandolier with the bullet pouch in front and the powder horn at the back; then with his huge hand he grasped the barrel of his trusty six-bore. 'With a gun like this,' he said, 'a man need never be afraid.'

'That is true, but has that gun killed any lions?' This was tantamount to asking whether the gun's owner had killed any lions, for a Boer would never lend his gun, any more than he would lend his horse, or his wife.

'You ask me whether this gun has killed any lions?' he said, smiling in disbelief; then, assuming a lofty and serious manner, 'Kotje Dafel is a poor devil, but he was not always as you see him today. He is not rich, but he would be if he had been paid 100 rixdollars for every lion he had killed'.

'Perhaps it would not take much to make you feel rich?'

'It would take quite a lot. Ten thousand rixdollars, or more, would suit Kotje Dafel well, for he has nothing, nothing at all since Massilicatzi robbed him of all the cattle he owned.'

'But, by your reckoning, that makes more than a hundred lions. Is that possible? And you have never been wounded?' 'Exactly so, that is quite true; it is an amazing thing, but I have never been wounded. My horses have not been as fortunate; more than one has been torn to pieces under me, which has meant that many a lion has got away without one of Kotje Dafel's bullets down his throat.'

'But you were born in the Cape Colony; there aren't any lions there, or at least only on the northern frontiers, in the Karoo country where buck are plentiful, or in old Hantam or the Rogge-Veld.'

'That's where I was born, in the Rogge-Veld. But you know, the inhabitants are obliged to drive their herds long distances in search of grazing, often beyond the frontiers into Bushman country. That's where it began for me. I was only a child, looking after my father's horses when, one day, I noticed a lion and a lioness prowling around in the vicinity. There was no doubt that one of the horses would be killed by the great predators. I regretted that I did not have a gun. Fortunately, that day the horses were not too far from the wagons, so I went to fetch my father's gun. He wasn't there and I took it down. Half an hour later, the male lion was lying dead with my bullet through his head. When I got back, my father accused me of being foolhardy but, as the other men joined in my praise, I realised that I had done well. I was excited now and began looking out for further opportunities, Whenever there was talk of lions, Kotje Dafel's name was mentioned. It all started a long time ago. I'm nearly fifty now, but whenever anyone wants to get rid of dangerous neighbours, they send for Kotje Dafel. You must have heard talk of the great number of lions killed by the Boers on the long trek from the great river to Natal. Three hundred and eighty is quite a number, don't you think. Well, Kotje Dafel played the biggest part in it.'

'That's a fine effort. I envy you your success at lion hunting, and I would happily exchange a few elephants for some of your lions.'

'You must be joking,' answered Dafel. 'I would exchange all of my lions, down to the last one, for your elephants.'

'Maybe. We all have our own view of things. The fact remains that, to shoot a lion is a great feat and he who has done so is justified in claiming some credit.'

'That is true, but it is also true that there is as much credit in killing an elephant, and sometimes also there is great profit. A lion skin has so little value that one rarely bothers with it, while an elephant's tusks are as good as currency. So, if you do not mind too much, Kotje Dafel would like to go with you when you return to Om-Philos. He promises to kill you some lions if you would like some, provided that you kill him some elephants, not too big, just a fair exchange. Kotje Dafel would be very pleased if you would agree.'

'We shall see Kotje. But tell me, do you always go out alone, or in company with others? I think seconds can be very useful; a man is stronger when he knows that he is not alone, and it could happen that, without a companion to spur him on, his resolve could weaken. What do you do?'

'My rule is to go alone. I do not prevent others from looking on to satisfy their curiosity, but I do not need others by my side. All you need is one man to lose his nerve. If he turns and runs away, the lion will chase after him and the order of attack is changed. Everybody now faces a danger that would not have arisen if the hunter had been alone. And what is more, where there are several, every man depends on his neighbour; I believe that one must trust only in oneself. A well-trained horse, a good simple heavy-calibre gun, with a single shot, a good eye and a firm hand, that's all you need. It is a duel to the death, in which man has the first shot and all the advantage. If he is calm and composed, nothing could be easier, but before attempting it, he must be sure of knowing himself. The slightest hesitation could mean death.'

'So Kotje, you prefer to go alone rather than to misplace your trust in others. I can understand that, because a man must be responsible for his own hand and eye, while he cannot answer for those of his neighbour. Then again, bad example may become contagious and affect even the bravest, even those who believe themselves immune. I am talking of fear, which I reckon should be listed among the infectious diseases. It is of short duration, but continually recurring, and it is incurable in certain cases where the carriers pass the infection on. But tell me, do you judge a horse to be indispensable? Why do you prefer a single-barrelled gun and only one shot? Why is your weapon not armed with a bayonet? Why do you not wear at least a dagger or a hunting knife on your belt?'

'That's a lot of whys and wherefores,' said Kotje, in his slow and unemotional way, so different from my own. 'You talk too fast, like all your countrymen. You want to know everything in two words, and I think you already know as well as I do what my reply will be. However, your questions are simple; if they were not, they would embarrass me as much as all those implements you want me to carry. First of all then, the horse is only indispensable out in the open where escape is easy, and when the lion is more than thirty-five paces away. A distance of twenty paces, for example, is too close; in a single leap, the lion, if he is not wounded, will leap on to the horse's hindquarters and, as the bridle is looped over the hunter's left arm, horse and rider run the same risk. In wooded areas, the horse is worse than useless. Secondly, it is natural to prefer to use the single-barrelled gun of heavy calibre because it has a more decisive effect. It is better to fire a single shot. If the situation is dangerous, requiring a second shot, this shot is always fired in haste and is therefore inaccurate. In this type of hunting, one strong shot is better than two weak ones. That is why we do not recommend double-barrelled guns. As for using a bayonet, believe me, they are better left to soldiers. Not only does a bayonet cause obstruction by catching on to low branches, but it gets in the way of the sights and, because of its weight, it produces a trembling of the hand which affects the aim. What is more, you feel compelled to use it when the lion is already upon you and what use will this match-stick be, stuck to the end of your gun? You cannot fail to be thrown to the ground by the impact and the bayonet will certainly not kill the lion immediately, even if it penetrates the vital organs. You would be torn to shreds long before the animal dropped dead. Now, as for daggers, I beg you to spare me, and this goes for pistols as well, which you left out of our inventory. The lion is strong, he needs something substantial which will produce haemorrhage as quickly as possible.

I have learnt from experience that even when he has been shot through the heart, the king of beasts still has enough strength to kill a horse and its rider. It was after witnessing such an incident that I became convinced that one should aim only at the head. That is a different matter; death follows a shot in the head almost instantly. There is no sign of life, except for a nervous reaction, a contraction of the leg muscles which lasts barely a second, and then the life of the great animal, with all its strength and all its fury, is extinguished.'

'Thank you very much Kotje. Now, here is the path we have to climb. Let's keep quiet now; we are getting close to the place. Careful, here's the dead cow; the lioness fell just near here.'

Alas, I saw only too well the place where she had fallen. The grass was flattened, but she had disappeared; there was not a drop of blood to be seen, only a few footprints remained which Kotje recognised as those of a strong lioness, and that was all. I began to feel the keen disappointment every hunter knows.

'Let us keep going,' said Dafel, 'we shall see what happens.' And we pushed on through almost impenetrable bush.

Two hours later, after a tiring search, we had found nothing; the tracks were too difficult to follow. We had to reconcile ourselves to returning empty handed. It was painful.

'Let's go,' said Kotje. 'Begin again tomorrow, perhaps you will be more fortunate.'

'Oh yes, tomorrow,' I said. 'Tomorrow will be no better than today.'

I was sunk in despair, and slung my gun carelessly over my shoulder. At that moment, a hyaena, *Hyaena crocuta*, started up almost beneath my feet and disappeared before I could load. 'All right, let's go Kotje. Luck is not with me today. Until tomorrow then. If it is only will power that is needed, I shall not let you down.'

But the following day, Kotje Dafel was not free to accompany me. I was nevertheless determined to continue my search. I needed a second but could not find anybody who was willing to come. Then, along came a hunchbacked German, full of enthusiasm because he had no idea of the danger. He offered his services.

'Can you fire a gun?'

'No.'

'What do you expect to do then?'

'Come with you.'

'But why?'

'To see a lion.'

'Just to look at it, not to kill it?'

'To kill it as well, if that is possible.'

'Won't you be afraid?'

'I don't think so.'

'Why don't you think so?'

'Because I am man enough to control my emotions.'

'That's fine, you can come then. Go and get ready, and be quick about it. We have no time to lose.' And I thought to myself that there is always some hidden quality in a hunchback.

A few minutes later, to the sound of mocking laughter, I set out, accompanied by the hunchback. I brushed aside a torrent of witticisms which I shall not repeat here.

In spite of the jeers, the German with his crooked spine managed to keep close at my heels, which augured well. We were soon among the trees and made our way with difficulty through an entanglement of roots and branches. I had to admit that the hunchback's handicap was proving to be an advantage. In that thick bush, I was obliged to crouch low in order to be able to see ahead; I was already quite exhausted from having to assume this uncomfortable position which constricts the lungs, while my hunchback, as fresh as when we started out, watched me with that strange smile that hunchbacks seem to have.

Two hours went by with no trace of our quarry, not even a footprint. My patience was wearing thin. Our two dogs had gone ahead We could not see them but we could hear them ferreting about. They had apparently not picked up any clues, for they gave no sign. The bush was growing less dense now, and we could see forty paces ahead. Suddenly, my attention was attracted by something tawny and white,

'Hush,' I said signalling behind me to my companion. 'It's my lion from yesterday. Careful!'

And I went forward five paces. There was no movement; I thought it was dead. 'That's it,' I cried, 'Its dead.'

Hardly were the words out of my mouth when the dogs, who had picked up the scent, began to bark.

The lion, which was not in the least dead, got up, gathered itself together and leapt, landing fifteen paces away and then leapt again. It seemed to be flying; it's mane looked like a pair of wings. It was a magnificent male whom we had inadvertently disturbed taking a siesta. I was so startled that it did not occur to me to take aim. In any case the speed of the animal's movements would have ruled out any chance of success. It seemed that no arrow, no bird gliding on outstretched wings, could surpass him. It was as if the lion left behind him in the air a semicircular trail in which his great image was repeated over and over, as if he were present everywhere at once, supporting himself aloft on his outstretched hind legs.

'Why didn't you kill him?' asked the German.

'Probably because I didn't think of it. It was the surprise; he was as quick as a flash, that's my reason. And what about you?'

Did you mean to?'

'No, not really. My greatest wish was to see him.' 'Well, you did see him, and you can consider yourself lucky, because a lion disturbed like that is usually terrified and runs away fast.'

We made our way back to Conguela, the German happy to be able to say that he had seen a lion, and I, regretting that I had not had just four more seconds to take aim and fire. At the camp, those who had mocked him gathered round the little hunchback to hear him describe, with great spirit, how the lion had jumped. He was paid due deference and praises were heaped upon him, for he had shown great resolution and firmness of purpose, in spite of his feeble, crooked body. A few doubting voices were raised but the German, sure of his facts, suggested a visit to inspect the evidence and offered himself as guide. His remarkable confidence silenced the criticism and won the jokers over to his side. Probably many of them did not feel inclined to exchange smiles with the lion, for lions are serious when they smile. They curl up their lips to reveal white teeth which are not in the least artificial, and they twitch their little black ears with a look which seems to say, 'Come on. I am ready. Are you?'

At that time, a body of men, all excellent marksmen, the pick of the Boers, were camped in the *leager* at Conguela. Some of them were resting, while others were busy in the trenches, digging or taking pot-shots at anything that moved in the English camp. The news of my ineffectual hunting expedition soon spread, but not a single man offered to help me. Kotje Dafel himself said that the dense, impenetrable bush was not a good place for lion hunting and anyway, as a sharp shooter, all his time was taken up and he could not spare even a couple of hours to accompany me. In the end I was obliged to give up my search. When he heard of it, Pretorius added his weight by expressing the opinion, which was passed on to me by some busybody, that 'at the present hour, one shot could decide our fate; powder is in short supply; it must be used sparingly; let not a shot be fired at anything which is not English.'

As lions do not come from England, there was nothing for it but to give up and devote myself, body and soul, to the boredom of the slowly moving events.

While still on the subject, I am going to give you a few descriptive details about the master of the forest. The lion, which in France enjoys such a great reputation for nobility and courage, probably owes it to the fact, firstly, that he lives far away and, secondly, that we are not in a position to observe his behaviour in his natural state. According to the South African hunters who live in these newly-inhabited lands where lions may be encountered every day, it is prudent to allow them to pass by unhindered. Lion hunting is dangerous and, as the skins only fetch from 50 to 75 francs, man's acquisitiveness is not sufficiently tempted. And so the lion often owes his life to the fact that his skin is not very valuable. But after some nocturnal plundering raid, when he has scattered the cattle and killed one of them, the anger of the Boer who has been robbed of one of his dearest possessions, knows no bounds and will only be appeased when the lion's skin is carried off to market and sold to defray part of the loss.

Our angry Boer will set off on horseback, usually alone, but sometimes accompanied by friends; company is not necessarily a good thing, for it gives the lion an advantage. The animal is spotted, he gets up slowly and proudly, walks away fifteen to thirty paces, glancing frequently behind him, then lies down again. His mind is made up; he intends to be kept at a respectful distance. If he is attacked, he will conquer or die.

The Boer approaches to within thirty paces; up to that point, there is no danger; he can choose to attack or retreat but he has made up his mind. He turns his horse about, so that the hindquarters now face the lion. He dismounts, keeping the bridle looped over his left arm; he aims and fires. If the bullet strikes the brain, death is instantaneous; the animal collapses without any sign of life, except for a trembling of the paws, as the muscles of the legs are briefly extended. But, if the hunter's bullet strikes the body, that is a different matter. It is impossible to know whether the wound is slight or mortal. There may be bleeding when the animal makes a violent effort to avenge himself. When the heart has been penetrated, and I personally have witnessed a case of this sort, it can happen that the lion lives long enough to leap upon the horse and tear it to pieces, before expiring beside the horseman who has been thrown to the ground by the impact.

If the animal is only slightly wounded, the hunter must expect a determined counter-attack; he will not be saved by galloping away on his horse for it cannot move fast enough; the lion will overtake it in two or three leaps. To attempt to repel the attack with a bayonet, an expedient invented by armchair hunters, would prove worse than useless, for even the most strongly built man will be unhorsed by the impact and, even were the lion to be pierced through the heart, this would not prevent the man's being torn to shreds by its claws or broken between its jaws.

The best thing to do in a situation like this, is to sacrifice the horse and step back to reload. Any hunter who is able to control his emotions may then approach the carnivore and finish him off point blank as he vents his fury on the horse, for the lion is so preoccupied with his gnawing, and his jaw muscles are moving so powerfully, that his other faculties are forgotten. With his eyes closed, the lion relishes his revenge and sees no more than if he were blind.

The Cafres living on the frontiers of the Cape of Good Hope are so well acquainted with this peculiarity that they base their method of attack upon this knowledge. One of their number, carrying an enormous shield of tough buffalo hide, fashioned into a concave shape, will approach the lion and boldly hurl an assegai at him. The lion leaps upon his attacker, but the man has dropped flat on the ground, pulling his shield over him like one of those conical shells which cling to the rocks and which are impossible to prise off. For a moment, the lion thinks he has triumphed over his victim; then he tries his claws and his teeth on the shield, but they simply slide off, producing no effect at all. As he redoubles his efforts, he is encircled by the rest of the band of armed men who hurl hundreds of assegais at him, their shafts shuddering as they pierce his body, while the lion believes that it is the man under the shield who has attacked him. His assailants withdraw; the lion grows weaker and weaker, until eventually he falls, while the man under the shield is careful not to emerge before the animal has ceased to show any signs of life.

In the sort of lion hunt favoured by the Boers, the horse has his uses, not so much in overtaking the lion, but in acting as a substitute and saving the rider from the terrible claws. As every South African hunter knows, the horse is always the first victim; he is a traitor to his kind and a slave to man; the lion does not fear him and easily overcomes his favourite prey. Man on the other hand, is different from the four-footed animals and the lion fears him, for he is a killer of lions. In no country where big game is hunted does the lion devour the man he has killed.

Certain animals, when they are mortally wounded, show a weakness which is due to their lack of means of defence, or to the gentleness of their character; some give plaintive cries which they utter only at that supreme moment, others weep tears; the canna, *Boselaphus oreas,* in particular, moves the hunter to pity when he seems to implore him for mercy, instead of attacking him with his formidable horns. Others again, are simply resigned, giving no sign of strength or weakness.

The lion differs from all of these; he seems more to resemble man, in that he gives evidence of despair when he is defeated. Perhaps he is aware of imminent death. While he retains the power of claws and teeth, his defence is as vigorous as his attack but, if he is frustrated and cannot reach his enemy, despair overwhelms him and he turns against himself, biting at his own paws as if he were trying to destroy himself, to become his own executioner. However, the weapons which nature has given him are inadequate for this task.

He displays great courage of this nature only in situations which he cannot avoid. Looked at from this angle, the king of beasts does not deserve his title and is not worthy of the respect generally accorded him. Many times have I seen a lion turn away and flee when unexpectedly confronted by a man, a child or even a dog. In a landscape furrowed by ravines and dotted with hills, where the thick bush provides refuge, the lion moves off and disappears at the mere sound of men's voices carried on the wind. Even though certain that he has not been seen, he is careful to get out of the way of danger, and his courage is not bolstered by the proximity of three or four other lions; they all move off slowly and silently, at first, and then more rapidly, in great leaps, as fear takes hold of them.

If an encounter occurs in open country where the ground is uneven, the lion takes advantage of the terrain. He does not dare turn and retreat, for he is afraid the man will think that he is running away. He seems to fear compromising his dignity. He turns and looks around, as if thinking of something else, while continuing to move away all the time. If the man wishes to stop him in his retreat, nothing could be easier; all he needs to do is wave his arms about and shout loudly and the lion will stand still and listen. When the man stops shouting, the lion goes on walking. If the man goes right up close to him, shouting all the time, the lion will stop once more and will often lie down immediately. In spite of himself, he takes up the challenge, for this time his honour and his reputation for courage are at stake. But if the hunter wishes, he can dislodge the animal from its position and the means whereby he does this are as simple as they are strange.

The land is covered in grass a metre tall; whether the man who is making his way towards the lion crouches or lies down, he becomes invisible and the animal grows anxious, because he can no longer see his enemy. Does he imagine that the man is planning to attack him from an unexpected quarter? I do not know what it is reasonable to believe, but I have tried it many times and the lion has always moved away. Even when I simply went down on my knees to avoid branches or to adjust my aim, lions standing thirty paces away were seized with panic and moved off. My experience is confirmed by a thousand stories told by hunters older and more seasoned than I.

Furthermore, one should not believe that it is dangerous to wound a lion taken by surprise, for his first reaction will always be to flee, if he is in a condition to do so. Whether a lion is dozing with his legs stretched out, or whether he is completely engrossed in stalking his prey, provided that he is unaware of the hunter, the latter must never hesitate to use his weapon. I have done this many times at very short range, without running into the least danger.

At night, the animal, along with the rest of the feline race, enjoys excellent sight and performs deeds of audacity bordering on the foolhardy. Man's domain, which he avoids in the daylight, becomes familiar territory in the dark. In spite of the dogs, which eventually wake and start barking, the lion will not hesitate to attack a horse tethered beside its sleeping master, or oxen with their horns tied to the wagon wheels.

But, let man switch roles, play the part of the aggressor and wound him, the lion, under cover of the dark, will withdraw, disappointed, ashamed and crestfallen, and will not dare to make another attack. In fact the game is up for him; the oxen are firmly tied and incapable of obeying their natural fear which urges them to flee, the dogs are barking, ready to follow up the thief, and the men are no longer asleep. If the moon and a few stars should appear and illuminate the lion, then take a shot at him; he will be abashed and go away: I did this once, firing from ten paces at a lion and then at his mate. As there was no other weapon to hand, I used my double-barrelled gun, loaded with birdshot, which made them snarl, the only evidence they dared give of their anger, and walk away.

In places where there is no easy game, the lion stalks the farmer's cattle; he watches them covetously by day and attacks by night, hoping to carry off a beast of which he will make more than one meal. If the hunter takes a few precautions, and if the lion is hungry, it is an easy enough matter to get within range of him. All that is required is to take up one's position in the vicinity of the kill and wait for His Majesty to appear. It is generally between ten and eleven at night that the hunter's patience is rewarded; the lion comes slowly along downwind; if he does not pick up the scent, the man is in luck, but he must take care to make no sound, whether of heavy breathing or the rustling of a leaf. Before the lion knows what is happening, he is wounded and will walk away; that is, if he is not already dead.

If, on the other hand, the lion has seen the hunter or even simply guessed his presence, the man is in danger for now the lion considers himself master of the situation, and he is not prepared to share the spoils. This is the moment when the hunter must keep perfectly calm; he must not equivocate, but most hold his ground and crouch down low. When he is under attack, it becomes very difficult for him to take accurate aim, and this crouching movement could save him from that attack. If the animal hesitates, it becomes vulnerable; the shot must be fired without delay and the animal killed stone dead, or it will have the upper hand and presently the moon, with its pale beams, will illuminate a terrible scene that is best left to the imagination.

This might be the moment to make an interesting observation: it sometimes happens that, on an inexplicable whim, which is usually described as generosity, the king of beasts does not kill the man whom he holds pinned beneath him, although that man has just wounded him. Sometimes he is quite content simply to inflict a few bites which crack the man's limbs, or he will deal a blow with his paw which ploughs four furrows across the man's chest. That is the limit of his revenge, and off he goes. I knew an intrepid hunter who, on two occasions in seven years, was pinned down in this manner by a wounded lion; on the first occasion he was left with two broken limbs, and on the second he suffered six fractures, as well as deep wounds inflicted by the lion's claws on several parts of his body. Another hunter by the name of Vermaes, no less brave, was pinned down for more than a minute by a famous lioness who let him go after she had inflicted four deep wounds with her canines, scars of glory which he displayed with fierce pride. The terrible animals held the power of life or death over their victims and so it is difficult, if not impossible, to understand the reason for their remarkable behaviour. It would appear then that the lion is gentler and less dangerous to man than is generally believed. It happens every day that unarmed Cafres and their families move about in country where lions are known to roam, but the presence of the animals apparently holds no terrors for the Cafres who go about their business unperturbed, and never have I heard of any unprovoked attack initiated by the lions. However, should these same Cafres be herding oxen or cows, the situation could be different. I would not care to be responsible for the cattle, or for the owners who try to protect them, but even then it is obvious that the lion is not primarily interested in attacking man.

It seems then that it is only pastoral people who need fear the lion. They are the only ones who take pleasure in his death. But I suppose that if the animal forfeits his life for some plunder he has committed, he deserves to pay the price. In all, the lion plays a useful role in these lands. If, from the Draakensberg and the source of the Touguela to the Tropic of Capricorn, not a single lion existed, it is certain that herds of gnus and quaggas (*Catoblepas gnou* and *taurina*, and *Equus burchellii*) which are all too numerous already, would multiply to alarming proportions. In less than ten years, the pastoral people would no longer be able to find a blade of grass for their cattle to graze on.

There must have been lots of lions when I travelled from Eland's Rivier to Vaal-Rivier, because we saw several every day and almost every night they tried to take our oxen. Their numbers must have been inadequate, for their mission was not fulfilled. Before reaching Vaal-Rivier, I journeyed six days without finding a blade of grass for my oxen to eat. It was winter-time and everything had been cropped by the gnus and the quaggas, whose teeth virtually shave the ground, while the imprint of their hooves is everywhere. When the earth is soft, these hoof prints give an impression of ploughed land. If there were no lions to reduce the number of wild herbivores, not only would the Cafres be unable to find grazing for their cattle, but the gnus and the quaggas themselves would diminish in numbers for they would die from starvation. When civilised man arrives with his gun the scene changes; the lion no longer has a mission to accomplish, because man has usurped his function and soon, both herbivores and carnivores disappear. But before this point is reached, the lion realises that his natural prey is becoming more and more difficult to find. He begins to prefer domestic animals; they are in better condition and they cannot escape. In fact he prefers them even when gnus and quaggas are in abundant supply. This would explain the attacks on travellers who rely for transport on great spans of oxen.

Peoples who, in the wake of disastrous wars, live simply, off the produce of the earth, or who, like the Boschjesmans, live only by hunting, are far from feeling any ill-will towards the lion He does them no harm; on the contrary he is useful to them in a thousand ways. As the method of hunting employed by these men promises rewards neither great nor certain, they are frequently reduced to scavenging in the bush and the left-overs from the lion's meal are not to be despised. Scouts go out each morning to watch for signals from the vultures, who never let them down. The cloak worn by more than one Makaschla is made from the skin of an animal which the lion has killed and which has been softened with the marrow of its own bones, after the man has satiated himself on the flesh. Naturally these people were in no great hurry to help me dispose of the neighbours whose services are so valuable to them.

It is only to be expected that the habits of the lion should vary according to where he lives. Thus the description I give applies only to those of southern Africa. It will differ perhaps from a description of the Saharan lion, but must, I believe, in principal, be the same. I have reason to believe that the lions of southern Africa must be the biggest and strongest of the species. The flattened and dried skin of one particular full-grown male, from the nose to the tip of the tail measured three metres fifty centimetres, the tail counting for one metre. They need to be strong here, more than in any other part of Africa. In Massilicatzi's country where I hunted for some time, buffaloes and rhinoceroses are more numerous than anywhere else, and their strength is in proportion to their size. It is difficult to convey adequately what this means, but I can swear to the fact that I once killed an old male buffalo *bos-cafer*, which bore, from the shoulder to the base of the tail, four furrows, four centimetres deep, gouged out by a lion's claws. Many a time have I come across the largest specimens of *Rhinoceros simus* which had been unable to survive the lion's attack, despite their weight, their strength, the toughness of their hide and the fury of their resistance. The site of the battle was always covered with imprints, those of the lion's paws being visible wherever one looked.

The little elephant, walking behind its mother, often falls victim to the lion which lies in wait for it, brings it down, throttles it and goes off without further ceremony, certain of finding it when he returns later. I have never heard of the lion attacking the hippopotamus which has the thickest hide of all known animals; perhaps it is because his jaws are so formidable that the lion does not risk an attack, although he finds the flesh very acceptable and similar to the *Rhinoceros simus*. I know this because lions often came after the remains of the hippopotamuses we had killed and left lying on the river banks.

His ability to leap astonishing distances is a testimony to the lion's great muscular strength. I once measured eighteen paces from the place where he had been standing to the spot where he landed. It is because he leaps upon his unsuspecting prey that he is able to kill it, for the lion is no runner and, were he to try and chase after the nimble antelopes, they would always escape him.

In November, December and January, which are the summer months in these latitudes, the grass is long and the lion goes hunting alone or, at the most, with his mate for company. It is at that season that he can expect to be successful in the daylight, for he excels at creeping up on his prey through the long grass. The herbivore, when he is grazing, keeps his head down, raising it only at regular intervals, when there is no noise to attract his attention. The lion calculates his distance, glances around, makes sure he is within range, gathers himself together and leaps; the prize is his. But if it should happen that he fails on the first attempt, he leaps again. Should the quarry escape once more, he makes one last attempt, which never turns out to be successful. The lion then changes his mind, turns his back on the antelope, and walks off in the opposite direction.

In the winter, during the months of June, July and August when the grass is trampled or burnt by fire, the lone lion can only hunt after dark and, even then, the rewards would not be great. The lions have found their own solution to this problem. They may be observed, during the day, gathering together to form a cordon with the intention of encircling the game and driving them towards the narrow gorges and wooded, tangled corridors where other lions lie in wait. This is one game drive which is carried out in silence, the scent of the lions borne on the wind being quite sufficient persuasion for the herbivores to move on.

On one occasion, my hunters and I found ourselves caught up in the midst of one of these cordons of 'beaters' When we first became aware of them there were twenty and the second time we looked, only a few minutes later, there were thirty, the low bushes of *jong-dorn*, young mimosa, having obscured some of them from our view. A rhinoceros which we were stalking appeared to be the object of their interest also. Unfortunately, just as *our* presence disconcerted them in their plan of attack, *theirs* obliged us to abandon our original objective, and so the rhinoceros owed his life to the conflicting interests of his two most redoubtable enemies. But what I most passionately desired to see was the rhinoceros coming to grips with a formidable pride of lions. I have often come upon the mighty heaps of remains resulting from one of these encounters in which the herbivore always finally succumbed, but never have I been granted the privilege of witnessing the thrilling scene.

One man, however, has seen and heard it all; alone in the dark, without arms or fire, abandoned by his Cafres, cowering in a *jong-doorn* bush because he had been unable to find a tree to shelter in, racked by thirst and beset by a thousand anxieties, his scent already picked up by the rhinoceroses, my worthy friend Mr Wahlberg, today professor of natural history at Stockholm, witnessed one of these encounters from a distance of only twenty paces. He is perhaps the only man in the world who can tell us of the primitive fury of the attack and of the despair and the anguish of the hapless victim. It is in a state of nature, in the midst of untamed forests, where they are unaware of the watching eye of man, that the unrestrained behaviour of these animals should be observed to be fully understood and appreciated.

After digressing to tell about the lion, I take up the thread of my narrative once more. Pray take note, reader, that it has never been my object to write a novel, in the style, for example, of *Voyage Autour du Monde* by Monsieur J. Arago, whose powerful imagination, as I have already said elsewhere[1] allowed him to see buffaloes in the skins of Cape oxen, lions at False Bay, where none had been seen for a century and a half, and a lion hunter in the shape of Rouvière, who was in fact only a wretched townsman, a baker whose horizons were limited to his kneading trough, a man who loaded his gun with an iron ball, a detestable object which scratches the barrel, a man who armed himself from head to foot with every sort of weapon, not excepting the trident, the sabre, the axe and even pistols, those playthings which are good for nothing more than to kill coxcombs arrayed in spurious honour and inflamed by insults; these weapons are unknown to the inhabitants of the Cape Colony. In writing, I have always had but one desire, which has been to introduce my reader to those things which I have seen with my own eyes, or have heard vouchsafed for as certain fact and, if these things have not enough drama to please the reader sitting comfortably at home in his armchair, the fault is not mine.

---

1 See Volume 1. *Translator's note*

But to repeat, is there anything more harmful than writings which, beneath an appearance of authenticity, distort with false information the thoughts of the man who is seeking to educate himself? Can anything be more ridiculous than to invent a story, when there is an abundance of interesting fact? Has the writer not failed in his task if he cannot say 'I saw'? In addition to this, he makes use of the most distinguished of names in order to disseminate untruths which I liken to women of shame, beautifully adorned.

The English camp had already been beseiged for a fortnight when my wagon arrived back at Natal, having finally succeeded in crossing the Touguela. Hardly had my specimens been unloaded, than my driver was taken from my service to fulfil his duty as a citizen; at that time nobody was his own master. A return to Om-Philos was impossible, so I waited. After Lieutenant-Colonel Cloete came, my Cafres, whom I had left to guard my possessions at Om-Philos, turned up unexpectedly.

'Master,' said Kotchobana, 'we heard up there from the Amazoulous that the English and the Boers were fighting down here. Some men told us that you had been killed; when you did not return at the appointed time, we thought it could be true, and so we decided to come and see. You are not dead; so much the better. It is right that you should know that things are going badly up there. Panda wishes to raise himself up in the eyes of the people. The Boers, occupied with their own war, are no longer present to control his actions and see that their rights are respected. The killings have become wanton; Panda's commando never rests. Every morning some *mouzi* or other is attacked, laid waste and burnt, while the inhabitants are mercilessly put to death. Souzouana has been killed, along with the principal members of his family and his followers; his four *mouzis* are now no more than heaps of ashes blown in the wind, and his people are scattered. The missionary Grout of Om-Schlatousse saw his servants murdered in his own house. We passed by that way and we saw the corpses of men and women who had just been killed. There was terror on every face, for no one knew whether their own *mouzi* would meet the same fate next day. Mr Grout fled, taking his wife, and all that he could carry of his most precious possessions; he is unlikely to return, for Panda does not like the missionaries. We have also heard tell that Panda refuses to allow white men to hunt in his country; if this is so, must we say goodbye to the elephants?'

Fear, more than any other cause, had driven my Cafres to leave the Amazoulou country, for they had witnessed the massacre of Souzouana's people; the bloody scene had made a deeply disturbing impression on them. As I was not with them, they did not feel safe. In their anxiety they had taken only four and a half days to cover almost seventy leagues on foot. I was concerned about my possessions, my ivory and my collection of bones which had been left unguarded on the banks of the Om-Philos, but on the other hand, it was as well for me to know that Panda was ill-disposed towards me and that I should have to deal with his changed attitude. Whatever the danger, I could not avoid returning in person and, in order to humour him as well as to sound him out, I loaded my men with gifts and ordered them to set out for Sképèle as soon as possible.

Hardly had I made these arrangements, when I saw the missionary Grout arriving, accompanied by his wife. He could not disguise his displeasure at having been obliged to abandon the agreeable situation he had created for himself in Zoulouland. His wife was reduced to tears as she told regretfully of the comforts they had lost. For people who claimed to be unworldly, I thought they cared a great deal about material things, which inclined me to believe that they themselves had not as much confidence in the life hereafter as would appear in their preaching to the Cafres. My own position at the time was perhaps worse than Mr Grout's, for my house at the bay had not been spared either and I had just been robbed of goods to the value of 6 000 francs, which I later tried to reclaim, but to no effect, for the English government declines all responsibility for losses incurred in time of war, however unjust that war might be.

Mr Grout assured me that, although he had left the country, he had not fled. He was convinced of Panda's ill-will, but he felt sure that the king would not lay hands on a white man. He strongly advised me to go back, probably so that he might discover, without any cost to himself, whether it would be possible for him to fetch the furniture he had left at his house at Om-Schlatousse. Although I saw through his ruse, I was obliged to take the only course open to me.

And so, as soon as Lieutenant-Colonel Cloete had returned my span of oxen, which he had requisitioned for service in his government's interests, I left Natal and made my way to Om-Philos where I arrived on 25 August, 1842, after an uneventful journey of fourteen days. I found all in order at my camp; nobody had thought of taking advantage of the absence of my guards, thanks to the severity of Panda's justice. Kotchobana and Boulandje, on their return from Sképèle, reported that Panda had accepted my gifts, although not quite so graciously as before. Behind the disjointed, clumsy phrases, they sensed that his heart was not well disposed towards me. They had heard along the way that secret meetings had been held, and were still going on, to decide what the attitude of the black man should be towards the whites of Natal, who were disputing the ownership of the land.

Three differing opinions had been expressed. The true politicians, the philosophers, were of the opinion that it was best not to take part, and proposed leaving the whites to cut each other's throats, for it did not much matter to them whether an Englishman or a Boer was killed, it was but one enemy the less. Those who were in favour of war, were equally divided as to which of the two warring parties to support. One body of opinion wanted to attack the Boers, whose great herds would be a rich prize, while the other thought it would be simpler to ally themselves with the Boers against the English, who possessed a thousand desirable things; by taking this easy course, they would preserve the friendship of the Boers from whom they had much to fear in a clash of interests. Panda himself sided with those who wished to attack the Boers, but there was strong opposition from the elders, who wanted peace. The deliberations went on too long and the treaty was signed before any decisive steps were taken by the Amazoulous. This tardiness preserved the peace, but passions had been aroused. It soon became apparent that there were those who were ill-disposed towards me, those who awaited only a word, or a sign, to thrust an assegai into me. Their eyes betrayed their feelings when they were near me; some of them behaved in an insolent manner, without provocation on my part. My situation demanded the greatest discretion, without any show of weakness, an attitude that was difficult to maintain.

I kept my patience for as long as I possibly could but when, emboldened by my silence, some who had begun by begging for certain possessions of mine, now had the audacity to demand them, and climbed into my wagon and helped themselves, I judged that the time had come to make them understand that I would not be intimidated. To the great astonishment of my Port Natal Cafres, I fell upon the Amazoulous who were responsible for stealing my things and rained such a shower of blows upon their heads and backs that their enthusiasm for theft was quite cooled. I was afraid of only one thing, and that was the need to have recourse to firearms for, had it come to that, I would never have been allowed to leave the country alive. It was as well to have done what I did for, from that moment, they were afraid to come near me; they backed away as I passed, and thenceforth I had no more dealings with the common people. From having been one of them, I now became an aristocrat and associated only with the important people who had been useful to me, re-doubling my attentions towards them.

Meanwhile Panda, who had received my proposals of barter, dispatched a headman to convey to me his wishes, and to negotiate in his name. But, from the start, insurmountable difficulties arose. Instead of a quantity of glass beads (*hamgazy*), worth ten rixdollars, for each cow, which was the going price, Panda demanded beads worth 125 rixdollars for young heifers with growing horns, only three inches long. I could not possibly agree to such an offer, and I rejected it out of hand. Then Panda's headman pronounced a few delicately phrased remarks which I interpreted as a declaration of intent; I did not suspect that it was an order.

'My master is considering sending his men to hunt elephant in the catchment of the two Om-Philos where you are hunting at the present moment.'

I asked for an explanation; the envoy gave it without deviating in any way from the sense of his master's words.

Three days later, another envoy arrived with this message: 'Panda, my master, plans an elephant hunt here, at this place. He commands me to tell you that in the south, yonder, at Om-Schlatousse, you will find many elephants; at least 200 have just been seen there; by going there you will oblige Panda.'

I begged for an explanation, but could discover no deeper meaning than the words themselves conveyed.

My Natal Cafres, whom I consulted about the meaning of these requests, were in agreement that it was Panda's intention to forbid me to hunt elephant in his country. I found his approach too subtle; his request was almost unintelligible and, had I not understood the true meaning of orders so delicately insinuated, I might well have called down his wrath upon my head. 'Well then,' I said, 'since he wishes me to go and hunt at Om-Schlatousse, and since by moving there I will oblige him, then tomorrow, when my wagonload of ivory sets off for Touguela, I will go with it as far as Om-Schlatousse.'

And that is what I did. Two days searching in the mountains of Om-Gohey produced only the dry old spoor of about 200 elephants which had passed that way more than a fortnight previously. I travelled for ten leagues along the northern slopes which were furrowed by pretty streams of limpid water running down into the Om-Schlatouzanne, a deep sparkling river bordered with tall green rushes which, like a daughter keeping close beside her mother, the Om-Schlatousse, would later join hands with her before they cast themselves together into the Indian Ocean.

On all these granitic mountains, where water is extremely abundant, the vegetation looks very like that of the plains; but the pasturage, although excellent for horses, does not suit cattle. Riet-booken, *Redunca eleotragus*, were frequently to be seen, singly or in small herds; the unevenness of the terrain, combined with their lack of fear, made hunting them an easy matter. The klip-springer, *Oreotragus saltatrix*, inhabited the most inaccessible places, where they perched boldly on flimsy outcrops, rather like birds of prey; but they were rare; this species is nowhere very prevalent. Occasionally, rockrabbits crept out of their holes. We saw no buffalo at all. Having made certain that there were no longer any elephants in the bush of the Om-Schlatousse basin, I lost interest and went back to my camp.

The following day, I was obliged to receive yet another of Panda's envoys, who insisted that the elephants were at Om-Schlatousse and that I must go there to hunt them. As I had just returned from there, I had seen enough to dismiss these claims.

'I understand,' I said, 'that Panda wishes to forbid me to hunt; he has the right to do so, and I submit to that. When my wagon arrives, I shall bid farewell to this country. Until that time, you may assure Panda that I shall hunt only for my daily needs. Buffalo, eland, rhinoceros, hippopotamus have not been included in the prohibition; I will confine myself to them.' And the envoy would surely have gone back to his master and said: 'The white man has understood; the white man will go away.' I fired shots at two *Rhinoceros simus*, a mother and her calf, which was almost as big as the mother herself, and ended up acquiring another skeleton.[1]

I went to say a last goodbye to the beloved, luxuriant banks of the Om-Philos, although they were less beautiful now, since the sombre events which had taken Souzouana from me. I felt my heart bursting with love for these scenes of many a hunt. My men, aware of my emotion, hastened to point out to me that there had been no definite order to leave and that Panda had not fixed on any particular date.

'Master you would be wrong to leave like this. Why not finish off with a last elephant hunt? There are still some elephants here, you saw them yourself. Two herds are grazing only half a day away, one of them ten strong and the other fifteen.'

'Yes I know, but they are wretched creatures, females with short feeble tusks. We'll have all the trouble, without hope of much profit. It would be best not to try anything more, but simply to pack up and go.'

Then the pleading and the entreaties began again; they would not have been at all pleased if I had denied them. And so, the following day was fixed upon to begin another hunt, whatever the weather might be. We had to get just one more, only one more elephant, and then we would go away content.

We were up and doing two hours before the dawn, which enabled us to get a glimpse of several straggling hyaenas who, after the bloody orgies of the night, were slinking home to their lair, looking rather like crest-fallen revellers, taken unawares by the cold before the dawn. They slunk past us, footsore and ashamed, trailing behind them their distinctive, disgusting stench. Although I kept them provided with food, I had no desire to see them, the vile things. Generally, one settled the matter with a shot, but this time, I

1 This skeleton today belongs to the gallery of comparative anatomy under the direction of Monsieur de Blainville at the Jardin du Roi.

refrained because our objective was elephants, which meant that no unnecessary shot should be fired at any other animal.

At about nine o'clock, we came upon a *Rhinoceros simus*, only eight paces in front of us, which was blocking our way. I was forced, in spite of my resolution, to rend the air with a powerful reverberating shot. The animal fell to the ground, stone dead, and we went on our way.

Round about eleven o'clock, when the heat was growing intense, we looked down over Om-Philos-Mouniama and saw the herd of ten elephants, with their feet in the water and using their trunks, like hands, to slap wet sand on to their bodies and then wash themselves with as much care as a dandy might apply to his toilet. As far as the direction of the wind was concerned, we were well placed; but the situation was too open, they must see us. I waited, hoping they would move on to a more favourable position. Henning, who was always impatient on these occasions, remarked that the elephants looked as if they were going through all the motions of performing a complete toilet.

'Are we going to wait for them to put their shirts on?'

'Of course, and only then will it be right for us to pin them down. But let us wait a little.'

A few minutes later, we divided up into two parties, Henning and his men going to the left, while my men and I turned right, our aim being to corner the elephants between us. Unfortunately, as soon as we tried to close in on them, one of the elephants raised its trunk, spread out its ears, and trumpeted a warning, whereupon they all bolted, climbed up the opposite bank and disappeared into the bush, where we searched for them for two hours to no avail. Their tracks led in the opposite direction from the one we wished to follow and so, having wearied ourselves to no purpose, we let them go.

By three o'clock, we were still searching, in the hope of finding the other herd. We were about to give up when one of my new Cafres, by the name of Kamdane, rushed up to me crying, 'They're here.'

'What did you say?'

'The elephants.'

'That's great news.'

I looked where he was pointing and saw, quite clearly, six or seven of them, peacefully moving about among the clumps of *Kruys-bezie* bushes which stood ten to fifteen feet high among a few taller trees.

The lie of the land was such that it seemed best for some of us to try and turn them, while the rest remained at the place from where we had first spotted them. Kamdane, carrying an enormous quarter-pounder, set off with two other Cafres. He succeeded perfectly in executing the plan and got within ten paces of the elephants. Then the shots all rang out at once but, as if they had guessed our intentions, instead of coming towards the place where we were waiting for them, the elephants turned on the men who had just attacked them. Kamdane sought refuge in a fallen tree which an elephant had uprooted and from which, later, we had infinite difficulty in extricating him. Boulandje lost his gun which, he said, had been snatched away by an elephant's trunk and which we found some distance off, quite out of action. The third man, when he saw the danger, disappeared out of sight into a nearby ravine; so suddenly did he vanish, that the elephant chasing him must have thought that he was pursuing a wizard.

Never before had my men been so completely outwitted by elephants. When the danger was past, we laughed about it. Even Kamdane laughed, although his back had been torn to ribbons by branches and thorns. Then we set off once more in pursuit of our prey, delighted to see their tracks leading towards our camp.

An hour later, we were alerted to the proximity of our elephants by the hollow rumbling sound which these animals often make, and which is apparently produced from their intestines. As the density of the low bushes prevented our seeing anything, we were obliged to listen very carefully to the rumbling noise in order to be able to calculate where it was coming from. Once again, the terrain was not in our favour and it needed particularly to be so, because the herd was a poor one.

We trod carefully, stopped and listened, edged forward, stopped again, all the while listening attentively; in a word, our behaviour was stealthy, cat-like. As there was no pattern, no order, in our advance, each man risked, in the event of having to retreat, trampling on the man behind him. One of my Cafres, who was to the left of me, was advancing in this fashion when the branches above his head started swaying, and out popped an elephant's trunk, followed by its head, which looked down, as if from a first floor window, to see what was going on below. Nose to trunk with the enemy, my Cafre raised his weapon and, without pausing to take aim, he singed the whiskers of the curious observer. The elephant spun around and took a line of retreat which cut right across ours, leaving one of my men flat on the ground, wondering how he had got there.

'It's not going well Kotchobana; we're not doing anything today.'

'Let us keep quiet master, perhaps success could be close at hand. Listen, the others are there; they are just not moving.'

As he said this, he pointed to where the rumbling noise was coming from. Four of us began walking towards the little clearing just ahead of us. Hardly had we reached it, when there was a crashing of branches and a large and furious elephant came charging towards us at great speed. His intentions were only too obvious for us to be in any doubt of the danger. Henning, Kotchobana and another Cafre did not hesitate, but turned and fled, quite forgetting about me. Anyway, I could never make up my mind to run away as long as there was a bullet left in the barrel. I stood my ground, and kept my sights trained on the swaying head of the animal as he readied himself for a headlong charge. He was thirty paces away when my bullet hit him. He changed his mind pretty fast, making the sharpest circular turn he possibly could. The bullet was all that was needed to deflate his blustering courage. He changed his mind about crushing us with his left tusk, just as a woman might squash a flying insect with her finger nail.

The elephant's rump could still be seen disappearing into the bush when another of my men, new to hunting, and fearless because he did not understand the danger, came upon the scene, and saw the fleeing animal. This man, a Provençal by birth, had been quartermaster on board the corvette *La Favorite*, and had deserted in Boston while the Prince de Jonville was stationed there; his name was Louis. Fearless to the point of insanity, he loved danger for danger's sake. Hell-bent on pursuing the fugitive, he set off after the elephant, who had better things to do than to stand and stare and continued on his waddling way. His long legs and the length of his stride stood him in good stead. His breathing was hard, like that of any other fleeing animal, but it was not laboured, and already Louis was losing ground. Louis, whose legs somewhat resembled those of the hippopotamus, ran fast for his size, but not nearly fast enough to win the race against an elephant. In addition, our man was carrying a gun weighing twenty-two pounds and Louis was not Roman enough to consider his weapon as part of his person. The gun was probably the reason why my intrepid Provençal was obliged to stop and rest for a moment.

His courage and his determination ensured that he soon regained his breath and then, quite unconcerned about getting lost and having to spend the night in the bush, he set off once more to follow the blood-stained trail. His perseverance was rewarded when a branch nearby cracked, and Louis found himself within arm's length of the elephant. An enormous shot rang out, the animal fell, and my Provençal was beginning to think of cutting off the tail as proof of possession, when he changed his mind and reloaded. He had not completed the operation when the wounded animal got up and walked away, much to the astonishment of the ex-sailor, who looked on open-mouthed as if he imagined he saw St Elmo's fire[1] flickering around the elephant's trunk, ears and tail.

Realising what had happened, Louis leapt about like the devil in holy water. In his fury, he tried to twist off the barrel of his gun; with

1 St Elmo was the patron saint of sailors. His protection was manifested in a luminosity around its object. *Translator's note*

the butt he beat the earth as if he wanted to open a crack 500 feet deep and bury himself in it. He accused himself of every stupidity in not carrying out his first intention. He would have grabbed the elephant by the tail, he would have cut a great hole in its stomach, he would have climbed through this lubber's hole[1] into this new kind of top, and then he would have tied all the rope it contained to an assegai, and shot it out on to the deck. He meant that he would liked to have yanked out its entrails. Oh, if only he had the chance again; Louis was not the man to let it pass, he would prove that!

A quarter of an hour later, along came another elephant. It passed by, right in front of Louis, who fired. The animal dropped just as the first one had done. This was a great consolation to Louis, and he savoured it as he reloaded his gun, thinking of the tail that he must not forget to cut off. But then the elephant got up, appeared to pull a face at the hunter and decamped, leaving no address.

This time the sailor, thunderstruck, stood gaping with amazement. Two hours later, at four o'clock, he was still rooted to the spot. He was talking to himself. 'I'm dreaming. Why should I tire myself out by climbing up there? I'm in my hammock; someone's on watch below; it's time to sleep.'

A kind of whistling sound roused him from his imaginary sleep; he thought he heard the quartermaster's whistle summoning the men of the starboard watch.[2]

This quarter-master turned out to be an elephant passing by, forty paces away; but Louis did not fire; he was by now certain that the third time wouldn't be any better than the first two.

Three hours after sunset, our hero arrived sadly back at the camp. He told us how he had managed to find his way through thick bush that was completely unfamiliar to him. The telling of the story of his misadventure kept us up all night; it was good to laugh, after all our adversity. Just imagine! Not a single elephant on my last day's hunting in the country of the Amazoulous.

The following day we rested, and the day after that we left Om-Philos-Om-Schlopu, knowing full well that we would not be allowed to set foot there again while Panda remained in power. We travelled in silence, each of us alone with his thoughts, full of regret that we could not spend the rest of our lives in that wonderful country. The hunting by which, and for which, we lived was at its best there. As it had depended on Panda's pleasure to permit it, so it depended on him alone to forbid it. We could do no other than obey the wishes of the despot. Four days journey, saddened by the

1   Lubber's hole: part of the top through which the topmen climb when they are afraid of climbing through the shrouds.
2   The crew of a ship is divided into watches; one starboard and one port.

knowledge that the beautiful country was receding further and further from us, brought us south of Om-Schlatousse to the banks of a lake where the hippopotamus had grown so cunning that they had learnt to avoid our bullets.

For some hours we'd had, travelling along with us, a man of all work, a sort of factotum, in the employ of the missionary Grout. He said that he preferred to travel in convoy, and when we outspanned, he drew his wagon up beside mine. At about midnight, there was some commotion; words were exchanged, then the voices grew fainter and disappeared into the distance, until silence reigned once more. When we arose the next morning, I learnt that the noise had been made by some deserting Cafres passing by. We crossed Om-Lalas at midday and outspanned on the bank so that we could put in some hunting. We had been there for a couple of hours, when eight Amazoulous appeared on the opposite bank. They hailed my men and asked them if they had seen the deserter, Unungongo. Upon receiving a negative reply, they began talking among themselves and gesticulating energetically. There was no doubt that this was a serious matter.

We were outspanned on low-lying ground where the mosquitoes were bound to attack us. I realised this, and my orders were being carried out to inspan again and move three kilometres away to higher ground where there were two or three huts, when we noticed, on the northern shore of the Om-Lalas, a gigantic hippopotamus, walking peacefully along. We fired fifty shots at it in less than two minutes. The echoes repeated the deafening noise of our rapid fire, giving the impression that we were four times more numerous than we really were. This chance circumstance was our salvation for I believe that my men and I would otherwise have been murdered that very night.

Once we had outspanned again, we all went off in different directions. Henning went straight to the place where the hippopotamuses were rising. My men and I took another direction, in search of riet-booken. By sunset, I had killed two of these antelopes and I returned to camp with some of my men. We were waiting for Henning and his people who were not yet back, when a Port Natal Cafre, who had been trading up near Om-Schlatousse, approached me in a state of agitation.

'Master,' he said, 'over there, on that mountain that I have just come down, I saw with my own eyes 600 Amazoulous lying flat on their shields, and surrounded by bundles of *om-kondos*. I made enquiries and found out that they are looking for Unungongo and his followers who are fleeing from Panda because he has threatened to kill them. Unungongo is somewhere nearby and, before the sun rises, he and his followers will be assegaied by Panda's men under their leader Magelebé.'

'Is this true, all that you are saying?'

'Yes, master, quite true, I swear by Farewell (Febana).'

'But I have had nothing to do with those people, I have never even seen them.'

'No, not you, but the missionary's man knows them well. These Amazoulous are deserting because of him; it is as if they are carrying out their desertion under the protection of the whites. From your camp to the *mouzi*, where they are, is no more than a step. To escape death, these deserters will take refuge in your wagons and the ruthless warriors will pursue them, in spite of your presence. Perhaps you will be killed in the confusion, either in trying to prevent one lot taking refuge, or in repelling the others; when one carries a gun it is very difficult not to use it in such circumstances, and to tell the truth, Panda has every right to believe that the whites are inciting his people to desertion.'

The man expressed exactly what I had been thinking. I decided immediately to move away from the centre of the scene of possible massacre, but I had to wait for my driver. It had been dark for half an hour when Henning returned at last, exuberant at having killed three hippopotamuses. 'That's more than we need,' I said. 'Anyway, we've got to inspan immediately; this place is no good. *'Bamba izinkabu!* Let's go!' Henning looked at me in open-mouthed disbelief. 'Come on, let's get a move on, Henning. I'll tell you about it on the way'.

We were putting on the yokes when along came the missionary's man. He suspected what our intentions were, and was anxious to come with us. Once we were on our way, I explained to my men what was going on. I handed out enough ammunition to fill each powder flask and bullet pouch, and then gave the order to follow behind the wagon in single file, keeping absolutely silent, while Henning was to refrain from cracking the great whip. We hoped to get far enough away to make it impossible for the Amazoulous to carry out their orders and attack us at their favourite time, the hour before the dawn. But the cause of all the unpleasantness began following us, in spite of our hostility. Unungongo and his people, feeling safer when they were near us, persisted in staying close. First they walked along beside us but I let them know that, as I was moving with the intention of getting away from them, I believed I had the right to drive them off. If they did not comply, I said I would be forced to fire on them as my personal safety and that of my men demanded that I resort to strong measures.

Then Unungongo and his followers fell back a little, and trailed along 100 paces behind us. But this did not suit my intentions either, for at that distance, it would have been impossible for me to distinguish whether they were deserters or Amazoulous. So I dispatched Kotchobana to tell them that I did not intend to be followed by anybody at all and that they must go away. Unongongo's party took heed of this warning, but in a manner which suited themselves best. As walking alongside us, or behind us, had been forbidden, they took up their position in front. But what can one do with people who are fleeing to escape death? My orders were already contrary to my real wishes. To tell the truth, I would like to have been able to help them, and I would have appeared less severe if they had first requested my assistance, instead of taking me unawares; in not consulting my wishes, these men were forcing me to confront the same dangers as they themselves were.

We made a halt at two in the morning, after travelling a long way over difficult terrain, where there were no tracks to be seen. Some of the men wanted to light fires, but I was against it for it was possible that, unbeknown to us, we had been followed, and we needed to be particularly vigilant just before the dawn. If the Amazoulous had arrived *en masse*, and armed, and had proceeded forcefully, in spite of our protests, to make a search, we would most certainly have opposed them with gunfire. I say most certainly, because I had convinced my twelve men that I was determined to blow myself up if a single one of them gave way. And I assured them that the explosion would spare no one. For the execution of this desperate measure, I told them that I had by me a double-barrelled gun which I would fire into my powder keg containing seventy pounds of gunpowder.

For the next few days, we made our way as quickly as possible towards Touguela and we felt safe only when we had put that river behind us. Having taken advantage of our company during the night, Unungongo disappeared, and was already at Port Natal while we were still in the Amazoulou country. Without my knowing it, it turned out that this man had compromised us in such a way as to give Panda's emissaries the right to murder us on the spot.

During the crossing of the Om-Vooty, I noticed that our herd of cows seemed more numerous than before. The herdsman, when I sent for him, informed me that, apart from my own cows and a few which belonged to Boulandje and Kotchobana, there were about fifteen others which must belong to Unungongo, as they had only been part of the herd since Om-Lalas.

This discovery made me realise that Magalebé's men would have been within their rights if, for no other reason than that these cows were in my herd, they had swooped on my convoy without warning. This was culpable evidence according to the way they think in these parts. In Panda's eyes I would without doubt have been seen as the guilty party. He could have reclaimed what he already considered as his own property, appropriated mine, and disposed of the lives of all of us. This had been brought upon me by Unungongo who, as he fled, could not drive his beasts fast enough. Wishing to get them safely to Natal, he had had the excellent idea of adding them to my herd. Without them, he was able to move rapidly and reach safety across the Touguela, while I, who moved more slowly, remained responsible for them and vulnerable, if the Amazoulous had proved bold enough to harass me. Fortunately, as I learnt later, Magabelé had reckoned on losing fifty men at least if he should attempt to overpower me and, disinclined to make so great a sacrifice, he had sent messages to the Princess Mahoha, instructing her to mobilise her men and prevent the *Oumlongo* from crossing the Touguela.

The *Oumlongo* was me, and Mahoha was one of my old friends. She did not receive the messengers very warmly, and finally she said to them: 'What is the reason for this? Since the *Oumlongo* is still in your territory, you have had all the time you needed. You did not dare to do anything, and the business that you failed to do you now want me to do. Mahoha will not do it and, if anyone has failed in his duty, it is your chief, Magalebé.' Thereupon, she dispatched a messenger to Panda and, while communications were in process, I had plenty of time to cross the border.

I was just about to reach Port Natal, having crossed the Om-Guinée, when two Cafres arrived to speak to me, one of whom claimed to be Unungongo.

'Master, master!'

As you may imagine, for some while I ignored him.

'Master, I have come to claim my cows.'

'Never seen them'.

'Master it is I, Unungongo.'

'Don't know him'.

'But of course you do; I was the one who travelled alongside you from Om-Lalas halfway to Oum-Matagoulou. I left my cows with your herd and now I've come to claim them.'

'Oh, so it's you, you rascal, *om-tagaty, om-koulou, kakoulu*, you rascally devil. Oh, so you took me to be your cattle herd, did you? And you left me to take responsibility for your actions when you and your men ran away from the laws of your land. Oh, so it was because of you that I had to abandon the three hippopotamuses we killed at Om-Lalas, so that we went hungry on the way home, and I had to suffer the wails of my people when they bound up their stomachs to still the pangs of hunger. It is just as well you came because my men and I have a bone to pick with you.'

I called my people together to hear the opinion of each man concerning the payment and the damages we should demand from Unungongo for the conduct of his cattle, and the inconvenience he had caused us. Everybody agreed on our keeping one of the young bulls, which we would feast on next day. I informed Unungongo of our decision, fully expecting his *vouma* (consent). After hesitating a while, he finally gave it, whereupon I invited him to take part in the feast, which duly took place next day. Unungongo did not come, although he had promised he would.

A fortnight later, I was much astonished to receive a letter from Captain Smith, the commander of the English forces at Natal, who also held the office of magistrate. He asked for an explanation of my relations with Unungongo. The latter had laid a charge against me, at the instigation of the missionary Grout, who was delighted to see me fall foul of the authorities against whose power there was no appeal.

Fortunately, most fortunately, I was dealing with a man of good sense, too much of a gentleman to allow this controversy to develop the way that the self-styled philanthropist had intended it should. I got off lightly, being required simply to recount the facts and then receive Unungongo's enforced thanks, for he had already forgotten that, had it not been for my fortuitous flight, both he and his men would have died by the assegai.

I learnt, at the same time, more about the offence that this man had committed, an offence which, although slight, is punishable by death. One day he had come across an elephant's tusk in the bush; the missionary's man heard of it, and desired it. The Cafre, who was rather weak-willed, had been tempted by the offer of a calabash of hippopotamus fat in exchange. Panda was no sooner informed of the transaction, than he ordered the thief to be punished. I say 'thief' because all ivory belongs to the king.

It is not surprising that the missionary Grout should have attempted to support Unungongo, and to stir up all kinds of trouble against me. The missionary Grout had doubtless not forgotten the manner in which I had received his first insult, as well as a subsequent occasion, when I submitted to him a demand for payment.

It may perhaps be of some interest to the reader to learn more of this incident, which throws some light on the machinations of these 'bearers of civilisation'. I was travelling on foot from Om-Philos to Natal and my way led me past Om-Schlatousse where the missionary lived in his very elegant and very white house. I was determined to avoid passing close by it, and so I took a long detour. An hour later, I came to a Cafre village where I asked for the chief and requested the usual hospitality. This man sniggered and said: 'You are a white man; it is strange that you do not ask the white man for hospitality and a place to spend the night.'

'It is possible that you are surprised, but I prefer a black man to that white man, and I will not go to his house'.

'But why not, what is your reason?'

'Because he is one of those white men who dress all in white, and who live in white houses, but whose hearts are black; while there are black men living in smoky black houses whose hearts are white. I believe that you are one of those black men, and I would like to ask you for a hut where I may spend the night, some maize to satisfy my hunger, and some *tchoula* to quench my thirst.'

'Some *tchoula*? How can a white man dare to ask for *tchoula*, the black man's beer, which the *om-phondiss* (missionary) forbids us to drink, because it makes men wicked, he says.'

'The *om-phondiss* lies; *tchoula* is the most innocent drink I know; it quenches the thirst, it strengthens a man when he is weak, and takes away fatigue; much more than this, it gives rise to a gentle gaiety and, for that alone, I swear by Dingaan, it makes one a better man.'

'Yes,' he replied, 'it nourishes and fortifies, but the *om-phondiss* told us that it makes the heart black and wicked; since then, we no longer brew it.'

'Oh, go on stupid Cafre, I pity you. Your ancestors drank *tchoula*, and they lived to a ripe old age. You yourself appreciate its benefits, the only comforts available to the black man, and you reject, without question, what God has given you, because an *om-phondiss*, of doubtful origin, tells you to do so. I pity you, you think like a crazy old woman. Give me anything you like, as long as I have something to eat and somewhere to sleep.'

At this point, my man excused himself and went off, eventually returning with a small quantity of dry maize. He offered me a wretched hut and a dirty sleeping mat, with a stone underneath, doing the office of a pillow. I fell asleep thinking that this bigot enjoyed none of the comforts of life because he sent his women off to waste their time praying, instead of cultivating the land.

When day broke, I was about to take leave of my hosts whose meagre services required few compliments, when the chief came along and asked me for payment for the food and the hut I had used. I must admit that I was filled with astonishment at this demand, which was unheard of among the Amazoulous. Was I to understand that hospitality, considered a virtue among the natives, had been given me in the expectation of reward? The thing seemed impossible, and I confronted my host. 'You want to be paid?' I asked. 'Your request would be the normal thing anywhere else, but you should respect the customs of your people. You alone are not in a position to change them. In your country, I have been welcomed everywhere; nowhere have I paid. In return, whenever Amazoulous have come to visit me, whether there were twenty or a hundred of them, I have given them as much meat as they wanted; each time I have had buffaloes killed for them, and the visitors have gone off with provisions for several days. This is what I have always done; I have

110

always returned hospitality with hospitality. I know of no other way of settling such a debt, and you must understand that, as I was relying on your generosity, I have brought nothing with which to pay for your services.'

'Master, it is true that these are not our ways; by asking for payment, I go against Zoulou custom, but the *om-phondiss* said that we have the right to demand recompense for all services we render to whites; that one must give nothing for nothing, and so you must pay for what you were offered.'

'You did wrong to listen to the *om-phondiss* because to listen to a bad man is wrong. The *om-phondiss* has shown himself to be bad, by destroying a good thing. Hospitality is a virtue which testifies to the brotherhood of men; it is the only great virtue you possess. The *om-phondiss* has done ill by not informing me of the changes he is trying to bring about. As a result of this negligence on his part, I find myself unable to pay you, as I did not foresee your demand. So the *om-phondiss* will have to pay you himself.'

Without further delay, I wrote with a piece of coal on a scrap of paper a demand for payment addressed to the missionary Grout, explaining to him that, although I was loath to do this, I had no alternative, and that it was all his fault. I have no doubt that the excellent and kind-hearted *om-phondiss* had this incident in mind when he set Unungongo against me, intending that the man's tongue would prove a terrible weapon with which to wound me. Unfortunately for him, his black heart did not have its revenge. For there are a few Englishmen of good sense who, understanding their methods and objectives, despise these agents of so-called evangelism.

CHAPTER XXVII

Customs of the Amazoulous — Physical appearance — Barefooted — Warriors with shaven heads and tufts of feathers — The young men keep their hair — Hard skulls — Men always go armed — Various sorts of arms — A single garment worn for the sake of modesty — Ornaments — Cloaks worn at night — Warriors in full dress — Merciless in war — Women do all the domestic and field work — Cloak worn by women — Their heads shaven like the men's — The pregnant woman — Young girl's scanty dress — Children completely naked — Tattooing — Polygamy — Marriage and ceremonies related thereto — Increased effort of each wife with a view to adding to the harem — Absence of jealousy — Attachment of children to their mothers — Breast-feeding keeps the wife apart from her husband — Qualities and faults of the Zoulou people — Government — Despotism — Frequent assassination of pretenders — Annual announcement of the state of the nation — Headmen — Guards — Taxes — Cultivation — Penalties — Sentences of death and confiscation which profit the king — No religious beliefs — Inianga and dead brothers — No funeral ceremony — Body of the deceased left for the hyaenas — Inheritance

Having lived almost a year among people as interesting as the Amazoulous, I decided to sum up all that I had learnt of them and I now offer to the reader an account of my findings.

The Amazoulou live in the south-eastern part of Africa; their country is bordered in the north by the *Om-Pongola*, river of the gnu, which empties its waters into Delagoa Bay, and in the south by the Touguela, called 'Fisher River' by English navigators; it is bathed in the east by the Indian Ocean and in the west, the tall mountains of Quathlambène separate it from the country of the Makatisses.

The climate of the Amazoulou country is generally hot, which is why the emigrant Boers call it 'Waarm-Veld'. It is situated between 27° and 29° south latitude, and its elevation above the Indian Ocean is not sufficient to produce a harsh winter climate. For this reason, and in spite of the fact that they live at the same latitude, the customs of the Amazoulou differ from those of peoples living further to the west.

The Amazoulous have the finest physique of all the Cafre races; their height which is rather less than that of the English, and quite considerably less than that of the Boers, is equal I think to the French, although their proportions are more graceful. The body is slim, without being too lean, strong and elegant, and the muscles are pronounced. There is strength allied with grace and agility; there is flexibility and ease in their bearing. The features share some of the characteristics of those of the negroes; for example, in the width of the mouth, the thickness of the lips, the length and whiteness of the teeth; the low-bridged nose with flaring nostrils, the woolly texture of the hair, the brown-black colour of the skin and its distinctive odour.

In all these features there are similarities, but none are as pronounced as they are in the negro. In fact, I was surprised to see that, in many cases, the faces were not unlike the European. I must admit that I have often found the Zoulou physiogonomy most attractive, while I never felt anything but repugnance for the negro faces which I encountered, whether in Senegal, Gambia, the Gulf of Guinea or all the Antilles, whether French, English, Spanish, Danish, Dutch or Swedish. I must mention that the progeny of unions between blue-eyed, fair haired Englishmen and Zoulou women are perfectly formed; their features, while not strictly according to our taste, are nevertheless very beautiful, and their gentle expression is immensely attractive. But the mulattos of our own colonies, whose mothers came from the Congo, are not at all like these.

One frequently notices among the Amazoulous, individuals with aquiline noses, thin lips, light complexions and long beards. Although there is no European blood in their veins, these men, seen in profile, have features exactly like ours. Their brilliant eyes, black in every case, are hooded, elongated in shape and so expressive that every humour is immediately apparent. One must except of course, those men in high places, who have early learned to deceive with their looks. Panda, king of the Amazoulous, whom I knew and observed for a long time, possessed to a high degree this ability. His eyes were never allowed to betray his thoughts. Almost invariably, an open-hearted friendly smile brightens the faces of these people and predisposes one to like them.

The Amazoulous have left off wearing sandals and walk barefoot, in spite of the cruel mimosa thorns and the sharp-edged stones which peppered the paths through the bush country. This is because Djacka, the builder of the nation, the contemporary of Napoleon, ordered that it should be so; he was convinced that barefoot warriors are swifter and more agile than the shod.[1]

---

1 Before Djacka's time, the Amazoulou were not numerous. They wore sandals and threw the *om-kondo* in battle as do the Ama-Kosas today. Where previously they had attacked in a disordered manner, Djacka formed them into regiments of 1 000 men; he forbade the wearing of sandals and stipulated that each warrior would carry only one *om-kondo* which was to be inspected after the encounter to ensure that it was stained with the enemy's blood. Fighting was hand to hand, and in the thick of battle every Zoulou warrior broke off the shaft of his assegai which made it possible to manipulate it more effectively. This new method of fighting, which was unknown to neighbouring nations, so much increased the destructiveness of the Amazoulous in battle that, during the twelve years that he was in power, Djacka succeeded in killing more than a million men. This is the figure given by Captain Jarvis who was busy with the history of these people at the time that I was living at Port Natal.

The Amazoulous have their heads shaved; only a ring of hair, five inches across and eliptical in shape, is retained on top of the head; this serves as a base for several circles of straw which are firmly stitched to the hair and smeared with a layer of black wax. This is done to hold the ceremonial plumes, the quills made of wood or iron, the snuff boxes made from the cocoon of the bombyx, the ivory snuff spoons and the plumes of war made from the tufts of touraco and widow bird tails; in short, all sorts of useful and decorative things. This is the insignia of the warrior; the *abafanas*, or young men, do not shave their heads.

As a consequence of this baldness, which is achieved by shaving with the untempered blade of an *om-kondo*, the bones of the cranium acquire remarkable thickness. This observation of mine, which I made on several occasions, is borne out by the Amazoulous themselves. In the wars against the whites, when the warrior has stabbed the enemy with an assegaai, he exchanges this weapon for the *tonga*, a sort of little club made of tambooty wood and rhinoceros horn. Its function is to crack the skull in order to ensure that the adversary will not rise again.

When they were dealing with people like themselves, the Amazoulou needed to inflict a violent blow to obtain the desired result, while in their encounters with the English or the Boers a much milder blow sufficed to shatter the skull. This amazed the Amazoulous and gave them further reason to despise the whites.

Warriors first and foremost, the men never go unarmed. They carry a great cow-hide shield, four and a half to five feet high, five or six assegais and a *tonga*. It is necessary to take these precautions, because the country abounds in great herbivores which are dangerous when encountered unexpectedly; buffalo, rhinoceros and elephant are more to be feared by day than lions and leopards. Even though the weapons are not powerful enough for the task, a man feels much more courageous when armed. To avoid being charged by wild beasts, and to frighten off those lurking in the bushes, it is the custom to make a great noise. This noise is produced by striking the shield with the shaft of the *om-kondo*.

The Amazoulous do not practice circumcision; they find it very distasteful and profess supreme contempt for the tribes that do. The *motgeas*, or modesty garments, are worn more for adornment than with the intention of concealment. This garment is composed simply of a dozen strips of genet fur, elegantly suspended from a narrow belt which encircles the loins at the pubic bone, holding in position a little skin cap which covers the foreskin. At the back, half way down the buttocks, five or six artificial tails two feet long, create a most picturesque impression, swaying attractively as the men walk or run.

114

It is perhaps worth observing that this custom of wearing the little cap produces quite the opposite effect to that of circumcision because the glans is never in contact with the air; hence the man retains throughout his life the same inclinations and the same sensitivity as the child before he becomes a man. Circumcision as an hygienic practice, although indispensable to the dirty Makatisses living in a cold country, would be perfectly useless to the Amazoulous, who are distinguished by a degree of cleanliness which is rare among the naked peoples.

The everyday dress of the Amazoulous consists simply of the *motgeas* which I have just described, and for the rest, a few articles intended for daily use or adornment. Around their necks, they wear necklaces of beads and the teeth and claws of lion, leopard, or eagle; there are also little bags containing simple medicaments, and pieces of root, but never any greegrees or amulets, for the Amazoulous do not value the talismans so prized by the negroes of the coast of Guinea and Senegal. Their arms are sometimes adorned with copper bangles, or armlets made from the intestines of animals, and their ears are always pierced, the large holes threaded through with sections of Spanish reed, closed up at each end and filled with snuff.

When evening comes and the land cools off, at milking time they drape themselves in night cloaks. This cloak is not in any way graceful and bears evidence of an industry which is but recent in origin. It is made from cow-hide, rendered pliable and soft by the application of fat; thorny aloe leaves are used to card the hair which is retained, and worn next to the body.

For those who have seen only the everyday costume, the sight of a troop of men dressed and armed for war comes as a great surprise. I myself was excessively astonished, but I fear I shall not be able to describe adequately what I saw, or rather I doubt that I am able to convey to the reader quite how picturesque and graceful they appeared. Well then, here is a warrior ready to salute his king as he leaves for battle.

His head is adorned with a pad of otter skin, reminiscent of a woman's boa, but this article of dress, which passes around the forehead and ties behind, is intended for practical purposes; it must parry the blows of the *tonga*, while its dark colour casts a shadow over the features and lends an implacable air to him who wears it. At the back of the head stands a Numidian crane's feather, its slender tip swaying in the breeze and trembling as if from impatience, while behind it, attached to the back of the Cafre crown flutters a bunch of feathers of many colours. On either side, two squares of jackal skin, six inches long, hang down from the pad to cover the ears. According to the Amazoulus, these lappets serve a useful purpose, for they ensure that the warrior will hear neither the curses nor the prayers of his foe, and will thus be influenced neither by fear or by compassion.

From neck to waist, in front and behind, the man is completely covered in the tassels of cow tails; his right arm is similarly adorned, but the left is bare, for it supports the shield.[1]

From waist to knee hangs the rich and graceful *symba*, the warrior's kilt, composed of 400 strips of genet skin, a heavy garment which parts, and closes again with the movement of the wearer. Lower down the leg, magnificent garters made from white tails protect the shinbone. Around the ankle are cuffs made from shortened cow tails, intended to afford protection from thorns or from bruising in the thick of battle.

This costume is worn only by the élite regiments. Other regiments do not wear the *symba*, but only the ordinary *motgeas*. They would appear to be trying to make amends for this by wearing on their heads globular tufts or balls, made of feathers, fixed to the back of the headring, and held in place on the forehead by bunches of swaying widowbird tails, *Emberiza longicaudata*, which create a wonderful effect when worn by a herald-at-arms, as he darts away like an arrow on his mission. At that moment too, his anklets, as he runs, bring to mind vividly the wings on the feet of Mercury.

I saw regiments which had adopted ostrich feathers as their insignia, but either because we associate them with women, or because their whiteness was dubious, I did not think them suitable for warriors. Others again were distinguished by horizontal plumes, three feet long, made of widow-bird tails, attached to a stalk. In the war dance, upon a certain pre-arranged beat, the line of men would lower their heads and by so doing, they raised the gigantic feathers upright into the air, thus adding greatly to each man's height. The effect was quite wonderful, but the extraordinary proportions of these wild-looking plumes gave the impression of overwhelming those whom they were intended to make more beautiful and more terrifying.

Slave traders have never come near these people, probably because of the Amazoulous' reputation for ferocity, and their conduct in war. They find it ridiculous that the victor should spare his enemy's life, and they kill everyone in their path; even women and young girls whom they would normally value, are not always spared.

They believe that man is born to make war and to hunt and, if it should happen that he builds huts or cuts wood, this is simply because male strength may be required for these activities and

---

1 The captains, the men of rank, and the women of the harem have the right arm encased in an arm-band of yellow copper, formed from a single piece and open along its entire length. It extends from wrist to elbow.

because the use of the axe is the prerogative of the man. But the Cafre-Zoulou would consider himself dishonoured if he touched the hoe used in agriculture; tilling the land, hoeing, sowing, weeding, harvesting, preparing food, fetching water, gathering wood, cleaning the hut, all these are woman's work. Any man who finds himself without wife and family, and thus obliged by dire necessity to handle a hoe, is given the name of *omphogazane*,[1] but he is not the only one to be called by this name.

Included are those who have eaten meat which is forbidden by foolish prejudice, even though the meat is perfectly wholesome and often very palatable, for example *Rhinoceros simus*, wild boar, *Sus lavartus*, and particularly fish of all kinds. The man who makes use of the fat from the intestine of the eland, *Boselaphus oreas*, according to their belief, is certain to lose his fertility. A woman fears the approach of her husband if he has touched a boa python, or a crocodile, or a hyaena, but this at least seems more reasonable.

The everyday apparel of the married woman is simply the *om-gobo*, which is rather like the night cloak worn by the men, but is more skillfully made; this garment is black, greased and often perfumed, and looks rather like shaggy black cloth. At night, the *om-gobo* serves as a blanket and during the day it hangs from the wearer's hips where the excess length is folded into a thick border or hem, while the length of the portion that forms the skirt varies according to the wearer's rank. Among ladies of quality, the skirt covers the feet. The garment crosses over and opens in front. These ladies wear an ornamental belt sometimes made of bark and sometimes of straw, which they place immediately above the fold of the *om-gobo*; around their necks they wear necklaces of beads, *makandas* (eggs) or *hamgazys* (blood pearls), and on their arms copper rings, polished by continual rubbing.

Their heads are shaved like the men's, except for a little topknot which they carefully dress with a pomade of red ochre. The more fashionable ladies have this tuft dressed and pinned every day. To this end, the one who is having her hair done lies flat on her stomach on a mat, while the hairdresser kneels, performing her office with complete absorption.

When a woman is pregnant, she covers her breast with an *om-doango* which hangs down to meet the *om-gobo*. Most often it is made from the skin of a gazelle, vaal-duyker (*Cahalopus mergens Burchellii*), artistically worked and probably intended to protect against the chill of the air. After the birth, the woman girdles herself with an apron which is draped around the small of the back, raised

---

1 *Omphogazane*: a man of no self respect, a poor devil, a wretch, a pariah.

117

in front, and tied at the throat, covering the shoulders; it is this garment which serves to hold the child on its mother's back for, however hard she must work, she will not be separated from her nurseling.

The costume of the nubile girls is even simpler still; a fringed belt, three inches wide, elegantly encircles the body; apart from this, she wears only a necklace of beads. When questioned about the scantiness of her dress, the young girl replies that an *intombu* must show herself as she really is, in order to find a husband. However, in spite of the virtual absence of clothing, propriety is satisfied because the movements of these girls are consciously adapted to their nudity, which is so well managed that the eye of the severest critic can find nothing to offend.[1]

The children are completely naked until the age of seven or eight; they frolic about in the sunshine and their bodies develop in all the freedom of their natural state. It is thus not surprising that they grow into strong, agile and, above all, healthy adults.

Some evidence of tattooing is found, but only among the women; it is usually in the form of two squares joined by their opposite angles, as in a checker board; these squares are made up of a number of incisions cut by a sharp implement; the scars which are darker than the skin, stand out in relief. Young girls marked in this way, on one side only, just above the pelvis, in the region of the kidneys, are more highly prized in marriage.

Polygamy exists in every sense of the word[2] among these people who believe that to have many wives is to possess the only true fortune, but under the rule of Djacka and Dingaan it was forbidden to the warriors of the élite regiments to possess even one wife. It is however true that these warriors were granted the privilege called *schlabonka*,[3] which allowed them only transient and incomplete liaisons.

A Zoulou finds a young girl whom he desires; he makes his intentions known to her, and then approaches her parents. Generally speaking, they will not oppose the match. Go-betweens then negotiate the price which the suitor must pay in compensation to his future

---

1   To make the matter even more intelligible, I give the assurance that the most searching eye discovers nothing of what should remain hidden and I say in all conscience, that these naked beauties, with their modest movements and gestures, are clothed in a garment as impenetrable as any ballgown worn by our European women. But these things must be seen to be believed.

2   I presume he is referring also to a figurative meaning of the word polygame : multiplicity of benefits. *Translator's note*

3   The *schlabonka* permitted to the warriors is an act unknown to us and which delicacy forbids me to define any further than I have already done, after it was explained to me by my Cafre Houahouaho. [See Vol. 1]

parents-in-law, for the cost of the girl's upbringing. Most often, ten cows are agreed upon, payable all together or on terms. If need be, five pregnant cows will suffice. The negotiations over, friends immediately demand that the day for the wedding dance should be named.

When the day arrives, groups of men start gathering together, not far from the bridegroom's *mouzi*; clusters of young girls form in the shade of a clump of isolated trees, with the bride among them. Her toilette is performed in the open, assisted by a thousand obliging hands while she is inundated by a tide of good wishes, poured upon her by her eager companions. Soon the sound of the beating of shields thuds out from the centre of the *mouzi*.[1]

This sound suggests warriors setting off for the hunt, or going to war, and one almost expects to see them appear, but instead, unbelievably, it is the old women of the *mouzi* who advance, matrons with their faces streaked red and white and their heads crowned with garlands of foliage; armed with shields and *om-kondos* they come, uttering sinister cries, simulating terror. They move off in different directions, weaving and swaying before they meet up again and return to their point of departure; veritable priestesses of Bacchus, they give vent to astonishing shrieks, which are taken up and repeated by the echoes. The silence which eventually falls is the signal for the dancing to begin.

At this strange summons, the various groups of dancers begin advancing towards each other. The men move into the centre of the enclosure, with the female contingent close behind. The singing begins, accompanied by the clapping of hands and the stamping of feet. Bodies sway, faces glow, limbs are soon shining with grease and sweat. The beer flows, sparkling and wine-coloured and agreeably pungent on the palate, spreading honest cheer. The cow destined to provide the feast for the guests, falls bellowing to the ground, felled by blows from an *om-kondo* and, before long, its flesh is sizzling over the glowing coals. Men and women eat and drink as they dance, until pleasurable fatigue obliges even the most enthusiastic to pause and take breath. At these weddings, which are beautiful in their simplicity, no priest is to be seen.

The bridegroom is the last to retire, with his young bride, but happiness is not yet to be his. In vain does he long, his desires are not yet to be satisfied; his bride, obedient to Zoulou custom, must make the first and second nights long and painful for him; the poor unfortunate bridegroom may claim his rights only on the third night! Now, if anything should excite our admiration, it must surely be

---

1 The *mouzi*, as we have already said elsewhere, signifies a collection of huts arranged in a circle; it is a kraal, a village.

the conduct of this first Zoulou wife. All her labours are directed towards making her husband rich enough to acquire a second wife; that is her chief objective, which will make it possible for her to lead a more comfortable life. The surplus of the produce from the labours of two women must soon bring about the acquisition of a third and, the more numerous the community, the greater the general ease, and the consideration in which the first wife is held. Chief Magalebé, whom I knew, had sixty wives; the first held the rank and title of *inkoskazi*, or princess.

The most perfect harmony reigns in these households; all these wives of one husband love each other, I would say even more than sisters do. There is never a quarrel, and why should there be, for these women are completely ignorant of the passion of jealousy.

Another strange thing, the children of one are the children of all; a boy has as many mothers as his father has wives. 'These are my mothers,' my tall Cafre, Nanana told me, when four old women embraced him with equal enthusiasm. 'Four? No that's impossible, each man has only one. Show me your real mother; I want to give her a present.' 'I've got many more than four,' replied the obstinate fellow. He never did answer my question, because he cherished them all equally and feared hurting their feelings if he singled one out.

Undoubtedly, if all nations practised polygamy as it is understood by the Amazoulous, it would be very much preferable to monogamy, as it is more in keeping with the dictates of nature and, as a result, is greatly beneficial to the human race. I must not digress, but I do feel that this is the moment to tell of what the Cafre women does during lactation. From the confinement until the weaning, a long period, a Zoulou woman will refuse her husband's advances; she devotes all her care, her whole being, to the development of the child; it is for him alone that she seems to live. The husband, during this time, has no rights over her, and so a Cafre who has ten wives considers that he is still too poor, and so he directs his efforts to acquiring twenty wives.

The character of these people has much in common with that of the French. If ever one needs to make comparisons between the Amazoulou and the Makatisse, who live more to the west, one may best do so by describing the Amazoulous as the French of south-east Africa, while the Makatisses, with their harsh language, and their divisions into a hundred different principalities, would represent the Germans. I would point out also that under Djacka the role played by the Amazoulous in these lands resembled that of the French in Europe under Napoleon. His victorious armies overran the land, wiping out peoples whose only memorial today is the crumbling stone walls of their circular huts.

The Zoulou is born proud and possesses to a high degree a sense of nationhood. He is courageous in war and would even be generous towards his enemies if his traditional methods of fighting allowed him to be so. In peace, he is kind, obliging and most hospitable, although very reserved with strangers. Once his confidence is won, however, he will put himself at the disposal of the traveller, although he will make an exception of tasks which he considers ignoble. In return, he will willingly accept gifts which are offered him and he will even solicit them to the point of importunity. He has a fund of good humour, which he spends in happy conversation and laughter. He gives himself body and soul, to the pleasures of singing and dancing. He is just as fond of war-dancing from which women are excluded, for he enjoys showing off his war-like passions. He is very responsive to music, although he has few instruments.

His emotions are easily aroused; he leaps about like a lion when he is stirred by political passions; it is then that the blood flows and brother stabs brother, heedless of the parents' anguished cries. He easily becomes fanatical and intemperate; devoted to the interests of his chief, he will boast of excesses committed in his service, yet his respect for discipline is a hundred times greater than is any European's. He will confront death without flinching, and he believes that there is nothing as fine as to die in the service of the king.

He is first and foremost a warrior; as he is not self-seeking, he is uninterested in offers of trade or barter; he might occasionally accept, but he never goes out of his way for gain. Endowed with sound judgement and astonishing acuteness, he is reluctant to believe all he is told, if the explanations are unacceptable to him. He might appear to be convinced, but even after listening for several hours to persuasive argument, he will remain sceptical. The Zoulou's manners are polished and urbane; his politeness and ease contrast strikingly with the churlishness, not only of some of the Cafres of the interior, but also of the Boers. He has a very high opinion of himself, which sometimes leads him to express a kind of contempt for everything European. He has no use for luxury.

He despises things that require little or no courage to handle, however useful they may be, for he believes they diminish the nobler qualities. This is why he rejects firearms. 'The weapons of a coward,' he says, 'which enable the chicken-hearted to kill the brave, from a safe distance'. He feels about wounds received in battle the same way as the Spartans felt; he proudly shows his battle-scarred chest, but a Zoulou warrior's greatest pride is an unmarked back; no French beauty could care more!

Every Zoulou is very jealous of his women, however virtuous they may be. The young girls are much freer than the married women, but they are restrained by the fear of forfeiting the ten cows anticipated by their parents; this is deterrent enough.

The government of the Amazoulous is based on the patriarchal system. This is the most natural of all social systems, but as it is open to wide interpretation, it may take on exaggerated proportions, and begin to wear the uglier attributes of despotism. The eldest son of the king's first wife succeeds his father, but there are so many children that, not infrequently, one who is more ambitious than the rest, will rise up and kill his brother and seat himself on the throne.

This is what happened in the case of Djacka, Dingaan and Panda, three of the sons of Synsakona. All of them climbed to power in the aftermath of an assassination or a war. Djacka killed his father, Synsakona, and was himself later assassinated at the hand of Dingaan, who was driven out by Panda. Each in his turn, upon grasping the reins of power, promised to exercise it in moderation, but each one of them, as soon as he felt securely enthroned, began to implement the cruellest measures, with the intention of spreading terror, and thus ruling largely by fear. Panda, the present king, who had fled from death at the hands of Dingaan, felt sufficiently secure once he was king, to order the massacre of his brothers, as well as of the headmen who might over-shadow him. Unfortunately, along with these political assassinations, went the killing of all the inhabitants of the *mouzis* where the victims lived.

The king, in the daily exercise of his duties, is always assisted by three counsellors whose advice he takes on matters of government. Unfortunately, placed as they are, so close to the despot, these men dare not oppose him. I have seen them tremble beneath Panda's gaze as they invariably defer to him, applaud his decisions and then flatter him. The king would be better served if he surrounded himself with upright, honest men; he would do well not to intimidate them, and to give them complete freedom of expression.

In spite of the most absolute despotism, for three days each year the nation has the right to demand of the king a strict account of all his dealings. It is at the gathering of the warriors, about 8 December, when the maize is ripe, that the lively debate takes place. Freely expressed challenges are issued, to which the king must reply immediately, and in such a way as to satisfy the people. On an occasion like this, I have seen simple warriors come leaping out of the ranks, transformed into fiery orators, unafraid to face Panda's daunting gaze, while attacking him before the eyes of all the people, condemning his deeds, calling them base, cowardly, demanding that he explain, and then rejecting his explanations, revealing the falsehoods, and finally threatening him proudly, before returning to the ranks with a last disdainful gesture. I have also seen, after these displays, arguments break out between the king's party and the opposition, which almost came to blows. I have seen how the voice of the despot was no longer heeded and how easily a rebellion could have erupted on the spot, if even one ambitious man had emerged to take advantage of the indignation of those opposed to the king. But what surprised me even more, was the way that order was immediately restored at the conclusion of this peoples' tribunal.

If a decision must be taken about declaring war on a neighbouring state, or when it becomes necessary to provide for the general security, the king summons all his commanders who number more than 3 000. He leaves out nobody. He considers the opinions of all, and then adopts the view of the majority. He is free to take command of his armies himself, to choose which of his royal residences he wishes to live in, and to go where he pleases. The land is divided up under the governorship of the great captains. These officials sometimes have under their jurisdiction sixty or eighty *mouzis*; they represent the king and make judgements in civil matters. It is their duty to inform Panda of all that is happening and they are responsible for the interests of their subordinates; the slightest negligence can mean death. They have no powers of punishment because, as death is the only method of controlling crime and misdemeanour, the king reserves to himself the right to pronounce sentence. In spite of this, the provincial governors are obeyed as implicitly as the king is.

There is always a corps of guards resident at the royal *mouzi*, which is maintained by the monarch himself. The king imposes taxes in kind on the nation, which are double the required amount. The gathering of taxes is carried out in an arbitrary manner. The tax is proportionate to the king's needs, without much consideration as to whether the people are able to pay.

The female population living in the vicinity of the royal *mouzis* is expected to devote several days each year to the cultivation of the king's lands. Those men living nearby who are too poor to give anything, whether grain or cattle, pay the king by performing whatever services he requires of them. Those living far away, in the region where iron is abundant, pay their dues in assegais and picks forged by their own hands, while those who live in the wooded areas and spend much of their time hunting, send the king bundles of animal skins.

When a particular region is known to produce excellent kaffir-corn or very good maize, the king instructs the inhabitants to plant additional crops so that, without depriving themselves they are able to contribute a certain quantity to the public treasury. If the population residing in these regions is not sufficiently numerous to perform the required labour, the king orders certain other *mouzis* to go and settle there.

The Amazoulous live primarily off their herds; milk, milk products and meat constitute their principal food. In times of peace, cereals provide important sustenance, but for long years the people were so constantly at war that they tend to think of their herds as their primary food supply. It is quite probably for these reasons that only the women are engaged in agriculture.

The plants most commonly cultivated by the Amazoulous are *ombyle*, or Turkish corn, *mabele*, or kaffircorn, different kinds of millet, pumpkins, watermelons, calabashes, little black beans, round beans which grow underground, and are something like the pistachio nut, and indigenous sugar cane, here and there. In addition, there are various roots but they do not resemble the yam which is so useful in Senegal and Guinea. Some of the gardens produce excellent little sweet potatoes, but the potato itself is unknown to these people. One sees tobacco plants, *gouaye*, which grow to a height of twelve to fifteen feet; the leaves are pulverised and taken as snuff. There is also *sango* which is no other than European hemp, and which they smoke through horns filled with water.

It is noteworthy that the Amazoulous do not cultivate any kind of tree. I believe that the most likely reason for this is that trees take a long time to reach maturity. They also never fertilize their fields; when the soil becomes impoverished they simply move the *mouzi* somewhere else; and so, if they planted trees they would have to sacrifice them to be destroyed by wild animals. There is however a large number of wild trees and shrubs whose fruit, although rather acid, satisfy the wants of these people. I believe that the vine and the fig tree would have enormous appeal if they were introduced, and the wild fruit trees of this land would thrive in Europe if they were gradually acclimatised. Do we not have our colony of Algeria where the climate is so similar? It seems to me that success would be certain. When I was out in Africa, I thought a lot about it, but the fortune, or rather the too modest resources, of the independent traveller did not permit such schemes.

When the food supply runs out, for example when the harvests have been destroyed by the enemy's cattle, or when the *nogotys* have been emptied by the conquering army, the Amazoulous turn to the produce of nature. If the season is right, wild fruit are gathered and dried; if it is too late, they look for bulbs which may be eaten right away or kept for several weeks. Later still, they must fall back on a certain woody plant, the roots of which are very distended, brownish-black on the outside and yellowish-white inside. When these are crushed, they are made into a sort of porridge, rather like the pulp from which cardboard is made. This pulp is bitter to a high degree, but as albumen is predominant, the stomach is able to support it, although only for a few days at a time.

I personally was obliged on several occasions to make use of this vegetable matter, when no animal products were available. As for dried bulbs, I found that mastication did not help, for the resultant substance simply deceived my stomach, and when I had to satisfy my appetite on ground-up roots, I felt that mastication contributed nothing, and that the stomach was loaded with food that wearied it to no purpose, indeed to its detriment, because of the contractions brought about by the tannin.

The inner bark and the gum of the *Mimosa nilotica* are used in dire necessity, but food of this sort only delays death by starvation for a short while. On occasion, I have cut pieces from the wild date palm and sometimes I took from inside the simple gladiolus, a few inches above the root collar, a tender white section that was quite tasty and not unlike the famous cabbage palm. I felt well after eating it, in spite of a tickling in the throat. This plant is not widely distributed; it grows near the sea or on the banks of a lake, areas where the hunter generally finds other means of subsistence, if he does not lack skill and ammunition.

The Amazoulus build hemispherical huts which are always arranged in a circle on a hillslope sufficiently steep to allow for drainage. From far off, these circles can be seen on the sides of mountains, surrounded by fields which are yellow or bare according to the season. The cattle are penned for the night in the enclosure, a circular hedge preventing them from too close contact with the huts, which in their turn are protected by an external fence from attack by hyaenas and panthers who are so bold that they dare enter man's abode and seize the dog sleeping at his feet.

It is in this cattle enclosure that the treasures of the harvest are buried. There is no external indication of the precise position of the different storage places, but the distance is reckoned from various markers; the owners take their bearings from these and it is where the lines intersect that they excavate. When the earth is cleared away down to one foot below the surface, wide flat stones and pieces of wood are revealed, lining the narrow orifice leading to a hole which grows wider and rounder down to a depth of eight or ten feet. Usually the inner walls are plastered with earth taken from termite heaps, which is also used for the floors of the huts. Water cannot penetrate, but humidity reacts rather unpleasantly on the grain which is simply thrown in pell mell. As a consequence of the exclusion of air, weevils, the scourge of Cafraria, breed less rapidly than usual, which means that the Amazoulous can depend on their supply of grain. And neither is there access for rats, which would devastate the harvest in a matter of weeks, particularly as there are no cats, which the Amazoulous refuse to accept as domestic animals.

If it should happen that the royal herds are being consumed at a greater rate than they are being replenished, messengers are sent out in the king's name to request the wealthy headmen to donate a certain number of cows. No hesitation is possible, refusal would mean death. The rich man must put on a gracious, smiling countenance and allow the king's collector to take his pick. When circumstances demand, the king takes from whomever he deems suitable, but most often, it is the rich who must bear the tax burden. In return, after a successful war, when the king has chosen his share of the booty, the remainder is divided up into large portions for the wealthy, and smaller ones for the ordinary people.

In times of peace and leisure, when the king is not concerned with external affairs, he turns his attention towards internal matters; it is then that the fear of death begins to haunt the rich and powerful of the land; for the king has no diversion other than counting his cattle, inspecting his warriors, listening to his wives sing; he does not even participate in the elephant hunt, but watches it from on high. So finally, the king is bored. Surrounded by flatterers, unable to depend on any real friend, he invents a thousand anxieties; this or that headman, who is living in grand style, seems to be threatening to overshadow him. He imagines that this man might be planning an attack on his life; his sleep becomes troubled, a terrifying nightmare weighs upon his breast. When he wakes, he names the man and pronounces the terrible sentence: '*Om tagaty boulala.*' A body of armed men is dispatched immediately. They surround the victim's *mouzi* and put all the inhabitants to death; they then set fire to the huts which, from afar, soon appear as no more than a great, charred, black circle. A report of the expedition is carried to the king, who now feels that he can breathe more freely. During the next few days the herds which have been seized are brought before him; no one contests his ownership of them because it is his sole right to inherit the wealth of those whom he has put to death; and so it often happens that a man has only to be rich for the king to proclaim himself his heir by these detestable means.

I have known Panda issue death warrants against men he did not particularly like merely in order to reward his favourites. The sailor's expression 'robbing Peter to pay Paul' exactly describes the situation. Far from feeling guilt-stricken, the king of the Amazoulous appears to pride himself on such deeds; after all, is he not known as '*Kos-omkoulou*, Great master, Om-tagaty[1] *Om-kouloa*, Great Destroyer?' He is great only because of the fear he inspires.

The Amazoulous have absolutely no religious belief and thus no form of worship. If their *iniangas* have been called priests, it is

---

1 *Om-tagaty* in the Zoulou language has a wide interpretation, but it is consistently pejorative. The South African Dutch translate the word as 'sorcerer' or 'witch'. I have almost always heard the Amazoulous using it to mean 'poisoner' or 'murderer'.

because these doctors claim to be capable, not only of curing the ills of the body, but also of the spirit. Nevertheless one does come across a few superstitions, which bear no relation to religion, and ceremonies which have sometimes been seen as worship, are in fact simply an extension of these superstitions. The *inianga* always attributes all his patients' ills to a 'dead brother' living under the ground, and he diagnoses that this dead brother must be appeased immediately by the sacrifice of a cow, which then provides a feast for the bystanders. What this really means, is that diversion is the best method of relieving anxiety or pain.

It was as a consequence of contact with whites, the first of whom was Farewell in 1824, that the Amazoulous learnt that God exists, but they were not at all perturbed by this discovery, and to designate this god, they still have a composite word, *Kospezou*, from *kos*, master, and *pezou*, on high. This clearly proves that the acquaintance is very recent.

The first man, according to them, came out of the rushes; he was a Cafre, *mounntou muniama*, a black man. In spite of all my investigations and questions, which they evaded, I was able to discover no more. They are quite unconcerned about things that do not relate directly to their daily lives and their material well-being. Wiser than the Cafres of the interior, they do not attribute the rain falling from heaven to any unseen power, although they frequently discuss this matter.

When a man dies, his relatives and friends pick up his body with the help of ropes or branches, taking care not to touch it with their hands. They then transport it several hundred paces beyond the *mouzi*. Generally, the corpse is deposited in a gully or in some bush or other; the next day it is no longer there; the hyaenas have dined well. Five or six weeks later, a skull, bleached by the sun, is all that remains, the only part of man's body which the vile carnivores respect.

Only male children inherit from their parents. Nevertheless wives who survive their husband continue to lead their communal lives. Generally it is the son who has not yet left his father's house who assumes the headship; his mothers then treat him with as much deference as they would a husband.

To these general remarks on the Amazoulous, I must add a few more to complete, as far as I am able, this picture of an interesting southern African nation. Each time that I have sought to establish some sort of comparison between the Cafres and the Europeans, I have always been surprised to find, in these less-developed people, a sort of average limit which they are never able to exceed and below which they never fall either. Their bodies are well-formed, while their faces, although agreeable to look upon, never display the elegance, the purity, the refinement of the most beautiful of European faces, but neither does one see among them those repulsively ugly countenances that are to be found in our towns, the product of poverty and licence.

It is the same thing with their moral character; their emotions are not excessive, except of course in time of war, when there is a collective passion inspired by war songs and manipulated at will by the leaders. Even love, that private passion, which among us gives rise to many beautiful acts, as well as to many odious crimes, has no effect on these people, whether good or bad. Love for them is a gentle feeling, like filial affection. For them, it is a physical condition imposed by nature whose demands they satisfy as soon as they are old enough to do so; thus it never becomes wildly exaggerated, as it does with us. Never have I heard that love caused the death of any man in the country of the Amazoulous. There is no record of any man going mad with unrequited passion, and certainly there are no suicides, for they are still in the fortunate position of being ignorant of this sad resort, or perhaps it is that they are more philosophical and understand better than we do how to bear present hardship and the prospect of future adversity.

But let no one expect to see deeds done which are inspired by intense devotion or heroic virtue. A Cafre knows wonderfully well how to die in battle; and if he is taken prisoner, and condemned to be shot, he is not afraid of death; in fact he faces the supreme moment with an equanimity which fills his enemies with admiration. Yet a Cafre will never sacrifice his life in order to save his captain. Warlike courage he possesses in abundance, while honourable acts of selflessness he appears to know nothing about.

Observing them in the bosom of their families, one notices that their feelings are controlled. They are fond of their parents, their wives, their children, but their feelings never degenerate into indulgence; they love reasonably, and more enduringly, than we do. They make no display of loving for they are content that this affection should remain within limits and, as it never becomes over-excited, so there are never the family quarrels which, alas, are so common in civilised countries. A Cafre has from one to fifty wives; frequently there are ten. The atmosphere of his household is one of peace; it is unheard of that a husband should strike one of his wives. The mothers do not slap their children as white women are apt to do; these women would not understand how a healthy mother could abandon her suckling child to the care of another woman. They are anxious to fulfil their maternal duties, and even to prolong the arduous task as long as possible; their children are never whimpering or demanding; they grow fast and soon become strong brave men.

When the Amazoulous have sworn hatred for someone, they wish him ill, that is only natural, but they do not kill him, not because they are liable to suffer the same fate in return, but rather because their hatred does not go that deep. There are exceptions, I know, but they are rare; murder when it is not committed by command of the king, is something that one may encounter perhaps once in five years.

The love of property is not a passion among them, as it is with us. In the first place, because of the great expanse of land and the relatively small population, the fields are communal; each man cultivates those which suit him, without experiencing the temptation to encroach on his neighbour. Ownership of land is thus almost unknown to the Cafres. But they do have a strong sense of ownership, first of all where their wives are concerned, secondly of their herds and thirdly of their harvests. They are very jealous of the first, numerous as they may be, they are much attached to the second and, as for the third, they will share with any stranger who asks for assistance, even if he is white, provided only that they retain for themselves a little more than they need. They are thus hospitable. They like to be visited, even though they see no possibility of returning the visit. Hospitality for them is a custom, hallowed by time, as old as the nation; according to them it is a service which men owe to each other; they make no particular virtue of it, for it is good and useful, practised by everyone and perfectly natural.

Civilisation, by establishing the principal that all service deserves payment, has destroyed hospitality, the virtue of the patriarchs. On this point, we differ completely, and to our disadvantage. Self-seeking is killing civilised man and, even if our vanity suffers, we must confess that civilisation robs man of qualities, virtues and practices which, though simple, are none the less fine and praiseworthy, for they directly affect the happiness of humankind.

In discussions about their material interests, whether individual or general, these people give evidence of great lucidity of mind and perfect rationality, for they never lose sight of their own integrity which they have no wish to abandon. Thus they are always on guard against the influence of European ideas; they are not in favour of allowing either missionaries or schoolmasters into their country and discourage even ordinary contact with whites. As they know that this contact is a source of misunderstanding and leads to a clash of interests, they endeavour to avoid it. This resolution on their part is a product of their discretion. But there are some who wish to moralise and who see this avoidance as a crime. If only one could convince these philosphers of their error by persuading them that contact would lead to the seduction of the Cafres, that war would break out, and that it would be waged all the more fiercely because it would be whites against blacks, or blacks against whites; what more reason does one need to convince them that they are wrong.

Dismissive of all that is imprecise or dubious or ambiguous, they reject the lessons one presumes to teach them. They do not readily accept new ideas; they show much scepticism and are always asking for proof, and when it is not possible to provide them with that proof, they think that we are liars. 'Kotlissa tena oum longo (the white man is deceiving us shamefully)', they say, laughing as if they had been the butt of some practical joke. The high opinion they have of themselves, the sort of scorn they profess for the Europeans, will not allow them to accept any of our ways. They believe that it was the poverty and sterility of the land of the whites which forced them to spread into Cafraria. Now, according to their reasoning, a poor, wretched country can only produce poor, wretched men; as poverty and wretchedness only engender wickedness, it follows that whites must be wicked; in short, the Cafres are prejudiced against them, they consider them their natural enemies, and they fear that the whites will poison their minds. They make no secret of these opinions, which I have heard expressed on several occasions.

The typical Amazoulou has an open countenance; the attractive, responsive smile lends a gentleness to the beautiful black eyes, shining, almond-shaped and edged with curved lashes, which reduces the severity of the forehead and softens the warlike expression. Their interest in discovering all they can without revealing much themselves, indicates a cautious curiosity and an impenetrable reserve. Far from importuning the traveller with their questions and then being obliged to reciprocate by answering questions about themselves, they are provokingly reticent. Their replies are calculated; if the subject is serious, they will artfully put the questioner off the track, but if the conversation is commonplace, their rejoinders are appropriate and witty and often give rise to laugher, which leads me to believe that the Amazoulous and the French share a similarity of temperament. They are invariably cheerful, although the love of war preoccupies them, and they will submit to the severest discipline to ensure victory over their enemies. They despise commercial dealings. Compared with all the other Cafre tribes, they are exquisitely polite; they certainly put the Dutch Boers to shame. Their admirable, harmonious language, which they speak with unbelievable rapidity, is far in advance, not only of the other Cafre dialects but, as the Hollanders themselves admit, of their own jargon. And if I have never yet heard an Englishman make a similar admission touching the inferiority of his own maternal tongue, which is so full of consonants, inharmonious words and harsh syllables, it is because I never met an Englishman who was not English.

Often, since the wars between Dingaan's subjects and the Boers, from 1837 to 1840, the Amazoulous have been accused of cruelty. It is a matter of general notoriety that at the Boschjesmans Rivier camp and at various other places, the Zoulou warriors behaved with great cruelty. As everybody knows, similar acts of cruelty occurred in our own recent history, in our own towns, which pride themselves on their advanced state of civilisation, acts in which motives which might serve to excuse the Cafres, could not be used to exonerate the whites. Everyone knows that, within a body of men fighting together in a common cause, the frenzy passes from man to man, that in these circumstances, he who appears detached falls under suspicion and that even the most reasonable must be swept away by the tide of violence. This is even more likely to happen to the Cafres than to us, for they know that the least sign of weakness means death. It is therefore not surprising that they acted as they did, particularly as they believed that they were wiping out the whole of the white race, for they had no idea of how numerous it was. And anyhow, they never take prisoners because prisoners are a hindrance and may betray one's position with their cries. To add to all this, the Cafres do not know the use of handcuffs, because they do not understand that a man may give himself up alive.

Please God that I do not play the apologist for all their wrong-doing, but I cannot resist saying that these acts of cruelty are short-lived, that they have been committed in exceptional circumstances, that they must be largely attributed to the character of the chief who commands, and not to the nation which obeys, for the chiefs of the Amazoulou tribe have been particularly bloodthirsty and since Synsakona, each one has given proof that he could reign only by terror. We all know how it sometimes happens that an opinion which is formed on the basis of an isolated incident will be unjustly extended to apply generally. I believe that it is appropriate to relate here how this happened in the case of an Englishman of my acquaintance.

'Look,' this man said to me, 'here is Panda's *om-douna* taking up his weapons to kill an ox. Just come and look, and then tell me that these Amazoulous do not enjoy the sight of blood.'

Curious to find out for myself, I followed the Englishman, believing that he might well be right. The *om-douna* ordered that the animal be driven until it stood with its back against a bush; then emerging from behind this bush on the animal's left flank, he thrust his *om-kondo* into its ribs. The ox tried to escape, but young men armed with sticks drove him back. The *om-douna* stabbed again, and the animal moved off, bellowing. I attributed the ineffectiveness of these blows to the clumsiness of the Cafre warrior, and I suggested to him that I finish it off with a shot.

'No, no,' he said, 'that would not do any good,' and the blood flowed copiously from the poor animal's wounds, as he was brought back once more to the bush. The *om-douna* waited patiently, like a man counting the minutes, instead of dealing the final blow.

'Well,' said the Englishman, 'are you still not convinced of the truth of what I told you just now? Is this man not delighting in the sight of blood? He could have killed the animal with one blow, but it will take more than a quarter of an hour for it to die.'

In fact, the Cafre took more than twenty minutes to complete the operation, and when at last it was done, I drew him aside and questioned him on the cruel pleasure he had taken in prolonging the death.

'But you are wrong,' replied the man, whose looks expressed great astonishment. 'I did not do it for pleasure. What can the blood of an ox mean to me? This is our method of slaughtering, because the meat is far better this way. It would not be very good to eat if we killed the animal with one blow.'

I thought that I should inform the Englishman of what I had discovered.

'Bah,' said the man, who was incapable of seeing the thing any other way, 'that is a miserable excuse, just another one of the thousands that the Cafres are always using.'

I was subsequently to witness this method of slaughter twenty times over. It is simply a custom, based on experience and consecrated by time – nothing more.

CHAPTER XXVIII

Hunting in the territory of Natal — An unlucky day — Customs of the bos-cafer — Another expedition to Om-Nonnoty – Crocodiles – The mamba of the Amazoulou.

On my return from the Amazoulou country, at the time when the elephant hunters had been told to leave, I found myself having to confine my activities within a much reduced area. I knew that I was likely to find elephant in the wooded parts near Om-Vooty's Poort, and that they would be difficult to reach, but having no alternative, I decided to go there.

Four days journey brought me to the banks of the Om-Vooty. When I came to the ford, I left the beaten track and continued beside the river as it wound through hills and gorges and unexplored forests. Two days later, in the company of Mr Wahlberg, I stood looking down on a country lying in a hollow 1 000 feet below, covered with trees of many kinds and dissected by numerous streams, the whole encompassing an area of about eight leagues in diameter. There was a grandeur in the aspect of the land which unfolded in a broad sweep far beneath us with the mountains tumbling away in picturesque disorder to the distant horizon, although the steep slopes, the deep ravines, the dense bush looked merciless and unyielding. I must admit that my first thought was about the hunting and how difficult it would be. The sight of buffalo moving peacefully about in the valley far down below only served to confirm my first impression.

Henning shared my view; an expression of sadness spread momentarily over his features, but then, growing hopeful again almost immediately, he said cheerfully, 'From what I've heard, this damned Om-Vooty's-Poort-Veld is absolutely swarming with elephants, just as Iniaty-Kase is a nest of buffaloes. By this time tomorrow we will have a better idea of what we're dealing with.'

We made ready for the hunt. Never had I been better prepared: I had eighteen men armed with guns, although most of them were inexperienced. Kotchobana and Boulandje, whom I had remunerated too generously, had recently acquired wives and preferred the charms of the idle life of the *mouzi*; the insidious influence of their wives had sapped their strength; their hearts were quite unmoved as they watched me go. These beloved companions of the hunt, these men who, in the face of danger, had become dear to me as brothers, had grown too soft to answer my call. The ingratitude! They, who knew me so well, preferred their new wives to old elephants, preferred

133

them even to me! And so, heavy-hearted, I set out without them, for those who now formed my party were as nothing compared with them. I was not counting on achieving much without them. The fact that they were not with me continued to torment me; I grew disheartened, my cheerful expectations deserted me, and what hunter can succeed without hope? There is a saying that happy expectations in the morning will surely be realised during the course of the day. I believed this hunter's creed and, had I only allowed myself to be guided by it and sacrificed the first day, I would have been spared terrible suffering.

I divided up my men into several parties, despatching them in all directions so that we could explore most of the territory in a single day. Henning, with two men, was to be free to move about from his position in the centre, while I kept to the right, close to the river where I expected there would be better prospects. Only the hunters in the party on the far left were to shoot buffalo, and then only as a last resort on the way back to camp. Mr Wahlberg left it to his driver Wilhelm, an excellent shot, to decide what action he wished to take, and Mr Wahlberg could not have made a better decision.

We slithered down into deep ravines and gazed back at the precipitous heights behind us. Only a great earthquake could so have rent the earth apart as to throw up these granite rocks, as sheer and as perpendicular as towers, with rockfalls of stone in between, forming the only possible pathways to the bottom. The inaccessible heights were haunted by birds of prey whose eerie cries were taken up by the echoes and repeated as a sinister warning directed at us, or so it seemed to me, as we buried ourselves deeper and deeper in that vast graveyard of the giants. The heat increased in intensity as we descended, for the breeze that was blowing on the high ground did not even condescend to rustle the tops of the bushes down below. Our faces streaming with sweat, we discovered the joy of resting in the cool shade beside a stream. At this point we separated, quite unaware of what was destined to befall us only a few hours later.

It was 30 December 1842, the anniversary of the day I killed my first elephant at Saint Lucia. I had with me only one armed Cafre, Houahouaho; two others, who were too young to use firearms, carried the ammunition; they were Djantje and Schlanvokane. We walked up hill and down dale for a long way, seeing nothing, only climbing and descending, negotiating obstacles, pushing our way with difficulty through thorn bushes which seemed determined to snatch souvenirs of me, shreds of my clothing or skin, and drops of blood.

However I was not so much preoccupied with these things that I failed to see the fresh spoor of rhinoceros. In the absence of elephant spoor, the imprint of a large foot with three toes seemed like a stroke of fortune. For a long while I followed, a very long while, until I came to the river. I inspected the tracks which emerged from the water on the other side to ascertain when they had been made. A glance at the sun, which was by then at an angle of 45° with the horizon, made me realise that we had not enough time. Nevertheless, I was still hesitating when an enormous black male buffalo, balding with age, came down to drink. I suddenly thought that I would kill him, simply to be able to take back a trophy, for the flesh of the old males is tough and unpleasant, even though that of the young females is quite delicious. In any event, the comparatively short distance to Natal would mean that I could take back the skin quite cheaply and the market price at the time, depending on the weight, was between thirty-six and forty francs.

I began crawling towards the animal, but when I still had forty paces to go, he picked up my scent and galloped off with his head down, taking short cuts by opening up pathways through the thick bush. I would probably not have given him another thought if Houahouaho, who was trying to be very helpful, hadn't set off immediately in pursuit. He was able to run fast enough not to lose the trail. Without thinking, I followed Houahouaho at some distance behind; a buffalo was not important enough for me to make the effort of running. Twenty minutes later I caught up with my man who had stopped at the edge of a ravine.

'Here,' he said. 'The buffalo was here, where the valley branches in two. If he took the right fork, it is too far for us to follow, but if he took the left, we just carry on from here, without going through the ravine.'

'That is so; in that case, let's go straight on.'

We had been walking for half an hour, when we heard a great noise fifteen paces to the right; bushes were being torn apart and there was a loud cracking of dry wood; it could only be something very heavy; it must be our buffalo making off at great speed. To judge by the muffled sound of the tread, the animal was crossing the gully and should not fail to reveal himself as he climbed the opposite slope. And this was exactly what happened. There was his blue-black back appearing out of the bushes, and then disappearing again. I had my gun trained on him. Finally, he presented himself broadside on, and stood quite still at 150 paces. This was the moment. I fired, Bang! The animal ran off and then stopped some 30 paces further away. The position was not unfavourable and I reloaded. Houahouaho was following silently behind. I decided to exchange my single-barrelled gun for an excellent double-barrelled one which had belonged to the famous Captain Alexander. 'Houahouaho, *upi na?*'

But there was no reply; he was no longer behind me. I was walking so fast now that Djantje and Schlanvokane had difficulty in keeping up.

135

When I heard a bellowing, I thought, 'That's fine; the buffalo must be about 200 paces away.' I began walking even faster, anxious to be done with the beast, but I had been strangely mistaken, for suddenly on my left, bushes were being torn apart and young trees broken as the monstrous animal came thundering towards the spot where I had just dropped to my knees. A rapid glance to the right, to the left and behind was enough to convince me that my position was hardly favourable; there was not a single tree strong enough to resist the charge or with branches I could leap into and hang from; nothing but thorn bushes, inextricably entangled with brambles and knotted creepers, those obstacles which are the despair of hunters in these lands.

In view of the lowness of the branches, to continue kneeling on one knee while my buffalo pounded towards me with his head lowered, seemed not to be a very good idea. The impetus of his charge was so great that if he fell he would plough into the spot to which I was rooted without my having either the time or the ability to jump out of the way. To remain where I was would mean that I would be likely to be cut in two. To stand my ground and to attempt at the last moment to leap over his withers, would have been preferable. By doing this I would avoid the terrible impact of his lowered head; I would slither on to his rump and fall behind him and, however difficult this might prove, it would be the least of several evils. But to do it, you needed legs that were not worn out from hunting.

All these thoughts, which have taken time to tell, flashed through my mind in those moments of imminent danger, before I decided to attempt a last desperate resort which would either leave me dead on the spot or let me off scot-free. I dropped flat on the ground, throwing aside my excellent gun, which had now become a useless thing, and I folded my arms one over the other to cushion my forehead. Inexorably, the buffalo came thundering on towards me; I caught a glimpse of his flaring nostrils, tinged with blood; seven more paces and I would be annihilated; his nose was buried in his chest, and his fearsome horned forehead was coming straight for my head, which would be shattered into splinters. How many thoughts flashed through my mind in that supreme moment. My whole life perhaps: twenty-six years in a single second. I said a last goodbye to this life and accepted that I was dead. I would not feel the crushing blow that was going to destroy me, for pain exists only when the soul is present, and mine was already floating above the scene of my death, anxiously watching over the destiny of its mortal remains.

Deafened by the pounding of the animal's hoofs which scattered a hail of stones over me, I gripped my head in my arms as if I were trying to condense it to make it stronger. Like the condemned man on the scaffold, I clung to the most fragile hope, because I wanted to live; but I was destined to die in this place; the 30 000 leagues I had travelled to many parts of the world were to culminate here. What a long way I had come to meet my fate.

His forehead crashed into mine, knocked off my hat, compacted my spine almost to annihilation; his four legs were the posts which, for a fleeting moment, held a canopy of death above me, and then he had passed by. Crumpled, bruised, hardly able to draw breath, I felt that I had just awoken from a dream. I leapt to my feet, listening to the noisy progress of the monster which was still in the vicinity. The animal must have been able to pull himself up in his headlong charge, for the noise stopped; then suddenly there was a great bellow; I could see a second charge coming, a charge to the death, for how could I expect the same good fortune a second time?

Indeed, the buffalo had fixed his sights on his objective; once more, he was trampling down everything in his path; he seemed resolved not to quit until he had torn me to pieces, until the tatters of my garments, along with the shreds of my flesh, adorned the thorn bushes all around. My only chance of salvation was flight but, in spite of my every effort of will, as so often happens in dreams, my body remained rooted to the spot. Three times I steadied myself, but it was to no avail, there was no strength left in my legs; the muscles were slack and would not respond. Never had I needed them more, and never had they been so completely useless.

At last, when barely seven paces separated me from the buffalo and I had given up all hope of moving, I was suddenly able to make a spring, and to take three leaps. To right and left of a great clump of nearby thornbushes that stood fifteen feet high, was an opening but it was too low for a man to clamber through with a buffalo in hot pursuit. So I stopped running, and hurled myself headlong into the midst of the branches which were tipped with thorns three inches long, and dangerous as a rapier. I was suspended in these branches when the animal crashed into the little opening on the right and gave me such a poke in the right side with his left horn that, in spite of the resistance of twenty branches as thick as an arm, I hurtled right through the thorn bushes and rolled out on the far side. My adversary, unable to check his speed, which was accelerated by the sloping ground, went thundering by. Disorientated from having spun around so much, I called to Houahouaho whose voice answered me from somewhere higher up the hillside. When I had climbed up to where the voice had come from, I hailed him again, but Houahouaho who had twice heard the sound of the charge and the bellowing of the buffalo, considered that to be near me was dangerous, and so kept on moving further and further away. I eventually managed to catch up with him and stop him.

I examined myself, and was reassured to discover that I was

suffering from nothing more serious than a few bruises and a number of punctures inflicted by the thorns. The back of my moleskin[1] hunting coat was spattered with the blood which the buffalo had snorted through his nostrils. I felt nothing as Houahouaho began pulling long thorns out of my clothes and my flesh. When, to reassure him, I removed my coat, I saw his expression of astonished disbelief that I had escaped, virtually unscathed, from such a terrible ordeal.

After first tending to the man, the next most important thing to consider is the gun. 'Where's your gun?' Houahouaho asked. 'Your cap also is missing, where is it?'

'It's all down there Houahouaho. I'll wait for you here. Go and bring back what you can find.'

'Does master not think that the buffalo might still be there and that it could be my turn next?'

'That's true. I wouldn't be tempted to go down myself. It can wait until tomorrow'.

So that I could recognise the exact spot again, I undid my neckcloth and tied it to the end of a branch, like a flag. A few moments later Djantje and Schlanvokane, whom fear had rendered as agile as monkeys, answered our call from the top of a tree, the first one they had been able to find strong enough to bear their weight. After the shock I had suffered, I was incapable of going on with the hunt; my men also were of the opinion that we should return to camp, which we hoped to do by the shortest possible route.

We started the laborious journey, climbing the first slopes along narrow buffalo paths which led us, an hour later, to rock faces that were as perpendicular as walls. As it was impossible to climb them, the best we could do was to follow along the foot looking for a way out. The only alternative was to go downwards again, thus losing the elevation we had so slowly and painfully attained.

Houahouaho, whom I had sent ahead to look for a path, thought that it would be easier to push through the undergrowth without his gun, so he threw it into a bush near where Djantje and Schlanvokane were standing. After searching for a quarter of an hour, Houahouaho called out to us joyfully that we could follow him; he asked Djantje to bring his gun. The latter, not taking all the precautions that he should have done, grasped the gun by the barrel and pulled it towards him; the shot went off and the bullet passed under his armpit and whistled past so close to my face that I felt the displacement of the air.

I was shaken when I realised that, within the space of two hours, I had escaped three times from dangers which could have cost me my

---

1 'Moleskin': name given to an English velveteen which is excellent for hunting garments.

A BUFFALO CHARGE

139

life, and it was no consolation to reflect that the sun had not yet set on this ill-fated day. Be that as it may, we succeeded at last in reaching the place where my oxen were grazing, not far from my wagon. The young herdboy came to meet me, looking contrite.

'Master,' he said, 'your best ox has just died.'

An hour later, when I had changed my clothes and was looking more like a human being than a porcupine, Mr Wahlberg came back from his insect hunting. My first concern, as one might imagine, was to tell him of my adventures and to seek from him some rational explanation. I needed reassurance, for man, left to himself in the wake of misfortune, falls into an indescribable weakness of mind, a state in which superstition is born. I swore that I would never touch a gun again, that I would leave the buffaloes to graze in peace, that I would even suppress my desire for elephant tusks. Even if this were to mean giving up the necessities of life, I would bid farewell to hunting whose indescribable joys were rendered void by the very thought of the dangers. Mr Wahlberg laughed heartily at this decision taken while recent events still possessed my mind. All he would say was, 'Within a week, Monsieur Delegorgue, my dear and worthy European compatriot, you will have forgotten these vows.' And indeed he was right.

The sun was setting when I noticed a file of men approaching from the distance. I trained my spyglass on them and recognised Henning in the lead; immediately behind him a body came swaying along which I could not identify. It was when they were only 300 paces away that I burst out laughing, a pleasant change from my gloomy thoughts, for it was a young elephant walking at the heels of my intrepid driver. When they got close to the wagons, the young animal lost Henning's scent for a moment and, picking up instead the scent of strangers, he rushed at us. Then, one after the other, he tumbled us head over heels. We were highly amused, for these attacks had no effect other than to send us flying. However, a quarter of an hour of this game was enough and Henning, who was holding his sides laughing, agreed to take control once more. The little elephant was soon following him as peacefully as he would have followed his mother. We tied him up for the night 200 paces from the camp for fear that the troop his mother belonged to would come and trample our wagons and oxen, and even ourselves.

Henning told us how unfortunate he had been that day; he had wounded four elephants in succession with bullets weighing a third of a pound which had been hastily made from pure lead, without the addition of tin. He explained to us how the little elephant, walking along behind the herd, had been cut off from the rest by my hunters; then he went into some detail about what he had done to make it lose its mother's scent and follow him instead. Several South Africans had, at various times, enlightened me on this subject but, quite honestly, I had always doubted that the method employed could have achieved much success. This time it was no longer a matter of hunter's tales, for there was the undeniable fact before our eyes; the little elephant was in our possession. Henning and his men had confirmed how simple it was to capture a young animal.

Certainly, nothing in the world could be easier. it is simply a question of passing one's hand over one's forehead, which is wet with sweat, and then rubbing the tip of the little elephant's trunk. Thereafter, deceived by the smell, I mean by the similarity of the smell he has just committed to memory, and that of the man, the little elephant follows that man as faithfully as he would his mother.

Mr Wahlberg, who had been greatly diverted by the scene, then confessed to me his fears regarding his hunters who had not returned; night had already closed in, and the sky was heavy with clouds darkening on the horizon. It was certain that a terrible storm was brewing; this had been evident for some hours and Wilhelm should have been back if some accident had not befallen him. We fired off a few shots intended to guide him to the camp and then, after we had quite given him up, and decided that he had taken shelter for the night among the rocks, Wilhelm's long, thin, impassive face appeared at the opening in the wagon tent. In general, Wilhelm spoke little, but this time he did not speak at all; his monosyllabic replies to our questions did not satisfy us. Silenced by exhaustion, the hunter drank his coffee, hung up his gun on one of the hoops of the tent and, only then did he reply to Mr Wahlberg's questions and give him the details of what had happened during the day's hunt.

We could see now that his clothes were even more tattered than usual and when we mentioned this, Wilhelm was not in the least embarrassed and gave vent to his anger in curses directed against 'this damned country full of thorn bushes'. 'Upon my soul,' he said 'they'll rip the breeches off us.' And then he told, in a few simple words, of an incident in which we realised he might well have lost his life had it not been for the cool presence of mind with which he was well endowed.

He had had his sights fixed on a troop of elephants which he was attempting to turn, when one of the animals, getting wind of him, detached itself from the herd and charged with lowered head. Wilhelm, realising the disadvantages of firing, cast a quick glance to his right, to find only a pit, twenty-four feet deep, with perpendicular sides. To take that way out would have meant danger equal to the one he was trying to escape, so Wilhelm decided to hold his ground, leap nimbly aside at the last moment, fire point blank, and force the animal into the hole. The elephant was upon him. In an instant they would collide. Wilhelm leapt to the right and, without taking aim, fired a shot which broke the elephant's second vertebra; as it crashed to the ground, it narrowly missed crushing the hunter who could find no refuge in the narrow clefts in the rocks and was forced to the edge of the precipice.

After much reflection on the events of that day, we retired to sleep; but the storm which had begun with a distant rumble, now rent the heavens, relentlessly attacking the high ground where we were camped and making sleep impossible. It was daybreak before the deafening onslaught abated and the sun restored order to the warring elements, revealing the numerous furrows ploughed up by the thunderbolts right beside our wagons and all around the camp.

My story of the encounter with the buffalo serves as an appropriate introduction to a description of this great quadruped and his habits, based on my own observations.

Naturalists have named the southern African buffalo *Bos cafer*. It differs from the Italian buffalo as well as from the Javanese by reason of its much superior size and strength, and even more so by its wild, indomitable, independent spirit. The sight of this animal is a particularly astonishing one because of its wild-looking eyes, an impression which is produced by the position of the horns which are curved backwards like the visor of a helmet. The shortness of the sinewy, vigorous legs, the thickness of the shaggy black body, often plastered with sun-baked mud, bear testimony to its muscular strength, which, in the male, is reinforced by a weight of more than 2 000 pounds.

Its external appearance is designed to suggest danger to the hunter. Its strength and speed are well known, as is its instinct for revenge. The men who most often hunt the buffalo are South Africans, who are used to taming oxen. They see a close resemblance between the ox and the buffalo, and behave towards the latter with reckless confidence which results in a thousand accidents, for these impressions of similarity are deceptive. If, indeed, there is little danger in firing on an isolated buffalo, to follow its blood trail, when it is wounded, is perilous.

These animals are to be found in the thick of the bush as well as on the edges of forests and in any country that is covered in shrubs six to ten feet high. Sometimes, one may find them out in the open, grazing, or near a spring where they go to drink or roll in the mud; however, there will always be thickets close by, where they can take shelter at the sound of the first shot. And so it is only in areas where the visibility is limited that the hunter begins his pursuit and therein lies the danger, for the nature of the terrain, allied to the speed of the buffalo, if he should charge, makes retreat virtually impossible. But in order that I should be properly understood, I must explain further.

Take the case of a buffalo wounded near the edge of the forest, with the wind blowing from right to left. No sooner is he hit, than the animal breaks into a run and heads for the line of trees. His speed, added to the weight of his body, endows him with enormous power; everything gives way before his horns. He forces his way through the undergrowth and young trees, forging gaps which close up after him. The line he follows is not a straight one, it curves to the left and has a tendency to form a spiral. But when the end of the spiral approaches the point from which he started out, he stops and lowers his head which enables him to see more clearly. He is now downwind from the pathway he himself has made. His nose, his eyes, his ears, all his senses are alert, but this is not the tension of the timid animal preparing for flight; on the contrary this is a furious animal, coldly calculating how best to take his revenge.

The hunter, anxious to know the outcome of his shot, ventures into the opening the buffalo has made. For the buffalo has pushed up the tangled branches overhead; he has broken everything that barred his way. But the resilient young branches immediately spring back, leaving an archway barely three feet high, so that the man is forced to crawl on his stomach, dragging his long gun after him. Such a situation makes it impossible for him to move with agility; even when the path is less difficult, he will never be easy when the buffalo charges, guided by the scent carried on the wind; he will never have the freedom of movement to be able to avoid the horns which will certainly crush him. This is how all the deplorable accidents have occurred in this type of hunting. Numerous sad accounts, however, have not served as an example to hunters, for they have not learnt greater prudence.

The impetus with which a buffalo moves when he is confronted, whether by a man or a lion, whether he is attacking or retreating, is so great that one cannot form an accurate idea of it. I will try to demonstrate by telling of an incident which I once witnessed.

With the assistance of my men, I had just killed an old male buffalo. He had only one horn, the left horn having been sliced off at the base by a piece of rock, as cleanly as an axe could have done, while the animal charged past. Now, the point where the horn had broken off was seventy centimetres in circumference, the horny substance covering the bony core being two centimetres thick. It follows that this portion required excessive force to break through, particularly as buffalo horn is the strongest and hardest of all, not easily broken like ivory; twenty blows with a sharp axe wielded by a strong man could, with difficulty, scarcely produce the same result.

The buffalo's charge is a premeditated, calculated act in which the intention of killing his adversary is quite apparent; for if he does not wound the man at the first attempt, or if the man is simply thrown down and his death is not certain, the furious animal, when he is able to pull himself up, wheels around, bellows, assures himself of the position of his enemy, and charges at him once again, just as energetically as he did the first time. I have very good reason for saying this, because that is exactly what an old male buffalo did to me and if, on his second charge, he had not been unable to stop because of the slope of the ground, he would have repeated his attack until he had achieved his objective.

The adult male buffalo equals our largest Dutch oxen in height, although he far surpasses them in breadth; his legs are short and powerfully muscled; his neck is enormous and well proportioned to carry his big ugly head with its green eyes. His horns which almost touch at the base, curve outward and sweep upward, the tips turning inward again towards the base which forms a sort of wide rough pad and protects the forehead like armour plate. Overshadowed by the horns, the eyes glow in a head which is too short from forehead to nostrils, often hairless in patches from rubbing on the branches, sometimes scarred, and distinguished by an unusual squareness of the muzzle.

Pieces of branch, broken off as the animal charges past at great speed, are often caught up in the angle between horn and temple, just above the eye. After gashing the surrounding parts, they remain embedded there, producing a festering from which I have several times extracted thick pieces of wood. Neither are their ears spared; funnel-shaped, and smaller than those of some of the great antelopes, they are often hairless and lacerated.

The body is covered in shiny black hair, rather sparse; rarely is a buffalo's coat in good condition because he wallows in muddy puddles, covering himself with a thick layer of clay which hardens in the sun, and when he rubs himself against rocks or tree trunks to scrape if off, the hair, and even the skin itself, are removed in wide strips, to the despair of the hunter-naturalist. At the end of the tail is a fine tassel of black hair which is much prized by the Amazoulou who use it as a shaggy garter to protect their shins from contact with grass and thorns.

The buffalo is covered in a great number of ticks, particularly in the lower parts of his body, where the skin is not so thick. He is happy to allow two species of *Buphaga* to roam about on his back and sides, searching out the ticks and thus relieving him. These birds behave exactly like woodpeckers; their claws enable them to cling to the animal, while they balance on their tails which support them admirably. It sometimes happens that a swish of the buffalo's tail, intended for a fly, will kill some *Buphaga* or other, but this is quite unintentional, for these birds are the guardian angels of the herbivores to whom they attach themselves. They are always first to sense the approach of the hunter and will fly off with shrill, staccato

144

cries. The buffalo does not wait for further confirmation of danger, but sets off after them.

The sudden, violent behaviour of this animal makes it a real danger to the hunter, and sometimes to the animal itself. I have already quoted the example of the buffalo which had broken off its horn. I saw another which had got itself so entangled in the branches of a great fallen tree that we had only to slit its throat and then extricate it in the only possible way – cut up in pieces. I have heard tell of a buffalo which broke its spine by crashing into a tree-trunk obscured by bushes which it had not seen. At Om-Vooty I saw a large old male, which had been wounded by one of my men, charge off and disappear over a cliff. We went down with the utmost caution and found that his charge had been arrested by a clump of trees 200 feet below the spot where he had first begun gathering speed like an avalanche; his weight had flattened or uprooted all the vegetation in his path; he had carried along with him large splinters of rock and when we examined him, we saw that his teeth were broken, his jawbone crushed, his spine dislocated, his ribs staved in. In short, the animal was mangled.

Like all heavy animals, the buffalo is not happy charging uphill. The hunter should take heed of this fact, for it could be useful to him as a last resort. Some people have suggested that a bayonet would protect the hunter from the full impact of the charge, but these people have not considered the manner in which the animal prepares himself; his nose is drawn back into his chest and the forehead, armed with its formidable horns, is all that is visible to the hunter. Our lead bullets, mixed with tin, would often rebound off the armour-plated forehead; bullets of pure lead would not penetrate at all, and what bullets cannot achieve, bayonets surely will not. Furthermore, an animal which weighs 2 000 pounds, which is able to bend or break trees as thick as a man's thigh, and carries his weapons on his head, far surpasses the easily injured horse in strength and endurance. There is no possible comparison to be made between the buffalo and the horse when it comes to strength and body structure. All the horse's vital parts are exposed, while the buffalo exposes none. If only it were possible to tame the animal, to teach him the art of war which the horse understands so well, to train him to tolerate a rider, for a squadron of buffalo would break all the squares drawn up by any army in the world, particularly as this animal is irritated by obstacles and is never discouraged.

When I first arrived, before I knew about buffaloes, I suggested that this might be done. The South African farmers just laughed, as they laughed when I said that I thought the same might be done with the lion. Their response was that you couldn't kill a hyaena or a ratel with a needle.

To attempt to run away when a buffalo is after you is not a good idea, unless you can find a slope which is sufficiently steep to slow him down, and force him to abandon the charge. The man who is trying to run away is usually obstructed by a thousand obstacles, tangled bushes, interlocking branches, long grass that trips him up, all of which are far from being obstacles to the buffalo but are rather to his advantage. Climbing a tree is not much good, one needs time to do it, and then there is rarely a suitable tree available; if it is too thick, the man cannot get his arms around it; if it is too slender, the buffalo will topple it over. In any case, the charge is so sudden and so unexpected that this means of salvation is practically impossible.

I had never given thought to the best method of avoiding the impact of the terrible horns and the crushing bulk of the enormous body, hurtling towards one like a projectile, but I decided that my best bet would be to stand firm and, at the last moment, to leap to one side, if the nature of the terrain allowed. I made this decision as I followed the tracks of a buffalo I had wounded, the one that I have already mentioned in this chapter.

A sudden bellowing revealed his position, followed by the crash of broken branches, and then he charged straight at me, his horns to the fore, and his blood-stained muzzle tucked into his chest. I realised that he was invulnerable, and that it would be impossible to fire with any hope of success; even if I killed him at seven paces, the impetus of his great speed would carry him right over the spot where I was standing, trampling me as he passed by. Unfortunately for me, I was trapped in a kind of cul-de-sac of bushes entangled with rattan cane, *wild rotang*, where to try and leap aside was out of the question. I was certain that I was going to be killed.

In less time than it takes to tell, I had weighed up the possibilities, which flashed before my mind with incredible rapidity. Those fifteen seconds seemed like hours, and it was more as a calculated risk than as an instinctive act of self-preservation that I threw my excellent gun, which was now useless, to one side as I flung myself flat on the ground, with my head turned in the direction from which the charge was coming. The gnarled forehead would crash into mine at any moment. I gripped my head even tighter in my clasped arms as if to strengthen my skull. A terrifying noise filled my ears and shook me to the core of my being. The animal passed right over me as I lay between his four feet. Unbelievably, my head was unscathed as my cap of single unlined cloth was whipped off my head, but my respiratory organs were badly compressed as my back took the enormous weight. But because he had not raked the ground with his horns, the buffalo had failed in his objective and, to my great astonishment, I was safe, thanks to the desperate measure I had taken, something which I had not previously considered and which I

146

realise I owe to the extreme lucidity of mind of a man in mortal danger.

However, I would not recommend this method as a general practice; it succeeded for me, perhaps because of exceptional circumstances, such as the uneven ground which forced the animal to keep his head up. I must say though that the best thing is to follow one's own intuition which will not fail one in moments of crisis. This is what has saved me in many a difficult situation and so I can recommend it. The following account will bear me out.

Hardly had the buffalo passed over my body than he began making desperate efforts to slacken speed. Stiffening his front legs had the effect of applying a brake, and he came to a halt twenty-five or thirty paces from where I had just scrambled to my feet, breathing with difficulty, amazed, disbelieving, overcome with emotion. But the buffalo wheeled around, bellowed and broke into a gallop, preparatory to beginning another charge. I tried to run away, I was swaying in readiness, my knees were flexed, but they were trembling, I stood rooted to the ground as my legs refused to move. Then in desperation I lurched sideways to where the ground sloped down an incline and my legs finally came to my body's assistance. In three bounds, I reached a clump of bushes fourteen feet high, the branches as thick as an arm, covered in white bark and full of thorns. To right and left of the clump, was a gap one metre high and thus too low for me to pass quickly through while the buffalo was hot on my heels.

Here again, as I have already told in less detail, I was saved by inspiration. I decided not to go for either gap but, at the risk of poking out my eyes or impaling my chest on the six-inch horizontal thorns, I leapt headlong into the midst of this dangerous bush. There I was hanging, suspended, when my furious adversary, passing to the right of the bush, stabbed me in the ribs with the curved part of his left horn. The force of the encounter thrust me right through the branches, so that I rolled out on the other side. The slope of the ground was too steep for him to pull himself up and he thundered past. I could hear him in the distance, crashing into bushes and setting stones rolling while I escaped, trembling and disheartened, towards the high ground where, very fortunately for me, the buffalo declined to pursue his revenge any further.

If it achieves nothing else, the account of these adventures will serve to inform others that, to escape the fury of the buffalo, it is best to make use of the advantages of the terrain. Even though buffalo hunting has produced a long history of misadventure, it is still one of the animals most often hunted by the South African Dutch. The skin has some value, as much for domestic use as for trade; it is sold by weight and the price varies between F18.75 and F33.75. The flesh, preserved as *beulton*, is very tasty, keeps for a long time and is much sought after.[1] The horns, because of their strength, the density of the grain, and the deep black colour would certainly have been valuable, except that their shape prohibits the extraction of the bony core which, if it cannot be removed, produces a fermentation that attracts insects the larvae of which bore into the horny matter in exactly the same way as do the larvae of the *Cossus Ligni perda* into the wood of the elm. It is for this reason that hunters never bring the horns to the market place. It would however be a simple matter to avoid this inconvenience by dividing each horn into three pieces. Nobody has thought of doing that until now; South Africans do not take readily to innovation.

This animal is becoming more and more rare in the territory of Natal, where the bush which protects it from man is being constantly invaded. But in the country of the Amazoulous it was very common; it could be found everywhere in the rainy season. On the other hand, in the dry season, it was difficult to find a single one. It was at this time that the animals gathered in herds of 1 000 to 1 500 at points where the rivers did not dry up, and where the adjoining pastures remained green, but it was difficult to make one's way through to these places. It once happened that one of my Cafres killed five of the animals in quick succession, simply to clear the way and save himself from making a long detour. I have seen buffalo contesting the ground they occupied, not condescending to move at my approach, growing irritated at the noise when a stone was thrown, and hardly bothering to move when I fired. I must admit though that nobody, before I came along, had used a firearm in that particular part of the Amazoulou country. Wherever animals are ignorant of the cause and the effect of gunfire, the sound of the shot does not frighten them. I think they believe it to be a thunderclap.

Seen in these circumstances, the animals seem less wild. Levaillant has expressed the opinion that it might be possible to domesticate them to the service of man, as in the case of the Italian buffalo in Rome and the Javanese buffalo in Batavia. I do not say that the thing would be impossible; there would almost certainly be results in a few cases, but it would take a great deal of effort, and it is doubtful that this taming of the natural instinct would be passed on from the mothers to their young. I believe one would have to begin all over again with each new generation, patiently trying to subdue the wild defiant character, so confident in its own strength, an enormous task which even after a century of endeavour, would probably not produce any real results.

The races of southern Africa have not the touch, which the Indians have, in reducing animals to servitude; they have in their country

1 *Beulton*: obviously biltong. *Translator's note*

species which are larger, more beautiful and gentler than the ox must have been in its natural state, and these species have always been shot dead without any effort at all having been made to train them as draught animals, or to husband them.

Take for example the *Boselaphus oreas* which is as graceful as a gazelle, as strong as an ox, as fleet as a horse and as gentle as a lamb, whose flesh is excellent to eat, whose skin makes the finest leather, yet it is left to roam the bush while its numbers diminish daily to the point of virtual disappearance from the land of Natal, after having already disappeared completely from the Cape Colony. To say that the buffalo cannot be domesticated because the South African Dutch, in 300 years, have not succeeded in doing so, would be ridiculous; they did not try with the *canna* or any of the other beautiful species. These examples are enough to condemn them as incompetent, or more precisely, as lacking in enterprise.

In their place, one needs shepherds from the Pontin marshes, or rather Indians, patient and intelligent men, who would begin with a herd of young animals taken from their mothers. Only then might there be some progress, although I doubt that there would be any real success. The buffalo has a cunning expression, he is as mistrustful as a savage; his head is designed entirely for attack, there cannot be much intelligence inside it. Vengeance is probably what he under-stands best, they say he never forgets the man who has wounded him and harbours a grudge against him so that days later, he will seek that man out, even in the midst of other men. He is also too strong and too excitable to be endowed with much patience. The strength of one male buffalo would equal that of three or four oxen, but the disadvantage would be that he would destroy the wagon he was intended to pull.

I should admit that we really do not have the right to blame the South African Dutch for having done nothing to tame the Cafre buffalo, for Europe itself possesses a kind of ox, closer to the domestic ox than is the buffalo; this is the *Bos urus*, big, strong and beautiful, designed to tempt man, which still runs free in the forests of the Krapack and the Oural mountains, and which has never been called upon to draw a wagon.

As the next few days produced nothing but more buffalo, for the elephants had deserted the valleys of Om-Vooty's Poort, I thought it would be best to go back to Natal and, even though I had no hides to take with me, I had a large collection of Coleoptera. As it was the most favourable season for the entomologist and, as the bay of Natal offered a great variety of fine specimens, I stayed a fortnight, endlessly collecting Coleoptera, Lepidoptera, Hymenoptera, Hemiptera and Diptera. I would like to have stayed longer at my country residence, to be able to devote myself to my interesting collections, but already my Cafres were casting scornful glances in my direction. They attributed my changed habits to the close encounter with the buffalo. They were saying that the fiery hunter, the *om-doda-kakoulou*, had ceased to be a man and was becoming a woman; gauze nets, little boxes, pins, insects, were the preoccupations of a woman, in their eyes. The attention I was devoting to these unimportant things, the meticulous care with which I collected them, bordered, in their opinion, on insanity. In fact I was losing their esteem and, as it was to my advantage to retain it, I was forced into setting the date for another hunting expedition.

This time I set off for the mouth of the Touguela, with the intention of selecting one buffalo and one hippopotamus; of all the buffaloes killed at Om-Philos, I never once thought of bringing back a single skin. I thought it was too commonplace an animal, and it was only after my encounter with one that it rose in my estimation. It was not long before I found a fine specimen, the very one in fact which is at present displayed in the Royal museum at Brussels. But, as for finding the hippopotamus I needed, to obtain the full skeleton which I wanted, that was another matter. Several weeks went by; I had given up all hope of finding what I wanted and had already left Touguela mouth when one of my men found and killed, at the mouth of the little Om-Nonnoty river, a superb male which must have weighed more than 4 000 pounds.

The day following the death of the amphibious mammal, at about four o'clock in the afternoon, I arrived with my wagon at a point overlooking the river where the enormous corpse was floating. All around it, thirty or forty crocodile heads were bobbing, looking as though they were getting ready for a feast. The sight did nothing to cheer Henning who had volunteered to go out alone and tie a rope to the hippopotamus's tail, so that we could haul him in. As the offer had been spontaneous, and as I had done the same thing myself on a previous occasion, and knew it to be possible, I insisted that he should carry it through. I was soon helping Henning construct a raft which I made as secure as I could. I did not spare him my advice and, like a latter-day Argonaut setting out to conquer an animal without a fleece, Henning was soon pushing off into the open water under cover of our guns which were aimed and ready to fire at the head of the first crocodile that took any liberties. But Henning was liberal with his blows; the heads ducked and reappeared at a safe distance, and my valiant driver was able, without further hindrance, to accomplish the onerous and painful task he had set himself to do.

A fierce squall came up, making the business even more difficult. As my men were determined to lose none of the excellent *zee-koe-spek* and would not be done with the cutting up before sunset, I pitched my tent in the shelter of the steep bank near the water's edge. The place was narrow but there was no choice.

The crocodiles hung about, watching us cutting up the carcass as we stood waist deep in the water. My men were much amused by their presence and made a game of throwing them pieces of meat, as one would do to the hounds after a hunt. In their haste to be done, my workers were throwing the meat rather wildly about, so that the rocks were covered with the debris and even my tent was spattered and surrounded by it. I was going to have to spend the night in this butcher's shop, but one will put up with anything in this sort of work. When the skeleton was in a fit state to be transported, we dragged it out of reach of the crocodiles, and laid it between my tent and the edge of the bank. To protect it further, we surrounded it with thorn branches; then, an hour after we had eaten, we all went to sleep in our canvas house, where I had reserved my place on the side nearest the river.

The plip-plop of the water as the crocodiles climbed in and out, searching for the pieces of meat that were lying about, kept me awake far longer than usual but, as the noise had a monotonous quality, I eventually fell asleep, while my Cafres were already snoring noisily.

It might have been midnight, or one o'clock, when I suddenly felt myself being shaken and my blanket being pulled off. What could it be? I had no idea. My first thought was to snatch up my gun, that faithful companion of all my African nights. A Cafre awoke; I was still confused. I questioned him; I accused him of having taken my blanket in his sleep. He was astonished and said he knew nothing about it. 'Let's go. Fetch a light and be quick about it'. He and I crept out of the tent. I groped about outside, and then my foot encountered my blanket which was about to disappear into the water had it not been for a sharp piece of rock holding it back. One corner was tinged with blood where the crocodile had snatched it up at the same moment as he took a mouthful of meat which happened to be lying near my feet. This discovery made my men laugh; they thought the crocodile story was a hoax.

In the morning we saw that our camp site had been cleared of all the litter of the night before. The laughter died away when we realised our good fortune in not being dragged out of the unguarded tent while we slept.

For the remainder of this little hunting trip, nothing much out of the ordinary happened, with the possible exception of our being chased by a snake, the one the Amazoulous call *mamba*, when I was out with Boulandje one day. The other thing was the desertion of two of my young Cafres who preferred to leave my service rather than carry out an order which, according to their Cafre superstition, would lead to their death during the course of the coming year. It was simply a question of walking three leagues to the mouth of the Om-Sinnquassy to find a crocodile we had killed and left in a muddy ditch, cut off the head, and bring it back to the camp. But, said the Amazoulous, whoever has touched the body of a crocodile, even with the tip of his finger, will soon die, either of an illness, or by accident. It was in obedience to these superstitions, rather than to my orders, that Djantje and Schlanvokana had slunk off. In spite of all these precautions which they took to stay alive, strangely enough, both were dead within a couple of months. I was just setting off to do the task which had so disgusted my servants, when I encountered the mamba, sunning itself on a narrow buffalo path. Boulandje, who was ahead of me, saw it first when it lifted its head and stood three feet from the ground. My man virtually sent me sprawling as he turned to run and I, with no idea of what was happening, turned and ran after him.

While we stayed on the narrow path, the mamba came after us at a speed that was almost equal to our own. 100 paces down the track Boulanje stopped, listened, and heard him coming; we leapt into the long grass at the side of the path, and made several detours before continuing on our way. Our guns were loaded with ball, which explains why we did not try to kill the snake, which we could easily have done with a charge of lead.

At that time, I thought I knew all the principal species of snakes with which that country is, unfortunately, so liberally provided. I plied Boulandje with questions concerning this one. What particularly astonished me was the speed and boldness of the reptile which is perhaps the only one in these parts that will attack a man. My servants told me all that the Cafres know about it. One of them assured me, and I believe it to be true for since then I have observed two others, that the mamba will not attack a man on the Achilles tendon or on the knee but rather on the back or even on the neck. His coils measure more than a metre and his speed is such that no other snake I know can compare with him. As for the wounds he inflicts, no remedy known to the natives is effective, not only because his venom is of the greatest acridity, but because it is injected into the upper parts of the body, where the vital organs are situated.

This dangerous reptile has a brownish skin, his body is very supple and measures between nine and eleven feet; his length is in no way proportionate to his breadth, for he is very slender, which is the reason why he moves so fast. Like the boas, he lives underground in termite holes, in fact as do all the species which cannot climb trees. In Natal, he is to be found at the edges of forests and on the banks of rivers, in particular the Om-Vooty and the Touguela.

When I had completed this last hunt, which took place within a radius of twenty leagues, too limited a space for my taste, I returned to the bay, without much idea of where I would go next. As a result of the sudden turnabout in political power since the English occupation of Port Natal, hunting in the Amazoulou country had been forbidden me by their king.

CHAPTER XXIX

Journey to the land of Massilicatzi — Preparations — Acquisition of a second wagon — Reasons why my first Cafres refuse to follow me – Route from Port Natal to Pieters-Mauritz-Burg — *Klaauw-Sickt* — Draaken's Bergen — Rivers — Pangolin — Winter — Kaasteel-Poort — Sudden appearance of two lions — Endless green grasslands — Ruins of a Cafre town — Gevecht-Kop — Method of lighting fires — Immense number of gnus and quaggas — Death of a lioness — Her despair — Time spent on the banks of the Vaal River — First encounter with a Makatisse *mouzi* — How a Cafre doctor silenced the pleas of a sterile woman — Departure from Vaal River — Sad state of my oxen — We are surprised to see snow — Potschepstroom — Zuiker-Bosch-Stroop

While I was hunting in the Amazoulou country, Mr Wahlberg had taken a long journey beyond the Makalis-Berg which is the most northerly point of white settlement. He went as far as the Aap-Rivier, the river of monkeys, thus named because of the presence there of Smith's *galago-makali* which the Boers call *Klein aappje*.

He collected many choice specimens. Although his hunting was not as exciting and lucrative as mine in Zoulou-Land, it had been more varied in that it had included all the antelopes of the plain, particularly the beautiful species described by Burchell, as well as Harris's remarkable antelope *Aigoceros nigra*.

To judge from my friend's description, there could be no more interesting sight than these vast open spaces, trodden by huge herds of wild animals of all shapes and sizes. He told of their peaceful unconcern as they watched the wagons go by, and I was reminded of the fable of the earthly paradise which increased my desire to go and see for myself. The thought of leaving Africa, perhaps never to return, without having taken my fill of such extraordinary sights, had become unbearable to me. I must confess that, as a result, my preparations for departure were made in great haste so that no untoward circumstance could possibly thwart my plans. I had a kind of dread of failing to carry out this self-imposed duty which I had made a matter of the first importance.

It was absolutely necessary to take a second wagon to enable me to bring back in one trip as many specimens as possible, in fact a small part of the interior of Africa, for no man is as covetous as a naturalist; he would, if he could, put a whole country into a few narrow boxes. The acquisition of the second wagon and a team of oxen was a simple matter. It was more difficult to come by the necessary quantity of gunpowder, for I could have done with 200 pounds. In spite of all my enquiries and the high price of twenty-five francs per kilogram, which I did not hesitate to pay, I could not find more than seventy-five pounds, due to the fact that at that time the importation of all munitions into Natal had been prohibited.

Neither was it an easy matter to find a driver. Two or three applied, but their expectations were so high that I had to keep turning them down until, the day before we were to set out, constrained by the demands of necessity, I accepted perhaps the most obnoxious man in the whole of Natal.

Those of my Cafres who had been with me during the elephant hunts, having grown rich on my generosity, now preferred the sweet life, and would not consider accompanying me to Massilicatzi's country. They thought me a fool for hoping to go so far, particularly as winter was coming to the highlands. They didn't think much of such a lengthy expedition, especially as it was my expressed intention not to hunt elephants. They said they had no desire to accompany me to the land of the circumcised, that no Zoulou, no Natal Cafre with any self-respect, would rub shoulders with the baser races whose language is so different from theirs that there can be no understanding.

However, I had to have helpers, six was the minimum I could manage with, and because I couldn't find mature men, I had to be satisfied with youngsters three of whom were barely fourteen years old. It wasn't much of a crew. There were nine of us in all and four were needed to attend to the wagon, but I could not do the impossible. I had many misgivings about setting off like this; I was already pessimistic about the way the expedition would turn out and if I had been able to foresee all that awaited me, I believe that I would have sacrificed satisfying my curiosity and taken to my heels.

It was the 22 May 1843 when I left Port Natal for Pieters-Mauritz-burg where I planned to spend a few days completing my preparations for the journey. Two days travel brought me to the newly founded capital where I managed at last to find a wheelwright to carry out some necessary repairs on one of my wagons. I spent a week in the house of Dr Portmann to whom I am indebted for a thousand obliging attentions. I finally left the town without having found all I needed.

In spite of my intention to travel fast, I found myself from the first having to limit our speed to half *skoften*. My oxen were in reasonable condition, although they suffered from *klauw sickt* which attacks the hoof and which made it almost impossible for them to walk, although it is not the custom in the circumstances to let them rest completely. It was distressing to see the poor beasts walking slowly and painfully on hoofs that were eaten away at the back, which made them look rather like slippers. Their feet bled at first, and then putrefaction set in between the horny matter and the flesh, giving off a foul stench.

To alleviate the condition, whenever we came to water we led them back and forth through it several times. This malady was prevalent at the time. Some of the farmers who were more observant than the rest attributed it to the severity of the winter which had deprived the grass of even the small amount of goodness which remained.

The enforced slowness of our progress meant that from Pieters-Mauritz-Burg it took us fourteen days to reach the foot of the Draakensberg range. We first crossed the upper part of the Om-Guinée near a beautiful waterfall, 180 feet high, where the river drops vertically over a sheer rock face into a wonderful and terrifying pool; then came Mooi Rivier with its gentle and tender coils; next was impetuous, boisterous Boschjesmans Rivier, lying in its hard stone bed where the crossings are a trial to oxen, wagons and drivers. Then came the turn of Klein-Touguela flowing across the open plain where, in spite of its youth, it has hollowed out a deep bed to lie in; further on was Touguela itself, tumbling down from the mountains, fresh as a child from the cool uplands, proud as a boy who, in discovering the nobility of his origins, guesses at the illustrious destiny which awaits him.

Now we found a very different challenge; it was no longer a simple matter like crossing a river, for which one needed only a little skill and patience; this was infinitely more difficult, for confronting us was the Draakensberg, the range of great blue mountains on the horizon which, for a week now, we had watched drawing closer and closer. At last we were there and we had to get across. But these mountains are so high; our wagons are so heavy and our oxen so weak! Come driver, use the whip, but go easy; see that the chains are slack enough to put on the drag; have the blocks ready on the back wheels for there are slopes so long and steep between the resting places that the wagon, if it is not restrained may well take the whole team down with it. And some of you men, look to the wheels and keep them balanced. Let's start with one wagon; the team of the other wagon must come to its assistance if one span is not enough. With twenty-four oxen in front it is unlikely that a wagon could be bogged down for long.

The crack of the enormous whip with its eighteen foot handle and its forty-five foot lash rends the air and the long haul begins. By God, how sad it is to have to watch the poor oxen struggle and to reflect that so often their efforts will be in vain. Advance ten paces, stop; go on another ten paces then stop again, and to have to climb 2 000 feet in this manner and then to keep going beyond.

To get a wagon up the Draakensberg is a tiring day's work; with what pleasure and relief one eventually reaches the top, and for those who are aware of the danger, what good fortune to have survived a journey which for more than 200 paces leads along a narrow track cut into the precipitous mountain side, with a terrible drop of 7 800 feet below. There must assuredly be a God who watches over the Boers when they travel, for never have I seen men more careless of danger, and accidents are rare.

If they should come across wheel tracks, these men say, 'Others have passed this way, we too will pass, if the space be wide enough.' And when they have successfully negotiated some hazard, one would imagine that their first concern would be to remove the obstacle or fill up the puddle that caused the problem; but not at all. A Boer would regret for the rest of his life having done something that was helpful to others. Too bad for those who didn't know about it. Each man for himself; God will provide.

Despite all the difficulties, the Draakensberg is crossed every day; shafts, wheels, axles are broken on its granite sides and drivers swear at the patient oxen, but as yet, no really serious accidents have taken place, in defiance of the difficulty of managing the long teams and in spite of the sheer cliff edges and the loose stones which could cause the wagons to skid and crash to the depths below. This is where the European cannot begrudge paying his tribute of admiration to the Boers, who are the bravest wagon drivers in the world, and to the oxen of southern Africa which are the most intelligent and docile and patient of their race. Although the ascent is arduous and excessively laborious, it is fairly safe. The descent is a different matter. The wagons, jolting down from stone to stone, rather in the way that a stream flows down a series of cascades, threaten at every moment to overrun and crush the wheel-oxen, and even the rest of the team which is forced to bunch together to prevent the wagon from hurtling downhill too rapidly in spite of the drags. The descent brings with it an infinite number of dangers which are always overcome with astonishing presence of mind. The ablest drivers from Paris or London would be quite incapable of managing this sort of thing.

Once we had all reached the top of the mountain, safe and sound, we expected that the other side would be just the same. Nothing of the kind; even though Draakensberg appears from the Natal side to be a great mountain range, its highest point being perhaps 5 000 to 7 000 feet above sea level, on the other side it becomes a vast plateau, where we travelled more than sixty leagues across great plains punctuated by solitary flat-topped mountains.

We had in fact arrived in another country, where the winter climate was harsh and the produce of the land different from what we had known. The sea might well once have beaten against its eastern side which is buttressed by arid ridges leaning slightly from the perpendicular. Today, Draakensberg is recognised as the spinal column of southern Africa, from which all the principal rivers rise and flow in different directions to irrigate this vast land. Flowing eastwards into the Indian Ocean there are Om-Pongola, Om-Philos-

Om-Schlopu and Om-Philos-Mouniama, Om-Schlatousse, Touguela, Om-Vooty, Om-Guinée, Om-Zimvobo, Om-Zimkoulou. In the west two great rivers, Vaal Rivier and Groote Rivier, to which the smaller rivers are tributaries, after a long journey finally reach a confluence and together, now called the Orange River, pour their waters into the Atlantic Ocean. This is the same Orange river, which Levaillant crossed near the mouth and which is today known by the Boers as Groote Rivier and not by its former name, which was given it by Colonel Gordon.

Groote Rivier is the greatest river in southern Africa but surprisingly it is deeper and wider and consequently contains more water during the first third of its course, than it does at the mouth. This is obviously because, in the last part of its course, its tributaries are fewer and weaker, while the land is drier and evaporation much greater.

Two days after crossing the Draakensberg I came to Eland's Rivier. It was here that I met an excellent settler by the name of Jacob Declerc. Not only did he receive me in a proper manner, but I owed to this worthy man the gift of the most curious of all the animals of this country; by this I mean the broad-tailed pangolin, *Manes Temminckii.*

This strange biped had been captured alive and, to prevent him from escaping, he had been firmly tied by the tail to a triangle of wood which he dragged round after him and which prevented him from going underground or moving very far, although he was able with his claws, which he used like hands, to demolish the hemispherical ant-heaps and eat his fill. His strength was far greater than I had anticipated. As soon as he was offered to me, my first concern was to untie him from his wooden triangle and to take him on a lead to his favourite pantry.

My pangolin always walked on two feet; with his curved body sup-ported by his tail, he folded his little arms across his chest and looked for all the world like an old man, bent with age, and shaking with the cold. He would often stop and seem to be listening; the rustle of his scales would stop too. These frequent pauses lasted only a moment and then he would set off again at the same slow, even pace.

When he came to an ant-heap his fore limbs went vigorously to work. It took him hardly a minute to demolish half the little mound, however hard it might be. The pangolin stuck his pointed snout against the opening of one of the galleries, thrust in his tongue, which measured forty or fifty centimetres, pulled it out again almost immediately, stuck it in again into the same gallery, or into a different one; suddenly he would grow impatient and furiously destroy the remains of the ant heap and then explore the holes which he believed contained food.

The second day I had him, I took him on his lead again; he did not want to eat but he made a hole in one of the ant nests and rolled himself into a ball inside it like a hedgehog, seeming to prefer a doze to a meal. His eyes were always watery, maybe because he was in the bright sunlight. I believe he normally goes in search of food during the night, rather than in daylight, exactly like the *orycterope* (aard-vark) which is his closest relative.

I do not know that this animal has any enemy other than man, and even man in these parts does not hunt him for his flesh or for his scales, although these could be put to some use if one only knew how. Far from being harmful, this toothless creature renders a service. In his own defence he has only his armour-plated shell inside which he curls up and remains motionless. It would need the strength of several horses to pull him out. Indeed, it is difficult to take hold of him at all; a man's hand would soon be cut and bloodied by the scales.

As he cannot escape unless there is a deep hole nearby, every pangolin that is found becomes a prisoner. Although he is not particularly rare, he only comes out after dark and so is not commonly encountered. The one that Jacob Declerc gave me was much admired by all who saw him, most of whom had never seen one before. He was a metre long, his tail accounting for half his length. A charge of hyaena shot would not penetrate his scales. If the bullet is not aimed at right angles to the scales, it will glance off. The self defence of this animal is more effective than that of any other. The excessive length of the sternum also sets it apart.

Although I trained my pangolin to sleep by my side, I felt that he was about as amenable as a tortoise by which I mean that he had poorly developed instincts and would set off at the first opportunity. And so, when I had studied him sufficiently, I reluctantly pierced him twenty times with a scalpel and then skinned him. His skin and his complete skeleton today belong to the Royal Museum of Brussels where scholars will be able to study at leisure the strange animal and discuss the classification 'biped' which I have ventured to give him.

That is what he is; a mammalian crustacean biped, one of the useful animals it would be in man's interests to conserve. I have heard that the negroes of Mozambique eat the flesh, in spite of the strong smell of formic acid; it is very similar to that of the *orycterope* which is eaten by the Boschjesmans and certain Hottentots but I do not think that the *Manes Temminckii* is worth the research being done in this regard. The Cafres of Quathlambène will not touch the flesh; it is for this reason that I refused to try it myself, although there was no disagreeable smell in the cooking and the particular animal was in good condition.

We began to feel the approach of winter; my men and I,

accustomed to a climate that was always warm, found the biting wind very harsh. Every morning the ponds were covered with ice two fingers deep; the thin dry grass was crisp with frost and my poor hungry oxen had no appetite for it. The outlook was bleak; the bare feet of my young Cafres developed deep cracks from the cold and, although they spent the night underneath the wagons, wrapped in excellent woollen blankets, they would have been much happier to be naked in a hut with a warm fire burning at their feet.

This is the moment to mention in passing the method the South Africans use to make fire. It is not as you might have believed. They do not use the first piece of wood they can find; on the contrary the two pieces of wood which must be rubbed together have to be of a certain type and degree of desiccation; and if all the conditions are not met – for example, if the weather is wet or they are far from home – these people are unable to procure the vital element, the friend of man and his protection against wild beasts. In the forests one frequently comes across trees, which have been struck down by lightning or age, whose wood has undergone changes that are not often seen in our temperate climate. Without being worm-eaten, this wood has completely changed character; the fibres are no longer connected and because it has lost its density one can pass a pin through it as easily as if it were cork. A species of mimosa without thorns called *plaat-kroon-boom* possesses these qualities when it has been uprooted for several years and this is what the Cafres of Port-Natal generally use. This wood provides the fixed base, or stationary piece, after it has been thoroughly dried out in the heat of the fire inside the hut. The size does not matter although the surface must be even. The fire stick is selected for its perfect dryness; it is cylindrical, straight and very smooth; it is forty-five centimetres long and has a diameter of six millimetres. Squatting on his heels, or kneeling, the man who is intending to make a fire places on the ground in front of him the piece of wood which serves as a base; he then pushes the rod into a little hole in the base which will hold it in place while it is rotated. Then, between the flat of his hands he rolls the rod which begins spinning like an arrow shot from the bow. In less than a minute of this exercise sweat is falling in great drops from the man's brow; he has to be relieved of his task or his hands will blister and he will probably not achieve his objective, but when there are several men to share the labour, the task is easy and success is assured. The fire is transferred to the soft wood base and then is picked up by the dry grass and is fanned and grows, much to everybody's satisfaction.

When one considers the difficulty of this method, one can understand the astonishment of many of the Cafres when they saw the ease and rapidity of my methods; the ignition of the powder by the flint, the percussion caps, the lucifer matches, which particularly delighted them, but they considered the burning-glass as sorcery; they could not begin to understand how it worked and I did not waste my time in trying to explain.

When the Boers have no tinderbox to hand, they use their flintlocks which will produce a flame without having to be fired. They close up the touch hole with a thorn and place near the fire pan a piece of cotton cloth impregnated with crushed powder which is intended to catch fire when the priming ignites. I have also seen them making fire another way. They mix a little crushed powder with a scrap of cotton cloth, then add a small quantity of ordinary powder and tie it all up like a bag. Then the little bag is placed on a stone and they take up another stone with sharp edges which they use to strike it. They base this practice on the knowledge that the impact of two stones will produce a spark.

Further along our way we passed through Kasteel-Poort, the gates of the castle, a natural passage between two great ramparts of stone, the disposition and shape of which are reminiscent of the citadel at the Cape. As they pass through, the wagon drivers crack their whips simply for the pleasure of hearing the echoes, or else they amuse themselves by firing off their guns, just to hear the noise of the detonation repeated by the bare perpendicular rock faces.

Two days later we came to the great plains which stretch unbroken as far as the Vaal Rivier. For the first time, the monotony of the journey was relieved by the sight of animals. There were quaggas, *Equus Burchellii,* in herds of three or four hundred and a smaller number of gnus, galloping round in circles.

Since leaving Natal I had killed only ducks which meant that I had by me in the wagon only a long gun loaded with ball; to hand was my double-barrelled gun loaded with no.5 lead. We outspanned for the night near a little stream where we made a fire from wild animal dung which produced hardly enough heat to cook our supper. It was eleven o'clock; everybody was asleep. Suddenly, our oxen all got to their feet and we immediately followed suit. What was it? The animals had smelled something; they knew before we did.

'Henning, What do you think? Is it a lion?'

'It must be.'

'Can you see anything?'

'Damnation! It's as dark as the devil's kitchen out there and there's fog. It's raining as well.'

I was sitting on the box at the front of the wagon holding my long gun; I peered into the dark.

Henning suddenly shouted 'Master, there he is, the lion is there, ten paces in front of you. That thin Zoulou ox that we didn't bother to tether is squaring up to him. But you'll see, the lion will get it,

161

he'll get it. A plague on it! my gun is in your wagon; fire, go on, fire.'

'Yes all right, but I can't see a thing from here and I've only got one shot.'

'Well then, pass me your gun.'

But it wasn't possible. I couldn't risk moving over to the other wagon. It would have required crossing the scene of action. My Cafres had scrambled into the wagons at the first sound of danger and we couldn't have got them out as long as the lion was there. My ox, although puny, was still standing up to him and the poor animal seemed even to be playing the part of the aggressor. Henning, growing impatient, and fearing for the life of our brave companion, shouted again, 'Go on, fire!' My shot went off; the ball hit the ground, glanced off, and whistled past the lion. 'Henning, grab your whip and crack it – let's frighten him off.'

As I said this, I took down my double-barrelled gun.

The lions, for there were in fact two of them, thought they were done for when the air was rent with a terrifying crack as the whip flicked past their noses. They began moving off and one of them got up on to a mound. There were only ten paces between us.

Bang! I peppered the lion with shot from my right-hand barrel; he grunted and slunk off. Hurrah! The thief had gone. I had fired only one shot, when the other lion which I hadn't seen until then, broke cover in time to receive my second shot. Like his companion, he growled and went away.

Quite honestly, if I had foreseen the situation, I could easily have picked off both the lions at the same time. In a case like this there is no danger for the hunter for, however hazardous it might be to approach a lion which has already seen you, there is little danger when he is taken unawares, for then he is governed by fear. If he is struck by a shot while his whole attention is engaged in attacking an ox which is tied by its horns to the wagon wheel, he growls resentfully, but cannot find the courage to attack the man. I have seen, and it was in the dark too, a brave little dog going for a lioness ten paces from the spot where she had attacked one of my oxen.

The further we advanced into the wilderness the more numerous the animals became, and the scantier the grass. We shot a few gnus and quaggas whose flesh was not to be despised. Springbooken were beginning to appear in timid little groups, then in herds of hundreds, and then in their thousands. As they were so readily available, we could expect to live off our hunting without having to slow down our progress. This was even more the case when the blue gnu, *Catoblepas gorgon*, began to appear as well, along with the antelope *albifrons*.

Two days after the nocturnal visit of the lion, I was out hunting when I came across piles of ruins, distributed over quite a wide area. This must certainly have been the *mouzi* of some Makatisse chief which had been destroyed, like so many others, by Djacka. The surrounding walls, contrary to Amazoulou practice, were made of stones, simply piled up, without any kind of mortar. The total absence of wood in these parts explains why the Cafres had built much more solidly than usual. Six or seven thousand people could have been accommodated in a Cafre town of this sort. Today, the walls provide a shelter for hyaenas. For my part, I killed a flock of partridges there.

We continued in short stages towards Vaal Rivier. Grazing became more and more sparse and when we found ourselves surrounded by enormous herds of gnus and quaggas, there was not a blade of grass to be seen. Everything that had not been cropped by their mouths was trampled by their feet. What could they possibly be feeding on, all these animals who frolicked and gambolled in the heart of the desert? I have no idea, and it is a problem which I have never been able to solve. However that may be, for five whole days my oxen had absolutely nothing to eat and I was resigned to seeing them collapse for want of food, when we arrived at Gevecht-Kop. We were not short of water though, for even if there weren't many streams, pans were everywhere to be found.

At Gevecht-Kop, so named because of the brilliant stand made there by thirty-six farmers against an attack by 10 000 of Massilicatzi's Cafres, we found mimosas with withered grass growing underneath and this appeared to satisfy my exhausted oxen. Not far away were marshes filled with all kinds of duck, and when we awoke in the morning, as far as the eye could see, were forty or fifty thousand gnus, leaping gazelles and quaggas filling the plain as far as the distant horizon.

On the evening of our arrival, I had brought down a gnu 300 paces from the wagon and had delayed cutting up the carcass until the next day. At about ten o'clock, we heard noises of a scuffle coming from the direction where it lay; there seemed to be sobs, then a death rattle, followed by diabolical laughter. I was beginning to suspect that I had been tricked, so before dawn I went to look, taking Henning with me. Seven hyaenas slunk off at our approach, their stomachs full of our gnu, except for a portion of the head and the horns. We greeted them with three gunshots. One of them dropped dead, and two others limped away. It was a just revenge for the loss of our dinner.

The skulls of many Cafres were lying about on the ground, all around the place where the Boer encampment had been. I selected eight from among the twenty finest ones and, intending to collect them on the return journey, I placed them in a crack between the rocks where the water could not reach them. Sadly, when I came back, I was too much preoccupied by my misfortunes to consider burdening myself with that sort of baggage. Those skulls are probably still where I left them.

We set off from Gevecht-Kop, taking with us an ample supply of firewood, for we knew that we would not find a single bush before we reached Vaal Rivier and experience had taught me how wretched it is to do without cooked food.

Wild animals appeared in even greater numbers, if that were possible; as a consequence, there was the same dearth of pasturage as before. Our teams were going to have difficulty in dragging their own bodies along, let alone in drawing the wagons; to try and force the pace would have been impossible while they were in this pitiful condition. During the day, I could think of nothing but their sorry state; it was only at night that I could drown my anxieties in sleep. But this sleep was sometimes troubled, particularly by lions who did not despise my emaciated oxen.

We were still three day's journey from Vaal Rivier and had outspanned in open country. We were sunk deep in well-earned sleep, when suddenly, men and animals all started up at the bellowing of an ox which was tied to the wheel of my wagon. At the same moment one of the dogs started barking close by, drawing our attention to a big, strong lioness just ten paces away.

Henning, who had been sleeping under my wagon, jumped up to assist the wounded victim, taking from its cover an enormous elephant gun, loaded with twenty buckshot, seventy to the pound.[1] The shot went off and the lioness retreated, struck in the groin and growling more from pain than from anger.

We spent the next half hour discussing the shot, then we went back to sleep and when daylight came, we looked about for the lioness who could not have been far off, whether dead or alive; but we could see nothing. We talked loudly as we made ready to search the vicinity and then, suddenly, we saw her getting to her feet, still proud and defiant, 100 paces away.

Lacking bullets of a suitable calibre for my double-barrelled gun, I loaded with slugs which meant that I could not expect great accuracy. One of my Cafres, trembling in every limb, carried a heavily loaded long gun. Another elephant gun had been loaded with fourteen large buckshot, ready for me to use. Henning and Isaac Niewkerk each had guns, but really there was nothing serious about what we were doing; it wasn't the lioness that was important. She was simply target practice.

We were eighty paces away from where she was standing, facing us. I used the elephant gun and got half the charge under her skin.

---

1 Bresler thinks that this gun was probably a four pounder. *Translator's note*

She gave a threatening roar, then lay down again, curling her lips and snarling, never taking her eyes off us.

When the first ball from my double-barrelled gun fell a foot short of her she gave a furious swipe at it, believing perhaps that she was attacking some part of me, a movement which she repeated when I fired my second shot with no greater success. Isaac Niewkerk fired a ball which whistled past her ears and the lioness seemed exasperated at having to deal with these invisible adversaries. She was getting to her feet and exposing herself sideways on, when I hit her in the shoulder with a ball which penetrated her body through and through; it was a death blow. The lioness, realising that there was no hope of salvation, began gnawing at her knuckles. Then Henning, who was preparing to fire his double triggered flintlock, lent me his weapon. I fired and she dropped stone dead. We skinned the body and left it to the vultures, as not one of us had the stomach to taste the flesh which had a very strong, repellant smell. The animal was very old with worn, rounded teeth, so my ox had received only a slight scratch which was not in the least dangerous.

Hardly had we completed our task then we noticed, among the herds of gnus, three male lions, looking very dignified and impressive. The closest was 250 paces from the wagons; he reminded one rather of a Cafre chief counting his herds. Some of the agile gnus, with no sign of fear, kept a distance of only forty to sixty paces from the king of beasts, while others pranced around him. I confess that I considered this sort of confidence as temerity, although I knew that the lion's only means of attack was to spring, and that he was unlikely to get the better of the nimble cloven-hoofed creatures. He watched them for more than half an hour and never once did the king of beasts compromise his dignity.

Two days later we arrived at the home of the Lynequey family and, together with the farmers who were going hunting, we crossed the Vaal Rivier that same evening. We camped on the northern bank under the mimosa trees for four days to rest our oxen and to give them time to graze on the grass shoots we expected to find there. Sadly, although slightly more plentiful, the grass was hardly green; everything was dead and dry. Added to this hardship was the intense cold which had no beneficial effect on my teams, coming as they did from warmer climes.

I employed this time of inactivity in acquiring several specimens of the species *Gazella euchore* and I made a point of visiting a Makatisse *mouzi* nearby. How different from the Amazoulous! What poverty exists among these people, manifested in the most disgusting state of filth which they maintain, I believe, to disguise their ugliness, and the imperfection of their bodies. There was not a single fine face to be seen; not one well formed man whom one could admire, not one open countenance upon which one could see the evidence of good will; there was nothing that was kind or agreeable, and the women, the fair sex, were hideous. Physically ugly, these Cafres were also morally base; defiant, lying, rascally, cowardly, it was a trial to be near them.

But they have been so hapless, they have experienced so many setbacks which have been almost impossible to overcome. In these vast deserted lands the man who possesses nothing cannot simply create for himself a cow, that source of all prosperity among the Cafres. In turn massacred by Djacka, overrun by Dingaan, scattered and ruined by Massilikatzi, the Makatisses are today dispersed over an area of almost 200 leagues from north to south. They are the Jews of the Cafre race,[1] and when one sees their pitiful condition, physical as well as moral, their disinclination to good, one cannot but reflect sadly that misfortune makes men ill-looking and wicked. One could thereby conclude that all men would be as brothers were it not for differences in their material conditions.

The first of these people to come forward was a man of some stature, but clumsy and stiff; his inexpressive face was pock-marked, to which he had added further embellishment. Muffled in the skin of *Canis melanotis*[2] he crouched before me; he had been at some pains to deck himself out; by this I mean that he had placed on top of his head more than a pound of soft mutton fat mixed with *sibilo* (antimony). His own heat was sufficient to make this fat trickle down in black rivulets over his face and the whole of his body. The Makatisse was careful not to wipe it away except when it got in his eyes. He preserved an expression of grave stupidity and did not utter a word, although I had the impression that he had come for that purpose.

I asked him some questions in Zoulou, which he did not understand any more than I understood his language which was Sissoutou or the language of the Bazoutous. I took an aversion to this harsh tongue in which Rs abounded, pronounced like the roll of a drum; it seemed to reflect the rigorous climate and the poverty of the people.

But among these Cafres were some who had lived under Massilicatzi who had brought the Zoulou language with him and had imposed it on the Makatisse tribes over which he ruled. We were able to converse freely with them, but they were not easy to find because many of them did not wish the whites to know that they had formerly been part of Massilicatzi's people, believing that the Boers had a right to ill-treat them for this reason.

---

1   A reference to the forced diaspora of the so-called Makatisse. *Translator's note*
2   *Canis melanotis* – jackal.

As I moved about the *mouzi*, observing and comparing, I noticed a woman, kneeling before a strange object. It was a calabash, surmounted by a carved head in which there were two eyes made from red seeds. A number of bead necklaces adorned the throat of this counterfeit creature and the Makatisse woman continued to embellish it with girdles and mutton fat. I was intrigued by the seriousness of the ritual for I had never heard that these people worshipped fetishes, and this object appeared to be one.

I called a Cafre who understood Zoulou to help me question the woman. 'This is my child which you see,' she said. 'I am taking great care of him so that he will grow.'

'Do you have many others like this one?'

'No, this is the only one.'

'Why do you take such care of a miserable old calabash?'

'The doctor said that I should do it.'

'I wager that you have never had a child, that it is not possible for you to have one.'

'That is so, that is exactly so.'

'And so you consulted the *inianga*, you wanted him to tell you what you needed to do to have a child; you asked him to give you one and the *inianga* made this one for you. A strange sort of child, I must say. May I pick him up? Is he heavy?' I picked him up; he weighed twenty-five pounds. The calabash was filled with iron ore.

The woman took him from me, put him on her back just like all the other babies and tied him on with an apron which went round her waist and was pulled up and knotted at her neck. Then she went on her way, burdened by the weight of her big healthy child. The *inianga* must have said to himself, 'Go woman, go on your way; when you know what a burden a child can be, you will no longer pester me to find the means of having one of your own, and then you will no longer be so unhappy about your sterile condition.' This is very likely what the doctor thought, and I find much good sense in it. This was the only sterile woman I came across in the course of all my travels in this part of Africa.

Vaal Rivier is big and beautiful and full of water, although not very impressive-looking at Linequey-Drift where her life is just beginning. By the time she reaches the lower drift known as Vaater-Val-Drift (Waterfall drift) she has grown beautiful, ample, strong, even frightening. There, where her deep waters sleep in a bed curtained by willows, Vaal Rivier could make poets dream; there she equals in beauty the most beautiful, as she moves a while with dignity, before wildly casting herself, tumbling and foaming and eager to lose her name, into the embrace of Groote Rivier.

After four days of rest and spare diet for my teams, I set off again, leaving behind one of my oxen which was worn out and exhausted; he had been a good servant but was now too feeble to move on. Alas, I hardly dare confess it for fear of being misunderstood and meeting with incredulity, but I was broken-hearted at the thought of leaving him there, knowing that the filthy hyaenas would come that night and tear at his throat, and I would have given ten times his value, not for services that he might one day render, but just to save him, for, by that time, I felt about my oxen the way the Dutch Boers felt; I loved them like good companions with many excellent qualities, and the unavoidable death of one of them was like the loss of a friend.

It took us three days to get to Mooi Rivier and six to reach the new Dorp de Potschepstroom, a name put together by the Boers of the district from the names Potgieter-Scheppers-Stroom, village of the stream of Potgieter and Scheppers.

It would have been difficult, if not impossible, for my teams to travel more than half a *scoften* a day for not only was the cold rigorous and the grass utterly destroyed but, to crown our misfortunes, two days before reaching Mooi Rivier we had woken up to a startling sight. Snow, like a white mantle, covered the plain and my Cafres who always went naked during the day had never before encountered it; their limbs froze and stiffened, and more than one of them fell to the ground as he tried to walk in obedience to my orders to keep moving. However, once they had had something hot to drink, my young men showed no ill-effects, and when the sun had warmed their bodies, they began to laugh at this new thing which is called 'cotton' in this part of Africa.

We had been led to believe that at Potschepstroom we would find warmer weather and a few blades of grass, so it was with a feeling of pleasurable anticipation that my men and I had our first sight of the scattered dwellings. Twenty Dutch families lived there, isolated from each other by quite considerable distances. They had a land-roost to settle their differences, and a veld cornet to police the community. This man lost no time in coming to ask me for my permit to cross Boer territory and, although it was perfectly in order, he found it necessary to refer it to the council, so that I should have to explain the reasons for my journey, particularly as I was not a Smause[1] and my intentions seemed rather unusual.

'It is not possible,' said this man, 'that you have come so far and that you intend going so much further, simply to find birds, which you then skin. Some political reason brings you here, no doubt. We have to be on our guard these days against the English and their dirty tricks. And so you say that you're a Frenchman; you'll have to prove it, and also that you are a naturalist. You see, I've got orders

---

1 Kaap's Smause, Jew of the Cape: name given to all merchants who traded beyond the town. *Translator's note*

not to let anyone pass without appearing before our authorities; it's up to them to decide.'

The next day was a Sunday; there was going to be a wedding; the landroost was sitting with his eymeraads.[1]

I approached him; I explained my reasons, taking great care to execrate the damned English, a precaution which was intended to ensure the sympathy of my listeners, and solemnly the landroost granted me permission to go where I pleased. I had decided that, had he refused, I would have made a pretence of complying with the injunction and then looked for another way round which would eventually have brought me back to where I wanted to go.

As I journeyed along, I came across a shrub which grows only in sandy soil and which is almost never encountered other than on hillslopes. Its produce is highly prized by the Boers. The shrub is called *zuiker-bosch*. Fairly common near the Cape, its height is usually from four to five feet; the leaves are rather rough, the wood which is useful only as firewood, is covered with rather thick bark and grows twisted in such a manner as to form an agreeable looking bush. The traveller may pass by without noticing the plant; this often happens when there are no flowers; but when the flowers appear, standing straight up at the end of the branch which they crown with their rough, dry, pink and white petals, not unlike the artichoke, the curiosity is awakened, the attention is caught, comparisons are made, and the Boer who is consulted, hastens to initiate the tourist into the mystery which takes place during the night in the heart of the crown of petals.

I believe that I have read the accounts of all the travellers who have visited the Colony of the Cape of Good Hope, and the strange thing is that nowhere have I seen the least mention of this useful and attractive shrub. I am amazed and incredulous, for the *Zuiker-bosch* grows very near Cape Town; on any visit to Constantia, one cannot fail to notice it; I do not believe it has escaped the attention of all these scholars; however I must confess that it is only in the early dawn that one may observe its distinguishing characteristic, and if I had not been told of this, I too, would probably not have discovered it for myself. What I am talking about is not exactly manna, but something very like it.

Let me show you this flower whose closely layered petals form an impermeable calyx. The sun has not yet appeared on the horizon, the air is peaceful, no breeze stirs, all nature is still asleep and, as the earth cools off, the grass adorns itself with dew. In the calyx, dewdrops left behind by the cold of the night tremble like little balls

1 Eymeraads – could this be heemraaden? *Translator's note*

169

of quicksilver. But how privileged these dewdrops are; especially chosen from among millions of others, all the sweetest qualities endow them at birth; their royal cradle sets them apart, and when their innumerable siblings, recalled by the sun, ascend into the clouds once more, they remain behind to be culled by careful hands, soon to sweeten the bitter black coffee which men will drink while they give thanks to the Creator for his providence. For the bee is not alone in producing nectar. The bee bears a cruel, harsh sting; some temerity is required to rob him of his treasure, but now, without danger or fatigue, a woman's hand suffices to tilt the graceful reservoirs which yield the sweetest, the most fragrant of nectars whose origin is so poetical that I fear being accused of fabrication in telling of it.

But if the seeker after *stroop* has had difficulty in overcoming sleep, if the sun has already risen above the horizon, the most favourable moment has passed, the calyxes are dry, the nectar has evaporated, although its essence remains in the heart of the flower. As the Boers have not the knowledge to make use of this, the late riser can do no other than wait for tomorrow.

We know that bees imbibe from deep inside the calyx the nectar which they need to transform into honey. This substance, which is abundant in the *Zuiker-bosch*, dissolves and mingles with the dew so that the droplets resemble those of a pleasant light syrup, imbued with the perfume of the flower and capable of condensation by boiling.

The Boers who are very precise about definitions, sought no other name for this nectar than *Zuiker-bosch-stroop*. The quantity that each careful gatherer is able to collect before the sun rises varies from six to eight bottles, so that in some places they make provision for the winter, but to do this the syrup must be boiled and condensed.

The *Zuiker-bosch* grows all over southern Africa, from the west coast to the mountains of Draakensberg or Quathlambène. The land of Natal seems not to suit it though, for it is only rarely seen there. I have only come across it in one place, not far from Meyer's Hoek; it does not thrive in heavy soil; earth covered with granitic sand seems to suit it best.

CHAPTER XXX

Mooi-Rivier — Vermaes — His adventure with a lioness — Rooye-Poort — Arrival at Makali's bergen — Makata — Description of his hut — Sloane, Oury — Camp at Klip-Dassen — Discovery of the battlefield where Barend-Barend, chief of the Griquas, was defeated — A few particulars about the Griquas, popularly called bastaards.

In the course of my journey I crossed Mooi-Rivier several times. Up near the source, I outspanned close by the dwelling of Mr Vermaes who was unfortunately away with his family. A stuffed lioness, standing on a section of unfinished wall near the house, had been put there to attract the attention of the infrequent passer-by. In common with other visitors, I was curious to discover the reason why, and this is what I was told by the farm manager who had been left in charge.

Within the space of three nights, Mr Vermaes had lost three oxen; the evidence suggested a lioness as the perpetrator of the crime. Annoyed at being robbed in this fashion, and intent on settling the debt, Vermaes took his eight pounder and called his young son to go with him to carry the powder and ball. He intended delivering two lessons in one; the first to the lioness and the second for the benefit of his son.

After spending an hour in pursuit of the formidable quadruped, Vermaes approached a clump of rushes where he rightly suspected that she was hiding. She presently emerged in full view. Vermaes, sixty paces away, fired and wounded her. He was waiting to see the outcome of his shot when she suddenly pounced, knocking him down and throwing him on his back. The terrifying animal, growling in pleasurable anticipation, opened her awful mouth which was filled with superb great shiny white fangs and encompassed the whole of the man's chest, engraving four bloody furrows over his ribs with her four canines.

The little boy fled from the spot and stood watching from 100 paces away as his father lay on the ground, with the lioness standing over him. The child trembled as he waited for the inevitable, horrifying end. But whether it was in error, or from generosity, or whether it was simply that the lioness intended only to exchange one wound for another, but slowly and gravely she turned and walked away, looking back frequently over her shoulder. Vermaes did not move; at least he could breathe now, but he lay like a corpse, for the lioness was not far off. A few minutes later she returned to her lair. Then the farmer got to his feet, picked up his gun, the butt of which bore the imprint of the animal's teeth, went over to where his young son was standing, reloaded the gun, and continued walking towards the clump of reeds.

'It's her or me my child,' said Vermaes to his little boy. One or the other of us will be dead within the hour inside this circle of 200 paces.'

'Yes father, but it is very provoking. If I'd had a gun, at least I could have killed the nasty animal while she was holding you in her claws. Just think, I had to stand still and watch! I want a gun father, d'you hear?'

'Yes son, next time.'

They walked along in single file, the son behind the father, not saying a word because they were very close now. Soon the father pushed his way boldly into the reeds where he expected that the lioness would be lying. 'Stay here my boy,' and he went on alone.

Ears and eyes straining, Vermaes heard the rustle of a reed; the next moment he came upon the lioness, only ten paces in front of him, lying there licking her wounds. She was taken completely unawares; the shot went off, hitting her in the chest. She rolled over on the ground, stone dead, and although there could be no possibility of doubt, Vermaes, maddened with anger, battered her with the butt of his gun.

Later, on my return journey, I had the opportunity of meeting Mr Vermaes in person. He confirmed the story and provided proof by showing me the splintered barrel of his gun, as well as the lion's skin, and by uncovering his chest to reveal the long deep scars. He was a respectable man, quick and lively yet stubborn, who proudly claimed French descent. He had sworn to hate all lions and all Englishmen because both had once lived, or were still living, at his expense. He was of average build but very strong, his black eyes and hair bearing incontestable witness to his origins. He was enterprising and industrious; he had built himself a windmill of tolerable size to which I was indebted for a bag of flour which was a rare gift at that time, and which pleased me very much.

After leaving the Vermaes dwelling, I found myself obliged to cross and recross the Mooi-Rivier several times. This is the only river in these parts which bears some resemblance to the rivers of northern France. Its waters are pure, limpid, cold and very deep in proportion to its width; the banks are covered in reeds whose trembling tips sway with the current. Ducks abound in the puddles where the river overflows, and the watercress which grows all around the two principal springs was very welcome, for we were constantly in need of fresh vegetables.

Two days later we had left the springs behind and were slowly making our way towards Makalisberg. Soon we were passing through Rooye-Poort, the red gates, a natural corridor, thus named because of the colour of the steeply hewn rock faces towering to left and right above the traveller. The next day we outspanned near a round lake, two kilometres in circumference, but no deeper than two or three feet; without realising it, we were approaching Makalisberg, which we reached the next day. By evening we were climbing the western approaches, a short distance from the dwelling of Veld-Commandant Henderick Potgieter, the most respected man in that country, the 'king of the Cafres' as he was derisively called by those Boers who did not like him.

For the first time since leaving Port Natal, we found that the country was wooded on the hill slopes, holding a promise of varied and abundant animal life. The first birds I saw were those grey, crested turacos, *Coliphymus concolor*, which the Boers incorrectly call 'cacatoes'; black and white shrikes with very long tails[1] nicknamed 'exter', and *Crateropus jardinei*. As far as animals were concerned, we saw only quaggas but it was because of the proximity of man that there were no others; three years previously the western slopes of these mountains had been swarming with buffalo and rhinoceros.

There could be no doubt that I was on the land belonging to Veld-Commandant Potgieter, at the very spot called Klein-Buffel-Hoek. As I was so close by, I could not neglect paying him a visit. In fact it was more than that; I was bound to call in order to deliver in person letters of recommendation from Pretorius, the Commandant-General of the Boers at Pieters-Mauritz-Burg.

It did not take me long to find the residence of Henderick Potgieter and his family. This consisted of a collection of buildings which served various purposes; most prominent among them was a white house, long and quadrangular in shape, with a thatched roof, like all the houses in these parts. Further off, were clustered the huts of the Cafre servants belonging to this noble and powerful lord of the manor. Nearby were various large cattle paddocks surrounded by hedges of thorns, and everywhere the ground was littered with whitened bones and stinking refuse which was being fought over by a pack of dogs of assorted sizes.

As I crossed the threshold I assumed a modest demeanour and removed my wide-brimmed straw hat which I had worn on purpose for the occasion. I greeted Mrs Potgieter, or so I took her to be, then her husband, then her brothers, sons, nephews, cousins etc. shaking each one by the hand as was the custom; this took at least five minutes. Once the formalities had been observed, I was invited to sit on a narrow stool. 'Zitten,' was the brief injunction, issued without the embellishment of 'Myn-Heer'.

1 *Lanius melanoleucus* which I first encountered on the banks of the Om-Kouzi in the Amazoulou country.

Nothing was said for some time while everybody seemed to be collecting his thoughts; the silence was eventually broken:

'What brought you here?'

'What is the news from Port Natal, Pieters-Mauritz-burg and the other places?'

'When are the English going home?' I had to answer all these questions before bringing out the letters from Pretorius.

At last, I had the opportunity of handing them to Henderick Potgieter who took them, turned them over and made a pretence of reading them. 'Yes, yes,' he said. 'I know Pretorius gives you a recommendation but I, Henderick Potgieter, commander-in-chief of this western part of the Draakensberg, no longer have anything in common with him. Pretorius betrayed our people; he sold us out to the English; you will understand how we feel about that. And so his protection is worth nothing to you. However, if you are a naturalist as you say you are, we will think about it.'

Potgieter fell silent. He had played his part quite well; he was determined to appear to be able to read, particularly in front of Europeans who would expect a man of his position to be literate.

I was not at first too optimistic about the outcome of my plans dependent as they were on the caprices of this man; but soon we began to talk about hunting; I told of my sojourn among the Amazoulous and of the success I had had; then I moved on to the war at Natal. I spoke of all that I had lost; I cursed the English, assuring the company that nothing in the world would please me more than a really good war between France and England. I had to talk this way to convince them that I was French; they believed me, and thereafter I was shown the best places and could soon begin my hunting and research in earnest.

The following day Henderick Potgieter set off for his second home and I took the opportunity to move on. In spite of his advice (which sounded more like a command) not to cross Makalisberg, but to proceed in a west north-westerly direction, by that evening I had put Makalisberg behind me, having crossed via the cuttings which truly deserve the name of Poort, for they spare the traveller the trials of a mountain crossing. As we passed through the Poort we had to contend with particles of burnt grass blowing into our eyes; this was due to the fact that Potgieter's son had gone off hunting in the mountains that morning, had decided that it was a good idea to revive the pasturage, and had set fire to the hillsides. Great swirls of smoke rose skywards as the flames laid waste the grass, leaving behind blackened slopes which soon took on a dismal and forbidding aspect.

I went on to spend the night near the *mouzi* of a Makatisse chief called Makata, a man of some importance. He was not at home so I

174

was obliged to present myself to his wives and headmen. I found the arrangement of the *mouzi* and the style of construction of the huts different from those I had previously known. The huts were circular in shape but not hemispherical, topped by a conical roof jutting beyond the hut itself and supported by wooden columns; the general appearance was similar to our beehives. Those belonging to men of distinction stood eighteen, twenty or twenty-two feet high. The floor of the surrounding area was made of hardened, beaten earth and kept polished with liquid cow manure.

The doorway, which was even smaller than that of the Zoulou huts, was no wider than the round shield of the Makatisses. The door itself was made from a thick piece of hard wood, carefully carved with an axe and sliding along a deep groove from which an assailant would be unable to extract it. The interior was plastered all over like the inside of an oven; the height inside was unrelated to the external height of the building, for the roof, and the straw which formed the foundation for the roof, accounted for twelve or fourteen feet. The walls appeared to be painted; there were drawings traced in diluted ochre and various other materials, such as white or bluish earth. These were representations of giraffe, rhinoceros, elephant, the inaccurate execution of which exactly recalled the hieroglyphic figures of Egyptian monuments.

The floor of this particular hut was black and hard, like polished marble. Because it served Chief Makata as a bedroom, there was very little in it except for weapons, mats and fur cloaks all rolled up in bundles, hanging from the walls. There was an air of great cleanliness, which surprised me, the more so as these people are generally very dirty. When I left, the door was pushed closed and for more than a minute the inside of the hut reverberated like a bell.

In view of the absence of the master, we were offered no refreshment. When I finally asked for some, we were given a little milk and some beer. I discovered that pumpkins were plentiful that year and suggested we might engage in some barter. I had with me, for the purpose, a stock of knives, seized from a Portuguese slave ship, which had sold for twenty-two and a half centimes at Natal, although they cost barely five in Europe. I offered one of these knives for every couple of fine pumpkins they brought. The offer was accepted, and within half an hour, my oxen were gathered around munching on a meal of a hundred *pampoenes* cut up into quarters.

Then along came some Makatisses, who expressed their astonishment that I was feeding my animals on food intended for humans. This was something quite foreign to them and raised a number of objections. I had the feeling that these Cafres, who were feeling affronted, were about to forbid me to continue what I was doing, so I hastened to inform them that it was everyone's right to dispose as he wished of goods which he had paid for, and that they had better be off now, because I wanted to sleep. A few who would not comply were persuaded by the menacing crack of the long whip. Our oxen could now continue to eat in peace; we too supped and fell asleep, happy in the thought that we were at last in real hunting country.

I was up at daybreak to survey the great plain, wooded in parts, which stretched away into the distance, extending from north to east-south-east. I had intended heading east-north-east, but according to the local Cafres, it was better to travel due south as far as the River Sloane, because water was too scarce going the other way. I took their advice, but later realised that the Makatisses were only serving their own interests. From the beginning, I regretted not having headed directly towards two or three isolated mountains which, from ten leagues off, looked like mere hillocks.

So we set off, led by some of Makata's Cafres, our self-appointed guides. The villainous wretches led us through precipitous valleys, assuring us that the wagons would easily follow and when I pointed out to them that the descent would be impossible without damage to the wagons, and that we'd never get out again, they were impudent and swore by Marimo, the evil spirit whom they fear, that the hunting Potgieters would not be deterred by such obstacles.

I was surprised at first by their odd manner and their boastful speech; I could not understand it. Soon I began to find them insolent. Eventually I realised that they were telling lie upon lie intending to lead me into making mistakes which would be advantageous to themselves. I tested them out and found them to be no more than prattlers, cowardly at the approach of the least danger, and I realised I was dealing with a very wretched sort of people. Although we had no formal agreement, I expected services in return for those that I rendered. When these were not forthcoming, and I no longer had any doubt of their ill-will, I showered blows upon their backs as though they were slaves. Those who had already grown fat on my hunting deserted that same night, while those who had just arrived, emaciated and weak, stayed on until they were sufficiently glutted. These new-comers were the most submissive. They had good reason to be so, for they were hungry, and I had plenty of meat. They could spend entire nights carving and roasting and munching with the expectation of continuing this delightful life until other needs became pressing. Then, laden with provisions, they were free to go back to their wives, who had been left behind at the *mouzi*.

Well, so much for that. Coming across a ravine with water in it, I was able to outspan without having to go as far as the Sloane, thus sparing my oxen unnecessary toil. The day was not yet advanced and we were at leisure to hunt the various species of antelope which were roaming about in great numbers. All we managed to get were *spring-booken*, but we had high hopes for the next few days when we expected to find the mimosa growing more densely. Indeed, the very next day, when we reached the banks of the Sloane, we found a line of trees of varying heights. We found rhinoceros spoor at several places, still fresh, and came across *Acronotus lunata* and *Gazella melampus*. It was not a difficult matter to hunt down these animals, but I must confess that our first attempts did not meet with much success. My hunters returned empty-handed that day. For my part, my love of beautiful birds had taken me a long way in pursuit of *Malaconotus Australis Smithii* but I was no more successful. The next day we followed the course of the Sloane as it flowed due east and then wound east-south-east. On the way, I killed a number of interesting birds and two gazelles. I even shot a hyaena in the rear as he was slinking off. In the evening, I added a quagga to my bag which I intended would provide dinner for my Makatisse Cafres. My Natal Cafres, now reduced to four by the desertion of two of their number near Kaastel-Poort, chose to eat apart.

Henning had had better luck: he had killed a *Rhinoceros Africanus bicornis* whose flesh, although much inferior to that of the *Rhinoceros simus*, was fatty enough to please us. He had also discovered an ostrich nest containing eighteen eggs which he and three Cafres carried back to the camp. We wallowed now in a sea of plenty: grilled meat of all kinds, omelettes, scrambled eggs, delicious cakes made from the Mooi-Rivier flour mixed with ostrich eggs and cooked in the fat from our rhinoceros. We ate like kings that day; our appetites were ravenous, real Cafre appetites sharpened by long deprivation of such fine fare and by the intensity of the cold.

We crossed the Sloane and two days later outspanned near an isolated mountain which was conical in shape and 250 feet high, the one which we had seen from Makata's place as we came through the Makalisberg. A few hundred paces from where we had camped, the Sloane flowed at right angles into a stream which the Boers called Elands-Rivier. Together they become the river the Cafres call Oury which, at its confluence with the Morikoey, becomes the Limpopo. This river, after flowing some distance towards the north-north-west, curves due north, then eastward before finally turning south to flow into Delagoa Bay which, it seems, the Portuguese called Lorenzo-Marques. On most of the English maps the river is called Manice at the point where it nears the mouth and flows into the sea.

We made an inspection of the rocky mountain; it was composed of stones which were often enormous; this meant that there were gaps where panthers could hide and which provided shelter for large numbers of *klip-dassen*, the natural food of these carnivores. This is why we called it *Dassen-Kop*. Tambooty trees and some mimosas were growing in the cracks between the rocks where a few birds lived. We startled *Melampus* and *Kobus ellipsiprymnus* which jumped out from the bushes that concealed them. Nearby there was an abundance of francolins, *Nudi collis Swainsonii* and troops of guinea-fowl, which ran off when they saw us.

All we had to do was to help ourselves to this bounty while keeping a sharp look-out for poisonous snakes which we encountered twenty times a day. The situation was so favourable, and my oxen so exhausted, that I thought it would be a good idea to spend a couple of weeks there, very profitable weeks as it turned out, for during that time I acquired eighteen large, or medium sized, antelope skins.

In the course of expeditions which we undertook in the vicinity of our camp in search of particular specimens of *Catoblepas-gorgon* or *taurina*, we discovered a large open space littered with bones, among which were skulls belonging to the horse genus. Our first thought was that the area had once been fenced with the intention of capturing whole herds of wild animals; this would explain the origin of the bleached and broken bones. We decided that the skulls belonged to the quagga, *Equus Burchellii*, but as there were no other skulls, we then thought that we were perhaps on the wrong track. A few days later we found human skulls. Henning made further investigations and brought back a gun barrel of English manufacture. We made enquiries of some Cafres who told us that it was here that Barend-Barend, in command of a force of 1 100 Griquas and 2 000 horses, had been completely cut off after dark and massacred at dawn by Massilicatzi's troops.

The Griquas are Hottentots of mixed blood who originated in the Cape Colony where they formerly lived in the village of Tulbach. White oppression had been the cause of their immigration; they chose to settle in the land where Theopolis and Philipolis stand today. As the jurisdiction of the Colony did not extend that far, they soon found the nucleus of their little settlement enlarging with the addition of a great number of deserters. These deserters took wives from among the Coranas, the result of which has been that many members of the tribe today resemble the Cafres as much as they do the Hottentots and the whites. The missionaries who worked among the Griquas, by nature a carefree people, made little or no progress, although they baptised them all. But when the infamous Dr Philip arrived on the scene, this commander-in-chief of all the missionaries in southern Africa made promises of such a nature to these people that they accepted the protection of the English government. Dr Philip certainly had some success among them, although I couldn't say exactly what, but there is no doubt that the Griquas believe that the reverend doctor is second in importance only to God: consider 'Theopolis', 'Philipolis'; how is that for a revival of Islam? God and his prophet.

Anyway, due to their situation and their needs, the Griquas were completely dependent on the Cape Colony. Dressing as they did in the European fashion, accustomed to sugar, coffee and tea and using firearms, it was in their interests to preserve a good relationship with the whites. They went to Colesberg with their wagons to buy supplies, or else the *smouses* would visit their country to trade, exchanging cheap merchandise for fine flocks.

But, humble and obsequious as their behaviour was towards their former masters, they were nevertheless proud and insolent in their dealings with the Cafre tribes who were their neighbours; what they lost on one hand they amply made up for on the other. Confident of impunity, and believing that the terror inspired by their guns would ensure success, the Griquas began glancing in the direction of Massilicatzi, the powerful Cafre chief who was immensely rich in cattle, and of whom their bravest men had brought back reports after venturing into his territory on hunting expeditions. Barend-Barend suggested the idea to his compatriots; as he had the reputation of being an enterprising and brave man, when an expedition was decided upon, command was entrusted to him.

And so he set off with 1 100 men, all mounted and most of them leading a spare horse. They crossed Makalisberg and falling upon some rich *mouzis*, they succeeded in terrorising the unsuspecting Amadébelés who allowed them to make off with enormous herds of cattle. The Griquas followed up with further conquests, their booty increasing each day, which hindered their progress. Each night they made merry and rejoiced as they considered the fine bargains they had acquired which had cost them no more than the inconvenience of leaving home.

When he heard the news, Massilicatzi immediately gathered together 10 000 warriors, lightly armed in the Amazoulou fashion; agile, fleet of foot, silent, skilful in tracking and concealment.

'Go,' said Massilicatzi, 'let no Griqua escape.'

All was done as he wished but, by chance, three Griquas got away. They took back the news which was to cast Theopolis and Philipolis into mourning. The dismay was so widespread that for a whole fortnight the sound of sobs and wailing filled the air, evidence of the wildest despair. The Griquas had learnt a terrible lesson which was nonetheless well deserved. Massilicatzi never forgot the attack on his people. It was the memory of this which led to the massacre by his warriors of the immigrant Boers who were encroaching in large numbers on his borders.

Lately the Griquas, humbly living under English protection, have behaved in the most puerile and hypocritical fashion, stirring up a thousand difficulties for the Boers. This has led to troops, recently disembarked from the mother country, being sent in. You may be sure that without the special protection of Dr Philip such events would never have taken place. It is painful to reflect how these men of God meddle in worldly matters, sow the seeds of strife and division, and incite to war and bloodshed, all with the expressed intent of making Christians. And what Christians they make! Christian morality certainly cannot be acquired simply by baptism, or by the wearing of clothes which they impose on these people whom they consider barbaric for the sole reason that they go naked or are clad only in cloaks made by their own hands.

I have never set eyes on this Dr Philip who oppresses me so; I know him only by his deeds, the scandal he has caused, and the hatred openly expressed by the whole of the South African Dutch population. A number of right-thinking English despise him even more, were that possible, for his vile character, and if I speak of him, very improperly no doubt, it is because of my astonishment at the extent of the evil which one man has the power to spread. This man, in executing his strange schemes, has made himself the bugbear of the people of the south; his name is everywhere abhorred and more than one individual has spat in his face or boxed his ears right in the streets of Cape Town.

What did Dr Philip do, then? Now, this is really curious; our man writes to the London Missionary society; he complains of his martyrdom; the courage which comes only from God is about to abandon him, he requests to be recalled. But, in England, money buys anything, even courage, which should come only from God. One thousand pounds sterling is then dispatched to the good father, who piously fondles the money murmuring, 'May the will of the Almighty be done.' Six months or a year later, the same comedy is restaged.

But I would much rather tell about my mountain and my hunting than of Dr Philip and his Griquas and, if I paused for a moment to philosophise on the battlefield; if I took the reader with me in order to tell him about these Griquas, if I put too much emphasis on Philip so that my reader might know him, I beg your forgiveness, although I must remind you that a traveller should tell all he knows, for it could be of the greatest importance to those who follow after to know his honest opinion about certain people.

CHAPTER XXXI

Aquisition of the *Catoblepas gorgon* — Description of it — The gazelle Melampus — Bots — The waterbuck [kobus] — A hoax — The agility of lions — The bee-eater *bullockoïdes* — *Lamprotornis Burchellii* – My traps – *Acronatus lunata* – The klip-springer

It was not difficult to find the *Catoblepas gorgon* which is the second species of the gnu genus. It is a curious animal which looks very much like the common gnu except that it is stronger and that its coat is of a uniform colour, a sort of dark grey turning to black and blue, depending on the condition of the animal, and the way the light is falling. There is the same long tail, but with the addition of coarse grey and black tufts. The head is armed with horns similarly positioned to those of the buffalo, turning up at the tip, but much inferior. This animal also has two manes, an upper, and a lower which adorns the neck like a beard and extends down over the breast but not, as is the case in the common gnu, as far as the chest itself. Its weight is probably 400 pounds or more, its flesh is fairly good with no distinguishing qualities other than the large amount of fat which is hard and of the same consistency as the thickest tallow. This animal lives in herds, although you will sometimes see one on his own, just as you will often see a lone buffalo, but the company of others of his own kind is not necessary to his existence. The first species of the common gnu appears to be much more dependent on society.

When I first saw them in the Amazoulou country, I was astonished by their similarity to horses in their general appearance, most notably in their gait, their spiritedness, the way they held their heads up high, their manes and the long tail which swished the air. All this conspired to confuse me and when I saw the horns, I was convinced that this was some mythical creature materialising before me. The hunter must beware of them; they will stand their ground against dogs and even attack them. The females also are horned and in appearance differ from the males only in that they are smaller. The Amazoulous know them as *ingogone* while the Boers call them *blaauw-wild-beest*.

They are rare in the Amazoulou country and are chiefly encountered north of Om-Philos-Om-Schlopu. In the land of the Makatisses one finds them in the Gevecht-Kop area. They are common on the banks of the Vaal Rivier while north-east of Makalisberg one finds them everywhere.

I discovered that all the wild animals in this part of Africa had one thing in common; they were all infested with great numbers of bots. The *catoblepas*, both gnu and gorgon, continually blew them out through their nostrils. When I sawed off the horns of the *Acronotus lunata* I always found, at the base, a cavity filled with these bots. The *Redunca Lalandii* harboured, just under its skin, insects in the form of a chrysalis the shape of which suggested a dipteran of large proportions. Each one was contained in a vesicle from which it was quite easy to remove it, revealing the insect attached by the anus to the skin, where a little hole provided access to the air. These chrysalises, thirteen millimetres long, were diaphanous and colourless in appearance; all one could see inside was the black viscera. A female *Redunca Lalandii* which I killed harboured thirty-four of the same species.

The *Rhinoceros simus* also had a few, not under the skin, but in its stomach. The *Rhinoceros Africanus bicornis* could well claim the title of foster father of bots. The imagination boggles at the quantity contained in his stomach; they could be shovelled out in bushels. This difference in the degree of infestation between the two species remains constant and I am very much inclined to think that the viciousness and ill-humour which characterise the *Rhinoceros Africanus bicornis* are due simply to the presence of thousands of these parasites and can be compared with the irritability of a man infested with a tapeworm. However, in spite of their numbers which sometimes seem to exceed all natural limits, bots do not, as far as I know, cause the death of indigenous animals.

I added the *Gazella melampus* to my collection, a creature with delicate legs and dainty feet, the male adorned with beautiful spreading horns, the female graceful and gentle. It seemed such a pity to kill these timid, charming creatures only to have them later displayed in an imperfect imitation of life. But what alternative is there for the naturalist without the considerable resources necessary to make a collection of living animals? What else can he do but observe them in the state of nature and then accept that their skins will provide the evidence which he owes to science and to public curiosity. And so he is obliged to be ruthless and destroy the things he most admires in nature's collection of masterpieces.

The melampus is about three feet high at the shoulder; its coat is an attractive pale red-brown in the upper parts, while the stomach is white. A brownish stripe curves around each side of the buttocks; the tail which is rather bushy, is composed chiefly of tawny hair at the root with white hair predominating towards the tip; a brown stripe runs from top to bottom, a faint patch of white surrounds the eye, the tip of the ears is brown.

The distinguishing feature of this gazelle, to which it owes its

AN IMPALA

name, is the elegant almost black tuft which adorns the back foot for ten centimetres above the hoof. Only the males grow horns which, in the adult animal, have sixteen rings. The longest I saw measured fifty-seven centimetres in a straight line; they are similarly positioned to those of the coudou.

The melampus lives in herds the most numerous of which never exceed 500. Its behaviour is similar to that of the *spring-book*, the only difference being that it never migrates. It is the most agile of creatures and has no difficulty jumping bushes ten feet high, giving an impression of diving as it comes down on the other side. However this agility does not save it from falling prey to the lion; nor does it help it escape from the covered pit traps of the Makaschlas. Its flesh, which is generally good, becomes quite delicious when the animal is plump. As with all the animals I know, the flesh of the female is superior to that of the male.

The Makalisberg farmers have two names to describe this animal: *groot rooye book*, big red buck, and *bastaard-spring-book*. It is not found in the Amazoulou country. I encountered it for the first time on the banks of the Vaal Rivier in the land of the Makatisses and it exists in great numbers beyond the Makalisberg. This antelope has never lived in the colony of the Cape of Good Hope.

The *Kobus ellipsiprymnus*, which I mentioned in the account of my early hunting expeditions on the banks of the Om-Philos, appeared frequently in the vicinity of my camp but in these parts the animal no longer deserves to be called *waaterbook*. The weather was cold and he preferred to keep to the mountains where the stones he displaced as he moved always gave us notice of his departure. I shot several, both male and female, and found no appreciable difference from those of the Amazoulou country, except that some of the males had longer horns.

There is, at the present moment, a male of the species living in the Jardin des Plantes in Paris. One is assured that he comes from Senegal. But, whether it is because he is still too young or that he has been injured, his horns have not grown to their full capacity; they also branch too much to give a proper idea of the living beauty of those whose skins I brought back. Anyway, all the animals which are maintained at great expense in the zoological gardens are in poor condition, or in a state of decline, for they lack sufficient fresh air and there is not enough space for the exercise which they constantly need.

I was able to prove how puny wild animals become in captivity by making comparisons with the quaggas *Equus Burchellii*, registered at the Jardin des Plantes under the name of *Dauws*. These creatures which originate from Upper Egypt or Abyssinia, are definitely of the same species as the ones I found in the Amazoulou and Makatisse countries. I know that I am not wrong in claiming that mine weighed

184

a third or perhaps even a half again more than these. The coat of the *douws* in the Jardin des Plantes has no richness of colour, no clear markings, no shine. On 15 July, when I saw them, they looked as though they were wearing their winter coats, but upon enquiring from a keeper, I discovered that this was their best season of the year from which I concluded that these animals which are studied live in France will never give a true picture of how they look in a state of nature. Besides, whenever a short-haired animal at the change of season does not display a shiny coat that changes colour according to the way the light falls on it, one may be sure that various conditions, whether of climate, nutrition or exercise, are not being satisfied.

When we wished to select certain species, Dassen-Kop, because of its height, was an admirable point from which to spot game grazing far away. One afternoon, after we had completed some work preparing specimens, I sent Henning off to this look-out point and waited for him to come back so that we could set out together for a couple of hours' hunting. He returned looking more joyful than usual saying that he had seen two wagons coming along, half a league away and that, in all probability, they belonged to Mr Wahlberg. Great was my joy at the prospect of such a happy encounter and without further delay I picked up my gun, my powder and my bullets. Henning and I set off, hurrying like men who expect to meet up in the desert with friends who, after long separation, have grown dear as brothers. We soon reached the place where Henning said he had seen them.

'It was here,' he said, 'right here that I saw them just now. They can't have gone far because they would be held up by bushes and fallen trees. Here's a rise; from there we must be able to see them and we're bound to come across their wheeltracks.'

From the top of the rise we scanned the country round about without seeing a thing. We looked for wheeltracks but it was a fruitless task. Finally, after going endlessly back and forth over the same ground we found, in the shade of some mimosas, what Henning had imagined to be two wagons.

Annoyed at having been so completely taken in, we killed one of them for, I have to confess, that it was nothing but two *Rhinoceros simus* walking along together, one behind the other, with the sunlight gleaming on their backs giving an impression of white tented wagons.

'Well, Henning,' I observed to my driver, 'it's all your fault that we started off with such happy hopes and that they turned to bitter disappointment. Now we are just as lonely as before, but I don't hold it against you. Let's just laugh it off and tonight I promise you some excellent wagon steaks.'

It rarely happened that Henning was mistaken about the identity of animals, and so he was embarrassed by our hearty laughter. The steaks provided by our enormous animal were declared to be delicious, which went a long way towards reconciling us to our disappointment.

Nevertheless, from that day on, I considered it advisable to lend Henning my field-glass on any occasion when errors could not be permitted. This little instrument, made by Dolland of London, was portable, light, took up little space and performed a great service by sparing us much searching and the consequent fatigue. The hunter in these parts should never be without one.

I had the opportunity, during my stay at Dassen-Kop, to see evidence of the agility with which lions are able to leap. We had just killed a *Catoblepas gorgon*; as evening was coming on I had time only to remove the skin and the head; my Cafres, who already had more than enough to carry, expressed the wish to put the meat out of harm's way for the night by placing it in the fork of a tree, fourteen feet above the ground. I helped them in this task and we returned to camp. The next day, when it was barely dawn, my men went back to their larder which they found empty. Not a morsel remained; everything had been pulled down from the fork and on the ground, under the tree, were the footprints of lions, evidence of the repeated leaps they must have made in order to get hold of our meat supply.

Every night the great carnivores disturbed our sleep with their roaring and frightened our oxen which were penned inside a hedge of dry thorn bushes. The powerfully vibrant voices seemed to strike the mountain rockfaces and rebound, producing an impression of circles in the air, much the way that a stone thrown into a pool will do on the surface of the water.

There was something terrifying about the sound, the only one that disturbed the night in this wilderness, a sound which forced one to recognise the lion as supreme in this land. We were not afraid for ourselves, but we feared greatly for our oxen which, untethered inside their circle of thorns, might be so transported by terror that they would break out through the hedge into the open, where the lions were lying in wait for them.

In the circumstances we kept great fires burning. Our long whips rent the night air; I blew blasts on a koudou horn which carried far into the distance and, with the additional help of loud shouts, we made as much noise as we could. But I have to admit that, either lions are deaf, or they just pretend they can't hear, for never once did we succeed in silencing one of them, however much noise we made. Even the loud gunshots which we fired had no effect.

Every evening, I decided it was time to strike camp, but when the next day dawned I changed my mind; there was so much still to be done and I felt that I must take advantage of our excellent situation. However, after fourteen days of research and diligent application to

186

work, I gave the order to pack up and our wagons started making their way slowly through the bush where we sometimes had to cut down trees to clear the way. Towards evening as I was planning to skirt the mountains which lay ahead, leaving them behind to our right, we came upon a deep ravine which barred our way. An additional difficulty was the scarcity of water in these parts, so we changed our plans and proceeded in the opposite direction which would bring us closer to the River Oury. After toiling for three hours, our oxen brought us finally to a tolerable spot, pleasant to the eye because of the greenness of the trees and the vegetation which covered the river banks. The Oury, which was deeply embanked, was already rising, although it was still possible at that time to cross at any point, its greatest depth in the dry season being no more than three feet.

Towards sunset, a thousand pretty bee-eaters, *Merops bullockoïdes,* began swooping and wheeling like swallows above a ravine only forty paces away from where my wagons were outspanned. Curious to discover what was attracting them, I walked over to the ravine, taking my double-barrelled gun. As my presence in no way inhibited their joyful flight, I was able to see that quite a number of them were settling on the vertical walls of the ravine. The clayey slopes were riddled with a great number of holes where the *bullockoïdes,* with their subterranean habits, went in and out.

These brightly-plumed birds which lived in the earth provided us with such interest that I could not bring myself to kill a single one of them. Francolins disturbed the peaceful air with their noisy, fitful cries, which were singularly audacious and discordant but none the less agreeable to the hunter's ear. The racket they made was followed by a chorus of sharp, impatient whistling. It was the first time that I had heard this particular sound: it must be something new and I pounded off in the direction it was coming from.

A clump of mimosas of the tall scrawny kind, with branches only at the top, provided a haven for the chorus. It was dark under the trees but that did not deter me. A few minutes passed and then my attention was caught by the noisy flight of a bird of average proportions. I fired my shot and picked up my quarry which I immediately recognised as a large blackbird. When I got back to the wagons, I fetched a light and had the pleasure of examining the superb glossy feathers and the glint of the long tail which was streaked like that of the *anhinga.* This bird was the *Lamprotornis Burchellii,* one of the most beautiful of African blackbirds. Its feathers gleam brightly when the light falls on them. The sound it makes in flight is sufficient to identify it; this sound is produced by the shape of its wings which are more concave than those of other birds.

The next day, when a wild cat started up under my feet, and I had already noticed the tracks of various small carnivores, I recalled with regret my snares which had been stolen in the Natal bush by Cafres who knew the value of the iron they were made from. I decided that I had to become a trapper, even though I had nothing to trap with. I started thinking about ways and means of making good this want by substituting for conventional, complicated traps, simpler ones of my own invention.

I remembered the trap I had seen Amazoulous set for francolins or civets. It consisted of a noose that tightened around the neck or the body of any animal which walked into a cage made for the purpose. A sapling served as a spring to activate the system which, on consideration, I rejected as requiring too much time. I tried the *quatre-en-chiffre*[1] but almost every time I had to replace the pieces which were broken when the stone fell. It would have been a day's work attending to twenty traps of this sort. Then I had the idea of replacing three of the four pieces with a simple forked branch which would support the stone on one side and on the other would hold the bait. I had thirty or forty of these forked branches cut, and at the tip of the lesser of the two branches a piece of meat was firmly fixed. As there were to be traps of all sizes, I needed four men with me to up-end stones as heavy as 400 or 500 pounds. The work took several hours, after which time thirty yawning traps had been set, many of them delicately poised with the upper extremity of the fork leaning on a little flat stone which was intended to give way at the slightest disturbance.

The next day I was up before dawn, as impatient as any other trapper. I had hardly slept for wondering how successful my traps had been. Upon investigation I found that they hadn't really been worth the trouble: a wretched hyaena had visited all the traps, one after the other. At the first one, she had pulled down the fork which carried the bait and calmly eaten up the meat on the stone. At the next one, she had been rapped over the knuckles, but had seized the reward nevertheless. At the third, her success had been easily won; she had pushed and turned the stone with her head. But good fortune did not continue to favour her. At the next trap, the block of stone weighed at least 500 pounds; we had had great difficulty in up-ending it and then we had reinforced it with other stones weighing an additional 300 to 400 pounds. Now, this was a different proposition. Madam Hyaena had found herself caught by the head; she had come to grief and to judge by her tracks I reckon she had made enormous efforts to free herself; bits of hair and blood still stuck to the massive stone which had fallen on her and her terror had been such that the bait was still in place.

1 Literally 'four in number'. *Translator's note*

This could hardly be reckoned as a great success, but I was undeterred. I stood all the stones up again and the next day I was fortunate enough to find a fox which had been completely crushed. The day after that, it was a white vulture, a percnopteran, caught by the feet, but unhurt, which I could have kept alive had I wanted to. Finally, I caught mongooses of various kinds, the acquisition of which rewarded me greatly for my patience; you need a lot of patience for trapping and without it you cannot hope to succeed.

Traps are not only an excellent means of collecting new specimens, but they are essential if the naturalist wishes to procure species which only come out at night to feed. It is the only way to obtain the numerous, little-known rodents which are so plentiful in these lands and which are currently the subject of so much interest among scientists.

I had been three days at the place when one of my oxen, grown thin because of fatigue and a diet of dry grass, sank to the ground, never to rise again. He had chosen as his last resting place, the edge of the ravine where the bee-eaters lived, only forty paces beyond our fires; this proved no deterrent to the hyaenas, which devoured him the first night. When they were still far off we heard their usual drawn-out whimpering cry – which always makes the Cafres laugh – but as they drew near the corpse, in their joyous anticipation of the feast, the hideous creatures broke into infernal laughter. They seemed to be frolicking about amidst the disgusting remains, shrieking with laughter, delighted at the abundance, in defiance of us men who were obliged to listen to the sound of their teeth cracking the bones of our old servant. Several times I went out to disturb these revolting dinner guests, appearing like a ghost only ten paces away from the feast, but quickly and quietly the guests slipped away, taking advantage of the dark which prevented me using my gun.

A guntrap would have caught at least one of them each night, but hyaenas are not worth the trouble, and I had no use for the skin. Anyway, the spotted hyaena, *Hyaena crocuta*, has its uses in this part of Africa, where it disposes of the debris left by the lion, for it feeds on dead prey rather than hunting for itself, and, if it occasionally kills an ox, one may be sure that only dire necessity has prompted the deed. The hyaena, then, stands in relation to the lion, the leopard and the panther as the vulture does to the eagle.

The *Acronotus lunata*, called *bastaard-haart-beest* by the Boers because of its relationship to the bubal *Ant. bubalus* or *Acronotus caama*, was the most frequently seen of all animals in the area where we were hunting and was therefore the most regular contributor to our food supply. At that season, the animals were fat, which pleased my men very well although the fat was a thick white tallow which solidified on our moustaches and beards making them look like candles. We slaughtered several every day and, as usual, the finest specimens became part of my collection.

The gait of the *Acronotus lunata* is the same as that of the *caama*, although he is less fleet of foot; he is also less shy. The *caama* keeps to the open plains where he can rely for protection on his great agility. The *lunata* prefers country which is dotted with mimosas. He rarely risks going into the forest where the trees are too dense. His head, though long, is less so than the *caama*'s; the positioning and shape of his horns is also less exaggerated; they reminded me of two croissants. The greatest length which they attain, in old males, is thirty centimetres, measured in a straight line and thirty-nine measured along the curve; the horns have ten rings. The females also have horns. The coat of this species is the colour which naturalists have agreed to call purple; it is rather like that of the *albifrons* but, at a little distance, it has silvery tones. One can still get some idea of this by looking at the dry skins which I brought back. The legs and the head are more deeply coloured, almost black; the stomach is paler, the tail is black.

Coming from Natal, you first find this animal on the banks of the Vaal Rivier, but it has become rare there. On the banks of the Oury, one sees it everywhere in herds of seven to fifteen. This is another animal which man could easily domesticate; it would pass from the wild to the domestic condition without much difficulty. Its flesh is good without being delicate; the fat would be valued for its solidity and its whiteness, just like that of the buffalo. The hide could be compared with that of the *caama* which is so much sought after by South African drivers to make whiplashes, which means that no other animal in southern Africa has so tough a skin.

While my men roamed the countryside, beating the woods and the clearings in search of unusual joints of choice meat for our table, as well as skins and heads for my collection, I often went ferreting about on a stony hilltop whose sharp ridge extended for almost a league to meet up with the neighbouring mountains. As my senses were always on the alert, nothing escaped my attention. One day, as I was walking along swearing about the sharp, angular stones which were cutting into my shoes and hurting my feet, I noticed something moving in the foliage of a little tree. Naturally I thought of birds; I approached the tree cautiously and stopped a short way off. The same movement was repeated. I glimpsed a brown body, and immediately fired a shot which brought a rock-rabbit tumbling down. Then seven, eight, ten of the little quadrupeds came hurrying down the tree, squeaking, and one after the other disappeared among the rocks.

I was very pleased to have witnessed this scene although it might appear to be of little interest, for otherwise I should never have known that rock-rabbits easily climb trees, that they like the foliage, and that they move about among the branches with extraordinary agility.

The klip-springer is almost always found where there are rock-rabbits. I saw a few which I killed but which I did not skin because this animal is plentiful near the Cape and anyhow, its hair falls out if one does not leave the body to cool before transporting it. This means having to sacrifice at least two hours travelling time. But, what is really discouraging, is the incredible quantity of hair which drops out when the animal falls, not to mention the hair destroyed by the bullet. It seems that the shock of a shot through the body is sufficient to cause a large amount of hair to fall out. When one of these animals drops dead on the very rock he is standing on, I swear a pound of hair falls out immediately.

I saw, gliding overhead at a great height among the mountains, a bird of prey which the Boers call *groot-berg-aarend*, great mountain eagle. I could do no more than watch him, for I was never lucky enough to get him within range.

CHAPTER XXXII

We find ourselves in a cul-de-sac which we call *Waayen-Poort* — Climate — *Ourityle* — Discovery of neighbours — These Cafres say that they are the last inhabitants that the traveller will encounter — A rhinoceros killed on a mountain top — Hunt for the black antelope – *Rhinoceros simus* killed for a steak — Giraffe — Excursion to meet Rabianne — Cafre children afraid of us — The Makaschlas — Porridge of kafir corn intoxicates — Bad method of grinding cereal — Henning kills a bastaard-guyms-book, the equine antelope — Rabianne's opinion of a wagon which he has never seen before — Great herds of cynhyaenas — I hit one on the head with a stone — Lightning — How a crocodile nearly snatched hunter and prey together

A week later, I set off again, heading for a site in the heart of the mountains which my men had previously discovered while out hunting. The Oury flowed through it and generally the situation could be considered a good one. In any case, I was obliged to take it, for a fire had destroyed the dry grass all around my last camp. We had been travelling for four hours when we were challenged by a *kop*[1] which rose up ahead of us. There was a pass on the eastern slope, but it was narrow and stony and sloped slightly downwards towards the river which flowed forty feet below. The least jolt would be likely to dash the wagons to the depths, dragging teams and drivers with them. I consulted my men and it was only when they had promised to increase their vigilance and to exert themselves to the utmost, that I agreed to tackle this Thermophylae. In the event, the pass was negotiated without accident, and I suffered no more than fear. But only South African drivers could have succeeded in a venture of this sort.

A mile further on, we reached a place where six huge trees were growing, equally spaced one from the other. Here I called for an outspan, leaving fifteen paces between the wagons which we would seal off with thorn bushes to make an enclosure for my oxen. Everybody immediately set to work and by evening we were able to sit back and drink our coffee, with the oxen asleep, free of their yokes, and a feeling of satisfaction that we had found an excellent rallying point and a new dwelling place. What helped particularly to create this comfortable illusion was an enormous tree, *kaamel doorn*, giraffe mimosa, at the foot of which our fire was burning. The smoke rising up the side of the trunk reminded me of a country fireplace at home, particularly as there were fine

---

1 They call *kop* any round isolated mountain which stands separately from those around it.

joints of meat hanging in the branches. With the intention of protecting ourselves from the cold air, we had improvised screens of dry branches, interwoven with straw. Our chamber was open to the stars; any canopy other than the sky would have been quite unnecessary; since we had left Vaal Rivier, the days had been constantly blue, dry and clear.

Nothing could be more predictable than the climate in this part of Africa. When the sun is in the northern hemisphere, the atmosphere is always clear; every day the sky is hazy blue, just as it is in the painting 'La Smala'. It is very similar to the sky in France on a beautiful autumn day, and it is invariably warm from ten in the morning until three. For six months you can be sure that the days will all be the same, although we did have a storm which lasted six hours, but this was considered unseasonal and due to a series of unusual circumstances, according to the Cafres.

For the other six months, with the sun in the southern hemisphere and hovering directly overhead at midday, water seems to be continually either rising up or falling down. Hardly has it fallen than it is in a state of suspension once more. The balance is broken when the storm bursts, pouring itself out in torrents until, once again, the heat is dominant; the pattern is repeated over and over again, without respite. Not a day or night goes by without a crashing succession of storms, seven or eight of them, each more thunderous than the last. This is summer in these parts, when the vegetation grows at an astonishing pace and the fringilla puts on its most beautiful plumage, while its nests are hanging everywhere from trees and rushes. Now is the time that the life force reawakens in all creatures, and each species must satisfy nature's great design by reproducing itself. But this hot, humid, steamy atmosphere is not congenial to man; it is as unwholesome as the dry season is salubrious.

The day after we arrived, we explored our surroundings and realised that we had entered into a cul-de-sac which offered no way out for our wagons. The Oury, because of the depth of its bed and the steepness of its banks, was impassable at every point. In fact, the river bathed the stony foot of a mountain which was so high and precipitous that it was inaccessible to man. All I could do was to follow the course of the river in the hope of finding an easier way out lower down stream. But, however hard we tried, we found none, and our last hope of advancing beyond the mountain was dashed.

And so I had no other choice than to make camp and continue my work while I waited for the end of winter. Besides, my teams were in no condition to take us any further. I had one consolation and that was being able to go wherever I wanted on foot. It was only the wagons which were held prisoner in that great, beautiful, rich valley, surrounded on all sides by mountains of varied shapes and sizes and inhabited by numerous wild animals. A little way downstream from my camp, the river was joined by the deep, lazy waters of a tributary called the Ourity}é whose banks were shadowed by willows, leaning across the water. The place was very attractive to the eye in spite of the bare mimosas, and gave promise of becoming even more pleasant in the leafy season. I lost no time in exploring the countryside in every direction.

My men made longer sorties than I did, for they were interested in exploring and there was no work to keep them in camp. On one of these excursions they killed a female canna; the noise of their firearms attracted a number of Cafres to the scene. These people, goaded on by their voracious appetites and guessing that there were advantages to be had, set to work without being invited, loaded the meat and the skin on to their shoulders, and headed for my camp. Henning, astonished at the goodwill of these strangers, shot a quagga for them as a gift and thenceforth we hoped to have neighbours we could depend upon in case of need. We expressed an interest in entering into some sort of agreement with them, but our suggestions were not welcomed, although they were not completely rejected either. However, as our intentions appeared honest, and we had approached them as friends, they decided to impart some important information.

Close to the banks of the Oury, right in the middle of the path we would have to follow to reach the *mouzi* where our visitors lived, were some covered pits, arranged quincuncially and intended to trap game. There were about twenty of them, covered over with such artistry that one required the most precise information of their situation to avoid falling into them.

We were careful to thank the Cafres for the kindness they had shown us and then we turned the conversation towards another matter; I mean towards a discussion of the black antelope with the white underbelly which I so much wanted to find. But it was all in vain; their response to our queries was no more satisfactory than any other we had yet obtained. According to them, no animal of that description existed in the whole of the country.

We also asked them what we were likely to encounter further north; if there were any inhabitants within a radius of twenty leagues; if the hunting was good up there etc. 'We are the last inhabitants within these borders,' was their only reply, and when I insisted that one would surely come across men, perhaps not within two days journey but at least within five or even ten, the only reply I could elicit was a unanimous 'We do not know.'

To judge by their demeanour, and their frank speech, one was easily led to believe that these men were telling the truth, but I was wary of their claims; I already knew that lying came easily to the

Makaschlas. Perhaps we would later get them to talk and if they would not, then we might meet others who would. My first concern was to win the trust and friendship of my neighbours so that they would have confidence in me and tell me all that I was longing to know. Unfortunately, my European reasoning proved quite ineffectual in the circumstances; had I proceeded in a completely different manner, much time, perhaps many months, could have been saved.

Some days after our first encounter with our neighbours, Henning killed a rhinoceros *Africanus bicornis* in the mountains which towered 500 feet above us on the opposite bank of the Oury. I had no use for the meat which was inferior to that of the *simus*, and the trees around my camp were already festooned with joints of the finest quality. It occurred to me that the Makaschlas would welcome the carcass as a godsend and I immediately dispatched one of my men to tell them about it. My only requirement was that they should cut off the head, remove the flesh from it, and bring it back to me in good condition.

My proposal was immediately accepted; thirty men and thirty women hurriedly left the *mouzi*, eager to get at the spoils; the mountain was soon climbed and the vultures, which had already gathered, were obliged to take their leave. The rhinoceros was lying there perfectly intact; the sight of the body excited the hungry visitors. Henning, who accompanied them, made them first remove and clean the head. Fires were soon burning and heaped with chunks of meat which were devoured almost before they had been seared by the flames.

When everybody was satiated, all that was left to do was to chop up the remains of the enormous body and carry the pieces down the mountain, which was almost completely composed of iron-ore. Henning pointed out that they could save themselves much of the burdensome task of getting down the mountain heavily laden. The odd creatures did not quite understand how this was to be done, so my driver told them to get to work and cut off the legs.

'Fine', said the Cafres 'and now what?'

'And now,' said Henning, 'some of you come around on this side. Come along now black vultures, all together now, push! hub-ho-hoye.'

The enormous legless trunk was moved into position and pushed. It rolled without difficulty; it rolled like a ball, bounding down from rock to rock, breaking and crushing the branches which stood in its way and came to a halt twenty paces from the edge of the river where the uneven ground brought it to a standstill, after its brisk descent of 500 feet.

The Cafres then understood the service which had been done them and they began to laugh at the originality of the device, intending doubtless to profit by it again in the future. They appeared so well disposed towards us that we could not let the opportunity pass. We tried to elicit replies to our questions, but they withdrew into a silence more absolute than before.

What was happening in fact was that the more useful we became to these Cafres, the more they were inclined to keep us in the vicinity so that they could profit by our services which, after all, cost us nothing. To this end, every *mouzi* claimed to be the last human habitation. They said that if we went any further we would find neither water nor game; the country was wretched they said. As nobody went there, nobody could give me the information I needed. This is exactly the same response given by all the Cafres in these parts, to the despair of the explorer; it means that he goes off into the unknown, risking privation from lack of water and increased fatigue occasioned by unforseen obstacles which might have been avoided if only they had been anticipated.

Be that as it may; for the moment I had more work than I could manage. Each day I came across mammals and birds which I had never seen before. I built myself a large hut to use as a laboratory and I worked in it until two o'clock in the morning. Time was passing too quickly and I feared being unable to make use of the abundance that was available to me. But all the while I could not forget the black antelope, and I eagerly questioned every Cafre visitor.

One day, four strangers came by on their way to the north. They told us that they came from a *mouzi* a day's journey distant and that they were going back there. I invited them to spend the night with us, putting at their disposal as much meat as they could eat and more to take away with them. Cafres are never able to resist an offer of this sort.

So they stayed; when they were satiated, when I had offered them some excellent snuff, when their eyes began to sparkle, I talked to them of the black antelope, taking care to describe the shape and the way the horns sloped backwards. They appeared to discuss the matter among themselves and finally said that they did not know the animal, 'But,' one of them added, 'we have in the mountains an animal with horns such as you describe, although the coat is not the same; from far away it looks white.'

'That's fine,' I thought, 'it's an antelope of the same genus, which is also extremely rare; it's the *Aigoceros equina* which the Boers call *bastaard-guyms-book* sometimes *bastaard-eland*; the *groot-blaauw-book* of the colonists of old Swellendam which Levaillant found and called 'great blue antelope', and which Buffon described under the name of *tzeiran*, after an animal which originated in Abyssinia. I decided·immediately to go in search of this remarkable creature. I made a point of remembering the name kakaraba by which the Makaschlas called it. It seemed like a discovery which could lead to others. I took this as a good omen and rewarded each of my visitors

196

with a knife and a wad of tobacco, but not before extracting a promise from them to accompany me in my search when we met again at the *mouzi* of Rabianne their chief.

Two days later, we were crossing the Oury, and then the Ourit ylé; for two hours we climbed up a long valley which would bring us out on the high ground. Henning and three Cafres were with me; it was dinner time and, as usual, we had brought nothing with us, for the way was long and we did not want to burden ourselves. Two peaceful-looking rhinoceroses appeared, thirty paces ahead.

'Henning, you take the one on the left, I'll get the other one.'

Our shots went off together and the two animals fell. One got up again almost immediately; the other rose more slowly, and then the two of them decamped, leaving us gaping in amazement.

'Devil take them, Henning, that's annoying! Our dinner's walking off.'

We reloaded fast and started running after them. We quickly caught up with the one which was staggering.

'Henning, you take a shot at him. If he doesn't drop, I'll put a bullet into him.'

Henning's shot went off; the animal dropped and in a couple of leaps I was alongside it; it was still moving, sunk down on its legs; its head was swaying and blood was pouring out through the mouth and nostrils.

'Watch out,' shouted Henning, 'he might get up again.'

The animal was in fact trying to get to its feet but I quickly grabbed a long assegai from one of my followers. I thrust it into the pelvis, piercing the kidneys and in a few seconds the animal was dead. We removed several pounds of meat streaked with fat from the ribs, just enough for our lunch, leaving the rest to the vultures and the hyaenas. We went on for a league until we found water and there we ate our steaks with the greatest relish. I have no hesitation in saying that this was one of the best meals I have ever eaten.

We had been walking again for a quarter of an hour; before us stretched a vast plain dotted with isolated trees among which were a lot of broken-off trunks, about eighteen feet high. I had begun to accept that they were a normal part of the landscape, when I noticed that one of them had suddenly turned into a giraffe which began running away in the oddest manner, its head swinging rhythmically back and forth through an angle of 40°–60°.

I confess I was so amazed that I did not even think of pulling the trigger. Henning, no less surprised than I was, had broken out into a sweat. 'That's a trick I've never seen before.'

The giraffe, whose head was peering over the mimosas, started off again on its fantastic progress, but seemed not to gain much ground. We set off in pursuit, expecting to catch up with it soon. This is a delusion experienced by every hunter; you believe that the giraffe is running slowly because of the slow swaying of its head, but this is a serious misapprehension. In fact, you need a fast horse to match its speed and as usual we were on foot.

Having had to abandon the giraffe, we walked on and soon came upon a burnt-out *mouzi*, the ruins of which contrasted oddly with the surroundings. Later in the day, having walked for four hours alongside a steep stony ridge, we saw on the horizon three blue hills which appeared to merge together. At the foot of these hills lay the *mouzi* of Rabianne. As we drew nearer, I killed an *Acronotus lunata* and Henning killed a quagga in order to ensure our welcome. One can be certain that a gesture of this sort will always be appreciated.

When we arrived at the *mouzi*, we were surrounded by men, women and children. At the sight of us, some of the smallest children shrieked and ran away; their mothers tried to calm their terror and aversion, but on that first evening they were unsuccessful. What most excited the curiosity of the women was my beard, which was seven inches long, and completely covered my mouth, the very existence of which these ladies questioned. They spent some time simply staring in silent astonishment, then they grew bold enough to hazard the suggestion that I must be hairy all over, like a monkey. I had to roll up my sleeves and undo my shirt to show my chest and back. I had to allow them to touch my skin whose whiteness they found fascinating. The complete satisfaction of their curiosity would have required further revelations, but I protested that contact with the air was bad for European bodies. I readjusted my dress, claiming that it was now my turn to inspect the ladies.

Very different from the Amazoulou women, the Makaschlas excited more revulsion than attraction. As they were dirty, generally ill-formed, and rarely pretty, I simply pretended to look them over; then, as if unaware of what I was doing, I turned away. The men did not interest me either, and if I had not needed to conciliate Rabianne, I would immediately have withdrawn to the huts which had been put at my disposal.

For supper, Rabianne offered us some pumpkin cooked in water, and a sort of cold thick porridge. This dish was new to me and did not recommend itself at all by its appearance. It was made of kaffir corn which had been fermented and then pounded in a hole dug in the earth and only thinly lined with clay, the result being that the final mixture was one-third sand. It had then been cooked and left long enough to ensure strong fermentation. This was the state in which it was offered to me; the taste was sourish, like that of kaffir beer made of the same ingredients. In a way, it was like solid beer which one ate with wooden spoons, rounded on one side, and flat where our spoons are concave. I might have found this concoction tolerable had it not been for the excessive amount of sand it contained, which made me swear whenever my teeth ground on pieces of grit. The Makaschlas laughed at me and said I must simply swallow the stuff and not try to chew it for it had already been crushed.

I noticed that the Makaschlas grind all their grain in this manner which could easily have been improved upon if only they had bothered. The porridge of whatever kind, is always full of gritty sand and this is the reason why the people have short teeth which look as though they have been filed. In Senegal I once saw negresses grinding couscous in wooden mortars. At the Cape, the Hottentots practise the same method in the preparation of their food. The Amazoulou women grind all their grains, whether cooked or raw, by means of a flat oval stone, weighing eight to ten pounds, using another stone, twenty inches in diameter, as a mortar. Held in both hands, with the weight of the body pressing down upon it, the oval stone does the duty of a rolling pin.

But during migrations or hunting expeditions, when suitable stones cannot be found, a hole is dug in the ground which is then lined with a dampened piece of ox-hide to cover the sides completely. There is thus no immediate contact between the sand and the grain; the stampers go to work and, if the flour is not very fine, at least it is not mixed with foreign matter like the flour of the dirty Makaschlas.

I decided to make use of Rabianne's hut to try to take a rest. My men, who had spent a succession of cold nights in the open, intended to taste the delights of sleeping under a roof, and came crawling into the hut after me. It was like an oven, completely cemented over, with light and air coming in only through an opening twenty-two inches wide. The heat grew intense and I could not tolerate it for more than a quarter of an hour; in spite of the cold night air, I went outside to sleep. My bed wasn't difficult to carry; a mat to lie on, a stone to put under my head, and a handkerchief rolled up to tuck under my cheek. Fatigue overcame me but I awoke later to find my men sleeping all around me. Their lungs, accustomed to the open air, would not allow them to rest while they remained inside the hut.

The hunting, which was our reason for being there, enticed us out early. In order to increase our chances of success, Henning went off in one direction, while I continued my search in the other. In fact, this was the only way of proceeding because, according to the Cafres, the *kakarabas* were sometimes to be found in one mountain, sometimes in another. By doing things our way, we were achieving two days' exploration in one. I have to confess that my quest for the unknown did not bring me happiness. I made too frequent use of my double-barrelled gun to shoot at birds which, at first sight, I believed were unknown to me. I walked the mountains, meeting only damned stones which tore my boots making my feet and legs bleed. But I did not lose my enthusiasm; perhaps it continued too lively. I found at Rabianne's *mouzi* an *aigocere* horn which confirmed the presence of the superb species, either *equina* or *nigra*;. I was too ignorant to be able to decide which of the two it was, for I had never been privileged to see either; but at least I was now certain that the finest specimens of one of the most distinguished of all species were somewhere in the vicinity.

Alas, if only I had been able at the time to recognise *Aigoceros nigra* by this horn which was flattened at the sides, curved backwards and had thirty annulations measuring seventy-five centimetres in a straight line and eighty-five along the curve. If only I had been able to recognise it, I could have bribed some Cafre to lead me to the place where the interesting creatures lived. This would have spared me five months of exhausting search, accompanied by anxiety and danger, not to mention the loss of a wagon complete with team, supplies, arms and ammunition, and the resultant shortage of clothing, arms, food followed by the loss of my second team, killed by flies, and of servants who could have been of assistance in helping me escape from this desert where I felt imprisoned, escape from a situation in which I was nearly murdered, and would have spared my family the distressing news which was too easily purveyed by newspapers in the Colony and which from there spread to London. But Destiny had decreed that I was not to find what I most desired, whatever the sacrifices I made.

I saw nothing on this outing, although I searched until nightfall. Exhausted, and down-hearted because the expedition had been fruitless, I lay down without eating; my brain, which was as tired as my body, finally allowed me to sleep. Two hours went by, two hours of happy oblivion. My men, stretched out to left and right of me, slept as deeply as I did. Suddenly, I felt myself pulled by the arm, called by name. I was so deeply asleep that at first I did not understand what was happening; at the very least the *mouzi* must be on fire to justify disturbing a man's first deep sleep, a sleep as well-deserved as mine was.

'What is it?' I asked without opening my eyes.

'It's me,' said Henning, 'get up. Come and see with your own eyes. Open them! It's a *bastaard-guyms-book*. I've brought you back the head and the skin.'

'Oh, pooh! It's only a dream.' I was about to lie down again when the indefatigable Henning pulled me up, saying, 'I'm going to have it put up on the roof of a hut and you'll only see it tomorrow.'

The prospect of a postponement of such delight roused me completely, and I was on my feet in an instant.

It turned out to be a superb male *bastaard-guyms-book*. I couldn't take my eyes off it. I particularly admired the beautiful annulated horns which sloped backwards, the long ears like sword blades, curving alongside them. The mane, tinged with tawny hair at the tip, set off to advantage the grey coat which appeared to be white from a distance. The size and the strength of the legs inclined me to classify it among the larger big game species. The more I looked at it, the more sure I was that my time had not been wasted searching for it. Under the eye, long, rough, white hairs formed a beautiful comma shape and embellished the face which is otherwise very similar to that of the guyms-book, *Ant. oryx.*

This animal lives only in rocky mountainous regions which are very hard on the hunter's feet. It is sometimes to be found alone and sometimes in small herds numbering three to seven. This one had been alone, and five times it had tried to flee before Henning got it within range; finally a shot fired at 300 paces had hit it behind the shoulder blade, and it had fallen just as the sun was about to set. This beautiful animal, the first of its kind ever to be taken back to Europe, is today in the collection of the Musée de Tournay.

I thanked Henning for the extraordinary pains he had taken and I did not fail to compliment him highly on his skill. We fell asleep side by side and at daybreak I got up and started work on the preparation of my treasure. The whole day was devoted to this task, except for an hour which I employed looking for a tiny species of bustard, two of which I killed, and two species of rollers with azure and purple-tinged plumage.

The next day, fearing that I would not have enough salt and alum for the preservation of my skins, I left the *mouzi* before dawn. Rabianne had offered me a porter and he himself said he wished to accompany me to my camp. This seemed strange to me, because I had not noticed much curiosity among these people. Rabianne had never before seen a wagon; he did not understand that a vehicle could travel along otherwise than by means of feet, as animals do. In vain I had tried to explain to him what a wheel was like and according to what principles it revolved. Rabianne, who was not a fool but who had nothing in his experience with which to make comparisons, could never grasp my explanations. But when he had seen for himself, even before the oxen had been harnessed, he exclaimed 'Ah, now that I have seen, I understand. Very good.' And his admiration was complete when two oxen paraded the empty wagon before him. He was delighted to climb aboard and I was highly amused by his air of immense satisfaction. For a man who had never even suspected its existence, my wagon was perhaps even more astonishing than the railways are to us.

Some days after my return from Rabianne's place, my second driver noticed a giraffe, which had been lying down, suddenly get to its feet. He immediately shot at it but as it appeared to run away, he did not follow it up. The next day, as he was ranging about in the same area, he saw some vultures flying off. Curious to find out, he went towards the place where they had been; there he found yesterday's giraffe, dead and eaten up, barely twenty paces from where he had shot it. He brought back a piece of skin with square markings which he intended to turn into soles for his shoes. This was his story anyhow, and to hear it you had the impression that he was sorry not to have followed up his shot. Unfortunately, I subsequently discovered that, to conceal the fact that he wanted to save himself a lot of hard work in acquiring some excellent shoes, Isaac-Abraham van Niewkerk had told me a lie; he had shot and killed the giraffe and had only told me about it on the evening of the second day when it had already been partially devoured.

I regretted this incident, not because giraffe were all that rare – we encountered them daily in herds of three, five or seven – but because, although I had taken a lot of shots at them from distances of 150 and 250 paces, it was very difficult to approach them closely enough to get as good a specimen as the one that Isaac Niewkerk had killed.

At this time wild dogs were causing us some anxiety concerning our oxen. Voracious even among carnivores, these indefatigable hunters appeared one morning just after my teams had gone out to graze. There were 300 to 400 of them, divided, it seemed, into gangs, each with a leader who picked up the scent when they were hunting and whose movements were imitated by all his followers. As the dogs came out of the bush, we watched these leaders stop in their tracks and raise one paw in the air; behind them, other dogs appeared and stood, also raising one paw in the air. My men and I watched with interest but not for long; we each grabbed a gun and rushed towards the ravenous beasts. My oxen were between us and the cynhyaenas; this reassured me because, in the event of an attack, our draught animals would be forced to back up towards us and, as we were advancing on them, it would be almost impossible for the wild dogs to seize their prey which would, in other circumstances, be easily overcome.

But, whether they had seen us first and were hesitating for this reason, or whether the vanguard was waiting for reinforcements in order to attack en masse to ensure greater success, the cynhyaenas gave us all the time we needed to overtake our oxen, to identify targets, to take aim and fire within range. They held their ground in an audacious challenge. Our first volley produced no results at all. Not a single cynhyaena moved, not an ear twitched. Following the example of their leaders, they all remained quite impassive until, having reloaded our guns, we gave chase with the assistance of our dogs which, rather over-confident at first, set off bravely, fifty paces ahead of us.

It was the sight of men swiftly approaching that determined the retreat, rather than the barking dogs which were easy game. When a cynhyaena was too closely harassed by one of the dogs, he stopped, wrinkling his nose and curling back his lips to reveal terrible sharp-edged canines. Our dogs stopped immediately, not daring to accept the challenge, showing the cynhyaena all the respect due to those stronger than themselves. A few bullets struck; there were broken legs and pierced stomachs, but not a single wounded animal was left on the battle-field; even those which had been seriously wounded had found sufficient courage and strength to leave the site of their bold stand and their defeat. And our oxen once again understood the advantages of the protection of man whom they serve with such patient resignation.

The next day, as we were finishing our midday meal, we became aware of barking, repeated at regular intervals, coming from the far side of the Oury. Our dogs jumped up and rushed off, throwing themselves into the river, where we saw them grappling with an animal. It was a koudou, a fine specimen, although not fully grown. This scene, which was never fully explained, interested us greatly and pleased us as much as it displeased another spectator standing on the opposite bank. This was a cynhyaena which, a moment before, had hoped to seize his prey as it leapt into the water. He was quite mystified to see his efforts turn to our advantage. He watched with sad astonishment as our dogs set to work. Alone, he would probably have taken on three of them, his courage equalling his voracity, and have got the better of them. But we men were there; he dared do nothing, not even make up his mind to go away.

As he stood there, crestfallen, watching the last hopeless struggles of the koudou, resigned to the loss of his meal, he appeared glued to the spot, condemned to the torture of Tantalus, when suddenly a bullet kicked up the dust under him. But what was the possibility of losing one's life compared with the certainty of having to say goodbye to a copious meal? Typically of a wild dog, our carnivore pretended not to notice the shot. Anyway, it had gone past, hadn't it? The danger was over. After the storm comes the calm. Unfortunately for him as he stood completely absorbed by gnawing regret, a second ball struck him in the femur and broke it before rattling away into the distance. Immediately, the foolish wild thing fell over, then, getting up again, he turned towards the place where my men and I were standing and strained his eyes, his ears and his nose in our direction, trying dimly to understand.

The time had come to put an end to the episode; I went quickly down the steep bank, crossing the river in two feet of water, and climbed forty feet up the opposite side. When I arrived on the level ground, the cynhyaena, which was twenty paces away, seemed about to retreat, but when my dogs came up, snapping at his heels, he turned his head to snarl at them and stood quite still in a deliberate display of defiance. Henning arrived with an empty gun.

'Shoot! Go on, shoot him,' he said. 'He'll play a nasty trick on our dogs, or on us.'

But I continued to walk towards him, as much to prevent making a hole in his skin as to study his method of defence; I was convinced anyhow that my dogs interested him more than I did. Barely six paces separated us; the slope giving me the advantage of height, I decided to make the most of my position by pelting him with pieces of iron-ore and trying to wound him. But whether it was because I was in too much of a hurry, or whether I used too much force, I could not succeed in hitting him, although I tried ten times over. Finally, giving up these clumsy attempts, I approached to within five paces and tried again; the piece of iron ore hit him at the back of the neck and he fell to the ground, stunned.

As soon as he was down, I held him with my left knee pressed against his lower jaw and my right knee weighing on his chest. Henning arrived and with a slash of his knife, slit the throat of the voracious creature. As for the koudou, we let our dogs keep it, for they had taken possession of it anyway, without our permission.

The cynhyaena was immediately flayed and his skin washed in the running water of the river to get rid of the obnoxious odour which it gave off, as well as to prevent infection. But this precaution proved useless; the skin swelled up around the ears just as it had done with the first of the species I had killed, which had also been pursuing its prey.

The season continued unchanging, except for the regrowth of pasture which had previously been burned; but these new shoots were still too short for our oxen to grasp in their tongues. One of them died and when large numbers of vultures settled on the corpse, I instinctively sacrificed a dozen of them to his departed spirit. This incident provided me with some rare insects which formed the kernel of the collection I made in Massilicatzi's country.

Despite the night cold, during the day a hot north wind brought us unaccustomed heat; the sky darkened with heavy clouds and then the rain pelted down, accompanied by furious claps of thunder. The temperature fell and my men and I began to shiver. Everyone had to occupy himself as best he could in this kind of weather. There was nothing for the men to do, although I had work enough. With no skins to prepare, I was busy assembling vulture skeletons, when there was a devastating crash which left us all stunned. The lightning had just struck a huge *kaamel-doorn* growing on the opposite bank of the river and had torn it from the topmost branch to the base of the trunk. The splinters of wood which flew 200 paces from the tree would have filled a wagon.

I considered myself very fortunate that chance had not chosen one of the tall trees which sheltered my wagons, my oxen and my collections. My losses would have been so great, that it would have been impossible for me to continue with my research. The storm, which raged for three days, poured an enormous quantity of water on to the land and the rivers were swollen; but afterwards everything soon returned to normal.

Because of the rain, it had not been possible to go out hunting and we began to feel the want of fresh food. As soon as the weather cleared, we hastened to take advantage of the respite. Henning killed a young rhinoceros which was walking behind its mother. We found the flesh inferior to that of an adult animal, but we agreed that the feet were better than anything we had previously had. The animal stood only eighty-five centimetres at the shoulder, but its skin was already fourteen millimetres thick.

After the rain, we found the earth freshly turned over each morning beside the river, ten to twenty paces from the bank, and almost always this work had been done to the detriment of the new grass shoots. It did not take me long to realise that the perpetrators of this destruction were the francolins in their search for buried seeds. Early each morning they made their way to the bank in troops of sixty to one hundred and fifty; as they passed, the noise of their feet on the dry leaves drew my attention to their presence. Their flesh was very good and provided us with welcome variety. When I hunted them I often used small shot for I had a good supply of it. I always shot more than we needed; I could have killed more than 200 in a single day if there had been any reason to do so, and if munitions had been in plentiful supply.

There were also lots of these birds on the banks of the Ouritylé, where they would try to escape from me by hiding on the horizontal trunks of the willows. In pursuit of them I almost fell victim to an accident which it was quite impossible to foresee, and I recount the incident in order to impress the fact that danger can be very close when one least suspects it.

I had just killed three francolins; I wanted a fourth; I fired a shot; the bird fell and floated on the surface of the water. I clambered along a willow branch so that I could fish the body out with my hand, as I had done with the others. I bent down, I was within reach of the bird, and with two fingers outstretched, I was trying to take hold of one wing, when my hand brushed against something green which disturbed the surface of the water for a moment, and then disappeared, dragging my francolin down with it. I have to admit that I was not quick enough and that I must consider myself fortunate to have suffered only shame-faced disappointment for I had been a mere two fingers away from joining my francolin in becoming a crocodile's dinner.

CHAPTER XXXIII

Departure from Waayen-Poort — Meeting with a Boer who tells me where to find Mr Wahlberg — This intrepid explorer persuades me to stay on — Necessity of sending one of the wagons back to Natal — Isaac Niewkerk leaves, never to return — *Mouzi* of Pilanne — Desertion of one of my young Cafres — Meeting with Pilanne — Information he gives me — A wounded rhinoceros revives — Monograph of the rhinoceros — A pipe — Thorns — Search for the black antelope — The inland sea — On the way again — Entry into a country of mountains — Delightful site

Each day my unremitting quest was rewarded with undreamed of success. I had collected all that I could possibly want, except for the black antelope with the white belly. A superb male kudu had been added to my collection, as well as a female of the same species which had horns, a rare irregularity. I had filled one of my wagons with the finest specimens of canna, caama, lunata, gorgon, ellipsiprymnus, melampus, and I was beginning to feel that these treasures should be sent back to Natal, along with 300 birds which I had acquired over a period of two and a half months.

A kind of intuition drew me back to the mountains which stood beside the Sloane. One of my hunters had caught sight of a creature, when we passed that way, which could well have been the black antelope. But whether I made up my mind to stay, or whether I returned immediately to Natal, it would be prudent to try to find some white settlement where I could replace the oxen which had died and the stragglers who could not recover their strength because of the lack of green grass.

And so I made preparations to move on. I personally took charge of the meticulous packing of my skins, carefully rolling them, with the hair on the inside to avoid friction. To this end also, pads stuffed with dry grass were wedged between them; the heads and the horns had been packed into straw-filled bags to protect all the projections. Furthermore, in order to prevent jolting, the load was secured with thongs which held each item in its assigned place. I only realised later that the thongs of buffalo hide, which tended to elongate, should have been replaced by ropes of vegetable origin, but unfortunately I hadn't any with me.

It was 1 October 1843 when my wagons started back along the road we had come. I greatly feared the rough and dangerous pass over the mountain side with its sheer drop down to the Oury. I went on ahead, not daring to look back, until I heard the crack of the long whips

206

announcing that the pass had been successfully negotiated. Only then did I breathe freely, greatly relieved to have come through without serious mishap. We named the pass Waayen-Poort because of the wind which rushed wildly through it, whatever the direction it was coming from.

Four days later, on the banks of the Sloane, I came across a Boer who was on a hunting expedition. We had spotted the white tent of his wagon from afar and hailed it as one would a ship at sea. Slowly we made our way towards it, alerting the occupants to our presence by firing several shots. He hove to, and we were able to exchange news. This man appeared to have some breeding, even a certain elegance. His wife was with him, and I discovered later that he was a bankrupt who had chosen to disappear into the desert, rather than face the creditors who were snapping at his heels.

He told me that, after he had left the Makalisberg area, he had travelled north along the Morikoey river until the densely growing trees on the bank had barred his way. Not having found elephant, he had then decided to head east-south-east into the land of Mammakaly to visit the chief Sibidely and further on, Queen Mammasetchy, whom he hoped to beguile into handing over a considerable quantity of ivory. But the most interesting news he told me was about his meeting with Mr Wahlberg, whose wagons were hidden away in the mountain gorges, not far from Maschlapine's *mouzi*. Mr Wahlberg had just acquired several specimens of *Aigoceros nigra*. This information was extremely gratifying; at last I was going to meet up with a man I could talk to. More than this, I saw myself within reach of possessing the object of my most passionate desire.

We communicated to the hunter all the information which we thought might be useful to him and then, as we were headed in different directions, we bid each other farewell. The next day we crossed the Sloane and came to the land of Pilanne. We heard two gunshots which were repeated by the mountain echoes. There was no doubt about it; they had been fired by Mr Wahlberg's party. Immediately, I fired a greeting shot from my enormous elephant gun. We listened, but there was no reply. Mr Wahlberg must have made his camp some distance away. We would need to find his tracks. That day and the next we pressed on. We found nothing, although we searched everywhere, and I was beginning to despair of ever overtaking my friend. I purposely outspanned in the open plain so that we might the more easily be seen, and the next day, when we heard shots high up in the mountains, we fired in answer. Our shots were heard by Wilhelm Neel, for it was he, Mr Wahlberg's tireless hunter, who was working the difficult terrain.

Shortly afterwards, Wilhelm appeared, perched on a rock 300 feet above us. He had no difficulty in finding our wagons and came down to shake us by the hand. We learnt from him that we had passed by the place where his master was temporarily encamped. He pointed it out to us but, as the tracks leading to it were right under the mountain and could not easily be found, I picked up my gun and prepared to follow him as soon as he had emptied his cup of coffee, that indispensable cup of coffee which is offered to every new arrival, as long as he is white.

An hour later, we came to a gap in the hills, quite hidden from view, where the white tents of Mr Wahlberg's two wagons could be seen lined up, one in front of the other. Always the observer, the patient naturalist was busy throwing stones at some kites. He was doing this in order to study the flight of these bold birds. When I drew near he said 'You must think me quite mad to amuse myself in this way, but you know, kites will try to seize the stone you throw at them as it drops. Do they take it to be a living enemy or prey? That is what I was trying to find out, but now that you have come, my observations can wait until another time.'

We told each other of our respective plans. The only thing I still wanted to do was to find the black antelope. As soon as I had done that, it would be back to Natal for me. As for Mr Wahlberg, he intended spending the summer in these parts, in order to collect all the varieties of fringilla which were at their most beautiful at that season. He also hoped to find Smith's famous rhinoceros *Quithloha*, and extend his research as far as he possibly could.

Alas, Wahlberg's plans were so vividly set forth that they found an echo in my heart, and my imagination conjured up dazzling possibilities. I had been undecided, but now I could not bear the thought that someone else would discover these unexplored lands. We were friends, Wahlberg and I, but I think that I would have begrudged him setting out without me, when I could easily have been there too. Now, as Wahlberg was the sort of man who did exactly what he intended, I could do not other than stay. Once I had decided, I needed to make certain arrangements. My collections were beginning to weigh me down and my munitions were running low. To solve these two problems I had no option but to send one of the wagons back to Natal, accompanied by a white man and two young Cafres. The white man had to be Isaac Niewkerk, because he had a wife in Pieters-Mauritz-Burg, and because Henning was too useful to me. So I would keep Henning and two young Natal Cafres, hoping to be able to take on some Makaschlas, in return for goats or sheep. I was about to start putting this plan into effect, when I thought of the possibility of finding some willing peasant who would undertake the journey for me. I made it known that I would pay 100 rixdollars and 150 for freight charges, but I found no one to accept my offer and regretfully I had to revert to my first plan.

Isaac Niewkerk left on 10 October, assuring me that he would not fail to carry out my instructions and, if swollen rivers did not delay him, he would be back within three months and ten days. His task should not be difficult. I had given this man permission to work the oxen to death, if he judged it to be necessary, on condition that he replace them, for it was absolutely essential that I should obtain supplies soon.

Mr Wahlberg understood the difficulty of my position and was kind enough to share with me the services of a mulatto, whom he had recently engaged. This young man was called Tom, and he was the son of an Englishman and a Hottentot woman. He was of gentle disposition, a passionate hunter, a good shot and very brave. He was a great acquisition and became indispensable to me; without him, I doubt that I would ever have come out alive from this land. Mr Wahlberg's kindness and helpfulness did not stop there; he gave me several pounds of powder and shot which were worth their weight in gold to me. He received from me in return a thousand thanks, but I never had the opportunity to repay him.

Mr Wahlberg moved camp in order to begin combing the mountains which lay to the north and north-east, his objective being to find a fine specimen of *Nigra*; my intention was the same. I retraced my tracks of a few days before. In two days, I arrived at Pilanne's kraal in the mountains. Unfortunately, he was away from home and his wives did not go out of their way to receive me. As I could find nobody who was deputising for the chief, I gave orders to leave again at daybreak.

When the call was made to inspan, a young Cafre from Natal was missing. He had expressed a strong desire to accompany Isaac Niewkerk, a request which I had refused, for I could not afford to lose another pair of hands. In spite of my refusal, he had had no scruple in leaving; he was undeterred by the fact that he would need to cross thirty leagues of country before overtaking that blessed wagon which was on its way home to the land of his fathers. An additional vexation was that Guimba, the only one left, would be deprived of a companion of his own age and might become very bored. Perhaps we would have to take turns in watching over the oxen. However inconvenienced we might be by the desertion, I was determined to proceed. Several hours later, our route curved towards the north as we followed the contours of the mountains of Pilanne. When evening came, we outspanned near a ravine not far from two *mouzis* belonging to the same chief. At sunset I noticed droves of grouse, *Gutturalis pterocles*, swooping over some little dams of water. I had no difficulty in bringing down twelve or fifteen, with a couple of shots.

It was 15 October, the time when the Makaschla women dig out the dry, dead plants from their gardens. When this is done, they scratch the earth with their wooden picks in preparation for the seeds which they plant every year in times of peace. The late growing season in these lands, which lie closer to the equator than does the bay of Natal, is proof of their great elevation above the waters of the Indian Ocean; ripe maize is being eaten at Natal, while it has not yet been sown by the Makaschlas.

The next day, we travelled north-north-east, across a plain full of mimosas in new leaf, towards an horizon of mountains. The density of the mimosas was such that there was hardly room for our wagons to pass through. Fortunately for us, we were able to follow in the tracks of Mr Wahlberg which saved us a great deal of time. We got through the trees in several hours, having passed a *mouzi* on our right. It was soon afterwards that we encountered Chief Pilanne who told us that he had been out hunting for three days with a hundred men. However noble a chief he might have been, Pilanne had a most strangely shaped head. He was said to be well-disposed and on the strength of that, I paid him many compliments and presented him with gifts accompanied by marks of deference. Instead of the distinguished appearance we expected, Pilanne looked rather demented; his skull, which was flattened at the sides, receded into a sort of cone. He spoke rapidly, without waiting for an answer; his movements were animated, but his physical strength appeared less than that of his ordinary subjects.

As I found him ready to talk, I asked him a number of questions, not all of which he answered, but I had reason to be satisfied, for Pilanne told me of white men living to the west-north-west in a country called 'Mandrisse'.[1] Pilanne should have said 'Manice'. He knew a Cafre who had made the journey there the previous year. The man had reached the Portuguese colony after travelling for a month; he had stayed two months and returned by the end of the fourth month.

I longed to meet this traveller; to question him about the details of direction and route, as well as about the site of the mysterious inland colony, which is today completely forgotten by Europeans. But to do this, I would have had to retrace my steps to the *mouzi* of Maschlapine and, having no horse at my disposal, I had to abandon the idea in spite of the immense interest there might be in what the man had to say.

However, any traveller wishing to cross Africa from one ocean to the other, could do not better than to make for Manice, where he would be sure to find caravans trading with the kingdom of Angola.

1   This is the direction I calculated by compass in accordance with Pilanne's description; however it does not accord with the position of the kingdom of 'Manica'. I thought however that it would be useful to give it just as I received it.

Starting from Port Natal and ending at Saint-Paul de Loanda, he would have cut across south-eastern Africa in a north-westerly direction, and covered more than 1 000 leagues, following the great contours. These whites, who are Portuguese of origin, are today more or less integrated with the natives. They are very ignorant and protective of their trade and are therefore extremely mistrustful of outsiders. I was told by Captain Azevedo, the son-in-law of the governor of Quilimane, that even a Portuguese could not venture without risk into the interior. Mr Azevedo also told me that in recent years two English naturalists had been assassinated because the creoles believed that their intention was to engage in trading in ivory and gold dust which were not in sufficient supply to satisfy the wants of the colonists themselves.

So, in addition to the numerous difficulties of such a journey, we now had to contend with fear of the men who had once been our brothers, but whose behaviour had been affected by the burning sun, as well as by ignorance and lust. Unfortunately, Manice appeared to be the only point where the lines of communication crossed. The worst of it is that, in exploration of this sort, the white man attracts a great deal of animosity. Because of his colour he cannot escape notice. He often arouses the suspicion of the chiefs, who have every reason to mistrust him.

If any government intends exploring the interior of this dark continent, the best thing to do would be to take black children from the four corners of the land, educate them, ensure that they understood their task, and then let them loose. Without a doubt, they would pass unnoticed and the nature of their skin would probably spare them from the ills which whites, for all of their love of science, cannot contend with.

I approached Pilanne to allow me to keep two of his men whom I would reward with a sheep each after six months service. He immediately agreed to my request, pleased, he said to be able to oblige me; then he indicated to me the route I should follow; and so I left him, and headed for the Sogoupana mountains.

The earth was now crumbling beneath our wheels; to our right, lay great stretches of land covered with *jong-doorn*, young mimosa. I was walking 200 paces ahead of the wagons, with a stick in my hand, beating the bushes from which I hoped swarms of insects would emerge, when I caught a glimpse of a reddish-yellow body, the colour of the earth, which I immediately took to be a canna. I walked quickly back to the wagon and signalled to Henning to pull in the oxen. Tom, Henning and I each grabbed a gun and advanced towards the animal, going round it to position ourselves down-wind.

As we drew nearer, we could make out several other bodies of the same shape, with their backs towards us. One of them turned round;

it was a rhinoceros *africanus bicornis*. There were four of them standing together; thirty paces further on, three others could be seen; all of them seemed very peaceful.

'Henning, we've been swindled,' I said. 'Rhinoceros instead of cannas; infamous! What're we going to do with them?'

'Might as well pot one off, while we're here.'

In no time, we were within thirty paces of the nearest one which was eating the slender tips of the young mimosa branches. A minute passed, and then he turned to present us with his flank. My ball struck the right shoulder blade, but the animal walked away. Henning followed him and fired, hitting him in the left shoulder and bringing him to the ground. Meanwhile, Tom wounded a young animal which was walking along behind its mother.

I had only one bullet left and I reloaded. Henning who was also short of ammunition, waited for me to finish the animal off, for it was making a tremendous effort to get to its feet. According to Henning, there wasn't a moment to lose because the rhinoceros had been knocked down by a *skraam schoot*[1], and he bet me ten to one that, once it got to its feet, it would be off just as fast as ever.

I walked over to the animal. 'Not a chance,' I said to Henning, noticing that the rhinoceros was lying on its right side, disgorging blood and struggling to get to its feet by supporting itself on its snout. 'Just let's leave him to die. His strength is running out anyway'.

'That's not so', replied Henning, 'you're quite wrong. Rather kill him, because I'm sure he's going to get up and run away. Watch it! Don't trust him.'

'Oh twaddle! Pass me your knife. It would be amusing if we could say we cut the tail off a rhinoceros while it was still alive'.

But for once, Henning did not have the indispensable implement with him. 'Wait,' he said, 'I'll get them to bring the wagon over; everything we need is there'.

At that moment, the young rhinoceros that Tom had wounded came flying past and my bullet struck it in the right foot. Tom went after it and I stayed behind alone; alone with an empty gun and an enormous beast whose struggles were becoming more and more frantic. What could I do? If only I had had a sharp hunting knife with me. I was beginning to realise that I had to finish him off. Then I remembered my iron ramrod, as thick as a finger. I leapt on to his right flank and I thrust the ramrod into the wound, tearing at the vital organs, intending to make a quick end of him. I was twice thrown off-balance by the wild thrashing of the great body. My ramrod was twisted; I pulled it out, straightened it with my foot as I would a

---

1 A glancing shot. *Translator's note*

fencing foil, and then began again, thrusting it in to its full extent, thinking all the while that it was possible the rhinoceros might run off with it stuck in his entrails.

Tom came back; he propped his gun up against a bush beside mine. 'Hold on,' I said, 'don't let us leave our guns there; let's take them, because if this devil of a rhinoceros runs off, he might trample them.' Hardly had we picked them up when I felt hot breathing on the back of my shirt and heard a sound which I recognised immediately. Quick as a flash I was off, leaping over obstacles, devouring the distance. I was being charged; perhaps it would be a charge to the death! Over a distance of forty paces, the animal did not gain an inch on me. Then the nasty brute turned on Tom, who streaked off as fleet as a deer. My ordeal was over. Suddenly, as if he realised that it was impossible to overtake either of us, the rhinoceros gave up chasing Tom, spun around in an arc, and disappeared among the young thorn trees, leaving us in a state of complete stupefication.

But for Henning, the scene had all the fascination of a bullfight. Perched on his driver's seat about forty paces away, he saw the animal get to its feet while my back was turned. He saw my astonishment and my headlong flight, followed by Tom's. He almost split his sides laughing. 'I told you so, I told you so.' And he was laughing so much he couldn't get another word out. Tom and I joined in the mirth, for we could laugh heartily now that the danger was past, especially as fear had contracted our muscles so much that we looked quite odd. It is at times like these that one experiences an inexpressible sense of joy, which is one of the charms of the dangerous life.

But the hunt was not over; the young wounded animal could not be far off. This time, we took the necessary ammunition and set out to look for it. It did not take us long; in that perfectly flat terrain, we soon came upon a large female with a young animal lying at her feet; seeing her distress, we could not doubt that this was her progeny. In circumstances like these, any attempt to remove the body would not be easy but, in spite of the danger, we could not accept losing our prey. The worst of it was that we hadn't the option of attacking from downwind, because in doing so, we would inevitably have driven her towards the wagon, and she would have trampled the yokes lying on the ground, which had to be avoided at all costs.

Henning and Tom shook their heads when I suggested approaching upwind, for she would immediately pick up our scent; their assurance seemed to have deserted them, and they were ready to run at the first threat of danger. For my part, I knew very well that I was going against all the rules, but I couldn't see any other way. When we were at fifty paces, I signalled to the others to fire. Tom fired the first shot which raised the dust on the animal's thick hide. She hesitated a second, saw us, and in a fury she charged. Henning, who was at the ready, fired his shot, forcing her to present broadside, whereupon my shot got her in the ribs and she trotted off like a pig, leaving us in possession of her calf which stood four feet high. I had its head cut off so that I could draw it.

This is the moment to give the reader a treatise on the rhinoceros, according to the observations which I had so many opportunities of making while I hunted the pachyderm, scientifically known as *Rhinoceros africanus bicornis*. This species of rhinoceros, the only one that Levaillant encountered in his exploration of the Cape of Good Hope, is no longer found today in the places where Sparmann once saw great numbers of them. The Sisikamma, now included in the territory of the Colony, has not had any for a long time. The land of the Ama-Kosa Cafres, that of the Ama-Pondos, and Natal itself, have also been depleted and, although the Amazoulou country provides a suitable habitat, the genus rhinoceros is only represented there by the species *Rhinoceros simus*, which has been described by the learned and brave English naturalist, Burchell. Nowadays, you have to look north-east of Makalisberg, that is north of 24° south latitude.

It is not surprising that man has driven this animal from his domains for, apart from the fact that it would be impossible to domesticate it, this *swart-rhenoster*, as the Boers call it, or *chokourou makaley*, as it is known to the Makaschlas, is a bad neighbour. The damage it causes in cultivated areas is immense. It frequently scatters the oxen by charging at them in a demented fashion, without the least provocation, and even man himself is not safe from its freakish and sanguinary humours. Its flesh, which the Cafres like to eat, and which the Boers find tolerable, is worth killing for, and the skin, strong and translucent when dry, is highly suitable for the making of *chambocks*, and so the gentleman hunter is tempted to take a potshot at it, if only for the sake of a dozen sharp and flexible riding-whips.

If you want to ensure that the animal is killed, you need a confident approach. If you keep downwind, you can get to within thirty, or twenty, perhaps ten paces, even if you cannot imitate the *By-Kruyper* (crawler). And pay no attention to the terrifying accounts of the South African Dutch hunters concerning the dangers which man risks in dealing with this stupid and ferocious animal. Certainly, danger does exist, I cannot deny that, in fact I know it only too well, but when the situation gets tricky, try to persuade yourself that the danger is much less than it seems, and you will get out of it much more easily. Confidence helps one to maintain composure, skill, agility and speed; it can save one from the most imminent danger. Fear, on the other hand paralyses all one's faculties, even one's legs, and seems to nail the feet to the earth; fear delivers one defenceless into the hands of the enemy. So if you are afflicted by that incurable malady, you would be well-advised to remain behind at the camp; take care to avoid the rhinoceros in particular, and you should content yourself with the exciting stories recounted by those nervous creatures who have been reduced to a state of trembling inaction by one single encounter.

The black rhinoceros is dangerous to man; that is a fact which is generally recognised. Nevertheless, in order to attack the animal successfully, one does not need to take the excessive precautions taken by Levaillant and, to be quite honest, I did well to forget Levaillant when I was obliged to kill these animals in order to eat. Quite simply, what you need to do to kill a two-horned African rhinoceros is this: approach him from downwind, crawling, so as not to be seen; carefully select the shoulder joint, and hit it with a ball weighing a sixth or a tenth of a pound, made of two parts lead and two parts tin.

Dogs are just as useless in this sort of hunt as they are in elephant hunting. As their teeth are ineffectual, a pack of fifty dogs can only excite the anger of these animals, an anger which may well turn to the disadvantage of the hunter. So when hunting rhinoceros, do not depend on the barking quadruped. This is particularly important when dealing with African packs which are difficult to control and which rush ahead and harass the quarry until the hunter arrives; often they will drive it a long distance off, which results in a great waste of time and energy.

Now, in southern Africa, where everyone hunts from necessity, and not simply as a pastime, there is too much at stake not to proceed by the shortest means, which are in my opinion always the best anyway. Even if it is a fine thing in France to count the number of dogs killed in a boar hunt, losses of this nature do not amuse the South African hunter, who would never consent to the death of a single one of his canine helpers in exchange for the death of several rhinoceroses. If one of these men, having suffered a disastrous loss of this sort, comes to you seeking consolation, you will invariably see tears shining in his eyes; it takes such a long time to replace the dogs which have died, and the first to be killed is almost always the best.

As far as I was concerned, no dog ever helped me in any sort of hunt whatever in Africa, and I was never moved to pity by the sad fate of any of their race. Early on I learnt to do without them, and I remain convinced that, in these lands, only small game hunting requires the involvement of dogs, which are completely useless or even a hindrance when it comes to the large pachyderms.

Measuring five foot at the shoulder, this rhinoceros, commonly called *swaart-rhenoster* by the Boers, has nothing at all black about his skin which, when compared with the skin of the white rhinoceros, *Rhinoceros simus*, casts doubt on the accuracy of the Dutch definition. While at close proximity, the difference is barely perceptible, at some distance away, it becomes more apparent and, from a long way off, every hunter will unerringly distinguish the white rhinoceros from the black, especially when the sun's rays fall directly on the body; in the shade, the difference is less obvious. As everyone knows, the coat of an animal which is in good condition has a bright shine on it so that, seen from afar, black oxen appear to be tinged with white. At least, I've often seen this in Africa, and I think that the amount of fat on the *Rhinoceros simus* is the reason for the difference; the fat layer in the black rhinoceros is usually only a third of the thickness.

The imprint of the feet, which have only three toes and are smaller than those of the *simus*, are to be found in all the swaart-rhenoster's favourite places. He frequents places where *rhenoster-boschis* grows in hard ground, or where *jong-doorn* is growing in crumbling earth; he likes to eat the tips of the branches and sometimes the roots. But this does not mean that you will not find him grazing on the long grass of the plains, or walking over the loose stones on the mountainside, where one would not expect him to be.

His snout is armed with two horns. The anterior horn, which is often square at the base, is long, more or less curved, and slopes backwards. The posterior horn is short, flattened at the sides, and looks as if it had been sharpened. Only the front horn seems to have any obvious use; it serves to dig up bulbs and roots, and even to uproot young trees. This horn is a terrible weapon which he aims with devastating skill; he implants it into the horse's belly, and thrusts it twenty times, like a lance, through the body of the man he has unhorsed.

These rhinoceros horns cannot be compared, it seems to me, with those of the ruminants. While lacking the bony nucleus they are nevertheless solid; they are independent of each other, and are not attached to the skeleton; they stand up like buttons on the skin and are part of it; consequently they are mobile. They are rough on the outside, and their composition can be seen with the naked eye. In most cases one can clearly see, eight inches from the base of the principal horn, unconnected fibres, rather like separate woody threads. Inside, the horn is made the same way, but the fibres are connected and the density is greater. Articles made from these horns polish up beautifully and are quite heavy. There is some transparency and variety of colour; sometimes it is tawny, sometimes amber yellow, occasionally pale white, or even lightish black, but each of these shades contains reddish threads, like hairs seen against the sun.

The upper lip, which is angular in shape at the centre, is capable of elongating and retracting as a trunk might. This lip grasps at things very efficiently, but it gives the mouth a vicious look. The eye, situated at an equal distance between the ear and the nostril, is so small that one would not see it at first, were it not for the wrinkles which surround and draw attention to it. The ear is shaped like a pig's ear, with a few bristles sprouting from the tip. The flare of the nostril is not unlike that of a man's. This then is the picture of the most stupid and hideous face I know.

In spite of the thickness and weight of the body which give the legs an impression of being slightly shorter than they really are, the rhinoceros is nevertheless much faster than one would expect. A man who is fleet of foot, and who runs in a straight line, could outrun the rhinoceros for a while, but if the animal persists and does not lose the scent, he will overtake the man, who is soon out of breath, while the rhinoceros, once he is under way, picks up speed rapidly. The hunter can nearly always save himself though by running downwind. The rhinoceros then loses the scent which is vital to him, for his eyes are weak and small. If, in attempting to escape, the man moves upwind, he will inevitably be overtaken. I have heard the story of a Cafre who was watching over some horses when he was taken by surprise. Hoping to escape by changing direction, he committed this serious mistake of moving upwind. Unfortunately for him, bushes were no obstacle to the rhinoceros which, charging in a direct line, soon caught up with him, trampled on his body, stabbed him with its horn, then repeatedly threw the corpse fifteen feet into the air; this was attested to by the tattered remains of intestine and hair left hanging in the branches of the mimosas. The tracks which the man and the animal left behind on the dusty path were examined with care and provided further evidence for this story. The Cafre had covered more than 200 paces, as though playing at a game of prisoner's base[1] with his ferocious adversary whose horrifying behaviour remains quite inexplicable. What interest can a herbivore have in killing a man if it is not to protect itself and, if it is not threatened, what can be its motive? Why does fury lead it to impale a man as though it were wreaking revenge, or is it simply for the pleasure of doing so? For the rhinoceros does not feed on dead men's bodies; nature offers him an abundance of food, including those which other herbivores reject. There is in his behaviour some secret cause, some hidden motive, which it would be difficult to discover and which distinguishes him from all other non-carnivores. I made a thousand conjectures, none of which I found completely satisfying, until one day I noticed something which gave me a clue.

We were beyond Makalisberg when I realised that I was infested with intestinal parasites. Their presence made my appetite even more voracious than usual, and produced in me an irascibility which astonished me, but which I attributed to the heavy demands of my

---

1 Prisoner's base: a very old game; the players are tagged as they attempt to run between bases. Webster's New International Dictionary. *Translator's note*

work. Some time went by; the segments of tapeworm increased, and so did my hunger, and the outbursts of anger, which were beginning to alarm me. Soon, to my great astonishment, I was consuming fifteen pounds of meat at a meal which lasted from six o'clock until midnight, and the least vexation caused my anger to become excessive; I was virtually foaming at the mouth.

When the torments of mind abated, I pondered on this extraordinary change of character, which I could attribute to more than one cause; for example, the extreme heat, the electricity in the atmosphere, and particularly my life of abstinence. My thoughts were becoming so confused at times that I began to fear hydrophobia until, one day, I discovered with certainty that I had been playing host to a *tenia solium*, four foot long, and as thick as a man's thumb. Immediately afterwards, I returned to my normal condition; the physical and mental symptoms did not reappear.

Now, on many occasions when I have been present at the dissecting of rhinoceroses, I have observed that the *simus*, which is quite peaceable, contained only a small quantity of bots, while all the specimens of *africanus bicornis* were infested with such numbers of these parasites that they could be measured in bushels. When I thought about these disparities, I was no longer in any doubt as to the cause of the implacable fury of the *bicornis*. Am I right or wrong? I don't know. I feel that I am right, even though I cannot explain this adequately. Science alone has the right to decide. I say once again that the observer must simply provide the facts, he may even express an opinion, but he cannot have the last word.

Whatever the cause of this fury may be, the *africanus bicornis* does not, as far as I know, attack other wild animals; man and his minions, horses, dogs and oxen appear to be the only objects. As for combats with elephant, these might well have taken place in the arenas of Calcutta or Bangolore, where the leopard, the royal tiger and the elephant were pitted against each other, but this animosity, which man has succeeded in provoking, is not habitual behaviour, and the antipathy between rhinoceros and elephant, the contest of herbivore against herbivore, seems to me to be falsely induced, for it can be based on no admissable grounds. In all the time that I hunted, I never saw any evidence to support a belief in this animosity. On the contrary, I often saw black rhinoceros grazing in close proximity to troops of elephant, without any aggression on either side and even more frequently, I saw *Rhinoceros simus* interspersed with elephant and seeming to enjoy equal rights with them, as if they all belonged to the same family.

It is worth observing here that the *africanus bicornis* is in no way covered in defensive armour, or creased wrinkled skin, as is the one-horned rhinoceros of Java. On the contrary, its skin is taut, which means that even the Cafre weapons, such as the *om-Kondos*, are easily able to penetrate, however thick the skin might be. As for what has been said about the invulnerability of these animals, of how bullets flatten out on their skins, one may be sure that this is not the experience of real hunters. If one hears of a ball being flattened so that it cannot penetrate beneath the skin, then I can assure you that this ball was made of pure lead and was of inferior calibre; but whenever a ball is made of ten parts lead to two parts tin, when the calibre is between a sixth and a tenth of a pound, the rhinoceros does not exist whose vital parts will escape penetration, without excepting the one-horned rhinoceros of Java; neither is there a crocodile in this world whose mosaic skull will not be pierced and shattered, for nothing can resist projectiles of these specifications.

So, whether a hunter makes excuses by saying that it was the head, or the body, of the crocodile which made his bullets ricochet, I feel confident of being able to prove to him that the surface of the water will have the same effect, as will all solid bodies which form an acute angle with the flight of the bullet, and the crocodile is almost always shot at as it rises above the water. Now this sort of shot presents difficulties and frequently the bullet does not reach its objective. As the spurt of water which the bullet produces at the point of impact becomes confused with the seething of the water produced by the submergence of the head, the hunter is almost always convinced of the excellence of his aim, although in fact the crocodile has escaped him.

The flesh of the *Rhinoceros africanus bicornis*, although superior to that of the elephant, is not as good as that of the hippopotamus, and much inferior to that of the *Rhinoceros simus*. It is covered by a thin layer of fat which is separated from the muscles by tough connective tissue which is very unpalatable. Nevertheless, the flavour is quite delicate; it makes excellent soup, and my men often preferred the *Rhinoceros africanus bicornis* to the antelopes, gnu, ellipsiprymnus, kudu, lunata, caama, because the delicate melting fat of the rhinoceros was much nicer to eat than the thick lard of the antelopes.

The rhinoceros, which is considered a noxious animal in the Makalisberg district, will soon have disappeared from the region. It has attacked and killed numerous men and horses which explains why hunters are wary of it. But the young men and boys of fourteen or so, who are already using powerful guns, do not have these reservations, for they are quite accurate marksmen and bold as are all children. They are eager for opportunities to hunt down the dangerous animal.

The female is a third smaller than the male; she produces only one young at a birth; the term of gestation, lactation, and the lifespan are unknown. This species is often found in isolation, but is sometimes seen in groups of three, five or seven individuals.

Let us take up the thread of our narrative once more. We

outspanned our oxen beside some leafy mimosas near a ravine, where there were pools of water in places. Flocks of birds rose, filling the air with their cries. I reached for my gun, hoping to discover among them some species previously unknown to me. I had already picked off a dozen or so, when I was attracted by the bright red plumage of *Malaconotus australis*. I fired and while I was picking up its body a *textor* fell on my head, followed by a pretty green snake, still wriggling. These three creatures had all been struck by the same bullet. The snake must have been about to pounce upon its prey which, transfixed with fear, was glued to the spot. The lead bullet spared neither the aggressor nor its victim.

The following day, we went on again towards the mountains. Not far short of them, we stopped for the night beside a long, deep marshland, bordered by rushes. We found ducks and sultan hen in abundance and I collected an ample supply of them. By next day, we were travelling alongside the Sogoupana range. It was becoming very difficult to make our way through the bushes and trees which obstructed our path, as did great blocks of granite which had rolled down from the mountain. Anxious about the jolting which threatened to overturn and destroy the wagon, I was thinking about altering direction when, on our left, a natural corridor opened up, about 200 paces long, and quite narrow. We were able to see, at the other end, what looked like a vast enclosure, with the mountains rising up at the far side, more towering than ever and the vegetation more beautiful than any we had yet seen. We were just turning to enter this corridor when I noticed that the stones had been recently broken by metal-rimmed wheels – we were once again on the tracks of Mr Wahlberg.

It was near this spot that Pilanne had lived two years previously when Massilicatzi unexpectedly fell upon his *mouzis*, stole his cattle, and killed 800 of his people, men and women of all ages. Pilanne abandoned the place and took refuge close to the white settlements. We found earthenware pots scattered about, burned-out *mouzis* and piles of bones, all of which confirmed what my two Makaschlas had told me. Pilanne had made a pretence of obeying, but in fact he had not followed Massilicatzi, his chief, in his retreat north after his defeat by the Boers and the Amazoulous; and so Massilicatzi had taken his revenge.

One of the Makaschlas whom Pilanne had lent me, taught me how to make a truly immovable pipe. This man carried a skin bag in which there were some pieces of earth taken from a termite heap. Now, to carry bits of earth around when one is already overladen seemed to me so strange that I watched attentively as he set to work. He went off to fetch some water, came back and then pounded the pieces of earth, which he sprinkled with the water; soon he had made a ball of pure clay. Then he made a hole in the ground big enough to accommodate it and he put the ball in the hole. Next he took two dry straws of *tambouki-gras* and pierced the lump of clay diagonally, intending that the two ends should meet. When he had succeeded in making a conduit communicating the two opposite ends, he fashioned a bowl at one end, and the other end he shaped into a sort of teat. Without further ado, my man stuffed the bowl with dried hemp, which the Boschjesmans call *dacka* and the Amazoulous know as *sango*; then he applied some burning coals to the bowl and, kneeling down, he began, with intense pleasure, to inhale the smoke which he sucked right down into his lungs. Then came the coughing fits, disturbing to those around him and prolonged beyond the natural limit. It is interesting to note that these men cough with as much pleasure as they sneeze when the attacks are brought on by hemp or tobacco. Some of the pleasures which are perfectly acceptable to foreign people seem very odd to us while we find our own, not dissimilar, habits quite natural. I left my Makaschla to cough to his heart's content, for I was grateful to him for demonstrating to me his simple method of constructing a pipe in the heart of the desert.

In spite of the beauty of the place, I stayed only one day. The mountains were stony and rendered further impracticable by the *haack-doorn* whose fang-like thorns tore pitilessly at the flesh, as well as at the clothing, just like fishhooks. With the best will in the world it was practically impossible for even the most patient of men to progress a mile without cursing this menace a hundred times over. In the Cape Colony, I had already made the acquaintance of the thorn bush which the Boers call *wacht-eine-beytje*, but that was nothing compared with this hooked thorn which was more treacherous than the claws of a cat.

Henning was particulary put out. 'The tears in my skin,' he said, 'will mend themselves, even if I do not attend to them, but what about my clothes? In Heaven's name where do we find cloth here to cover the holes?'

Indeed our supply of clothes was running out, we hardly had enough to protect ourselves from the burning sun.

We emerged from the great enclosure in the north-east, near the *mouzi* where Pilanne had lived before the destruction of his people by Massilicatzi. I met up again with Mr Wahlberg who had camped a mile beyond.

On the first day we did no more than investigate our surroundings. On the second day Tom went off alone to explore the gorges and the mountains. When evening came he found an inhabited *mouzi* where he spent the night and made some enquiries. On the third day he had the good fortune to encounter a herd of twenty-eight black antelope which were very shy and ran off. His first concern was to come back and tell me the news. I set out immediately, taking Henning and Tom with me, the proximity of Mr Wahlberg's camp enabling me to leave my property in the care of two simple Cafres.

Six hours later, we had passed the *mouzi* and were perched on top of the last foothills of the mountain chain which looks out over an immense wooded plain. The fatigue of our climb in intense heat demanded that we rest, and our elevated position enabled us to contemplate vast, unknown Africa which stretched before us to the distant blue horizon, where the peaks of two faraway mountains reached for the sky. The immeasurable wooded plain concealed among its forests great hollows, rough terrain, gorges, but all was rendered smooth and even to the eye by the vastness of the expanse. At least twenty leagues separated us from the distant peaks which our Cafres said marked the junction of the Oury and the Morikoey rivers, and the country between so resembled the sea that one was almost deceived into thinking it to be so. It was blue as the ocean's horizon, the blue we call cerulean. It was level as the ocean and had that same immensity which makes man feel so insignificant. To all appearances it *was* the ocean and each of us, independent of the others, baptised the great plain Aardsch-Zee – the inland sea.

Could we dare risk going down into this great wilderness, the extent of which we were beginning to comprehend. I asked myself the question, but could find no answer. And what lay beyond? What white man had ever set foot there? It seemed that there was no doubt Mr Wahlberg and I were destined to be the first. This great privilege had been reserved for us for centuries, a favour which might have been regarded by some as a terrible punishment. But every man sees things from his own perspective; for Wahlberg and me this terrifying prospect of great new lands made us tremble with joy.

My men and I remained rooted to the spot, taking turns with the field glass, while the Makaschlas, who thought only of their stomachs, played heads or tails with stones to discover whether or not we were likely to kill a black antelope that day.

Perhaps we had taken up too much time gazing at the grandeur of the scene, for we spent only two hours following tracks, which turned out to lead nowhere. Everyone was complaining of the difficulty in walking on the cursed stones, so we decided to return to the *mouzi* where we would find shelter and something to eat for, in all the vastness of these mountains, we had not encountered any game.

We had to be satisfied once again with the nasty concoction of kaffir-corn mixed with sand. Henning coped as badly as I did, but Tom, who was more philosophical, consoled us by saying that we would be comfortable again once we got back to camp. He said that we were wrong not to do as he did, that we should try not to close our eyes and hold our noses, but should just forget about it and simply get on with chewing the stuff.

In spite of our willingness to endure such privation, perhaps even because of such privation, we were no more successful the next day. We saw absolutely nothing, and evening found us back at the camp, weary and disappointed. However, the time I spent in this place was not entirely wasted as far as natural history was concerned; I got some fine bustards, a *Ploceus ignicephale* and a tiny squirrel, *Sciurus cepapi*.

Mr Wahlberg, who preferred to pursue his research without foreign competition, decided to look for other places which might prove more fruitful. The north-western side of the range tempted him greatly but to get there was no easy matter. Whatever the obstacles, he was determined to go ahead; his oxen were inspanned and off he went. Since that day we have never set eyes on each other again.

As I also felt that it was necessary to move on, but without going beyond the mountains, I headed towards some high peaks which the local Cafres called Mourikeyley. The direction we took was north-north-east, with Sogoupana on our left. After two days of slow travel, an opening presented itself like a gateway to a great, beautiful, diverse land. I went through and found beneath the thickly growing mimosas a shelter from the sun's rays and from the storms which were beginning to rumble threateningly.

Bister-Veld, my best wheel-ox, had died on the journey without showing any signs of suffering. Along with Holland, he was my oldest servant, a superb animal and an excellent companion, intelligent and mild, who seemed to hold a position of leadership in the team. Bister-Veld's qualities could never be matched, even had I gone to the Boers in search of a replacement. And the Makaschlas had no oxen, so I could not find a replacement there. I was very anxious; Holland himself was not well, and if he died I would have no ox good enough to take his place in the team. How much greater my apprehension would have been had I foreseen the fate which lay in store for us all.

CHAPTER XXXIV

We stay for a month — Acquisition of five specimens of the black antelope — Description of this animal and its habits — My oxen stuck fast in the mud — Excellence of the flesh of *Rhinoceros simus* — Illness of my oxen — Crossing to the right bank of the Oury — Camp on the banks of the Mokoha — The river rises — We escape from danger — Visit to the *mouzi* of Schloschlomé — Spring of sweet water — Pit traps of the Makaschla Cafres — Arrangement of the conducting hedges — The game they bring in — Silence of nature on the hottest days — Arrival at Schloschlomé's place — How the Cafres answered my questions — Venomous arachnids — Fruitless hunting — Henning sets out for Makalisberg to buy a new team

No sooner had I settled in, than I became completely fascinated by the beetles; the flowering shrubs were covered in rose-chafers, the blades of grass were weighed down by numbers of curculionids, buprestids flashed through the air, while on the ground crawled the carabids, among which I must mention the beautiful big *Anthia Burchellii* and the new *Tefflus* which M. Guérin Menneville has named in my honour.

The numbers grew daily and I can say without fear of exaggeration that one could have collected sackfuls of rose-chafers. Unfortunately, in order to be able to bring back a greater number of varieties, I was obliged to select fewer individual specimens, for I had not enough boxes and pins. There was yet another obstacle, and this was the presence of a host of larvae in the bodies of my beetles only two days after they had died. These larvae were deposited around the anus by a minute dipteran which was unaffected by the camphor and the concentrated turpentine in the boxes. And so I found myself having to prepare all my big insects individually, as I did with my ornithological collection, and this method was detrimental to some of them, for the colours were altered by the action of the arsenical soap. The buprestid *Delegorguei*, which was closely related to the *Squamosa*, although glossy, always suffered this effect.

Meanwhile, Henning and Tom were goading each other on to hunt the black antelope which we knew lived in the nearby mountains and, from time to time, I went along with them if I felt like it. Henning had no luck, but Tom the dawdler, Tom who often got home at eleven o'clock at night after making his way through lion country with the utmost unconcern, Tom, as a consequence of the unusual hours he kept, encountered one of these animals. He killed it and decided to spend the night watching over the body to ward off the carnivores, for there were in the vicinity lions, leopards, hyaenas and jackals. Tom soon realised that the black antelope, which had taken up so much of our time and energy, was different from the other antelopes in that it moved about at dusk, and even after dark. So he sent me back the skin, and spent the day sleeping while he waited for his Cafre to return. Then at dusk, he began his search once more, continuing until nine or ten o'clock, just as long as he could distinguish objects at eighty paces.

As on the previous night, he was again successful; he killed another female, and then the next night a young one. All of this led Tom to conclude that these black animals only came out to graze when it was dark enough for them to be barely visible. This unusual behaviour sufficed to explain why all our efforts had been unsuccessful for so long.

Henning, who did not care to be outshone by Tom, then made such an effort that he ended up by killing a fully-grown male. This is the very specimen, which can be seen today, together with a female and her young, in the Jardin des Plantes. They were the first of their kind to be sent back to France. Described in 1840 by Captain Harris in his work entitled *Wild-Spoort* [sic] *in Southern Africa*, this animal, the king of antelopes, is nearly the size of an average horse. The adult male is black, with the exception of the belly which is white, and the ears which are reddish-brown. A white 'comma' of thick hair underlines the eye. The fine mane is composed of straight hair, eleven to fourteen centimetres long, and there is sometimes a tawny tinge, but only in the centre. The horns are a metre long; flat, annulated, sharp, curving backwards and diverging only slightly; they are so perfectly uniform that, found in isolation, they could not be distinguished as belonging to the left or the right side. The female also has horns; her coat is, in every way, just like the male's, but she is a third smaller than he. The coat of the young animal is tawny-brown.

These important acquisitions filled me with joy. I wanted more but, too much preoccupied by my insects and birds, I left my men to do as they saw fit. Absorbed in my work, I spent the days alone in the bush, without company of any sort except, in the evening, that of my young Cafre, Guimba, who watched over my oxen all day. Of course this was entrusting too much to him. but an explorer must have the freedom to get on with his work.

On the last day, as a result of an unexpected incident, I came to realise how important it was not to be dependent only upon oneself. Guimba came sidling up to me, looking sheepish and making excuses.

'Master, four of your oxen have got stuck in the river where I took them to drink.'

I ran with him to the place. It wasn't far, and I found four of my poor beasts floundering in the water which came up to the chests of some of them, and to the necks of the others. They were trying desperately to extricate themselves, but they were achieving the opposite effect, for their efforts made them sink even further.

'This is bad,' I thought, 'one of them is about to drown, and the others are floundering about so much that they too will soon go under.' To lose four oxen when I was so far from anywhere that it was impossible to make good the loss, would put me in desperate straits. But what could I do to prevent it? I had not enough manpower, no kind of mechanical support, no pulley or tackle, but I had to do something, and I sent Guimba running to fetch some thongs.

As soon as he arrived with them, I tied them to the horns of the ox that was about to drown and, with the added assistance of Guimba's puny strength, I got his head above water. After ten minutes of indescribable effort, the animal managed to extricate his legs from the mud and then fell on his side where his body, by reason of its breadth, remained lying on the surface of the quicksand. We began dragging him along slowly and I was pretty relieved to see him gain a footing at last on solid ground. The second ox was entangled in some roots which I hacked through with an axe; then we hauled him in, tied by the horns, until he finally found a footing. As for the other two, I was considering tying thongs around their horns and attaching them to a yoke of two fresh oxen, even though there was a risk of dislocating the vertebrae as they were dragged out, but there did not seem to be any other way. Guimba was already setting off to fetch the yoke when I heard men's voices. It was Henning and Tom, with their Cafres, who were arriving in the nick of time. A quarter of an hour later, the last two oxen had been freed.

These sands which are washed down by the floods have not time to settle before being covered by vegetation. A man would not be sucked under as fast as an ox but, if he had not something stable to cling to, he would be unable to extricate himself. Several days later, a kudu leapt into these quicksands. It had been put up by some wild dogs which had then been routed by my own dogs. While the kudu was caught in the quick sands, my dogs attacked it and although they were not heavy, they had difficulty in keeping from sinking. The worst of it is, that close by these shifting sands, where the water is barely a foot deep, crocodiles lie in wait for any creature which is trapped. I saw them in the sort of places where one would never expect to see them because I was able quite easily to jump over the stream. I did not spare these traitors; within a period of two weeks I shot six of them at point blank range.

In spite of their long absence, my hunters returned empty-handed. Incessant rainstorms had forced them to remain inside their improvised hut where, for days on end, to pass the time, they had grilled and eaten huge quantities of meat, a popular recreation in southern Africa, which Europeans readily adopt even if they live only a comparatively short time in the bush. So, they all came back looking plump. The Cafres were particularly stout, their skins glowing like polished boots; their excellent constitutions were able to withstand excess as well as privation; they would be the envy of our over-indulged millionaires.

It was about this time that we shot a *Rhinoceros simus*. The flesh was so remarkably good that we decided we preferred it to buffalo and that, henceforth, we would hunt rhinoceros for the pot. And that is what we did. As decay set in rapidly, each day one, or even two, rhinoceros were killed to feed seven men, for a third Makaschla had recently come to join us.

After we'd spent a month in this place, rhinoceros were becoming rather scarce, and Henning pointed out that our oxen weren't getting any fatter, in spite of the rich grazing. Besides I was growing weary of going over the same old ground. Then, Holland lay down and died. That decided it; I gave orders to inspan and we left.

As we went along, two other oxen began showing a reluctance to pull, which was a clear indication that they were ill. Henning shook his head and muttered to himself. 'This doesn't look good,' he said over and over in the tone of a man who foresees great tribulation.

Since these oxen were mine, their loss would not lighten Henning's purse; on the contrary, losing them would make the journey longer, and he would earn more wages, but their condition saddened him. Henning loved them like his own family. Bisterveld the black, Holland the blue, his two best friends were dead. For three years he had driven them; his life had been inextricably linked with theirs, he understood them wonderfully well and knew how to make them understand him; he found in them so many good qualities that his heart melted at the mere thought of them. Henning's only consolation was the knowledge that men too must die just as oxen do.

With our shortened team and our lack of experienced wheel-oxen, we travelled slowly. The Sogoupana mountains were still on our left; we hoped to cross the river two or three leagues further on at the place where it flows through the mountains. As we had expected, the Oury soon came into view. It flowed through green plains, attractively dotted with mimosa, and its deep bed was outlined with trees of another kind, which appeared to form a canopy over the water to protect it from drying up in the heat of the sun. Its appearance was that of a great river; its red-brown waters told of the rainy season; perhaps it would not be fordable at the only point where we could get down into the river bed, a place that the Makaschlas had told us about.

We were following the river along the left bank, when the man we had sent ahead to check on the lie of the land, shouted back to us that there were some covered pits close by. When he signalled to us to stop, I caught up with him. The covering of two of the pits had been staved in. In one of them was a young melampus, alive and unharmed, which leapt up upon seeing us so that we could touch its head, in spite of the pit being fifteen feet deep and very narrow at the bottom. On the edge of the other pit, which was empty, we saw the footprints of a lion which had almost certainly helped itself to another melampus before the arrival of the owner of the traps. I had no more conscience than the lion, and I took possession of the young animal, regretting only that I could not keep it alive.

Eventually, half a league further on, we went down to the ford which we found near the confluence with the little Mokoha river. Fortunately, the water was only three feet deep. We crossed, climbing the opposite bank with some difficulty, and headed towards three *mouzis* which were situated two miles from the Oury and which were ruled over by three different chiefs; Mapooney, Om-Sitanne and Rhemkoka. When we were 400 metres from these villages, our progress was arrested by the Makoha river. We had to outspan on the bank under the curious gaze of the whole population which had come running to see us, or rather to see our wagon, that strange moving contraption having excited great interest.

Mapooney, accompanied by his family, hurriedly left the *mouzi*. Whether it was because of puerile fear, or whether it was from uneasy conscience, I had no idea and, although I remained in that place a long time, I never saw him. I went to pay my respects to Om-Sitanne and Remkoka who both struck me as sorry specimens which was due as much to their demeanour as to the dirt they wore in place of shirts. Their attitude to me was cold and aloof, no matter how I approached them, and I could get nothing out of them. However, I took comfort in the thought that they could hold nothing against me personally, because this was the first time we had met. Let me say right away for the information of the reader that I learnt later, on my return to Potgieter's house at Makali's Berg, that it was because they lived a long way away from the whites, and close to Massilicatzi, that these Cafres needed to be cautious. Had it come to his ears that a white man had been made welcome, it seems that this terrible chief would have had them all put to death, if one is to believe what the whites say about the local Cafres spying for Massilicatzi.

I could therefore not expect much in the way of service from these men, but the time would come when I would need their assistance. So I resorted to winning them over with presents of animals I had shot. This meant that we had to kill quite a number of buffalo and rhinoceros. Even if we did not make friends of them, they became indebted to us.

The fourth night, which we spent on the banks of the Makoha, was almost a disaster. A terrible storm burst over the mountains where the river has its source, with the result that in less than half an hour the water level rose nine feet, overflowing the banks so that my oxen were up to their knees before the noise awakened us. We had just enough time to inspan and drive the wagon to high ground 100 paces away. The water swept away a lot of our equipment which was stowed under the wagon, but in circumstances like these one makes light of such losses, particularly when one calculates that half an hour's delay would have resulted in our being washed away too, along with our goods.

Tom, during an excursion lasting several days, had gone as far as the foot of the high peaks of Mourikeyley where he had encountered and wounded a number of *Aigoceros nigra* and *equina*, but had killed nothing. This he attributed to the poor quality of his powder. He had come upon a *mouzi* whose chief was called Schloschlomé; but had not much to say about the reception he had received. Along the way he had seen many giraffe and also a fine herd of elephant which he admitted he had not dared attack. Although he was brave, this was the first time he had seen these giants and every hunter is deeply moved when he first sees elephants, much more so than when he first encounters lions, which are so easy to kill if one has bullets mixed with tin.

I had such wonderful memories of hunting in the Amazoulou country that the word 'elephant' rang in my ears with an indescribably beautiful sound which found an echo in the depths of my heart. I couldn't sleep, and when day was just beginning to break, Tom, one of the Cafres and I were already on the way to the *mouzi* of Schloschlomé. As the distance was great, we had to make frequent stops to rest. We saw those creatures of fantasy, the giraffes, with their necks swaying like elastic springs, and the heads and rumps of about ten hippopotamus which did not interest us for the moment. We were about to start climbing down into a great plain wedged in between the mountains, when we were tempted to stop once again by a spring bubbling up through the stones. It was the last water we would find until we got to the foot of the mountains.

'That's funny,' said Tom, who was the first to drink, 'we must be on a sugar mine. Just taste this water, it's sugary like the kind you give me to drink sometimes.'

Not only was I curious, but I was thirsty too, and I took a large gulp of the liquid, the first taste of which was indeed sweet, but which then turned bitter on the palate, and then very insipid. It might have been pleasant to drink but it did not quench the thirst. Tom, who could only taste the sugar, said that he could easily do without the sugar the *smouses* sold, and cow's milk too, if he lived near a spring like this one, with another one close by, such as we had once encountered, which bubbled out of a chalky bed and whose white water gave us coffee with mineral milk not unlike coffee with real cow's milk. I did not want to disillusion him, and we went on in the intense heat.

A quarter of an hour later, we were forced to make a detour to avoid some pit traps with fences made of branches leading to them. Not far off, we could see some hastily constructed huts and heaps of bones. We inspected the pits, which were all intact. I had never before seen anything quite like them and I thoroughly approved the Makatisse method of construction, although it would only be appropriate in wooded areas.

They choose a trail which herbivores of all kinds would be likely to use. It is a good thing when this trail leads to water and it is excellent when it is the only pathway through steep rocks. When these two advantages are combined, pits are dug at the point where funnel-shaped hedges will form an angle. These pits are twelve feet deep, twenty feet long and twenty feet wide; the sides are raised by means of horizontal branches firmly secured and interlaced with additional dry branches, intended to cover over the top of the pit, but not strong enough to support the weight of an animal, even one the size of the melampus.

The hedges are then set up, generally standing twelve or fourteen feet high and their sides are stuck full of thorny mimosa branches; they are intended to be strong enough to resist a herd of buffalo. To create an impression of solidity, light is blocked out by filling up the gaps with grass. I saw a corridor 100 metres long which led to seven pits; the total length of all the hedges was no less than 1 200 metres. From whatever direction the animals came, they ended up at the apex of one of the seven angles where the comparatively low barrier seemed to offer them the hope of escaping in one leap. When they attempted to do this, they fell through the horizontal branches into the trap from which they struggled hopelessly to escape; the most agile species hit their heads on the transverse branches forcing them into submission when their strength was finally exhausted.

This system of traps brings in quite a good haul, sometimes daily, sometimes only weekly, but if the need arises, the Makaschlas will drive the game into these runs from which they cannot escape. I will always remember an astonishing incident which I witnessed at Rhemkoka's.

Thirty buffalo were grazing in the bush, 300 paces away from the hedges. A child discovered them and ran to the *mouzi* with the news. Immediately all the men, women and children formed themselves into a long, rapidly-moving line. In ten minutes, the buffalo, surprised from behind, had been partly encircled. A confusion of shouts arose, and the herd tried to escape from the noise. As a result, they were all cornered and trapped in one of the corridors where, crowded together, they made for the far end as fast as they could. When they got there, four abreast, without hesitation, they leapt and disappeared into the pit. The second row, arriving hot on their heels, jumped in on top of them, followed by the third row; all of them disappeared. Then came the bellowing! Unable to stop themselves, the fourth row landed on top of all the others, which they trampled. When the fifth row arrived, there was a hellish chaos of buffaloes. They bellowed and writhed as they were trampled and suffocated. By now, the hole was filled up and the last to arrive went over the top unharmed. The ten which formed the top layer, recovering from their astonishment, managed to get out, although rather lame and bruised, but the first ten to fall into the trap remained there, killed, not only by the fall, but by the weight of their peers which had crushed the life out of them. How singular it was to see these fine animals which weighed more than 2 000 pounds, being pulled out of the pit their necks fractured, their spines crushed, their legs broken, their horns bloodied and their eyes frantic.

This great stroke of good fortune for the Cafres brought in its train so much dissent over the sharing of it, that the extraction from the pit of all the bodies, and the carving up, took three days which meant that the last to be served had to be content with rather 'high' and gamey buffalo. But it is not easy to disgust a Makaschla, for their tastes are closely related to those of the hyaena.

When we had inspected the pits to make sure that there was nothing in them, we went on our way across the plain which was almost completely covered in trees whose foliage was very much like that of the makano. We walked with difficulty, for the granitic sand gave way beneath our feet, making our footprints look smaller. As the heat grew more and more intense, without any suggestion of a breeze, we struggled to breathe, bathed in our own sweat. When it was time for all creatures to retire to sleep in the shade, the hour when the sun overwhelms the land with his ardour, we were probably the only living things brave enough to move. Not a mammal could be seen, not a bird, not even a beetle; they were all lying down, hidden away, each in his sheltered retreat. It was the stillest time in the daily revolution of the earth, for the night has its players, some of them very noisy ones. Although the rodents are quiet then, the carnivores make the air tremble with the sound of their voices in concert, majestic and impressive, reverberating or hoarse, harmonious and fluty or whining – this strange chorus troubles the sleep. So, between mid-day and two o'clock the sacred hours of siesta are observed by all those upon whose heads the sun darts his rays; these blessed hours we too could have spent joyfully lying cool in a bed of sand.

But we were short of time, we had to keep walking if we were to arrive before nightfall at Schloschlomé's kraal, for he did not know us, and the isolated *mouzis* are always on their guard against attack. To spare ourselves the risk of being taken for enemies in the dark, it was worth the sacrifice of pressing on in the heat.

At about five o'clock, we came upon a foul, stinking pool where millions of aquatic insects and larvae swarmed in the muddy water that bubbled on the surface. I was terribly thirsty, but I dared not drink. My Makaschla, putting down his load, got into the pool up to his knees, stirred the water with his arm, as if to get rid of all the animalcules, and scooped some water into his mouth, which was eight to ten inches away from his hand; it was rather like a dog lapping. I imitated my man; a few drops were quite enough, for the water was disgusting, the sulphurous taste made me want to vomit.

Two hours further on, we met a Cafre who led us to Schloschlomé's wretched *mouzi* which was situated on a slope at the edge of a gorge and at the foot of towering stratified peaks. The nearest one, conical in shape, rose up like a tower with crumbling walls; on the rocky ledges baboons loped about, calling out to each other in their gruff voices.

'Water, water,' we gasped by way of introduction when we arrived. They poured us some, into dirty little clay pots, just like the ones all Cafres make. The water tasted good, and, only when we had drunk our fill did we question Schloschlomé, who was squatting on the ground like a mountain baboon.

Surrounded by the elders, Schloschlomé never once replied directly to my inquiries. At each question he applied to the elders as to how the answer should be given. Suspicious, crafty and dishonest like the Makatisses, the Makaschlas, who are an offshoot, behaved in exactly the same way towards me as the Makatisses had done. Now, as each phrase was composed, arranged, formulated with careful intent, just as though we were playing a game of chess, it seemed to me that it contained only falsehood, for truth had no need of such artifice. I lost my temper several times; lashing out at their damned advice which I did not want, I assured these knaves that they had a perfect right not to receive me, but that I did not accept their right to deceive me. However I must admit that these men never showed any desire to know what my intentions were, or anything at all that related to the whites. This reserve could of course be interpreted as a show of contempt.

All this, added to their disobliging manners – I might even call it insolence – gave me an aversion for these disgusting people who, in spite of their wretchedness, have the effrontery to believe themselves superior to the whites. At the time when I was living at Natal, I had had practical lessons on how to treat the Cafres from the English, who were the first white inhabitants in those parts. This method consisted simply in affecting an air of supreme superiority towards the chiefs, so that they would get the impression that one was oneself a great white chief. One commanded, rather than entreated, taking care only to show some deference to the headman of the *mouzi* who would thus have difficulty in opposing one, even though he was in fact being superseded. All the underlings were as obedient as if they were taking orders from their own chief. I would like to have been able to assume this grand manner, but it was quite out of the question. In the first place, I was dressed in rags and I had nothing to offer; apart from this, chiefs are not much respected among the Makatisses, an attitude which I attribute to a spirit of independence prevailing in the race. It is this same spirit which is responsible for the excessive division among the Makatisses, a numerous nation scattered over a wide area and divided into a great number of chieftainships which, because they are disunited, are incapable of offering the least resistance.

Even though I was not in a position to woo him, Schloschlomé offered me a hut and some quite odious food. The night was unbearable; I was plagued by unknown insects and, unable to close my eyes, I waited with the greatest impatience for the coming of the dawn. I was particularly interested to find out what parasites had attacked me, because never had I been so tormented, even by mosquitos or fleas, since I had been in Africa. My legs were covered with blisters which looked like bunches of grapes on a bas-relief, and the unbearable itching led me to entertain the idea of putting my legs into the fire, simply to change the nature of the pain.

I found the insects I was looking for in my woollen blanket; there were a great number of them clinging to the blanket in a state of torpor which resulted from the excellent nourishment they had had during the night. They had the general appearance of ticks, although their shape and their behaviour was different. They were rounder and grey in colour and they did not cling by their feet, nor did they attach themselves to the flesh by suckers, as is the case with ticks. Apart from all this, they were quite rapid in their movements, and their bodies were soft.

I have no doubt that this terrible species belongs to the arachnid family, but what the species can be, I just do not know. The first thing I did when I got back to camp was not to preserve my specimens, but to boil my blanket and my clothes, although this did nothing to lessen my suffering which continued for a week. I have never encountered this insect anywhere other than at Schloschlomé's *mouzi* where it was to be seen running about on the ground in the sunlight, as well as in the shade, and it was active by night as well as by day, when it was particularly numerous. But whether these

Cafres were inured to the sting, or whether the thickness of their skins made them insensitive, or whether they were simply spared; whatever the reason, none of them complained. But they were so wretched anyway, that one more misery could well have been added to a hundred others and pass unnoticed.

Schloschlomé, however much ill-will he felt towards whites in general, and me in particular, did not hesitate to put several men at my disposal to help in the hunting. This gesture was obviously in his own interests. We set out in a northerly direction, with a range of inaccessible mountains on our right. It took us two hours before we discovered a practicable way up to the first stratum where we found ourselves on a fairly large expanse of land with sandy soil, enormous blocks of stone, and stunted trees. Before us, one of the highest peaks of the Mourikeyley sloped gently upwards, covered with mimosas up to the point where it began rising steeply, laying bare its bony ribs. Its shoulders were covered in sparse vegetation, but its stony head was bald. This peak made me think of a Titan seated on the ground, resting after his heavy labours, and then slowly turned to stone by the revolutions of the earth.

To our right were other granitic mountains, stretching away to the horizon. Between them and us lay four leagues of country where the black and equine antelopes lived.

A search which lasted four hours yielded nothing, and then one of the young men came to report finding the fresh spoor of seven black antelope of different ages. Taking every precaution in my approach, in less than twenty minutes I had come within sixty paces of them. They were standing or moving about; through the leafy branches I caught glimpses of a hindquarters here, a head or a pair of legs there. I could have fired, and wounded one, but this is just what one must never do. To make sure of getting a fine specimen, I waited. He appeared at last, presenting his shoulder towards me. I stood up and a pebble rolled away beneath my feet; the noise was sufficient to give the alarm and the herd moved off.

This animal certainly has a wonderful sense of hearing; in this he resembles the kudu. We followed them from cover to cover but in vain; it was impossible to approach them. The next day we began our search once more, but it was even less fruitful than that of the day before, and we left Schloschlomé's place, promising ourselves never to sleep there again if circumstances took us back that way.

By now it was 30 December, that day which will always be engraved on my memory above all the other days that I journeyed. My oxen all went down with the sickness which the people here attribute to flies; but I continued to doubt the cause, preferring to believe that it was poisonous grass, or perhaps the unhealthy climate. I instructed Henning to take the oxen to a *mouzi* ten leagues away,

234

which had an undisputed reputation for being wholesome. Alas, I was never to see them again, for they all died and from that moment, the desert became my prison, as confining in its immensity as the narrowest cell.

The Oury barred our way. She was thirty to forty feet deep at the time, and not content with filling her own bed, she poured out into the two riverine beds which lay alongside her and were characterised by the absence of trees. Often, Oury expanded even further by overflowing into the plains, which were only too happy to drink their fill; here she warmed herself in the sun and provided a home for millions of ducks.

I had to accept the fact that I was unable to move, whatever the danger might be from Massilicatzi. There was no way of transporting my collections and I could not possibly leave them behind. In any case, I was collecting more and more rare insects and with this to occupy my thoughts, the days passed swiftly enough.

I learnt of the death of the last of my oxen just as the level of the Oury was going down, so I sent Henning off on foot to Makalisberg to buy a new team to pull us out of our unfortunate situation. Impediments to my success were, first of all the great distance that had to be covered, and the time it would take; secondly the lack of money, because nobody burdens himself with this useless commodity on long journeys, and the farmers of Makalisberg did not recognise my solvency, considering a promissory note as a mere worthless piece of paper. I instructed Henning to go in search of a certain trader from Natal who could well be fifty leagues beyond Makalisberg. This was Mr Michel van Breda, the only man I knew who was capable of doing me this service without taking advantage of my misfortune to make personal gain. I gave Henning authority to buy at any price and if he could find nothing at Makalisberg or at Mooi Rivier, he was to go to Pieters-Mauritz-Burg but he was not to return without a team.

He started out, and I made a note of each passing day, thinking to shorten the time he would be away and hoping to predict exactly the day of his return, just as though Henning had power to surmount all obstacles, as though the rivers would dry up in the middle of the rainy season, as though strangers would care about my fate, putting aside their own selfish interests with the sole object of attending to mine.

The man who is down on his luck is surely the most sanguine of all men; the most unlikely ways out of his predicament will occur to his imagination, and he clings to these fragile vines, shallow rooted in sand, taking them to be a strongly secured lifeline. He believes that he will be saved by clinging to them. He is almost out of the abyss, when suddenly the fragile creepers give way, and he falls back into the depths of his wretchedness but, if he is man enough, he will gather up his dreams again and make a ladder out of them.

CHAPTER XXXV

Reasons for an excursion into the north — My mistakes and Tom's — Danger avoided — A deputation — Precautions — Rhemkoka the rainmaker — I supplant him — I leave the banks of the Mokoha on foot — Route towards the north-north-east — Stream of Mourikeyley-Amaboa — Two waterfalls; Om-Schlabatzi Om-Tounène — Cafres who see a white man for the first time — Route to the north-east — Echo *mouzi* deserted — Wild bulbs — Wretched people — The inhabitants of a village flee at our approach — My men do not hesitate to loot — Their arrogance and love of plunder — *Aarde-Bontjes* — We find human remains — Tom's idea — Impossibility of going any further — Route towards the south-west — Sunny banks of the Om-Schlabatzi — *Rhinoceros simus* — Pink bee-eaters with green heads — *Merops nubicoïdes* — We continue towards the south-east — Thirst — The delights of water — The banks of the Oury where hippopotamus still abound — Impossibility of crossing this river — Opposition from my men — Innumerable fringillas — What one needs in order to reach the Equator — The things Cafre kings are capable of doing — Return south-easterly direction — We enjoy the remains of the lion's feast — I kill him as he flees — Route south-south east — Optical illusion — Flooding of the Oury — Bronze goose — Rhinoceros — Crossing of the Sogoupana mountains — Darkness — Lions — Arrival at the camp — Henning's return after forty-one day's absence — Crossing the Oury — Speed of the current — Difficulty — Final departure — Pilanne — Makata — Mooi-Rivier — I learn of the theft of my wagon with oxen and load — Vaal Rivier — The ford at the waterfall — I try to cross further up-stream — Useless endeavour — Detour to Lyneque-Drift — Tom leaves me — Alone with Henning and Guimba I go on my way back to Natal — Cannibals — Pygmies

As I was now deprived of the company of Henning and rarely had occasion to be with Tom, the indefatigable hunter, I was becoming very bored. The excessive heat forced me to spend three hours every day in the little Makoha River in spite of the crocodiles which, though they regularly took dogs from the *mouzi*, seemed nevertheless to respect humans. Extreme lassitude resulted from this routine which was the complete opposite of the one I should have followed. I frequently lay down during the day, particularly as I could not sleep at night because of the incessant terrible thunder storms. On top of this I felt an indefinable sense of malaise. My men also were not well. Of my three dogs, only one was still alive, and when I looked at the people living in the three *mouzis* I became convinced that the situation must be unhealthy.

We had to have a change of air. There was nothing to stop me going, and there were other reasons which made it imperative that I should move on. It all started with an unfortunate matter which arose, firstly because of my unusual situation, and secondly because of my dedication to science. From the outset, I had proceeded by the most honest means in my attempts to get from Rhemkoka the information which I needed. Without in any way going against the customs of his people, Rhemkoka in his position as chief, could easily have satisfied my demands. He made empty promises which I later realised had not been given in good faith, so I had no hesitation in informing him that I intended to do without his co-operation.

True to my word, I presented myself at the *mouzi* where some forty men were in attendance. Tom was with me and thoughtlessly committed a small blunder for which I immediately reprimanded him. As a result of Tom's heedlessness, one of the Cafres saw fit to direct some insolent remarks at me. As I insisted on an apology, I asked this man if perhaps he had not been mistaken, and whether his heart spoke the same language as his tongue.

'Certainly,' he replied with an air of complete confidence.

'Well then,' I replied, 'if you will repeat, word for word, what you have just said, so that my ears may hear it for a second time, I will fill you with lead as I would a bird.'

As I said this, the catch of my trigger clicked sharply in the silence; my gun was cocked.

The Cafre, reading in my eyes that I dissembled, made a grab at my double-barrelled gun while my finger was on the trigger. Fortunately for him, my composure was such that I was able to keep hold of the barrel in my left hand, while I pounded his head with my fist to force him to let go.

It is well known that Cafres have skulls of steel. This one at first seemed not to feel a thing but eventually he gave up and, letting go of my gun, he ran off. I pretended to take aim at him, but I did not fire although I could just have nicked him because my gun was loaded with birdshot. However, this would have been misconstrued; I would have been suspected of malice aforethought which was certainly not the case.

With only Tom beside me, I could have done nothing against forty savages who were voicing their irritation in no uncertain terms, so I assumed an attitude of stony silence. When Tom had tried to come to my assistance, he'd got a blow on the head from the butt of my rifle as I turned it suddenly to wrench it from the Cafre's hands. Tom was stunned for a moment, and when he managed to gather his thoughts together, he said 'Just look at these damned Cafres leaping about and howling. Does this matter concern them all? Don't you think it's a plot against us? There's a call to arms; five of them are already armed. Master, what are we going to do? We're as good as dead.'

Tom was unarmed and he was afraid.

'Let's go,' he said, 'let's go home, at least we've got guns and powder and bullets there. Let them come and get us there if they dare. I'll flatten ten of them. In God's name master, let's get out of this place.'

I sat down on a mound of earth, holding my gun upright. 'You can go Tom, if you want to, for my part, I'm staying.'

'But why stay?'

'I'll tell you why. If I go, they'll think I'm afraid; if I stay they'll see that I do not fear them.'

'That's all very well, but just look at that man over there waving his assegai about and hitting his shield with it. He's the orator and he's trying to stir up their courage. Can you understand what he is saying? He's saying 'How is this? How can so many black men bow to the wishes of a single white dog? But the white dog will eat up your harvest and you will die of hunger. How much longer will you black men suffer this? Where are the men, the real men? Let them come forward and kill the white dog, for if they do not, they themselves will die by famine or the gun.'

As I had every reason to fear the effect of these words, I beckoned to one of the elders and asked him to explain the aggressive behaviour of the Cafre who had started the trouble. Either he feared compromising himself, or perhaps it was that he simply wished to express his own ill-will, but the old man replied with an insolent shake of the head, and took no further notice of me. This annoyed me exceedingly; if only I'd had a whip, I'd have shaken the dust from the filthy skin cloak which crackled between his legs as he walked away, and the ancient perambulating pest would have paid the price of his contempt.

As he walked away, another came to take his place. I informed this man of how I felt about the wrongs which had been done me, taking care to make him understand that the life of my attacker had been in my hands. I said that a white man is a lion who kills only when he has been wounded, but that he kills until he is satiated.

'It is true,' said the old man, 'I saw the mouth of your gun turned towards this man and if the fire did not come out, it is because you did not wish it.'

'That is exactly so. I did not wish it, because I am right in this matter and I expect to see your countrymen coming to me and admitting their wrongs. Until then there will be no more ties of friendship with your people. You have darkened my heart; there will be no more hunting together; there will be no more meat. And so I bid you farewell.'

Slowly and deliberately, Tom and I walked away. Tom would have liked to run, but I restrained him. He was pale, and beads of cold perspiration stood out on his forehead. The crisis was over, at least for the time being, and I tried to raise his spirits by forcing him to laugh, although I was far from laughing myself. But his face remained yellow and waxen until after he had consumed several cups of coffee.

We took out all my clean guns and loaded some of them with ball and the others with buckshot. Then we cleaned the dirty guns and loaded them. Finally we laid them all out in the wagon, some to be fired through the front opening, others through the back. At the slightest threat of danger, Tom and I were to leap into our fortress and take up our positions. We were quite aware of the impossibility of fending off our attackers for long, for they could easily run us through with their long spears by piercing the canvas of the wagon tent which was inadequately reinforced with my mattresses and woollen blankets. Our only consolation for the loss of our lives would be to dispatch forty or fifty of them into eternity before they finally got us.

I admit that I carried my precautions to excessive lengths but I was loathe to accept the idea that these disgusting Makaschlas would deal me the mortal blow. To avoid this, as well as to do my enemies the greatest possible injury, I placed my powder box which now, alas, contained only seven pounds of powder, in such a way that my last despairing shot would explode the gunpowder, taking Tom and me with it, as well as the boldest of our assailants.

Once we had made our arrangements, our attitude changed. We were so buoyed up by the idea of the havoc we could wreak that we almost hoped the attack would come soon. Tom was joyful. When he was armed, he feared nothing and, if he had appeared ready to collapse at the *mouzi*, it was the prospect of going down without firing a shot that had almost prostrated him. What more desperate situation for a man than to be exposed to attack without hope of retaliation!

The coming of night gave me cause for some anxiety. Without doubt, my plans of resistance, however well conceived, would come to nothing in the dark. I could see only one solution; we would have to take our guns every evening and conceal them in a field of maize, thirty-five paces from the wagon, where we would sit on them. If the enemy came, they would find themselves attacked from the rear at the very moment when they believed their objective had been won.

Tom thought it an excellent means of deceiving them, and we had already chosen our spot, when a deputation of elders arrived from the *mouzi* of Om-Sitanne. When these men asked to speak with me, I responded coolly. They squatted on their heels and then one of them began slowly relating the whole story of the unfortunate incident, casting all the blame on the insolent fellow who had been so lacking in respect towards us. When he had finished, one of the others recounted the same story in almost the same words, adding that the actions of one man should not bring harm to the majority, particularly as the majority did not approve of this behaviour. A third speaker praised the great benefits my hunting had brought them. He enumerated the advantages of an abundance of meat and fat, begging me to allow my heart to turn white again towards them. In fact, each spoke with the intention of cooling my anger, the effect of which they feared, not only because I would cease to hunt for them, but also because I might withhold the rain which I claimed was at my disposal.

It was not possible for me to give complete credibility to their words, for I knew the Makaschlas too well; lying is so inherent to their nature, that this time, as on a thousand other occasions, what they said could well be the opposite of the truth. More than that, it was not unlikely that their words served to cover some sinister intent. Nevertheless, I pretended to believe them and thanked the deputation for their goodwill and the manner in which they had approached me, assuring them that I would render them every service in my power in the future, as I had done in the past. As it was of vital importance to give them a false idea of the power of my guns, I did not allow them to leave before I had achieved this objective.

'I knew very well this morning when I left the *mouzi* that the Makaschlas would admit their wrongs, that their hearts would swell with sorrow, and that they would make every endeavour to turn my heart white again, for the Makaschlas are not less good, their hearts are not less white, than the hearts of white men. All that has passed I knew of before; everything was destined to happen this way, for no other way was possible. The bad feeling could not have continued, or blood would have flowed on both sides. But what chance have men against *me*, when they are armed only with sharpened iron. These men must approach close to their enemy, but for me, how easy it is to kill at 500 paces; at 500 paces my guns can even break pieces of rock. In case you doubt the truth of my words I shall do this thing, and your eyes shall see.'

I picked up an elephant gun loaded with a ball weighing a fifth of a pound; the gun weighed twenty-five pounds. I lined up the eight emissaries facing the rock which I had chosen for my demonstration, and I fired at the point I had indicated. They all watched as the piece of stone flew into the air. Their ears were deafened by the hellish detonation and in utter amazement they all put their hands over their open mouths.

'This is the way we shoot during the day,' I informed my Makaschlas, 'but at night I do better. At night, if twenty or forty men come, I kill them all with one shot. Let me show you.' I went behind the wagon to reload my gun and poured in twenty-four buckshot, weighing 120 to the pound. This done, I returned to my visitors and, indicating to them a mound of sand about 110 paces away on the other side of the little river, I asked them to take note of the distance. 'Just imagine,' I said to them, 'twenty men on that mound. Whether it be day or night, it matters little, darkness does not take away the strength from my bullets. Well now, about these twenty men, I'll pierce them through with a single shot'.

240

I fired, the buckshot kicked up the sand. I don't think one pellet missed the mound, and the astonishment of the Makaschlas reached new heights.

'You will say to those who sent you,' I told them, 'that if their intention is to do me harm, my greatest desire is that they should come and attack me at night.'

Then, to be rid of them, I handed out half-a-pound of snuff which elicited civilities I could well have done without.

Perhaps I was unintelligible to many of my readers just now when I mentioned the rain which it was in my power to dispense. I owe an explanation; let me now explain.

Among the Cafres, as among other African people, certain men are believed to be endowed with the power of making rain; often it is the *iniangas*, the same ones who practise medicine; sometimes it is the chiefs who hope in this way to increase their influence over their people. As these chiefs have no greater magical powers than have those who consult them, their talent consists in giving evasive answers, or in promising rain within a certain time, if there is a reasonable expectation that rain will fall at that period; or else they reply that they will see what can be done, and when heavy clouds blow up, a certain sign that a storm is about to break, they do not hesitate to announce publicly that the requested rain is about to fall. They exhort the people to sing their loudest songs to help bring down the rain and when it falls in torrents, shot through with lightning, these men never fail to accept praise for it, and will often also accept promises of offerings from the harvest to come.

One night, when I needed more rest than I usually did, my sleep was continually interrupted by infernal chanting and terrifying yells; it was the doing of Rhemkoka the rainmaker who, for ten days, had been trying in vain to persuade the heavens to produce a decent storm. Annoyed at having my sleep disturbed by these stupid goings-on, rituals Rhemkoka no more believed in than do all those others whose business it is to exploit superstition, I began cursing him, and the idea came to me to discredit him in the eyes of his tribe and to turn matters to my own advantage.

I looked at the weather; there was not the slightest sign of rain. I called Tom and instructed him to go to the *mouzi*, bearing a few words from me to Rhemkoka. Tom was to address him in the presence of others, so that there would be witnesses to what I had to say.

This is what Tom, the messenger, said, 'Rhemkoka, it is you I seek on behalf of my master. Let your ears hear and your spirit understand. How the devil, Rhemkoka, dare you claim to make rain while the white man, my master, is here among you. How can you hope to succeed without asking his consent. Do you believe you have sufficient power to do this on your own, while the white man is here? Do you not know that the whites have superior power to call down from the heavens the rain which feeds the earth? Rhemkoka, have you not been trying now for ten days, without producing a single drop? Do you not tire your people out every night with all that bawling? It is all so useless, so harmful even, and it makes my master down there laugh. Because you see, Rhemkoka, this is the way of the black man, and it is the worst way. The white man, my master, can make rain fall from the sky without all that noise. Do you want torrents of rain, do you want your gardens flooded? Well then, get your people to stop that infernal racket, then come and talk to my master and you will see.'

'What?,' said Rhemkoka with a crafty look. 'Your master can make great rains, and he told us nothing of it? Tomorrow morning I shall go speedily to find your master, for the earth is so dry that it is cracking. Ah, so the white man knows how to make rain, does he?'

'Does my master know how to make rain?' answered Tom with amazing confidence. 'I want you to know that he made so much of it when he was with the Amazoulous that Panda did not want him to go away because he was afraid of a drought the next year.'

This cunning reply, which Tom invented, seemed to convince Rhemkoka of my powers, particularly as he had not much confidence in his own. The clamour ceased, silence descended, and everyone went to bed.

The following day, Rhemkoka came as he had promised and, without interrupting my work, I conversed with him. I thought of lighting up my pipe. A Cafre was near the fire grilling a piece of meat; I called to him to bring me a light but, as it did not suit him to do so, he did not move.

'Guimba,' I shouted in Dutch to my young Cafre, 'Take a bucket of water, throw it on the fire and don't give that man the time to remove his meat. My order was carried out immediately, to the astonishment and mortification of the man who had been so unobliging. He swore at me but I interrupted him, 'Miserable scum, go and roast your meat in the fire of the sun, the same way that I'm going to light my pipe, and don't you set foot here again.'

Picking up my burning glass and turning to Rhemkoka, 'You see the sun,' I said to him. 'I want fire from it, and I will get it.' I held out my pipe to the sun's rays and, naturally, nothing happened. 'Devil take it,' I said, stamping my foot, 'what's the matter with the sun today? Is it no longer made of fire?'

And Rhemkoka smiled a smile that expressed doubt and disdain.

'Rhemkoka, has the sun never burnt you?'

'No, never,' he said. 'The sun is warm but it does not burn.'

'Oh yes it does, for it's made of fire, and the great *iniangas* of my country light their pipes by it. All those *iniangas* who make thunder, rain, drought, gunpowder, guns, they who call all the stars by name, they all do it.'

'Yes all right, but are *you* one of those great *iniangas*?'

'Who me? Yes of course. My father, my grandfather, the ancestors of my ancestors, were all great *iniangas*, as I am for I am descended from them, just as you are descended from your ancestors who, I am obliged to tell you, seem to me not to have known very much.'

'But your father, your grandfather, the ancestors of your ancestors, did they all draw fire from the sun?'

'Yes always, when they wanted to.'

'Well, you wanted to, but you could not do it, so you are not a great *inianga* like your ancestors.'

'I beg your pardon, *greater* than they were Rhemkoka, for I know many things which they did not know.' I adjusted my burning glass so that it caught the sun's rays, and my tobacco began to smoke, although the flame was imperceptible. 'This is fire, Rhemkoka; touch it with your finger. What do you think? Oh excellent sun, you know who your friends are.'

Rhemkoka's emotions would be difficult to describe; first it was perfect satisfaction that I saw painted on his face, followed by open-mouthed admiration. He did not know how to express himself and, after much exclamation, he finally asked me for some of this fire, which I brought down from the sun, to ignite a little gunpowder in order to set alight some twigs. It was obvious that Rhemkoka imagined that this fire must be different from ordinary fire, and must have astonishing properties. He wanted to take some home. There was much at stake for me in encouraging this belief. I assured him that he was right, and then I brought this farcical scene to a close by telling him that, in the same way that I was able to command the fire from the sun, I could call down water from the heavens.

Rhemkoka believed this, and why should he not believe what seemed to him to be a miracle, for after all, we ourselves wonder at the achievements of science. Up until then, everything had been going well; I had supplanted Rhemkoka; he had publicly admitted my superiority, and thenceforth I was accepted as an *inianga*. At first Tom and I had a good laugh over the comedy that we had improvised, but then I began to feel more than a little terrified when I contemplated the consequences of all this. What would these savages think if the rain failed to appear when they asked for it? This was the whole point and I hadn't thought of it. Would I not be accused of malicious deception? Was it not likely that I would be exposed and destroyed as a noxious object? However, I consoled myself with the idea that the rain *did* fall occasionally.

As I should have anticipated, it was not long before I was importuned. Rhemkoka came in person, followed by the élite of his society, to request me to make some rain as soon as possible. I quickly collected my thoughts then, raising my eyes to the heavens; 'My dear Rhemkoka,' I said to him. 'I perceive that there is not a cloud within a radius of twenty leagues. Henderick Potgieter over at Makalisberg has taken them all to water his own country. You will have to wait. When there are some available, tomorrow perhaps, I will bring them over here and the rain will fall.'

Two days later, by pure chance, we had a beautiful rainy day, and I received thanks for it. Then for ten days on end there was nothing. People complained, and an official deputation came over to see me one evening. I told them that the rain would certainly fall, but that we had to wait for a considerable gathering of the clouds; an ordinary little rain was hardly worth the trouble, and that if a thing was worth doing it was worth doing well.

The next morning, one of the petitioners of the day before, having had the unfortunate idea of coming alone to see me about the rain, arrived while I was busy. I had no hesitation in packing him off without ceremony. The repercussions could have been unpleasant. I was thinking about this rather anxiously when, towards sunset, I noticed that big clouds were blowing up.

'Quick Tom, go to the *mouzi*. Tell Rhemkoka that I am very sorry that I spoke roughly to that man this morning, but why did he come asking for rain when he could see I was busy making some. I was working hard this morning in their interests. Rain is going to fall in floods, if it responds to my efforts. Go on, run and tell them.'

Tom fulfilled his charge with distinction; a whole week later it was still raining. All communication was cut off[1] because the Mokoha river had risen ten feet but, from the far bank, came shouts of congratulation and thanks, and invitations to pick from their gardens whatever I fancied.

'Yes, yes,' Tom replied to all the praise 'there is no more famous *inianga* in the world than my master. When *he* makes rain it is quite different from Rhemkoka's rain. But ask him to make it stop now, because it's been going on for a long time and your fields are flooded and full of ducks. If you don't say anything, it will fall forever.'

'When are you going to make some fine weather for us?' shouted Rhemkoka. 'When the rain is finished,' I shouted back and everybody seemed satisfied.

I am well aware that my conduct in this matter will be condemned by the philanthropists who are trying, with all the means in their

---

1 No Makaschla Cafre can swim.

power, to substitute Christian belief for the faith which these people have in their *iniangas*. I am not unaware of the reproaches which could be levelled against me for behaving like this, but I would invite those people who condemn my behaviour to come here and find themselves in a position like mine. My clothes were almost worn out, my skin was blistering in the hot sun, there was nothing but meat to eat, and even that was becoming scarce because my supply of powder was almost depleted; I was at the mercy of these Cafres who were ill-disposed towards me. Was I not justified in using extraordinary means to ward off present and future suffering, a sorry picture which I prefer to spare my reader. In spite of everything, I gave these people a high opinion of whites, something which those whose whole mission it is to do just that, rarely succeed in doing.

Henning had been gone twenty-eight days when I left my camp on the banks of the Mokoha to proceed on foot towards the north. Rhemkoka had given me two men and I took along one of mine. Tom was with me, and once more we set out for Schloschlomé's *mouzi* which we reached the same evening at sunset. But this time, the memory of the terrible insects which had attacked me on my first visit made me decide to camp 200 paces away from the huts, where the long grass offered a soft bed.

These precautions proved almost fatal to me and, had it not been for the moon shining brightly overhead, I would have fallen victim to a small but highly venomous snake. My bed consisted of a mat and a woollen blanket, spread out three paces from the fire. After my first sleep, at about eleven o'clock, I got up. A few minutes later, just as I was about to stretch myself out again, I noticed something shaped like an S lying in the middle of my sleeping mat. I was more than a little surprised to recognise the triangular head; it was a *nacht-adder* lying on its back, which had come to find a bed in the folds of my blanket before the cold of the night numbed it. I used my ramrod to break its spine, and then cast it fifteen paces away, after which I lay down again, without giving much thought to the possibility that others could have taken its place.

As soon as day broke, we set out, accompanied by the two men Schloschlomé had lent us as guides. We were no longer heading due north; our direction varied between north-east and east-north-east. It was 10 February and although the rainy season was not yet quite over, the weather was fine and seemed set to continue: a blessing for which I considered myself very fortunate. After walking for two hours we reached a pretty stream called Mourikeyley-Amaboa which we crossed and, at about midday, we reached a *mouzi* which everybody said was the last we would find.

We were received into a sort of caravanserai supported on wooden pillars and open to the wind. This was the public enclosure where the men held their meetings during the day; this is where they talked of what had been done, and what was still to do; here they planned hunts and discussed private business. It was not the cleanest place, there was nowhere to sit but on the dusty earth. The dry grass which was strewn about the periphery had served as bedding for visitors. Here and there piles of ashes with three stones in the middle were visible, providing evidence that food had been cooked there. The roof was higher than is usual; the building was round as always, and with a capacity of 100 people, it was the biggest building constructed by Cafres that I ever saw.

The wretched looking *mouzi* was built on a gentle, narrow slope which formed a sort of pedestal to the enormous stratified peaks all made of granite. The eye was drawn to admire what looked like two long silvery ribbons falling straight down from the summits of these mountains, with their red and green slopes in such contrast to the surrounding countryside. One could have likened the mountains to vast pieces of furniture encrusted with filaments of mother-of-pearl, 1 000 or 1 200 feet long. These filaments were the rivers of Om-Schlabatzi and Om-Tounène which had their beginning in this great leap into the plain. Whether I wanted them or not, the headman insisted on giving me some guides to lead me to the next *mouzi*, although he would not admit in so many words that there were in fact other *mouzis*. With these men added to mine, I hoped to have a more impressive retinue for the rest of the journey. We soon crossed Om-Schlabatzi at a point where big black rocks filled the river-bed and, after a thousand detours, probably intentionally taken by our ill-disposed guides, we reached the *mouzi* as evening was falling. I named it *Gradin mouzi* because of its situation on a stratified mountainside which gave the impression of the steps of a staircase. As we had not seen even the shadow of a gazelle, I had to be satisfied with a few pieces of sugarcane for supper, offered me by the chief, who seemed to be a reasonably good man although rather reserved. I paid him for his services with some metal buttons but, judging by the indifference with which they were accepted, I suspected that something more practical would have pleased him better.

On the 11th, at about nine o'clock in the morning, we crossed the Om-Tounène river whose limpid waters, five feet deep, slumbered in the shade of green rushes. We did not leave again until we had drunk our fill, for according to indications, the day would be very hot, and the ground we had to cover held no promise of water. As our guides continued to deceive us about distances, it was impossible for us to know when and where we would come across a river, a pool, or a *mouzi*, and so it was a good idea to consume enough liquid for the whole day, particularly as it is not customary for Cafres to carry water in a calabash.

246

We were by now getting into the mountains. A short *poff-adder* slithered between my legs; I killed the dangerous reptile with my ramrod and we went on our way until about midday, when we were happy to come upon a *mouzi*, yet another which the inhabitants claimed was the last.

I was the first white man whom the chief of the *mouzi* had ever seen, but he showed no surprise at the sight of me, and no deference either. I was offered nothing to eat until I assumed a masterly air and demanded something. It turned out that I need not have bothered, for these men had only sugar cane to give, which had turned pink because of the presence of white larvae. Besides, as we came along, the wild medlar trees of the mountains had provided us with an abundance of fruit.

After resting for an hour, we left this place and made our way towards the north-east, arriving at Echo *mouzi* as the sun was setting. We had caught sight of three *melampus* gazelles; I had wounded one of them, but it had escaped, and once again, we had to make do with the wretched food of the Makaschlas. One of my servants, fearful that he would find nothing to eat, had provided himself with some bulbs he had found growing in low-lying damp ground. He cooked these bulbs, some in water and others in the ashes. I tried some, but they had a very disagreeable, earthy taste and I couldn't masticate them properly. The bulbs were very solid and stringy; even the Makaschlas could hardly chew them.

Echo *mouzi* was not easy to find, for it was tucked away in a tortuous valley which was steep and difficult of access and, without guides, we would have passed it by. As we approached, our voices echoed in the strangest manner; one voice alone sounded like ten, as it reverberated against the rocks and we thought we had arrived, when we were still 200 paces away.

The situation had been especially chosen so that the inhabitants would escape Massilicatzi's raids, which were carried out by his army with instructions to purge the country of any Makaschlas who might still be there. There were only old men, women and a few children at the *mouzi*, all men capable of bearing arms having been killed two years previously by Massilicatzi's warriors. When we arrived we could find nobody to talk to; everybody had fled into the rocks and the nearby bushes. Eyes watched us from hiding places, but my men were undaunted; on the ground lay watermelons dropped by a woman as she ran; two big flat stones were covered with kaffircorn, a little further on was a fire with loaves cooking in boiling water. My starving fellows grabbed everything and, as if they needed me to condone their actions, they deposited their loot at my feet. I had no hesitation in allowing them a free rein; I was as hungry as they were and I felt entitled by the wild exodus of the inhabitants to dispose of their goods. For myself, I kept a watermelon and some flour which I made into loaves and cooked on the burning coals.

It was only after we had eaten our fill that several of the inhabitants risked coming out of hiding. It had been reported by some scout or other that we did not look at all like terrible conquerors. The inhabitants had rather bad-tempered expressions on their faces, probably because they realised that they need not have fled. My fellows took a certain pleasure in ridiculing these ancient wrecks who looked very shamefaced.

One woman had more determination than all the rest of them put together. She ranted and railed, hurling abuse at us until after midnight. She was the very one whose flour I had taken. It was probably precious to her, for I noticed that cereals were not cultivated in these parts, to prevent discovery. The inhabitants lived on gourds and, in winter, on dried wild fruit.

Early on the 12th we crossed a long valley which later opened out into a marshy plain. There, in the green grass, grew numerous little yellow flowers at the sight of which Tom was unable to restrain a cry of joy. He said he was so happy to see these *booter-bloem* which reminded him of the Binnen-land (the interior of the Cape colony where he was born). According to him, and he was a competent judge in these matters, the presence of these flowers was a certain indication of the excellence of the pasturage.

Not far from here we encountered two young women walking along in company with a man. Their astonishment and their fear were extreme when Tom and I appeared from behind our black servants. As it was by then too late to run away, these poor women were obliged to show some spirit. We learnt from them that their *mouzi* was no more than an hour distant, and we left them considering themselves very fortunate that they had got off so lightly. My Makaschlas, the very ones I had taken against their wishes, now began saying openly that we should take prisoner any man or woman we came across. They said we needed to increase our numbers so as to be able to impose our will wherever we went.

At first I took this for a joke, but then I realised that these scoundrels had thought up this scheme to take advantage of the terror which my guns could inspire in order to rob the local population; to steal skins and pelts, and to abduct women and children to serve them, while making me responsible for their reprehensible deeds.

Before we had even reached the *mouzi* they had told us about, black bodies came flying out in every direction. Women, children, even men, were scuttling off all over the place. More than 300 panic-stricken people abandoned all their possessions as they saw us coming, although there were only fifteen of us. Did they believe that

248

we were the advance party; were they expecting to see more of us appear? I really do not know, but when we arrived the village was deserted.

My men, emboldened by the faint-heartedness of the inhabitants, and encouraged by their love of furs, pushed their way into the huts on the pretext of looking for food. I condoned this behaviour because I was unable to do otherwise. All of them, without exception, laid hands on the most desirable of the furs; the skins of tiger-cat, genet, *canis melanotis* were appropriated as soon as they were discovered. Four men would take hold of a large bundle to get a better grip on it. It was only when they all had their share of the booty that they even thought of food. In vain I reproached them for their behaviour; I had no power to enforce my will.

The headman of the *mouzi* who had not fled as far off as the others, returned half an hour after our arrival. He saw the bundles my men had piled up, and showed no signs of displeasure. Then my insolent Makaschlas went even further; they demanded provisions for the journey and men to carry them. This was the height of audacity; not only had the inhabitants to consent to being robbed, but they had also to assist the thieves in carrying away the booty. I was so indignant that I did not calculate the danger which might threaten me when I sided with the chief and set about punishing some of the more determined of the looters. I laid about them with a short stick and raised welts on their backs and their ribs.

During the short stay I made at *Pillage mouzi*, I found again the beans which in Natal they call *aarde-bontjes*, which grow under the earth from the neck of the root. They differed from those in Natal only in their superiority of size and excellence. The seeds were round and two centimetres in diameter; the skin that covered them was a deep red colour; a bivalvular pod, which cracked open when dry, contained one or two beans. The bean has a mealy texture, like that of the chestnut and might be confused by the uninformed with the pistachio nut. It would be an excellent thing to introduce this vegetable into Algeria.

We continued towards the north-quarter-north-east, but this time without guides, because I had opposed the demands of my Cafres. Overloaded as they now were with the fruit of their plunder, these men did not much care to go north, for it was completely the opposite direction from the one they wished to take. There were objections: 'What're you going to look for there?' 'What do you expect to see?' 'There are no more people there; there's no water, no game.' 'What do you think you're going to do there?' I was besieged by questions but irritated, annoyed, wearied, I said nothing. I realised that they were trying to force me to change my plans. My savage companions, who were determined to return home, were quite capable of abandoning me during the night while I slept. Tom was in agreement with me, and with his support, I decided I would impose my will upon them.

'You belong with me,' I said 'and I swear by this gun that you will stay with me. I shoot any man who tries to leave. Look sharp and forward march.'

The complaints immediately ceased and we set off, making our way along the mountainside. Everytime we made a halt, we looked down on the great plain where the Oury and the Morikoey met and considered the vastness of it. There were endless forests of huge *kaamel-doorn*, interspersed with other species of beautiful strong trees. Underfoot was the coarse granitic sand favoured by the larger plants, but there was no water and I bitterly regretted not having adhered to my original plan of following the Oury.

Soon after getting down into the wooded plain, we came upon elephant spoor; unfortunately it went off in too westerly a direction for us, and we pressed on towards the north. As the sun was setting we came upon a pool of stagnant water. We lit our fires beside it and prepared to spend the night there. My first object was to find myself some supper. I was depending on the grouse which came at twilight to drink. I fired a few shots and bagged about fifteen of them, as well as two ducks which rather stupidly came within fifteen paces of where I was lying in wait. My servants, whose fate did not much concern me, also found something to eat which they owed to their keen observation, for these savage people are able to read the tracks in the sand of every creature that has passed by. They found the imprint of a human foot on the edge of the pool; it was a woman's foot. This clue was sufficient for them to discover a little path which they supposed would lead to some habitation, and they were right, for they found a cluster of three huts only ten minutes away. Here they robbed the inhabitants of all their meat which was drying in long strips in the wind. When I returned I was not a little astonished to find my pirates making merry around great fires laden with abundant food.

'Master Delegorgue,' Tom said to me as he plucked, roasted and ate the ducks and the grouse 'it all depends on you, don't you see. When you consider the greedy and adventurous character of these scoundrelly Makaschlas, nothing could be easier.'

'What couldn't be easier Tom?'

'Well you see now, when this lot here were forced to do what they didn't want to do, they got upset about it. But now, since the love of plunder has got into them and they can see how easy it is with the protection of a white man . . . I'm sure whole populations would follow us.'

'And what would we do with all these people?'

'What would we do?' exclaimed Tom 'Why, plunder of course, strike terror, live off the booty, win over the leaders of the tribes which would then surrender to avoid being robbed, and then we'd found an empire. You'd be king, just think of it – a king with 500 wives and 100 000 head of cattle – what a fate! And all you've got to do is take it.'

'I'm just as sure of it as you are Tom. The thing wouldn't be difficult to do. But what would I do with a throne of this sort? It wouldn't make me happy. The 500 wives and the 100 000 cattle would be fine, but God help me with 200 000 subjects like the ones we've got here. The first thing we'd have to do would be to kill off half of them in order to make things better for the other half. We'd have to do exactly the same thing that Djacka, Dingaan and Panda did with the Amazoulous; it's a hard thing to have to impose discipline over a nation by sacrificing fifty per cent of the people. If I had any hope that the cost would be less, I'd give it a try, but *you* know the Cafres and *you* know that I'm not wrong when I talk about the difficulties.'

Tom had come up with a curious idea, which I found intriguing and, to be sure, the more I thought about it the more I could see how easy it would be to put it into practice. The reputation of the white man had reached these remote parts although the Cafres had not seen any until I arrived. The fear which a few guns could inspire would be quite sufficient for this sort of conquest and it would only take a couple of months for me to become more powerful than most of the petty kings in Germany.

The success of such a venture would be all the more certain because of the lack of unity among the various population groups. These groups, when attacked, would put up little or no resistance, and would be forced to join the conquering band which would grow like a snowball. Massilicatzi, at the head of a faction of Amazoulous, had done no more than this, and his conquest had been rapid. Soon, he had at his disposal 25 000 warriors. But for the reasons I have just mentioned, I abandoned the idea of acquiring a kingdom.

Unfortunately, Tom did not share my views and he was very loath to sacrifice the thousand cattle and the twenty wives which would have been his portion as a great captain. For a long time his sleep was troubled by thoughts of them.

The weather was kind and the night was beautiful, although the mosquitoes, attracted by the pool, tormented us to some extent. We were up early and our first concern was to pay our neighbours a visit. They ran away when they saw us, all except for one man whom my fellows pounced upon and forced to carry a bundle of stolen pelts. Further on, the man who carried my box of munitions and preservatives, came upon a woman and made her carry his load for him. He followed behind her, keeping a close watch on her, so that she had no chance of escape. Once again, my efforts to intercede on behalf of these unfortunate strangers were in vain. To ensure that my orders were respected I would have to have blown out the brains of a couple of my own men. The remedy was worse than the complaint. We continued on into the immense plain, heading always in a northerly direction. When we made our first halt, we were all thirsty but we were short of water. We held a council. Our prisoner was emphatic that we would not find a drop of water in three days if we continued on the way we were going. According to what he said, we would only find it where the Makatous lived and near the kraals of the Amadebés or Amadebelés three or four day's journey towards the north-east. The Makatous received visitors at the point of an assegai; the Amadebés[1] were the people of Massilicatzi and I knew that there could be no possible compromise with this chief if my servants or I were discovered in his territory.

As I knew the approximate course of the Oury, I suggested we follow it and head due west, but my men wanted to go back towards Om-Schlabatzi because they knew what the distance was, and where we would find plentiful game. I gave in to them, while secretly intending to get to the banks of the Oury and travel downstream for several days. From now on we set course towards the south-west, and after walking rapidly for ten hours, during which time we found nothing but a vast *zout-pan* whose saline water was quite undrinkable, we at last looked down on the green banks of the Om-Schlabatzi. It didn't take us long to cross the river and find a place to make camp. Then we plunged into the limpid waters to bathe. The river was so beautiful, her bed so soft and pure that our extreme fatigue of the day was washed away in a few minutes, and rewarded a hundred times over. While we were playing at being crocodiles and taunting the real ones lying on the banks under the reeds, one of the Cafres suddenly called out to us to be silent. He pointed to the opposite bank where something a clayey-red colour was moving about.

'Tom! rhinoceros! let's go!.'

In just a quarter of an hour we had shot three, one of them a large female covered in fat which gave us hopes of a delicious supper. All my Cafres were enthusiastic about helping with the cutting up. They were right to want to hurry, for the night was coming on fast, and it would have been a shame to leave too large a piece of so excellent a beast for the hyaenas.

---

1   One usually says Amadèbés, sometimes Amadébelés. Captain Harris writes Matabili. These people also had the name Ama-Balekyle which means not the Invisibles but literally the Deserters because of their desertion from the Amazoulou tribe to which they belonged.

Clouds were building up in the south, which made me fear that heavy rains were coming. Rapidly we put together a sort of hut covered in tufts of grass so that we might have at least the semblance of a shelter for the night. The Makaschlas can put up a roof of this sort in a quarter of an hour. As soon as the provisions were under shelter, the fires were stoked until the flames leapt fifteen feet into the air. When they died down they left us a tablecloth of glowing embers upon which strips of superb fat-streaked meat writhed and twisted like snakes. What a pleasure it was for me to see these men as they crouched around the fire, as they pulled out a portion of grilled meat, carried it to their mouths, took hold of it in their teeth and, with their assagais, cropped off the meat close to their lips. They were able to do this because of the protrusion of their lips and the flatness of their noses. However great their enthusiasm, it did not exceed mine; I finished off my supper at midnight, by which time I had consumed no less than fifteen pounds of meat; but by six o'clock I was hungry again. Without knowing it, I was playing host at that time to a four-and-a-half-foot long tapeworm which had declared its presence with the appearance of numerous segments which I must confess I did not recognise.

This condition explains my astonishing, although passing, voraciousness. The cruel and insatiable parasite inflicted various sorts of indigestion upon me when I had eaten something that did not please it. Meat, however great the quantity, was quickly digested, but Indian curry and rice and *aarde-bontjes* brought on cramps or vomiting.

The tapeworm I describe is well known and very prevalent among all the Cafres, whether Zoulou or Makatisse. These people do not seem to mind it much. The Makaschlas have no remedy, but the people of Port Natal use the root of a fern which grows in the fields near the bay and the present English camp; it is called *om-komo-komo*. They pulverise it in a mortar and make little cakes which they eat. When I later became infested with a second tape-worm, I tried this remedy but the bitterness and the woodiness of the medication prevented me from taking a sufficient quantity, and so it had no effect on me, although the Cafres believed in it. This remedy is much inferior to that made from the root of the pomegranate.

Having been inconvenienced for so long by these insatiable parasites, segments of which came away in great quantities, eighteen or twenty of them every twenty-four hours, I was determined to discover how the infection passed from one person to another. My investigations led me to believe that the eggs which are tiny, light and powdery, after remaining a short time in the lower intestinal passage, break off and fall away, not to be transported by the wind like pollen but, when certain conditions are right, to penetrate man through the nose, the mouth or any other organ which suits them best.

On the 14th, while my men were sleeping off the meal of the previous night, I took my double-barrelled gun and went off to look for some pretty birds which were more plentiful there than at Sogoupana. There were mostly widow birds, the longtailed and the royal (four-pronged). I also found a variety of hobby and an adult male blac. Big, pink, green-crested bee-eaters were quite common, but I already had some from my camp at Mokoa and the plumage of these was, as usual, not very fresh.

This species which I have not previously mentioned, and which I was the first to send back to the collection at the Jardin des Plantes in Paris, is not found in great numbers on the banks of the Oury before its confluence with the little Mokoha, between 24° and 25° south latitude. The birds are only to be seen here towards the end of December and the length of their stay depends on the duration of the hot weather. As many amateurs will confuse this new bee-eater with the pink bee-eater of Senegal, I feel it would be useful to give measurements and a description.

Of a total length of thirty-six centimetres five millimetres, the beak measures four, the body twelve, the tail ten, and the two wing feathers project ten centimetres five millimetres. The beak, the feet and the claws are black; a crest, the colour of which is a mixture of green and seaweed-blue, covers the head; a beautiful black line of feathers passes under the eye, projecting at the back of the head for the same distance as the cap and underlining it. The rump is of a lighter and more definite blue than the head. The wings, the covering of the wings, and the back are brick-red mixed with pink. The tips of all the feathers darken into a deeper shade and, from the beak to the rump, over the whole breast and abdomen, the colouring is the softest pink. The bird from Senegal is smaller and the green or seaweed-blue colour covers the head and the neck.[1]

Levaillant tells us that he found, among the Kabobiquois on the west coast, a pink bee-eater which was already known and named 'bee-eater of Nubia'. If Levaillant is correct, he did not find the species I am talking about. Dr Smith, during his travels, did not find it either, which must be attributed to the season. Because these birds spend the winter at the Equator, that is where one must go to find them at their best. During the three summer months, I killed forty-five specimens of which only five or six were acceptable. At this

1 The specimens which I collected for the Jardin des Plantes are those described by Messrs Desmurs and Pucheran in their interesting work on these birds. These are the naturalists who named the bee-eater *Merops nubicoïdes*.

period, many still had their first feathers which are sufficiently different to deserve a mention. The colours were not yet very pronounced; the head was more green, the body was an equal mixture of green and red; the breast, a dirty pink, had at its base a blue strip which extended in a bluish tinge over the whole abdomen. The tail did not yet have the two feathers which project only two centimetres. This bee-eater is a bird of passage in these lands as is the *Merops apiaster* and *M. Savignii*, while the *M. minulus* and the *M. bullockoïdes* spend the winter there and are seen at all times.

At the site we had chosen for our camp there grew the most beautiful grass – long, fine and sweet. Tom thought it would be an excellent place to graze flocks and herds. One day, if he had the means, he intended to carry out such a plan for he was determined to procure a piece of land free from European control where he would be able to live in fine independent style, but not without a sizeable population under his command. Such, unfortunately, are the desires of man; we all want to be free, but we also want power to rule over our inferiors. In every age and in every land, man has had one burning ambition – to live the comfortable life. The first step towards this end, is to free himself of all fetters. No sooner is he free, than he wants more; it is luxury that he is now after and, to satisfy this desire, to enable him to live the life of ease as he sees it, he requires that ten, or a hundred or even a thousand men should devote themselves to his service. These tastes are so universal, they have such deep roots that even if there were to be a clean sweep and all made equal, it would be of no use, for the very next day differences would start to appear again.

Further along the banks of the Om-Schlabatzi we found vast tracts of land covered with *haack-doorn*. The bushes grew close together with their branches intertwined so that no other woody plant could survive there. It would have been madness to try to get through, so I had to give up my idea of following the river down to its confluence with the Oury. On the 15th we struck camp before daylight and went on towards the south-west. Each Makaschla, in order to be able to carry his ration of rhinoceros meat more easily, had arranged it in twisted strips, rigged around his neck; the thickness of this new kind of hawser was not less than fifteen centimetres. Our prisoners were still with us; they had had a good share of the feasting at the rhinoceros's expense, and their looks had improved. Diversion was provided during the early stages of the journey by an incident which involved these prisoners.

As the woman had tried to escape in the darkness of the previous night, the man whose burden she was carrying, in a determined effort to keep her by him, had tied her legs to his with a thong in such a manner that the woman, who had neither knife nor sharp stone,

255

could not untie herself without waking her jailer. In revenge for the cruel treatment, she pulled on the thong every time that the man was about to drop off to sleep. So the Makaschla paid with a sleepless night for the privilege of having a prisoner. The recounting of this story, with the additional seasoning of witticism, served to shorten the long morning hours.

How far we were from the Oury, nobody appeared to know. Our prisoners claimed that they had no idea either, and still we went on, across the limitless plain. At two o'clock in the afternoon we rested and, to quench our thirst, we chewed bitter leaves in an attempt to stimulate the saliva. There was no sign of game of any sort to distract us. A buffalo would have been a great prize because we could have opened the belly and squeezed out some water from the masticated grass which it contained, as the Cafres do. Unfortunately, there was neither buffalo nor any other living animal to be seen.

My eyes and my brain were growing weary with searching for a change in the vegetation which would indicate the presence of water, and with trying to determine whether any change were real or merely an illusion created by my inflamed imagination. Whenever I examined the wooded plain, it seemed to me to be gently sloping, which gave me reason to believe that a river bed could not be far off. When we had covered the distance to where we hoped the river bed might be, it was the same scene all over again; the gently sloping ground with the promise of a river bed not far off and the same disappointment, repeated over and over again, like a candle flame reflected in mirrors. But even though I was deceived a hundred times, I could not give up hope. Increasingly tormented by thirst, we hardly thought of resting, although we did make two stops during which nobody exchanged a word, for our tongues were sticking to the roofs of our mouths. The only thing I could think of to relieve this was to suck a lead bullet; this got my saliva flowing again. But that was not much consolation when one dreamt of great quantities of water into which one longed to plunge body and soul.

How varied are perceptions of the element in which the man who is tormented by thirst longs to immerse himself. Roused by the needs of the body, what exquisite delight the imagination feels as it slips into that moment of oblivion.

Then what bitter despair, what consuming heat, what agonizing disappointment when the imagination is recalled to reality. Man writhes in agony; he would drink his own blood, if blood had the freshness and taste of water. Oh the impossibility of describing the experience of thirst, for only he who has known it can understand. However distinguished and talented the writer, his talent will desert him when he tries to put into words the wild fancies the imagination indulges in as it pursues this consuming objective – the quest for water.

My own imagination drilled artesian wells in the granitic sand; it turned back water from springs which poured too soon into the bed of the Oury; it created long ducts to carry water everywhere so that there would be no lack of the indispensable element; and in an excess of dementia, it blocked up rivers at the mouth, because floods would be better for human kind than burning sterile drought. Oh blessed New Holland, why was it not my lot to travel that damp land instead of this hateful Africa, where the burning sand bakes the feet of the traveller and where not even creatures which require the merest drop of water are able to survive. Wild schemes, futile regrets, pursued each other through my fevered brain, interwoven with the constant thought of water. This incessant nightmare turned a few hours into eternity, for the slowness of time is measured in suffering and this suffering is increased tenfold, even a hundredfold, when hope is gone.

That time was very long; that single day was several months long. I have forgotten many of the months of my life, but that day will never be erased from my memory. By five o'clock nothing had changed, there was no water; and before us lay the interminable monotonous plain. Even a stagnant, muddy puddle would have been enough. There was not the slightest trace of an animal, nothing, nothing but sand, bitter leaves, dry air and those clear blue skies so much favoured by painters and poets, who are too foolish to know the value of big black clouds. I began then with bitter regret to yearn for my native Flanders' skies, overcast with a cold grey cloak of clouds, which so clothes the earth that no man there has ever known thirst. But regret will kill if you allow it to get a hold on you, so I tried to sing to drive it away. Sadly, the attempt was a failure; it was impossible for me to utter a single note, for my tongue, my palate, the whole inside of my mouth, all were inflamed.

It was about eight o'clock; twilight was falling; nobody was in a fit state to go a step further. A halt was called, and every man dropped his burden and collapsed on the ground. After a few moments of complete silence, I delegated five or six Cafres to go off and look for wood in the vicinity and I was going to add, to look for some water too, but I was so certain of the impossibility of this, that I did not even bother to complete my sentence. They returned, bearing only dry wood with which we made a great fire and we prepared to lie down and sleep, for we could not eat. But then one of my famished Cafres began cooking some meat for himself; I followed suit and I was glad I did. Sleep came soon after I had eaten, and took such possession of me, that the racket my Cafres made trying to kill a snake which had taken refuge in a bush I was leaning against, failed to disturb me. I awoke at daybreak, and although my thirst had not been quenched, at least I felt fresher and more cheerful than I could have hoped.

On the 10th we set forth again; the first hours were less painful than those of the day before, but towards the middle of the morning, thirst once again preoccupied us completely. The accursed delusions of the previous day began again, adding to our physical suffering which was only too real and which was now becoming quite unbearable. We dared not even encourage one another; each man walked isolated in silence, in an effort to conserve his saliva. But apart from this, if under the circumstances anybody had tried to raise spirits with a flicker of hope, grim reality would have made a mockery of the attempt and added insult to our misery.

And so, in dejection, we trudged on. Our legs, which had become the machines of our salvation, moved of their own accord, unrelated to our will. The distance behind us grew rapidly greater, but before us stretched a vast expanse of space whose unknown boundaries promised us nothing but emptiness. It was fortunate that I had an understanding of the geography of the region. That morning I decided to head due west, rather than south-west; this way we must reach the river sooner. Hope brought some balm to my soul; the saving of a few cruel hours would be an immense relief to us all.

Just as the heat was becoming so intense that the torture of fatigue and burning thirst was unbearable, just as we were cursing the sand which slowed us down as it disintegrated into intolerable dust beneath our feet, I suddenly gave a great yell which electrified every one of those men who were stumbling along, ready to drop from exhaustion. 'There's the Oury! There it is!' Although it was 600 paces away, the taller trees and the darker foliage had given me advance warning. But more than that, I had felt the proximity of water by some indefinable instinct. We began running with the greed of misers in pursuit of some rich treasure, until our feet were wading through the marshy banks and we were finally convinced that it was not all a dream.

We wallowed and drank; for two hours we frolicked and fooled, exhilarated by the cool pure water. Never in all my life had any pleasure party given me a hint of the indescribable delight of those moments. We had walked for twenty-one hours, we had covered more than twenty-four French leagues, and for thirty hours we had drunk nothing. My men had earned a rest, but for my part it was important that I should get to know the river and its banks.

The red-brown waters had abated to half their former depth leaving behind fallen reeds covered in silt. The trees were bent and their muddied bark bore witness to the recent flood. Everywhere there was confusion, litter and dirt, in complete contrast to the scene I had gazed down upon a fortnight previously as I sat on a little hill-top, admiring the majesty and tranquillity of the Oury as it spread out over the countryside. The numerous tracks of hippopotamus, rhinoceros, buffalo and canna explained why we had seen no game in the dry country we had been through. The trees were full of birds, filling the air with a thousand cries; pink bee-eaters skimmed our heads in the noon-day sun; little quails, unique to these lands, called out to each other continually as they rose up from under our feet, and the voracious fringillas, flying in flocks of hundreds of thousands, made so much noise with their wings as they took flight that one was reminded of distant cannon fire.

Happening to stop in a thicket, I witnessed a scene that would have beguiled any hunter's idle moments. There were thirty species of birds each volubly expressing in his own language his sharpest defiance. Prominent among them was the garrulous *Crateropus jardinei*, a sort of fishwife among birds, and the *Irrisor capensis*, this comic actor with his long red nose, his long blue coat gleaming with gold and purple, mocking at his peers, this marquis of the Ancien Régime making a showing of his Gallic wit. Then there was *Rhinopomastus Smithii*, similar in shape although smaller, but just as much of a joker. Added to these, were the blackbirds, the orioles, the weavers and they were all shouting abuse at a placid bird, perched modestly at the centre of the hubbub. He was the pearly sparrow-owl, the object of all this name-calling by the diurnal birds.

What is he accused of then, this poor wretch with so gentle and peaceful a demeanour that one would be tempted to acquit him without witnesses. What resignation! See how he puts his trust in his innocence. Does he not seem to ward off the storm by his silence, and compel the respect which is due to misfortune. The poor little thing is blind in the daylight; the warmth of the sun glows on his feathers which were made for the night. Peacefully huddled, who could he possibly have disturbed or offended in any way? What could they accuse him of? The poor wretch belongs to a strange breed, spurned by their peers, pariahs which come out only at night to look for the food which they cannot find when the sun is high. Some of the bigger ones, when there are no snakes, lizards or mice to be found, are goaded by hunger into disturbing the sleep of the parent birds and carrying off the downy young. This then is the reason why the whole race has become the object of abuse among the winged denizens of the daylight hours. There is nothing to compare with this furious animosity directed by the whole community against one of its members. Hunter, select a victim. Aim, fire! Reload, fire again! But the feathered tribe has strong passions in cases of this sort; gunshots will not deter them. If by chance the birds all suddenly disappear, it is simply that the sparrow-owl has disappeared also.

The east bank, which I explored, presented a picture of untamed nature, and was unimaginably wild. Enormous fallen tree trunks were hidden under long matted grass which entangled one's feet at every step. Great cracks and ravines barred the way, making it impossible to walk close to the river. The left bank, on the other hand, was rather bare; the animals seemed to have flattened everything. I had a strong desire to cross over and I went back to my men to suggest that we try to do this. In order to get across the river we had to find an easy ford, for my Makaschlas, like all their compatriots, were ignorant of the art of swimming. Parts of the river bed where we could see deep trenches dug by hippopotamuses did not suit us at all. We went further downstream to where the river curved between two steep sand banks. Tom and I got into the water to test the depth.

After half an hour's investigation, we discovered that the water was uniformly three metres deep which meant that we had to abandon the idea of crossing on foot. When our Makaschlas saw us gathering dead trees to make a raft, they were overcome with terror and some of them ran away, believing that they were in great danger. I tried every means of persuasion and when I had exhausted them all, I allowed my temper to have a free rein and expressions like 'miserable scum', 'stupid idiots', 'useless good for nothings', flowed profusely, but the wretches just laughed, counting themselves fortunate that, instead of forcing them to take to the water, I did no more than swear at them like dogs.

Having been obliged to abandon my plans because I could not undertake any serious work without the help of my servants, I made up my mind that, in spite of the difficulties, I would go down the Oury. The day was by then too advanced; it would be better to wait until tomorrow. In the meanwhile, every man employed himself according to his own interests. I saw Tom go off to where some tall, strong grass was growing, grass which would be superior even to wheat if it were properly cultivated. Tom was carrying a stick with a knob on it, the Amazoulou *tonga*. He bent down low, only to stand up again suddenly as an enormous flock of birds rose into the air. He threw the *tonga*, which flew in an arc and was lost to sight among the dense mass of birds. Tom ran after it and picked up twenty fringillas which the *tonga* had killed as it whirled past.

'You see,' said Tom, proudly carrying back his numerous little victims, 'a man could very well live here without powder or ball; that's twenty birds killed with a spinning stick.'

Curious to discover how many I would get with two shots, I picked up my gun loaded with no.5 and no.7. I took ten paces and fired into the flock, which was more compact and more numerous than a cloud of locusts. A hundred and sixty four birds fell, but a great number of the wounded escaped into the matted grass, which formed a layer two feet thick. I felt certain that at thirty paces a double-barrelled gun loaded with no.9 would certainly bring down five or six hundred birds. Flocks like these are often 100 to 120 paces long, by thirty or forty deep. They settle in places where they can find mature grasses. The numbers which a single shot will kill give some idea of the total.

These fringillas are to be found near the *mouzis* of Maponey and Rhemkoka. Although they are far less numerous there, a constant battle is waged against them by men posted on guard in huts, standing on stakes fourteen feet high. But with all their clamour and their scarecrows, they have great difficulty in driving the birds away. Near the confluence of the Oury and the Morikoey, there is no grain to be found. The continual visits of these birds have caused devastation comparable only to the ravages of locusts.

That night as I lay down to sleep by the glow of the great fires, a galago began hopping from branch to branch in a neighbouring tree, but he disappeared before I could get my gun. An hour later, I heard the hippopotamuses snorting as they heaved out of the water. One of them came to within fifty paces of our fireplace and began grazing without the least suspicion of our presence. When a gunshot warned him that the place was occupied, the heavy animal lumbered off. A little later the air was rent with the terrifying roar of lions but, as we had neither oxen nor any other sort of prey which might attract them, we slept comfortably in close proximity to the great masters of the nocturnal forest.

At daybreak, I gave the order to prepare for departure and I began looking for an easy way to follow the Oury downstream. In spite of my orders, my Makaschlas remained seated on their bundles. Upon enquiry I discovered that during the night, our prisoners had taken their leave without permission. I thought that it was because they did not intend carrying the extra load that my men had not obeyed my orders and I went back to find out. I was mistaken; it was something else. The refusal to proceed was unanimous and the reason they gave was fear of the Makatous whom we were about to encounter. I tried to calm this fear. My words, carried away on the wind, had no effect. I tried flattering my cowards but to no avail. Finally, losing all patience, I threatened that I would use firearms against them if they would not obey me, but even this had no effect; not one of them moved. What was I to do with these mummies who used their inert weight to oppose my will? What could I do with men who were not in my service and thus in no way at my disposal. It is true that they had allowed me some sort of authority over them when they chose, but they could also choose not to obey. And this is what they did now, with the greatest obstinacy combined with the most placid manner in the world. I wanted to exert my will, but I had no power to do so and once again I was forced to sacrifice my wishes to their intransigence.

Certainly it was very painful for me to have to give in to the will of others; to have got thus far, with my mind made up to achieve certain objectives, just to have these plans wrecked by the ill will, the complete indifference, the cowardice, of base and ignorant men. I had made the serious mistake of not anticipating what was inevitable, but even had I foreseen it, I would have found myself in the same position and unable to act otherwise. The difficulties I faced were those of every traveller in these lands. More than one such traveller, filled with enthusiasm and devotion to the interests of science, has set out with the avowed intention of pushing back the frontiers reached by his predecessors. More than one has had the determination to cover great distances, but a traveller is not alone, and his attendants, who do not take the same interest in exploration and do not have the same moral strength, refuse to go on because they foresee endless privation and danger, and once they have compared the unknown territory which stretches ahead and the distance they have already covered, there is not a moment's hesitation; it becomes a matter of urgent necessity to go back. Under these circumstances, what does the leader of the expedition do? For he is isolated and power lies in the hands of the masses. Let us suppose that he succeeds in forcing them to follow him, what will be his position if things turn out for the worst? Will he be able to bear the reproaches of his companions since he has accepted responsibility for them. In their eyes, he alone is seen as the author of all their misfortune; vowing hatred, they turn against him and soon the society of his own men is more intolerable to him than that of savage tribes.

Crossing southern Africa from 34° south latitude to the Equator would not be so very difficult a journey if the explorer had at his disposal a suitable means of transport such as camels, for example, as well as fifteen or so men accustomed to the climate and to privation, in whom he had complete confidence. Wagons drawn by long teams of oxen are only of use as far as 24°, beyond that, a thousand obstacles impede or delay their progress. Oxen, which are so easily stricken down by illness, are of no use either as beasts of burden, and horses are even more susceptible than oxen. But the camel, which is an eminently African animal, would certainly be more suited to the work. Apart from this, a beast of so strange a shape would excite the interest of tribes which the explorer might encounter and would guarantee him a welcome wherever he went.

As far as the men are concerned, I still do not know where one would find them. Europeans are soon debilitated by the heat, and nothing which Africa can offer provides sufficient compensation for the privation of all kinds. These privations soon weaken morale, until even the smallest danger takes on terrifying proportions. In a short time these Europeans are emasculated. They fall an easy prey to illness which sometimes leads to death within a few days.

The Boers are by nature too indolent and too used to the comfort of their wagons to accept travel by any other means. Apart from this, the sight of their oxen has become indispensable to them, for wherever they go, these men feel at home as long as they have their favourite animals with them and they will not venture beyond a certain radius which is familiar to them. Their co-operation could not be relied upon, particularly as they are conditioned from childhood to recognise only their father as lord and master. The grown men have no idea of how to conform, although, when young, they certainly do good service. However it would be very difficult to gather together sufficient numbers of them for an undertaking of this nature, and then the price one would have to pay them would be three or four times as much as one would pay the most capable Hottentot. As for the Hottentots, they are great talkers and consequently great cowards. To rely on their services would be unwise, for they make far more promises than they could possibly keep. Insubordination is also one of their vices. Hottentots are too much inclined to lead the easy life and insist on bringing their wives along with them. In any case, travelling does not appeal to them very much.

Cafres would be more suitable, if one could only engage their interest and somehow overcome the aversion certain tribes have for others. How does one make them understand the importance of one's mission, so that they will persevere until it is accomplished. This is an impossible task for a white man. But there is a man who is able to impose his will upon them in the complete certainty of being obeyed, whatever might happen. This man is a Cafre despot; this man is Panda. If some explorers' society were clever enough to gain the support of such a leader, this chief would simply designate the men he wanted for the expedition. One word from him would suffice; they would go where he ordered them to go, no matter how far.

When Djacka was king of the Amazoulous, Farewell had an audience with him. He showed the King beautiful articles of English manufacture which these people, who were new to European contact, had never seen before. Farewell, encouraged by Djacka's enthusiastic response, described to him a thousand things, each more wonderful than the last. He told him of English towns, in particular of Cape Town, of the white men's houses, their comfort, the luxury, the carriages, the beauty of the women, the great powerful cannons, the abundance of goods, the different races of men, the great ships; and he told of all these things without departing from the truth. In the end, Farewell astonished Djacka so much with his wonderful accounts that the latter began to doubt that they were true, and ordered two of his great captains, men of wit and judgment, to go and see with their own eyes whether the town at the Cape of Good Hope did, in fact, contain the extraordinary things which Farewell had described.

'Go,' he said 'look well at all things and return to me.' And his order was immediately executed.

Massilicatzi, when he foresaw that he might one day be forced to flee towards the north, thought that it would be a good idea to obtain some information relating to these lands. To this end he dispatched a small band of men which did not return for five months. This means that they must have walked for more than two months in search of the information they needed, and so one may reasonably say that they covered a distance of more than 500 French leagues. They discovered a great lake, but it is impossible to say whether this was the lake of Maravi, Aquitunda or Quiffua.

If, as it seems, the Cafre kings are the only ones whose orders are obeyed with the most admirable alacrity, ought we not to attempt to make use of this power which they wield over their people, when organising expeditions of great interest to science and trade?

Because of the opposition of my Makaschlas, I decided to delay our departure for a little while longer and I used the time to continue searching the environs. It was only towards midday that we left, making our way south-south-east. It was 17 February, a day of no particular interest. I was in a bad mood and out of my ill humour grew the idea that I would not allow any animal to be killed; this was to teach my savages that they were completely dependent on me for their sustenance. This prohibition was very painful to them. When night fell the fires burned bright and clear but not a single piece of meat dripped fat into the flames.

On the 18th, while we were still following the Oury which was some distance off to the right, a lone elephant came into view. The animal was grazing on mimosas not far from the river and he was completely unaware of our approach. I reached for the biggest gun and, with Tom behind me, I made use of the bushes and gullies to get up close. But while we were stalking him, the elephant had moved on and was now 100 paces further away. The approach was easy. We got to within thirty paces of the giant and shouldered our guns. We took careful aim and our two shots struck simultaneously, kicking up the dust from the animal's hide, which was caked in dried mud. Both shots hit the mark, but in spite of that, the elephant fled across the marsh and disappeared into the bush where for two hours we followed his blood-stained tracks. Eventually, heat and the lack of water forced us to give up the search. It was not without difficulty that we found our Cafres again.

Two hours after this vain attempt, Tom and I decided to take revenge for our fruitless endeavours on a rhinoceros *africanus bicornis*. The animal was in open country, making his way along a rhinoceros path. The wind was blowing directly away from him and towards us. With this factor in our favour, we began following him along the rhinoceros path, intent on catching him up. When we were only ten paces behind the stupid, though formidable beast, I had the wild idea of going up close and touching him. I made a sign to Tom, who immediately understood what I intended doing. I crept closer, determined to play a schoolboy's trick on my rhinoceros. Now, this animal might not see very well, but his hearing is much better than his sight, and he smells perfectly. I was at his heels when he became aware of me and tried to turn around. Halt! Aim! Bang into the ribs. Suddenly overcome by fear, the animal was breaking into a run when Tom's bullet hit him in the rump and brought him down. He got up again immediately, spun around to face us, and charged us for fifty paces. As we fled, I thought that we were going to have to pay dearly for the pleasure of our prank. But we gave him a run for his money. When we looked at each other, and saw that our foreheads were streaming with sweat, Tom and I had to admit that we'd expended a great deal of energy on escaping from the fury of our enemy.

At about midday, we wounded two other rhinoceros but although our shots were not long ones, we did not kill them. This made me think that the powder had been spoilt when we spent cool nights in the dew-laden grass.

It was at about one o'clock that I noticed that the top branches of a number of trees seemed to be turning white; this was caused by a gathering of vultures, whose arrival never fails to awaken curiosity, for somewhere in the vicinity there must be something which has attracted them; there must be dead game, a buffalo, a rhinoceros or a canna killed by lions; sometimes it might be an elephant, wounded by hunters, which has fallen, never to rise again, and which is of interest because of the tusks. 'We will soon see what the attraction is,' I said to one of my men who, spurred on by hunger, was running off to joint the others who had already gone ahead.

As they rounded a clump of bushes, they came upon a muddy ravine. Suddenly a lion jumped out of it and tried to run away. Although he was more than 100 paces away from me, I took aim, my shot went off, he rolled over and lay motionless. Almost at the same moment, and close to the place from which the lion had emerged, a buffalo got up and rushed past Tom who wounded it without bringing it down.

I thought that my followers would applaud my shot, but their passion for carrion was such that they were not interested in anything else. At the bottom of the ravine, they found a male *melampus* with half its body stuck into the mud. The animal had apparently been killed by the lion the day before; already the flesh was turning green and gave off a foul stench which did not in the least repel my Makaschlas. They cut up the body and portioned it out into bundles. Then an altercation arose over the skin and, as no one would make concessions, it was shared out equally which made it completely useless to anybody.

I then went off to inspect my lion. My bullet had hit him ten inches below the shoulder and death had been almost instantaneous. He was a large male with a tawny mane and I would like to have kept his skin, but the difficulty of preservation, the impossibility of drying it out as we went along, the problem of persuading my men who were already loaded with booty, to carry it, all these reasons conspired to persuade me to give up the idea. Then my Makaschlas thought that they would like to take away bits of the lion; one cut off the tail, another took a piece of the skin, and the claws were shared out to be hung round the necks of warriors, as a token of bravery.

Although we had had no luck hunting that day, evening found us sitting around great fires crackling with dripping fat. In spite of the repugnance we had shown when the melampus was being cut up, we now joined our happy followers without too much distaste. It had been Tom's idea, because the flesh of the melampus was nice and fat. Although it had been green and very strong smelling in a raw state, it was rendered delicious by cooking. Never had I eaten anything more choice.

On the 19th, as we followed the river closely, it led us south-south-east directly towards the Sogoupana mountains which we had been able to see since the morning of the previous day, and which we felt we were rapidly approaching when we inspected them just before sunset. We compared this apparent proximity with the distance we had calculated in the morning, and were not a little surprised; our reckoning of the distance varied between three and eighteen leagues. But this phenomenon is easily explained. As the range extends from the south towards the east and then east-north-east, early in the morning the outlines were clear but the slopes were still in darkness and none of the features were apparent. At midday when the light fell directly on the peaks, the outlines of the mountains were no longer clearly defined against the sky, the contours were hazy and indistinct. which made it quite impossible to calculate an approximate distance; but towards evening, when the setting sun shone directly on them, the projections, the clefts, the forests, the bare rock, all were clearly visible; the mountains appeared higher, and consequently closer. We said to each other 'Tomorrow, about ten o'clock in the morning, we'll be there, exploring the gorges.' But for two whole days our calculations proved false.

During the morning, I shot a few ducks and to do them honour we made a halt. About midday we came to a place where the Oury overflowed its banks producing wide stretches of water two or three feet deep, where there appeared to be a fair number of aquatic birds. But when a shot was fired, the air resounded with the deafening clamour of hundreds of thousands of beating wings. The most numerous of the birds were ducks, of which there were three species. There were also brilliant bronze caruncular geese which were so beautiful that I very much wanted to add several to my collection, but they were also so fat that it would have been impossible to preserve them. However there was a simpler use to which the gourmets among us intended to put them.

Without any regard for the crocodiles, I moved about all over the place and in twenty minutes I had ten or so brilliant specimens. The males were more rare, but they had the shinier plumage and on their beaks the strange oily caruncle. Shortly afterwards I discovered a curlew *falcinellus*, or something closely related to it, which I had not yet come across. I fired, and when I went to pick up the body I found, lying all around it, thirteen plovers and lapwings which I had not even suspected were there. Aquatic birds were in such abundance that it seemed that they must have gathered there from fifty leagues around, and what better place for them. All about me tall grasses stood in the water; so tall that they covered my head and hid me from both swimming and flying birds. Everywhere there was an abundance of food and few enemies. As the overflow of the water invaded more and more of the land and the river made a bend, we took to the bush, where we walked in single file.

It was probably about four o'clock; we were lulled into somnolence by the silence. As often happened in these conditions, I had relaxed my vigilance and was thinking of nothing at all when, fifty or sixty paces to my left, something moved. It was an earthy red colour and its height made me think it was an elephant. Tom and the others who had stopped when I hissed a warning, were convinced that it must indeed be an elephant, although they had seen only a small part of its back.

Tom removed his percussion cap and inspected his gun. I picked up the big gun, convinced that I could not use too great a force in view of the poor condition of my powder. We advanced, one behind the other, crouching low and walking slowly to avoid breaking the dry twigs which snapped loudly. It took us only a few minutes to get within sixty paces of the animal which, to our great surprise, we discovered to be a large female *Rhinoceros simus*. It wasn't nearly as exciting as an elephant, but the encounter was opportune; everybody was hungry and we needed to make provision for our supper.

Resting the barrel of my gun on a convenient branch, I waited for the animal to present broadside. We could only see her rump, but soon another body appeared; it was her calf, three and a half feet tall, with his snout turned towards us as if to pick up our scent. Wretched child! He was perhaps about to give the warning to his mother. I aimed at him. Come on, turn around! There you are! My shot went off, toppled him, and the little rhinoceros was soon writhing in the dust, squealing like a pig. Anxiously the mother turned and tried to help her child to his feet with her horn.

Tom had not fired.

'Let's go,' I murmured to him, 'this isn't over yet.'

Noiselessly we retreated eighty paces so that I could reload, for the bullets were a tight fit and needed to be packed in with the ramrod. When this was done, I said, 'We're going to have to dislodge the mother – that's my business, but as soon as I've fired, you must run after the young one and finish him off. But look sharp; if he sees his mother going, and if he can possibly make the effort, he will follow her. Understand? Let's go.'

I took up my position once more, with the barrel of the big gun resting on the same branch. The female was moving around her young, unconcerned about what danger might be lying in wait for her. I waited for the moment when she presented her left flank; it was impossible not to put a ball within a radius of six inches. 'Bang!', my shot rang out. The badly wounded mother retreated and the calf followed, for Tom was too astonished to fire.

'What's the matter Tom, what happened?'

'Ah master, nothing happened; no supper tonight, he's gone.'

'But what the devil were you thinking about?'

'I thought he would've stayed, but I think he's shamming. You see, that youngster was just trying to soften his mother's heart; he wanted her to carry him on her back, but then he got frightened and he forgot about shamming and he ran away.'

'But Tom, this is no joking matter, its very serious for our men. Remember we've only got enough ducks for the two of us. Our Makaschlas haven't got anything; we need at least a rhinoceros. Go on, the young animal can't be far off. The mother's a different matter.'

Tom followed the bloody tracks, soon losing those of the young rhinoceros, but at 250 paces he saw the mother staggering along like a drunkard. Tom fired, and a second later the heavy animal dropped down dead. His ball had penetrated four inches; mine had lodged in the lungs. The animal was cut up immediately. On the way back, Tom was bitten on the little toe by a *poff-adder* and I had to spend the evening tending and comforting him, for his suffering was acute and his anxiety even more so.

On the 20th my men were busy drying their meat in the wind and Tom felt unable to move because of excessive swelling and pain in the groin, so I busied myself preparing specimens of birds. Early in the afternoon I took two men with me and by four o'clock we were moving about on the mountain, between the valleys and in the bush. It was eight o'clock and completely dark when we emerged. We soon realised that it would be impossible to continue much longer, for darkness shrouded everything and we could easily have mistaken ravines for pathways. Apart from this, lions were roaring all around us and although my Cafres showed no signs of fear, I thought it best to make a camp on the bank at a bend of the Oury.

A big fire was soon burning, cheering our spirits with its brightness and comforting us with its warmth, while it cooked our food and protected us from the great carnivores by repelling the dark which favoured their attacks. What an excellent thing fire is for man, a gift given only to him above all other creatures. If a man is all alone in a desert which is inhabited only by animals, he is safe at night if he has a fire. If he is taken, while he sleeps, by a lion or a hyaena, this is certainly because he has allowed his fire to go out, but as long as there is the flicker of a flame, only the rhinoceros is a danger, probably because the flames irritate him, the way a red flag irritates a bull.

As soon as it was daylight, we set off again and in two hours we had reached our camp to find that Henning was back after forty-one days absence. He had met Mr Michel van Breda from whom he had bought a superb team of oxen which, in an excess of caution, he had left at Makalisberg. To my great regret, Henning had heard nothing of my second wagon which Isaac van Niewkerk was to have brought back from Natal. Anxiety was added to impatience, for our needs were becoming pressing; it was not only that we lacked clothes, but more important still, our stock of ammunition was running low.

It was by then 24 February. Isaac Niewkerk had been gone since 10 October; it was unlikely that the usual predictable causes could have kept him so long, without news reaching the Boers of Makalisberg. I could wait no longer and I sent Henning off immediately to fetch the team of oxen.

On 2 March he was back, but the Oury had swollen during his absence and was still nine feet deep at the wagon drift. I had not foreseen this new obstacle. Henning swam over from the far bank to discuss with me how to overcome the difficulty. We decided that the oxen would swim across the river, that they would draw the wagon to a ford further upstream which could only be crossed on foot; that there we would transport the whole load manually to the other side, that the empty wagon would go down again to the wagon drift, to be towed across by the oxen, which would have to swim with some of us leading them.

The first part of this plan was carried out in a day and a half in the most difficult circumstances because, heavily burdened, we had to cross and recross on foot 100 paces of swirling water flowing over the drift. The rest looked easy but when we tried, alas, the men delegagated to lead the oxen were unable to hold them in the strong current. The wagon drifted on to a bank, where it sank into two feet of sand, while under the shaft there were still five feet of water which meant that the oxen had to keep swimming. The whole team floated out in a long line on the current, struggling to keep their heads above water. The terrified animals became so entangled in their harness that the only way to save them was to cut the traces, and to cut them fast. Henning and Tom, swimming in among the horned heads, slashed about to left and right, cutting them free, until finally the team drifted downstream on the current. But where would it stop in God's name, for there was no foothold. Fatigue would soon overcome the poor beasts and I was convinced that I would lose every one of them.

Then, 200 paces downstream from the confluence with the Mokoha, I saw my animals run aground. The current would soon carry me down to join them. I was overjoyed to think that they had got a foothold, without in the least knowing how I was going to get them off. My joy was short-lived, for I landed on shifting sand where I sank in up to my knees. When Henning and Tom reached the sandbank we dislodged our oxen whose wide bellies had kept them from sinking. We found a suitable bank on the other side of the river and after a long rest we guided the oxen across, while the wagon was still embedded 500 paces away on the opposite bank. Wearied by all our efforts and our failures, we could do no more that day. We were too few to be able to drag the wagon out of the mud, although nothing would have been simpler, if only we had had a length of cable the width of the river to which we could have secured our oxen harnessed to the main shaft. But on these journeys the necessities are almost always lacking and for months on end, when rivers are in flood, for want of a little boat or half a cable's length of rope, thirty or forty or even sixty families are stranded in their wagons on the bank. But time means nothing to the Boers, who do not do a great deal and feel at home wherever they find themselves, as long as they have their women, their wagons and their oxen close by them. For them the English proverb 'Times is money' [sic] is completely meaningless.

Only the Cafres could get me out of the present difficulty. I needed lots of them and I sent a message to Rhemkoka who, instead of the twenty-five I had requested, sent me seven miserable looking wretches, the dregs of the *mouzi*. There were now fourteen of us, all counted. We had to try and lighten the wagon so I had the tent taken off; we floated it down the river like a boat and it soon arrived at its destination. Then came the turn of the wagon itself with its heavy iron-banded wheels. We managed with our combined strength to dislodge it and to our astonishment, it rolled along the bottom with the greatest of ease. In no time at all we had reassembled it and with inexpressible joy we left the place which had been the scene of such misfortune and trials of patience.

As my oxen were in excellent condition, we were able to travel ten leagues a day in spite of the difficulties of the terrain, although these were fewer this time because we now knew of a series of clearings we could use. By the evening of the fifth day, we were at Pilanne's *mouzi*. I returned his men to him and at the same time did some business transactions concerning oxen because I needed to make provision for accidents along the way. But Pilanne wanted more than I had bargained for. He would not be satisfied unless two guns were included in the deal. He offered me an elephant tusk weighing forty to fifty pounds for each of them. I knew that the Boers would not like it; they had made laws forbidding Cafres the possession of firearms, but Pilanne was so insistent and I was so much indebted to him and, after all, hunting was his only object, so I gave in to his demands and bade him farewell.

The next day we arrived at Makota's place; he also had a strong desire to obtain firearms. Makota was an excellent man, but I knew that he already possessed two guns and I did not want to become involved in bargaining which would compromise me in the eyes of the whites who lived not far off. The following day we put Makalisberg behind us and soon H. Potgieter's dwelling came into view. I found there his son-in-law who was full of admiration for the fact that I had lived so long among the Cafres. In his opinion this was proof of reckless daring, and he was amazed that I had survived.

Three more days' journey brought me to Mooi Rivier where I was very properly welcomed by the Vermaes family. It was here that I became convinced that I could no longer hope for the return of my second wagon which it had been my intention to use for several months more to continue my explorations. Isaac van Niewkerk, in whom I had so ill-advisedly placed my trust, had made his way to Zand-Rivier and all along the way he had sold off goods which had been sent to me by my correspondent, and had reserved for himself the option of disposing of the rest of my possessions further on.

This news sent me into a rage. The value of the stolen goods, not including oxen and wagon, mounted to more than 200 pounds sterling which would have been very useful to me. I had waited such a long time for my goods and now, without ever having possessed them, I was going to have to pay for them as soon as I got back. Worse than this, Niewkerk had letters for me from Europe which I would never now be able to read. Oh! my letters. This thought exasperated me to such a degree that I decided to set off and try to find him with the intention of stopping him in his tracks with a well-aimed bullet. And then I would read those letters which brought me kisses from 3 000 leagues away. But when I got to the lower drift on the Vaal Rivier where the water foams and thunders over a fall, I found the river three times wider than before, as wide as the Seine in Paris, and

271

twelve feet deep. Forty wagons were drawn up on the banks; some had been there for three weeks.

I could not bear the prospect of waiting, each minute was an hour of torture for me, plagued as I was by a thousand thoughts each more disagreeable than the last. I heard talk of a man who transported wagons by means of a raft made of barrels tied together, at a place higher up the river where the water was more peaceful and where the crossing should be successful. In spite of having to lose a day because of difficult rough terrain, I went to this place but the man was drunk. He made promises, wasted my time and did nothing. I left him and went further upstream to a point where the water was so still it seemed to be asleep, and I tried to make myself a raft. Unfortunately, the only wood I could find was green willow and green rushes and I wasted three days stubbornly working to no avail.

The last resort was the upper drift known as Lynequey-Drift, two days away. This was going out of my way, but to turn back through extremely difficult terrain was too daunting and, as the delay at the wagon drift must be even greater than before, I had no choice but to give up the pursuit of Niewkerk. Henning agreed and we did the only reasonable thing – we continued on our way.

As soon as we had made the crossing of Vaal Rivier, Tom asked permission to leave me and return to *Bastaard-Land*. I gave him the two guns I had promised him in return for his services and added whatever else I could manage to spare. It was not without emotion that I watched the brave and honest boy walk away. Henning and my young Cafre Guimba were now the only men I had left to make the long journey back to Natal.

The journey did not produce anything unexpected except that, the day before we tackled the descent of the Draakensberg, I met a Boer called Neethling who, by way of being agreeable, talked at length of the fossilised head of an animal that had been found in the bed of Moeder-Rivier, the muddy river. According to Neethling's description, this animal must have been a ruminant of the largest kind. The head which he had seen was something like that of a hippopotamus except that there were two bony cores which, when they were covered in horn, must have been excessively long; the distance between the two tips might reasonably be expected to have been eleven feet, which is to say two feet more than is the case with the biggest South African ox. When we had exhausted this topic of conversation, Neethling, who knew I had just returned from lands where the Boers do not go, asked me, 'You have been far into the interior, you have been all over, but have you seen cannibals?'

I admitted that I had never seen any, although I had heard of them from my Cafres at the time when I was living among the Amazoulous. I told him about this.

It concerned the Amazimos, a small, unimportant tribe massacred by Dingaan on the pretext that they were seizing men, women and children from among his people for the purpose of eating them. Dingaan's act of justice happened a long time ago. For a while, no one heard anything more about the Amazimos, a few feeble remnants of whom had taken refuge, so it was said, among the Makatisses where, to avoid persecution, they had been careful not to show their preference for human flesh. They had become absorbed into the Makatisses and could no longer be distinguished from them, but they continued to be talked of as having teeth which they sharpened with little stones until they resembled the teeth of a saw. It was said also that they had a characteristic which was peculiar to them: their hair grew down very low, close to their eyebrows, which was as good as saying that their foreheads were not much developed.

'It's true,' Neethling said to me, 'I have heard the same thing, and people say that whole tribes of them live in the territory which adjoins ours.'

'But has anybody seen this? Was it a Boer? I would very much like to meet such a man, for the information is valuable to me.'

'No,' replied Neethling, 'as far as I know, not a single Boer has met a cannibal and we have been in this part of the country since 1836. But since you are so keen to find out, I will tell you that we Boers did not know of the existence of cannibals here until we had newspapers from the Cape in which we read of them. It was one of your compatriots, a Protestant French missionary who was the author of the article.'

I have not the shadow of a doubt that Dingaan used this story of cannibalism to justify the massacre of the Amazimos. It is very much what a king of the Amazoulous would do to achieve his own ends. Although it is possible that the Amazimos really were man-eaters, I find it difficult to believe because of the horror these Cafre people have for the dead, whom they do not even dare touch with the tip of their fingers. This practice of the Amazimos, if it really existed, would only have been a rare exception, in cases of extreme hunger, although I find even *that* difficult to accept because in all these lands there are bulbs and wild roots and sometimes fruit which the Cafres know, and eat with pleasure.

Imagine my astonishment when, on my return, I glanced at the map of the journey taken by Messrs Arbousset and Daumas to find the horrible, unbelievable word 'cannibals' written in six different places. This is enough to repel any explorer who is travelling in the interest of science, and is bound to produce the sort of isolation in which Paraguay has slumbered so long under the Jesuits. But, rest assured; although the mission stations Moridja, Motito, Thaba-Uncha, Thaba-Bossiou and others are, according to the map, situated among cannibals, up until now, not a single missionary has been eaten. Cannibals in this part of Africa are therefore nothing more than terrifying phantoms produced by the fevered imagination of the good missionaries, who are either too gullible themselves, or believe that they are dealing with men of inexhaustible credulity.

They ask for money, and they are right to want money; without money nothing can be done; but you have to give a reason for asking for it. However kindly the donor, he will want to know how his contribution will be spent.

'Over there,' they cry, 'men eat each other. Be generous, help us to civilise them, allow your hearts to be touched, and support our endeavours.'

The worthy and credulous man opens his purse, his heart fills with a glow of satisfaction, for he feels that he has done a noble thing. But a little later, from the depths of Africa a laugh can be heard; it is the hearty, complacent laugh of a white man living very comfortably indeed among the cannibals, who exist only on maps. And who would have known of this laughter if I had not chosen to tell of it?

My love of the truth cannot fail to make me many enemies. I welcome them with open arms, for at least I will have fulfilled my mission. No one will ever find in my writings a single untruth with which to reproach me; errors are possible, but not calculated mistakes. I believe that very few travellers could say as much. So many lies have been told and written about this part of Africa that it would take me six months to produce a great volume of refutation. It should be noted that more than half of the claims of which I speak have been circulated with the intention of achieving some particular objective.

I received some interesting information from a Cafre headman called Matouana who lived at the foot of the Draakensberg mountains, the same Matouana I have mentioned before at the time of the war between the Boers and the Amazoulous. If this information is true it would be of much interest to ethnology but, as I cannot vouch for it, I communicate it only with the greatest reservation. However, I can certainly say that there is perfect agreement between Matouana's claims and those of a man who hunted with me at the time that I was in the Amazoulou country. Until now, I have never mentioned these things.

This information concerns a race of men whom no traveller has yet described. I refer to those men whom the Amazoulous call Kossobalas and sometime Ikoey. They live in isolation to the north of the country of the Amazoulous in the land of the Amassouazis, commonly called at Port Natal, the country of Sapoussa, where at the present moment his son Massousse is king. These men are only one metre tall; their skins are a dirty, tawny bronze colour; they have black, bushy hair and thick, strong beards. Their sense of hearing is poor, but their eyesight is perfect, surpassing even that of the Cafres. Because of their habitual use of termite heaps to make fires in, the front part of their legs is almost always singed, and so they are in a permanent state of suffering. When there is no game, they feed on insects. They have complete liberty of movement among the Amassouazis who fear to harm them because of the ability they have to poison all the springs in the country.

I was quick to give Matouana my opinion that these men could be no other than Boschjesmans; but the Boschjesmans are well known to the Amazoulous who call them Amayaho or Mayaho. He explained the difference to me, and even if I did not accept this explanation, I had no convincing argument against it. Matouana had lived a long time in the country of Sapoussa and had no interest in fabricating myths. Apart from that, the two places where I heard these accounts, the first from Kamdane and the second from Matouana were 100 leagues apart.

I must mention that there was once talk of a similar race living in Madagascar; the famous Buffon refers to them by the name of Quimos. Research which was undertaken to determine whether they really existed produced no evidence; perhaps today there is not a single Quimos alive in Madgascar, but I do not see why the fact that there are none now, should prove that they never existed. Once man reaches the last degree of degeneration, through poverty or deprivation, it is possible that he will lose the ability to procreate. I suspect that this is the reason why the Kossobalas are so few in number in the land of the Amassouazis where they live on friendly terms with their neighbours. However, not having personally seen this race of extraordinary people, and having only received from others this description of them, it is not possible for me to state with any certainty that they exist.

I arrived back at Natal during the last days of April 1844, at the end of my journey which I had not intended should last longer than five or six months. I returned, partly because of the lack of ammunition, which was virtually unobtainable in Natal at that time, and partly because of the great expense which an undertaking of this sort entails. My readers will have observed that, contrary to the general practice of explorers, I never dared make the bold claim that I would set out from Port Natal to cross the Tropic of Capricorn. I did better than make promises. Allowing myself simply to be carried along on the stream of events, which were often disastrous, I managed to penetrate a good distance beyond the beacons planted by the English travellers, Smith and Harris, ten years before. For this achievement, I feel the greatest satisfaction. My estimate is that I had reached 23°18 south latitude when the lack of water, added to the cowardice and ill will of my servants, forced me to turn back against my wishes.

But let me hasten to say that perhaps I am not the only European to have penetrated thus far. My worthy and esteemed colleague, Mr Wahlberg of Stockholm was on the left bank of the Oury while I was on the right. Would the deep water at the confluence of the Oury and the Morikoey have prevented the brave and patient Swedish explorer from crossing? I do not know, but whatever happened, this reliable witness of my own endeavours was only a short distance away and I would be very wrong indeed if I neglected to mention the proximity of my friend, a man to whom natural history will one day be indebted for great enlightenment.

CHAPTER XXXVI

Retrospective glance at the customs of the Makatisses — Arrival at Port Natal — Departure for the Cape — I leave the Cape — Visit to Saint Helena — Return to Europe

Now that my expedition is ended, and before I return to Port Natal, I must cast a retrospective glance at the people who live west of the Draakensberg, by this I mean those who call themselves Makatisses, which I have always taken to include all the Sissoutou[1] speaking tribes, all those who practise circumcision and all those whose men wear a strange, uncomfortable-looking modesty garment, a sort of suspensory bandage made of softened leather.

I have already dealt with their cowardice, lying, and deceit, their gluttony, dirtiness and arrogance. There remains for me to tell of their customs, to describe their persons, and to compare them with the Amazoulous. Shall I describe to you the Makatisse in transit, the way I saw them on several occasions, travelling in caravan with their cattle and their wives, on a bartering expedition. Imagine thirty, forty, or fifty individuals, preceded by a herd of laden oxen which were not harnessed in any way except for a length of rope attached to a small piece of wood passed through the dividing membrane of the nostril.

This troop of animals, walking silently ahead with a somewhat philosophical air, is in striking contrast to the humans who chirp and twitter incessantly, like a flock of birds, although the accent is harsh, with repetitive sounds and bristling with Rs. Even a lively political discussion could not produce so much verbosity. What topic could excite so much talk? What matters of state can they be discussing; what important point does the main speaker wish to make? I hardly dare to reveal it. One man maintains that the flesh of the female quagga is the best of all meat; another prefers rhinoceros; a third claims that he has eaten very fatty hyaena which was superior to thin black rhinoceros. This then, was the substance of their animated discourse. What amazing interest in so insignificant a subject!

One man leaves the group and comes towards us. To tell the truth, he is less a man than an ambulating wardrobe, for he wears a fur *kros* with the hair turned inside, goatskins, sheepskins, jackal skins,

---

1 Some say *izoutou* or *zoutou*. When the Amazoulous want to ask 'Do you speak the language of the Bazoutous?' they say 'Koluma ni Zoutou?'

each one superimposed upon the other like a coachman's cape, but in extraordinary disorder. These outer garments cover a body which is disgusting in its habitual filth, added to, in this instance, by the grease which is applied on festive occasions. A pointed hat in the Malay style, shaped rather like the bell of a trumpet, covers the thick hair which is dripping with grease mixed with *sibylo* (antimony). The feet, which are the ugliest I have ever seen, are shod in sandals and support a body which is very narrow in the hips. As the Makatisse comes closer, our attention is drawn to his neck and chest, where a hundred assorted objects are suspended, all threaded together; claws of lion, leopard and eagle, crocodile teeth, vertebrae of snakes, pieces of roots and wood, and a dozen little skin bags containing roots, or bark, or powdered leaves – in all, a collection of curios such as might be sold by vendors on the Quai Voltaire. The reason for all this you see is that the Makatisse fears death; he is cautious, and wears his pharmacy about his person.

Each man carries a round shield made from giraffe skin. In general, one or more assegais, eight or nine feet long, are attached to this shield, as well as empty calabashes, and dozens of wooden spoons artistically carved, with designs burnt into the wood, and various little skin bags containing tobacco or hemp. All these trading goods make an irritating clatter as the men walk along, which is compounded by the sound of the skin cloaks flapping against their naked bodies and their ugly legs. It is immediately apparent that a band of Makatisses is infinitely more noisy than an equivalent number of Amazoulous, who go naked and who do not journey about on trading expeditions laden with goods.

When I considered their commercial instincts and certain of their customs, I often wondered whether the Makatisses were perhaps a more ancient people than the Amazoulous. It occurred to me that some of their customs might probably have originated in Abyssinia. The only traditional practice which has survived is that of circumcision, although I believe that this alone is insufficient to prove that there was once contact with the people of central and north Africa.

The skin cloaks in which these people drape themselves, are always worn with the hair on the inside. The everyday cloaks are made from antelope skins, and the special ones from the pelts of carnivores – jackal, genet, leopard or cheetah, which without the use of needles are held together by flat stitches, made from animal sinews, passed through holes pierced by a little spike.

The skins are transformed into amazingly soft leather by a process of greasing and pounding, followed by tanning with several applications of a decoction of bark which stains reddish-brown. The Makatisses, who are considered to be excellent leather workers by those competent to judge, could well give a few lessons to our leading Parisian furriers. It was upon inspection of some of their work, which I took home with me, that this opinion was expressed. The price of a cloak varies according to the skin; four made of antelope-hide but only one of jackal skin can be bought for one cow. Three or four cows is the going rate for a headman's cloak, made from the skins of cheetah and leopard.

The Makatisses have a quite different style of headgear from the Amazoulous, for they make a straw hat which is woven in rather the same way as the hats our sailors wear, although the shape is more like the pointed hat of the Malays. This headgear, perched on top of their thick, black, tufted hair which sticks up in a thousand little spring-like curls, strongly emphasizes their barbarous features. In the matter of dressing their hair they do not all follow the same fashion. Some never cut their mops but others, who live at latitudes of 25°, shave around the temples and the back of the head, leaving a section of hair which looks rather like a headless tortoise or else an elliptical citadel with four rectangular bastions.

The great many skins which they habitually wear to ward off the cold, added to the thick hair, are partly to blame for a lack of cleanliness which one does not find among the Amazoulous. They are commonly infested with human parasites, with the exception of Latreille's *Pediculus pubis* which they appear not to know. It is to be rid of these parasites that they anoint the top of their heads with a pound of fat mixed with *sibylo*[1] and sit for hours on end in the sun waiting for the fat to melt into their hair and stifle the little creatures.

Besides the *om-gobo*, the women wear a belt from which are suspended twelve or fifteen strips of hide, rather like the Zoulou *motgees*. These thongs, arranged to form a sort of modesty garment, are intended, in case of need, to protect the woman from a man's advances. In this way, art makes up for what nature has not seen fit to grant to the coloured races of tropical lands.

These ladies, or rather these females, deck themselves out in cloaks similar to the male cloak; more often than not, the head is bare, although sometimes it is covered with a cap made of fox skin. On their legs, beneath the knee, they wear several circlets of brass wire or beads, like the ones around their necks. They wear the same sandals as the men do.

As is the way with all women, however ugly they may be, and however dirty, a little touch of coquetterie is apparent. They love finery, and they take great pleasure in adorning their bodies, but I

---

1   Antimony, which Monsieur Arbousset took to be platinum.

don't think that the idea of washing themselves ever crossed their minds; they seem to leave the performance of this task to nature – I mean, to the rain which falls from heaven, or to the river which they are obliged to cross on foot. In this matter they are completely different from the Zoulou women.

In spite of the winters which last four months, the Makatisse mothers have no more idea than have the Zoulou women of clothing their children, for they are completely naked. But, as they are nearly always carried on the mother's back, the proximity of her body must be all they need to keep them warm.

When I enter a Makatisse village with its cone-shaped roofs rising to a height of fifteen to twenty-two feet, what strikes me most is the disorder, the confusion, the complete absence of any plan. The plan of an Amazoulou village is invariably based on an elipse, while in the case of the Makatisses, it would appear that the intention is to create a maze so as to confuse any enemy who might try to find his way in. As an added defence against attackers, the thoroughfares, edged with enormous pieces of wood or unhewn trees, are so wretchedly narrow that it is virtually impossible for three men to walk abreast. Neither is the direction of these thoroughfares very precise, for they are as tortuous as possible, so much so that, having visited one of these villages on three consecutive days, I still needed a guide to enter and to leave. Such a village was Makate which housed about 500 inhabitants.

The visitor's sensibilities are offended by the disorder and the piles of rubbish dumped at the approaches to the village and he gains a sorry impression of the inhabitants, an impression which is, however, somewhat ameliorated by the sight of the courtyards which adjoin the huts, and which are formed by screens of rushes, providing a place for housewives to prepare the food. The huts are rather better built than those of the Amazoulous.

They are rounded in shape with a pitched roof which juts out four feet all around and is supported by columns three feet high. Beneath the shelter of this extended roof, household goods are piled, which would otherwise clutter the interior of the hut. These huts are usually raised so that the rain water circulates around them without finding its way inside. The walls are built of strong wooden beams, filled in with clay, and smoothed over. There are often drawings on the walls, done in red, blue and white, which are the artist's impression of giraffe, rhinoceros and elephant. Tidiness is the rule, both within and without. Provisions are stored in great earthenware pots, often as much as eight feet high which are fixed to the floor, and therefore immovable. Skin bags are to be seen, artistically worked and stuffed brimful with maize or kaffircorn. Only the basic essentials of furniture are to be found inside the huts, along with a conglomeration of farming implements, household utensils and weapons. But all this is barely distinguishable without a light, for the only aperture is the entrance door which is no wider than the round shield used by these people – that is to say about sixty centimetres. The interior is so thoroughly plastered that, when the sliding door is slammed, the vibrations echo for more than a minute. Nothing could be easier than to keep this kind of building heated. I grant that the Makatisses have perfectly understood how to protect themselves from the cold.

I have often seen clay pots that were spherical in shape, which seems to prove that they have some knowledge of the potter's art. The red-brown colouring is reminiscent of Etruscan vases, and the design, although primitive, does not lack a certain taste.

The only musical instrument which I have heard them play, and that was rarely, consists of an empty calabash attached to a bow with a single string, rather like the *izimkopo* of the Amazoulous, but with the difference that the cord is tightened around a quill which is fixed to the point of the bow. The musician applies his lips to the quill and blows. The vibrations are hollow-sounding or shrill, depending on the artist who modulates the sound by using his fingers, but who is incapable of producing a single exciting note. In spite of what some travellers have said about it, this is really a string instrument, although it depends on air to produce the sound.

The character of the Makatisses is illustrated in their dances, just as the particular qualities of the Amazoulou nation are expressed in theirs. The bellicose spirit of the Amazoulous is reflected in war dances which require the wearing of ornaments and the carrying of arms of war. The Makatisses, on the other hand, who are bourgeois in the extreme, perform only the most sedate of dances in which the women also take part. They do not indulge in over-ornamentation, their bearing is that of a people long civilised; they assume graceful poses and twist and turn with elegant ease. But above all they compose their features to give an impression of agreeable smiling countenances. In short they conduct themselves in a manner which is quite contrary to their habitual behaviour. Very little energy is expended on the dance. The women group together in a semi-circle; they stamp their feet and clap their hands, singing all the while. This singing, or perhaps I should call it shouting, is sometimes soft and low, sometimes very loud, and sometimes an ear-splitting shriek, while at certain moments, the red tongues vibrate inside the open mouths to produce a tremulous sound, the effect of which is quite monstrous, and which carries far into the distance. From time to time, the women intermingle with the male dancers but they are not endowed with the same elegance, grace and agility. These dances, whether they are intended simply for pleasure or designed to persuade the clouds to give up their rain, provide a unique opportunity of observing a great number of Makatisses gathered together.

These people have no religious beliefs; I never heard them speak of a supreme being. They swear by Morrimo, who is perhaps some sort of evil spirit, but there is no trace of any form of worship.

Circumcision is practised simply as an hygienic measure and distinguishes the race from others. Young girls, as well as boys, are subjected to this ordeal. When the time comes, all those who are to be circumcised leave the *mouzi* under the supervision of an operating doctor, and go off to spend three months in an isolated place, at least a league away from the *mouzi*. After three months, when all is over, the group returns home. When they approach the village they look for a detour, for they will try to avoid the beating which awaits the initiates. This is the traditional baptism which all must accept, although they may try to avoid it by reaching the centre of the village unseen. I had known about male circumcision; that of females intrigued me greatly. I tried to discover something about it; I asked many questions, but I learnt nothing. The laughter and the ribald remarks of my men reduced the Makatisses to silence, and by the time I left, I knew no more about it than when I arrived. But, further south, there are French Protestant missionaries who dwell in the midst of circumcised people. If only these gentlemen would be more explicit, science would benefit from some very interesting information. I leave it to them to report on this intriguing matter, for they are adept at close investigation and are always peering into local customs.

The Makatisses I encountered had no more respect for their dead than did the Amazoulous; they exposed the bodies to be eaten by hyaenas. I say nothing of the system of justice or of the laws of inheritance because the Makatisse customs relating to these matters are similar to those of the Amazoulou.

The packing up of my specimens and the final preparations for departure took me six weeks, at the end of which time I set sail for the Cape. A fortnight later I arrived in Cape Town. Despite my impatience to be gone from the capital of southern Africa within the shortest possible time, the scarcity of ships bound for Europe at that season kept me two long months. During this enforced delay, I enjoyed the hospitality of Monsieur Rocher, the doyen of the French community, an excellent and worthy man, with the manners of the simple, unsophisticated Dutch whose way of life he had adopted many years before. I had also the privilege of meeting a no less worthy compatriot, known to all French travellers who called on their way to and from India. This man was a nephew of our celebrated naturalist Delalande. Monsieur Alexis Verreaux, when he learnt of the losses I had suffered during the looting at Port Natal, was quick to put a sum of money at my disposal in spite of the fact that we had only just met. Monsieur Verreaux was not concerned as to whether I would be in a position to repay him some day. 'No, no,' he said, 'you will perhaps come across some Frenchman over there who is in need of assistance.' I was soon in receipt of a letter containing his generous gift. This sort of thing does not require any comment; I simply mention the incident in praise of that brotherhood which, across the world, unites Frenchmen who have never met before. It would be even more remarkable if this sentiment took root in the metropolitan earth!

At last, a ship being ready to sail, and the wind favourable, I bade farewell to Cape Town, nestling like a child in its mother's lap, beneath that strange mass of mountains which receded slowly into the distance.

Thirteen days later, Saint Helena appeared on the horizon, a rugged stony outcrop which seemed to have been cast carelessly into the vastness of the seas. I bared my head with patriotic pride at the sight of this island which had witnessed the extinction of the mortal life of the greatest general in the world. Island with a heart of stone, sterile, hideous in the extreme, Saint Helena offered us a view of its craggy slopes corroded by the sea and the wind. In vain did we search for signs of some living creature upon the inhospitable shores. The only birds we could see were phaetons, their white plumage vivid against the grey of the bare rocks as they flew by. Great was my surprise when, imagining that I saw a black vulture perched on a jutting piece of rock, I discovered that it was in fact an English cannon. The capital, James Town soon came into view, lying in a narrow sloping valley at the foot of which a formidable row of yawning cannons watched over the vessels lying at anchor.

But what we all found most remarkable was a fort built on a flat piece of ground 1 000 feet above the town, which was reached by a terrifyingly long white ladder, leaning against the rock, and which provided the only possible communication between the fort and the town. To the left, we could see more cannon positioned at different levels, and aimed in every direction, perched like birds of prey among the rocks. Beneath them was a zig-zag path cut into the stone which was the only access to the interior of the island, to the grave, and to Longwood.

It was the English who hewed this rock, the English who opened up the road, who brought in the cannon and made accessible that accursed place, lying beneath the most beautiful skies in the world, a place intended by nature simply as the haunt of seabirds. Hewn from rock, Saint Helena will resist for hundreds and thousands of centuries the onslaught of the ocean, and for these hundreds and thousands of centuries it will stand like a tombstone, the greatest tombstone in the whole world, reminding all the nations of the earth of Napoleon's glory and of England's shame, a shame which she brought upon herself when she sanctioned the deeds of Hudson Lowe.[1]

After visiting the valley of the Tomb, empty now of the mortal remains of the colossus of glory, after surveying the vault and the gaping grave which had given back to France the treasure that was hers alone, after listening to the stories told by the old English sergeant, the keeper of the place, and receiving from the hands of his young daughter a bouquet of field flowers, after drinking a cup of pure water from the spring which quietly bubbles twenty paces from the grave, after inscribing my name, like every other traveller, in the register handed to me by Madame Torbette, I set sail from Saint Helena and watched its 2 000 feet of stone disappear beneath the horizon.

The albatrosses, the Cape petrels, the *manches-de-velours,* the shoemakers, those light-hearted birds which bring cheer to the southern seas, were now more rarely to be seen. Soon they were no longer following in the vessel's wake. Once we had crossed the line, a cooling of the air indicated that we were approaching Europe. At last, after a journey of two months and a week, the *Sarah Charlotte* entered the strait which the English presume to call the British Channel. Here the winds thwarted us; we lay to for three terrible days and witnessed more than one shipwreck before there was a change in the weather. We weighed anchor and crossed the Pas de Calais, and the next day entered the Thames Estuary. Within a few more days, towards the end of November 1844, I was once again in France and surrounded by friends and family. At last I tasted the sweetness of homecoming, a delight which may be savoured only by those who have been a long time gone.

1 Sir Hudson Lowe the English general who was Napoleon's jailer on St. Helena. *Translator's note*

284

VOCABULARY OF THE ZOULOU LANGUAGE

Adulphe Delegorgue's *Vocabulaire de la Langue Zoulouse* is a remarkable find of particular interest to Bantu philologists. Part of its value is in its age: it is one of the earliest lists of vocabulary in the Nguni languages, and most probably the earliest Zulu list. The accounts of other early travellers do not include lists of vocabulary as Delegorgue does, though they often provide Zulu words and phrases, particularly the names of places, individuals, and clans. For example, in Nathaniel Isaacs' *Travels and Adventures in Eastern Africa* the phrase *'In yar mogoss imponte moonya'* = *'inyamakazi empondo munye'* [sub standard Zulu] = *'an antelope with (only) one horn'*. Another valuable aspect of the *Vocabulaire* is its length: this list totals more than 650 items, an impressive number for the first half of the nineteenth century, the more so in that these were collected by a naturalist explorer, who, we assume, was not a trained linguist.

At the time Delegorgue was writing, Zulu had never been written in a standardised form, and he has listed the Zulu items as they would have been spelt were they French. In other words, he has assigned letters to the various Zulu sounds on the basis of French sound/letter correspondence. At first glance the Zulu appears ludicrously inaccurate, but once one has worked out Delegorgue's system, one finds that not only was he extremely consistent in his rendering of Zulu, he also had a very good ear. Even subtleties (such as the formation of identificative copulatives) have been marked.

Of interest to students of language contact in South Africa is Delegorgue's inclusion of various Dutch words in the list of Zulu items. Some of these he has identified as adoptives ('loan words') by writing *'du Hollandais'* in brackets after the item. Others he apparently assumed to be Zulu words.

Of particular interest is the inclusion of phrases which are unquestionably examples of early 'Fanakalo'. This confounds current theories that Fanakalo was developed in the mines at the end of the nineteenth century, or that it was developed in the sugarcane fields in Natal from 1870 onwards.

Professors A.S. Davey and A. Koopman of the Department of Zulu, University of Natal, Pietermaritzburg, are at present doing an intensive analysis of the Delegorgue *Vocabularie*. They intend presenting papers on their research at a conference on African languages, and later publishing their findings.

A. Koopman

INTRODUCTORY REMARKS

It is very difficult to hear the vowel sounds at the beginning and, particularly, at the end of many words in the Zoulou language. To illustrate this, let us take the word *impoff* which can mean either the colour yellow or the antelope canna. This word may also be pronounced *impoffo, impoff, ompoffe, um poff, um poffo.*

I was given many different names for certain things; for example the word for 'river' could be any one of the following: *om-phlène, om-fèlene, om-philos, um-filos, om-volos, folos* or *volos,* and *volosie* or *om-pholosie.*

It would seem that many Amazoulous are principally concerned with euphony but this presents us with the enormous problem of too much latitude in interpretation.

A. Delegorgue

(The vocabulary was originally listed in alphabetical order of the French words. When the English equivalents were arranged in alphabetical order we found many duplications which we have attempted to rationalise.—*Translator*)

Zoulou	English
abantou maninkié	crowd of people
abantou zonké	the people
ahé mahmé!	alas!
ahi	no
ahi mounié	more, not one, none
ahi sinnda	easy
aibo	no
akôna kôna lapa	yonder
amaas, maazi	sour milk
amanga	to lie
amannzy	water
amâs, amaazy	fresh (soft) cheese
amba	to go, to walk, to depart
amba amannzy-ny	to bathe
amba apetcheïa	to cross (over), go the other way
amba fouty pezoulou	climb up again
amba gouschleg	farewell, goodbye to one who departs
amba insjhlé-ny	to walk, to proceed
amba kôna	to lead or tend to
amba kotjima-na-hache	to gallop
amba na hache	to ride a horse
amba pagaty	to enter
amba pannzy	to go down, descend
amba pannzy	to crawl

286

amba pezoulou	to climb
amba souty ka pagaty	to re-enter, return
ambasam	to accompany
ambylé	absent, away
amenschlo	a glance, look, stare
amenschlo	eyes
amphazy	woman, female
apetcheïa	that side
apetcheïa	after, behind, rear
baba	papa (father)
baba ka baba	forefather (fathers' father)
baléka	to decamp, to escape, to run away
balékylé	fugitive
bamba	to hold back, detain, confiscate
bamba (bambylë)	to catch, seize, grasp (caught)
bamba fouty	to catch again
bamba inïaho ka knouelé	to put the drag on a wagon wheel, to brake
bamba py mazignio	to bite
bassa om-lulo	to light the fire
baye-baye	cannon
bloulou	puff adder
bona	to see
bona fouty	to see again
bona kaschleg	to consider
bona mangapy	to measure
bôna pambylé	to foresee, to forecast
bonvo	red
bôpa	to tie up, knot
bosouko	night, darkness
bouïa	to come back
boulala	to murder, to kill, destroy
boulala	to crush, overpower, break
boulala py mouty	to poison
boulala py tonga	to fell, kill with a stick
boulongo	cow dung
bounn, amabounn	Dutch farmer, farmers
chiamounié, minamounié	nine
duur makar (from Dutch)	a mix-up
ébabale	antelope: *Sylvatica*
ebobiss	lion
édoubé	quagga
ekoikoye	green-crested touraco
elanga makaza	winter
empyss, empyssy	hyaena
etambo	bone
etambo laté pouma	to debone
faga	to take, hold, touch
fiaga, figylé	to arrive, come
figa fouty	to rejoin, to catch up
founa	to seek
founa tabata	to go and fetch
founa zonké kaschleg	to examine
foutimélé	hot, heat
foutiméle inkouzana	warm
foutimélé kakoulou	boiling
fouty	again
fylé	to pass away, to die

fylé	to decay, to decline
fyle amannzy-ny	to drown
galogo, tchouala ka amaloungo	brandy
gama	name, nickname
Ghismann	English
ghlébé	ear
gouassa	combat, fight, war
gouassa (gouassylé)	to wound with weapons (wounded)
gouassa py om-kondo	to thrust in an assegai
gouaye	tobacco
goudé	far
goula	sick, weak, ill
goumsso	the next day, tomorrow
goussassa	morning
goussina	chirping, warbling
goussina	to sing
hache	horse, pony
hamgâzy	blood
hamgazy pouma	to bleed
himphée	sugar-cane
hinndaho	form, shape
hinndaho	manner, custom, practice
hinndaho imbu	derangement
hinndaho ka koluma	dialect
hinnhiaho	track, footprint, foot
hinyaho	wheel
hyazy	power, force
hyazy	to know
hyazy	memory
hynzoey	country, land, region
hynzoey ka téna, hynzoey ka abantou Mouniama	Africa (our land, the land of the black men)
Hynzoey ka abaloungo	Europe
hyophéha	gonorrhea
hyshlizio	heart, conscience
hyshlizio goula	affliction, distress (emotional)
hyssla	to graze, to feed, to eat
hyssla	feast
hythié	wish, consent, inclination
hythié	rock, stone
hythié mouschlé: om-schlopu, bonvo, impoffo	agate: white, red, yellow
hyza, hôza	to come
hyzoua	to understand, to hear
ibaye *ou* embaaly	plant
iebo	yes
ïena	he, him
ignama	meat, flesh
ignamazane	wild animal, game, meat
ikoalakoala	pheasant, francolin
ikoé	ostrich
ikomba	skin
ikomba ka inglobu	pork rind (or skin)
ikomba sebensylé	sheepskin
ikota	seven
imbâly	flower
imbaly founa	to gather plants

imbu	puny, worthless
imbu kakoulou	horrible (very ugly)
imbu, mombu	bad, evil
imphana (abafanas)	son, boy (young men)
imponnzy	he-goat
indihi	thin
indja	dog
ingané	child
ingané nonina	suckling child
inglobu	wild boar, pig
ingoniama	lion
ingouenïa	crocodile
inianga	diviner, soothsayer, doctor, wizard, sorcerer
inianga	moon, lunar month
iniaty	buffalo
inié	alone, single, only
inioucé	honey
iniouka	turning, circuitous road, bend (of river)
iniouka	snake
iniouné	bird
inkâbu	ox
inkinani moutou mannschla	strapping, vigorous
inkinany	little [adj], thin, fine
inkinany	small, inconsiderable
inkinany-pannzy	low, down
inkomo	cow
inkomokazy	cattle, heifer
inkoniana	calf
inkonnzy	bull
inkoskazy	princess, wife, lady
inkossiny	prince, king
inkossy, om-kos	chief
inkouné	log, fire-wood
inkouzana	singular, scarce, little [adv]
innaoé	pipe
inndaho	manner, style, way
inndjalo	always, still
inngua	panther
innza	to make up, to form, to do
innza fouty	to begin again, to do again
innza souty	to fill
innza souty fouty	to recharge
insjhlé	road, way
insjhlé amannzy na ka omphléne	ford (in a river)
intombazane	little girl
intombu	young girl
inzindgé	thus, like this
iploup-loulou	masked barbet (*Pogonias personnatus*)
ischlâno	five
ischlou	room, house
ischlozy	porcupine
isithia	dish, cup
isseboom	gun
isseva	calabash (for eating)
istoupa	six
itchouba	fowl
itchoumé chiamounié	ninety

itchoumé cobambili	eighty
itchoumé istoupa	sixty
itchoumé izambili	twenty
itchoumé izitatou	thirty
itkaguety	mongoose, weasel
izikomba	pelts, furs
izikova	owl
izimkopo	cafre guitar
izinianga tchoumé izambili mouva	year (ten moons plus two)
izithia	dish
izolo	yesterday
izolo pambylé	the day before yesterday
ka	no
ka	of
ka	nothing
ka amanga	to lie, to contradict (no, it is not true)
ka panslé/pannzlé	outside, beyond
ka téna	our
kaïa	house, hut
kalogo	now
kam-kam	rain, shower
kam-kam om-schlopu	snow
kant	face, head
kaschleg	enough, well [adv]
kaschlegh	fair, proper, exact
kaschlegh	peaceful, peacefully
kaschlegh	thanks
kinngane, tchoumé	ten, about ten
kissa (kissylé)	to flame, to burn, burnt
kissa ignama mafouta ny	to fry
knaba	a refusal, to refuse
knaba	to disown, to retract
knala	antelope: *Redunca Lalandii*
knema	to divide, separate
knema	to slice, cut, gash
knema	to knock/strike down, to fell
knema ikomba ka om-tondo	to circumcise
knema kant ka moutou	to decapitate
knema py zympy	to chop, to hew
knouélé	carriage, wagon, cart, vehicle
kodouka	to return
koluma	speech, address, discussion
koluma (kolumylé)	to confer (discussed)
koluma	account, story, language, a speech
koluma	to talk, chatter, prattle
Kos-Pezou	God
kôta	copper
kotchima, kotjima	to hasten, come running
kotjima	rapid, fast
kotlissa	to coax
kotlissa (kotlissylé)	to deceive, catch out, deceived
kouatylé	angry
kouko	bed, mat
koulou	a hundred
koulou mouné	four hundred
lala	sleep, to doze
lambylé	hungry

landa	egret: *Ardea bubuleus*
langa	sun, day
langa ambylé	evening
langa pezoulou	midday
langa pouma	dawn
lâpa	here
laté	to leave, quit
laté bôna	to show
laté izinkabu pouma	to unyoke
lâté schlala	to leave, leave alone, remain
lo	the, this, that, which
loanslé	sea
louto	baggage, bagage
mabelé	cafre corn
mabelé om-schlopu	rice
mabily, izambily	two, both
madada	duck, teal
madada om-koulou	goose
mafouta	tallow, fat, lard
mafouta	grease for the face
mafouta	fat, corpulent, obese
mafouta ka inkomo	butter
mafouta ka etambo	marrow
mafouta ka mounty	oil
mafouta ka om-lulo	candle
mafouta ka schlannza	soap
mahlé	money
mahmé	mama, mother
makakoye	leguaan, lizard
makanda	egg
makanque	antelope: *Strepsiceros coudou*
makaza	cold
makazane	tick
mananty	delicious
mangapy	how much
manghetjanne	wild dog, cynhyene
Mangish	English
maninkié	plenty, many (hundreds)
maninkié kakoulou	considerably
mannschla	strong, firm, muscular, vigorous
mannschla ka gouassa	warlike (adept at stabbing)
matatou	three
mazignio	tooth, jaw
mazima	cultivated field, garden
ména	me
mena ahi schlala na lo	to have: this verb is not used as we [the French] use it. 'I have not got that' would be expressed as 'I do not remain with that'.
menschlo	eye
mlomo	mouth
moïa	air, breath, wind, puff
moïa om-koulou py kam-kam	storm, tempest
mombu, imbu	ugly, misshapen
mombu om-phogazane	mean/contemptible
monkomb	antelope: *Cephalopus natalensis*
monkomb	hare

monkongo	oriole
montou, abantou	man, men
montou fylé	dead, defunct
montou om-koulou kakoulou	giant
motgea	cafre garb
mouné	salt
mouné iné	four
mouniama	black
mouniama	dark, dim
mounié	one
mounié tchoumé mounié mouva	eleven (ten plus one)
mounty	tree
mouschlé	easy, accommodating, pleasing
mouschlé	beautiful, fine, nice, pretty
mouschlé kakoulou	wonderful, admirable, superb
mouty	medicine, poison, drug
mouzi	homestead
nannzy, nangou	here, there
nemschla	today
niannaty	letter (a message)
nika	to grant, give
nika betaye (from the Dutch)	to pay
nika fouty	to give back
nika hyssla montou	to feed a man
ninkié	several
niouka	mother
nogoty	hole, cave, chasm
nogoty	underground
nogôty hythié ny	cave (hole in rocks)
nohounnda	giraffe
ny	in
oâmi, sâmi	my, mine
om-betjanne	rhinoceros
om-bïha, om-byla	maize
om-dala	old (or old man)
om-doango	cloth, rag, handkerchief
om-doango	linen, cotton cloth
om-doda	man, husband
om-doda mannschla	courageous
om-douna	headman, captain, officer
om-douna ka inkossiny	king's aide de camp
om-gâane	sir, master
om-gobo	clothes, dress
om-kaho	monkey
om-koloani	hornbill
om-kômas	buffalo female
om-komo	whole
om-kondo	assegai, javelin, knife
om-kopo	calabash (as container)
om-kos, om-kossy	master
om-kouko	hen, fowl, cock
om-koulou	large, spacious, huge, wide
om-koulou, kakoulou	immense, enormous
om-koulou	rich, great
om-kouschlouane	wild fig
om-kuytchélo	bow, arch
om-lomo	mouth (animal)

om-lulo	fire
om-lulo ka pezoulou	lightning
om-luloana	fire (colour of fire)
om-pêto	worm
om-phéne	baboon
om-phléne, om-philos	river
om-phogazane	wretch, outcast
om-phondiss	preacher
om-poff	blond, fair
om-poff, om-poffo	African eland
om-poffane	yellowish
om-poffo	yellow
om-pomolo	nose, nostril
om-pomolo	trunk of an elephant
om-pondo	horn
om-pondo ka uncklove	ivory
om-pouko	rat
om-poulou	flour
om-schlaba	soil, earth, ground
om-schlaba bonvo	clay
om-schlabatsi	sand, grit
om-schlanga	shield
om-schlanga	reed
om-schlango	antelope: *Eleotragus*
om-schlanvo ka baye-baye	bullet, cannon ball
om-schlanvo	bullet
om-schlâzy .	sweet potatoes
om-schloaty	wild celery
om-schloazy	green
om-schlobo	cafre bean growing underground
om-schlohahy	bird-shot
om-schlopu	white
om-schlouno	genitals of female, vulva
om-tâba	hill, mountain
om-tagaty	murder, homicide
om-tagaty	tyrant, wizard
om-tagaty	to murder, murderer, killer
om-tagaty	villain, scoundrel, traitor, spy
om-tagaty	destroyer, ravager
om-tagaty boulala	to curse, to sentence
om-tagaty	massacre, slaughter
om-tini	louse
om-tondo	genitals of male, penis
om-vobo	hippopotomus
om-vooty	otter
om-zizy	gun powder
om-zizy ka pannzlé	priming of gun
omoucé	Le Vaillant's caterpillar destroyer
omounié mounié	each one
omounié, omounié fouty	the one, the other
omounié pambylé	first, foremost
omounié montou	someone
omounié fouty	another
ou bani?	what? which? which one?
ou-bany	who, which

293

ouako	your
oubiss	sweet milk
ouéna	you
pagaty	inside
pambylé	former, previous, formerly
pambylé	in front of, before
pambylé filé	to be at the point of death
pannda	food
pannda kakoulou	excellent, best
pannzlé	outside
pezou	above, on
pézou, pézoulou	above
pezoulou ka mouty	tree top
pongolo	box, chest, cask
pongolo	bucket
ponnzy	gazelle
ponsa	to throw
pouma	to go out
pouma ka lala	to awake
poussa	to drink
py	with
saba ka makaza	susceptible to cold
sango	hemp for smoking
sani gouschleg	goodbye to one who remains
scap (from Dutch)	sheep
schlaba	to prick, to sting
schlabonka	to copulate, copulation
schlala	to live in, to inhabit, to stay, to remain
schlala pannzy	to lie down
schlannza	to sweep, to wash, to clean
schlannza fouty	to polish again
schlannza py mafouta	annoint
schlaty	a wood, the bush
schloutann-zébé	a bat
sebensa	to make, to fashion
sebensa	work, to work, labour, toil
sebensa	to operate, to perform
sebensa om-koulou	to enlarge, augment
sebensa py tambo	to sew up
sebensa zonké	to govern, manage
sibylo	antimony
sina	song or dance
sina	festival, holiday
singuela	hunt, to hunt, to go hunting
sinnda	solid, massive, heavy
sinnda	well, healthy
sinnda	dense, thick
sinnqua	bread, biscuit
sitébé	plate of plaited straw for serving meat
sondagh (from Dutch)	Sunday
souty ka isséboom	charge of a gun
souty	full
suepp (from Dutch)	whip
sylo	panther
symba	genet

symba	warrior's dress
tabata	to take away, to bring
tabata fouty	to bring back
tabâta	to supply, procure
tambo	thong, strap
tambo	rope, string
tambo	thread, wire
tanta	to desire, to want
tanta	to love dearly, to cherish
tanta	to like, love
tchiahia	to beat, hit, strike
tchiahia	to strike a blow, beat
tchiahia isseboom (or better) tobouïa	to shoot with a gun
tchïahia, tobouïa	to fire a gun
tchouala	beer
tchouala ka abaloungo	wine, brandy
tchouala ka inioucé	mead (for drinking), liqueur
tchoumé-ischlâno	fifty
tchoumé istoupa mouva	sixteen
tchoumé matatou mouva	thirteen
tchoumé mouné mouva	fourteen
tèla	to say
téla amanga	to deny
téla (dankie) (from Dutch)	to thank
téla fouty	to repeat, to recount, tell
téla gama	to name
têla imbu ka montou	to speak ill of a man
téla pambylé	to warn, to precede, to inform
téna	we
thiathia	to hurry
thiathia kotjima	to make haste
tinga	a purchase, to purchase
tinga (tingylé)	barter, trade, exchange (exchanged)
tinga	to sell, sole
tinga-intombu	to marry (to buy) a young girl
tingou	drongo
tola	to gather, to find, to obtain
tola	to put
tôla, (tolylé)	to raise, raised
tola ka pannzy	to pick up
tôla pannzy	to lower, put down, to drag
tonga inkinany	rod, stick
tonga	wooden rod, staff, stick
touboula	to pound, to crush
toula	to silence, silence
toula	to hide
tounga	wooden milk pot
uncklove	elephant
uncklovedoane	boar of the plain
vaala	to close
vaala fouty	to close again
vaâla	door
vouma	consent, to consent
vouma	to assert, declare
vouma	to confess, confession, consent

yako	his, hers
yebo (Dingaan!)	surely, certainly (by Dingaan)
yssyo	panther
zannzy	beneath
zannzy	this side
zonké, zonka	all
zonké	entire, whole, complete
zonké mouniama	complete darkness
zoulou	to thunder, thunder-bolt
zympy	iron
zympy ka knema mounty	axe (to cut trees)
zympy ka om-schlanvo	lead

TAXONOMIC SECTION

A NOTE ON THE LISTS OF SPECIES

INSECTS AND BIRDS

There are no extant lists of the various vertebrate species, let alone of the hundreds, perhaps thousands, of vertebrate specimens – reptilian, avian, mammalian – with which Delegorgue returned to France. The lists appended here include only insects, followed by descriptions of two bird species.

Those with an interest in ornithology – especially those to whom the name Delegorgue was hitherto associated only with 'Delegorgue's pigeon', that is, the bronzenaped pigeon, *Columba delegorguei*, will wish at once to turn to the birds (p329). Although specialists may already have gone to the original and translated for themselves Delegorgue's descriptions of the pigeon (his 'dusky turtledove') and of the harlequin quail, *Coturnix delegorguei* (the 'Oury quail'), these will have been unavailable and/or inaccessible to the general reader, and for this reason have been rendered in English. The descriptions appear to have been intended as preliminary notes, written in Delegorgue's typical discursive style, blending detail and reminiscence, and, though colourful, without great regard for taxonomic exactitude or completeness. He apparently expected an authority (unnamed) to prepare definitive descriptions later on, and so cheerfully named the birds after himself in anticipation. Unfortunately, once a description, however sketchy, is in print, it stands. The birds could never again be described and named for the first time, and Delegorgue is thus the authority for these two species which carry his name – paradoxically breaking and upholding the rules of nomenclature at one and the same time.

Although Delegorgue refers several times in the text to intense periods of insect collecting, and mentions at least five of the major insect orders, the appended lists are of only three of these. The lists of beetles (*Catalogue des Insectes Coléoptè*res, some 1400 species, p317) and of two-winged flies (*Diptères,* 37 species, p328) are presented in facsimile: there is no associated descriptive material and they will probably be of interest only to specialists – and even to the latter they may now have little more than curiosity value; they are included for the sake of completeness.

The Catalogue of Lepidoptera (p300) may have wider appeal for two reasons. First, there are detailed descriptions of many butterflies and moths, a number of which include comments on distribution and biology, as well as some references to relevant local customs. In translating the descriptions into English the greatest care has been taken to preserve the style and character of the original as well as the pictorial quality of the writing. The reader may initially be irked by the absence of illustrations, which would have enhanced understanding and perhaps elucidated some of the lepidopteran terminology, but the writing is clear and colourful enough for this not to be a serious disadvantage.

A second point of interest relates to authorship. For as one reads one apprehends that these descriptions are stylistically very different from the main body of the text, from the bird descriptions mentioned above, and even from the remarks introducing the entomological section (p300). The language, while it is by no means modern, is that of a practised taxonomist – terse, precise, at times almost telegraphic. Further, the author consistently uses names and terms that never appear elsewhere in the work: for example, where the text always, and incorrectly, refers to 'Mimosa', the Catalogue correctly uses Acacia. In short, there are strong indications that the author of the Catalogue was not Delegorgue.

If Delegorgue did not prepare the Catalogue of Lepidoptera that appears under his name, who did? The author is not far to seek: his is the name which appears most frequently as authority, the oft-mentioned 'we' who refers to 'our' Faune de Madagascar (in which Delegorgue had no part), and who actually reveals himself at the end of the description of Saturnia Wahlbergii. This is Jean Baptiste A.D. de Boisduval (1799–1879), in the Catalogue usually abbreviated to 'Boisd.'. Serious students of the history of southern African entomology, especially lepidopterists familiar with the rest of Boisduval's work, have apparently long recognised him as the author of the Delegorgue Catalogue. It is both entertaining and satisfying, however, to have arrived at the same conclusion via a different, more literary and more generally biological route. It is also tempting, but beyond the scope of this note, to speculate upon how and why Boisduval's descriptions of Delegorgue's insects came to be published under Delegorgue's name.

It is hoped that this may pique the interest of the non-specialist reader, who, in dipping into the Catalogue, may begin to wonder about other enigmatic-looking names, some of them abbreviated. 'Linn.' and 'Fab.', for example, are abridgements of two names fundamental to taxonomy in general and that of insects in particular: Linnaeus and Fabricius are given separate entries in the Natural History Index. 'Cram.' is Pieter Cramer, who, with Caspar Stoll (also listed), published a major work on exotic Lepidoptera in Dutch and French (1775–1782).

Jacob Hübner ('Hub.': 1761–1826) described many African Lepidoptera and published a large work on the subject, while Johann C.F. Klug (1775–1865) of the Naturkunde-Museum in Berlin described *inter alia* Lepidoptera collected by Ludwig Krebs at the Cape. 'God.' was probably Jean Baptiste Godart (1775–1825), who collected and described Lepidoptera from all over the world. The three English authorities mentioned are one Drury (1725–1803), a wealthy London court jeweller, who collected and described mainly West African Lepidoptera, and also Henry Doubleday (1809–1875) and William Chapman Hewitson (1806–1878). The former is noted for his *List of Specimens of Lepidopterous Insects in the Collection of the British Museum*, and *The Genera of Diurnal Lepidoptera*, with plates furnished by Hewitson. Other authorities are less easy to identify. 'Ehrenberg' may have been C.G. Ehrenberg (1795–1876) who collected insects in North Africa, while 'Goudot' was probably Justin Goudot (dates unknown) who both made and dealt in insect collections. Only 'Sganzin' remains untraced. Other abbreviations are of the titles of various publications, and letters and numbers refer, presumably, to illustrations in those works.

It is hoped that, with the aid of this explanatory note, the Catalogue of Lepidoptera will afford the general reader a glimpse into the world of taxonomy, the orderly arangement, division and subdivision of living things based upon characteristics they consistently possess. This will, perhaps, be assisted by the more expansive style of an earlier time, unconstrained by problems of space and expense. Modern taxonomic writing is governed by strict formal economy of expression and employs a technical argot and conventions which may render it virtually incomprehensible to the uninitiated.

S.J.A.

ENTOMOLOGY

The study of the collections, the fruits of my travels, not being yet complete, nor likely to be so soon, I have included here only a list of a number of the insects so as to provide, in a synoptic tabulation, a brief account of the species living in eastern and southern Africa, which may assist the studies of entomologists who follow me.

An account of the birds, of which I collected a large number of specimens, will be the subject of a separate publication, one too large to be included here as an appendix. I have therefore limited myself to descriptions of two new species, both called after me by the authority whose studies of this material have yet to be published.[1]

A.D.

CATALOGUE OF THE LEPIDOPTERA

Collected by M. Delegorgue

during the years 1838 to 1844
at Port Natal, in the land of the Amazoulous
and in the country of Massilicatzi

Descriptions translated from the French
by
D.W. Ewer

Formerly Professor and Head of the Department of Zoology and
Entomology, Rhodes University, Grahamstown, South Africa, and of
the Department of Zoology, University of Ghana, Legon, Accra.

RHOPALOCERA[2]

1. **Papilio Lalandei** Boisd., *Sp.*, p. 326 — Port Natal.
   Found by the late M. Lalande[3] in the Land of the Hottentots and also in
   Madagascar by M. Goudot.

2. **Papili Demoleus** Linn.[3] Very common everywhere.

3. **Papilio Brutus** Boisd., *Sp.*, p. 221 — Bay of Port Natal.

4. **Papili Lyaeus** Doubleday *Nireus*, Cram. 378, F. G. — Bay of Port Natal.
   Already known from the Cape of Good Hope.

5. **Papilio Nireus** Linn. — Port Natal.
   Common on the west coast, but not extending as far north as Senegal.

6. **Papilio Antheus** Cram. 234, B. C. — Bay of Port Natal.

7. **Papilio Policenes** Cram. 37, A. B. — Bay of Port Natal.

8. **Papilio Cenea** Stoll, pl. 29. — Bay of Port Natal
   The specimen figured by Stoll was brought back from Cafrerie by Levaillant.[3]

9. **Papilio Zenobius** Boisd., *Spec.*, p. 366 — Country of the Amazoulous.
   Also found in the land of the Ashanti.[4]

10. **Pontia Narica** Fab.[3] *Ent. syst.* — Country of the Amazoulous
Common in *mimosa* woodland.

11. **Pieris Gidica** God. — Bay of Port Natal
In most of the specimens collected in Natal, the underside of the wings in both sexes is a uniform yellow. In some females, however, the upper surface of all four wings is a bright yellow-ochre, while in females from the western seaboard of the African continent[5] it is almost always white.

12. **Pieris Calypso** Cram. 154, C. D. E. F. — Bay of Port Natal.
The females are highly variable.

13. **Pieris Creona** Cram. 95, C. D. E. F. — Bay of Port Natal.
Common on the western seaboard especially in Senegal.

14. **Pieris Zochalia** Boisd., *Sp.* Country of the Amazoulous.
We have also received specimens from the country of the Hottentots.

15. **Pieris Severina**. Cram. 338. G. H. — Bay of Port Natal.
This species shows colour variations similar to those found in *Gidica*.

16. **Pieris Mesentina** Cram. 270. A, B.
This species appears to occur throughout inter-tropical and southern Africa.

17. **Pieris Agathina** Cram. 237, D. E. — Bay of Port Natal.
Also found on Zanzibar.

18. **Pieris Phileris** Boisd., *Sp* — The land of Massilicatzi.
Found on Madagascar by the late M. Sganzin.

19. **Pieris Charina** Boisd., *Sp.* — Bay of Port Natal.

20. **Pieris Chloris** Fab. — Port Natal.
Also found over the greater part of the west side of the continent.

21. **Pieris Hellica** Linn. — Bay of Port Natal.

22. **Pieris Pigea** Boisd., *Sp.* — Land of the Amazoulous.

23. **Anthocharis Evarne** Klug., *Symb. phys.*
The specimens from the land of the Amazoulous differ from those described by Ehrenberg from Dongola[6] which are similar to those from Senegal. The present specimens are much bigger and the background colour of the wings of both sexes is a brilliant sulphur-yellow. The markings on the female are also more pronounced than on those from Senegal and Dongola. This species is not uncommon.

24. **Anthocharis Danae**. Fab. — Land of the Amazoulous.
The specimens we already have from the land of the Hottentots are about one-third bigger than those found in Bengal; the base of all four wings is dusted in grey as in the specimen illustrated by MM. Doubleday and Hewitson in their *Genera*.

25. **Anthocharis Achine** Cram. 338, E. F.
This attractive species is distributed from the Cape of Good Hope to Delagoa Bay. The specimens from Natal are in no way different from those illustrated by Cramer and Hubner.

26. **Anthocaris Omphale** Boisd., *Sp.*, p. 575. — Land of the Amazoulous.

This is slightly more abundant than *Achine*, although the latter is by no means rare. The female, so far not described, differs from the male in so far as the black colouration is stronger, while the red band at the apex of the forewings is slightly paler and divided by a transverse black streak.

27. **Anthocharis Ione** Boisd., *Sp.* — Bay of Port Natal.

Before this expedition, this species was poorly represented in collections. The few known specimens had been taken in Ethiopia and Senegal. It is quite common throughout Natal.

The female is markedly different from the male: not only are the wings more extensively edged in black, but the apex of the forewings shows a tawny stripe formed from five rectangular spots, separated from each other by black streaks. On the under-surface, the hind-wings are of a yellow ground colour, as are the tips of the forewings, while the costa is saffron; there is a black spot on the discoidal cell. Further, on all four wings, a continuous, sinuous, blackish streak runs from the black spot to the wing tip; this streak is rather like that in *Eris* but less broken.

It is convenient to mention here another female *Anthocaris* collected along with *Ione* at the same times and in the same places, but far more abundant than the one we have just described. We have seen no males which can be related to these specimens. This leads us to conclude that they should be regarded as a variety of the female of *Ione* which they resemble as far as the lower wing surfaces are concerned. The upper surfaces, however, more closely resemble female *Eris* in lacking any tawny marking at the tips of the forewings which are completely black, apart from three or four small white or whitish yellow spots.

28. **Anthocharis Eris** Boisd., *Sp.* — Land of the Amazoulous.

This species is slightly less common than the preceding one. The individuals we have examined are similar to those from Nubia and Senegal.

29. **Idmais Vesta** Boisd., unpublished. — Land of the Amazoulous.

The female of this beautiful species was illustrated by MM. Doubleday and Hewitson in their *Genera*, pl. 7, f. 5, as the female of Klug's *Chrysonome*.

30. **Dryas Leda** Boisd., unpublished. — Land of the Amazoulous.

This charming species is at the moment the sole representative of a new genus between *Anthocharis* and *Eronia*. This new genus displays the fragile structure of species of the former genus and some of the generic characteristics of the latter from which it does not differ except that the hairs of the palps are denser and the wings are entire.

Dryas Leda is about the same size as *Callidryas Marcellina*. All four wings are of a bright yellow, especially striking in the male, with a large triangular marking of a bright, tawny red at the apex of the forewings. The under-surface of the wings is of nearly the same yellow as that of the upper surface, with some brown streaks and marbling on the hind pair, both more marked on the costa and near the middle. In some specimens there is a small round brown spot with a white centre near the anal angle of these latter, as well as at the apex of the forewings.

The female is a light sulphur-yellow with the apex of the forewings a pale tawny colour, broken by six rust-coloured spots.

This most attractive species is found also in Abyssinia, but the specimens from this latter country are about a third smaller than those we have received from Natal.

31. **Eronia Cleodora** Hubn. — Bay of Port Natal.

Very common in *mimosa* woodland.

32. **Eronia Buquetii** Boisd., *Sp.* — Land of the Amazoulous.

33. **Callidryas Florella** Boisd., *Sp.* — Bay of Port Natal.

34. **Callidryas Rhadia** Boisd., *Sp.* — Bay of Port Natal.

35. **Colias Electra** Boisd., *Sp.* — Bay of Port Natal.

36. **Terias Brigitta** Boisd., *Sp.* — Land of the Amazoulous.

37. **Zeritis Manticles** Boisd. — Land of the Amazoulous.

38. **Lycaena Lingeus** Cram. — Land of the Amazoulous.

39. **Lycaena Thespis** God. — Bay of Port Natal.

40. **Lycaena Asteris** God. — Bay of Port Natal.

41. **Lycaena Parsimon** God. — Bay of Port Natal.

42. **Lycaena Gambius** Boisd. — Bay of Port Natal.

43. **Lycaena Emolus** God. — Land of the Amazoulous.

44. **Lycaena Boetica** Linn. — Land of the Amazoulous.

45. **Lycaena Delegorguei** Boisd. — Land of Massilicatzi.
    This delightful species, which will unquestionably be a new genus, is of about the same size as the European *Polyom.*[7] *xanthe.*[8]
    The upper surface of the male is a uniform brown but with a grey edge. That of the female is also brown but with a whitish spot in the middle of each wing and the discoidal cell a more or less violet grey; the edge is whitish with a few flecks of brown. The under-surface of the wings is a greyish brown in the male, a whitish grey in the female, with a brown pattern formed of spots, each of which is flecked by tiny dots of silver at the edges. This pattern on the hind wing is partly formed of a transverse band running from the outer margin to the middle of the inner margin, but also of two spots on the costa and a row of more clearly defined marginal spots lying within some other very indistinct brown markings. The pattern on the forewings consists of three or four discoidal spots and a row of marginal dots. The legs are very hairy; the antennae short, with an elongated club, while the palps are concealed and strongly divergent.

46. **Tingra Tropicalis** Boisd., unpublished. — Bay of Port Natal.
    This species, found also in Ashantiland, forms the type of a new African genus of Lycaenid.
    It resembles *Acraea punctatissima* from Madagascar both in appearance and size. All four wings are of yellow-ochre, with a round, dark brown spot on the discoidal cell, often with smaller spots of the same colour just in front. The forewings have, moreover, a black edging at the apex and the costa is more or less dusted with brown. In one specimen from Ashanti the apex and outer margin are completely edged in black; in the specimens from Natal, the edging is shorter and broken up into spots near the internal angle. The under-surface of the wings is of a yellow ochre, with scattered black dots and dusted with particles of the same colour. It is possible that the specimen from Natal is different from that from the West Coast of Africa; but this cannot be resolved with two individuals of different sexes. The one here described is female.

47. **Euploea Ochlea** Boisd. — Bay of Port Natal.
    This species is also found in Zanzibar. It is slightly smaller than *Niavia*. The

304

upper surface of the wings is black, with a large white spot on the discoidal cell of the hind-wings and two or three small spots of the same colour on the outer margin. The forewings have a large white mark in the middle; this extends neither to the costa nor the inner margin and is divided into three almost equal parts by the median vein. At the tip of the wing there are three further white spots which are joined transversely, two white dots near the costa and three marginal spots, likewise white. The pattern of the under-surface is very similar but the hind wings have a basal white spot and two marginal rows of white dots.

48. **Euploea Echeria** Stoll — Bay of Port Natal.
The specimens collected in Natal differ from those brought back from Cafrerie by the late M. Levaillant in so far as the markings on the front wings are always white and not a pale ochre yellow like the stripe on the hind wings.

49. **Acraea Petraea** Boisd., unpublished. — Port Natal.
This is of the same size as *Horta*. The upper wing surfaces are of a slightly pale brick-red, with black margins, which colour extends over the veins. The costa and veins of the forewings are black; a sinuous transverse black band lies between the middle and the apex and, running from the costa to the base, which is more or less smoky, are five or six spots of the same colour. On the upper surface of the hind-wings are, extending from the base to the middle, about 20 black dots, some of which are joined together. On the undersurface the wings are paler and more roseate, with black veins; the margins of the hind wings are divided by a series of whitish spots, lying behind a row of tawny spots. Further, among the black dots at the base, there are some tawny spots. The female is much duller than the male and on the forewings, between the apex and the sinuous band, there is a white oval spot divided up by the veins.
This species is very common around Port Natal.

50. **Acraea Sganzini** Boisd., *f. de Mad.* — Port Natal.
This species is as common in Natal as in Madagascar. However, instead of being of a pale yellow ochre, as in the latter country, it is invariably of a tawny yellow, with a very white apical band.

51. **Acraea Stitica** Boisd., unpublished. — Land of the Amazoulous.
This *Acraea* is probably only a local variety of *Punctatissima* from Madagascar. It differs only in that the spots are larger.

52. **Acraea Cynthia** Drury — Land of the Amazoulous.

53. **Acraea Serena** Fab. — Port Natal.

54. **Acraea Nohara** Boisd., unpublished. — Port Natal.
This is of about the size of *Horta* while it resembles *Rahira* in appearance. We have seen only a single specimen. The upper surface of the wings is of a dark, tawny yellow with a black margin edged with white; this margin is very narrow on the front wings and extends along the veins to the middle. The front wings have also, lying between the middle and the apex, a short, black, transverse band arising from the costa, while on the basal side there are three black spots over the discoidal cell. The hind-wings carry, between the base and the middle, a dozen scattered large, black spots. The lower surface is paler than the upper, especially that of the hind-wings which are of a yellowish hue with the edging broken by a row of spots of the background colour and also tawny marks between the black spots.

55. **Acraea Rahira** Boisd., *f. de Madag* — Port Natal.

56. **Acraea Hypatia** Drur. — Port Natal.
The specimens collected in Natal are paler than those from the west coast of

Africa: they are close to a variety illustrated by Stoll, pl. 25. fig. 4, given the name of *Artemisa*.

57. **Acraea natalica** Boisd., unpublished. — Bay of Port Natal.

This has the same appearance as the preceding species, but is larger. The upper surface of the four wings is darker than that of normal specimens of *Hypatia*; that is, more or less reddish-brown except for the apex of the forewings where the coloration is paler. The pattern of the upper surfaces is rather like that of *Hypatia*. Although the spots on the hind-wings are rather more numerous than those on the forewings, they are distributed in a similar fashion; they form, however, only two arrays while on the costa of the forewings there is a narrow, black, rectangular mark. The lower wing surfaces are much lighter in colour than the upper, being of a pinkish hue, with spotting similar to that on the upper surfaces. Here, however, the rectangular mark is absent and the margin of the hind wings is divided by a set of seven white spots next to a row of tawny, wedge-shaped marks. There are also tawny spots near the base of these wings.

We have seen only a single specimen and would not be surprised if the rectangular marking we mentioned were only accidental.

58. **Acraea Violarum** Boisd., unpublished. — Port Natal.

This is of the same colour as *Violae* from Bengal but has the appearance and wing-shape of *Hypatia*. The spots on the forewings are more abundant than in *Violae*. They form, near the apex, a row which is not found in that species, and there is no saw-toothed border as in *Violae*. The hind-wings have a black margin, rather as in *Violae* but somewhat crenellated and broken by a row of spots of a yellowish white. On their surface there are about a dozen large, scattered, black spots of about the same size as those on the forewings. The lower surface is of about the same colour as the upper and shows the same pattern. The spots which divide the marginal marking of the hind-wings are, however, larger and whiter and the apex of the forewings is marked with two of three small, white spots. Thus, although this species has some resemblance to *Violae*, it is distinct from *Hypatia*.

59. **Acraea Horta** Linn. — Port Natal.

60. **Acraea Amazoula** Boisd., unpublished. — Land of the Amazoulous.

This acraeid, the smallest that we know, differs from all other African species in the absence of spotting. The antennae are very short and thick and the discoidal cell of the hind-wing has a shape not found in any other of the species from this ancient continent. We think that it should form the type of a new genus which we will call *Aloena*. It is of a uniform ochre-yellow with the costa, the margin and the veins black, more markedly in the male than in the female. The margin is saw-toothed with an edge of whitish grey. The lower surface of the wings is a whitish yellow ochre, with all the veins black; but there is no black margin, only a narrow stripe which separates the edge which is of the background colour. The discoidal cell of the front wings is less pale and almost as yellow as the upper surface. In the male, which is slightly smaller than the female, the body is blackish, but the abdomen and [prothoracic] collar are yellow-ochre.

61. **Hypanis illythia** Cram. — Port Natal.

62. **Hypanis Anvatara** Boisd., *f. de Madag.* — Land of the Amazoulous.

63. **Eurytela Hyarba** Cram. — Port Natal.

64. **Eurytela Dryope** Cram. — Port Natal.

65. **Cynthia Anacardii** Linn. — Port Natal.

66. **Salamis Cloantha** Cram. — Land of the Amazoulous.

67. **Salamis Archesia** Cram. — Land of Massilicatzi.

68. **Salamis Ceryne** Boisd., unpublished. — Land of the Amazoulous.
    This species has almost the appearance and size of our *Vanessa urticae*. As to facies, it resembles the female of *Andremiaja* described on p. 45 of our *Faune de Madagascar*. The front wings are dentate, slightly pointed; the hind-wings are similar but lack the prolongation in the form of a tail as in related species. The upper surface of both wings is brown and crossed close to the apex by a continuous stripe which is a pale yellow ochre on its inner side and tawny on the outer. On the forewings this stripe is bifid anteriorly, enclosing four white spots, while the tawny edge bears a row of black spots. The hind-wings have two whitish or rather pale yellow-ochre spots near the base. The margin on both surfaces is divided by a series of bluish white lenticular marks. The under-surface of the wings is a tawny yellow brown with the stripe much paler, almost white, as are also the spots at the base and the marginal lenticular marks.

69. **Salamis Pelarga** Drury — Port Natal.

70. **Vanessa Cardui** Linn. — Everywhere.

71. **Vanessa Amestris** Drury — Land of Massilicatzi.

72. **Vanessa Oenone** Linn. — Found everywhere.

73. **Vanessa Clelia** Cram. — Found everywhere.

74. **Vanessa Octavia** Cram. — Land of Massilicatzi.
    We have seen only three specimens of this beautiful species.

75. **Argynnis Phalanta** Fab. — Port Natal.

76. **Adolias Meleagris** Cram. — Land of Massilicatzi.

77. **Euriphene Coerulea** Boisd., unpublished. — Port Natal.
    This new species has the appearance and size of *Guineensis*; the colour of the upper surface of its wings is a deep blue, as in the species illustrated by Cramer pl. 323, F.C., under the name *Veronica*. The pattern near the tips of all four wings is formed, as in *Guineensis*, by a row of oval markings which are darker than the background and lead to a marginal streak of the same colour. From the base of the wings as far as the middle the colour is darker than that of the background and here the forewings have two or three round spots of a paler blue, lying transversely between the costa and the median vein. The under surface of the wings is of a brownish red as in *Veronica* with some transverse bands which are paler than the background. Here also, as in *Veronica*, there is a transverse row of small, whitish spots beyond the middle.

78. **Diadema Bolina** Linn. — Common everywhere.

79. **Diadema Salmacis** Drury — Port Natal.

80. **Crenis Natalensis** Boisd., unpublished. — Bay of Port Natal.
    This is slightly smaller than *Madagascariensis* described on p. 48 of our *Faune de Madagascar* which it closely resembles. The upper surface of the wings is of a dull, somewhat ochre yellow, especially on part of the discoidal cell of the forewings and with a submarginal line of small black dots, separated from the edge by a row

of more or less distinct small lenticules of the same colour. The undersurface of the forewings resembles the upper surface but the background colour is yellower and tinged with a whitish grey near the apex; the undersurface of the hind-wings is ash-grey, crossed by two very sinuous, rust-coloured lines separated by a stretch of background colour, followed by a series of abutting eye-spots, of equal size; each with a black pupil and tawny iris. As on the upper surface, there is a marginal row of small, black lenticules, forming an almost unbroken line. The female is slightly larger than the male; the upper surface of the forewings shows two short, oblique bands of an ochre yellow and separated by black; these are yet more marked on the lower surfaces.

At the time of publication of the *Faune de Madagascar* in 1833, we knew of only a single species of this genus. Now we have four; three from Madagascar and one from Port Natal.

81. **Charaxes Xiphares** Cram. — Port Natal.

Cramer has illustrated the female under the name *Xiphares*, coming from the Cape of Good Hope, and Stoll the male, as *Thyestes*, based on a specimen which Levaillant brought back from the Country of the Cafres.

82. **Charaxes Tiridates** Cram. — Land of Massilicatzi.

The specimens are identical with those from the western seaboard.

83. **Charaxes Ethalion** Boisd., unpublished. — Port Natal.

This is slightly smaller than *Tiridates*. The upper surface of all four wings is a blackish brown with a continuous white stripe which is maculate on the forewings as far back as the first branch of the median vein and then extending entire and wider to a point near the anal angle of the hind-wings. This stripe is tinged with azure blue. The forewings show further, between the continuous stripe and the apex, a sinuous row of seven or eight small bluish-white spots. The hind-wings are marked by a row of seven white, more or less distinct lunules, running parallel to the costal margin, and followed between the outer margin and the first tail by three tawny, marginal lunules. From that tail round to the anal angle is a row of three, large, black spots, of which that nearest the anal angle is dusted a violet blue. These black spots are separated from the edge by a greenish line; the first tail is streaked a tawny colour, while the inner, which is very small, is greenish. The under-surface is a pale reddish brown and crossed near the base by three continuous, very sinuous black lines; the white line on the upper surface is found only on the forewings; on the hindwing it is almost of the background colour, but its outer margin is defined by a sinuous black streak followed by a sort of tawny band; the lunulae are more or less as on the upper surface. Further, the forewings have three black spots encircled in white at the base and on the internal angle two large black marks.

84. **Satyrus Natalii** Boisd., unpublished. — Land of the Amazoulous.

This satyrid, like the one which follows, belongs to the Division A of our genus *Satyrus*, a division which includes those species from Southern Africa which might at first glance be taken to be *Erebia*.

It is of the same size as *Erebia OEme*. All four wings are brown, each showing near the tip a fairly large tawny mark. On each forewing is a black eye-spot with a white double pupil and a yellow, tawny iris, while on the hind wings there are two or three eye-spots of the same coloration. The under-surface of the forewings is like the upper; that of the hind-wings is brown with two transverse, parallel, sinuous, rust-coloured lines, followed by an almost marginal row of four black eye-spots with white pupils and encircled in a tawny shade; of these, the anal is slightly smaller. Behind these eye-spots, parallel to the edge, are two small lines, darker than the background.

Only the female is known.

85. **Satyrus Panda** Boisd., unpublished. — Land of the Amazoulous.
The upper surface of this fine species is rather like our *Erebia* Ceto. It is of a dark brown with a marginal row of five, abutting, tawny eye-spots with black pupils but lacking any iris. The under-surface shows a matting of yellow and black streaks with an almost marginal row of abutting eye-spots of an attractive tawny shade with silver pupils; there are five on the forewings and six on the hind, of which the most anterior is slightly larger and clearer, while the anal is smaller and commonly double. The name *Panda* given to this species is that of the reigning king of the Amazoulous.

86. **Satyrus Corynetes** Boisd. — Port Natal.

87. **Satyrus Narcissus** Fab. — Port Natal.

88. **Cyllo Leda** Linn. — Port Natal.

89. **Thymele Florestan** Cram. — Everywhere.

90. **Thymele Ratek** Boisd., *f. de Madag* — Port Natal.

91. **Thymele Ophion** Stoll — Common.

92. **Hesperia Havei** Boisd., *f. de Madag* — Port Natal.

93. **Hesperia Poutieri** Boisd., *f. de Madag.* — Port Natal.

94. **Steropes Metis** Cram. — Port Natal.

HETEROCERA[2]

95. **Macroglossa Hylas** Fab. — Port Natal.

96. **Macroglossa Apus** Boisd., *f. de Madag.* — Port Natal.

97. **Macroglossa Trochilus** Hubn. — Bay of Port Natal.

98. **Pterogon Nanum** Boisd., *synops.* — Land of the Amazoulous.

99. **Pterogon Pumilum** Boisd., *synops.* — Land of the Amazoulous.

100. **Lophuron Brisaeus** Boisd., *synops* —

101. **Lophuron Dicanus** Boisd., *synops.* —

102. **Lophuron Dorus** Boisd., *synops.* — Port Natal.

103. **Lophuron Tyrrhus** Boisd., *synops.* — Land of the Amazoulous.

104. **Choerocampa Capensis** Boisd., *synops.* — Port Natal.

105. **Choerocampa Eson** Boisd., *synops.* — Bay of Port Natal.

106. **Choerocampa Charis** Boisd., *synops.* — Bay of Port Natal.

107. **Choerocampa Celerio** Boisd., *synops* — Everywhere.

108. **Choerocampa Epicles** Boisd., *synops.* — Land of the Amazoulous.

109. **Choerocampa Megaera** Boisd., *synops.* — Port Natal.

110. **Choerocampa Idriaeus** Boisd., *synops.* — Bay of Port Natal.

111. **Zonilia Oenopion** Boisd., *synops* — Port Natal.

112. **Sphinx Juniperi** Boisd., *synops.* —
We have given no descriptions of the new species of *Sphinx* collected during this expedition as they will shortly be described in the general *Synopsis* which Dr Boisduval is publishing in the *Annales de la Société entomologique*. Nevertheless, since there is but a single specimen of the present species, we thought that it would be desirable to publish a short description. This was found at Port Natal, resting on the bark of a gummy-resinous tree.
It is slightly smaller than the North American *Sphinx plebeja* which it closely resembles, although paler. The forewings are a pale ash-colour with some longitudinal black streaks, of which many are close to the apex. The edge is a whitish grey, broken by black. The hind-wings are black with a whitish edge. The body is pale ash-coloured, the inner margin of the tegula being black. The upper surface of the abdomen shows a black streak in the midline and on either side a *single*[9] row of black spots. The undersurface of the four wings is of a greyish brown; the antennae are pale grey.

113. **Sphinx convolvulae** Linn. — Everywhere.

114. **Acherontia Atropos** Linn. — Occurs everywhere.

115. **Agarista Echione** Boisd., unpublished. — Port Natal.
This is of about the same size as *Glycinoe*. The upper surface of the four wings is a brownish black, with spots of a very pale sulphur yellow. There are five spots on the forewings, of which two are larger, namely the one in the middle of the inner margin and that at the apex which is bilobed. Further, these wings show at the base four or five spots of the same colour and these are crossed by streaks of steel blue. The hind-wings show five or six spots of different sizes. The abdomen is brown and the thorax tawny. The lower wing surfaces show the same arrangement of spots as the upper surfaces but the streaks of steel blue are absent.

116. **Agarista Decora** Linn. — Land of Massilicatzi.

117. **Egybolis Natalii** Boisd., unpublished. — Port Natal.
Very common in the daytime on flowers around Port Natal. This species most closely resembles *Egybolis Vaillantina*, illustrated by Stoll, Pl. 31, and described on p. 142 of his work. But if the illustration and description he has provided are correct, as there is every reason to expect, our species must be new. The one illustrated by Stoll was brought back from Cafrerie by Levaillant; it is of a deep, glossy green, with *black* antennae; ours is of an attractive steel-blue with *orange coloured* antennae. Stoll says further that the under-surfaces of the wings differ only slightly from the upper surfaces. In our specimen, on the other hand, the lower wing surfaces are of a brilliant deep blue with no trace of the orange lines on the upper surface of the forewings.

118. **Arthileta Cloekeneria** Cram. — Land of Massilicatzi.

119. **Zygaena Namaqua** Boisd., unpublished. — Land of the Amazoulous.
Of about the size of *Lavandulae* and the appearance of *Anthyllidis*. The

310

forewings are a slightly green, deep black with five pale sulphur yellow spots. Of these, one is at the base, two in the middle and two near the tip. The hind-wings are of a bright yellow ochre with a black marginal band showing a tooth- or hook-shaped notch near its middle.

120. **Naclia Puella** Boisd., unpublished. —
This resembles and is of the same size as *Punctata* from the south of France. The upper surface of the forewings is brown, with four small, translucent, white spots of which the two in the middle join to form a short transverse stripe, while the other two, near the apex, are unequal and close together but not joined. The hind-wings are of a yellow ochre with a small black, discoidal spot and a black, sinuous margin. The abdomen is yellowish, being darker on the upper surface. The female hardly differs from the male.

121. **Naclea Gnatula** Boisd., unpublished. —
This species is as small as the one before, but its wings are larger and it has a different appearance: further we assign it to this genus only provisionally. The forewings are brown with three pale, yellow ochre spots. Of those, one near the base is triangular; there is a second, small one in the middle close to the costa and the third, slightly elliptical, is near the wing tip. The hind-wings are of a yellow ochre, with a black margin. The abdomen and the tegulae are of a yellow ochre.

122. **Syntomis Cerbera** Linn. — Land of the Amazoulous.

123. **Syntomis Natalii** Boisd., unpublished. — Port Natal.
This closely resembles the European *Phegea*, but is much smaller. The upper wing surface is blue-black. The forewings of the male have five or six small white translucent dots and, in the female, six similar spots. The hind-wings of the male usually have a single white spot close to the base; in the female there are two small spots: one is near the base and the other near the apex. Further, the edge is white near the apex of the forewings in both sexes. The body is blue-black with a tawny red spot on the upper surface of the base of the abdomen.

124. **Thyretes Hiphothes**[10] Cram. — Land of the Amazoulous.
The specimens collected here are slightly larger than those from Bengal.

125. **Thyretes Montana** Boisd., unpublished. — Land of the Amazoulous and of Massilicatzi.
Of the same size as the *Hippothes*[10] of Cramer and with the wings showing the same pattern, but of a yellow ochre rather than white. The body is more distinct; the head is black with a tawny front; the thorax is also tawny, while the patagia, a dorsal line and the inner and outer margins of the tegulae are all dark brown. The abdomen is black with closely set rows of tawny spots; three on the dorsal surface and one on each side. This species might be a variety of the former. Its prefered habitat is the mountains of the land of Massilicatzi.

126. **Thyretes Amazoula** Boisd., unpublished. — Land of the Amazoulous.
This species has the antennae of a *Thyretes*, but the wing pattern is like that of *Syntomis cerbera*. The wings are of a brownish black with the edge slightly whiter. The forewings have six translucent white spots; one at the base, two in the middle and three towards the apex. The hind-wings have two similarly coloured spots of which the larger is near the base. The colour of the body is a dark greenish brown with the abdominal incisions[11] edged by yellow ochre above and below. The patagia also carry some ochre-yellow hairs. Only the male is known.

127. **Glaucopis Formosa** Boisd., *f. de Madag.* — Port Natal.
In March thousands of this species hover, along with *Egybolis Natalii*, over the flowers of a spineless *Acacia*.

128. **Glaucopis Madagascariensis** Boisd., *f. de Madag* — Port Natal.
Rarer than the previous species.

129. **Lithosia Eborella** Boisd., unpublished. — Land of the Amazoulous.
This resembles *Gilveola* but is smaller. The upper surface of the forewings is completely white; the hind-wings are of a pale ochre yellow on both surfaces. The under-surface of the forewings is also of a yellow ochre but darker over the discoidal cell. The thorax is white and the head tawny. The abdomen is of a yellow ochre tinged with white on its upper surface near the base.

130. **Lithosia Pandula** Boisd., unpublished. — Land of Massilicatzi.
Of the same size as the preceding species. All four wings are of a pale ochre-yellow on both surfaces with a well-marked black border. The forewings are black at the base, except near the costa. The thorax is black both dorsally and ventrally, as are the four front legs; the abdomen is an ochre yellow.

131. **Euchelia Pulchella** Linn. — Everywhere.

132. **Euchelia Formosa** Boisd., *f. de Madag* — Bay of Port Natal.

133. **Euchelia Amanda** Boisd., unpublished. — Land of the Amazoulous.
This species is fairly close to *Pylotis*, but about a third larger and the spots on the forewings of both sexes are clearly encircled in white. Found also on the Guinea coast and in the land of Galam.[12]

134. **Chelonia Madagascariensis** Boisd., unpublished. — Bay of Port Natal.
This handsome species, also found on Madagascar by M. Goudet, is close to *Mauritia*, illustrated by Cramer, pl. 345D, and should form, along with some other related species, the basis for a new genus close to *Arctia*. The forewings are of a ruddy grey, with a large translucent area, sinuous on the outer side and crossed by veins of the background colour. Further, near the base, there are two small black dots. The hind-wings are a pale red on their inner half but paler on the outer where they have a longitudinal, translucent area. Both thorax and head are of a pale ruddy grey with small black spots. There is one of these on each tegula, one on the occiput, a small one on the front and two on the mesoscutum. The body and the legs are red; the undersurface of the abdomen is white with two lateral rows of black dots which are not visible from above. The antennae are black and filiform in both sexes.

135. **Chelonia Erythronota** Boisd., unpublished. — Land of Massilicatzi.
This has both the appearance and size of *Sanguinolenta* of Fabricius. The forewings are white and without markings; the hind-wings are of a pale yellow ochre, marked on both surfaces by a large, black lunula. The undersurface of the forewings is a pale yellow ochre, with a large, black lunula at the tip of the discoidal cell. The thorax is white and separated from the head by a small, red, transverse line. The body is red on the upper surface and white below. The first pair of legs are red in front and white behind. The antennae are filiform and the same in both sexes.

136. **Chelonia Phedonia** Cram. — Land of the Amazoulous.

137. **Chelonia Sylviana** Stoll — Land of Massilicatzi.
This attractive species forms, with another found in the land of Galam, the foundation of a small genus which we place provisionally among the chelonids, but which might nevertheless belong with the notodontids.

138. **Liparis Subfusca** Boisd., unpublished. — Land of the Amazoulous.
Provisionally, and without knowing the females, we assign this species and the

312

one which follows to the genus *Liparis*. It is as big as an ordinary *Bombyx Trifolii*. The front wings are of a slightly glossy brown glazed with a whitish grey towards the costa and marked with a small, central brown dot. They are crossed by two very fine, saw-toothed lines of the same colour; one is near the middle, the other near the wing tip. Between these two lines can be seen a third, transverse line which is of a clear white, well-marked and lacking toothed margins, while towards the base is a slightly oblique, transverse line of the same colour. The hind-wings are of a reddish grey, crossed by two darker, sinuous lines. The under-surface of all four wings is cinnamon red with two parallel, confluent, saw-toothed, brown lines.

139. **Liparis Lutea** Boisd., unpublished. — Land of the Amazoulous.
  This is of the same size as the preceding species. The upper surface of the four wings is yellow ochre. The forewings have a broad, brown, oblique marginal band which arises as a spot at the apex and broadens towards the internal angle. Ahead of this marginal band, yet joined to it posteriorly, is a more deeply coloured, transverse, spotted line, which is sinuous. Further, in the middle of these wings, there is a transverse line of a yellow darker than the background. The hind-wings have at the edge of the inner margin a small brown mark. The undersurface of all four wings is uniformly yellow.

140. **Liparis Crocata** Boisd., unpublished. — Land of the Amazoulous.
  This is slightly smaller than the European *Dispar*. Its four wings are of a fine, almost tawny yellow with no markings on the lower surfaces. The forewings have a small rust-red mark in the middle. In newly emerged specimens this gives rise to a small, almost effaced, slightly maculate, transverse blackish streak. Also, near the apex, are two ill-defined black marks; one of these is near the internal angle. There are no markings on the lower surfaces.

141. **Liparis Picta** Boisd., unpublished. — Land of Massilicatzi.
  This small species is of about the size of the smallest of our *Orgya*[13] and perhaps belongs rather to that genus than to *Liparis*. The background colour of the forewings is white with three tawny bands, of which two are near the base and the other near the wing tip. These bands are separated from each other by a black, slightly spotted stripe, dotted with white; the stripe between the two basal bands is very reduced and may be expressed simply as a few black spots. Between the most apical band and the edge of the wing is a row of well-marked black spots. The hind-wings are of a pale yellow ochre with a marginal row of black dots. The female differs from the male only in not having pectinate antennae.

142. **Bombyx Patens** Boisd., unpublished. — Land of the Amazoulous.
  This has the appearance of *Trifolii* and related species, but it is at least as big as the female of *Quercus*. The four wings are, on both surfaces, pale cinnamon red with no markings. The female is slightly paler and also lacks markings.

143. **Bombyx Thunbergii** Boisd., unpublished. — Land of the Amazoulous.
  This has the appearance of the preceding species but is slightly larger; it is of the same cinnamon red. The four wings are crossed, slightly before the apex, by a confluent, saw-toothed, brown line. The forewings also show, between the middle and the base, a sinuous streak of the same colour. The female is not known.

144. **Bombyx Montana** Cram. — Land of Massilicatzi.

145. **Bombyx Edulis** Boisd., unpublished. — Port Natal.
  This *Bombyx* is almost as big as *Erebus Bubo*. Its four wings are entire and well-rounded. It is of a brownish grey with confluent streaks or bands, some of which are paler, others darker than the background colour. They are arranged as follows: right at the wing tip is a well-marked brown band, dentate and crenellated;

then, nearer the base, another of the same form and colour, but, on the hind-wings, more clearly distinguished from the background, here browner, by a streak of whitish grey. Behind the darker shade we have mentioned are two confluent, parallel brown streaks, close together and saw-toothed; then a whitish band, followed within by a dark colour which is crossed by a sinuous white streak. The base of the hind wings is whitish and crossed by a row of black hairs. The thorax is of the same colour as the wings. The female is unknown. The caterpillars of this big *Bombyx* are black and marked by red spots; they aggregate on a tree in the neighbourhood of Port Natal. They are eaten by the Cafres after having been roasted; this is why we have given this species the trivial name *Edulis*.[14]

146. **Bombyx Panda** Boisd., unpublished. — Port Natal.
This species belongs to the division of the *Processionaries*[15] and is close in size to the processionary of Madagascar (*B. Rhamada*). It somewhat resembles *Chelonia Villica*. The upper surface of the forewings is white with two transverse bands and two longitudinal streaks, both brown; these intersect so as to form rectangular white patches. The hind-wings are of yellow ochre, paler in the female, with a darker transverse streak. The thorax is brown, with two white spots on the patagia; the abdomen is slightly red and, as in other related species, carries a bundle of hairs of the same colour at its tip.

147. **Saturnia Mimosae** Boisd., unpublished. —
This big *Saturnia* is most closely related to *Saturnia Cometes*, brought back ten years ago from Madagascar by M. Goudot, and forming a small, distinct group including *Selene* from Bengal, *Luna* from North America and *Isis* from Java.[16]
Our *Saturnia Mimosae* has wings which are far more dentate than in *Cometes*; the background colour is an attractive green and not yellow; the tails are, proportionally, slightly longer. As for other characters, the specimens brought back from Natal are in too poor a condition to make it possible to provide here an exact description. This lovely species is quite common on *Mimosa* at four or five places in the interior of the country. The Cafres use the cocoons, which are very large and very tough, as snuff boxes. They make a hole to extract the pupa and then close the cocoon with a wooden plug.[17]

148. **Saturnia Wahlbergii** Boisd., unpublished. — Port Natal.
This is slightly bigger than the European *Saturnia Pyri* and its appearance is quite distinct. The upper surface of the four wings is yellow, generously sprinkled with specks of brown and with a straight, narrow, brown, confluent band, lined on its inner side by a violet-grey; this starts near the apex of the forewings and ends at the inner margin of the hind-wings, just level with the tip of the abdomen. At the bases of the four wings there is another very sinuous, irregular and confluent band of a violet shade; just ahead, on the base of the forewings, is a sort of mark of this colour. The eye-spot on each forewing is small and transparent, encircled in yellow surrounded by a slight violet hue, especially in the male. The eye-spot on each hind-wing is bigger, yellow with a diaphanous pupil and the black iris encircled in violet. Named after M. Wahlberg, one of M. Delegorgue's companions. Boisd.

149. **Saturnia Tyrrhea** Cram. — Port Natal.

150. **Saturnia Caffra** Boisd., *Caffraria*, Stoll — Land of the Amazoulous.
This species, with Cramer's *Alcinoe* and another as yet undescribed species from Madagascar, form a small group which links Drury's *Phedusa* with other *Saturnia*.

151. **Saturnia Cynthia** Fab. — Land of Massilicatzi.

152. **Saturnia Delegorguei** Boisd., unpublished. — Land of the Amazoulous.
This has both the appearance and size of *Grimmia* illustrated by Hubner and

forms with this species a small unit which could become the type for a new genus. The wings are slightly sinuous; the forewings are brown with an irregular ash-coloured space along the length of the costa and an almost terminal band of the same colour, clear on its inner edge and merging with the brown colour of the wing tip along its outer side. Further, on the brown area, beyond the centre and running towards the apex, there is a small, translucent, silvery zig-zag streak, almost as in *Grimmia*. The hind-wings are reddish at the base and along their outer margin, brown at the apex, darker and almost black in the centre where there is a narrow, steel-blue lunula resembling a reversed C. Further, the darker part in the middle of the wing is separated from the lighter area at the wing-tip by a transverse, whitish line. The lower surfaces of the wings are brown, with a paler band near the apex, and the base of the forewing tinged with rose. Only a single female, collected in the land of the Amazoulous, is known.

153. **Saturnia Apollinaris** Boisd., unpublished. — Port Natal.
This species will be a new genus when we know the female. It is as much a *Liparid* as a *Saturnid*. It is about the size of the female of *B. Quercus*, but in texture it is thin and delicate. The four wings are white with dark veins, especially near the apex. This latter has a brown border, broken by a row of marginal yellow spots. Ahead of the tip is a straight brown streak, crenellated on the outer side and saw-toothed on the inner so as to enclose between the veins spots of the background colour. The forewings have, further, at the tip of the discoidal cell, two yellow spots encircled by a little black; one of these is near the costa. The lower wing surfaces are like the upper.
The antennae are black and strongly pectinate. We have a variety in which the background colour is yellow ochre.
This species flies in broad daylight. One year, in the environs of Port Natal, it would have been possible to collect hundreds in a few hours. Two or three days later, they had vanished. The female, which we do not know, does not fly. It may be apterous, and all the fluttering males were doubtless seeking mates.

154. **Ophideres Imperator** Boisd., *f. de Madag.* — Port Natal.

155. **Ophiusa Magica** Hubn., *Zutr.*, 535-536. — Port Natal.

156. **Ophiusa Klugii** Boisd., *f. de Madag.* — Port Natal.

157. **Ophiusa Delta** Boisd., *f. de Madag* — Massilicatzi.

158. **Ophiusa Rubricans** Boisd., *f. de Madag.* — Massilicatzi.

159. **Ophiusa Repanda** Fab. — Land of the Amazoulous.

160. **Polydesma Nycterina** Boisd., *f. de Madag* — Port Natal.

161. **Cycligramma Latona** Cram., 13. — Land of the Amazoulous.

162. **Cycligramma Joa** Boisd., *f. de Madag.* — Port Natal.

163. **Erebus Bubo** Fab. — Port Natal.

We do not discuss the Geometers[18] or the Microlepidoptera[19] although these lands produce many species. These families were omitted because specimens were too difficult to preserve on long and arduous journeys. The few specimens which were collected were lost or destroyed before reaching Europe.

Notes

1. There is no indication in the literature that this unnamed 'authority' ever published the work. Delegorgue thus remains the authority in both cases (*see* p329, and the Natural History Index for *Columba Delegorguei* and *Coturnix Delegorguei*).
2. Rhopalocera (butterflies) and Heterocera (moths), though once used as a convenient means of dividing the Lepidoptera, are terms lacking any taxonomic value (S.J.A.).
3. *See* Natural History Index: Delalande, Fabricius, Levaillant, Linnaeus.
4. Gold Coast, i.e. modern Ghana (S.J.A.).
5. 'West coast' of Africa in the late 20th century refers to the region bordering the Gulf of Guinea and so is here used specifically when that seems to be indicated. When A.D. clearly means the western coast of the southern and central African regions, this has been rendered 'western seaboard' (D.W.E.).
6. A locality on or near the Nile, northern Sudan (S.J.A.).
7. *Polyom.* is an abbreviation of *Polyommateus* (D.W.E.).
8. The lower case *x*, though in accordance with modern taxonomic convention, is surely a typographical error in the original; several similar errors occur in the catalogue (S.J.A.).
9. Emphasis in the original.
10. Two different spellings of the same species name (D.W.E.).
11. 'Incisions', now as then, refers to the intersegmental grooves (D.W.E.).
12. Probably Senegal (S.J.A.).
13. Probably *Orygia* (D.W.E.).
14. *Edulis*, Latin: edible; *see* Natural History Index: *Bombyx Edulis*.
15. Not, as this seems to indicate, a taxonomic grouping. Processionary caterpillars are those which exhibit gregarious habits and which march in columns (S.J.A.).
16. The only known specimen of this latter is to be found in the fine collection of M. Robyns in Brussels (note in original).
17. *See* Natural History Index: *Bombyx*, cocoons of.
18. Moths of the very large family Geometridae. They are small to medium, slender moths with relatively large wings (S.J.A.).
19. The old divisons of Lepidoptera into Macro- and Micro-lepidoptera, founded mainly on the criterion of size, are convenient, but do not represent definable natural groups (S.J.A.).

CATALOGUE OF COLEOPTERA

Genres.		Espèces.
Mauticora latipennis Wat.		1
Cicindela fatidica Laferte.		
— natala Dup.		
— clathrata Dej.		
— brevicollis Wid.		
— candida Dej.		
— espèces non détermi-		
nées.	5 —	11
Dromica tuberculata Kl.		
— vittata Kl.		2
Cymindis ebenina Dup.		1
Dromius, espèces non déterminées.		2
Lebia Dregei Dej.		
— espèces non détermin. 2 —		3
Arsinoe quadriguttata Chev. . . .		1
Thyreopterus flavosignatus Dej. .		1
Catascopus algoensis Dup.		1
Graphepterus cinctus Dup.		
— cordiger Klug.		
— cinctipennis Dup.		
Bohem.		
— Westwoodii Brême.		
— frontalis Dup.		
— vittatus Klug. . . .		6
Piezia axillaris Dup.		
— basalis Dup.		
— limbata Dup.		
— laticornis Dup.		
— lineolata Dup.		5
Anthia cinctipennis Dup.		
— id var. marginip. Delaporte.		
A reporter. . .		34

Genres.		Espèces.
Report. . .		34
Anthia Mellyi Brême.		
— omoplata Dup.		
— massilicata Guer.		
— Burchellii Hope.		
— anthracina Kl.		
— lævicollis Schon.		
— cruenticollis Mannerh.		
— villosa Thumb.		
— biguttata Wied.		
— limbata Dej.		
— uniguttata Dup. Guer.		
— sexnotata Thumb.		
— Delegorguei Dup.		
— rugosopunctata Thumb.		
— sulcipennis Dup.		
— albolineata Guer.		
— alveolata Brême.		
— stigmatipennis Dup.		
— Dregei Dej.		
— macilinta Ol.		
— gracilis Dej.		20
Scarites Delegorguei Dup.		
— brontes Kl.		
— rugosus var. Wied.		
Scarites Boisduvalii Dej.		
— elongatus Kl.		
— espèces non déterm. 5 —		6
Clivina, espèces non déterminées.		4
Morio nemestrinus? Dup.		1
Tefflus Delegorguei Guer.		1
A reporter. . .		66

Genres.	Espèces.
Report. . .	66
Colosoma hottenlottum Dup.	
— rugosum var.	2
Panagæus natala Dup.	
— longipennis Dup.	
— ebeninus Dup.	3
Chlænius cinctipennis Boh.	
— posticus Dup.	
— cylindricollis Kl.	3
Dolichus caffer Wied.	
— rugipennis Dej.	
— rufipes Dej.	
— badius Wied.	4
Distrigus natalensis Dup.	
— algoensis Dup.	2
Nov. genus castaneus Dup.	1
Steropus lænis Illiger.	1
Hypolythus tomentosus Dej.	
— espèces non détermi-	
nées. . . . . 2 —	3
Selenophorus ochropus var.	1
Hydaticus leander Aubé.	
— bivittatus id.	2
Dineutes africanus id.	1
Gyrinus algoensis Dup.	1
Sternocera oryssa Bq.	1
Jaladis natalensis Boh.	
— bivittata Boh.	
— compressicollis Guer. . . .	3
Acmæadera gibbosa Fab.,	
— xanthotænia Wied.	
— carbonaria Dup.	
— aspersa Fab.	
— quadrivittata Dej.	
— cribricollis Dup.	
espèces non détermi-	
nées. . . . . 6 —	12
Chrysochroa natalensis Dup. . . .	1
Steraspis Delegorguei Reiche. . . .	1
Lampetis amakosà Dup.	
— cæruleipes Dup.	
— consanguinea Dup.	
— cæca Dup.	
— cataphracta Dej. (Psilop-	
tera Dej.)	
A reporter. . .	108

Genres	Espèces.
Report. . .	108
Lampetis vespertilioides Dup.	
— fasciatocollis Dup.	
— espèces non détermi-	
nées. . . . . 5 —	12
Strigoptera miliaris Dup.	1
Chrisobothris spinimana.	1
Belionata madagascariensis Dup. .	1
Authaxia, espèces non détermi-	
nées.	13
Sphenoptera mazilicatziana Dup.	
— espèces non détermi-	
nées. . . . . 6 —	7
Agrillus coarctatus Kl.	
— ferrugineoguttatus.	
— exasperatus Scho.	
— femoratus Dup.	
— nodicollis Gory.	
— espèces non détermi-	
nées. . . . . . 11 —	16
Aphanisticus truncatipennis Dup.	
spinola Dup. . . .	2
—	
Tetralobus Hopei Guer.	
— amakosús Dup.	
— flabellicornis Fab. . . .	3
Dicrepiduis non determinis. . . .	10
Dicronychus serraticornis? var.	
Dej.	
— algoensis Dup.	
— cruentatipennis Dup.	
— castaneipennis Dup.	
— badius Dup.	
— espèces non détermi-	
nées. . . . 2 —	7
Crepicardus senex Dup.	1
Alaus vetustus var. Dej.	
— Reichei Dej.	
— phalenoides Dup.	
— espèces non détermi-	
nées. . . . . 4 —	7
Cardiophorus, espèces non déter-	
minées.	5
Oophorus, espèces non détermi-	
nées.	2
A reporter. . .	196

Genres.	Espèces.
Report. . .	196
Ectinus natalensis Dup.	1
Rhipicera? Delegorguei Dup. . . .	1
Cyphon figurata Dup.	1
Lycus rostratus Fab.	
— palliatus Fab.	
— pasticus Dej.	
— espèces non détermi-	
nées. . . . . 6 —	9
Dytiophorus bipartitus Dup.	1
Pygolampis, non déterminée. . . .	2
Melyris viridis Fab.	
— abdominalis Fab.	
— lineata Fab.	
— caffra Dup.	
— sanguineo-cincta Dup. . .	5
Callitheres, espèce non détermi-	
née.	1
Tillus terminatus Kl.	
— espèces non détermi-	
nées. . . . . 5 —	6
Trichodes, espèces non dé-	
terminées.	6
Corynetes collaris, et autres. . . .	4
Mastigus, espèce non détermi-	
née.	1
Silpha capensis Dej.	
— punctulata Olivier.	2
Scaphidium caffrum Dup.	1
Malachius, espèces non détermi-	
nées.	3
Dermestes vulpinus Fab.	1
Histerites, espèces non détermi-	
nées.	20
Hyporagus giganteus Dup.	1
Cercyon, espèces non déterminées.	4
Ateuchus guineensis Dej.	
— religiosus Dej.	
— satanas Dup.	
— caffer Dej.	
— intricatus Fab.	
— convalescens Wied.	
— espèces non détermi-	
nées. . . . . . 4 —	10
Gymnopleurus caffer Reiche.	
— splendidus Dej.	
A reporter. . .	276

Genres.	Espèces.
Report. . .	276
Gymnopleurus Wahlbergii Boh.	
— amazoulotianus	
Dup.	
— severus Dup.	
— chrysithis Dup.	
— atratus Fab.	
— espèce non déter-	
— minée. . . 4 —	12
Sisyphus Heissii Illiger.	
— crispus Dej.	
— deutipis Dej.	3
Circellium Bacchus Fab.	1
Chalconotus capreus.	1
Coptorhinus africanus Westwood.	1
Epirinus scabrosus Dup.	
— olivieri Megerle.	
— Æneus. . . *. . . . . , .	3
Chœridium pullum Boh.	
— gemminatum Dej.. . .	2
Copris hamadrias Fab.	
— infernalis Dup.	
— Jachus Fab.	
— Œdipus Fab.	
— Nemestrinus Fab.	
— Empedocles Dej.	
— Plutus Fab.	
— latifrons Dej.	
— satyrus Boh.	
— espèces non détermi-	
nées. . . . . . . 2 —	11
Onthophogus Reichei Dej.	
— aciculatus Dej.	
— sericans Dup.	
— lanista Kl.	
— corruscus Dej.	
— flavocinctus Dup.	
— fissus Dup.	
— nasutus? var. Dup.	
— girafa Hoff.	
— elegans Hope.	
— catta Fab.	
— espèces non détermi-	
nées. . . . 11 —	23
Ouitis pecuarius Burchell.	
A reporter. . .	333

Genres.	Espèces.
Report...	333

Onitis sobrinus Dup.
— Alexis *var*. Dej.
— bos Dej.
— intermedius Dej.
— espèce non détermi-
née. .... 1 — 6
Oniticellus squalidus Dej.
— planatus Illiger.
— ciliatus Dej.
— militaris Illiger.
— medius Boh.
— pumilus *var*. Dup.
— fuscomaculatus Fab.
— Kirbii Hope.
— Natalensis Dup.
— pictus Kl.. 10
Aphodius rútilipennis Germ.
espèces non détermi-
nées. ..... 14 — 15
Terox caffer Dup.
— ordinatus Dej.
— luridus Fab.
— incultus Dej.
— natalensis Dup.
— horridus Fab.
— espèces non détermi-
nées. .... 3 — 9
Geobatus squalidus Ch. 1
Bolbocéras algoensis Dup. 1
Hybosorus, espèce non déterminée. 1
Oryctes boas Fab. 1
Heteronychus syrrichtus Fab.
— digitalis Kl.
— Licas Dej. 3
Coptorhinus Diana P. B.
— espèce non détermi-
née. ..... 1 — 2
Phænomeris Delegorguei Dup. .. 1
Schizorhina? senegalensis Dej.
— espèce non détermi-
née. ..... 1 — 2
Anomala nitens Burchell.
— basalis Dup.

A reporter... 385

Genres.	Espèces.
Report...	385

Anomala suturalis.
— espèces non détermi-
nées. ...... 5 — 8
Leucothyreus ictericum Dej.
— espèces non déter-
minées. ... 3 — 4
Trigonotoma setulosa Boh.
— testacea Dup.
— brunnea Kl. 3
Popillia bipunctata Fab.
— espèce non détermi-
née. .... 1 — 2
Lagosterna flavofasciata Dej. ... 1
Ægostheta maritima Burchell.
— longicornis Fab. 2
Leocæta alopex Fab. 1
Ablabera splendida Illiger.
— suturalis Dej. 3
Rhizotrogus, espèces non déterminées. 3
Omoloplia costata Dup.
— fulgida Boh.
— abbreviata Dup. Reich.
— cruentata Dup.
— subænea Kl.
— sericans Dup.
— espèces non détermi-
nées. ..... 7 — 13
Chasme decora Wied. 1
Lepisa rupicola Fab. 1
Dichelus hypocrita Dup.
— Reichei Dej.
— rufipes Dej.
— carbonarius Dej.
— rufinus Dup.
— atratus Dej.
— trivittatus Dup.
— espèces non détermi-
nées. ..... 22 — 29
Hoploscelis Dregei Dej.
— fuliginosus Dup.
— capucinus Dup. 3
Monochelus, espèces non déterminées. 5

A reporter... 464

Genres.	Espèces.

Report. . . 464

Microplus, espèces non déterminées. 3
Anisonix ursus Fab.
— crinitum Fab.
— lepidotum Wied.
— ignitum Kl.
— lynx Fab. 5
Lepitrix nigripes Fab.
— suturella Reich.
— espèces non détermi-
nées. . . . . . 2 — 4
Pachycnema striata Drege.
— erythropus Dej.
— nigromaculata Dej.
— espèces non détermi-
nées. . . . . 4 — 7
Hypselogenia concava G. P.
— geotrupina Schon. . 2
Cerathorina Derbyana Westw.
— Smithii Mac-Leay. . . 2
Cheirolasia Burkei Westw.
— Passerinii Westw. . . 2
Heterorhina plana Wied.
— trivittata Schaum. . . 2
Mystroceros algoensis Westw.
— amakosus Dup.
— natalensis Hope.
— flavomaculata Fab.
— umbonata Gor. P. . . 5
Clinteria discophora Reich.
— permutans Dup.. 2
Gametis balteata Degeer.
— subfasciata Swed. 2
Odontochina hispida Ol.
— pubescens Fab.
— fascicularis Fab.
— signata Fab.
— albipicta G. P. . . . 5
Taphræa dichroa Schaum.
— lutulenta Schaum.
— amazoulousiana Dup.
— cruenticollis Dup. . . . 4
Oxythyræa rubra G. P.
— koras Dup.

A reporter. . . 509

Genres.	Espèces.

Report. . . 509

Oxythyræa massilicatziana Dup.
— fasciatocollis Dup.
— thoracica? Schæn.
— æneicollis Schaum.
— adspersa Fab.
— marginalis Schæn.
— Peroudii Schaum.
— amabilis Schaum. . . 10
Anoplochilus odiosus G. P.
— tomentosus. 2
Protæcia amakosa Dup. 1
Pachnodia monacha G. P. Dup.
— sinuata Fab.
— flaviventris Hope.
— impressa Gold.
— cincta Degeer.
— leucomelana G. P.
— aulica Fab.
— semipunctata Fab.
— chalcea G. P.
— funeralis Dup.
— consanguinea Dup.
— espèces non détermi-
nées. . . . . 2 — 13
Elaphinis cinerascens Fab.
— (irrorata Fab.
— (ulcerosa Dup.
— contemptus Fab.
— furvata Fab.
— espèces non détermi-
nées. . . . . . 2 — 7
Ischnostoma cuspidata Fab.
— nasuta Boh.
— tristis.
— patera G. P. 4
Rhinocæta cornuta Fab.
— sanguinipes G. P. . . . 2
Diplognatha quadrisignata G. P.
— silicea Mac-Leay.
— hæbrea Olivier.
— carnifex Fab. 4
Macroma cognata Schaum. 1
Ptycophorus, espèces non déterminées. 4

A reporter. . . 557

Genres.	Espèces.		Genres.	Espèces.
Report. . .	557		Report. . .	617
Ceutrognathus maculosus Boh.			Gonopus ventricosus.	
— scutellaris Dup.			— espèce non détermi-	
— signatulus Dup. . .	3		née. . . . . . 1 —	2
Haplostomus fuligineus G. P. . . .	1		Psorodes tuberculata Dej.	
Pilinurgus, non déterminée. . . .	1		— granulata Wied.	
Cænochilus hottentotus Fab. . . .	1		— calcarata Fab.	3
Scaptobius caffer Schaum.			Heteroscelis exasperatus Dej.	
— espèce non détermi-			— espèces non détermi-	
née. . . . . . 1 —	2		nées. . . . 5 —	6
Valgus fascicularis Schæn.	1		Eurynotus muricatus Kirby.	
Stringophorus zebra G. P.			— tuberculatus Dej.	
— niger G. P.			— exasperatus Mannerh.	
— longipes Swed. . . .	3		— tenebricosus Dej.	
Dorcus senegalensis? Dup.	1		— marginatus Wied.	
Figulus vervex Dej.	1		— brunnicornis Dej.	
Zophosis testudinarius Illiger.			— espèces non détermi-	
— espèces non détermi-			nées. . . . . 2 —	8
nées. . . . . . 8 —	9		Selenepistoma longipalpes Wied.	
Adesmia, espèces non détermi-			— acutum.	2
nées.	4		Platynotus gigas Dej. Wied.	
Moluris striata Fab.			— perforatus Dej.	
— scabra Fab.			— Rabourdinii Petit.	
— pilosa Thumberg.			— excavatus Fab.	4
— semiscabra Dej.			Blacades brunnipes Dej.	
— lævicollis Reich.			— vertagus Illiger.	2
— globulipennis Dej.			Opatrum crenatum Fab.	
— melanaria Dup.			— lugubre var. Dej.	
— espèces non détermi-			— holosericeum Dej.	
nées. . . . . . 8 —	15		— espèces non détermi-	
Eurychora, espèces non déter-			nées. . . . . . 3 —	6
minées.	3		Leichenum, espèces non détermi-	
Cyrthodes discoidea Guer.			nées.	2
— cancellata Dup.			Phaleria lævigata Schüppel. . . .	1
— crispata Brême.			Neomida, espèces non détermi-	
— variolosa Brême.	5		nées.	2
Dicrossa lutulenta Dej.			Aniara maura Dej.	1
— maculata Dej.			Hypophlæus capensis? var. Dej. .	1
— murina Kl.	3		Eustrophus axillaris Dup.	
Melancrus capensis var. Dej.			— signatus Dup.	2
Machla polygona Brême.			Imatismus patruelis Dej.	
— coarctata Dej.			— espèces non détermi-	
— villosa Oliv.			nées. . . . . 2 —	3
— espèces non détermi-			Iphthinus, non déterminée.	1
nées. . . . . . . 4 —	7			
A reporter. . .	617		A reporter. . .	663

Genres.	Espèces.
Report. . .	663
Toxicum vitulum Erichson.	
— bubalus Dej.	2
Heterotarsus, espèces non détermi-	
nées.	2
Særangades? espèce non détermi-	
née.	1
Adelphus, espèces non détermi-	
nées.	7
Stenochia caffra Dej.	
— espèces non détermi-	
nées. . . . . . 8 —	9
Eupezus amakosus Dup.	
— sublineatus Reich.	
— espèce non détermi-	
née. . . . . . . 1 —	3
Oplocheirus upioides Dej.	
— carbonarius Dej.	
— tenebrioides Dup.	
— algoensis Dup.	
— espèces non détermi-	
nées. . . . . 2 —	6
Cistela, espèces non déterminées.	11
Eutrapelia lateralis Dej.	
— vittata Illiger.	
— gracilis Kl.	
— porrecta Fab.	
— erythrodera Dej.	
— espèces non détermi-	
nées. . . . . . 4 —	9
Lagria flavipennis Dej.	
— columbina Dej.	
— fuscipennis Kl.	
— puberula Dej.	
— foveicollis Dej.	
— janthina Dup.	
— espèces non détermi-	
nées. . . . . 6 —	12
Monoceros pilosus Dej.	
— scenicus Dej.	
— espèces non détermi-	
nées. . . . . . 2 —	4
Anthicus, espèces non détermi-	
nées.	8
A reporter. . .	737

T. II.

Genres.	Espèces.
Report. . .	737
Acosmus capensis var. Dej.	1
Mordella, espèces non détermi-	
nées.	7
Meloe, espèce non détermi-	
née.	1
Dices decoratus Dej.	
— espèce non détermi-	
née. . . . . 2 —	3
Decatoma lunata Fab.	
— lœtum Dej.	
— quadriguttatum Bil-	
berg.	
— africanus Olivier.	
— decipiens Dej.	
— undatum Bilberg.	
— espèces non détermi-	
nées. . . . . . 5 —	11
Mylabris transversalis Dej.	
— myops Dej.	
— oculata Olivier.	
— lavataræ Fab.	
— ophthalmica Dej.	
— Dregei Dej.	
— cœcigena Dej.	
— 16-guttata Thumberg.	
— tripunctata Thumberg.	
— binotata Dej.	
— cœca Bilberg.	
— caffra Dup.	
— capensis Fab.	
— connexa Dej.	
— Thumbergi Bilberg.	
— espèces non détermi-	
nées. . . . . . 9 —	25
Eletica rufa Fab.	
— id. var. nigra.	
— id. var. lateralis.	3
Lyta nitidula Fab.	1
Epicauta brevipennis Dej.	
— espèces non détermi-	
nées. . . . . . . 5 —	6
Zonitis hœmatoptera Dej.	
— rufipennis Dej.	
— crebricollis Dej.	3
A reporter. . .	798

39

323

Genres.   Espèces.
                   Report. . . 798
Nacerdes capensis Dej.
    — espèce non détermi-
        née. . . . . . 1 — 2
Asclera lineata Klug. 1
Bruchus, espèces non déterminées. 11
Phlœotragus amakosus Dup.
    — espèces non détermi-
        nées. . . . . 2 — 3
Anthribus capensis Dej. var. . . . 1
Xylinades, espèce non déterminée. 1
Apoderus, espèces non détermi-
        nées. 3
Rhynchites protæ Lichtenstein.
    — espèces non détermi-
        nées. . . . . . 2 — 3
Apion, espèces non déterminées. 5
Arrhenodes vulsellatus Schon. 1
Ceocephalus picipes Olivier.
    — espèce non détermi-
        née. . . . . 1 — 2
Taphroderes, espèces non déter-
        nées. 3
Brachycerus apterus Fab.
    — Boisduvalii Dej.
    — serricans Dup.
    — imperialis Dej.
    — obesus Fab.
    — scalaris Fab.
    — angulatus Dej.
    — verrucosus Olivier.
    — semi-ocellatus Chre-
        vrolat.
    — cornutus Fab.
    — reticulatus Wied.
    — venustus Wied.
    — exasperatus Dej.
    — paganus Dej.
    — hirtellus Dej.
    — reticulosus Schon.
    — cavifrons Illiger.
    — fascicularis Olivier.
    — piger Chevrolat.
    — espèces non détermi-
        nées. . . . . 11 — 30

                   A reporter. . 864

Genres.   Espèces.
                   Report. . . 864
Microcerus lividus Dej.
    — retusus Fab.
    — espèce non détermi-
        née. . . . . 1 — 3
Hipporhinus Gyllenhalii Schon.
    — severus Schon.
    — carinatus Dej.
    — productus Dej.
    — furcatus Dej.
    — albovittis Wied.
    — nivosus Sparrmann.
    — sexvittatus Fab.
    — nodulosus Fab.
    — infacetus Schon.
    — costatus Dup.
    — verrucosus Fab.
    — satanas Dup.
    — tenebricosus Dej.
    — granulosus Wied.
    — granulatus Dej.
    — espèces non détermi-
        nées. . . . . 7 — 23
Gneorhinus, espèces non détermi-
        nées. 12
Sciobius dealbatus Schon.
    — espèces non détermi-
        nées. . . . . . 9 — 10
Anæmerus, espèce non déterminée. 1
Polychleis equestris Schon.
    — plumbens Dup.
    — espèce non détermi-
        née. . . . . 1 — 3
Polydrusus, espèces non détermi-
        nées. 3
Cleonis caliginosus Schon.
    — glacialis Herbst.
    — puncticollis Schon.
    — lacrimosus Schon.
    — gibbicollis Dej.
    — espèces non détermi-
        nées. . . . . . 5 — 10
Byrsops sulcicollis Dej.
    — inæqualis Dup.
    — triangularis Dup.

                   A reporter. . 929

324

Genres.		Espèces.
	Report. . .	929
Byrsops, espèces non détermi- nées. 3	—	6
Myllocerus, espèces non détermi- nées.		2
Odontomerus bidentatus Chevro- lat.		1
Cosmorhinus cristatus Bilberg. . .		1
Phlyctinus callosus Schon.		
— obesus Dup.		
— hariolus Schon.		
— espèces non détermi- nées. 3	—	6
Perytelus, espèces non détermi- nées.		14
Psomeles? espèces non détermi- nées		4
Lixus spectabilis Klug.		
— lividus Fab.		
— auriculatus Schon.		
— tabulus Dej.		
— caffer Herbet.		
— espèces non détermi- nées. 5	—	10
Aclaes, espèces non détermi- nées		2
Balaninus alternans Dej.		
— espèces non détermi- nées. 2	—	3
Tychius, non déterminé.		1
Ithyponis capensis Dej.		1
Alcides brevirostris Dej.		
— hæmopterus Sturm.		
— espèces non détermi- nées. 8	—	10
Baris, espèces non déterminées. .		4
Brachypterus, espèce non déter- minée.		1
		1
Cyrtomon,	—	1
Cœlosternus,	—	5
Cryptorhynchus,	—	7
Anacles sulcipes Schon.		
— crenicollis Dup.		
— espèce non détermi- née. 1	—	3
Desmiphorus,	—	1
	A reporter, . .	1013

Genres.		Espèces.
	Report. . .	1013
Ceutorhynchus.		8
Cionus,	—	2
Calandra zamiarum Perret.		
— espèces non détermi- nées. 3	—	4
Cossonus capensis Dej. var.		
— espèces non détermi- nées. 6	—	7
Hylesinus senex Dup.		1
Apate cornuta Fab.		
— reticulata Dej.		
— capucina Dej.		
— postica Dup.		
— espèces non détermi- nées. 8	—	12
Xylographus,	—	1
Trogosita opaca Klug.		
— espèce non détermi- née. 1	—	2
Gymnocheilis vestita Dej.		
— espèce non détermi- née. . . . 1	—	2
Acanthophorus Delegorguei Dup. .		1
Mallodou miles Dej.		
— Delegorguei Dup..		2
Calpoderus caffer Klug.		
Macrotoma amakosa Dup.		
— carbonaria Dup.		
— natala Dreigi.		
— espèces non détermi- nées. 3	—	6
Aulecopis amakosa Lac.		1
Erioderus lanuginosus Dej.		1
Dorcasomus ebulinus Fab.		
— Delegorguei Guer. . . .		2
Amphidesmus quadridens Fab. . . .		1
Hamaticherus Klugii Dup.		
— natalensis Dup.		
— viridipennis Dup.		
— depressus Dup.		
— vespertilionoides Dup.		
— caffer Dup.		6
Jontho des cruentata Chevrolat.		
— caffra Dup.		
	A reporter. . .	1072

325

Genres.	Espèces.
Report. . . 1072	
Jonthodes cærulea Dup.	3
Callichroma Latreillei Dup.	
— opulenta Dup.	
— natala Dup.	
— splendicollis Dup.	
— latipis Fab.	5
Litopus femoralis Dup.	
— dispar Chevrolat.	
Promeces longipes Fab.	
— cyanicollis Dup.	
- espèces non détermi-	
nées. . . . . . . 3 —	5
Polyzomus clavicornis Fab.	
— crassicornis Fab.	
— scalaris Dej.	
— tricinctus Dej.	
— Delegorguei Dup. . . .	5
Nouveau genre, nouvelle espèce. .	1
Closteromerus cyanipennis Dej.	
— sexpunctatus Fab. .	2
Sericogaster argentatus Klug. . . .	1
Xystrocera imperialis Dup.	1
Stromacium caffrum Dup.	1
Callidium Delegorguei Dup.	
— espèces non détermi-	
nées. . . . . . . 3 —	4
Clytus cruenticollis Dup.	
— hottentotta Dej.	
— espèces non détermi-	
nées. . . . . . . 4 —	6
Odontocera ? funeralis Dup. . . .	1
Ancylonotus Dejeanii Dup.	1
Lasiodactylus Buquetii *var.* Dej.	
— luctuosus Dup. . . .	2
Chætosoma pilosum Dej.	2
— elegantulum Dup. . .	2
Cloniocerus opulentus Dup.	
— histrix Fab.	
— nebulosus Dup. . . .	3
Monohammus natalensis Dup.	
— Delegorguei Dup. . .	2
Amblesthis alutaceus Dej.	1
Anoplosthæta lactator Fab.	
— *id var.* radiata Dup.	2
A reporter, . . 1122	

Genres.	Espèces.
Report. . . 1122	
Phryneta spinator Fab.	1
Pachystola griseosignata Dup. . .	1
Ceroplesis caffra Dej.	
— marginata Boh.	
— brachypterus Dup.	
— bicincta Fab.	
— cruentata *var.* Dej.	
— Klugii Dej.	6
Tragocephala dynasta Dup.	
— similata Dup. . . .	2
Zographus nivisparsus Chevrolat.	1
Sternodonta amabilis West. . . .	1
Prosopocera interrupta Dup.	
— armifrons Dup.	
— espèces non détermi-	
nées. . . . . 2 —	4
Xylorhiza —	1
Nyphona caffra Dup.	
— natala Dup.	2
Crostsopus sexpunctata Klug.	
— similatus Dup.	
— ægrotus Dup.	
— curtus Dup.	4
Cotops subhamatus Dup.	
— funereus Dup.	
— cicatricosus Dup.	3
Mastigocera barbicornis Fab. . . .	1
Acmocera compressa Fab.	1
Sophronica carbonaria Dej.	1
Apomecina sulphureo-signata Dup.	1
Hathlia doreadioides Dej.	1
Nouv. genre, apomecinoides Dup.	1
Oberea, espèces non déterminées.	14
Sphænura Westermanii Dej.	
— espèces non détermi-	
nées. . . . . 2 —	3
Hippopsis, espèces non déterminées	3
Nemotragus helvolus Klug.	2
Sagra, espèces non déterminées. .	4
Pæcilomorphus atripes Lacordaire.	1
Megalopus, espèces non détermi-	
nées.	4
Lema,	10
Hispa,	11
A reporter. . . 1206	

Genres.		Espèces.
	Report. . .	1206
Deloyala,	—	2
Cassida vigintimaculatu Thumberg.		
— amakosa Dup.		
— excavata Dej.		
— punctata		
— espèces non détermi-		
nées. 11	—	15
Basipta palleus Klug.		1
Polyclada nigripes Dup.		1
Cælomera, —		5
Aleruca linteata Fab.		2
Aulacophora, —		2
Diacantha algoensis Dup.		
— espèces non détermi-		
nées. 2	—	3
Malacosoma vertebralis Dup. . . .		1
Oligocera, espèces non déterminées.		3
Apophylia, —		7
Monolepta, —		3
Apteropeda, —		3
Argopus semi-rufus Dej.		
— indicus *var*. Fab.		
— espèces non détermi-		
nées. 2	—	4
Blephorida catenulata Dej.		
— Dreigei Dej.		
— espèce non détermi-		
née. 1	—	3
Chrysomela, —		5
Centroscelis castanea Dup.		
— macularia Dej.		2
Plagiadera rufocincta Dej.		
— espèces non détermi-		
nées. 2	—	3
	A reporter. . .	1271

Genres.		Espèces.
	Report. . .	1271
Strongylotarsa,	—	1
Thysbe algoensis Dup.		
— laticollis Dup.		
— espèces non détermi-		
nées. 6	—	8
Acis velutinus Dup.		
— espèces non déterminées. . .		2
Thypophorus, espèces non déter-		
minées.		7
Euryope bucephalus Dup.		
— Dregei Dej.		
— thoracicus Dej.		
— formosa Dup. Boh.		
Platycorinus Dejeanii Dregei.		
— auripennis Dup.		
— espèces non détermi-		
nées. 2	—	4
Heteraspis.		1
Eubrachis.		11
Nerissus lineatus Dup.		
— strigatus Dej.		2
Clythra, espèces non déterminées.		14
Cryptocephalus.		16
Triplax.		3
Tritoma.		3
Coccinella.		5
Exoplecta lunata et *var*.		3
Epilachna.		7
Chilocorus.		2
Micraspis vittata.		1
Hyperaspis.		5
Espèces non encore rapportées à		
leurs genres.		42
	Total. . .	1408

DIPTERA

New species recorded by M. Delegorgue, and described by M. Macquart, director of the Museum of the town of Lille.

1. Pachyrhina Delegorguei.
2. Tabanus fraternus.
3. Tabanus subelongatus.
4. Tabanus fallax.
5. Sargus ruficornis.
6. Microstylum flavipennis.
7. Microstylum pica.
8. Dasypogon lymbithorax.
9. Discocephala tibialis.
10. Discocephala caffra.
11. Laxenecera andrenoides.
12. Trupanea caffra.
13. Asilus nigribarbis.
14. Asilus dubius.
15. Asilus forficula.
16. Damalis hirtiventris.
17. Damalis hyalipennis.
18. Gonypes albitarsis.
19. Empis incompleta.
20. Exoprosopa costalis.
21. Exoprosopa dimidiata.
22. Anthrax aurata.
23. Hystricephala nigra.
24. Hoplacephala tessellata.
25. Lamprometopia caffra.
26. Masicera caffra.
27. Idia punctulata.
28. Idia albitarsis.
29. Spilogaster hirtipes.
30. Sapromyza guttulata.
31. Sapromyza obliquepunctata.
32. Heterogaster fascipennis.
33. Herina vicina.
34. Epidesma fascipennis.
35. Dichromyia caffra.
36. Sphœrocera hyalipennis.
37. Phytomyza caffra.

ORNITHOLOGY

The dusky turtledove – *Columba Delegorguei* ♂

This pigeon[1] inhabits the forest at the bay of Port Natal. It is solitary and extremely rare. I killed it there in June.

The length from the tip of the beak to that of the tail is 30cm. The outermost wing feathers are slightly shorter than the inner ones. The general colour of the plumage is a deep slate grey, grading to burnished purple, except for the tail and wing feathers which are slightly darkened. The nape of the neck below the occiput is white, looking so much like a bird dropping that it may deceive the eye of the observer.

Above, this unpretentious bird is distinguished by a beautifully hued metallic sheen, from anterior to posterior and from the eyes down onto the breast. This hue is a blend of emerald, amethyst and purple, and seems to be a purplish golden green highlighted with red and green. Turned one way it appears pure green-gold; turned the other it is brilliant amethyst. Proximally the beak is black for half its length. Distally, beyond the medial swelling, it is yellow. The feet are also yellow.

The female differs from the male in that the head is reddish brown grading into amethyst. The white at the nape of the neck is completely absent.

The Oury quail – *Coturnix Delegorguei* ♂

In its migrations from the north this species[2] travels little further than 25 south. Flocks are encountered in February and are extremely abundant. At about 10 o'clock in the morning the birds are very vocal: there are so many of them that the clamour is quite exhausting. The grass is so long on the banks of the Oury, which is their favourite haunt, that we would not see them until they rose up unexpectedly three paces in front of us or sometimes even from under our feet. My men would throw tongas at them to kill them and I could have shot several hundred in a day.

The bird is 15cm long from the tip of the beak to the end of the tail. Its dorsal surface is very like that of the common quail – a deep brown, mingled with fawn, with small transverse streaks broken by dirty white lanceolate patches marking the centre of the primary feathers. From above male and female are alike. Below, however, the throat of the male is distinguished by a black anchor on a white background, and by a completely black breast, with spatulate black areas extending to the abdomen, which is tawny brown. The beak is black, the feet are a yellowish brown.

The underparts of the female have no more than a rather indeterminate blend of fawn, brown and dirty white – a livery similar to that of the juvenile.

Notes

1. Columba delegorguei, Delegorgue's pigeon or bronzenaped pigeon.
2. Coturnix delegorguei, the harlequin quail.
   (and see Natural History Index.)

Number and A.D.'s name	Present scientific name	Common name
1. *Elephas Africanus*	*Loxodonta africana*	African elephant
2. *Rhinoceros Af. Bicornis*	*Diceros bicornis*	Black/hooklipped rhinoceros
3. *Rhinoceros Simus*	*Ceratotherium simum*	White/squarelipped rhinoceros
4. *Rhinoceros Quetloha**	*Diceros bicornis*	Black rhinoceros
5. *Rhinoceros Lelongouanne**	?	?
6. *Rhinoceros Unicornis**	?	?
7. *Hippopotamus Amphibius*	*Hippopotamus amphibius*	Hippopotamus
8. *Sus Larvatus*	*Potamochoerus porcus*	Bushpig
9. *Sus Phacochaerus*	*Phacochoerus aethiopicus*	Warthog
10. *Bos Cafer*	*Syncerus caffer*	Cape buffalo
11. *Equus Zebra**	*Equus zebra*	Cape mountain zebra
12. *Equus Burschellii**	*Equus burchelli*	Burchell's zebra
13. *Equus Couagga**	*Equus quagga*	Quagga
14. *Camelopardalis Giraffa*	*Giraffa camelopardalis*	Giraffe
15. *Catoblepas Gnou*	*Connochaetes gnou*	Black wildebeest
16. *Catoblepas Gorgon*	*Connochaetes taurinus*	Blue wildebeest
17. *Boselaphus Oreas (seu†Canna)*	*Taurotragus oryx*	Eland
18. *Strepsiceros Condoma*	*Tragelaphus strepsiceros*	Kudu
19. *Acronotus Caama*	*Alcelaphus buselaphus*	Red hartebeest
20. *Acronotus Lunata*	*Damaliscus lunatus*	Tsessebe
21. *Aigoceros Nigra*	*Hippotragus niger*	Sable antelope
22. *Aigoceros Equina*	*Hippotragus equinus*	Roan antelope
23. *Kobus Ellipsiprymnus*	*Kobus ellipsiprymnus*	Waterbuck
24. *Oryx Capensis*	*Oryx gazella*	Gemsbok
25. *Gazella Euchore*	*Antidorcas marsupialis*	Springbok
26. *Gazella Albifrons*	*Damaliscus dorcas phillipsi*	Blesbok
27. *Gazella Pygarga*	*Damaliscus dorcas dorcas*	Bontebok
28. *Antilope Melampus*	*Aepyceros melampus*	Impala
29. *Tragelaphus Sylvatica*	*Tragelaphus scriptus sylvaticus*	Bushbuck
30. *Redunca Eleotragus*	*Redunca arundinum*	Reed buck
31. *Redunca Lalandii*	*Redunca fulvorufula*	Mountain reed buck
32. *Redunca Capreolus*	*Pelea capreolus*	Grey rhebok
33. *Redunca Scoparia*	*Ourebia ourebi*	Oribi
34. *Oreotragus Saltatrix*	*Oreotragus oreotragus*	Klipspringer
35. *Tragulus Rupestris*	*Raphicerus campestris*	Steenbok
36. *Tragulus Melanotis*	*Raphicerus melanotis*	Grysbok
37. *Cephalopus Mergens**	*Sylvicapra grimmia*	Grey duiker
38. *Cephalopus Burschellii**	*Sylvicapra grimmia*	Grey duiker
39. *Cephalopus Natalensis*	*Cephalophus natalensis*	Red duiker
40. *Cephalopus Coerulea*	*Philantomba monticolor*	Blue duiker
41. *Felis Leo*	*Panthera leo*	Lion
42. *Felis Leopardus*	*Panthera pardus*	Leopard
43. *Felis Jubata*	*Acinonyx jubatus*	Cheetah
44. *Felis Serval*	*Felis serval*	Serval
45. *Hyaena Crocuta*	*Crocuta crocuta*	Spotted hyaena
46. *Hyaena Fusca*	*Hyaena brunnea*	Brown hyaena
47. *Cynhyaena Venatica*	*Lycaon pictus*	African wild dog
48. *Manes Temminckii*	*Manis temmincki*	Pangolin/scaly anteater

* For explanation or comment see Natural History Index
** Not shown on the original map
† = or; also

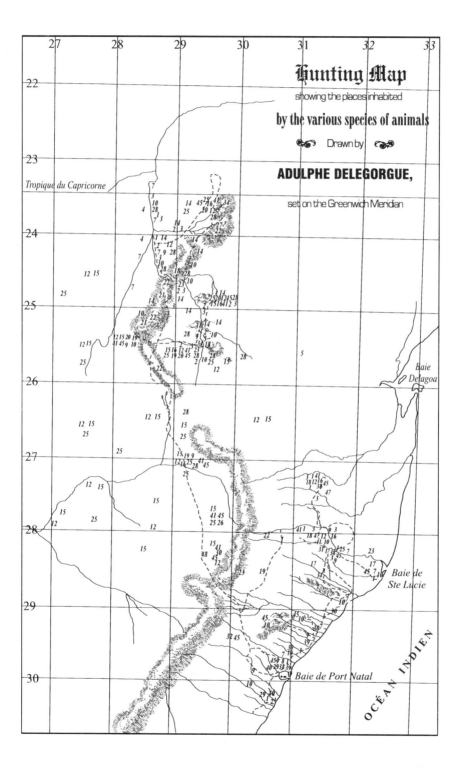

Hunting Map

showing the places inhabited

by the various species of animals

Drawn by

ADULPHE DELEGORGUE,

set on the Greenwich Meridian

Tropique du Capricorne

Baie Delagoa

Baie de Ste Lucie

Baie de Port Natal

OCÉAN INDIEN

NATURAL HISTORY INDEX

This index has the same purpose as that which accompanied Volume I: it is a guide to the plants and animals mentioned in the text, as well as to an assortment of items of scientific interest. As before, although the facts required by the biological scientist are deemed important, the intention also is to inform and divert the general reader. To this end, besides pointing to material in the text, entries include supplementary information and, wherever possible, discussion or comment enabling the non-specialist to put facts into a wider biological context and also into social and historical perspective.

Adulphe Delegorgue's *Travels* is a continuous narrative, broken in two at a point more likely to have been decided on by the printer than by the author. At first, it seemed artificial to create two separate indexes for what is a single book, but as the work of compilation proceeded advantages became apparent. A single index would have been extremely long, and those entries with page references and commentary relating to both volumes might have become so unwieldy as to sap the reader's interest. Separate indexes keep page references under control and permit the focusing of attention on the volume in hand – yet a sense of continuity from Volume I to II may be achieved by referring from the latter back to the former where appropriate. Although some entry words are duplicated in the two indexes, the entries themselves are not: every effort has gone into making them complementary. However, even though readers will gain most from using the two indexes side-by-side, all of the information necessary for an understanding of the natural history of Volume II is available in the Volume II index, and the book may be read and enjoyed as complete in itself.

The index includes:

(a) Brief notes on the lives of scientists, travellers and collectors mentioned in the text. Special attention is given to influential 19th-century figures and to those who have contributed to our knowledge of the southern African fauna.

(b) Commentary on topics of scientific, medical and veterinary interest raised or suggested by the text. Parasites, pests, viral and bacterial infections, as well as the techniques of specimen preparation, all receive attention, as do relevant practices of indigenous peoples and, occasionally, matters bordering on fantasy and myth.

(c) The identification and a brief classification of every plant and animal mentioned in the text. The entry word is the name first given by Delegorgue, whether this be a scientific, common, Dutch or vernacular name, and each is given precisely as Delegorgue gives it, idiosyncratic as this may be. His alternative names are given with each entry and explained where necessary (and where possible); all forms are cross-referenced, as are useful modern common names – and, as before, no common name carries an initial capital. Where identification has had to be based on deduction, lines of reasoning are summarised, and where exact identification has been impossible, the merits of different possibilities are argued.

Identification proceeds as far as species whenever possible, and generic and specific names are italicised and abbreviated in the accepted fashion (by contrast with which Delegorgue's often looks highly eccentric), thus, *Hippopotamus amphibius*; *H. amphibius*. Authorities are omitted unless they are essential to an argument. For each plant only the family name is given, in brackets, e.g., (Euphorbiaceae), but animals are usually given two taxonomic subdivisions, those which seem most immediate and most useful in pinpointing identity and position. Thus, for example, while it would be superfluous to note for every mammal that it belongs to the Phylum Chordata, Class Mammalia, for one it may be important to give Order and Family, while for another, Family and Subfamily may be more significant and useful. Less common subdivisions, such as Tribe, are given in full. Otherwise, abbreviations are used, as follows, listed in descending order: P.~ Phylum; S.P. ~ Subphylum; C.~ Class; S.C. ~ Subclass; O. ~ Order; S.O. ~ Suborder; F. ~ Family; S.F. ~ Subfamily.

Other abbreviations include sp and spp ~ species in the singular and plural; subsp ~ subspecies.

Regrettably, apart from some arthropods (mainly insects), invertebrate animals hardly feature at all in Delegorgue's narrative. Invertebrate classification, a delight to the orderly specialist, is complicated, and it was decided to treat this as simply as possible, bypassing a host of groupings which, to most readers, would seem both confusing and unnecessary. It is hoped that those few which have been included (e.g., P. Platyhelminthes, P. Chelicerata), will excite, rather than dampen, interest.

Again, Delegorgue mixes metric and imperial measures. The index gives preference to metric measures but includes feet, inches, etc., with the metric version when appropriate. And, once again, for the benefit of the general reader, metric measurements are expressed not in millimetres, but in metres and centimetres.

An asterisk (*) after the name of an animal indicates that it is listed in the key to the hunting map, p330; some of the listed animals, however, did not appear on the original map. These are marked with a double asterisk (**).

Stephanie Alexander

Aarde-bontjes ~ 249 ~ *see* Beans, underground.

Aarde vark also ant-bear, *orycterope* ~ 159 ~ *see also* Vol I
Orycteropus afer, the antbear, the only living representative of O. Tubulidentata, F. Orycteropodidae.

Acronotus caama see Caama

Acronotus lunata* *also Bastaard-haartbeest*, Lunata ~ 177, 182, 189–90
The tsessebe, *Damaliscus lunatus* (F. Bovidae, S.F. Alcelaphinae: Afrikaans, *basterhartbees*, Tswana, *tshêsêbe*). Large antelope which were plentiful in the north of South Africa. Now, tsessebe occur in the Kruger National Park, mainly north of the Letaba River. Otherwise they occur in private game reserves and have been reintroduced into various other reserves.

Tsessebe are ungainly in appearance, but swift on their feet, faster than the red hartebeest (*see Caama*), despite A.D.'s assertion to the contrary (190), and faster also than most other antelope. A.D.'s lively description of the tsessebe is marred by slight confusion, for the dark reddish brown of the coat, with its distinct iridescent purplish sheen, resembles that of the bontebok (*see bonte-book*) and not that of the blesbok (*see Gazella albifrons*). This is a reminder that his identifications, especially of antelope, should be treated with caution.

Acronotus was never a generic name given to tsessebe, but was used as a substitute for *Alcelaphus* by H. Smith (1827). *Alcelaphus buselaphus* is the red hartebeest (*see Caama*). For parasites of tsessebe *see* Bots.

Africanus Bicornis see Rhinoceros

Aigoceros Equina see Bastaard-guymsbook

Aigoceros nigra* *also* Black antelope, kakaraba ~ 154, 194, 196, 199, 200, 206–9, 221–2, 224–5, 229, 234
A.D.'s first mention of the sable antelope, the animal which was to become something of an obsession for him, is as 'Harris' remarkable antelope...' Indeed, Cornwallis Harris (q.v.), whose portrait of the sable, *Hippotragus niger*, adorns the cover of this volume, collected the original type specimen in the Magaliesberg west of Pretoria. It was described in 1838, and was for some time afterwards called 'Harris' buck' (for further comment, *see* Harris; Verreaux).

'Sable' is really a misnomer, because only old adult males are gleaming black in colour, with white underparts and characteristic black and white face patterning. Old adult females may be very dark brown, but younger animals are reddish brown. Sable are more lightly built and less robust than the closely related roan, *H. equinus* (*see Bastaard-guymsbook*, which includes comment on nomenclature). It is a savanna woodland species confined to the central and eastern parts of Africa, and although there has been local retreat in the face of development, the overall distributional range is little changed.

The origin of A.D.'s obsession with the antelope is not entirely clear. The sable is, certainly, of extraordinarily noble appearance, with splendid, sweepingly curved horns in both sexes. These are deadly weapons: territorial bulls may fight to the death, and unwary hunters approaching too closely to wounded bulls have been seriously injured. To its beauty (which A.D. vigorously appreciated, *see* 225) may have been added a certain rarity value, for though sable congregate in moderately large herds (20+ animals) their numbers had already been depleted and they may have become shy and more inclined to confine activity to early morning and late afternoon. A.D. was certainly also influenced by Wahlberg (q.v.),who conceived almost a passion for killing as many sable as possible in the Magaliesberg, as his memoirs show (*and see* 207): perhaps there was an element of competition to see who could kill and thus possess more of these rare and beautiful 'things'.

A.D.'s 'kakaraba' is his rendering of a vernacular (? Sotho) name for the sable. Wahlberg gives *kaharaba*. Both might have joined with the paean of praise implicit in the longdisused generic name *Ozanna* (F. Bovidae, S.F. Hippotraginae).

Albatross *also Manches des velours* ~ 285 ~ *see also* Vol I
Large marine birds (O. Procellariiformes, F. Diomedeidae). The commonest albatross of the south-west coast of Africa is the blackbrowed alba-

tross, *Diomedea melanophris*. A.D.'s '*manches de velours*' (French, literally = velvet sleeves) probably refers to the beautiful darkmantled sooty albatross, *Phoebetria fusca*. It is a medium-sized, slenderly built bird whose long wings are slender also. The body is all dark, and the feathers are softly velvety (*fusca*, Latin = velvet). *P. fusca* is a rare vagrant to all southern African waters.

Albifrons see Gazella albifrons

Aloe ~ 115 ~ *see also* Vol I
The word 'aloe' has long been a catch-all for spiny or fleshy-leaved plants with a real or fancied resemblance to *Aloe* spp (Asphodelaceae) such as species of *Agave*, *Dracaena* and even *Euphorbia*. The spiny leaves used to card the hair of cowhide may have been aloe leaves – or they may not.

Alum, as preservative *also* Salt and alum ~ 201 ~ *see also* Vol I
A mixture of burnt alum and saltpetre was rubbed into mammal skins to preserve (or cure, or tan) them. *See also* Arsenic; Corrosive sublimate

Anhinga ~ 187 ~ *see also* Vol I
Anhinga melanogaster, the darter or 'snakebird' (O. Pelicaniformes, F. Anhingidae: darters). For details of habits and habitat *see* Vol I. Here, A.D. likens the transversely-barred tail to that of a starling (*see Lamprotornis Burchellii*).

Animalcules ~ 232 ~ *see also* Vol I
Very small animals – here, aquatic insects and other small creatures inhabiting a brackish or polluted pond which may have been drying up. *See* Insects and larvae, aquatic

Ant. An abbreviation for *Antilope*, a generic name no longer in use.

Ant. bubalus see Caama

Ant. canna see Eland

Ant. melampus* also Bastaard-spring-book, big red buck, *Gazella melampus*, *groot-rooye-book*, *Melampus* ~ 177, 178, 182–4, 206, 228, 230, 247, 265–6 ~ *see also* Vol I
The impala, *Aepyceros melampus* (F. Bovidae, S.F. Aepycerotinae), a graceful antelope with a shiny, reddish coat and long, slender legs. Although it must have been abundant in Natal A.D. hardly mentions it in his account of that stage of his travels: it seems to have caught his eye and his imagination only later when (182–4) he gives

a graphic and accurate description. As he indicates, the black tuft on each hind foot is the source of the name: *melampous*, Gk = black-footed.

Ant. oryx see Guyms-book

Antelope, black, with white underbelly *see Aigoceros nigra*

Ant-heap *see* Termites

Anthia Burchellii see Carabids

Antimony *see Sibilo/sibylo*

Ants ~ 23 ~ *see also* Vol I
Insects belonging to O. Hymenoptera (q.v.), F. Formicidae.

Arachnids, venomous ~ 224, 233–4
Although the arthropods which attacked A.D. in such numbers in Schloschlome's hut may have been bedbugs (*Cimex lectularius*, O. Hemiptera) this seems unlikely. There is evidence (*see* Bugs, Vol I) that A.D. had made the painful acquaintance of bedbugs during his short sojourn at the Cape, and he must have seen – and experienced – them many times since then. Although he at first calls these arthropods 'insects' he later decides that they are enough like ticks to be called arachnids. Indeed, his description accords with that of the soft tick (F. Argasidae) *Ornithodorus moubata*, which commonly lives with people and their livestock, and feeds almost preferentially on human beings. Much like bedbugs, these are temporary ectoparasites, feeding at night and crawling away to hide at dawn. A.D. reports that they ran about on the ground by day, in sunlight and shadow, but he may have misidentified some other arachnid or insect. He was, after all, weary, frustrated and in enough discomfort for his observations to have been less than acute (P. Chelicerata, C. Arachnida, O. Acarina: ticks and mites).

His reaction to the bites (as to the tapeworm, – q.v. – and to bedbugs and other ticks, *see* Vol I) was extreme. It was not that the soft ticks were 'venomous', but that he was hypersensitive. He experienced a severe skin reaction – not only 'unbearable itching', but also pain – and became overwrought, though not as seriously as he did in response to the presence of the tapeworm. Clinicians would find A.D. a fascinating subject and, of course, it would be interesting to know if his erratic and often heavily carnivorous diet was in any way related to the intensity of his reactions to both ecto- and endoparasites.

Arago, Jacques Étienne Victor ~ 95–6 ~ see also Vol I
In Vol I A.D. writes slightingly of Arago's fanciful account of his South African exploits in his *Voyage Auteur du Monde* (Voyage around the world). Here he continues to pour scorn on Arago's extravagantly incorrect impressions of the Cape, and on the pathetic Rouviére – a 'lion hunter' whose description reads like that of a character invented by Lewis Carroll.

It is pleasing, though, to see this far into the narrative a return – though sadly brief – of the instructive, didactic A.D. who so enlivened the early chapters of Vol I.

Arsenic, arsenical soap, used in taxidermy ~ 43, 44, 224
After preservation (curing or tanning), animal skins are cleaned. Modern workers use formalin for tanning (*see* Vol I: Alum, for A.D.'s method) and a proprietary detergent to clean, whiten and soften. Until the 1950s and 1960s arsenical soaps were used: arsenic ('white arsenic', i.e. arsenious oxide or arsenic trioxide, As_4O_6) was combined with soap and other ingredients and repeatedly rubbed into the skin. Arsenic is highly poisonous, and these days museum workers who handle old specimens prepared in this way wear gloves and other protective clothing.

Arsenic was known to the ancients and used as a caustic. In the 19th century it would have been readily available at any druggist and sold as rat poison. It is not surprising, therefore, that A.D. carried as much as seven pounds of arsenic with him, and that he was willing to 'scatter it to the wind' rather than allow it to be used to poison the water supply as the Boers planned: it would have been easy enough to replace.

Arsenic was used well into the 20th century as a weed killer and, in arsenical flypapers, as an insecticide, and it would be interesting to know what effect, if any, the scattered powder had on the vegetation and its inhabitants. It is difficult to imagine how A.D. used arsenical soap in the preparation of (presumably) dried insect specimens (224), and is not surprising that they were damaged in whatever the process was. *See also* Alum; Camphor; Corrosive sublimate; Turpentine

Baboon *also* Mountain baboon ~ 232 ~ *see also* Vol I
Papio ursinus, the chacma baboon (O. Primates, S.O. Haplorhini, F. Cercopithecidae: monkeys and baboons). There are six subspecies in the southern African subregion, and A.D. probably saw the largest, *P.u. griseipes*, in the Transvaal. The chacma baboon is gregarious and lives in troops – up to 130 individuals in exceptional cases. As the context indicates, availability of water is important in determining home ranges; it also dictates the movements of baboon troops. The calls A.D. heard were the bisyllabic warning barks of large male baboons on the look-out, alerting the troop to the approach of danger.

Baboons are omnivorous, though the single most important item of diet appears to be grass, the more succulent parts of which enable them to supplement their water requirements in the dry season. Insects, other arthropods and even molluscs are eaten, but predation on other vertebrates (e.g. birds, rodents, newborn small antelope, free-ranging domestic stock), while it does occur, is relatively rare.

Badger *see* Ratel
Bastaard-eland see Bastaard guyms-book
Bastaard-guyms-book *also* Aigoceres, *Aigoceros equina*, bastaard-eland, equine antelope, great blue antelope, *groot blaauw-book*, *tzeiran* ~ 196, 200–1, 229, 234 ~ *see also* Vol I
The roan antelope (Afrikaans: *bastergemsbok*), *Hippotragus equinus* (F. Bovidae, S.F. Hippotraginae). A large antelope with distinctive pelage: greyish brown, with a slight strawberry tinge in certain lights. The face is black or very dark brown, with a strongly contrasting white patch from the top of the muzzle to the chin. Both the male and female roan carry horns, strongly ridged and rising from the top of the head in an even backward

336

curve. These curved horns were the source of a number of 19th century spelling variations on a generic name meaning 'goat-horned': *Egocerus, Aegocera, Aigocerus, Oegocerus, Aegocerus* and *Aegocoerus*. A.D. adds his own variants.

This large and noble antelope was once plentiful in the subregion, but with human encroachment and their critical habitat requirement of lightly wooded savanna, distribution has become patchy. A.D.'s enraptured description of the animal – actually of a head and skin which eventually found its way to a museum in France (200–1) is not only graphic but conveys the old excitement of discovery and delight in animal beauty, common in Vol I, but on the wane in Vol II. The origin of *'tzeiran'* is unknown.

Bastaard-haart-beest see Acronotus lunata
Bastaard-spring-book see Ant. melampus
Beans, small, black ~ 124

Perhaps the seeds of *Tyloma fassoglensis*, the marama bean or gemsbok bean: they are well-flavoured and are used as a foodstuff in some parts of southern Africa. Otherwise the beans may have been seeds of a species of *Vigna*, perhaps *V. unguiculata*, the kaffir bean or cow pea, a versatile crop prepared in various ways and eaten alone or mixed with grain.

Shoots and leaves may be prepared as a side dish, or steamed and sun-dried until crisp and very tasty (Fabaceae).

Beans, underground ~ 124, 249, 253 *also Aarde-bontjes*

Not, as might be expected, the ground nut (Afrikaans: *grondboontjie*), *Arachis hypogaea*, even though this had been cultivated in Natal since 1830. The description is clearly that of *Voandzeia subterranea*, the African ground bean, bambarra groundnut, jugo bean or Madagascar pistachio nut (Fabaceae). This is a prostrate annual herb whose ovoid pods form subterranean clusters round the central root or along the secondary roots. Widely cultivated in many parts of the tropics, the plant was introduced into South Africa several times – the Lovedu, Venda and Shangaan all claim credit – and has been cultivated by the Zulus. The bean is versatile, and is ground into flour which, after boiling, is eaten with meat, fat or maize; sometimes it is boiled with maize or millet-meal into a stiff dough, which keeps well when salted and pounded into balls. It is high in protein and is used as a substitute for meat.

A.D.'s description (249) is eloquent, but there would be nothing 'uninformed' about one who confused the bean with a pistachio nut: they are closely related.

It is remarkable that so nutritious and drought-resistant a crop has received so little attention from science and commercial agriculture.

Bee-eaters *includes Merops apiaster, M. bullockoïdes, M. minulus, M. nubicoïdes, M. Savignii, also* pink bee-eater of Senegal ~ 187, 189, 254–5, 259 ~ *see also* Vol I

Bee-eaters are birds of O. Apodiformes, F. Meropidae, a family characterised by bright plumage and confined to the Old World. They all breed in holes, whether on level ground or in sandbanks or similar situations: A.D. describes the nesting of one of the South African bee-eaters in the walls of a ravine (187), and also their characteristic 'wheeling and swooping like swallows' at sunset.

The European bee-eater, *Merops apiaster* (255), is a breeding migrant which spends the summer months in the southern hemisphere. Like all bee-eaters it hawks for insects in the air from a perch or in flight pursuit, and is most gregarious. Although the bird has the cheerful, mainly blue-and-yellow coloration of several species, its back is uniquely brown. A species of woodland, savanna and scrubby grassland, it is widely distributed in South Africa.

M. bullockoides is the whitefronted bee-eater (187, 255) distinguished by its red and white throat, with crown and breast cinnamon, otherwise predominantly green with bright blue undertail coverts. This is a common resident, as A.D. observes, found in the north and north east of South Africa. A.D.'s *M. minulus* (doubtless a misprint of *minutus*) is surely the little bee-eater, *M. pusillus* (255). This is a small (17–18 cm) bird with distinctive bright yellow-ochre underparts and green above. It, too, is a common resident of the north and north east, preferring bushveld, open woodland, savanna, streams and reedbeds.

The carmine bee-eater, *M. nubicoides*, is large (33–38 cm) and predominantly rose red to crimson, with cobalt blue crown and undertail coverts, and light green rump. The bird was first described by Desmurs and Pucheran (1846; q.v.), as A.D. mentions (254), from the material he supplied as well as from the Limpopo Valley. Some authors believe this to be the most beautiful of all South African birds. It is a locally common migrant, found, when breeding, only along major lowveld river valleys and floodplains, usually those with vertical banks. It is very gregarious, roosting by day, emerging at evening to skim over the water after insects. The birds are attracted by veld fires and descend in large numbers to snap up insects disturbed by the flames. *M. nubicoides* is widely distributed in Africa and this may, therefore, despite A.D.'s disclaimer (254), also be the identity of the Senegalese bird.

A.D.'s *M. Savignii* (255) is *M. persicus*, the bluecheeked bee-eater, a fairly common palaearctic non-breeding migrant which occurs in northern Natal, Transvaal and northern Cape and Free State. It is found along larger rivers and in woodland around pools and vleis; it is gregarious in small flocks. A medium-to-large bird (30–33 cm), it is predominantly green in colour, with blue cheeks and shades of brown, yellow and rufous-cinnamon below.

A.D. has not tried to describe in lyrical language the incomparable richness and overwhelming colour (and enormous numbers) of the riverine avifauna of the northern Transvaal. Perhaps he is wise: the task might defeat writers far more literary than he.

Beetles *see* Coleoptera
Big red buck see Ant. melampus
Blaauw-wild-beest see Catoblepas gorgon
Blac *see* Kite
Black antelope, with white underbelly *see Aigoceros nigra*
Blackbird ~ 259
The 'blackbird' at the Limpopo was not, of course, the European blackbird

Turdus merula, but, presumably, a smallish bird resembling it, and (since it was 'shouting abuse' at a 'sparrow-owl' – q.v.) one with loud and aggressive vocalisation.

The forktailed drongo *Dicrurus adsimilis* (O. Passeriformes, F. Dicruridae) is black with a purplish sheen all over, frequents riverine *Acacia*, and is a versatile and strident vocalist. In groups it mobs larger raptors, other birds and small mammals. A less likely candidate would be the black cuckooshrike, *Campephaga flava* (F. Campephagidae) which, though it may certainly be vocal, also tends to be quiet and unobstrusive, perching in dense vegetation.

Blue gnou/gnu *see Catoblepas gorgon*
Boa python *see* Python
Boar*, wild *also Sus Phacochaerus*, ~ 117
~ *see also* Warthog, Vol I
Phacochoerus aethiopicus, the warthog. For description *see* Vol I. In Vol II it is mentioned only in passing.
Bombyx, cocoon of ~ 114
Although the oriental silkworm, i.e.,the moth *Bombyx mori*, has long been widely distributed in the world, it is highly unlikely that silken *B. mori* cocoons were used to make snuff boxes. The Catalogue of Lepidoptera (313) refers to the making of snuffboxes, sealed with a wooden plug, from the large, firm cocoons of '*Saturnia Mimosae*', an emperor moth (F. Saturniidae), listed by Pinhey (1975) as *Argema mimosae*. Otherwise the firm, oval cocoons of moths of the genera *Pachypasa*, *Gonometa* and *Trabata* (F. Lasiocampidae), may have been used. The hairy larvae of these moths weave large (20 mm long) cocoons of dense silk mingled with hairs from their bodies, and plastered inside with a paste of saliva and fine-ground sand particles. These may be used as ornaments or containers – with a few small stones they become fine wrist or ankle rattles. The cocoon is slit open neatly and the pupa is not discarded, but cooked and eaten (O. Lepidoptera). *See also Bombyx Edulis*
Bombyx Edulis ~ 313
Although this insect is referred to only in the Catalogue of Lepidoptera, it is appropriate to comment on it here. First, as indicated in the previous entry, *Bombyx* is not a southern African

genus, and the former *B. edulis* is not a bombycid moth. The moth in question is *Striphnopteryx edulis* (F. Eupterotidae, S.F. Striphnopterygina). The common name for eupterotids is 'monkey moths', and Pinhey (1975) calls *S. edulis* an 'edible monkey'. There seems to be no recent evidence, however, of the human consumption of the spotted caterpillars near the Natal coast as described, and the *edulis* (Latin = edible), while it may be taxonomically valid, may have no basis in fact.

Bonte-book* also Gazella pygarga ~ see also Vol I *Damaliscus dorcas dorcas*, the bontebok (F. Bovidae, S.F. Alcelaphinae). For comparison of coloration with that of the tsessebe *see Acronotus lunata; see also Gazella albifrons*

Booter-bloem ~ 248

Although the Dutch first gave the name *boterbloem* to *Ranunculus multifidus* at the Cape (Ranunculaceae) presumably because of its resemblance to the richly yellow European buttercup, this *'booterbloem'* is probably *Gerbera discolor* (Asteraceae, formerly Compositae).

C.A. Smith (1962) writes, 'Delagorgue (sic), who visited the Voortrekker country north of the "Makalis Berg" in 1840–41, records *booterbloem* for what can only be *Gerbera discolor* for which the common name still holds. . .'. This golden daisy is a close relative of *G. jamesonii*, the Barberton daisy, and the rare Hilton daisy, *G. aurantiaca*.

These flowers reminded Tom of other golden daisies in the Cape, probably *Gazania* spp. These acquired *boterbloem* or Afrikaans *botterblom* as common name, and the name gradually embraced more and more species as the Boers moved through the interior of Natal.

Borers, buffalo horn ~ 148

A.D. gives what seems to be a clear description of the larva of the 'horn moth', *Ceratophaga vastella*, which burrows into old horns of buffalo and rhinoceros, feeding on the keratin of which the horns are composed (*Ceratophaga* is from Gk *keratos* = of horn; *phago* = to eat). The remains of pupal cases jutting out from the horns is the usual sign of their presence (O. Lepi-

doptera, F. Tineidae: an enormous family of small moths, many of whose larvae are scavengers and some of which – the clothes moths – are of economic importance). A.D.'s comparison of the habits and destructive effects of *Ceratophaga* with those of carpenter moths (*see Cossus Ligni perda*) shows insight, and that A.D. was no mean entomologist. His assertion that 'fermentation' attracts the moth is questionable, however.

Borers, into dead beetles *see* Saprophagous fly larvae

Borers, sugarcane *see* Sugarcane borers

Bos Cafer see Buffalo

Boselaphus oreas see Eland .

Bos urus ~ 149

The 'wild and beautiful' buffalo-like animal of Europe to which A.D. refers is *Bison bonasus*, the wisent or European bison. These would still have been plentiful in his time, though numbers were dwindling as natural forests, their preferred habitat, were destroyed. Small populations remained in Poland, Lithuania, the Caucasus and what was Byelorussia, but many were exterminated during and after the First World War. Careful management of zoo animals has permitted the building up of herds in reserves, but *B. bonasus* is again under threat because, through the depredations of war in Central and Eastern Europe in the 1990s, many animals have been lost and scientists believe the gene pool of those few remaining in the Caucasus may be too small for the species to survive (F. Bovidae, S.F. Bovinae).

While *Bos urus* was never a name that could be applied to *Bison bonasus*, it could have been an incorrect version of *Bos taurus*. *B.t. primigenius*, the aurochs or urus, once widely spread in Europe and Asia, and domesticated very early, well before 2500 BC. The wild aurochs became extinct in 1627, but as all western domestic cattle are descended from it, it has been possible to breed back and produce an animal resembling the aurochs physically as well as in agility and temperament.

Bots ~ 182, 218

Flies (O. Diptera) of two families, the Gasterophilidae and the Oestridae, have adults which do not feed: the mouthparts are reduced and non-functional. They live only long enough to deposit their eggs on the host (or, more rarely, a vector, i.e. a living go-between) which will house and feed their long-lived larvae, or bots.

As A.D. describes, the rhinoceros is susceptible. *Gyrostigma* spp (F. Gasterophilidae) have life cycles similar to those of horse bot flies: eggs are laid on hair shafts, and hatch when licked off by the host. The larvae burrow into the tissues of the mouth cavity and, later, pass into the gut where, attached by strong mouth hooks to the wall, they feed on blood and mature over several months. Once mature, they detach themselves, are ejected with the dung and pupate in the soil. The adults are giant (25mm) wasp-like flies. A.D. describes particularly heavy infestations (182).

However, it is probably not worth taking too seriously A.D.'s suggestion that such heavy infestations were the cause of irascible behaviour in black rhinoceros (217–8, *see also* Rhinoceros). *Diceros bicornis* is known to have a fierier temperament than does *Ceratotherium simum*, and there appears to be no evidence that this difference is related to differences in parasitic infestation. *D. bicornis* does tend to react violently to harassment (in this case, of course, harassment by the hunter who would later dissect the carcase and discover the bots), and rapidly learns that human harassment is especially dangerous, requiring swift and decisive fight or flight.

At the time A.D.'s suggestion would have been acceptable. It would also not have seemed far-fetched to compare the emotional state of a human being harbouring a tapeworm (q.v.) with that of a bot-infested rhinoceros. Before one dismisses the argument it is worth recalling that scientists of every age have always used the information and tools available to them at the time and that personal sensations, reactions and intuitions may be important in helping solve problems and finding the answers to questions, while even errors may have some scientific use.

Flies of the F. Oestridae are stout, hairy and rather bee-like. They fall into two groups: those whose larvae live in the nasal and pharyngeal cavi-ties of certain animals, and the 'warble flies' whose larvae develop in skin boils, each of which has a breathing hole.

A.D. encountered both kinds, describing vividly infestations of nasal bot fly larvae (*Oestrus* sp or *Gedoelstia* sp) in wildebeest, which are often seen sneezing out the stout, barrel-shaped maggots which have been maturing in the nasal passages over several months. In some antelope the sinus cavities extend into the horns and, as A.D. describes for '*Acronotus lunata*' (tsessebe), masses of large larvae may be found in these cavities(182). Warble flies may attack several smaller antelope species. A.D.'s descriptions of the boils and their contents are clear: he writes only of '*Redunca lalandii*' (the mountain reed buck) but must surely have encountered *Strobiloestrus* in the skins of a number of other species (182).

Broad-tailed pangolin *see* Pangolin

Bubal *see* Caama

Buffalo* *also Bos Cafer* ~ 11, 13, 25, 93, 99, 100, 114, 133–8, 141, 142–9, 150, 173, 228, 230–1, 256, 259, 265 ~ *see also* Vol I

Syncerus caffer, the Cape buffalo (F. Bovidae, S.F. Bovinae). A large, ox-like animal, heavily built, with massive shoulders and curved horns arising from bulky bosses on the forehead. Under normal circumstances this gregarious bovid is not aggressive, but if panicked it is very dangerous, displaying a speed and ferocity extraordinary for its great size and mass. As A.D. comments (148), it is a poor candidate for domestication, unlike the more docile Indian buffalo and its descendants (*see* Buffalo, Italian; Javanese). Herds may charge if panicked, and a single agitated animal may fearfully injure a victim by goring and trampling, as A.D. discovered. He also learned that a wounded buffalo exhibits behaviour that in a human being would be called vindictive, doubling back on its tracks and hiding in bush or other shelter. It is not deliberately waiting in ambush, but is so inflamed that the very sight of its pursuer following its trail is sufficient to make it charge forth and attack.

A.D. gives a wonderfully spirited

account of the animal's appearance, temperament and habits (142–9), as well as of his own narrow escape (136–8). The accompanying illustration is equally vigorous in intent, although it is presented as a somewhat static set-piece: the huge bulk and exaggeratedly-drawn horns give an impression of solidity rather than of power and fury.

Buffalo horn, borers *see* Borers, buffalo horn

Buffalo, Italian ~ 142, 148–9
The European domestic buffalo is of a type very similar to, and probably derived from, the Indian buffalo, *Bubalus bubalis* (F. Bovidae, S.F. Bovinae). For centuries it was widely spread and used in many countries of Europe and the Middle East. Buffalo were probably introduced into Italy from Hungary in the 6th century AD. In 1900 there were 50 000 there; by 1930 the number had dwindled to 15 000. The draining of the Pontine Marshes virtually eliminated the animal, and there was little incentive to keep it, as its state of domestication in Italy was never as close as it is in India or the Far East. In effect, Italian buffaloes were semi-wild and considered rather dangerous. From Italy they were, incidentally, introduced into Guyana, Trinidad and Brazil, and also into the lower Congo. *See also* Buffalo, Javanese

Buffalo, Javanese ~ 142, 148–9
The Indian buffalo, *Bubalus bubalis* (F. Bovidae, S.F. Bovinae), commonly known as the water buffalo, has long been domesticated as a working animal, and for its milk. There are different breeds: the swamp buffalo is much used as a draught animal in oriental paddy fields including those of Java, but suffers in hot sun and must bathe or wallow regularly. River buffaloes prefer dry pastures, and clear rivers and canals. They are used especially in India and Pakistan, are very docile, and are kept for their milk. The present distribution of domestic buffaloes in the world is centuries old, although in recent decades mechanisation will have caused a decline in numbers in some countries.

Buffon, Georges Louis Leclerc, Compte de (1707–88) ~ 196, 275~ *see also* Vol I for comment on Buffon's life and the scientific significance of his work.

It has not been possible to track down Buffon's *'tzeiran'*, an antelope from Abyssinia, stated by A.D. to have been a roan. (*See Bastaard-Guyms-Book*)

Buphaga ~ 144–5 ~ *see also* Vol I
A.D. writes of two species of *'Buphaga'* in Natal. Sadly, now, *Buphagus africanus*, the yellowbilled oxpecker, is no longer recorded there, while *B. erythrorhynchus*, the redbilled oxpecker, comes no further south than northern Zululand (O. Passeriformes, F. Buphagidae).

Buprestids *includes Delegorguei; Squamosa* ~ 224
Nearly always metallic or bronzed, hardbodied, elongated beetles: they do indeed 'flash through the air', and some are so beautiful that they may be incorporated into items of jewellery. The larvae of most buprestids bore into wood. It is not possible here to identify the genera attached to the species names *Delegorguei* and *Squamosa* (O. Coleoptera, F. Buprestidae).

Burchell, W.J. ~ 154, 214 ~ *see also* Vol I
Renowned traveller, naturalist, collector and author of *Travels in the Interior of South Africa* (1822, 1824). A.D. often spells his name 'Burschell'.

Burchell, beautiful antelope described by ~ 154
Possibly *Silvicapra grimmia*, the common or grey duiker, formerly *Antilope burchellii*, etc., dignified by A.D. as 'Burschell's leaping antelope' (*see* Duyker). It is more likely, however, as A.D. is writing of the 'antelopes of the plain', beyond the 'Makalis-Berg' to the north, that this was the tsessebe, *Damaliscus lunatus* (Burchell, 1823), called elsewhere by A.D. *Acronotus lunata* (q.v.)

Bushbaby, lesser *see* Smith's *galago-makali*

Bushpig* *also Sus Larvatus, Sus lavartus* ~ 117 ~ *see also* Vol I
A.D.'s *Sus larvatus* (*'lavartus'* is a misprint in the original) is the bushpig, *Potamochoerus porcus* (O. Artiodactyla, F. Suidae). For comments on biology *see* Vol I. It is mentioned only in passing in Vol II.

Bustard *also Groote-kuyf-pauw, Otis-kori* ~10, 28, 201, 223 ~ *see also* Vol I
The large bustard A.D. shot in north-

ern Natal was surely *Ardeotis kori*: this is confirmed not only by his '*otis-kori*' but by '*groote-kuyf-pauw*' (Afrikaans: *grote kuif pou* = great crested peacock) (10, 28). The 'tiny species' of bustard A.D. sought and killed during his northern travels (201) was probably the redcrested korhaan, *Eupodotis ruficrista*, which weighs under 1kg (cf *A. kori*: specimens of 19kg have been recorded) (O. Gruiformes, F. Otididae).

Caama* also Acronotus caama, Ant. bubalus, bubal ~ 189–90, 206, 219 ~ *see also* Vol I

The red hartebeest, *Alcelaphus buselaphus* (F. Bovidae, S.F. Alcelaphinae). The vernacular (probably Khoi) name, *caama*, is retained and distinguishes the extant *A.b. caama* from the extinct *A.b. buselaphus*. The ungainly appearance of this large antelope is deceiving, for it is fleet of foot. The body colour varies from red-brown to yellowish fawn, with lighter rump, blackish or plum-coloured legs and other dark markings on the face and shoulders. The red hartebeest is gregarious, occurring in herds of about 20 which coalesce with others to form aggregations of 300 or more. It is suprising that A.D. so seldom mentions this animal, for at that time it would have been one of the commonest antelope. It might possibly be that he mistook herds with the paler coloration for some other large antelope, e.g. eland (q.v.). The red hartebeest is now confined to the north-west in southern Africa. *Acronotus*, *Bubalus* and *Bubalis* are all former generic names for *Alcelaphus*, and *A.b. caama* has also been known as *Antilope caama* and *Bubalus caama*. The red hartebeest was not called the bubal, however, as A.D. asserts. This was the name given to the now extinct North African hartebeest, *A.b. buselaphus*, known many years before the red hartebeest.

Also, A.D. incorrectly places the red hartebeest and the tsessebe (*see Acronotus lunata*) in the same genus. The tsessebe is *Damaliscus lunatus*.

Cabbage palm ~ 125

The cabbage trees of genus *Cussonia* (Araliaceae) have a palm-like habit, with succulent stems and very large leaves clustered at the tops of branches. Indigenous people use the roots as a source of food, often peeling and eating, or just chewing, them raw. The common cabbage tree, *C. spicata*, is a conspicuous component of the coastal scrub forest of Natal, but A.D. would have encountered several other edible species also.

Cacatoes *see* Touraco/ Turaco

Calabash ~ 124 ~ *see also* Gourds

Lagenaria siceraria (Cucurbitaceae), known as the bottle gourd, calabash gourd, or white pumpkin. An annual herb bearing fruit varying in shape and size, usually oblong, green at first and turning white or yellow at maturity. Orginally from South America; cultivated by the indigenous people of South Africa for the fruits and especially the leaves, eaten cooked with porridge.

Camel ~ 24, 262

'Eminently an African animal . . .' writes A.D. of the camel (262). Numerically this is true, but not historically – or, perhaps, prehistorically.

For camels originated in North America and, although many early species died out, gave rise (via two migrations) to both the South American llamas and the Asiatic camel. From the latter, the two-humped bactrian camel (*Camelus bactrianus*) was derived, over thousands of years and by processes of domestication, the single-humped *C. dromedarius*, which did not reach North Africa until the first millennium B.C. (O. Tylopoda, F. Camelidae).

The camel is specialised for survival with minimal food and water in the driest habitats, and is physiologically equipped to withstand extremes of temperature (circadian in deserts) with ease. It combines an extraordinary ability to conserve water within the body with an extremely high tolerance of dehydration; it is able, also, to replenish water lost through dehydration very swiftly. Thus, a camel may go for a week without drinking, but when given access to free water will restore the loss in a few minutes: a 400kg camel which has lost water equivalent to 20% of its body mass will imbibe the necessary 80–100*l* in about 10 minutes in a single spell of drinking. Absorption and distribution of the water in the body are as rapid: as it drinks the wrinkled, wasted outward appearance of dehydration disappears, and the body plumps out to its usual smooth contours.

Clearly, the camel is both physiologically and behaviourally incapable of wasting water, and it is interesting to speculate upon the reasoning behind A.D.'s assertion that it uses a similar water-cooling device to that of the elephant (q.v.) in similar circumstances (24). Perhaps A.D. compares the long, flexible neck of the camel to the trunk, which is the elephant's built-in hosepipe or douche. Perhaps, too, he recalls stories of spitting camels. Possibly, also, he believes, as many still do, that the camel's hump, which in reality is a fat store, is a water reservoir, a kind of tank into which the animal can tap in conditions of water shortage. Whatever the reasoning, the argument is spurious.

Still, he rightly recognises the camel as a superb long-distance traveller (262). The oldest of all working animals, it is a beast of burden capable of carrying a load of 180kg for 18 hours at a time without strain; an animal which can be ridden and which will draw a conveyance or a plough. In addition, it transplants well to other parts of the world, not only to desert regions such as Arizona, Namibia and parts of Australia (where several thousand camels currently work and flourish), but to various African countries, where it is increasingly used in small-scale agriculture. Seen in this light, A.D.'s idea that camels, so very much hardier than oxen, would be ideal for African expeditions, is an intelligent one. Its expression, however, brings forth an aspect of A.D. that is hidden for much of Vol II: the showman, delighted at the thought of the exotic spectacle his camel caravan would afford, and the admiration (and awed benevolence) it would excite in indigenous peoples.

Camelopardalis Giraffa see Giraffe
Camphor ~ 224

Camphor is a general term for the organic chemical compounds occurring in association with volatile oils in many plants. The white crystalline solid we know as camphor is produced by a distillation process. *Cinnamomum camphora*, a tree abundant in the Far East, is the source of common camphor (once known as Japan or Laurel camphor). The camphor, and the aromatic wood of the tree, are moth repellants, and camphor wood chests also impart an agreeable fragrance to clothes, blankets, etc., stored in them. A.D. clearly did not have insect storage boxes or cabinets of camphorwood, but placed pieces of crystalline camphor in the boxes he had, together with turpentine (q.v.). Besides being an insect repellant, camphor is an antiseptic (and was so used in medicine) and preservative (it was often a component of embalming fluid) and should have helped prevent damage by fungi, bacteria, etc.to dried or drying insect specimens.

The entomological use of camphor and turpentine persisted well into the 20th century: a paste of camphor and turpentine was painted on the inside surfaces of insect storage boxes, especially along their open edges. Modern insecticides, bactericides and fungicides have made this practice obsolete.

Canis melanotis see Jackal
Canna *see* Eland
Cannabis see *Sango*
Cape petrel *see* Petrel
Carabids *includes Anthia Burchellii, Tefflus Delegorguei* ~ 224

Beetles (O. Coleoptera) of the large (over 25 000 described species) Family Carabidae, the ground beetles. Many are important predators in all terrestrial habitats. Among the ground beetles are many with notable chemical defence mechanisms, best known of which are the European bombardier beetles which discharge, with an audible report, a foul-smelling mixture of chemicals from the tip of the abdomen. Members of the African genus *Anthia* and its relatives also have chemical weaponry. These large (24-50mm) black beetles squirt formic acid (up to 35cm and in any direction) when threatened – very painful and, of course, dangerous to human eyes. This defence mechanism is linked to the fact that although the beetles can run swiftly, they cannot fly: the wing cases (elytra) are firmly joined together and the membranous wings beneath have disappeared (*see* Coleoptera). They are fierce hunters with strong, sharp jaws. *A. Burchellii* is but one of the 20 species of *Anthia* listed on p317. Only one species of *Tefflus, T. Delegorguei*, is given.

Carnivore
Any flesh-eating animal. A.D. uses the term more specifically to refer to mammals belonging to the Order Carnivora, with powerful jaws and teeth specialised for stabbing, tearing and cutting flesh. These include among others, the Families Hyaenidae, Felidae (cats), Canidae (foxes, wild dogs, jackals), Mustelidae (otters, polecats, weasels, honey badger) and Viverridae (mongoose, civets, genets, suricate). The fur seals (F. Otariidae) and true seals (F. Phocidae) belong here also. No page references are given here as the word occurs widely in the text.

Cat *see* Wild cat; Tiger cat
Catoblepas gnou see Gnu/Gnou
*Catoblepas gorgon** *also Blaauw-wildbeest*, blue gnou, ingogone, taurina ~ 162, 178, 181, 182, 186, 206 ~ *see also* Vol I
Connochaetes taurinus, the blue (i.e. silver-grey) wildebeest or brindled gnu (F. Bovidae, S.F. Alcelaphinae). Vol I includes comments on the vernacular name (*inkonkoni*) and modifications of it in scientific nomenclature. *C. taurinus* is an animal of savanna woodland, and requires shade and available drinking water. Its habitat does somewhat overlap with that of *C. gnou* (black wildebeest) and A.D. often appears to have encountered groups (mixed herds?) of both. A.D.'s short but spirited account of the appearance, temperament and habits of *C. taurinus* shows him at his acutely observant best (181). For parasites of blue wildebeest *see* Bots.
*Cephalopus** spp *See* Duyker ~ *see also* Vol I

Chafers ~ 224
The French word *cétoines* apparently identifies chafer beetles of the Subfamily Cetoniinae (O. Coleoptera, F. Scarabeidae). These brightly coloured, diurnal and strong-flying insects often frequent flowers as adults.

The genus *Pachnoda*, coloured green and yellow, can devastate cultivated roses. Two other subfamilies are commonly called chafers. The Rutelinae, which are diurnal and brightly coloured, feed on leaves. The Melolonthinae are mainly nocturnal, and brown or black in colour; the adults eat young leaves, and in abundance may defoliate a grape vine or rose bush overnight. One small group of Melolonthinae, however, is diurnal, and frequents flowers. This, the Tribe Hopliini, is unique to South Africa.

Cheetah** *also Felis Jubata* ~ 16, 278, 279 *see also* Vol I
Acinonyx jubatus (F. Felidae, S.F. Felinae) the fastest animals on earth over short distances. They are elegant cats with beautifully spotted coats, and it is hardly surprising that their skins were used by the Makatisse (278, 279) to make cloaks. Equally at home in savanna woodland and open plains, cheetahs were relentlessly hunted because of exaggerated ideas about their predation on stock, as well as for their skins. Their distributional range has shrunk alarmingly.

Chokourou makaley see Rhinoceros
Civet ~ 188 ~ *see also* Vol I
The African civet, *Civettictis civetta*, a small, doglike carnivore (q.v.) patterned in grey, black and white (F. Viverridae, S.F. Viverrinae).
A.D. apparently disdained to mention small mammals unless they occurred in large numbers or were in some way exceptional, and this gives a misleading impression of their distribution and abundance. Civets were not uncommon, as he reveals through his comment on trapping.

Coffin flies *see* Saprophagous fly larvae
Coleoptera ~ 149, 224, 317
The largest order of insects – and indeed, the largest order in the entire animal kingdom: some 300 000 species of beetles have been described and named, and more are discovered all the time. Included here are some of the largest and some of the smallest of all insects. Many are of economic importance. *Coleos* Gk: a sheath, referring to the hard or leathery forewings (the elytra) which ensheathe the membranous hindwings; *Pteron* Gk: wing. *See also* Borers; Buprestids;

Carabids; Chafers; Sugarcane borers; Weevils; *and* for fly larvae which bore into dead beetles, *see* Saprophagous fly larvae.

Columba Delegorguei also Dusky turtle dove ~ 328

Not a turtle dove but a pigeon, *Columba delegorguei* is still known as Delegorgue's pigeon or the bronze-naped pigeon.

C. *delegorguei* is discontinuously distributed in certain forest patches in Transkei, Natal, possibly Transvaal and along the Zimbabwe–Mozambique border. It is a rare resident, fairly common only in the Ngoye and Dlinza forests. It is shy and elusive, perching in the tops of tall trees and foraging for fruit morning and evening, mainly in the upper branches. A.D.'s description is lyrical. Modern descriptions describing 'maroon-brown' back and wings, with 'white collar on mantle of male' and head 'bronzy-grey', etc., seem prosaic by comparison. Curiously, A.D. gives the feet and beak tip as yellow, whereas the former are purplish pink and the latter slate. It is, in fact, the rameron pigeon, C. *arquatrix*, which has bill, legs and feet of chrome yellow. C. *delegorguei* sometimes feeds in company with C. *arquatrix*, which has a much more continuous coastal distribution from the Cape to Southern Mozambique, and into the Transvaal and further north, where it continues to overlap with C. *delegorguei*. (O. Columbiformes, F. Columbidae – pigeons and doves).

It is incidentally, a taxonomic impropriety – strictly no longer countenanced – for the authority who describes a species to name it after him- or herself. It may be that the intention to have the bird more fully described by an appropriate authority was genuine, but that once this book was published A.D.'s description became definitive. *See also* p297.

Common gnou *see also* Gnu/Gnou

Corn, Turkish *see* Maize

Corrosive sublimate, use in taxidermy ~ 43, 44

Mercuric chloride (HgCl$_2$), called corrosive sublimate because of its poisonous properties and its volatility. Paracelsus (1493–1541) introduced the medicinal use of HgCl$_2$ and other mercuric compounds. In the late 19th and early 20th centuries it was used as a bactericide and, in 0.1% solution, for sterilizing hands and instruments in surgery. Although arsenic (q.v.) is effective against some insects, the use of it in the preparation of animal skins did not protect them from the so-called 'museum beetles' and other insects that feed on skin, hair and feathers. Treatment with a solution of HgCl$_2$, though dangerous, was very effective. The practice has been obsolete since the 1950s and 60s, with the introduction of insecticidal materials and insect repellants that are not harmful to human beings.

It is surprising that A.D. should have found it necessary to carry with him as much as two pounds of HgCl$_2$, but it was easy to come by and and would have been readily available from most druggists. As with arsenic, the wisdom of scattering this virulent poison 'to the wind' is questionable. It would be interesting to know just how the Boers learned that A.D. was in possession of large quantities of these particular poisons (*see also* Alum; Arsenic; Camphor; Turpentine).

Cossus Ligni perda ~ 148

Carpenter moths, *Cossus* spp (O. Lepidoptera, F. Cossidae) are medium-to-large and heavy-bodied as adults, with long, narrow wings. Eggs are deposited on the bark of quince, apple and pear trees (not, in South Africa, on elms as A.D. states). When the larvae hatch two months later they feed at first on the bark before burrowing into the wood: they may inflict serious damage during the 18-month larval life. A.D. likens their depredations to those of insects which bore into buffalo horn. This was an astute observation, for these borers are also the larvae of moths (*see* Borers, buffalo horn).

Coturnix Delegorguei also Oury quail ~ 259, 328

Coturnix delegorguei, the harlequin quail (O. Galliformes, F. Phasianidae, francolins, quail, pheasants, etc.)

Widely distributed south of the Sahara, except in forested areas (and, in southern Africa mainly absent from the dry west and south west) this bird is a locally common breeding migrant, from September to early May. It migrates in large flocks, but is otherwise gregarious in coveys of 6–20 birds when not breeding: A.D.'s account of very large groups or flocks in February is confusing. He also indicates that their noisy activity occurs in the morning only, whereas this is a twice-daily event, morning and evening. His measurement of length seems on the small side at 15cm (length currently accepted is 16–18cm), but his description is otherwise accurate enough. The underparts look dark in flight: Wahlberg (q.v.) refers to the 'black underside' – and also to their very large numbers at a locality near the Pilanesberg. Wahlberg, something of a taxonomic stickler (and very properly so) would have disapproved of A.D.'s naming of the bird after himself. *See also Columba Delegorguei* and for further comment *see* p297.

Couagga *see* Quagga

Coudou *see* Kudu

Crane ~ 115 ~ *see also* Vol I
Very large, long-legged birds (O. Gruiformes, F. Gruidae).

Crateropus jardinei ~ 173, 259
Turdoides jardineii, the arrow-marked babbler, a very common resident of northern Natal and further north into Mozambique and Zimbabwe (O. Passeriformes, F. Timaliidae: babblers). The birds prefer thickets with long grass and bushes in woodland, riverine reedbeds, etc. They are gregarious, in noisy groups of up to 10 birds, foraging for insects, seeds and fruit on the ground, or in lower bushes and undergrowth. Wings and tail dark brown, breast brownish streaked with white 'arrow-markings'.

Crocodile ~ 36, 117, 150–1, 152, 205, 219, 226, 236, 252, 267 ~ *see also* Vol I
Crocodylus niloticus, the Nile crocodile (O. Crocodilia, F. Crocodylidae), widely distributed in Africa and once very plentiful in southern African rivers, as many river and place names attest. Although A.D.'s familiarity with these animals has clearly bred, if not contempt, a remarkably blasé attitude towards them since his earlier days (151, for example), anthropomorphism is seldom far away. Hence, they can be shot execution style, as 'traitors', (226).

Curculionids *see* Weevil

Curlew *also falcinellus* ~ 267
A.D. is uncertain of the identity of this curlew- or sandpiper-like bird. It probably was not *Limicola falcinellus* the broad billed sandpiper, a rare, non-breeding palaearctic migrant found far nearer to the coast when it is observed. Had he not commented that this was his first sighting of the particular species, the obvious candidate would have been the curlew sandpiper, *Calidris ferruginea*. This bird is so common, however, that A.D. must have seen it many times. Identification remains open, therefore (O. Charadriiformes, F. Scolopacidae).

Cynhyaena, *Cynhyaena Venatica see* Wild dog

Dacka, dagga see Sango

Dauws see Quagga

De Blainville, H.M.D. ~ 100
In 1793, the legendary Lamarck, who had been 'Botanist to the King' at the Jardin du Roi, the pre-revolutionary name of the Museum d'Histoire Naturelle, Paris, was given the newly founded chair of invertebrate zoology. On his death (1829) the chair was divided between P.A. Latreille (q.v.) and De Blainville, whose area of responsibility included Molluscs, worms and 'zoophytes' (animals with a superficial resemblance to plants, such as sea anemones). A.D. indicates that he retained an interest in and responsibility for vertebrate specimens at the museum into the 1840s.

Delalande, Pierre-Antoine (1787–1823) *also* Lalande ~ 282, 301
It is hardly surprising that A.D. refers to Delalande as 'our celebrated naturalist' for this great traveller, natural historian and taxidermist was surely the finest possible example of all a 19th century natural historian and collector should be. He was the son of a taxidermist at the Museum d'Histoire Naturelle, Paris, and he himself trained there under Geoffroy Saint-Hilaire. The most important of his collecting missions for the Museum was to South Africa in 1818, accompanied by his 11-year-old nephew, P.J. Verreaux (*see* Verreaux). During the next two years,

based in the Cape, he undertook three South African expeditions, collecting 131 405 specimens, including hundreds of mammals, reptiles and fishes, and thousands of birds and marine invertebrates. A valuable collection of human skulls and skeletons was included, and also many geological specimens. Much of his plant material perished, lost at sea, but his meticulously prepared, described and illustrated zoological specimens greatly enriched the museum and the Jardin des Plantes. His death was, it was said, the result of an infection contracted while he was dissecting decomposing whales at the Cape. His notes were still sadly incomplete, but his renowned *Précis d'un voyage au Cap du Bonne Esperance* was read posthumously to the members of the Academy of Sciences, and some of his fine landscapes and animal paintings were exhibited at the Paris Salon. Delalande's zeal and dedication were unflagging, underpinned always by great technical skill and scrupulous honesty. He appears, too, to have had extraordinary stamina.

This 'most considerate and modest man' made a remarkable contribution to the study of southern African fauna and flora, and his name lives on, most often as an authority, but also in the nomenclature, e.g., *Jasus lalandei*, the Cape rock lobster. The abridgement to '*Lalande*' is used by A.D. in the text, and also in the Catalogue of Lepidoptera.

Delegorguei ~ 224 ~ When on its own, this is the specific (trivial) name of a beetle: *see* Buprestids. *See also Columba Delegorguei, Coturnix Delegorguei*

Delegorgue's pigeon *see Columba Delegorguei*

Desmurs and Pucheran ~ 254n
French ornithologists, the authorities for *Merops nubicoides*, the carmine or carmine-throated bee-eater, which they described in the *Revue de Zoologie* of 1846 (*see* Bee-eaters). The name of Pucheran is commemorated in that of the crested guinea fowl, *Guttera pucherani* (*see* Guinea fowl). Biographical details are not readily available.

Diptera ~ 149, 224
The highly successful insect order Diptera includes the two-winged flies,

many of which are familiar to every South African – houseflies, bluebottles, horseflies, craneflies, sandflies, midges, mosquitoes. The order is large and includes over 35 families. *Di-* Gk: prefix meaning two; *Pteron* Gk: wing. *See also* Bots; Mosquitoes; Saprophagous fly larvae.

Dipteran, minute, with boring larvae *see* Saprophagous fly larvae

Doorn-veld, dorn-veld see Mimosa

Drongo, forktailed *see* Blackbird

Duck ~ 161, 163, 172, 220, 235, 244, 250, 266, 267, 268 ~ *see also* Vol I
Waterbirds (O. Anseriformes, F. Anatidae).

Medium to large aquatic birds found mainly on inland waters. They are excellent swimmers – the toes are webbed – and dive or dabble for food using the flattened bill which has inner lamellae for filterfeeding.

In the Transvaal A.D. would have encountered numerous species, including several of *Anas*, and one or two species of at least six other genera (O. Anseriformes, F. Anatidae: ducks, geese, swans). For the knobbilled duck *see* Goose, caruncular, bronze.

Dusky turtle dove *see Columba Delegorguei*

Duyker* (*also Ant. mergens Burschellii, Cephalopus Coerulea, C. Burschellii, C. Mergens, C. Coerulea*, Burschell's leaping antelope, vaal-duyker) ~ 117 ~ *see also* Vol. I.

The only duiker (A.D.'s 'duyker') mentioned in the text is the common or grey duiker, *Silvicapra grimmia* (his *Ant. mergens Burschellii*). It also appears twice in the key to the hunting map (330) as *Cephalopus Mergens* and *C. Burschellii*, perhaps reflecting some of the then prevalent confusion over colour varieties (shown in the proliferation of genus, species and subspecies names). A.D.'s *C. Natalensis* is the red or Natal duiker, while *C. Coerulea* is *Philantomba monticolor*, the blue duiker (all F. Bovidae, S.F. Cephalophinae).

All are small to medium-sized antelope, with plain coloured, unpatterned bodies. They have short tails and tufts of hair on top of the head between the ears. The horns are short and simple. The discontinuous but widely distributed *P. monticolor* is the smallest of all Southern African antelope (adult males stand sbout 30 cm at the shoulder): they are seldom seen, being confined to forest, thickets or dense coastal bush. *C. natalensis*, richly red in colour, stands 42 cm at the shoulder and is associated with forest and dense thicket. In Natal, now, it occurs south only as far as Umzumbe. *S. grimmia* stands 50cm at the shoulder: it is very widely distributed in Africa south of the Sahara, but does not occur in forest or in desert regions.

Eagle *also* Great mountain eagle, *grootberg-aarend* ~ 115, 191, 278 ~ *see also* Vol I

Large raptors, the diurnal birds of prey (O. Falconiformes, F. Accipitridae).

The '*groot-berg-aarend*' (191) is surely the black eagle, *Aquila verreauxii*, which not only chooses rocky hills, mountains and gorges for its habitat, often soaring to great heights, but shows a preference for areas where dassies are plentiful (*see* Rock rabbits).

Ectoparasites *see* Arachnids, venomous; Parasites, of human beings; Ticks

Eland* *also Ant. canna, Boselaphus oreas*, canna ~ 7, 8, 12, 25, 89, 100, 117, 149, 194, 206, 211, 212, 259 ~ *see also* Vol I

Taurotragus oryx, the eland, is the largest of the African antelope (F. Bovidae, S.F. Bovinae). For comment on appearance, distribution and nomenclature *see* Vol I. Eland are now restricted to the northern, central and north eastern parts of southern Africa, but whereas they were frequently mentioned as A.D. travelled in the Cape and Natal, their treatment as he went northward seems cursory. In the key to the hunting map (330) the eland is listed as '*Boselaphus Oreas* (*seu Canna*)', indicating that *Canna* was an alternative species name. In fact there seems to be no record of the use of '*Boselaphus*'. *Oreas* as genus, and as species, crops up several times from 1777; *canna* (as *Damalis canna*) occurs once (H. Smith, 1827).

Elephant* *also Elephas Africanus, Uncklove* ~ 1–9, 10, 11, 13, 19–26, 83, 93–4, 99, 100–4, 109, 114, 133–4, 141–2, 229, 250, 264, 265, 280–1 ~ *see also* Vol I

The African elephant, *Loxodonta africana*, the largest of the terrestrial mammals (O. Proboscidea, F. Elephantidae). The Zulu word is *indhlovu* or *indlovu*: A.D.'s *uncklove* is a fair phonetic spelling. For comment on elephant biology and distribution, and on the distinction between *L. africana* and the Asian *Elephas*, *see* Vol I: there are few new insights in Vol I. A.D. does, however, refer again, and in a different context, to the cooling device whereby water from the stomach is sprayed onto head and shoulders – and other individuals – in conditions of crowding and stress at high temperatures (23–4), a phenomenon still poorly understood and worthy of investigation. The comparison with the camel (q.v.) is not valid.

Once again, also, there is reference to a tuskless specimen as '*poeskop*' (21), translated by Le Vaillant (q.v.) as 'snubnosed'. In fact the Afrikaans *poenskop* = pollarded, which, although it strictly applies to animals which have lost or cast horns (not tusks), comes closer to describing the tuskless condition, whether it be congenital or accidental.

The frontispiece shows a most curious and doubtless imaginary elephant procession, only very loosely based on the account in pp 20–1, as it were passing in review before A.D. and his elephant gun and appearing to make serial obeisance as each succumbs, having been mortally wounded by that same gun. Clearly, the artist had never seen the chaos that is large-scale big game hunting.

Elephas Africanus see Elephant
Ellipsiprymnus *see Kobus ellipsiprymnus*
Emberiza longicaudata see widow bird
Equine antelope *see Bastaard guyms -book*
Equus: Burchellii/Burschellii; Couagga; Zebra see Quagga; Zebra
Euchore see Spring-booken
European hemp *see Sango*
'Exter' *see* Widow-shrike

Fabricius, Johann Christian (1745–1808)
~ 301 *et seq.*
Danish entomologist and economist, a
pupil of Linnaeus (q.v.) at Uppsala. In
1775 he was appointed professor of
natural history, economy and finance
at Kiel. It is as an entomologist that
his memory survives, and for many
years his reputation rested on the system of classification which he founded
upon the structure of insect mouthparts rather than that of wings. Reference to his *Systema Entomologiae*
(1775) occurs in the Catalogue of Lepidoptera (301), abbreviated as 'Fab.
Ent. syst.': this work demonstrated
Fabricius' keen eye for specific differences, and his mastery of terse, accurate description. He is not to be
confused with J.H. Fabre (1823–
1915), the prolific French entomologist and polymath whose original approach to experimental biology was of
such lasting significance.
Fairy shrimps *see* Insects and larvae,
aquatic
Falcinellus see Curlew
Felis Jubata see Cheetah
Felis Leo see Lion
Felis Leopardus see Leopard
Felis Serval see Tiger-cat
Fern root, as anthelmintic *also Om-komo-
komo* ~ 253
Probably the rhizome of *Dryopteris
athamantica* (Pteridophyta, Polypo-
diaceae). Long used by indigenous
people as an anthelmintic/vermifuge,
especially against tapeworms (q.v.). If
this is the plant in question, A.D.'s
mention of it predates the 1857 'first'
record from Natal. The rhizomes
were, and perhaps occasionally still
are, exported from Natal under the
pharmaceutical name 'Pannae radix'.
It is probable that the active principle
in the rhizome is similar to that in the
European *D. filix-mas* or 'male fern'.
Had the remedy been less crudely prepared A.D. might have been able to
take an effective dose.
  While the locality suggests *D.
athamantica*, it should be noted that
the powdered rhizomes of the parsley
fern *Cheilanthes hirta* are also used
by Zulus as an anthelmintic. Both *D.
athamantica* and *C. hirta* are known
in Zulu as *inkomakoma.*
Fig tree ~ 124 ~ *see also* Vol I
Many species of fig tree are indige-

nous to southern Africa (*Ficus* spp:
Moraceae).
  A.D. suggests that cultivation of
(presumably) the domestic green fig,
F. carica, in South Africa, would be
highly desirable. In fact *F. carica*, the
fig of classical times, had been introduced from south Europe in about
1700.
Fleas *see* Parasites, of human beings
Flies ~ *see* Diptera ~ *see also* Vol I
and, for flies with a parasitic stage in
the life cycle, *see* Bots; Saprophagous
fly larvae
Fossil *see* Ruminant, fossil
Four-pronged widow bird *see* Whydah;
Widow bird
Francolin *also Nudi collis Swainsonii* ~
178, 187, 188, 205 ~ *see also* Vol I
Swainson's francolin, *Francolinus
swainsonii*, is distributed mainly in
the north and north east of South
Africa, and in the Namibian highlands. It is a shy bird, despite its
harsh, crowing call; swift to seek cover
in dense vegetation when disturbed,
fast and manœvreable in flight. '*Nudi
collis*' (Latin = naked neck) refers to
the bare facial and gular/throat skin,
which is red, but whether *nudicollis*
was ever an accepted trivial name is
not clear. 'Noisy' and 'fitful' describe
the cries of many different species of
francolin (187), and do not help in
identification. It may be that A.D.
quite often encountered groups of
mixed francolin species. 'Troops of
sixty to one hundred and fifty' (205)
are unlikely to have been of a single
species, for most francolins are found
in pairs, family groups, or coveys of
6–18 birds, depending on the species.
Possible species are the coqui francolin (*F. coqui*), the crested francolin
(*F. sephaena*), Shelley's francolin (*F.
shelleyi*), the Natal francolin (*F.
natalensis*), the redwing francolin (*F.
levaillantii*) and, of course, Swainson's
francolin. Chunky, somewhat chicken-
like birds, many cryptically coloured,
many with loud, harsh, cackling or
crowing calls – though *F. shelleyi* has
a musical whistle. (O. Galliformes, F.
Phasianidae: francolins, quail, pheasants, etc.).
Fringillas *includes Ploceus ignicephale*,
weavers ~ 193, 208, 223, 259 ~ *see also*
Sparrows, Vol I
  In Vol I A.D. used 'sparrow' as a gen-

eral name for any small, passerine bird with a conspicuous and well-shaped nest. Here '*fringille*' (= finch) is a similar omnibus name for colourful, gregarious, seed-eating passerines nesting in reeds or riverine bush or forest, and it seems best to use the English 'fringilla' in the same way. Some of A.D.'s fringillas may actually have been members of F. Fringillidae some of which occur in the Transvaal and are gregarious and moderately colourful. Most, however, appear to be weavers (193, 259), and possibly bishops, as well, perhaps, as some sparrows, and sparrowweavers, queleas and widows. *Ploceus ignicephale* (= fiery-headed) cannot be an older name for the firecrowned bishop, *Euplectes hordaceus*, which does not occur further south than northern Mozambique. It may refer to the redheaded weaver, *Anaplectes rubriceps*, or the red bishop, *Anaplectes orix*. It may be also that '*P. ignicephale*' and '*Ignicolor*' of Vol I are variant versions of the name of the same bird (O. Passeriformes).

'Fringilla' cannot, incidentally, refer to the European chaffinch, *Fringilla coelebs*, for this was not introduced into South Africa until c. 1898, by C.J. Rhodes.

Galago *see* Smith's *galago-makali*
Gallinule, purple *also* Sultan hen ~ 220 ~ *see also* Vol I

Porphyrio porphyrio, the purple gallinule (swamphen, king reed hen) is widely distributed in southern Africa and elsewhere, including Asia, Australasia and extreme southern Europe. The bird prefers reedy swamps and marshes, where it conceals itself by day and emerges at dawn and dusk to forage. It swims well and often climbs trees, where it may roost. The colour is mainly deep, purplish blue, and greenish on the back. The large, bright red bill and frontal shield are instantly recognisable and diagnostic. The use of 'sultan hen' (q.v. for a more modern application) for this bird has long been obsolete. Cuvier (q.v. Vol I) referred to the 'common sultana' *Fulica porphyrio*, and other 19th century authors used,

variously the 'hyacinthine gallinule or sultana fowl', the 'sultan gallinule', and '*Sultana porphyrio*'. The origin of 'sultan' or 'sultana' is obscure, but the words may have indicated a real or fancied resemblance of the red frontal shield to some form of turban or other oriental headgear (O. Gruiformes, F. Rallidae: rails, crakes, gallinules, etc.).

Gazella albifrons* *also albifrons* ~ 162, 190 ~ *see also* Vol I

The blesbok, *Damaliscus dorcas phillipsi*, formerly *Antilope albifrons* (*albifrons* describing the white face blaze) (F. Bovidae, S.F. Alcelaphinae). The blesbok, unlike the bontebok, *D.d. dorcas*, still occurs marginally in Natal, and is lighter in colour than the bontebok. Both have the white blaze, so that the old name supplied by A.D. is not conclusive on its own. Fortunately, in Vol I the locality tends to confirm the identity of his first sighting. There is some confusion, however, when he compares the colouring of his *albifrons* with that of the tsessebe (190, *see also Acronotus lunata*). In fact it is the bontebok and not the blesbok which has a purple gloss similar to that of the tsessebe (*see Bonte-book*).

Gazella Euchore see Spring-booken
Gazella melampus see Ant. melampus
Gazella pygarga* *see Bonte-book*
Gemsbok *see* Guyms-book
Genet (*also Symba*) ~ 114, 116, 249, 278 ~ *see also* Vol I

The small-spotted or feline genet, *Genetta genetta*, and the large-spotted or blotched genet, *G.tigrina*, are both decoratively spotted and banded . It is interesting that the Zulu name for the animal, *insimba* (A.D.'s *Symba*) should have been transferred to the military kilt of genet fur (114) which still forms part of ceremonial dress. (O. Carnivora, F. Viverridae).

Giraffe* *also Camelopardalis Giraffa* ~ 175, 197–8, 201–2, 229, 278, 280 ~ *see also* Vol I

Giraffa camelopardalis (O. Artiodactyla, F. Giraffidae). The tallest animal – with the longest neck – reaching an average height of 5m in males and 4.5m in females. The familiar patched pattern in shades of brown (from cream to almost black in some) contributes to *camelopardalis*, a blend of

Greek and Latin = big as a camel, spotted like a leopard. Distribution in sub-Saharan Africa has shrunk dramatically, but it remains wide if discontinuous, from the eastern Transvaal to West Africa. Le Vaillant (q.v.) noted the occurrence of giraffe in the northern Cape near the Orange River, as did other travellers in the first two decades of the 19th century. It has long been absent from Natal and A.D.'s only sightings (e.g. 197–8, 202) were in the Transvaal. Otherwise he mentions them only in passing, and makes interesting references to the wall painting of giraffe in Makata's kraal beyond the Magaliesberg (175, 280).

Giraffe are found in dry savanna associated with scrub and woodland, not in forest or on open plains. The preferred and most important food is *Acacia* shoots, on which they browse: in A.D.'s most vivid encounter the giraffe was 'peering over the mimosas' (197), presumably having been interrupted while feeding.

As A.D. notes, giraffe do move at some speed (up to 56km/h) and in fact 'giraffe' is from Arabic *xirapha* = one who walks swiftly. Television and the cinema have made their extraordinary rocking movement at speed familiar to us, the legs on each side moving almost in unison at times and the head swinging back and forth, the angle of swing changing with the length of stride. To A.D. (and to every first-time observer) the gait seemed both awkward and astonishing (197–8). There are two subspecies, *G.c.capensis* from South Africa, south west Mozambique and south east Zimbabwe, and *G.c. angolensis* from northwest Zimbabwe, northern Botswana and northern Namibia.

It is interesting to read of giraffe-hide shields carried by the Makatisse: A.D. does not indicate if these were decorative or actual accoutrements of war (278).

Giraffe mimosa *see* Mimosa

Gladiolus, wild ~ 125 ~ *see also* Vol I
Various species of gladiolus are variously edible – e.g. the corms of *G. permeabilis* var. *edulis*, and the flowers of *G. cruentus*, *G. eckloni* and *G. dalenii*. A.D. appears to have used neither corms nor flowers, but rather what seems to have been a leek-like section of the lower stem. This sounds too substantial to have come from a wild *Gladiolus*, especially as A.D. compares it to a cabbage palm (q.v.) root (Iridaceae).

Gnu/Gnou* *also Catoblepas gnou*, common gnou ~ 92, 161, 162, 163, 165, 181, 182, 219 ~ *see also* Vol I
Connochaetes gnou, the black wildebeest (F. Bovidae, S.F. Alcelaphinae). The colloquial name is well entrenched, even though the animal is not black, but buffy brown: it does seem darker than the blue wildebeest, which is silvery-grey (*see Catoblepas gorgon*). The tail is white, and they are often referred to as white-tailed wildebeest. *Gnu* is a Khoikhoi name referring to the bellowing snort they emit when alarmed. They are endemic to the southern subregion but their range, once wide, has shrunk to a tiny fraction of its original size. *C. gnou* is a species of open plains, once found in the Karroo and also the grasslands of the Free State and Transvaal.

A.D. often reports sighting the two wildebeest at the same time even though the blue wildebeest is associated particularly with savanna woodland. For parasites of black wildebeest *see* Bots.

Goose, caruncular, bronze ~ 267
Not a goose at all, but the knobbilled duck, *Sarkidiornis melanotos* (O. Anseriformes, F. Anatidae). This is a large bird, average length of the male 75cm, mass up to 2.6kg. The back and wings are black, glossed with purple, green and coppery metallic sheen on the scapulars, wings and tail (A.D.'s 'bronze' seems both inadequate and misleading). Below, the body is white, the undertail is yellow and the head is yellowish when breeding and otherwise white, speckled black. There is a laterally compressed black knob (A.D.'s 'caruncle') on top of the bill which enlarges conspicuously during the breeding season. The female is smaller than the male and lacks the knob.

S. melanotos is mainly a summer visitor and is widely distributed but nomadic, more common to the north and north east of South Africa. It is found on lakes and dams in woodland, and along larger rivers – here, the Limpopo. A.D. was not the first, and certainly not the last, hunter to find it extraordinarily good eating.

Gouaye see Tobacco

Gourds ~ 248
For communities to be 'living on' gourds, these would need to be both plentiful and nourishing. *Acanthosicyos naudiniana*, the Herero cucumber or wild melon, would qualify, as would the pumpkin, *Cucurbita pepo* (*see* Pumpkin). However, A.D. mentions this separately. Although many other cucurbits are eaten, it is usually not the fruit ('gourd') which is used for food, but the leaves (Cucurbitaceae). *See also* Calabash

Grape, grapevine *see* Vine

Great blue antelope *see Bastaard guymsbook*

Great mountain eagle *see* Eagle

Groot-berg-aarend see Eagle

Groot-blaauw-book see Bastaard-guymsbook

Groot-kuyf-pauw see Bustard

Groot-rooye-book see Ant. melampus

Grouse *also Gutturalis pterocles* ~ 209, 250
Sandgrouse are medium-sized birds of pigeonlike appearance. The legs are short and the plumage is elaborately patterned in soft colours, providing excellent camouflage: the birds inhabit open areas from deserts to dry savanna, and nest on bare ground. A.D.'s *Gutturalis pterocles* (209) is *Pterocles gutturalis*, the yellow-throated sandgrouse, a compact bird about the size of a rock pigeon. It usually occurs in pairs or small groups, but there may be 1000 individuals in a migrating flock. Large flocks gather at water in the morning, and sometimes also in the afternoon. A localised, probably now rare, resident in the west Transvaal: some birds remain all year, while others migrate to Zambia for breeding. The 'grouse' of the northern Transvaal (250) was doubtless the doublebanded sandgrouse, *Pterocles bicinctus*. *P. bicinctus* occurs from southern Namibia, northern Cape and Transvaal to southern Angola, Zambia and Malawi. It is a common resident in *Acacia* and other savanna, dry bushveld, stony areas and on rocky hills with scrub and grass tussocks. A.D. was indeed in *Acacia* country when he shot *P. bicinctus*, and knew its habits well enough to wait until dusk when the bird, flying low and silently, and often in large flocks, goes to its drinking places, often nesting in shade during the heat of the day. A.D. uses the French word *ganga*, which translates as 'pin-tailed' grouse and might be thought to refer to the Namaqua sandgrouse, *P. namaqua*, the only sandgrouse in the region which has a long, pointed tail: that of *P. bicinctus* is rounded. However *P. namaqua*, which avoids mountainous regions, is found in the dry west, from the Cape and and Karroo to southwest Angola. It does not occur in the Transvaal. Clearly, A.D. is using 'ganga' loosely to include all sandgrouse. (O. Pterocliformes, F. Pteroclidae).

Guérin-Méneville, Félix Edouard (1799–1874) ~ xxv, 224
French entomologist who collected mainly Coleoptera (q.v.), but also other insects. He described *inter alia* Lepidoptera (q.v.) from French colonies in West Africa (Senegal) and Madagascar.

Guinea-fowl ~ 178 ~ *see also* Vol I
Numida meleagris, the helmeted guineafowl, common in all but the dry west of southern Africa, and *Guttera pucherani*, the crested guineafowl, confined to the north east (O. Galliformes, F. Numididae).

Gutturalis pterocles see Grouse

*Guyms-book*** *also Ant. oryx, Oryx Capensis* ~ 201
The gemsbok, *Oryx gazella*, a most handsome antelope, with its long, straight horns, strongly marked face and body and the long, flowing black hair of the tail. (F. Bovidae, S.F. Hippotraginae). This is a species of arid terrain, confined to Namibia and parts of Botswana in the south, and no longer present south of the Orange River, although they were once recorded in the Karroo. It thus seems unlikely that A.D. ever saw a gemsbok in the wild, and this may account for his likening of the face patterning to that of the roan (*see Bastaard - guyms-book*): any similarity there may be is superficial at best. A former name is *Antilope oryx* Pallas, 1777.

Confusingly, *A. oryx* Pallas, 1766, was the eland: fortunately both appellations are obsolete. It should be noted that in Vol I A.D. uses '*Oryx capensis*' as the name of a 'hawfinch', perhaps *Euplectes orix*, the red bishop, or *E. capensis*, the Cape bishop or yellowrumped widow.

Haack-doorn see Mimosa

Harris, W. Cornwallis ~ 154, 225, 275
Captain William (later Sir William) Cornwallis Harris, an Indian army officer, who led a party into the interior of southern Africa in 1836. He was an observant and reliable naturalist, a competent wildlife artist and writer, and a dedicated hunter.

He published *Portraits of Game and Wild Animals of Southern Africa* (1840) and *The Wild Sports of Southern Africa* (1852).

A.D.'s reference to an 1840 publication, *Wild-Spoort in Southern Africa*, (sic), probably indicates that he received some rather garbled information at second hand.

Hartebeest, red *see Caama*

Hemiptera ~ 149
Order of insects commonly called bugs and characterised by specialisations for piercing and sucking. Most are plant feeders and some (e.g. aphids, scales, etc.) are serious pests. The bedbug, *Cimex lectularius*, would have been familiar to A.D. as it still is to many South Africans today. *Hemi-* Gk: inseparable prefix meaning half; *Pteron* Gk: wing. The name refers to the half-sclerotised/ tanned forewings of some bugs. *See* Insects and larvae, aquatic

Herbivore
Herbivorous animals feed only on plants. In herbivorous mammals such as antelope, buffalo, zebra, etc., meat cannot be utilised as food because the structure and function of the alimentary system, including digestive and absorptive physiology, are specialised for dealing with plant material.

Contrast this obligate herbivory with human vegetarianism. This is a conscious choice made by a physically and physiologically omnivorous mammal to eat plants and plant products while avoiding meat and (but not

always) fish, eggs and milk. No page references for Herbivore are given because the word is used widely in the text.

Hippopotamus* ~ 94, 105, 106, 108, 150–1, 229, 258, 260, 261 ~ *see also* Vol I
Hippopotamus amphibius (O. Artiodactyla, F. Hippopotamidae): very large mammals of amphibious habit. They feature at some length in Vol I, where appropriate comment may be found.

Hobby ~ 254
Possibly the European hobby falcon, *Falco subbuteo*, a migrant to Africa and south Asia. Otherwise, and more interestingly, because A.D. was at the southernmost limit of its range, this could have been the African hobby falcon, *F. cuvieri*, a smallish, slender bird found in tropical Africa and southward to the extreme north of South Africa. It prefers moist savanna and woodland and is solitary or found in pairs – rather more gregarious elsewhere in Africa (O. Falconiformes, F. Falconidae: falcons and kestrels).

Hyaena* *also Hyaena Crocuta* ~ 9, 10, 11, 28, 85, 100, 117, 125, 127, 145, 163, 177, 188–9, 224, 252, 269, 277, 282 ~ *see also* Vol I
The hyaena referred to throughout Vol II is *Crocuta crocuta*, the spotted hyaena (F. Hyaenidae, S.F. Hyaeninae). For comment on distribution and aspects of biology *see* Vol I. A.D. adds little to our understanding of hyaenas in Vol II, but does give insight into the anthropomorphic and prejudiced mindset of the time (*see*, e.g., 188–9).

*Hyaena Fusca*** For text references *see* Vol I.
Hyaena brunnea, the brown hyaena (F. Hyaenidae, S.F. Hyaeninae).

Hydrophobia ~ 218
Rabies, a virus infection unusual in its severity. Human rabies is relatively rare, even in countries where the virus is common in wild animals: it is almost always the result of a bite from an infected dog. The virus enters the skin and slowly travels – during the incubation period of from 10 days to several months – along nerves to the spinal cord and brain. The illness itself, once symptoms appear, is fatal within a few days. There is typically

fever, accompanied by delirium, muscle spasm and eventually paralysis and death. Painful throat spasms may prevent drinking – hence the alternative name 'hydrophobia'.

A.D. must have been familiar with the symptoms of the disease, which was once not uncommon in Europe: no treatment for it was possible until Pasteur developed an effective vaccine in 1855. Because it was invariably fatal, rabies was regarded with superstitious dread and it was no doubt out of alarmed atavism that A.D. tremulously associated his own tapeworm-induced irritability and mental confusion with the disease. Had rational thought been possible at the time he would have recalled the usual course of events, from the bite by a rabid animal to the development of the fever and the neuromuscular symptoms that were all absent in his case. *See also* Tapeworm

Hymenoptera ~ 149
The insect order which includes wasps, bees and ants. When wings are present there are four of them, all membranous, the forewing interlocked with the hindwing of the same side by tiny hooks.

Hymen Gk: a parchment or membrane; *Pteron* Gk: wing.

Impala *see Ant. Melampus*
Indian hemp *see Sango*
Ingogone see Catoblepas gorgon
Insecticides and insect repellants, use of in specimen preparation *see* Arsenic; Camphor; Corrosive sublimate; Turpentine
Insects and larvae, aquatic ~ 232
The aquatic insects may have included, among adult forms, various water bugs (O. Hemiptera), such as water striders (F. Gerridae), backswimmers (F. Notonectidae), water boatmen (F. Corixidae), and others. There may also have been aquatic larvae of mosquitoes (q.v.) and water midges.

Under the blanket term 'larvae' may have been included amphibian tadpoles (though A.D. would surely have recognised these) and some small (developing and adult) freshwater crustaceans, which are very likely to have

been present. There are many species of fairy shrimp found in southern African temporary pools, some of which occur in polluted water (O. Anostraca), as well as tadpole shrimps, *Triops granarius* (O. Notostraca) (all arthropods of P. Crustacea, C. Phyllopoda).

'Insects', biting *see* Arachnids, venomous
Irrisor capensis ~ 259
The redbilled woodhoopoe, *Phoeniculus purpureus* (O. Alcediniformes, F. Phoeniculidae: woodhoopoes). A medium-sized bird, black with a blue iridescence, blue on throat and wings, purplish on wrist and tail. The long, slender, decurved bill is red, as are the legs.

To A.D. it is a 'comic actor . . . mocking at his peers' and indeed, the former name, *Irrisor* is Latin = one who mocks. The mockery is in the call, a loud cackling, starting off slowly and building up, often with several birds calling together. Le Vaillant (q.v.) actually coined the trivial name *moqueur* for the bird, while the Afrikaans name *gewone kakelaar* (common chatterer or cackler) is expressive. The Zulu *inhlekabafazi* = cackles like a woman, is colourful enough, perhaps, to be forgiven its political incorrectness.

Izi-mango see Monkey

Jackal *also Canis melanotis* ~ 115, 166n, 224, 249, 277, 278, 279 ~ *see also* Fox, Vol I
The black-backed jackal, *Canis mesomelas* (F. Canidae, S.F. Caninae).

Although *melanotis* means blackbacked (Gk *melas* = black; *notos* = the back), there is apparently no record of the taxonomic use of the name: the '*meso*' of *mesomelas* is Gk = middle, referring to the dark saddle on the back, from the neck to the base of the tail. Silvery hairs are sprinkled in the saddle, and in winter males may develop a rich red colour which is very handsome, and accounts for the Afrikaans name *rooijakkals*.

Although *C. mesomelas* is widely distributed in South Africa, and although it was probably the source of the skins used by the Makatisse (277

354

ff), it should not be forgotten that *C. adustus*, the side-striped jackal, occurs in the far north and east of the country. The coat is drab compared with that of *C. mesomelas*, however, and never has the red coloration.

Jong-doorn, jong-dorn ~ 94, 95
Two spellings of what in Afrikaans would be *jongdoring* = young thorn. '*Doring* ' is often used almost as a suffix in common names given to many thorny plants, not all of which, by any means, are *Acacia* spp. This one, called by A.D. 'young mimosa', is, however. *See also* Mimosa

Kaamel doorn see Mimosa
Kaffircorn *also* Mabélé, mabele ~ 14, 124, 198, 222, 247, 280
Both *Sorghum caffrorum* and *S. dochna* (Poaceae) are commonly known as Kaffir corn, and as 'great' and 'giant' millet (q.v.) respectively. In Zulu both are *amabele*. The grain is still used as a staple food in areas of very low rainfall, because sorghum is extremely drought-resistant. However, the main use of sorghum these days is in making beer. The stalks of some varieties of *S. dochna* are chewed for the sweet juice they contain, like sugar cane (q.v.): it is not clear to which of these plants A.D. refers when he uses 'sugar cane' (e.g., 23).

The name Kaffircorn (as Dutch: *kaffer koring*) was first recorded by Thunberg (q.v. Vol I). He noted in 1773 that specimens were cultivated as a rarity in several Cape gardens.
Kakaraba *see Aigoceros nigra*
Kite *includes* Blac ~ 208, 254 ~ *see also* Vol I
Smallish to medium sized and slender diurnal birds of prey (O. Falconiformes, F. Accipitridae).

The Transvaal kites (208) were probably yellowbilled and/or black kites, formerly subspecies of *Milvus migrans*, now generally considered to be two species, *M. parasitus* (yellowbilled) and *M. migrans* (black). The yellowbilled kite, a breeding migrant from equatorial Africa (July to March), is very common, especially in the east. Wahlberg (q.v.), here throwing stones at kites in the interest of science, frequently records in his own journal the presence of yellowbilled

kites and comments briefly on some of their habits. He does not, however, describe the stone throwing-experiment or record its results.

The 'adult male blac' A.D. noted at the Limpopo (254) was *Elanus caeruleus*, the black-shouldered kite. '*Blac*' was, apparently, the French common name for this bird from the 18th until well into the 20th century. A.D. may have known this species from Europe. It is also the commonest raptor in most parts of southern Africa and it is extraordinary that he should not have mentioned it earlier.
Klaauw-Sickt, Klauw-sickt ~ 155–6
The Afrikaans name for this ailment of cattle is *klouseer*, more rarely *klou siekte* (*klou* = hoof; *seer* = sore; *siekte* = illness, disease). Known in English as foot rot, the condition is caused by a bacterial infection common where cattle are kept in wet conditions or track repeatedly through mud or moist manure. The micro-organism enters through any break in the skin of the foot or between the toes – and the feet of draught oxen trekking over rough terrain would have been especially vulnerable. An abscess develops, and the pain causes an alteration in gait. As a result the hooves, which grow continously, are not worn down, and the overgrowth does indeed make them look like oriental slippers (155).

Although bathing in water (156) may have soothed the infected feet temporarily, it will obviously not have encouraged healing. Effective treatment is in fact simple. The abscess is drained and cleaned and may then be disinfected by bathing in a solution of potassium permanganate ($KMnO_4$) or copper sulphate ($CuSO_4$). Overgrown hooves are reshaped by cutting or filing.

Untreated, the infection invades the joints of the feet. Rarely, there is more widespread internal damage.
Klein aappje see Smith's *galago-makali*
Klip-springer* *also* Oreotragus saltatrix ~ 99, 191 ~ *see also* Vol I
Oreotragus oreotragus, the klipspringer (F. Bovidae, S.F. Antilopinae). Small antelope standing about 60cm at the shoulder. '*Klipspringer*' (Afrikaans: rock-jumper) describes their extraordinary – indeed, unique – agility in their preferred and often steep

rocky habitat, where they may perch, all four feet together, on a rock pinnacle (99). The most important adaptation for this way of life is the shape of the hooves, which are cylindrical-oval with blunt tips on which the animal both stands and walks. Old names reflect the leaping habit, e.g. *Antilope saltatrix*, *Oreotragus saltator* (L. *saltus* = leap; *saltator* = dancer; *saltatrix* = dancing girl).

The structure of the hair is unique among southern African antelope. Each hair is hollow, flattened and spiny, and this makes the coat springy. The hairs adhere very loosely to the skin, and it is suggested that while the almost mossy springiness cushions the animal against rocks and protects it from thorns, the ease with which it breaks off – noted by A.D. (191) – ensures that nothing can snag in the coat and so impair the agility on which the klipspringer's life depends. The coarse, springy hair was much prized as stuffing for saddles.

Because klipspringer have such specialised habitat requirements their distribution within their range (Cape to East Africa) is discontinuous. They were hunted for their skins, and were also deliberately eliminated from sheep farming areas of the central Karoo.

Kobus ellipsiprymnus* also Ellipsiprymnus, *waater-book* ~ 178, 184, 206, 219 ~ *see also* Vol I
The large and handsome waterbuck, *Kobus ellipsiprymnus* (F. Bovidae, S.F. Reduncinae): easily distinguished by the white ring round the rump. Comment on the animal's appearance and on nomenclature are given in Vol I.

There are two species of *Kobus*, *K. ellipsiprymnus* and *K. defassa* (the defassa waterbuck), although not all taxonomists are agreed on this because distribution overlaps and animals may interbreed. For convenience, therefore, they are treated as two groups of subspecies, the *K.e.* group from Somalia southward (four subspecies, of which only *K.e. ellipsiprymnus* occurs in the southern subregion), and the *K. d.* group, none of whose nine subspecies occurs in southern Africa. The Senegalese specimen in the Jardin Des Plantes

(184) must therefore have been a member of the *K. defassa* group.

In southern Africa distribution is now restricted to the northern and north eastern parts, though they are present in game reserves elsewhere.
Kooker-boom see Milk tree
Koudou *see* kudu
Kruys-bezie bushes ~ 101
The cross-berry, (Afrikaans: *kruisbessie*), *Grewia occidentalis*, is a shrub or small tree abundant in forest and scrub from the Cape Peninsula to Ethiopia. The finegrained wood was used by Bushmen for their arrows, and also for assegai shafts. The common name refers to the fruit, a fourseeded edible drupe whose seeds are arranged in a miniature cross.
Kudu *also* koudou, *Strepsiceros Condoma** ~ 203–4, 206, 219, 226, 234 ~ *see also* Vol I
Tragelaphus strepsiceros, the kudu, a large antelope noted for the handsome corkscrew horns of the male (*strepsis* Gk: twisting; *keras* Gk: horn) and, in both sexes, the broad, spoonshaped ears (F. Bovidae, S.F. Bovinae).

Lalande *see* Delalande
Lamprotornis Burchellii ~ 187
The metallic or 'glossy' starlings of the genus *Lamprotornis* all have black plumage with intense green, blue and purple lustre (O. Passeriformes, F. Sturnidae). Burchell's starling, *L. australis*, is heavily built, splendidly coloured in black and iridescent blue-green, with a long, heavy, rounded tail which is purplish and barred black – in good light much resembling the *Anhinga* (q.v.) pattern as A.D. indicates.
Lanius melanoleucus see widow-shrike
Lapwing *see* Plover
Latreille, Pierre André (1762–1833) ~ 279
French naturalist who, following admission to priestly orders in 1786, devoted all of his leisure time to the study of insects. After various vicissitudes, including imprisonment during the French Revolution (as a priest with conservative sympathies), he was given the task of arranging the entomological collection at the Jardin Des Plantes in Paris: this was on the

strength of his 1796 publication, *Précis des caractères génériques des insectes, disposés dans un ordre naturel* (Summary of the generic characteristics of insects, arranged in a natural sequence). In 1830, aged 67, Latreille was appointed professor of zoology (of crustaceans, arachnids and insects) at the Muséum d' Histoire Naturelle, Paris, and said gloomily, 'They give me bread when I've no longer any teeth'. His numerous publications include a 14-volume contribution to an edition of Buffon (q.v., Vol I), many taxonomic works, and the whole of the section *Crustacés, Arachnides, Insectes* in the *Règne Animal* of G. Cuvier (q.v., Vol I). It seems somewhat neglectful that A.D. should mention this illustrious scientist by name only once, and that when citing him as the authority for the human body louse.

Leaping gazelles *see Spring-booken*

Leopard** *also Felis Leopardus*, panther ~ 11–12, 15–16, 80, 81,114, 115, 125, 177, 224, 278, 279 ~ *see also* Vol I
Panthera pardus (F. Felidae, S.F. Felinae), the largest of the African spotted cats. Curiously, A.D. never writes descriptively of this beautiful animal.

Lepidoptera ~ 149; 300–15
Butterflies and moths belong to the order Lepidoptera, characterised, among other things, by the presence of tiny scales on the wings which give them their typical velvety texture and appearance. *Lepidion* Gk: a scale; *Pteron* Gk: wing. *See also Cossus Ligni perda*; Sugarcane borers; borers, buffalo horn

Levaillant ~ 21, 148, 158, 215, 254 ~ *see also* Vol I
Francois Le Vaillant (1753–1824), great traveller and collector, author of volumes detailing his southern African *Travels*, and the magnificently presented *Histoire Naturelle des Oiseaux d'Afrique* (1796–1808). These works, and the flamboyant and colourful personality they seemed to reflect, were a major source of delight and inspiration to A.D., and were in large part instrumental in bringing him to South Africa. Alas, within a very short time of his arrival he began to discover Le Vaillant's shortcomings as an observer and recorder, and his disappointment, disillusion and vexa-

tion are expressed several times in both volumes. That he was dismayed is clear from his revisiting of particularly irksome notions or assertions of Le Vaillant such as the possibility of domesticating the Cape buffalo, a notoriously dangerous and certainly untameable animal (148), in temperament resembling the tractable Italian and Javanese buffaloes (q.q.v.) not at all.

Several times A.D. hints at Le Vaillant's carelessness or inaccuracy. Once (25n), without mentioning him by name, he makes what must surely be a reference to Le Vaillant, who doubtless will have been one of the travellers needing to be asked if he really had made the journey he had described. Here, too, A.D. explains how he himself has taken pains to avoid doubt and scepticism by being precise about matching localities and species. Modern readers may wish for far greater cartographic exactness than he supplies, but the tone of his writing, and the evidence of a number of taxonomic authorities, indicate that although his knowledge may have been frustratingly skimpy in some areas, he was fundamentally honest. In fact, discovery of Le Vaillant's cavalier attitude may have spurred A.D. to strive for accuracy and truth. For biographical details, *see* Vol I

Lice *see* Parasites, of human beings

Linnaeus ~ 301 *et seq.*
Carl von Linné (1707–78) whose name, abridged to Linn., appears as the authority for a number of Lepidoptera. In the fashion of the day, his name was Latinised to Carolus Linnaeus. Linné, a Swedish botanist (incidentally also a physician: he pursued his vast botanical studies while employed as a professor of medicine at Uppsala), had a passion for arranging and classifying which eventually led him to systematise the plant and animal kingdoms. The *Systema Naturae*, outlining the system which made him famous, first appeared in 1737: it was seven pages long. When the 10th edition appeared, the work had expanded to 2500 pages. It embodied and elaborated the binomial system of nomenclature (first devised in the 16th century by one

Bauhin, a Swiss physician) which is still in use. Linné introduced the astrological signs ♂ and ♀ to indicate male and female.

Lion* ~ 4, 6, 7, 8, 11, 16, 78–95, 114, 115, 161, 162, 164, 165, 171–2, 186, 224, 228, 265–6, 269, 278 ~ *see also* Vol I
Panthera leo (F. Felidae, S.F. Felinae): the largest of the African carnivores. A.D. appears to have lost some of his awe of the animal. Amid accounts of sightings, woundings, killings and hunting lore, may be found some interesting observations, albeit with an anthropomorphic slant, on lion biology and behaviour (78–95).

Long-tailed shrike *see* Widow-shrike
Longtailed widow *see* Widow bird; Whydah
Louse *see* Parasites, of human beings
Lunata *see Acronotus lunata*

Mabélé, mabele *see* Kaffircorn
Maize *also Ombyle*, Turkish corn ~ 23, 110, 124, 239, 280
Zea mays (Poaceae) which is considered to have reached Africa from America soon after AD1500: Van Riebeeck recorded its cultivation at the Cape in 1653 and was the first to use 'mielie' (spelled 'mily') for the fruit or cob. Zulus first used a small-cobbed, yellow, quickly ripening variety. A wide assortment of dishes is made from the maize meal, which may vary from coarse to very fine, depending on the method and style of grinding. Maize was often known in English as Turkish or Egyptian corn. In Zulu it is ummbila.

Makano ~ 1, 231 ~ *see also* Vol I
The marula or cider tree, *Sclerocarya birrea caffra* (Anacardiaceae), renowned for its versatile and nutritious fruit.
The Transvaal tree whose leaves resembled those of *S. birrea* (231) may have been the related *Lannea schweinfurthii stuhlmannii*, the false marula. The overall resemblance is superficial, but the compound leaves are similar: those of *L. schweinfurthii* have fewer leaflets, however.

Malaconotus Australis Smithii ~ 177, 220
The '*Australis*' suggests that this bird is the southern boubou, *Laniarius ferrugineus*, but this does not have the bright red plumage of the bird shot by

A.D. (220). One must therefore deduce that this was *L. atrococcineus*, the crimsonbreasted shrike, which he presumably observed from below: its upper body (head, back, wings, tail) is jet black, relieved only by a white wing stripe. It flies fairly high between patches of bush or trees, although it forages on the ground or searches rough-barked tree trunks and branches for insects. (O. Passeriformes, F. Malaconotidae: bushshrikes). *See also* Shrike, Widowshrike

Mamba ~ *see Memba*
Manches des velours see Albatross
Manes Temminckii * *see* Pangolin
Mangroves ~ 40, 41 ~ *see also* Vol I
A.D. means both the mangrove swamp forest as a whole, and the plants called mangroves, belonging to the Families Rhizophoraceae and Verbenaceae.

Medlar, wild ~ 247
Probably *Vangueria infausta* (Rubiaceae) the wild medlar, a small tree (3–7m), which is widely distributed in the eastern and northern parts of South Africa and on into Zimbabwe. The almost spherical fruit, 2.5–3.5 cm in diameter, is yellowish to brown when mature (January to April). They are sweetish but acid in flavour and are eaten raw, but also can be dried and stored, to be used as flavouring for porridge, etc. Farmers' wives still use the sweetened pulp in puddings or as a substitute for applesauce, and in the western Transvaal a brandy is distilled from the fruit. Remedies for various ailments, including pneumonia and malaria, are made from the roots, but indigenous people will not use the wood, even as fuel, because they believe it possesses evil powers: this belief is reflected in the scientific name – *infausta*, Latin = unlucky.

Melampus see Ant. melampus
Melanoleucus see Widow-shrike
Memba also Mamba see also Snake, arboreal, green, ~ 151–2 ~ *see also* Vol I
Both the black mamba (*Dendroaspis polylepis*) and the green (*D. angusticeps*) occur in Natal (S.O. Serpentes, F. Elapidae).
The black mamba is never jet black but is brownish above (light or dark) over much of its range, and a uniform lead grey (A.D.'s 'metallic grey

358

brown') in humid coastal areas; the belly is pale grey-green, sometimes blotched. It does rear high to strike, sometimes to 5–6 ft (1.5–1.8m), which accounts for the bites high up on human beings unfortunate enough to be struck. The venom is neurotoxic and cardiotoxic, and the yield is 100–400mg. Since 10–15mg will kill a man, it is hardly surprising that there was no remedy known to the indigenous people: up to 10 ampoules of antivenom are required to counteract the effect of the venom. As A.D. describes, *D. polylepis* lives underground in a favoured home – a termite nest, hollow log or rock crevice – and is territorial. It is confident in defence, but will retreat unless cornered.It is probable that the specimen surprised by A.D.'s party was not chasing after them, but pursuing prey, which includes birds and small mammals such as rats and dassies.

Merops spp, *including M.apiaster, M. bullockoïdes, M. minulus, M. nubicoïdes, M. Savignii (and* pink bee-eater of Senegal) *see* Bee-eater

Milk tree *also kooker-boom* ~ 64
The locality excludes the *kokerboom* or quiver tree, *Aloe dichotoma* (*see* Vol I), but the fact that A.D. equates this with his 'milk tree' indicates that it was a fleshy, relatively leafless plant. This in turn indicates that of the various trees which exude a milky latex and are found in Natal and Zululand, the most likely is the common tree *Euphorbia* (or naboom), *E. ingens* (Euphorbiaceae). Were it not for the *kooker-boom* clue, however, there would have been several other possibilities, such as the white milkwood, *Sideroxylon inerme* (Sapotaceae), and various species of *Ficus* (Moraceae).

Millet ~ 124
A general term for several species of *Panicum, Pennisetum, Setaria* and *Sorghum,* cultivated for their grain (Poaceae).

Mimosa *also Doorn-veld, dorn-veld, Haack-doorn,* giraffe mimosa, *jongdoorn, jong-dorn, Mimosa nilotica,* thorn bushes, thorn trees, thorn veld ~ 8, 10, 14, 94, 95, 113, 125, 134, 136, 137, 138, 163, 177, 187, 192, 194, 197, 204, 210, 211, 216, 220, 221, 227, 230, 234, 250, 255, 264 ~ *see also* Vol I
A.D.'s 'mimosa' almost always refers

to species of *Acacia* (Fabaceae) (For historical comment, *see* Vol I). Most often he mentions the thorn trees and thorn bushes that dominate in various areas, either alone, or mixed with other plants, but several times he refers to particular acacias which have especially notable features. The 'tall, scrawny mimosas' with branches only at the top (187) may have been   *A. xanthophloea,* the fever tree, so called by travellers who associated the tree with malaria – a superstitious belief, related to its preferred habitat in swampy, fever-ridden localities. It grows to 16m, with a trunk diameter of 45cm, and the bark is covered with a yellowish-green powder, which gives it an unhealthy appearance.

The 'giraffe mimosa' or '*kaameldoorn*' (192, 204) is *A. erioloba,* formerly *A. giraffae,* known among other things as the camel or giraffe thorn (Afrikaans *kameeldoring*). This tree grows to 15m and has a spreading but rounded crown. It was once very common between Kimberley and Mafikeng and it was there, in 1811–12, that Burchell (q.v.) noted it and, aware that young shoots were browsed by giraffe, bestowed on it the trivial name *giraffae.* It is still fairly plentiful further north (as far as Angola and Zambia), but has dwindled considerably. Much of the damage was done early on, when the long, straight and very hard trunks were used in enormous numbers as mine props as well as for wagon manufacture and fuel. The gum was highly esteemed by indigenous people, and the seeds have been used by some as a coffee substitute.

Acacia barks and gums are used medicinally (Vol I), but it must indeed have been 'dire necessity' that drove A.D. to eat the inner bark and gum of '*Mimosa nilotica*', an old name for *A. karroo,* the most widespread *Acacia* species in southern Africa (125): the gum of this small, much-branched tree is copious: children enjoy it as a summer sweet, but it is hardly a sustaining food.

A.D. comments that young *Acacia* plants ('*jong-doorn*') were used as shelter by rhinoceros (q.v., *and see Rhenoster-boschis*): *Acacia* shoots are also a favourite food of these large herbivores.

The *haakdoring* (A.D.'s *haack-doorn* 221) is probably *A. mellifera detinens*.

Burchell became so exasperated by repeated entanglement in thickets of this 10m deciduous tree, with its paired, recurved thorns, that he coined *detinens* (= detaining) and bestowed it as species, later subspecies, name. *A.m. detinens* is one of several thorny plants known as the *wag-'n-bietjie*, but when A.D. refers to the *wacht-eine-beytje* (q.v.) he clearly does not mean *A.m. detinens*.

Mimosa nilotica see Mimosa

Mongoose ~ 189 ~ *see also* Vol I

Mammalogists will find A.D.'s 'mongooses of various kinds' deeply frustrating. As he moved northwards he could have trapped, besides *Mungos mungo* (the banded mongoose), any or all of the following: *Paracynictis selousi* (Selous' mongoose), *Cynictis penicillata* (yellow mongoose), *Gallerella sanguinea* (slender mongoose), *Rhynchogale milleri* (Miller's mongoose), *Ichneumia albicauda* (white-tailed mongoose), *Atilax paludinosus* (water mongoose) and *Helogale parvula* (dwarf mongoose) (F. Viverridae, S.F. Herpestinae).

Monkey *also Amakaho, izi-mango, om-kaho, Simia monoides* ~ 80, 81, 81n ~ *see also* Vol I

The vervet monkey, *Cercopithecus aethiops* (O. Primates, S.O. Haplorhinae, F. Cercopithecidae), which would have been so abundant in coastal bush and inland that it is surprising A.D. so seldom mentions it. His *Amakaho* and *om-kaho* are from Zulu *inkawu*, the blue, i.e. vervet, monkey (pl not *amakawu* but *izinkawu*). His *izi-mango* is the samango monkey, *C. mitis* (Zulu: *insimango*), darker in colour than the vervet, and with a narrower habitat tolerance, being more rigidly attached to forest areas. Different predators (e.g. leopard, martial eagle) evoke different alarm calls and other behavioural responses in the vervet monkey. A.D.'s account of their reaction to the presence of a lion is vivid. *Simia* is one of several former generic names; *monoides* is obscure.

Mosquitoes ~ 105, 232, 251 ~ *See also* Vol I

Delicately built true flies (Insects: O. Diptera) with long legs, narrow wings, and mouthparts adapted for piercing and sucking. It is possible that mosquito larvae, which are aquatic, were among the millions of 'aquatic insects and larvae' swarming in the 'foul, stinking pool' of water in the Transvaal (232). *See also* Insects and larvae, aquatic

Mountain baboon *see* Baboon

Mountain reed buck *see Redunca Lalandii*

Nacht-adder ~ 245 ~ *see also* Vol I

Either *Causus rhombeatus*, the common night adder, or *C. defilippii*, the snouted night adder (S.O. Serpentes, F. Viperidae). Both are small adders, and both have the characteristic **V** on the back of the head, as well as blotches: rhomboidal blotches on the body and tail (*C. rhombeatus*), and blotches on the back and tail (*C. defilippii*). The common night adder has a rounded snout; the snouted night adder is so-called because the snout is upturned. Neither is 'highly venomous', and therefore neither is 'fatal'. *C. rhombeatus* has large venom glands which produce 20–30 mg of mild, dilute venom. Though a bite causes pain and swelling, no fatalities have been recorded. Antivenom is effective but rarely necessary. The symptoms and toxicity of *C. defilippii* venom are much the same, though the volume produced is smaller.

Nagapie see Smith's *galago-makali*

Night adder *see Nacht-adder*

Nudi collis Swainsonii see Francolin

Ombylé see Maize

Om-kaho see Monkey

Om-komo-komo see Fern root, as anthelmintic; Tapeworm

Oreotragus saltatrix see klip-springer

Oribi *see Redunca scoparia*

Oriole ~ 259

Small to medium-sized birds of O. Passeriformes, F. Oriolidae, the Old World orioles. Those A.D. encountered at the Limpopo were among other birds 'shouting abuse' at a 'sparrow-owl' (q.v.). All three possible species have harsh alarm calls, but of these three the European golden oriole, *Oriolus oriolus,* tends to be shy and secretive, keeping to the tops of trees. This leaves *O. auratus,* the African golden oriole, and the black-headed oriole, *O. larvatus.* Although the beautiful, liquid calls of these two birds are indistinguishable, they are different in appearance, most notably by the predominance of bright yellow in the former, and the black head in the latter, with greenish back and some black in the wings and tail.

Oryx/*Oryx Capensis see Guyms-book*
Ostrich ~ 177 ~ *see also* Vol I
Struthio camelus, the largest living bird, which is flightless and at times nomadic (O. Struthioniformes, F. Struthionidae).

Although ostrich farming is carried on in the south of the country, the ostrich now occurs wild only northwards and on into Namibia, Botswana, Zimbabwe and west Mozambique.

Otis-kori see Bustard
Otter, South African ~ 115 ~ *see also* Vol I
Lutra maculicollis, the spotted-necked otter (F. Mustelidae, S.F. Lutrinae).

Oury quail *see Coturnix Delegorguei*
Oxpeckers *see Buphaga*

Pampoenes see Pumpkin
Pangolin* *also* Broad-tailed pangolin, *Manes Temminckii* ~ 158–9
Manis temminckii (O. Pholidota, F. Manidae), the pangolin or scaly ant-eater, is the only one of the four African species of pangolin to occur in the southern subregion. 'Pangolin' derives from the Malay *peng-goling* = roller, from their habit of rolling up in self-defence, with vulnerable parts concealed and protected. Pangolins grow to about 1m in length, with a mass of up to 18kg. The head is small and the muzzle pointed and covered with small scales, while the upper body and tail have an armour of heavy brown scales. The underparts and sides of the face lack scales, and the skin is tough but pliable. The limbs are covered with small scales.

M. temminckii is a savanna species. It is a nocturnal, solitary forager, feeding predominantly on formicid ants. As A.D. describes, it opens ants'

nests with the curved front claws, inserts the narrow head and uses the long, rounded and highly extensible tongue to reach into the inner tunnels. When the tongue is withdrawn the sticky surface is covered with ants, pupae and larvae. Pangolins have no teeth, and the food is ground up in muscular regions of the stomach.

Although pangolins do usually walk on their hind legs, with forefeet and tail clear of the ground, they are certainly not 'bipeds' as A.D. asserts, and his use of 'crustacean' (159) is zoologically irresponsible, indicating as it does a relationship between these mammals and the invertebrate Crustacea. It would have been more appropriate to use descriptive words such as *cuirassé* = armour-clad, or *recouvert de plaques* = plated.

Although there are morphological and functional similarities between the pangolin and the aardvark (A.D.'s *orycterope: see Aarde-vark*), these are convergences related to habit and habitat and not evidence of close relationship as A.D. suggests (159).

Panther *see* Leopard
Parasites, of human beings *includes Pediculus pubis* ~ 279
A.D. writes disapprovingly of the dirtiness of the Makatisse, and associates this with the parasites common among them. These may have included ticks and bedbugs (*see* Arachnids, venomous, *and also* Vol I). They certainly included fleas and lice.

Fleas (insects, O. Siphonaptera) are small, wingless, laterally compressed, bloodsucking ectoparasites of mammals and birds. Those most commonly found in human dwellings are the human flea, *Pulex irritans,* found also on pigs; the cat flea *Ctenocephalides felis,* and the dog flea, *C. canis.* Fleas are voracious blood feeders, piercing the skin of the host with lancet-like mouthparts. The use of insecticides has helped control human fleas, as has improvement in human hygiene. A.D. doubtless made the connection between squalid conditions and disease, even if there was at the time no understanding of the pathogens, the hosts and the vectors involved For this reason, despite his understanding of insect life cycles, he may have shared the widely held notion that ectoparasites, especially lice, were generated in and of dirt.

Lice (insects, O. Phthiraptera) are small, wingless and flattened permanent ectoparasites of birds and mammals. Those parasitic on *Homo sapiens* belong to the S.O. Anoplura, and are sucking lice with hollow, piercing mouthparts and legs whose claws are adapted for gripping hair. The eggs (nits), often very numerous, adhere firmly to individual hairs. *Phthirus pubis* (A.D.'s *Pediculus pubis*) is the crab louse, which lives in the coarse pubic hairs – but not, apparently, those of the Makatisse: there is a hint (279) that their pubic hair may have been sparse. They were, however, susceptible to the head louse, *Pediculus capitis*. This is largely restricted to the scalp, where each adult sucks blood, clinging to a hair. It spreads readily by close body contact, but is easily controlled by an application of an insecticidal shampoo. In the Zulu tradition there are several plant-based washes for dealing with it, but the Makatisse had a different approach (*see Sibilo/sibylo*).

The body louse, *P. humanus*, concentrates in the body areas constricted by clothing, such as the armpits. It breeds rapidly, and large infestations cause intense discomfort. It is of medical importance because of its role in the spreading of relapsing fever and typhus, which latter still occurs in overcrowded and deprived conditions, e.g., during war and famine.

The fact that A.D. himself reacted so very badly to both ecto- and endoparasites (*see*, e.g., Arachnids, venomous; Tapeworm) probably heightened his repugnance for both dirt and parasitic insects. He would have been as repelled as we are by the mediaeval association of sanctity with lousiness: after the death of Thomas à Beckett, for example, it was noted with reverent admiration that the lice in his haircloth garment 'boiled over like water in a simmering cauldron'.

Partridge ~ 24, 163 ~ *see also* Vol I

The identity of A.D's 'partridges' is uncertain: he seems to use the word loosely to refer to several different kinds of game birds.

Pediculus pubis see Parasites, of human beings

Percnopteran *see* Vulture

Petrel *includes* Cape petrel, shoemakers ~ 285 ~ *see also* Vol I

Marine birds (O. Procellariiformes, F. Procellariidae): see Vol I for general comments on habits and nomenclature. A.D.'s 'Cape petrel' is *Daption capense*, the chequered pintado petrel. His 'shoemaker' is the Cape hen or whitechinned petrel, *Procellaria aequinoctialis*. It is doubtful if such birds may be described as 'lighthearted', but no doubt A.D. was cheered by their gregarious and lively presence, and by their adroit manœuvres as they followed his ship.

Phaeton ~ 284 ~ *see also* Vol I

Large marine birds of the genus *Phaethon* (O. Pelicaniformes, F. Phaethontidae), known in English as tropicbirds. Possibly the redtailed tropicbird, *Phaethon rubricauda*, which is white (sometimes washed pink) and has two long red central streamers extending straight back from the white, wedge-shaped tail. It is a very rare vagrant, usually to the south coast of southern Africa, and not, usually, to the Atlantic. The precise identity of this bird at St Helena must remain open to question, therefore.

Plaat-kroon-boom ~ 160

Not as A.D. states, a 'mimosa' (i.e., *Acacia*), but another member of the same family, *Albizia adianthifolia*, the flatcrown (Afrikaans: *platkroon*). A large, splendid deciduous tree with conspicuous spreading flat crown, common in eastern coastal forest. The light, pale brown wood is used for parquet flooring, and poles are used for hut building, and for firewood (Fabaceae).

Platinum *see Sibilo/sibylo*

Ploceus ignicephale see Fringillas

Plover *also* Lapwing ~ 267 ~ *see also* Vol I

A.D. is referring to birds inhabiting the shores of inland waters, of O. Charadriiformes, F. Charadriidae.

By 'plover' he probably meant species of *Charadrius* of which at least four would have been present at the Limpopo. 'Lapwing' is not a South African common name – it applies to *Vanellus vanellus*, which he would have known from Europe. Plovers of the genus *Vanellus* are larger than

Charadrius spp, with longer legs, and *V. albiceps*, the whitecrowned plover, is a well-known Limpopo species. The blacksmith plover, *V. armatus*, might also have been present, but as A.D. knew this well (Vol I) he might have mentioned it separately and by name had he seen it.

Poff-adder ~ 247, 268 ~ *see also* Vol I
The common puffadder, *Bitis arietans* (S.O. Serpentes, F. Viperidae) which is, as A.D. records, 'short': 70–90 cm, maximum 120 cm. It is thick and heavily built, and moves caterpillar fashion with the aid of strongly-keeled scales: it would thus have slithered straight between A.D.'s legs. The venom is cytotoxic, causing extensive swelling, pain and necrosis: bites are common but relatively few are fatal.

Pomegranate, as anthelmintic ~ 253
Punica granatum (Punicaceae). A native of south-west Asia introduced into South Africa apparently before 1700: now widely distributed. The fruits are large and the bitter rind contains tannin and gallic acid. It was this rind, and not the root (as A.D. states), which was used in early days as vermifuge/anthelmintic. A.D. found it effective against tapeworm (q.v.) – more effective than the more commonly used preparation from the rhizome of *Dryopteris athamantica* (*see* Fern root, as anthelmintic).

Pucheran *see* Desmurs and Pucheran
Puff adder *see Poff-adder*
Pumpkin *also Pampoenes* ~ 124, 175–6, 198
Cucurbita pepo (Cucurbitaceae): a vine-like annual herb, with fruit usually large, hard and thick-skinned, and with orange flesh and numerous flat white seeds; probably South American in origin but long cultivated around the world. Indigenous people eat, besides the fruit, roasted seeds, stem tips and leaves, the tops of young pumpkins, and often the male flowers. The Afrikaans word is *pampoen*.

Python *also* Boa python ~ 12, 12n, 117 ~ *see also* Vol I
Python sebae natalensis, the African rock python and the largest snake in southern Africa. It is restricted mainly to the lowveld, reaching the Natal south coast and extending along the Limpopo Valley into Botswana and into the northern Cape. It

is surprising that A.D. so seldom mentions these snakes. (S.O. Serpentes, F. Bovidae: includes the egg-laying pythons – S.F. Pythoninae – and the viviparous boas – S.F. Boinae. Only pythons are found on the southern subcontinent, and A.D.'s 'boa' is both superfluous and incorrect).

Quagga** *also* Couagga, *Dauws, Equus Burchellii, E. Burchellii, E. Quagga* ~ 25, 92, 161, 162, 163, 173, 177, 178, 184–5, 194, 198, 277 ~ *see also* Vol I
Equus quagga (O. Perissodactyla, F. Equidae): extinct. The anterior half of the body was striped; posteriorly it was brown and white. They did not, reportedly, survive longer than about 1878. However, there is an increasing tendency among mammalogists to treat the quagga and the zebra (q.v.) as conspecifics, separated as subspecies only by differences in colour pattern and in details of skeletal structure.

Early travellers appear to have used 'quagga' and '*Equus Burchellii*' interchangeably, and A.D. often does this, even though he distinguishes the quagga from both *E. burchelli* and *E. zebra* (the Cape mountain zebra) in the key to his hunting map.

The '*Dauws*' label given to the Jardin Des Plantes specimens (184–5) is obscure: it is worth noting that in some later works there are scathing comments about the way in which a number of museums and zoos in France presented and labelled their specimens.

Quail, Oury *see Coturnix Delegorguei*
Quetloha / Quithloha see Rhinoceros

Ratel *also* Stinking badger ~ 2, 145
Mellivora capensis, the honey badger or *ratel* (an Afrikaans name often used in English texts). One of the most widely spread species of small carnivores in the subregion. It is stocky, with, above, a broad, light-coloured saddle from the eyes to the short tail; underparts jet black. It uses its powerful, knife-like foreclaws to dig refuges and excavate the hives of wild bees. Food includes honey, bee

larvae, various land arthropods, small vertebrates, and fruit.

A.D.'s 'stinking' refers to the foul-smelling secretion from paired anal glands, released defensively as a repellant, as well as for territorial marking and as a stimulus to courtship (O. Carnivora, F. Mustelidae, S.F. Mellivorinae).

Rattan cane *also Wild rotang* ~ 146
Rottang is the vernacular name of *Calamus rotang* (Restionaceae) – both vernacular and specific names appear to derive from the Malaysian name of the plant. The culms were and are still cut into walking sticks, canes, etc., and the thinner parts used for various kinds of wicker-work. A.D. may, of course, have mistaken one of the larger indigenous reeds (q.v.) for rattan cane.

Redunca capreolus* ~ *see also* Vol I
Pelea capreolus, the grey rhebok (F. Bovidae, S.F. Peleinae).

Redunca Eleotragus* see Riet-book

Redunca Lalandii* ~ 182 ~ *see also Vol I*
Redunca fulvorufula, the mountain reed buck (F. Bovidae, S.F. Reduncinae).

The earlier name commemorated that of P.-A. Delalande (q.v.). For comments on biology and nomenclature *see* Vol I. In the present volume *R. fulvorufula* appears only as the host of dipteran parasites (*see* Bots), and there is a possibility that A.D. confuses the mountain reed buck with the reed buck, *R. arundinum* (*see Riet–book*).

Redunca Scoparia** see also Vol I
The oribi, *Ourebia ourebi* (F. Bovidae, S.F. Antilopinae).

Reedbuck *see Riet–Book*

Reeds ~ 172, 246 *also* Rushes
A.D. never describes or gives even a common name to the reeds he notes in rivers, vleis etc., of which those cited here are but two examples. There are many different reed- or rush-like plants indigenous to South Africa, including Juncaceae (*Juncus* spp), Cyperaceae (sedges, etc.), Restionaceae (*Restio* spp and many other reeds) and Typhaceae. Strictly, 'rushes' is used only for Juncaceae, but 'bulrushes' are *Typha* spp (Typhaceae) and, like 'reeds', 'rushes' has now come to be used loosely to mean any tall, grasslike aquatic plant.

Rhebok *see Redunca capreolus*

Rhenoster-boschis ~ 216
Elytropappus rhinocerotis, the *renosterbossie* (Asteraceae, formerly Compositae), a bushy shrub about 1m high, with closely grouped, greyish to bluish green leaves. Van der Stel was the first to set down this name – the oldest known vernacular name of a Cape plant – in his *Journal* (1685), as 'Rinocerbosch'. He commented that rhinoceros often lay among these bushes: they in fact seek the shade of any bushes or low trees during the heat of the day. *E. rhinocerotis* is a Cape plant: it began to spread from the Western Cape as land was cleared and cultivated, and Sparrman (q.v. Vol I) noted that considerable encroachment had occurred by 1775, while 19th century travellers, including Burchell (q.v.) remarked on its continued expansion in the Cape. The vernacular name is a sorry reminder that rhinoceros once roamed on the slopes of Table Mountain and were common on the Cape Flats. *See also* Rhinoceros

Rhinoceros* *also Africanus Bicornis, Chokourou makaley, Quetloha*, Quithloha, Simus, Swart-rhenoster, and includes R. Lelongouanne*, R. Unicornis*** ~ 13, 19, 93, 94, 100, 114, 117, 134–5, 173, 177, 182, 185, 195, 197, 205, 208, 211–19, 227, 228, 252, 255, 259, 264, 267–8, 269, 277, 280 ~ *see also* Vol I
The two rhinoceros species of southern Africa are *Ceratotherium simum*, the squarelipped or white rhinoceros (A.D.'s *R. simus*), and the hooklipped or black rhinoceros, *Diceros bicornis* (A.D.'s *R. Africanus Bicornis*, swart rhenoster, etc). A.D. knew both well, but at times does not distinguish between them. However, as he moves northward, he records *D. bicornis* almost exclusively. Interestingly, he never uses the then current synonym for *C. simum*, *C. oswelli*, and most of his nomenclatural oddities apply to *D. bicornis*. Thus 'Smith's famous rhinoceros *Quithloha*' (208, spelled *Quetloha* on the hunting map) recalls that A. Smith (q.v.) in 1836 assigned the name *Rhinoceros keitloa* to a specimen of *D. bicornis* from Zeerust in which the posterior horn was longer than the anterior; the following year

he listed a more northerly specimen as *R. ketloa*, and later *D. bicornis* was briefly given the generic name *Keitloa*. Wahlberg (q.v.) uses both *Keitloa* and *Keithloa*. In fact horn length is variable and cannot be used as a taxonomic character (*see* Rhinoceros horns). No doubt, therefore, A.D.'s *R. Unicornis* was an invention of his own, based on a specimen which had lost a horn, while '*Lelongouanne*', said aloud, sounds like nothing so much as 'the long one'. Deliberate 'Franglais'? A joke by some English-speaking acquaintance? We shall never know. While A.D.'s '*chokourou*' is probably his version of the Tswana *tshukudu* = rhinoceros, his *makaley* is obscure. One suggestion for it is *bogale* = fierce. (O. Perissodactyla, F. Rhinocerotidae).

For comment on the structure of the horns *see* Rhinoceros horns; for habits and temperament *see Rhenosterboschis* and Bots, which deals with parasites; for Asiatic genera and species, *see* Rhinoceros, of Java

Rhinoceros horns ~ 216

A.D.'s description is admirable. The horns are composed of a mass of tubular filaments similar in substance (i.e., keratin) to hair, and, like hair, are continuously growing outgrowths of skin. They are therefore not attached to the bone of the skull – although their position is marked on the skull by elliptical and slightly swollen rugose areas permitting firm attachment of the skin to the bone. The anterior horn is almost always longer than the posterior in both *C. simum* and *D. bicornis*, but, whether through wear or accident or inheritance, there is variability. The record length of a horn in *C. simum*, the white rhinoceros, is 1.58m.

Rhinoceros Lelongouanne, R. Unicornis see Rhinoceros

Rhinoceros, of Java ~ 218–9

There are five species of rhinoceros, of which three are Asiatic: the Sumatran rhinoceros, *Dicerorhinus sumatrensis*, the Indian rhinoceros, *Rhinoceros unicornis*, and the Javanese or Javan rhinoceros, *R. sondaicus*, all more closely related to one another than to the two African species (*see* Rhinoceros). All three tend to be hairy, even in the adult; the horns are short; the lower canines are long and tusklike; the skin is thrown into folds superficially like armour-plating – especially marked in *R. unicornis* where the skin is studded with raised knobs. The Javan rhinoceros, *R. sondaicus*, has a heavily folded skin, broken up by a network of cracks into mosaic-like polygons, with a short hair in the centre of each, at least in the young. It has only one horn, which is very short and may be lacking in the female. Both Javan and Sumatran rhinoceros were once found throughout much of south east Asia: like the Indian rhinoceros they were ruthlessly hunted for medicinal, magical and religious purposes as well as for food and for sport. A.D. must have seen a Javan rhinoceros, either live in the Jardin des Plantes, or a mounted museum specimen (O. Perissodactyla, F. Rhinocerotidae).

Rhinopomastus Smithii ~ 259

The scimitarbilled woodhoopoe, *Rhinopomastus cyanomelas*, formerly *smithii*. Smaller than the redbilled woodhoopoe (*see Irrisor capensis*), this bird is black with a metallic blue sheen, tinged violet above, green below (no metallic sheen below on the female, whose underparts are dark brown). In flight, which is buoyant and graceful, a white bar on each primary forms a distinctive white stripe. It is found usually singly or in pairs (not in parties like the redbilled woodhoopoe), frequenting forest as well as thorn country, where it runs up and down the trunks and branches of trees in search of the insects that are its main food source. Sometimes it will creep head downwards down a perpendicular tree trunk, and will also cling beneath a branch examining flower buds for insects. Perhaps it was this agility which seemed clownish to A.D. It has a peculiar plaintive coo, which can be heard at a distance, but also has a variety of noisy, chattering calls (O. Coraciiformes, F. Phoeniculidae: woodhoopoes).

*Riet-Book also Redunca Eleotragus** ~ 99, 105, *see also* Vol I

The rietbok or reedbuck, *Redunca arundinum* (F. Bovidae, S.F. Reduncinae). A.D. may be confusing this animal with *R. fulvorufula* (his *R. Lalandii*, q.v.), the mountain reed buck.

Roan antelope *see Bastaard-guyms-book*
Rock rabbits *also Klip-dassen* ~ 99, 177,
190 ~ *see also* Vol I
The rock dassie, a small, compact, agile and surefooted mammal also known as hyrax, rock-rabbit and stone badger (O. Hyracoidea, F. Procaviidae: *Procavia capensis*). The English 'dassie' comes from the Dutch *das*: badger. *P.capensis* is still widely distributed in South Africa: it occurs in colonies where there are rocky outcrops with crevices for shelter and suitable plants for food. Colony size is related to the size of the habitat. While the *klip-dassen* recorded on the rocky mountain to the north (177) may have been *P. capensis*, it could also have been the yellow-spotted rock dassie, *Heterohyrax brucei*, which extends from the Transvaal northwards.

Habits and habitats of *P. capensis* and *H. brucei* are very similar, and where ranges overlap the two species may live on the same rocks, use identical crevices, and bask alongside each other in the sun.

Rodents ~ 231
Any mammal of the Order Rodentia, with a pair of strong, ever-growing, chisel-sharp incisor teeth on the anterior part of the upper and lower jaws. Canine teeth and anterior premolars are missing, leaving a toothless area, the diastema, between the incisors and the cheek teeth. Rodents, which gnaw their food (the name is from Latin, *rodere* = to gnaw), are the most successful of all living mammals. The group includes rats, mice, porcupines, molerats, the springhaas, squirrels, etc.

Roller ~ 201
Medium-sized birds with long wings, bright blue in patches, and plumage usually with blue coloration associated with purple, green or brown (O. Coraciiformes, F. Coraciidae).

It is not clear from the original text if A.D. killed birds of two blue-and-purple-tinged species, or if one was predominantly blue, and the other mainly purplish. The European roller, *Coracius garrulus*, is mainly sky blue. Otherwise the purple roller, *C. naevia*, has both blue (rump,tail) and light purple (wingcoverts, underparts), while the broadbilled roller (*Eurystomus glaucurus*) has blue

(wings, rump, tail) and deep violet-purple (below). *C. caudata* has blue (rump, belly, tail) and lilac (breast, hence: lilacbreasted roller). Without more details of colour pattern it is impossible to go further, but at least the blue-and-brown rackettailed roller, *C. spatulata*, can be excluded. It is very rare in the extreme north of South Africa and is distributed mainly from Zimbabwe and Mozambique northwards.

*Rooye-booken** (*also Cephalopus natalensis*) ~ 79 ~ *see also* Vol I
The red duiker, *Cephalophus natalensis* (F. Bovidae, S.F. Cephalophinae).
Rotang see Rattan cane
Rouviére *see* Arago
Royal widow bird *see* Whydah; Widow bird
Ruminant, fossil ~ 272
The fossilised skull from the bed of the Modder (A.D.'s 'Moeder') River in the Free State was surely that of a specimen of *Pelorovis bainii* (F. Bovidae, S.F. Bovinae). This was a large buffalo-like animal of grassy plains, related to the Cape buffalo *Syncerus caffer*, but of a separate lineage. A.D.'s calculation that the wide-spread horns would have been 11ft (ca 3.3m) from tip to tip, is reasonable: there are museum specimens which have an even wider span. *P. bainii* became extinct 10 000 –12 000 years ago, an event which coincided with, and may have been related to, major climatic changes.

The long, sideways projecting horns of *P. bainii* would have been a liability in woodland, and it is useful to compare them with the horns of the savanna to savanna woodland species, *S. caffer*. These are massive and curved, but arise centrally and project relatively little *(see* Buffalo).

A.D.'s (or rather, Neethling's) use of a hippopotamus as a means of comparison (of size? shape? mass?) is misleading. Had A.D. seen the specimen for himself the comparison would never have occurred to him, for he was schooled in vertebrate comparative anatomy, osteology and morphology, and was well aware of the diffences between Bovidae and Hippopotamidae.

Rushes *see* Reeds

Sable antelope *see Aigoceros nigra*
Salt and alum *see* Alum

Sandgrouse *see* Grouse

Sango also Dacka, European hemp ~ 124, 221, 278

Not *Leonotis,* the wild dagga or hemp, but *Cannabis sativa* (Urticaceae), thought to have orginated in Siberia, and one of the earliest introduced plants brought from the East by the Dutch, probably during the time of Van Riebeeck. Early Cape writers commented on the popularity among the indigenous Cape people of smoking the leaves, and on its induction of carefree euphoria followed, in excess, by wild intoxication.

The Dutch also apparently introduced the plant to India (hence 'Indian hemp', not 'European'), taking with them the KhoiSan name *dakab.* This was transmuted to *dacha* in India and returned with the Dutch, now pronounced *dakka* (or A.D.'s *dacka*). Used also medicinally by various peoples, the plant spread rapidly, and was often found growing as a weed around Zulu kraals in Natal, where it was called *insangu* (A.D.'s *sango*).

The dagga pipe A.D. describes (220–1) is an interesting variant, with its ball of moist clay, of the more traditional form in which the hole in the ground was dug near water. It is interesting also to compare it, as well as the simpler waterfilled horn pipe (124), with the more elegant but essentially similar hookah or 'hubble–bubble' of Arab countries.

Saprophagous fly larvae ~ 224

Coffin flies (O. Diptera, F. Phoridae) are small to minute insects with a humpbacked appearance. They have maggot-like larvae which live in decaying vegetable matter or carcases. The common name derives from the habits of certain species that feed on human corpses and emerge from graves. As many South African Phoridae are of the genus *Megaselia* it is likely that the larvae which bored into and damaged A.D.'s beetle specimens were *Megaselia* sp. Although phorid larvae are often found on decaying invertebrates, it is possible that the interesting behaviour described here has not been recorded elsewhere. Occasionally A.D.'s acute and detailed observations (as also, e.g., with Bots, q.v.) are startling.

Saturnia Mimosae see Bombyx, cocoons of

Sciurus cepapi see Squirrel

Serval *see* Tiger-cat

Shoemakers *see* Petrel

Shrike ~ *see* Widow-shrike, *Malaconotus Australis Smithii* ~ *see also* Vol I

Sibilo/sibylo also Antimony ~ 166, 278, 279

In both the text and his glossary of Zulu words (294), A.D. repeatedly gives the meaning of *sibilo* or *sibylo* as antimony. However, the Zulu *isibilo* means a magic spell or preparation, and several related words from other siNtu (Bantu) languages refer or apply to the administering or taking of medicine. It therefore seems probable that the black powder blended with fat and applied so liberally to the heads of the Makatisse was either the pulverised ash of some medicinal plant, or else a powdered charcoal with medicinal or insecticidal properties. Thus, the thick greasy black mixture was an ointment used not so much to suffocate head lice, as A.D. suggests (279) – although the huge quantity of it might have had that effect – as to help loosen both nits and adult parasites and, perhaps, poison them (*see* Parasites, of human beings). Although the preparation of insecticidal washes for the elimination of ectoparasites is well documented, there appears to be little information about ointments used for this purpose.

Why does A.D. identify the black powder as antimony? One possible clue comes from the story of his first encounter with the Makatisse custom (166). There he presents it as cosmetic – an adornment in the form of a grotesque pomade – and not as the medicament it probably was. He was almost certainly aware of *kohl*, the black pigment used to darken the eyelids, which is the oldest cosmetic known (in use for more than 5000 years). Kohl is a fine black powder which may be blended with grease or waxes for ease of application. Chemically it is stibnite (Sb_2S_3), the naturally occurring sulphide of antimony. Hence, antimony may have suggested itself to A.D. through cosmetic use.

There is also the possibility that he was aware of the medical uses of antimony and antimonial compounds, and of their irritant and poisonous attributes. Metallic antimony (sometimes in the form of pills, recoverable and therefore 'everlasting'), was used medicinally as an emetic and purgative, and tartrate of antimony was sold as 'tartar emetic'. While the irritant properties of such preparations were useful, there were dangerous side-effects: antimony is a cardiac and nervous depressant. In large doses it produces symptoms similar to those of arsenical poisoning, and is equally fatal.

It seems not unlikely that it was this kind of information which led A.D. to give *sibilo* a 'chemical' identity. He was probably scientist enough not simply to apply an arbitrary label (as, apparently, did Arbousset who identified the black powder as 'platinum', i.e., probably finely divided platinum black).

Simia monoides see Monkey

Simus see Rhinoceros

Smith, Andrew (1797–1872) ~ 154, 208, 254, 275

The first superintendent of the South African Museum (founded in 1825), and a naturalist, taxonomist and prolific author, from 1826 (*A Descriptive Catalogue of the South African Museum*) to 1849. In 1836 he published his *Report of the expedition for exploring central Africa, from the Cape of Good Hope... under the superintendence of... A. Smith*. He was the author of a massive five-volume work published between 1838–49, *Illustrations of the Zoology of South Africa*, consisting mainly of collections made during the expedition, which had run from 1834–36. His work earned him the title of 'Father of South African Zoology'.

He described and named many South African mammals, so that his name often appears in taxonomic works as an authority, e.g. *Oreotragus* A. Smith, 1834; *Kobus* A. Smith, 1840 and, of course, *Galago moholi* A. Smith, 1836 (*see* Smith's *galago-makali*).

Smith's *galago-makali also klein aappje* ~ 154, 261

The South African lesser bushbaby or lesser galago (Afrikaans: *nagapie* = night monkey; *klein apie* = small monkey), *Galago moholi* A. Smith, 1836 (O. Primates, S.O. Strepsirhinae, F.

Lorisidae, S.F. Galaginae). The generic name *Galago* was adopted from Senegalese: there are close similarities between *G. moholi* and *G. senegalensis*.

Lesser bushbabies are attractive small mammals, with soft, furry bodies, long tails, huge eyes and very mobile, large and membranous ears. *G. moholi* is a savanna-woodland species, and in the more arid parts of the range is confined to *Acacia* woodland, rich in insects and a source of the gum which is an important component of the diet. It is nocturnal and arboreal, resting by day in small groups, in hollow tree trunks, or in disused birds' nests or clumps of foliage: it may also build platform-like nests of its own. Animals forage singly for some hours after sunset and again before sunrise. They are noted for their principal mode of locomotion, spectacular leaps. Even on the ground they usually hop bipedally and seldom move quadrupedally. The bipedal stance is also adopted for (often vicious) fighting, with fists raised to deliver a cuff. Live insect prey is caught in the hands. *G. moholi* appears to be independent of drinking water, obtaining sufficient moisture from its food.

Snake, arboreal, green ~ 220

The text suggests that this 'pretty green snake' was an arboreal bird-eater, a description which perfectly fits the agile (but shy and seldom seen) green mamba, *Dendroaspis angusticeps* (O. Serpentes, F. Elapidae) (*see Memba*). In southern Africa, however, *D. angusticeps* is restricted to Natal coastal regions and forests along the eastern escarpment of Zimbabwe.

The snake in question, therefore, may have been one of the so-called green snakes, *Philothamnus* spp, probably *P. semivariegatus*, the spotted bush snake (S.O. Serpentes, F. Colubridae).

This graceful, slender snake is an expert and speedy climber, hunting among shrubs and bushes for geckos, chameleons and tree frogs (but not for birds). The body is bright green to olive, usually with dark spots and bars on the forebody (sometimes absent in eastern Transvaal specimens), becoming grey-bronze towards the rear. The head is green or blue-green. Its 'prettiness' is indisputable.

Snuffboxes *see Bombyx*, cocoon of; Spanish reed; Tobacco

Spanish reed ~ 115
Arundo donax (Restionaceae): the giant reed. The name (Afrikaans *spaanse-riet*, Dutch *spaansche riet*) indicates its South European origin. It was introduced as a garden plant in about 1660, and by 1800 was to be found all over the Cape Colony and elsewhere. It had many uses, from Khoi musical instruments to the building of huts and sheds. Sections of hollow stem would make excellent small containers – in this case, snuff boxes. It is a story reminiscent in a modest way of that of the bamboo of south-east Asia.

Sparrman, Andrew *also* Sparmann ~ 214 ~ *see also* Vol I
Swedish naturalist and author among other things of a two-volume travel memoir including an account of his journeys '*into the country of the Hottentots and Caffres from 1772 to 1776*'.

Sparrow-owl, pearly ~ 259
Glaucidium perlatum is the smallest of the southern African owls (O. Strigiformes, F. Strigidae). The pearl-spotted owl lacks eartufts, and is coloured brown and white – brown spotted with white above, white streaked with brown below. On the back of the head are two dark spots surrounded with white: a false face. It is common in riverine woodland north of the Orange, and is at least partly diurnal. Thus, as A.D. records, it may be seen in bright sunlight, and may during the heat of the day sit perched in the shade of a thick tree, usually flying off when disturbed. The food consists mainly of insects and the occasional mouse or lizard. Yet although it poses no threat to smaller birds, they often mob the owl, just as A.D. describes. He uses the fact as a basis for some very anthropomorphic philosophising, amusing, perhaps even containing a germ of truth, but not an insight of any real help in the understanding of animal behaviour.

Specimen preparation see Alum; Arsenic; Camphor; Corrosive sublimate; Turpentine

Springbok *see Spring-booken*

Spring-booken* *also* Euchore, *Gazella Euchore*, Leaping gazelles ~ 162, 163, 165, 176–7 ~ *see also* Vol I
The springbok, *Antidorcas marsupialis* (F. Bovidae, S.F. Antilopinae): a beautiful and lively antelope of medium size. For comments on its appearance, distribution and biology, *see* Vol I. The early name *Antilope euchore* was given by Le Vaillant (q.v.), who was impressed by the springbok's vertical leaping or 'pronking': *euchore*, Gk = fine dancer. A.D. gives a heartstopping picture of the huge herds of antelope that once populated large areas of South Africa: '*Springbooken* were beginning to appear in . . . groups, . . . in herds of hundreds, and then in their thousands' (162).

Squamosa ~ 224
Specific name of a beetle: *see* Buprestids

Squirrel *also Sciurus cepapi* ~ 223
The tree squirrel, *Paraxerus cepapi* (F. Sciuridae). Widespread from Angola to Mozambique and north to south eastern Zaire, it occurs only in the extreme north of South Africa'.

It is a savanna-woodland species, which uses holes in trees as resting places. It is small, as A.D. records, with body length about 35 cm and tail about half as long. Generally solitary, it is extremely agile in feeding, hanging by its feet to reach the flowers, seeds and fruits which are the main food source – though insects are an important secondary component of the diet.

St Elmo's fire ~ 103 and footnote
'Elmo' is a name derived from Erasmus, the 3rd century saint and martyr. Legend has it that he was put to death by having his intestines wound out of his body on a windlass. Perhaps because of the resemblance of a windlass to a capstan, he became honoured as the patron saint of sailors. 'St Elmo's fire' refers to the electrical discharges sometimes seen at mastheads of ships: the light was taken as a sign of St Elmo's protection.

Stinking badger *see* Ratel

*Strepsiceros Condoma** *see* Kudu

Sugar bushes *also Suiker-bosch, Zuyker-bosch* ~ 54, 169–70
A.D.'s detailed, almost lyrical description (169–70) is probably of *Protea*

caffra (Proteaceae) the Natal or common sugarbush (Afrikaans: *suiker-bos*), the most widespread South African protea.

It occurs in a variety of veld types, usually on the southern aspects of mountainsides. The flower bracts (A.D.'s 'petals') are deep pink-cream; the mass of flowers surrounded by the bracts is white.

Several *Protea* spp are called sugarbushes because they secrete copious sweet nectar, which is scented in *P.caffra* and is secreted from October to March: it attracts birds and beetles. The woody stems have thick, black, fissured bark and make excellent firewood, as A.D. records. He is astonished that earlier travellers to the Cape did not mention the plants, yet he himself says they are rare in Natal, where they are, in fact, not uncommon, especially at higher altitudes. It seems that A.D. himself was guilty of the fault he ascribes to other travellers (169). He noted what was colourful and extraordinary (in this case, summer proteas in flower and exuding their 'manna'); he ignored what seemed drab (winter proteas).

Suikerbosstroop, the fragrant sugarbush syrup, is still made in parts of South Africa.

Sugar cane ~ 23, 124, 246, 247

The sugar cane A.D. was given to eat (23) may well have been *Saccharum officinarum* (Poaceae), long cultivated as a source of sugar in many parts of the world. The identity of the 'indigenous' sugar cane (124) is uncertain: it appears to have been distinct from *Sorghum dochna* (see kaffircorn), often chewed for its sweet juice.

Sugar cane borers ~ 247

The white larvae could have belonged to a variety of insects. They were probably the larvae of one of the two lepidopteran stalk borers, *Eldana saccharina* (F. Pyralidae – a large and almost ubiquitous family of small, drab moths, many of which are pests), or *Sesamia calamistis* (F. Noctuidae, the largest lepidopteran family, which includes cutworms, bollworms and army worms as well as stalk borers). The information A.D. gives is insufficient for precise identification, and it may even be that these were the larvae of a stalk boring bee-

tle (F. Scarabeidae). The pink colour imparted to the sugarcane by these pests may have been caused by their frass (excretory products) or by bacterial or fungal invasion following the disruption of the plant tissue by the feeding and growing larvae.

Sultan hen ~ 220

A.D. uses this common name for the purple gallinule (see Gallinule, purple), but this usage has long been obsolete.

Since the 1930s 'sultan hen' has referred to a small, crested variety of white domestic fowl, originally from Turkey.

Sus larvatus / lavartus see Bushpig

Sus Phacochaerus see Boar, wild

Swart-rhenoster see Rhinoceros

Sweet potato ~ 124

Ipomoea batatas (Convolvulaceae), the sweet potato, is a prostrate, ascending and sometimes twining perennial whose stems arise from a yellow or reddish ellipsoid or fusiform tuber.

Probably a native of tropical America, it has long been widely cultivated in the tropics and may now be found growing wild as a culture relic. It is easy to grow and is a staple crop in Natal. The tubers are boiled, roasted or baked; boiled sweet potatoes may be mixed with maize meal to form a porridge.

Tadpoles; Tadpole shrimps *see* Insects and larvae, aquatic

Taenia; T. solium, T. saginata see Tapeworm

Tambouki-gras ~ 221 ~ *see also* Vol I

Tambookie grass is a general name given to several species of tall, coarse grass used for thatching, etc., including *Cymbopogon*, *Hyparrhenia* and *Miscanthidium* (Poaceae). A.D. describes the ingenious use of a dry grass stalk in the smoking of '*dacka*'. *See also sango*.

Tambooty trees ~114, 177 ~ *see also* Vol I

Spirostachys africana, the tamboti tree (Euphorbiaceae).

Tannin *see* Woody plant, edible root of

Tapeworm *also Tenia solium* ~ 182, 217–8, 253–4

Tapeworms have been known for millennia: first documented in 1500

BC (the Ebers Papyrus), the parasites are mentioned by many ancient authors, including Hippocrates, Aristotle and Pliny the Elder, as well as writers in the Middle and Far East. A.D.'s first experience as host to a tapeworm impressed him so deeply that he tells the story twice, with embellishments. For example, from having been four feet long (218) it later (253) grows to four-and-a-half feet (about 1.35m – not very long really, as worms in excess of 10m are not uncommon). He names the parasite as *'Tenia' solium*, but *Taenia solium*, which is almost cosmopolitan and was certainly well known in Europe, is the pork tapeworm, and is ribbonlike and translucent. A.D.'s was 'as thick as man's thumb', which would describe *T. saginata*, the beef tapeworm (P. Platyhelminthes, S.O. Cestoda). As he does not mention the consumption of pork, but certainly included beef in what now seems an excessively carnivorous diet, *T. saginata* is even more likely to have been the tapeworm concerned.

The life cycle of tapeworms is more complex than A.D. imagined (253–4), involving as it does two hosts, primary (human) and secondary or intermediate (cow or pig). The adult worm attaches itself to the human intestinal wall by means of hooks, suckers (or both) on the anterior end, the scolex. The elongated body absorbs nutrients from the digesting food in which it is bathed, and is divided transversely along its length into separate units (A.D.'s 'segments'), the proglottids, each of which is sexually complete. When fully developed and replete with fertilised eggs, gravid proglottids break off and are passed out via the anus: A.D. reports seeing but not recognising these for what they were – though he recorded their appearance at the rate of 18 – 20 each day. Growth of the body is from the anterior end, behind the scolex, which means that as fast as proglottids break off they are replaced, so that tapeworms can live in the human host for some years.

Eggs on grass or in soil are ingested by the intermediate host, in whose gut they hatch into larvae which make their way to the body tissues by entering the bloodvascular system. In the tissues, especially muscle, they encyst as bladder worms. When the infected beef (or pork, known as 'measly pork' because of the spotted effect created by the cysts) is eaten, the bladder worms develop into tapeworms and the cycle begins again, with eggs being produced after two or three months. Thorough cooking kills the bladder worms: the partially cooked slabs of meat A.D. and his men habitually devoured made infection almost inevitable and, apparently, people living in Natal and the Transvaal were accepting of this and prepared for it with various well known remedies.

Often, apart from the appearance of released segments, frequently at night during sleep, infection is virtually symptomless, even when more than one worm is present. There are, however, anecdotal reports of varied symptoms, from lack of appetite to ravenous hunger (like A.D.'s), and including general indisposition, anxiety, weariness and emaciation. The latter, incidentally, prompted the deliberate swallowing of tapeworm cysts as aids to slimming in earlier and more ignorant times. A.D.'s extreme agitation, his irascibility and mental confusion, seem exceptional and it is understandable that he believed himself victim of some dread disease (*see* Hydrophobia). However, the possibility cannot be excluded that some individuals are especially sensitive to one or more by-products of the parasite's metabolism (a subject on which even now little information is available) which, able to traverse the 'blood-brain-barrier', disturb central nervous function in some way. This possibility is supported by the apparently trustworthy story of a sufferer who became intensely agitated, but only when he heard music; it is supported, too, by the fact that as soon as A.D. had rid himself of the parasite his mental (and physical) condition returned almost magically to normal. The cramps and vomiting (253) brought on by eating curry and ground beans (*see* Beans, underground) were probably less a symptom of the presence of the tapeworm than the despairing peristaltic and antiperistaltic efforts of an alimentary canal strained and irritated beyond endurance by the consumption of huge quantities of food: 15 1bs (almost 7kg) of meat at a sitting is a staggering quantity, especially for a man of small build.

We are not specifically told how the first tapeworm was persuaded to make its exit, although his reference to the reliability of pomegranate root (253) may be significant (see Pomegranate, as anthelmintic, for comment on the properties of, not the root, but the rind of the fruit). The time-honoured method is twofold: a vermifuge or anthelmintic is given to cause the worm to detach from the intestinal wall, together with, or followed by a purgative to hasten its removal. Effective plant-based vermifuges and purgatives had been known for centuries, and the commonly used European remedy, the rhizomes of 'male fern' (*Dryopteris filix-mas*), must surely have been in many a traveller's medical kit, together with such a common purgative as senna or castor oil. A.D. was apparently not so prudent, and had to turn to local remedies, of which that prepared from *Dryopteris athamantica* should have been effective but was, in its manner of preparation, unpalatable (see Fern root, as anthelmintic, for comment on both *D. filix-mas* and *D. athamantica*).

That tapeworms – and several other intestinal worms – were a common problem is attested to by the number of indigenous and Boer remedies for them and the various irritant plant preparations and decoctions that were recommended (or touted) as specifics: see e.g., *Wacht-eine-beytje*.

Interestingly, there is, even now, minimal evidence of *Taenia saginata* bladder worms in antelope and other wild bovids, confirming that A.D. was not infected by what he had shot for the pot, but by beef.

Taurina, Catoblepas taurina see Catoblepas gorgon
Taxidermy *see* Alum, Arsenic, Corrosive sublimate
Tefflus Delegorguei see Carabids
Tenia solium see Tapeworm
Termites *also* White ants ~ 7, 125 ~ *see also* Vol I
Social insects living in colonies of hundreds of thousands of individuals (O. Isoptera). Nests may be subterranean or else visible as clay mounds of cement-like hardness and consistency.

Textor ~ 220
Possibly the cloud cisticola, *Cisticola textrix* (O. Passeriformes, F. Sylviidae: warblers, apalises, cisticolas). However, cisticolas are difficult to identify precisely by sight alone: they are small, sombre-coloured warblers of grassy habitats, from semidesert to moist woodland edges and vleis. A.D.'s Transvaal specimen may have been *C. textrix*, but other species are possible, including *C. juncidis* (fantailed cisticola) *C. chiniana* (rattling cisticola), *C. erythrops* (redfaced cisticola), *C. aberrans* (lazy or rock cisticola), *C. fulvicapilla* (neddicky), or *C. tinniens* (Levaillant's cisticola).
Thorn bushes, tree, veld *see* Mimosa
Ticks *see* Arachnids, venomous ~ 144, 233–4
Arthopods of P. Chelicerata, C. Arachnida, O. Acarina, which are usually temporary, sometimes permanent, ectoparasites, clinging to a host, piercing the integument and withdrawing the host's body fluid on which the tick feeds. For comment on the species of ticks infesting bovids (144) and rhinoceros *see* Vol I
Tiger-cat** *also Felis Serval* ~ 249
The serval (Afrikaans: *tierboskat*, from the Dutch *tyger bosch katten*), *Felis serval* (O. Carnivora, F. Felidae). An elegant animal, with long legs and neck, small head, large ears and beautifully spotted and barred coat, the black bands and spots standing out against a background which may vary from off-white to shades of golden-yellow. The tail appears to be ringed with black. The ears are large and rounded and are especially noticeable because of the relatively small head. The height at the shoulder is about 60cm. The serval is widely distributed south of the Sahara, but in South Africa occurs mainly in the eastern Transvaal and in much of Natal – but not at the coast.
Tobacco *also Gouaye* ~ 124, 221, 278
Nicotiana tabacum (Solanaceae), the tobacco plant. The species is said to have originated in South America, and to have been brought to Europe in 1586 by one Ralph Lane from Tobago in the West Indies (or Tobasco in

Mexico). Sir Walter Raleigh first introduced the smoking of the leaves. From 1652 onwards almost every expedition to and within southern Africa carried a good supply of tobacco for barter. It is hardly surprising that indigenous people were growing tobacco by the 19th century, and it does indeed seem certain that the plant in question was *N. tabacum*. So-called 'wild tobacco', *N. glauca*, was not introduced from South America until about 1845, when Baron von Ludwig did so 'to supply this treeless country with an ornamental tree'.

A.D.'s *'gouaye'* is his French phonetic rendering of Zulu: *igwayi* = snuff. Snuff is, of course, powdered tobacco which is sniffed up the nostrils. The stimulating effect of the nicotine is achieved more swiftly in this way than through smoking, and the practice is less harmful to the lungs. There may be deleterious consequences for the epithelium of the naso-pharynx and the sinuses, however.

Touraco/Turaco *also* Loury; *includes*: *cacatoes*, ~ 104, 173 ~ *see also* Vol I
Touracos or louries are medium to large birds, often with bright plumage and a conspicuously crested head (O. Musophagiformes, F. Musophagidae). They feed mainly on fruit, seeds and buds.

The 'incorrect' Boer name for the grey lourie, *cacatoe* (173) (from Dutch, *kaketoe*, cf English, cockatoo) refers strictly to parrots of F. Cacatuinae: ultimate origin of the name the Malay, *kakatua*.

Tsessebe *see Acronotus lunata*
Tragelaphus Sylvatica** ~ not mentioned in text
The bush buck, *Tragelaphus scriptus sylvaticus* (F. Bovidae, S.F. Tragelaphinae). This medium-sized antelope, whose distribution has been remarkably little affected, does not occur in arid areas. In South Africa it occurs in riverine woodland to the north, as well as in coastal bush of the southeast and south.

Tragulus Rupestris**; *T. Melanotis*** ~ not mentioned in text
Raphicerus campestris, the steenbok, and *R. melanotis*, the grysbok (F. Bovidae, S.F. Antilopinae).
Both are small antelope. The steenbok (named for its reddish colour, from

Afrikaans *steen* = brick: N.B., not 'steinbok', which is the German name for the ibex), inhabits open country and is widespread through most of the southern subregion. The grysbok is rufous-brown above, sprinkled with white hairs giving it a grizzled appearance. It is endemic to the south western and southern parts of the Cape Province.

Triops *see* Insects and larvae, aquatic
Turkish corn *see* Maize
Turpentine ~ 224
Turpentine is the name given to oleoresins exuded from certain trees, especially from conifers and also the terebinth tree, *Pistacia terebinthus*, a native of Mediterranean islands and shores. Although the association between painting and turpentine is well known, few will be aware, in the late 20th century, that it was once used as an insecticide, and also was noted for its antiseptic and mildly anaesthetic properties. It was in medical use as a disinfectant, a parasiticide (e.g., for ringworm and other dermal fungal infections) and as a component of liniments. Its use as a disinfectant and insecticide or insect repellant in insect collecting boxes is thus easy to understand. A.D. used 'concentrated' turpentine, presumably a viscous oil in some kind of non-spill container, in his insect boxes.

In combination with camphor (q.v.) the disinfectant effect should have been reinforced. Until relatively recently, it was common to blend the two as a paste which was painted on the inner surfaces of the boxes.

Tzeiran see Bastaard-guyms-book

Uncklove see Elephant

Vaal-duyker *see* Duyker
Verreaux, Joseph Alexis ~ 282–3
The youngest of the three noted brothers who took over and ran Maison Verreaux in Paris, which had been started by their father, and which dealt in natural history specimens, especially rare birds. The eldest, Pierre Jules, in 1818 and at the age of

11, accompanied his uncle, P.-A. Delalande (q.v.), the naturalist, to the Cape. Delalande trained him in taxidermy and natural history, and he trained further with the great Cuvier (q.v. Vol I) on his return to Paris. P.J. Verreaux later returned to the Cape (1826) for further collecting, and offered his help to Andrew Smith (q.v.) in stocking the newly-founded South African Museum. In 1830 he was joined by his younger brother, J.B. Edouard, who helped mount and pack the first Paris collection. In 1832 the youngest brother, Alexis, arrived. He assisted in the mounting of Smith's specimens and, after his brothers returned to France to run the Paris business, stayed on at the Cape and supplied them with specimens. It seems almost certain that he mounted the sable antelope brought to Cape Town by Captain William Cornwallis Harris (q.v.) – perhaps the very specimen whose portrait distinguishes the cover of this book. Unlike his brothers, who were, especially Pierre, prolific authors of mainly ornithological works, Alexis seems not to have been an intellectual: in Cape Town he ran a gunpowder shop. He does, however, appear from A.D.'s encounter with him to have been both generous and thoroughly gentlemanly.

It is P.J. Verreaux's name that is commemorated in the nomenclature. Examples are *Aquila verreauxi*, Verreaux's eagle, and *Myomyscus verreauxii*, Verreaux's mouse.

Vine ~ 124

A.D. suggests that cultivation of grapes, *Vitis vinifera* (Vitaceae), in South Africa would be successful and, probably, lucrative. In fact *V. vinifera* had been introduced by Simon van der Stel, who had early recognised the wine-growing potential of the western Cape. A.D. appears not to have noticed the several indigenous species of wild grape, especially *Rhoicissus tomentosa*, *R. rhomboidea* and *R. tridentata*: all bear clusters of edible fruit, though the flesh is usually acid or astringent.

Vulture also White vulture, percnopteran ~ 93, 189, 195, 202, 204, 265 ~ see also Vol I
Large diurnal birds of prey (raptors) which prefer carrion to live prey (O. Falconiformes, F. Accipitridae). As he

travelled northward A.D. noted a white vulture which he called a 'percnopteran' (189), surely the Egyptian vulture, *Neophron percnopterus*, distinctive for its white body and white, wedge-shaped tail, and the all-black primaries. The bird prefers grassland, savanna and semi-desert, and was formerly a localised breeding resident. It is now a rare vagrant with most recent sightings in Transkei, Namibia and Transvaal.

Waater-book see Kobus ellipsiprymnus
Wacht-eine-beytje ~ 221
'Wag-'n-bietjie' (Afrikaans: wait a bit) is the name applied to several species of plants with strong, spreading, usually recurved spines, causing one to pause to disentangle oneself when clothes are hooked. In the Cape the name is given to several species of *Asparagus*, but further north the name may be used for, among other things, some species of *Acacia*, including the *haakdoring*, *Acacia mellifera detinens* (see Mimosa). A.D. indicates that his *wag-'n-bietjie* is not *A.m.detinens*, and, as it is a bush rather than a tree, species of *Ziziphus* may be suggested (Rhamnaceae). *Z. mucronata*, the buffalo thorn, is known in Afrikaans as the *blinkblaar* (shiny leaved) *wag 'n bietjie*: this is a small to medium-sized deciduous tree with paired thorns, one straight and the other recurved. This, together with the elasticity of the twigs, ensures that the unwary will become seriously entangled in a clinging and savagely prickly embrace which must have prompted several indigenous names meaning (surely in ironic vein) 'come and I'll kiss you'. The plant is useful – for protective fencing, for its wood and for its fruits, eaten fresh or dried and ground to a meal or roasted as coffee substitute. The roots are used medicinally: chewed as an anthelmintic (see Tapeworm) or in decoctions taken for skin diseases and swollen lymph nodes.

The *klein wag 'n bietjie*, *Z. zeyheriana*, is a dwarf, bushy, deciduous perennial growing socially: A.D. may have encountered thickets. The branches are armed with strong re-

374

curved prickles. They tend to overrun bare ground, especially on hard, gravelly red soils.

Wahlberg, Johan August (1810–56) ~ 95, 133–4, 140–1, 154, 185, 207–10, 220, 222–3, 276 ~ see also Vol I

Natural historian and collector chosen by the Swedish Academy of Sciences to visit South Africa, to which he came in 1839. Interestingly, he completed most of his education at Uppsala, renowned as a centre for the study of aspects of natural history (see also Fabricius; Linnaeus), qualifying in forestry, surveying, agronomy and engineering. He also taught – physics, chemistry, natural history and agronomy.

Wahlberg's southern African travels, during which he collected with ruthless single-mindedness, provided the Stockholm Natural History Museum with large numbers of meticulously prepared specimens. These included 2527 birds, 533 mammals, 480 reptiles and amphibians, and 5000 species (and many more individual specimens) of insects, many of which may still be seen and studied.

His travel journal is succinct and his records and methods are regarded as more consistent and precise than were A.D.'s. This was partly because of his strict academic and technical training, and partly because of what seems to have been a rather chilly but obsessive (or perhaps passionately aquisitive) disposition. He appears to have preferred to travel alone, with just his employees, and to have made his aversion from foreign competition clear. A.D. writes of him with warm affection, but although Wahlberg records that he made use of A.D.'s hospitality, such personal feeling does not enter his own writing. However, while modern commentators present Wahlberg as aloof and remote, the eagerness with which A.D. greets him, his repeated use of 'my friend', the hints that they enjoyed each other's company, and his evident sadness at his last sight of Wahlberg (222–3), all speak of a genuine friendship.

To A.D. Wahlberg was the object of great affection and deep respect (276): he clearly recognised in the Swede outstanding ability as a scientist. If asked, he might, for once self-deprecating, (if not humble), have admitted that by comparison he, A.D., was something of an amateur or dilettante.

Warthog see Boar, wild

Watercress ~ 172

Probably *Rorippa nasturtium-aquaticum* (formerly *Nasturtium officinale*), an aquatic or semi-aquatic herb often found growing in springs as A.D. describes, as well as in rivulets and along the banks of streams. It was early introduced at the Cape to supply ships on the East India route with 'greens' for combating scurvy. It spread rapidly and was reported to be plentiful in a Mooi River spring in 1841. It is now a common weed all over South Africa, and is eaten as salad or as a vegetable (Brassicaceae). In Afrikaans watercress is *bronkos* or *bronkors(t)*: literally, spring food, or salad. The word has been incorporated into at least one South African place name.

Watermelon ~ 124, 248

Citrullus lanatus (Cucurbitaceae), the common wild melon of South Africa, also known as colocynth, wild watermelon, desert melon. The Afrikaans *bitterappel* describes the sometimes bitter taste, but usually the white flesh of the fruit, though crisp and juicy, has little flavour. It is indigenous to south-west Asia and Africa, and is found in a semi-wild or cultivated state elsewhere. Under American cultivation many edible varieties of watermelon have been produced, with sweet pink or reddish flesh.

Weavers see Fringillas ~ see also Vol I, Sparrows

Weevil ~ also Curculionids ~ 125, 224

Beetles (O. Coleoptera) of F. Curculionidae, the largest of all insect families: more than 60 000 species have been named so far. Weevils have the front of the head prolonged into a snout or rostrum, which may be short and broad or long and narrow. All weevils feed on plants, and the group includes a number of serious agricultural pests.

White vulture see Vulture

Whydah *includes* royal, four-pronged *and possibly*, longtailed widow bird ~ 254

The words 'royal' and 'four-pronged' indicate that this bird from the far northern Transvaal was not a widow bird (q.v.) but a whydah (O. Passeriformes, F. Viduidae). In this family the four central tail feathers (rectrices) of breeding males may be greatly elongated in ways which are diagnostic. In the shafttailed whydah, *Vidua regia* (*regia* perhaps the source of A.D.'s 'royal') these rectrices are very long and thin, with broadened ends. A.D. would not have seen this bird during his travels in Natal: he would first have encountered it as he moved northward in the Transvaal. A second possibility is the far more widely spread pintailed whydah, *V. macroura*, whose long rectrices are very noticeable, if less striking in appearance than those of *V. regia*. An Afrikaans common name for this bird is *koningweduweetjie* = king (or royal) widow.

Although A.D.'s longtailed widow bird is usually just that, i.e. *Euplectes progne* (*see* widow bird), there is some confusion about the identity of the 'longtailed widow' in the northern Transvaal (254), because *E. progne* is not recorded this far north. Although other, shorter-tailed widows may be found there, this particular bird's bracketing with a whydah may indicate that it, too, was a whydah – although the differences in colour between the very long-tailed paradise whydah, *Vidua paradisaea* (chestnut breast and ochre belly, with broad ochre collar), and *E. progne* (underparts black, bend of wing scarlet with a white band) are such that the identification must remain uncertain.

Widow bird (*also Emberiza longicaudata*, longtailed widow) ~ 114, 116, 254 ~ *see also* Vol I
The genus *Euplectes* (O. Passeriformes, F. Ploceidae) includes both bishops and widows, but while bishops have short tails at all times, most widow males develop long tails in the breeding season.

Long black widow tail feathers added great elegance to Zulu ceremonial dress and may have been the extremely long feathers of *Euplectes progne*, the longtailed widow. Presumably, '*Emberiza longicaudata*' (116) refers to *E. progne*: the use of '*Emberiza*' is puzzling as only buntings, which are relatively short-

tailed, belong to this genus.
In the northern Transvaal (254) A.D. again reports the presence of longtailed widows, as well as of 'royal, four-pronged' widow birds. In fact the locality is further north than one would expect to find *E. progne*. This, and the 'four-pronged', are clues to the probability that these were not widows, but whydahs (q.v., and for other Ploceidae, *see* Fringillas).

Widow-shrike *also* 'exter', *Lanius melanoleucus*, long-tailed shrike, *Melanoleucus* ~ 25, 25n, 173, 173n ~ *see also* Vol I, shrike
A.D. gives a clear and accurate description of the appearance and some of the habits of the black and white longtailed shrike, *Corvinella melanoleuca* (O. Passeriformes, F. Laniidae) (25), distributed in southern Africa from Zululand to Zimbabwe and southern Mozambique, and from the northern Karroo to the north and north west of the subregion. A.D.'s use of 'widow-shrike' is understandable: the long tail does somewhat resemble that of the breeding widowbird (q.v.). His use of 'exter' as a common name or nickname is enigmatic, but may be a misrendering of the German *Elster*: magpie. Indeed, the full German common name for the longtailed shrike is *Elsterwürger* = 'strangler magpie': cf the English 'butcherbird' and 'Johnny ' or 'Jackie hangman' and Afrikaans '*laksman*' = hangman. All refer to the predatory behaviour of shrikes: they swoop after small animals (in this case, insects and small reptiles), strike them with their feet and carry them away in their claws. The prey is often, especially in the breeding season when it is most useful to have a 'larder' of food, impaled on thorns, barbed wire, etc. The bad reputation of shrikes, as birds which kill and impale for pleasure, is, of course, undeserved, as is the belief that they torture their victims. The shrike kills only for food, and does so swiftly and cleanly by biting the neck, aided by a toothed area (similar to that in falcons) on the bill.

Wild cat ~ 187
The African wild cat, *Felis lybica* (O. Carnivora, F. Felidae), which has a wide distribution on the continent, being absent only in tropical and mon-

tane forest. In the southern subregion it occurs in all but the eastern, low-lying coastal regions.

F. lybica is almost entirely nocturnal, secretive and cunning and difficult to trap, and it is remarkable that A.D. actually surprised one.

Wild dog* *also* Cynhyaena, *Cynhyaena Venatica* ~ 202-4, 226 ~ *see also* Vol I *Lycaon pictus*, the African wild dog (F. Canidae, S.F. Simocyoninae), a ferocious diurnal carnivore, living and hunting in packs. The Vol I index entry comments on aspects of the biology and behaviour of this animal, and some of this is confirmed by A.D.'s observations (202-4). Only recently has *L. pictus* received serious study and been revealed as an animal with a remarkable social structure and of great ecological importance. Unfortunately, because of the generalised contempt for it (and A.D.'s attitude is typical), the wild dog has been treated as vermin and may well now be endangered.

Wild-dattle-boom (*also* Wild date palm) ~ 125 ~ *see also* Vol I *Phoenix reclinata*, the wild date palm or *wildedadel boom* (Arecaceae). Confined to the eastern coastal and sandy regions of South Africa from the Eastern Cape to the eastern Transvaal. The fruit is edible, but it was not, apparently, the fruit that A.D. consumed when in desperate straits: perhaps the trees were not carrying ripe fruit at the time.

He does not state precisely which pieces he cut from the palm trees.

Wildebeest, black *see* Gnu/Gnou

Wildebeest, blue *see Catoblepas gorgon*

Wild rotang see Rattan cane

Willow ~ 194

The willows shading the banks of the Ourityle may have been the indigenous Vaal, wild or river willow, a tree which grows up to 15m and is found in various forms in different parts of South Africa. It cannot be excluded, however, that the plants were *Salix babylonica*, the weeping willow, said to have been imported in the time of Simon van der Stel (1679–99), and long naturalised, growing readily from cuttings along river banks.

Woody plant: edible root of ~ 124–5

In time of famine the roots of the woody shrubs *Boscia albitrunca*,

Maerua caffra and *M. racemulosa* (all Capparaceae) may be used, especially in Natal and Swaziland, for food, usually to make bread or porridge.

Treatment of the usually very fibrous roots is elaborate and time consuming. It seems possible that A.D.'s own preparation was overhasty. This would account for his experience of indigestibility, discomfort and hyperperistalsis. He must surely have been guessing in his citing of 'tannin' as the irritant component.

Zebra** *also Equus Burchellii / Burschellii, E. Zebra* ~ 130

Burchell's zebra, *Equus burchelli* (O. Perissodactyla, F. Equidae) is named for W.J. Burchell (q.v.), the great traveller and naturalist who brought the original specimen from South Africa and presented it to the British Museum.

A.D. gives to the quagga (q.v.) the name of *E. burchelli* (as *E. Burchellii* and *E. Burschellii*), and, as he does not describe the animals he sees, often in large herds, it is impossible to tell whether he is recording quagga or zebra or both. Many early travellers used 'quagga' and *E. burchellii* indiscriminately.

The text is confusing and the hunting map (331) is unhelpful. The key to the map (330) does, however, list separately *E. Burchellii, E. Quagga* (*E. quagga*: quagga), and *E. Zebra* (*E. zebra*: the Cape mountain zebra): perhaps A.D. was aware of the distinction after all.

Zuiker-bosch, Zuyker-bosch see Sugar bushes

GENERAL INDEX

In compiling this index, I have followed the style used by Colin Webb in Volume
I. It is appropriate, therefore, to reproduce his introductory notes.

In the interests of conciseness and economy I have frequently referred the
reader to the previous volume, rather than repeating the detailed information
given there. I have not indexed scientists or animals (except for Zulu cattle and
cats), plants or minerals as these have been dealt with by Stephanie Alexander
in the Natural History Index.

Bill Guest

Idiosyncratic and often inconsistent renderings of personal names,
place-names, and Zulu and Dutch/Afrikaans words and phrases are a feature
of Delegorgue's text. While these oddities and anomalies give to the work its
own particular flavour, they also raise special problems for the indexer and
annotator.

Where the text carries different spellings of the same name or word, page
references are given under the orthographic form in which the name or word
first appears, but in all such cases alternative spellings are shown alongside
the main entry, thus: *Abanto also Abantou*. Where different names or words
are used for the same subject, page references are given under the name or
word which appears most frequently in the text, and the alternatives are shown
thus: Amazoulou country *also* Zoulouland. In all cases, cross-references are
provided where appropriate. Where Delegorgue's rendering of Zulu or
Dutch/Afrikaans woeds is likely to obstruct comprehension of the text, these
terms have been included in the index together with explanatory notes.

In the annotations and in sub-entries, modern orthography is used in respect
of proper nouns and Zulu and Dutch/Afrikaans words and phrases, and A.D.'s
orthography is given in parentheses where this will assist the reader to identify
the relevant passages in the text, thus: Bushmans (Boschjesmans) River
massacres. Where there is a well-accepted alternative modern spelling of a
name, as for example Mlandela and Myandeya, the variation is shown thus:
Mlandela/Myandeya. Since the rendering of place-names, especially those of
Zulu origin, is confusingly varied and inconsistent, the modern orthography
used in the annotations and sub-entries is that which appears on recent official
topographical maps.

Sub-entries are odered alphabetically without regard to intial prepositions
and conjunctions. In cross-references, sub-entries are shown in parentheses,
thus: *see* Amazoulous (food and drink).

The following abbreviations are used in the annotations: A.D. ~ Adulphe
Delegorgue; km ~ kilometres.

C. de B. Webb

378

Aap-Rivier ~ The Aap (Apies) River, upon which Pretoria was later established, was named after the numerous vervet monkeys which the Boers encountered on its banks. Further north it converges with the Pienaars River to form the Moretele. ~ 154 ~ *see also Moretele*

Abafanas also *Imphana, Imphanas* ~ 63, 114 ~ *see also* Vol I

Abyssinia ~ A reference to present day Ethiopia in north-east Africa, an independent African kingdom prior to Italian domination (1936–41). ~ 184, 196, 278

Achilles tendon ~ The tendon at the back of the heel, named after Achilles who, according to classical mythology, had been rendered invulnerable by being plunged into the Styx River as an infant except for the heel by which his mother had held him. ~ 152

Adams, Char. ~ Charles Adams was one of the less well-known early settlers of Port Natal. ~ 58

Adams, *Revd Dr* Newton ~ A missionary physician of the American Board Zulu Mission. ~46 ~ *see also* Vol I

African-Dutch ~ *see* Boers

Africans ~ *see* Amazoulous; Boschjesmanes; Cafres; Cafres of Natal; Hottentots

Afrikaners~ *see* Boers; Emigrant Boers, Natal; Cape Colony

Albany district ~ A part of the Uitenhage district on the Cape Colony's eastern frontier. Formerly known as 'Zuurveld', Governor Sir John Cradock named it 'Albany' in January 1814 following the expulsion of its Xhosa inhabitants north-eastwards across the Great Fish River. ~ 6

Alexander, *Captain* James Edward ~ Served in the English East India Company and in several military campaigns abroad before arriving at the Cape in January 1835 where he was aide-de-camp to Governor Sir Benjamin D'Urban. After action in the Cape frontier war of that year he explored the western Cape coast into present-day Namibia on behalf of the Royal Geographical Society and gave his name to Alexander Bay on the Atlantic coastline. He subsequently attained the rank of general and was knighted in 1838. ~ 135

Algeria ~ The north African territory which the French began to colonize with the occupation of Algiers in 1830. ~ 124, 249

Ama-Balekyle ~ *see* Ndebele

Amadebeles/Amadebés ~ *see* Ndebele

Amadouna ~ *see Om-douna*

Ama-Kosa(s) ~ The Xhosa are southern Nguni-speaking people who originally followed the Tshawe royal clan which claimed an ancestor named Xhosa. The Tshawe established themselves in the northern Transkei prior to 1600, gradually expanding their control from the Mbashe River in the north to the Sundays River in the south by the late eighteenth century. In the process numerous autonomous sub-chiefdoms emerged, divided roughly into two sections, the Gcaleka in the east and the Rharabe in the south-west. The latter were the first to clash with white settlers advancing in a north-easterly direction from Dutch Cape Colony in the late eighteenth century. By 1878 all the Xhosa had been defeated and subjected to white authority. ~ 113, 214 ~ *see also Cafres*

Ama-Pondo(s) ~ The Mpondo were the followers of Faku who lived between the Mtata and Mzimkhulu Rivers on the eastern seaboard of southern Africa. ~ 29, 214

Ama-Souasis ~ Members of the Swazi kingdom. ~ 15, 73, 274, 275 ~ *see also* Vol I

Amatikulu ~ *see* Om-Matagoulou

Amayaho ~ The Zulu word *Amalawo* means Hottentot. ~ 275

Amazimos ~ The Zulu word *Amazimu* means cannibals. ~ 273

Amazoulou country *also* Zoulouland ~ 112, 153, 173, 181, 184, 214, ~ *see also* Vol I

Boer annexations of Zulu territory 1840 ~ 97 ~ *see also* Vol I

Amazoulous *also* Cafres of Amazoulou country ~ Amazulu means members of the Zulu nation or state. ~ 13, 49, 56, 57, 277, ~ *see also* Vol I

arms ~ 18, 113–14, 179, 260 ~ *see also* Vol I

avoidances and taboos ~ 117 ~ *see also* Vol I

at Blood River battle, 1838 ~ 70–2 ~ *see also* Vol I

and Boer annexation of territory, 1840 ~ 73–4 ~ *see also* Vol I

and Boer invasion, 1837–8 ~ 56–74, 274 ~ *see also* Vol I

Amazoulous ... /cont
and cats ~ 125
cattle enclosures ~ 125
cattle, method of slaughter ~ 132
circumcision, contempt for ~ 114–15,
155
compared with the Europeans ~ 127–9
compared with the French and the
Makatisses (Mantatees) ~ 120, 130,
165, 278–82
courtship ~ 118–19
cruelty ~ 130–2
dancing and singing ~ 64, 119,121, 281
~ see also Vol I
division of labour ~ 116–17, 124
dress ~ 114–16, 117–18, 144
and emotions ~ 128–9
and execution ~ 32
fear of water ~ 36
food and drink ~ 36, 123–4, 199 ~ see
also Vol I
food conventions ~ 117 ~ see also Vol I
food gathering ~ 124
food storage ~ 125
footwear, lack of ~ 113
friendliness of ~ 113
funerals, absence of ~ 127
good humour ~ 121
government ~ 122–3,126
habitations ~ 175 ~ see also Vol I
hairstyles and headdress ~ 114, 115,
116, 117,
honesty ~ 12
hospitality ~ 110–11, 121, 129 ~ see also
Vol I
hunting practices and techniques ~ 188
~ see also Vol I
huts, construction of ~ 14, 125, 163
inheritance among ~ 127, 282
iron smelting ~ 16–18
jealousy amongst ~ 120, 121, 129
justice ~ 29–32, 109, 123
kingship ~ 122–3, 126, 131 ~ see also
Vol I
language ~ 130, 166, 167
marital relations ~ 119–20, 121, 128
medicine ~ 253
military tactics of ~ 113,116
motherhood ~ 120
murder ~ 129
nudity ~ 114, 118 ~ see also Vol I
outcasts ~ 117
ownership of property ~ 129,
physical attributes and beauty ~
112–13, 118, 130, 198 ~ see also Vol I
politeness ~ 121, 130
polygyny ~ 118, 120 ~ see also Vol I
pride of ~ 121, 155
regimental dress and insignia ~ 63,

115–16 ~ see also Vol I
regiments, i.e. amabutho ~ 71, 113 ~ see
also Vol I
religious beliefs, lack of ~ 126–7
resistance to foreign influences ~
129–30
and smoking ~ 221
and snakebite treatment ~ 151–2 ~ see
also Vol I
spoils of war ~ 126
superstitions ~ 11–12, 117, 127, 151–2
tattooing ~ 118
taxation ~ 123
warlike disposition ~ 121, 128
wedding ceremonies ~ 119
and whites ~ 39, 130 ~ see also Vol I
Amazoulous ~ see Amazoulous
Amba ~ A.D.'s version of the Zulu word
hamba, meaning go away. ~ 7
America ~ A.D.'s term for the United
States of America. ~ 77
Ancien Régime ~ The social and political
order in France prior to the Revolution of the late 18th century. ~ 259
Angola ~ A reference to the vast territory
between the Kunene and Congo Rivers
on the west coast of Africa which was
colonized by the Portuguese. ~ 210
Antilles ~ the Archipelago comprising the
Caribbean Sea and Gulf of Mexico. ~
113
Aquitunda ~ A reference to one of the great
lakes of east central Africa. It is not
clear whether A.D. is referring to
Lake Tanganyika or Lake Victoria. ~
264
Arbousset ~ The Revd (Jean) Thomas Arbousset (1810–77) was a French Protestant missionary in southern Africa
who in 1836 undertook an exploration
of the territory between the Orange
and Vaal Rivers with his colleague the
Revd Francois Daumas on behalf of
the Paris Evangelical Missionary Society. They were honoured by the Société de Geographie de Paris and their
book, Narrative of an exploratory tour
to the north-east of the Colony of the
Cape of Good Hope, published in 1842,
was later translated into English. ~
273, 279
Argonaut ~ The Argonautae were companions of Jason who, according to classical mythology, sailed his ship the Argo
in quest of the Golden Fleece which
was kept by King Acetes of Colchis and
guarded by a dragon. ~ 150
Arms ~ see Amazoulous (arms); Shields;
Tongas

Assegais ~ *see* Omkondo

Azevedo, Capt. ~ A Portuguese military official. It is not clear where A.D. met him, possibly at Port Natal. ~ 211

Bamba Izinkabu ~ The Zulu words *Bamba izinkabi* mean inspan the oxen. ~ 106

Bacchus ~ The god of wine, known to the Greeks as Dionysus. ~ 119

Badenhorst, L. ~ Lourens Badenhorst (1800–?) arrived in Natal with the Maritz group of trekkers in 1838 and after being put in charge of the Boer camp at Port Natal was appointed heemraad there and later landdros. In 1840 he became a member of the Volksraad of the Republic of Natal and served briefly as its chairman. His fiery diposition led to clashes with other members of that body and he was temporarily suspended from its sittings for using insulting language. ~ 70

Barend-Barend ~ In the late eighteenth century Barend Barends (1770–1839) first emerged as leader of migratory Griqua groups who were persuaded by members of the London Missionary Society to adopt a more settled lifestyle. He consistently refused to recognize the authority of Andries Waterboer after he had been chosen as chief at Griquatown and moved away from the orbit of the Cape Government and the LMS missionaries. In about 1827 he established himself at Boetsap, where he encouraged the Wesleyan Missionary Society to work among his followers. After abandoning Boetsap in the face of a threatened Ndebele raid, he subsequently joined the Wesleyans at their mission station at Nuwe Platberg, near Ladybrand, settling at Groenkloof (Lishuane), close to the Basutoland border. He was defeated during a raid on Mzilikazi's Ndebele in 1831 and eventually killed by them in 1833. ~ 178–9

Barye bronze ~ A reference to Antoine-Louis Barye (1796–1875), a French sculptor who devoted himself almost entirely to animal sculpture after making models of animals for a goldsmith in the Jardin des Plantes during the 1820s. ~ 8

Bastaards ~ *see* Griqua; Half-castes

Bastaard-Land ~ The territory settled by the Griqua along the middle reaches of the Orange River. ~ 272

Bastinado ~ A gaol or public prison ~ 32, 272

Batavia ~ 148 ~ *see also* Vol I

Bay, The ~ *see* Port Natal

Baye-Ban(k)g ~ 11, 34 ~ *see also* Vol I

Bazoutous ~ The Basotho or southern Sotho-speaking inhabitants of what came to be known as Basutoland (Lesotho). Their loosely-knit federal state was built between the 1820s and 1840s by Moshweshwe (Moshoeshoe). After surviving many threats to their independence, including Boer expansionism, the Basotho submitted to British annexation in 1868 and annexation by the Cape Colony in 1870, before their state became a High Commission Territory in 1884 and eventually regained its independence in 1966. ~ 166, 277 ~ *see also* Sissoutou, Thaba Bossiou

Bedouins ~ Arab inhabitants of North Africa and Western Asia, many of whom were subjected to French rule during the nineteenth century. ~ 50

Beer *also Tchouala* ~ 13, 31, 33, 34, 64, 110 ~ *see also* Vol I

amaBele ~ *see* *Mabéle*

Bengalore ~ Bangalore is a city in Mysore state, India. ~ 218

Berea ~ Ridge of hills overlooking Port Natal where Capt. A.F. Gardiner established his mission station in 1835. ~49 ~ *see also* Vol I

Bester, P. ~ Paul Michiel Bester (1811–76) arrived in Natal with the group of trekkers led by P.L. Uys. He acquired property in the Port Natal, Umkomaas and Klip Rivier districts, and was appointed field-cornet and heemraad for Pietermaritzburg before serving on the Volksraad from 1842 onwards. He left Natal in 1844 and played a prominent role in the public life of the Orange Free State before settling on the farm Spitzkop in the Ladysmith district in 1858. ~ 48

Beulton ~ 147–8 ~ *see also* Vol I

Biggar, Mr A. ~ Alexander Biggar (1781–1838) had previously served in the British Army and arrived in South Africa with the 1820 settlers. He worked in the Kareiga Valley near Theopolis before moving to Port Natal as one of the earliest white settlers there in 1824. He was killed in a Zulu ambush following the Boer victory at Blood River in 1838. ~ 57, 58

Biggar, George (1820–38) ~ He was an early Port Natal settler and the son of Alexander Biggar. He died in 1838 during a Zulu attack on the Boer laager at Bloukrans, shot by a Boer who thought that he was collaborating with the Zulu. ~ 58

Biltong ~ see Beulton

Bisterveld ~ The name of one of A.D.'s trek-oxen. ~ 223, 227

Black Mfolozi/Umfolozi ~ see Omphilos Mouniama

Blaw-Kranz Rivier ~ The Bloukrans river in northern Natal, where more than five hundred recently arrived Boers were killed by Zulu impis in February 1838, following the deaths of Pieter Retief and his negotiating party at King Dingane's capital, Mgungund-lovu. ~ 66

Bloed Rivier ~ 70–2 ~ see also Vol I

Bodenstein, J. ~ Johannes Bodenstein (1796–1848) arrived in Natal from the Beaufort district of the Cape in 1838 and established himself as a farmer in the vicinity of the Bay before being elected to the Natal Volksraad and made harbour master and landdrost at Port Natal in 1842. He served as secretary to the Volksraad between 1842 and 1845 when it was dissolved, and left Natal for the Transvaal in 1847. ~ 48

Boers also African-Dutch, Peasants, Hollanders ~ 29, 166, 169, 170, 191, 196, 214, 215, 221, 262, 269, 270, 271, 272, 273 ~ see also Vol I
  causes of their trek from the Cape Colony ~ 52–53
  controlled by Cape of Good Hope Punishment Bill ~ 74–6
  at Magaliesberg ~ 269, 271,
  defeat of Mzilikazi ~ 55–6
  fire-making ~ 161
  hunting and trapping ~ 89, 181 ~ see also Vol I
  negotiations with and defeat of Dingane ~ 56–74
  and oxen ~ 168, 263, 270
  and plants and animals ~ 169–70, 191, 196, 214, 215, 221
  struggle against the British for Natal ~ 36–51
  wagon-driving ~ 157, 168 see also Vol I

Bolandje ~ see Boulandje

Boschjemanes also Boschemans, Bosch-

jesmans ~ The San hunter-gatherer people of southern Africa. ~ 82, 93, 159, 221, 275 ~ see also Vol I

Boschjesmans Rivier ~ 65, 66, 130, 156 ~ see also Vol I

Boshoff, J. ~ Jacobus Nicolaas Boshof (1808–81) settled in Natal in 1839 and was elected chairman of the Volksraad of the Republic of Natalia. Following the British annexation of the territory he became Registrar and Master of the Supreme Court. He moved to the Orange Free State in 1854 when offered the presidency of that Boer republic but resigned office in 1858 and returned to Natal where he served in the Legislative Council for several years. ~ 48

Botma, L.S. ~ Stephanus Botma was wounded in the conflict with the British at Port Natal. ~ 48

Bottomley, W. ~ William Bottomley was a hunter and trader based at Port Natal in the 1830s. He was a member of the settler commandos sent against Dingane in March and April 1838 following the murder of Piet Retief and his followers. Bottomley was killed on the second expedition in a battle on the Thukela River. ~ 58

Boulandje also Boulantje, Bolandje ~ 4, 6, 19, 20, 23, 25, 33, 97, 102, 107, 133, 151, 152 ~ see also Vol I

British Channel ~ A.D.'s reference to the English Channel (La Manche), or narrow sea separating England from France. ~ 284

British occupation of Port Natal, 1842 ~ 36–52, 153, 155

Brussels ~ The capital city of Belgium. ~ 150, 159

Bruwer, J.H. ~ He was a member of the Volksraad of the Boer Republic of Natal. ~ 48

Burgher, J.J. ~ Jacobus Johannes 'Kootjie' Burger (1795–1849) joined Piet Retief on the Great Trek in 1837 and drew up the treaty between him and King Dingane. He became Secretary to the Volksraad of the Republic of Natalia and in 1840 requested recognition of Boer independence which was rejected by the Cape Governor, Sir George Napier. He subsequently moved to the Transvaal and died of malaria. ~ 49, 51

Bushman ~ see Boschjemanes

By-Kruyper ~ Crawler, meaning stalker. ~ 214

Cafrerie *also* Cafre Land, Land of the Cafres ~ 53, 125, 130 ~ *see also* Vol I

Cafres ~ 75, 76, 121, 127, 128, 129, 130, 131, 132, 163, 193, 194, 195, 234, 237, 238, 241, 263, 264, 269, 271, 273 ~ *see also* Vol I
  clash with the Boers ~ 52–3, 55–6
  hunting practices ~ 89, 219, 231 ~ *see also* Vol I

Cafres of Natal ~ 66, 98, 99, 105, 108, 109, 150, 151, 152, 155, 159, 160, 168, 177, 188, 189, 209 ~ *see also* Vol I
  and English ~ 46–7, 49 *see also* Vol I
  fire-making ~ 160
  in service of whites ~ 39, 68 ~ *see also* Vol I

Calcutta ~ A large sea port on the coast of West Bengal in India. ~ 218

Cane, John ~ John Cane (c1800–38), trader and adventurer, left England for Batavia in 1813 but disembarked at the Cape where he subsequently joined Lieutenant F.G. Farewell's expedition to Natal. On good terms with Shaka, he was sent on two overland trips to the Cape Colony by him in 1828 and 1830. He subsequently joined the settler opposition to Dingane and was killed at the battle on the Thukela River in 1838. ~ 58

Cape Colony ~ The Colony established by the Dutch in 1652 and permanently occupied by Britain in 1806, to which Natal was attached in 1843. ~ 82, 95, 149, 169, 178, 179, 184, 199, 200, 214, 221, 248, 273, 282 ~ *see also* Vol I
  British administration ~ 52–4 ~ *see also* Vol I

Cape of Good Hope *also* Cape of Storms ~ 214, 263, 285 ~ *see also* Vol I

Cape of Good Hope Punishment Bill ~ This act of 1836 was an attempt to extend British jurisdiction in southern Africa beyond the frontiers of the Cape Colony, as far north as latitude 25° S, without the formal annexation of territory. It led, *inter alia*, to the appointment of a British magistrate at Port Natal in 1842 though Natal was not annexed until 1843. ~ 74–5

Cape Town ~ Seat of government for the Cape Colony. ~ 169, 189, 263, 282, 284 ~ *see also* Vol I

Capricorn, Tropic of ~ At 23° 27' south latitude the Tropic of Capricorn marks the southerly extremity of the world's so-called tropical regions. ~ 92, 275

Carden, Thos. ~ Thomas Carden was a

hunter and trader in Natal, with black hunters in his employ. He attended the meeting in June 1835 at which the town of Durban was founded, was a member of the defence force organized at the Bay in 1837 and as a participant in both commandos sent against Dingane in 1838, was killed that year in the battle on the Thukela. ~ 58

Chambock ~ 214 ~ *see also* Vol I

Charter, *Major*. ~ Major S. Charters commanded a British detachment which occupied Port Natal in 1838. ~ 70 ~ *see also* Vol I

Charybdis ~ *see* Scylla and Charybdis

Cloete, *Lt.-Col*. ~ Colonel Josias Cloete commanded a British force sent to Port Natal from the Cape in 1842 to relieve a garrison beseiged at the bay by the Boers. ~ 46–51, 96, 97 ~ *see also* Vol I

Congh (Conch) ~ A British schooner which brought reinforcements to the relief of the British garrison at Port Natal in June 1842 and was fired upon by Boer forces. ~ 45

Colesberg ~ The northern Cape town, situated near the Orange River, previously known as Toverberg (Witch Mountain) until that name was prohibited under penalty of heavy fine by Cape Governor Sir Lowry Cole (1828–32). ~ 54, 179

Congo ~ Central Africa, a large part of which, mainly south of the Congo River, was colonized by Belgium and north of the River by France. ~ 113

Conguela ~ Site of a major Boer encampment on the western shore of the bay of Port Natal. ~ 37, 39, 41, 42, 46, 87 ~ *see also* Vol I

Constantia ~ 169 ~ *see also* Vol I

Coranas ~ *see* Koranas

Council ~ The Volksraad of the Boer Republic of Natalia, which had been established with Pietermaritzburg as its capital in 1839. ~ 48

Creoles ~ A West Indian and Spanish American term for those born in the country but of foreign parents. In this context A.D. applied the term to those of Portuguese origin who had been born in Africa. ~ 211

Dafel, Henning ~ Wagon driver employed by A.D. ~ 1, 9, 82, 101, 102, 105, 106, 133, 134, 140, 141, 150, 161, 162, 163, 164, 165, 177, 178, 185, 186, 194, 195, 197, 199, 200, 201, 204, 205, 208, 211, 212, 213, 214, 221, 222, 224, 225, 226, 227, 234, 235, 236, 245, 269, 270, 272 ~ see also Vol I

Dafel, Kotje ~ The father of A.D.'s wagon driver, Henning. ~ 4, 82–5, 87

Dakra ~ Somewhere in what was then French North Africa, probably in Algeria. ~ 50

Dambuza kaSobadli ~ see Tamboussa

Dancing ~ see Amazoulous (dancing and singing) and Makatisses (dancing)

Dassenkop ~ meaning hill or mountain of the dassies. There is no geographical feature bearing that name in the vicinity today. A.D. was probably referring to what is now known as Bulkop. ~ 177, 185, 186

Daumas ~ The Revd Francois Daumas (1812–71) was a member of the Paris Evangelical Missionary Society who, with the Revd Thomas Arbousset, explored the region between the Orange and Vaal Rivers and named Mont-Aux-Sources. He established a mission-station near Ficksburg and published several religious works in Sotho. ~ 273

Declerc, Jacob ~ Jacob Declercq (1791–1881) farmed at present-day Beaufort West before joining the Great Trek in 1837. He fought at the Battle of Blood (Ncome) River in 1838 and in the following year was appointed landdrost of Potchefstroom, settling in the vicinity of Schoonspruit. He helped to lay out 'Oude Dorp', renamed Klerksdorp in 1853 in his honour. He moved to Ohrigstad in 1846, where her served on the Origstad and Lydenburg Council between 1847 and 1852. He also helped in planning the town of Lydenburg, where De Clercq Street was named after him. ~ 158, 159

De Jonville, Prince ~ Francois, Duc de Joinville was a son of Louis Phillipe, King of the French (1830–48) at the time of A.D.'s sojourn in southern Africa. ~ 103

De La Caille ~ 112, 177 ~ see also Vol I

Delagoa Bay ~ On the Mozambique coast of East Africa, its natural harbour became an important port of call for Portuguese shipping on the Cape sea route between Europe and India. ~ 112, 177

Delegorgue, Adulphe ~
and the black antelope ~ 194, 196, 199–201, 206, 208, 221, 222, 224–5
and Boer annexation of Zulu territory ~ 73–4 ~ see also Vol I
and Boer campaign against Dingane (Dingaan), 1840 ~ 74 ~ see also Vol I
on the Boers ~ 14, 40, 42, 43–4, 53, 54, 73, 78, 149, 157, 262–3, 270
and buffalo ~ 142–9
on Cafres ~ 5
on cannibals ~ 272–3
career as sailor ~ 78 ~ see also Vol I
on civilization ~ 32–3, 93, 129, 131
on colonialism ~ 74–7 ~ see also Vol I
and crocodiles ~ 36, 205, 219, 226
and Emigrant Boers ~ 29, 39–40, 78–9 see also Vol I
on England and the English ~ 33, 40, 47, 53, 60, 74, 76–7, 97, 130, 169
expedition beyond the Vaal River ~ 154–282
on exploration ~ 222, 262–3, 275–6
food-gathering ~ 124–5
on Hottentots ~ 263
on hunting ~ 3–4, 140, 213, 215, 229, ~ see also Vol I
hunting on Black Mfolozi (Omphilos-Mouniama), 1842 ~ 100–4 ~ see also Vol I
hunting on lower Mfolozi (Omphilos), 1841–2 ~ 3–9, 150 ~ see also Vol I
hunting on the Mvoti ~ 134–8, 146–7
hunting on Om-Kouzane ~ 18–23
ill-health ~ 217–18, 236, 253 ~ see also Vol I
on integrity in writing ~ 95–6, 274
on lion ~ 87–95
love of his oxen ~ 168, 223, 227
on Makaschlas ~ 194–5, 198, 199, 232, 239, 240
on Makatisses (Mantatees) ~ 165–6, 233
on missionaries ~ 58–9, 60, 97, 180, 274
and Mpande (Panda), 1839 and 1841 ~ 9, 28–9, 32–3, 97, 98–100, 104, 106–8 ~ see also Vol I
on philanthropists ~ 75–6
on racism ~ 208
and rain-making ~ 241–5
and rhinoceros ~ 182, 195, 197, 205, 208, 212–19, 227, 228, 252, 264–5, 267–8, 269
scientific activity ~ 87–95, 142–9, 158–9, 163, 181–5, 186, 187, 189, 190, 200–1, 206, 235, 236, 254, 255, 259, 268 ~ see also Vol I
servants and employees, relations with

384

~ 96, 98, 99, 276 ~ *see also* Vol I
on Sir George Napier ~ 50, 70, 76, 77
and snakes ~ 151–2, 245 ~ *see also*
Vol I
and thirst ~ 256–8
and wild dogs ~ 202–4
on the Zulu ~ *see* Amazoulous; *see also*
Vol I
Deserts ~ Presumably a reference to the
unexplored region north of the Orange
River. ~ 54
Dingaan/Dingane ~ Zulu king, 1828–40.
~12, 73, 110, 118, 122, 166, 251, 273
~ *see also* Vol I
attack on Boer encampments at Bushmans (Boschesmans) River, 1838 ~
65–6, 130–1 ~ *see also* Vol I
Boer plans to overthrow, 1839 ~ 66 ~ *see*
also Vol I
and elephant (ivory) hunting ~ 8 ~ *see*
also Vol I
and emigrant Boers, 1839–40 ~ 56–74
see also Vol I
flight, 1840 ~ 73 ~ *see also* Vol I
and Mpande (Panda), 1839–40 ~ 73–4
murder of Retief, 1838 ~ 63–5 ~ *see also*
Vol I
Djacka ~ Zulu king, *c.* 1816–28. ~59, 113,
118, 122, 163, 166, 251, 263 ~ *see also*
Vol I
and iron-smelting ~ 17
compared with Napoleon ~ 120
Djantje ~ A.D.'s servant. ~ 33, 134, 135,
138, 152 ~ *see also* Vol I
Dorp de Potschepstroom ~ *see* Potchefstroom
Draaken's Berg *also* Draak-Berg, Quath-
lambéne mountains ~ 56, 63, 92, 112,
156, 157, 170 ~ *see also* Vol I
inDuna ~ *see* Om-douna
du Plessis, J. ~ Possibly Jan Harm du
Plessis who trekked from Colesburg
in the Cape Colony in 1840 and eventually settled on the farm 'Klipvoor' on
the Apies River. ~ 48
D'Urban, *Sir* Benjamin ~ D'Urban
(1777–1849) had a distinguished career in military and colonial service
before arriving as Governor of the
Cape Colony in 1834. His previous
experience in British slave-owning
colonies was invaluable to the Colony
at a time when its slaves were being
emancipated but his attempt to stabi-
lise the Cape's eastern frontier following the 1835 frontier war was
unacceptable in London. His newly
created Queen Adelaide Province was
disannexed and, despite his promo-

tion to Lieutenant-General in 1837
and his personal popularity in the
Colony, he was relieved of the governorship in 1838. He remained in
South Africa in a military capacity
until 1846 and subsequently served
as commander-in-chief of British
forces in North America. ~ 53, 76
D'Urban, *Major* W.J. ~ William James
D'Urban was the son of Sir Benjamin
D'Urban, governor of the Cape Colony. A participant in the British occupation of Natal in 1842, he later joined
his father in Canada, where the latter
commanded the British troops, serving him as deputy-master general. He
returned to South Africa in the 1860s,
commanding a British force in the
Ciskei. ~ 49, 50

Echo *mouzi* ~ So named by A.D. and situated in the present-day Northen
Province, somewhere north of the Waterberg mountains and north-east of
the Mokolo River. ~ 247 ~ *see also*
Om-Tounène (Mokolo)
Edict of Nantes ~ 53 ~ *see also* Vol I
Egypt ~ Situated in north-east Africa and
site of one of the ancient civilizations
of the world. ~ 184
Elands River ~ A.D. encountered two rivers known as the Elands. The first
rises near Mont-aux-Sources in the
Drakensberg, cascading northwards
onto the highveld where it eventually
flows into the Wilge River north-west
of Warden. ~ 92, 158
The other Elands River (*also*
Kgetleng River) flows through modern South Africa's North-West Province, eventually merging with the Hex
and then the Crocodile River near
Bulkop. ~ 177
Emigrant Boers, Natal also African-Dutch, Peasants ~ Dutch-speaking colonists who, after
abandoning the Cape Colony, crossed the
Drakensberg into Natal in 1837 and subsequently. ~ 112 ~ see also Vol I
at Blood River (Bloed Rivier) battle,
1838 ~ 70–2 ~ *see also* Vol I
campaign against Dingane (Dingaan),
1840 ~ 73–4, 274 ~ *see also* Vol I
and English ~ 36–52, 66 ~ *see also*
Vol I
massacred at Bushmans (Boschjesmans) River, 1838 ~ 65–6 ~ *see also*
Vol I

massacred at Mgungundlovu (Unkunglove), 1838 ~ 63–5 ~ see also Vol
massacred by Mzilikazi ~ 179
Emigration of Boers also Retief emigration ~ 52–77 ~ see also Vol I
England and the English ~ see also Vol I
Boer attitudes towards ~ 168 ~ see also Delegorgue on England and the English
Etruscan ~ The Etruscans invaded the Italian peninsula in the 9th century B.C. from Asia Minor and exerted an enduring influence on local art forms, including pottery. ~ 281
Eymeraads ~ A.D.'s rendering of heemraden, meaning members of the district council. ~ 169

Farewell (Febana) ~ Lieutenant Francis George Farewell (1793–1829) served in the Royal Navy and, following his arrival at the Cape in 1822, travelled to Port Natal where he decided to settle. In 1824 he visited the Zulu king Shaka, from whom he acquired a large grant of land round the Bay. After a visit to the Cape in 1828 to collect trading merchandise, he was murdered on his return in the following year, by followers of the Qwabe chief Nqeto. ~ 106, 127, 263
Flanders ~ A part of Belgium close to the village of Courcelles, near Douai in Picardy, where A.D. was born. ~ 257
umFokazana ~ see Om-phogazane
umFolozi mnyama ~ see Omphilos Mouniama
umFolozi omhlophe ~ see Omphilos-om-Schlopu
umFundisi ~ see Om-phondiss
Fusiliers ~ Captain T.C. Smith arrived at Port Natal with a force of 237 men drawn from the 27th Regiment and the Royal Artillery. ~ 40
Fyle ~ A.D.'s rendering of the Zulu word ifile meaning dead. ~ 5
Fynn, F. ~ Henry Francis Fynn (1803–61) arrived at the Cape in 1818 and lived on the Colony's eastern frontier for some years before travelling up the eastern seaboard of southern Africa as well as inland. In 1824 he was sent by a Cape commercial syndicate to establish a trading post at Port Natal, and subsequently negotiated with King Shaka and his successor King Dingane on their behalf. In 1834 he

returned to the Cape as an expert in frontier negotiations and in 1852 was appointed assistant magistrate in Natal. His writings on conditions in the Natal-Zululand region, on its indigenous population and on the Zulu kings, had extensive influence on white settler opinion and on subsequent assessments by historians. He died at Fynnlands, where he had settled on the shores of Durban Bay. ~58

Gambia ~ The West African territory colonized by Britain. ~ 113
Gardiner, Capt. ~ Capt. A.F. Gardiner, missionary to the Zulu, was active in the years 1835 and 1837–8. ~ 63 ~ see also Vol I
Gazelle ~ 182, 183
Germans at Port Natal ~ 38, 43, 85–7
Germany ~ The German-speaking world in north-central Europe was still a medley of major and minor states prior to their unification under Prussian leadership in 1871 ~ 251
Gevecht-Kop, Vegkop (Vechtkop) ~ Previously known to the Boers as Doringkop, was the site of the first major battle in October1836 between them and Mzilikazi's Ndebele. The Boers withstood the attack and in January 1837 defeated the Ndebele, capturing their stronghold Mosega and driving them northwards. ~ 55–6, 163, 164, 181 ~ see also Massilicatzi
umGodi ~ see Nogoty
Gordon, Colonel ~ Robert Jacob Gordon (1743–95) was a Scottish employee of the Dutch East India Company who in 1777 named the Orange River (q.v.) in honour of the Prince of the Dutch House of Orange. ~ 158
Gouaye ~ see Tobacco
Gradin mouzi ~ So named by A.D. and situated somewhere north-east of the Motlhabatsi River in the present-day North-West Province of South Africa. ~ 246
Graham's Town ~ Eastern Cape town founded in 1812. ~ 43, 52, 54 ~ see also Vol I
Greyling, A.C. ~ Abraham Greyling died with Piet Retief at the hands of Dingane's Zulu warriors. He and other members of the Boer party were advised by the Revd Owen to leave the

Zulu capital the evening before their death but Retief declined to do so. ~ 73

Griqua ~ 178–80 ~ *see also* Vol I

Groote Rivier ~ *see* Orange River

Groote-Vish-Rivier ~ The Great Fish River had been declared the eastern frontier of the Dutch Cape Colony by Governor Van Plettenberg in 1780. The original Khoikhoi name for the river was retained in translation. ~ 52

Grout, *Dr* Aldin ~ Member of the American Board Zulu Mission. ~ 96, 97, 105, 109–11 ~ *see also* Vol I

Guimba ~ A young servant of A.D.'s. ~ 225, 226, 242, 272

Gulf of Guinea ~ A general name for the West African coastline from the Gambia to the Congo River. ~ 113, 115, 124

emGungundlovu ~ *see* Unkunglove

uGwayi ~ *see* Tobacco

Hahy om pondo ~ *Hayi mpondo* means 'no teeth'. ~ 20

Half-castes *also* Bastaards, Mulattos ~ 76, 113, 209 ~ *see also* Vol I

Hamgazy ~ A small river south of the mZimvubu in Mpondoland. Captain Thomas Smith encountered it en route from the Cape Colony to Natal in 1842. ~ 29, 36

Hamgazy ~ The Zulu word *umgazi* for an opaque, dark blood-red bead. ~ 98, 117

Hantam ~ 82 ~ *see also* Vol I

Headman, Zulu ~ *see* Om-douna

Hebrews ~ A.D.'s allusion is to the Biblical reference to the parting of the Red Sea which enabled the ancient Hebrews to escape from bondage in Egypt before the waters closed again to engulf their Egyptian pursuers. ~ 42

Henning ~ *see* Dafel, Henning

Hieroglyphic figures ~ Hieroglyphics are the earliest known form of pictured symbolic expressions, and are believed to have originated with the ancient Egyptians. ~ 175

Hlatikulu ~ *see* Om-Schlaty-Om-Koulou

umHlatuze ~ *see* Om-Schlatousse

ukuHlobonga ~ *see* Schlabonka

Holland ~ 74 ~ *see also* Vol I

Holland ~ The name of one of A.D.'s trekoxen ~ 223, 227

Hollanders ~ *see* Boers

Holstead, Thos. ~ Thomas Halstead was a teenager when he arrived with the first group of white settlers at Port

Natal in 1824. He was a member of Piet Retief's party that was murdered by King Dingane in 1838. ~ 58

Hottentots ~ 66, 68, 159, 178, 199, 209, 263 ~ *see also* Vol I

Houahouaho ~ A servant of A.D.'s. ~ 27, 34, 35, 36, 39, 118, 134, 135, 137, 138 ~ *see also* Vol I

Hudson Lowe ~ *see* Lowe, Hudson

Hunting ~ 1–7, 10, 19–26 ~ *see also* Vol I; *see also under* Delegorgue

Hut ~ *see* Mouzi

Huys, Pieter ~ *see* Uys, Pieter

Huys Doorn ~ Uys Doorns, just south of Pietermaritzburg, now known as Thornville. ~ 57

Hyza lapa ~ A.D.'s rendering of the Zulu expression *yiza lapha* meaning 'come here'. ~ 6

Ignamazane ~ Inyamazane is the Zulu word for wild animal, game. ~ 4

Illovo ~ *see* Lofa

Indian Ocean ~ Sea extending from the eastern seaboard of Africa to Australia, the Malay Archipelago and southern Asia. ~ 99, 112, 157, 210

Ingogone ~ The Zulu word *inkonkoni* means blue wildebeest. ~ 181

Inianga ~ 12, 126, 127, 167, 241, 243, 244 ~ *see also* Vol I

Iniaty-Kase ~ A.D.'s rendition of the Zulu word for *inyathikazi* meaning female buffalo or huge buffalo. ~ 133

Inkoey ~ The Zulu word isichwe means dwarf or Bushman. ~ 274

Inkonnzy *also* *Inkounzi* ~ 11 ~ *see also* Vol I

Inkosikazi also Inkosikazy ~ 120 ~ *see also* Vol I

Intombu ~ 118 ~ *see also* Vol I

Inyaty also Iniaty ~ 135–8, 142–9, 181, 228, 230–1, 265 ~ *see also* Vol I

Islam ~ The religion founded by Mahomet (AD 570–632). ~ 178

Izimkopo ~ The Zulu word *izingubhu* means musical bow and resonator. ~ 281

James Town ~ The capital of the island of Saint Helena. ~ 283

Jardin Des Plantes ~ The Botanical Gardens of Paris on the River Seine include a menagerie and large natural history collection. They were founded in the 17th century, during the reign of Louis XIII, and opened to the public in 1650. ~ 184, 185, 225, 254

Jardin du Roi ~ The Royal Gardens in Paris ~ 100

Jarvis, *Captain* ~ A British commander at Port Natal in 1839. ~ 113 ~ *see also* Vol I

Java ~ A major Indonesian island, situated between the Indian Ocean and the Java Sea. ~ 148, 218, 219

Jesuits ~ The Society of Jesus, a Roman Catholic teaching order founded in 1534 by Ignatius Loyola. The Society played a major role in teaching, missionary work and politics in Europe and abroad. ~ 273
see also Loyola, Ignatius

Juliavius ~ One of Dingane's *izinduna*; his name Julawoshiya is said to have meant 'he who throws away and leaves behind'. ~ 73

Kabobiquois ~ A reference to the Coboqua, a Khoisan clan situated on the south-west coast of southern Africa. ~ 254

Kafirs ~ *see* Cafres

Kakoulou ~ 150 ~ *see also* Vol I

Kamdane ~ A servant of A.D.'s. ~ 101, 102, 275

Karosses ~ *see* Kros

Karroo *also* Karrou ~ 82 ~ *see also* Vol I

Kasteel-Poort ~ meaning Castle Gate, in the eastern Orange Free State. ~ 161, 177

Kemble, John ~ A Port Natal settler, John Kemble was a lieutenant in the defence force organized there in 1837 and was killed in the battle on the Thukela in 1838. ~ 58

umKhonto ~ *see* Omkondo

inKhosi phezulu ~ *see* Kos-Pezou

umKhulu ~ *see* Om-Koulou

King, Richard ~ Richard (Dick) Philip King (1813–71) arrived at the Cape as a child with the 1820 settlers and moved to Natal in about 1828. He worked there as a wagon driver, hunter-trader and transport rider. His familiarity with the terrain between Durban and Grahamstown served him in good stead when, in May 1842, he completed the ride to the eastern Cape in a record ten days to summon help for the British garrison besieged at Durban by the Boers.

King subsequently farmed near Isipingo in Natal where he died. He was a hunting friend of A.D.'s. ~ 43, 58 ~ *see also* Vol I

Klein-Buffel-Hoek ~ The farm of Veld-Commandant Hendrik Potgieter was situated on the south-western slopes of the Magaliesberg range, across the hills from Phokeng and present-day Rustenberg. (The farm Buffelshoek now forms part of the Magaliesberg Nature Reserve). ~ 173

Klein-Touguela ~ The Little Thukela is a tributary of the Touguela/Thukela River with which it merges north-east of present-day Winterton and west of Colenso. ~156 ~ *see also* Touguela

Knema py omkondo ~ A.D.'s rendering of the Zulu words *nquma pi umkhonto* or *nquma ngomkhonto* meaning severed or cut by an assegai. ~ 28

Koluma ~ In this context, A.D.'s word for noise or hubbub. ~ 23

Koluma ni Zoutou ~ A.D.'s version of the Zulu words *Nikhuluma(isi) Sotho?* meaning 'Do you speak Sotho?'. ~ 277

Koranas ~ Remnants of Khoikhoi peoples living north of the middle reaches of the Orange River. ~ 178 ~ *see also* Vol I

inKosi phezulu ~ *see* Kos-Pezou

Kos-Omkoulou ~ 126 ~ *see also* Vol I

Kos-Pezou ~ *Inkosi/inkhosi phezulu* literally means king on high. ~ 127 ~ *see also* Vol I

Kossobalas ~ A.D. is probably attempting the Zulu word *abathwa* meaning Bushmen. ~ 274, 275

Kotchobana ~ African hunter employed by A.D. ~ 4, 5, 6, 7, 8, 9, 19, 20, 21, 22, 23, 24, 25, 26, 33, 96, 97, 102, 107, 133 ~ *see also* Vol I

Kotlissa tena oumlongo ~ A.D.'s rendering of the Zulu *uyasi khohlisa umlungu* which means 'he deceives us, the white man does'. ~ 130

Krapack Mountains ~ A reference probably to the Carpathian mountains in eastern Europe, or possibly to the Caucasus range between the Caspian and Black Sea. ~ 149

Krockmann ~ A Port Natal resident called Krogman was sentenced to hard labour by the Boers for allegedly aiding the British. ~ 43

Kros ~ 277 ~ *see also* Vol I

Kuruichane ~ Karechuenya (Karetshwenya) in South Africa's present-day North-West Province is situated west of the Pilansberg mountains and was originally established as the capital of the Hurutshe people. ~ 56

umLalazi ~ *see* Om-Lalas

Landroost ~ A local official with administrative and judicial functions. ~ 168, 169 ~ *see* Vol I

La Smala ~ A painting, possibly by Delacroix (1798–1863), which was apparently well-known in the late 1830s and early 1840s but is less so today. ~ 193

Leager ~ A.D.'s rendering of *laager*, meaning a circle of wagons drawn up in defensive formation or an otherwise fortified position. ~ 82, 87, 158

Liebenberg, B.J. ~ Barend Liebenberg was among the first party of trekkers to arrive in Natal and was killed with Piet Retief at Dingane's capital. ~ 73

Limpopo River *also* Magnice, Oury ~ 56, 177, 187, 190, 192, 193, 194, 195, 197, 203, 206, 222, 227, 228, 235, 250, 252, 254, 255, 256, 257, 258, 260, 261, 264, 266, 269, 276 ~ *see also* Vol I

Linequey-Drift ~ Lindeque's drift on the Vaal River, situated west of present day Vereeniging and north-east of Parys. ~ 167, 272

Linequey family ~ The Lindeque family farmed on the southern bank of the Vaal River, at the drift which bore their name. This was probably the trekker G.P. Lindeque and family, a descendent of the Swedish immigrant Barend Lindequast. ~ 165

Loanda ~ Luanda, as it is now known, was established in 1576. It was the centre of Portuguese colonial administration and commerce in Angola and subsequently became the capital city of that territory. ~ 211

Lofa ~ 46 ~ *see also* Vol I

Lombardt, H.P. ~ Hermanus Lombardt suffered a hand injury from an exploding gun during the conflict at Port Natal and had to have the limb amputated with a carpenter's saw. ~ 48

London ~ The capital of England and centre of the British Empire, situated on the River Thames. ~ 157, 186, 200

London Missionary Society ~ The Society's first missionaries had arrived at the Cape in 1799 and within a few years had established mission-stations within and well beyond the Colony's frontiers. ~ 180 ~ see also Philip, Dr J.

Longwood ~ The home which Napoleon Bonaparte occupied during his exile on the island of Saint Helena. ~ 283

Lorenzo Marquez ~ A.D.'s rendering of Lourenco Marques (now known as Maputo). It was named after one of the earliest Portuguese seamen who landed there in 1544. A fort was built there in 1787 and a town in 1887, which became the capital of the Portuguese colony of Mozambique. ~ 177

iLovu ~ *see* Lofa

Lowe, Hudson ~ Sir Hudson Lowe was appointed governor of Saint Helena during Napoleon Bonaparte's exile there and imposed various restrictions upon his lifestyle and movements. ~ 284

Loyola ~ Ignatius Loyola (1491–1556), founder of the Society of Jesus, better known as the Jesuits. ~ 77

umLungu ~ *see* Oum-Longo

Lynequey ~ A.D.'s rendering of Lindeque. ~ *see* Linequey Family

Lynequey-Drift ~ *see* Linequey-Drift

Mabhubu Tsonga ~ *see* Makazanes

Madagascar ~ A large island situated off the east coast of Africa, now known as Malagasy. ~ 275

Magalébe ~ A homestead head visted by A.D. ~ 105, 107, 108, 120 ~ *see also* Vol I

Magaliesberg ~ *see* Makali mountains

Mahoha, Princess ~ Mawa ka Jama was Mpande's aunt, the sister of his father (and that of Shaka and Dingane) Senzangakhona. In 1843, shortly after A.D.'s visit, she fled Mpande's rule settling in the Dakuza district of Natal, near present-day Stanger and later at Ndwedwe, near Verulam, where she died. ~ 108

Makali mountains *also* Makalis-Berg ~ 154, 172–3, 174, 177, 179, 181, 184, 207, 214, 217, 219, 228, 235, 244, 269, 271 ~ *see also* Vol I and Mohale

Makandas ~ The Zulu word *amaqanda* means eggs. ~ 117

Makaschla(s) ~ A.D.'s rendering of Bakgatla, the followers of chief Pilane. ~ 194–6, 198, 208, 214, 220, 221, 222, 223, 227, 231, 239, 240–1, 244, 245, 247, 248–9, 250, 251, 253, 255, 256, 261, 264, 265–6, 268, 270

dishonesty of ~ 232, 240,

dress ~ 93

farming ~ 209–10

food ~ 199

inability to swim ~ 244, 260

Makaschla(s) .../*cont*
smoking ~ 220–1
use of pit traps ~ 184, 230
Makata ~ A.D.'s rendering of Mokatlhe, the Ba Fokeng chief who ruled from 1836 to 1891 and resided at the traditional capital Phokeng, called Magato-Stad by the Boers. It is now adjacent to Rustenburg, the Boer settlement of Magaliesberg that was founded by Hendrik Potgieter in 1839 and so re-named in 1850. ~ 174, 175 176, 177, 271
Makatisses ~ A corruption of Mantatees. The name derives from that of a chieftainess, 'MaNthatisi, regent of the Tlokoa/Tlokwa whose people were driven off their lands in what is now the north-eastern Free State. ~174–7, 233, 253, 273, 277 ~ *see also* Vol I
arms of ~ 278
attributes and misfortunes of ~ 165–6, 176, 232, 277, 281
circumcision practised by ~ 115, 278, 282
clothing of ~ 278, 279, 280
compared with the Germans and the Zulu ~ 120, 165–6, 278–82
dancing of ~ 281–2
fertility doll ~ 167
food ~ 175
hairstyle and headdress of ~ 278, 279
huts of ~ 163, 165, 175, 280–81
justice ~ 282
language of ~ 166, 277
musical instruments of ~ 281
physical dirtiness of ~ 278, 279, 280
pottery of ~ 281
religious beliefs, lack of ~ 278, 282
tidiness of ~ 280
use of mutton fat and *sibilo* ~ 166, 279
Makatous ~ According to A.D.'s information, the Makatous whom his retainers so feared lived to the north-east of the Mokolo (Om-Tounène) River in South Africa's present-day Northern Province. ~ 252, 261
Makaza ~ He was chief of the Maputo people in present-day northern Zululand/ southern Mozambique. ~ 21, 23, 25, 26
Makazanes ~ The Mabhudu-Tsonga people living south of Delegoa Bay. ~ 15 ~ *see also* Vol I
Makoha River ~ *see* Mokoha River
Makota ~ *see* Makata
Malappo, Springs of ~ The Molopo spring or 'Molopo Oog' (eye) is forty kilometres east of Mafikeng. ~ 55

Malay ~ A reference to the Malay population of the Cape Colony, who originated from the Malayan peninsula, the most southerly part of the Asian continent, which was also colonized by the Dutch. ~ 278–9
Mammakaly ~ Mohale (Mogale), chief of the SeTswana-speaking BaPoo, whom the Boers had earlier encountered in the vicinity of the Magaliesberg, which derive their name from him. ~ 207
Mammasetchy ~ A female potentate who lived somewhere north of the Magaliesberg range. ~ 207
Mandrisse ~ *see* Manice
Manica ~ Situated in the west central part of present-day Mozambique, Manica's gold and ivory resources attracted the Portuguese, who declared it a district of their colony on the eastern seaboard of Africa in 1884. ~ 210
Manice ~ The Manice or Manhica River constitutes the lower reaches and mouth of the Nkomati River in southern Mozambique and not that of the neighbouring Limpopo as suggested by A.D. ~ 177, 210, 211
Manna ~ Food on which the Israelites survived during their biblical journey through the wilderness; now anything that is pleasant and unexpected. ~ 169
Manondo ~ Mandondo ka Dube was one of Dingane's *izinduna* and chief of the Khanyile, who were closely associated with the Chunu chiefdom. ~ 73
Mantatees ~ *see* Makatisses
Mapo(o)ney ~ A local chief or homestead head who lived on the Mokoha (Sand) River, slightly north-east of its confluence with the Crocodile River. ~ 228, 261
Maputa ~ Maphitha was chief of the Mandlakazi branch of the Zulu royal house. ·- 13, 14, 16, 26
Marais, M.H. ~ A lesser known member of the Natal Boer community. ~ 48
Marao ~ Mawola was one of Dingane's *izinduna*. His name is said to have meant 'the collector'. ~ 73
Maravi ~ A reference to one of the great lakes of east-central Africa, probably Lake Malawi or Lake Mweru. ~ 264
Marimo (Morrimo) ~ A malevolent power or force in which, according to A.D., the indigenous people of the region north of the Magaliesberg mountains believed. He may have been referring

to Modimo, the supreme being recognised by the Sotho-Tswana. ~ 176, 282

Maritz *also* Mauritz, Gert ~ A Trekker leader. ~ 55, 66 ~ *see also* Vol I

Maschlapine ~ A chief who lived somewhere north of the Magaliesberg and west of the Hex River, in the vicinity of the Pilansberg. ~ 207, 210

Massilicatzi *also* Moselekatse ~ 55–6, 60, 61, 63, 82, 93, 163, 166, 178, 179, 204, 220, 221, 228, 235, 247, 251, 252, 264 ~ *see also* Vol I and Ndebele

Massousse ~ Mswati was the son of King Sobhuza I of Swaziland and reigned over the kingdom in succession to him from 1838/9 to 1865, with the queen mother Thandile serving as regent until 1846. ~ 274

Matabili ~ *see* Ndebele

Matigulu/eMatikulu ~ *see* Om-Matagoulou

Matiwane ~ *see* Matouana

Matouana ~ A chief living near the Biggarsberg. ~ 274, 275 ~ *see also* Vol I

Mayaho ~ *see* Amayaho

Mazeppa ~ The schooner *Mazeppa*, under the command of Captain Tait, was owned by the Port Elizabeth merchant John Owen Smith. It brought A.D. and the Swedish naturalist J.G. Wahlberg to Port Natal in 1839 and was later chartered by the trekkers to fetch survivors of Louis Trigardt's trek party from Delagoa Bay. ~ 42, 43

Medusa's head ~ Medusa was one of the Gorgons, killed by Perseus, whose face, according to classical mythology, turned those who gazed upon it to stone. ~ 7

Mena tanta boulala yena ~ The Zulu words *mina thanda bulala yena* mean 'I (mina) want to kill him'. ~ 6

Mercury ~ In classical mythology he was the son and messenger of Jupiter, the lord of heaven, who wore a winged cap, had wings on his feet and could move with the speed of the wind. ~ 116

Meyer Howek *also* Meyer's Hoek ~ 170 ~ *see also* Vol I

Mfolozi ~ *see* Omphilos

Mgeni ~ *see* Om-Guinée

Mgojane ~ *see* Om-Ghetjanne

Mgungundlovu ~ *see* Unkunglove

Mhlali ~ *see* Om-Schlala

Mhlatuze ~ *see* Om-Schlatousse

Mina ~ *see* Mena

Missionaries ~ 58–9, 60, 61, 63, 64, 96, 97, 105, 109–11, 273, 274, 282 ~ *see also* Vol I

Mkomazi ~ *see* Om-Komas

Mlalazi ~ *see* Om-Lalas

Mlandela ~ *see* Om-Landelle

Mlazi ~ *see* Om-Las

Moeder-Rivier ~ Probably the Modder River, which flows through the Orange Free State north of present-day Bloemfontein before merging with the Riet and Vaal Rivers. ~ 272

Mokoa ~ A.D.'s camp on the Sand (Mokoha) River. ~ 254 ~ *see also* Mokoha River

Mokoha River ~ A.D. refers to what is now known as the Sand River, which rises in the Badsberg north of Warmbad and flows into the Crocodile River south of Thabazimbi. ~ 228, 229, 236, 244, 245, 254, 270

Mona River ~ 13, 14 ~ *see also* Vol I

Mooi Rivier ~ 156 ~ *see also* Vol I

Mooi-Rivier (North-West Province) ~ The Mooi River rises in the Koster district south of the Magaliesberg and flows into the Vaal River south-west of Potchefstroom. ~ 168, 171, 172, 177, 235, 271

More Graig, J. ~ A government official in Cape Town. ~ 51

Moridja ~ Moridja was established in 1833 as the headquarters of the Lesotho Evangelical Church, 43 kilometres south of Maseru. ~ 273

Morikoe(y) ~ The Marico or Madikwe River is a tributary of the Limpopo River, situated in present day South Africa's North-West Province. ~ 55, 177, 207, 222, 250, 261, 276

Morrimo ~ *see* Marimo

Mosega ~ The large Ndebele settlement and Mzilikazi's base west of the Magaliesberg where he was attacked and defeated by the Boers in January 1837. ~ 55 ~ *see also* Massilicatzi, Ndebele

Moselekatse ~ *see* Massilicatzi

Motgeas ~ *Umutsha* is the Zulu word for loin-cover. ~ 114–15, 116, 279 ~ *see also* Vol I

Motito ~ The first mission station established, in 1832, by the Paris Evangelical Missionary Society in southern Africa, north-east of Kuruman. ~ 273 ~ *see also* Moridja

Mouniama ~ 127 ~ *see also* Vol I

Mounntou Mouniama ~ The Zulu words *umuntu omnyama* mean a black person. ~ 127

Mourikeyley ~ Judging by A.D.'s advance into the interior with the Sogoupana (Mokopoaniberg) or Witfontein Rand on his left as he travelled north-north-east, the peaks of Mourikeyley must be at or near the western end of the Waterberg range, just east of the Crocodile River. ~ 223, 229, 234

Mourikeyley-Amaboa ~ A.D.'s movement northwards from the Mokoha (Sand) River suggests that this stream is in or just beyond the Waterberg range, north-east of present-day Thabazimbi, and is possibly an upper tributary of the Motlhabatsi (Om-Schlabatsi) River which he crossed soon afterwards. ~ 245

Mourikoey ~ *see* Morikoe(y)

Mouzi ~ 124 ~ *see also* Vol I
of Bayé-Ban(k)g ~ 11
of Dingaan ~ 72
of Maputa ~ 13, 14
of Om-Ghet-Janne ~ 2, 6 ~ *see also* Vol I

Mozambique ~ The vast territory on the eastern seaboard of Africa, to the north of present-day KwaZulu-Natal, which was colonized by the Portuguese from the sixteenth century onwards. ~ 159

Mpande kaSenzangakhona ~ *see* Panda

Mulattos ~ *see* Half-castes

Muniama ~ *see* Mouniama

Munywana ~ *see* Mouniama

Musée de Tournay ~ The Museum of Tournai, a town on the River Scheldt in Belgium. ~ 201

Mvoti ~ *see* Om-Vooty

Myandela/Myandeya ~ *see* Om-Landelle

Mzilikazi ~ *see* Massilicatzi

Naba ~ The Zulu word meaning to remain unresponsive. ~ 31

Nacht-adder ~ Night adder ~ 245

Nanana ~ 27, 34, 120 ~ *see also* Vol I

Nannzy, bona lapa ~ The Zulu words *nansi, bona lapha* mean 'here it is, see here'. ~ 6

Nannzy Ebohiss ~ The Zulu words *nansi ibhubesi* mean 'here is the lion!'. ~ 6

Napier, Sir George ~ Governor of the Cape, January 1838 – March 1844. ~ 42, 50, 51, 52, 70, 76, 77 ~ *see also* Vol I

Napoleon ~ Napoleon I, (Bonaparte) (1769–1821) was born in Corsica and rose to prominence through the French army as a brilliant military commander before effecting a *coup d'état* in 1799 and subsequently crowning himself Emperor of the French (1804–15). His enduring domestic reforms were accompanied by a series of military victories elsewhere in Europe until he was eventually defeated by a coalition of European powers and exiled, initially to Elba and, after the battle of Waterloo in 1815, to the island of St. Helena where he died. ~ 113, 119, 120, 284

Natal ~ 148, 149, 152, 155, 170, 210, 214, 249, 275 ~ *see also* Vol I
given to the Boers by Dingane ~ 73

Ndebele ~ The Ndebele (Matabele) led by Mzilikazi were originally members of the northern Nguni-speaking Khumalo chiefdom who fled northwards out of Shaka's sphere of influence. In the late 1820s they settled near present-day Pretoria and absorbed many of the Sotho-speaking peoples of the central Transvaal into their state before moving, in about 1832, into the western Transvaal (present-day North-West Province). They continued to be threatened by the Zulu under Shaka's successor Dingane, and were also challenged by the Griqua and by the Boers advancing out of the Cape Colony to the south. Following their defeat by the latter in 1837, the Ndebele followed Mzilikazi northwards, eventually forming a new state that came to be known as Matabeleland in present-day south western Zimbabwe. ~ 56, 179, 252 ~ *see also* Massilicatzi

Ndlela kaSompisi ~ *see* Schlala

Nee baas ~ meaning 'no master'. ~ 6

Neel, Wilhelm ~ A hunter in the employ of J.G. Wahlberg, the Swedish naturalist. ~ 207

Neethling ~ A Boer whom A.D. encountered while descending the Drakensberg mountains to Natal on his return from the interior. ~ 272, 273

New Holland ~ A reference to Dutch settlements on the New England coastline of North America. ~ 257

umNgeni ~ *see* Om-Guinée

Ngolothi ~ *see* Om-Grooty

oNgoye ~ *see* Om-Goey

eNgqolothi ~ *see* Om-Grooty

iNgubo ~ *see* Om-gobo

Niewkerk, Isaac ~ Presumably Izak van Niekerk, a Boer spy on the 1840 expedition against Dingane. ~ 164, 165, 202, 208, 209, 269, 271, 272 ~ *see also* Vol I

iNkosi phezulu ~ *see* Kos-Pezou

iNkunzi ~ *see* Inkonnzy

Nogoty ~ 124 ~ *see also* Vol I

Nongalaza ~ *see* Nonglas
Nonglas(s) ~ One of Mpande's *izinduna*. ~ *see also* Vol I
hospitality of ~ 34, 35 ~ *see also* Vol I
Nonoti ~ *see* Om-Nonnoty
iNtombi ~ *see* Intombu
Nzobo kaSobadli ~ *see* Tamboussa

Ogle, Henry ~ One of the early hunter-traders at Port Natal. ~ 58, 68 ~ *see also* Vol I
Om-doango ~ A.D.'s rendering of the Zulu word *indwangu* meaning cloth. ~ 117
Om-doda-kakoulou ~ A.D.'s version of *indoda kakhulu* meaning, freely translated, real man. ~ 150
Om-douna ~ A.D.'s rendering of *iduna* or *induna*, a man of high position. ~ 60, 131 ~ *see also* Vol I
Om-Ghetjanne *also* Om-Ghet-Janne ~ 2, 7, 13, 26, 27 ~ *see also* Vol I
Om-gobo ~ *Ingubo* means clothing. ~ 15, 16, 117, 279 ~ *see also* Vol I
Om-Goey *also* Om-Gohey ~ 99 ~ *see also* Vol I
Om-Grooty ~ Possibly a corruption of Ngolothi, a mountain near the White Mfolozi. ~ 28 ~ *see also* Vol I
Om-Guinée (river) *also* Omguinée ~ 42, 49, 68, 108, 156, 158 ~ *see also* Vol I
Om-Kamtinganne ~ The father of Pheteganne (Phathekani) who was executed for ransacking and robbing A.D.'s tent; he was probably a household head rather than a chief, as suggested by A.D. ~ 31
Om-Komas (river) ~ 46 ~ *see also* Vol I
Omkondo also Assegaai ~ 7, 15, 18, 71, 113, 114, , 219 ~ *see also* Vol I
Om-Koulou ~ Great, big. ~ 126 ~ *see also* Vol I
Om-Kouzane ~ A tributary of the Mkhuze River. ~ 18 ~ *see* Om-Kouzi
Om-Kouzi ~ The Mkhuze River rises 24 kilometres east of Vryheid in northern KwaZulu-Natal and flows eastwards through the Ubombo Mountains before turning southwards and disgorging into the northern extremity of Lake St Lucia. ~ 13, 15, 18, 19, 25, 27, 173
Om-Lalas (river) ~ 107, 108 ~ *see also* Vol I
hunting in vicinity of ~ 105 ~ *see also* Vol I
Om-Landelle ~ A Mthethwe chief. ~ 9, 32 ~ *see also* Vol I
Om-Las (river) *also* Om-Lasy, Om-Laas ~

46, 49 ~ *see also* Vol I
Om-Matagoulou (river) *also* Oum-Matagoulou ~ 108 ~ *see also* Vol I
Om-Nonnoty (river) ~ 150 ~ *see also* Vol I
Omphilos (river) *also* Omphilozie, Ompholozie ~ 3, 34, 39, 44, 83, 96, 97, 99, 100, 109, 150, 184 ~ *see also* Vol I
Omphilos-Mouniama (river) ~ 2, 13, 26, 101, 158 ~ *see also* Vol I
Omphilos-om-Schlopu (river) ~ 10, 104, 158, 181 ~ *see also* Vol I
Om-phogazane ~ *Umfokazane* means a person of no account. ~ 117 ~ *see also* Vol I
Ompholozie ~ *see* Omphilos
Om-phondiss ~ *Umfundisi* means a teacher or preacher. ~ 110, 111 ~ *see also* Vol I
Om-Pongola (river) ~ 25, 112, 157 ~ *see also* Vol I
Om-Schlabatzi ~ The Motlhabatsi River rises north of the western end of the Waterberg mountain range and flows in a north-westerly direction into the Limpopo River some distance to the north of the latter's confluence with the Crocodile River. ~ 246, 252, 255
Om-Schlala (river) ~ 60 ~ *see also* Vol I
Om-Schlanga-Mouniama ~ The Zulu *isihlangu esimnyama* means black shield. ~ 63
Om-Schlanga-Om-Schlopu ~ The Zulu *isihlangu esimhlophe* means white shield. ~ 63
Om-Schlatousse (river) ~ 72, 96, 97, 99, 100, 105, 109, 158 ~ *see also* Vol I
Om-Schlatouzana ~ The Mhlathuzana River is a tributary of the Mhlathuze, entering it some eight kilometres south-west of Empangeni. ~ 99
Om-Schlaty-Om-Koulou ~ A forested area adjacent to the White Mfolozi. ~ 10 ~ *see also* Vol II
Om-Sinnquassy ~ The Zinkwazi River flows past the present town of Darnell and into the Indian Ocean at Zinkwazi Beach, 10 kilometres south-west of Thukela mouth. ~ 152
Om-Sinyate (river) *also* Om-Siniaty ~ 70 ~ *see also* Vol I
Om-Sitanne ~ A local chief, possibly only a homestead head, who lived just beyond the Mokoha (Sand River), slightly north and to the east of its confluence with the Crocodile River. ~ 228, 239
Om-Sovoobo ~ 73 ~ *see* Om-Zimvobo
Om-Tagaty ~ Often translated as 'wizard' though A.D. usually heard it used to

mean 'murderer'. ~ 108, 126 ~ *see also* Vol I

Om-tagaty boulala! ~ The Zulu words *umthakathi bulala!* mean 'kill the wizard(s)/killer(s)!'. ~ 28, 32, 64, 126

Om-Tounène ~ A.D. probably refers to the Mokolo River which flows from north of the Waterberg mountains in a northerly direction to its confluence with the Limpopo River. ~ 246

Om-Vooty (river) ~ 107, 133, 145, 152, 158 ~ *see also* Vol I

Om-Vooty's Poort ~ A deep valley on the Mvoti River, north-west of Stanger. ~ 133, 149

Om-Zimkoulou ~ The Mzimkhulu River rises in the Drakensberg near Lesotho and flows south-east past Underberg before reaching the Indian Ocean at Port Shepstone. ~ 158

Om-Zimvobo ~ The Mzimvubu River has its origins in the Drakensberg near Mount Macdonald and flows south and south-east from there to disgorge into the Indian Ocean at Port St Johns on the Transkei coast. ~ 29, 59, 63, 158

Oosthuisen, M. ~ Marthinus Oosthuizen, a friend of the Trekker leader Gerrit Maritz, died with Piet Retief at King Dingane's capital. ~ 73

Orange River ~ also known as the Groote Rivier and as the Gariep (Great River) by the Nama and Korana people. It is the longest of South Africa's rivers (approx. 1920 kms) from its source in Lesotho to the Atlantic Ocean. ~ 158, 167 ~ *see also* Gordon, *Colonel* ~ 54

Otto, P.A.R. ~ Petrus Albertus Ryno Otto (1810–90) served in the Natal Volksraad from 1842 to 1845 and was a prominent member of the Boer community in Natal. He was more sympathetic towards the British than most of his compatriots and subsequently developed his properties 'Otto's Bluff' and 'Upper Saxony' to become one of the Colony's pre-eminent farmers, renowned for the quality of his livestock. ~ 48

Oud-Keerl ~ meaning old fellow ~ 40

Oum-Longo also Oumlongo ~ *Umlungu* (pl. *abelungu*) is the Zulu word for a white person. ~ 108 ~ *see also* Vol I

Oum-Matagoulou ~ *see* Om-Matagoulou

Oural Mountains ~ The Ural mountains are 3280 kilometres long and separate Asia from Europe. ~ 149

Ourityle ~ Known to the northern Sotho-speaking peoples as the Moretele River, and also known in part as Pienaars River, this watercourse flows north past the town of Pienaars-rivier, due north of Pretoria, and then westwards before joining the Crocodile River at Buffelspoort. ~ 194, 197, 205

Oury River ~ *see* Limpopo River

Owen, *Dr* ~ The Revd F. Owen was a missionary doctor. ~ 59, 60, 61, 63, 64 ~ *see also* Vol I

Panda/Mpande ~ Zulu king, 1840–72. ~ 16, 28, 31, 32, 68, 73, 131, 251, 263 ~ *see also* Vol I and A.D. ~ 9, 28–9, 32–3, 35, 97, 98–100, 104, 106–8, 242 ~ *see also* Vol attempts to kill Unungongo and followers ~ 105–9 and Boers ~ 98 ~ *see also* Vol I capriciousness ~ 13–14, 29, 34, 96, 126 and Dingane (Dingaan), 1839–40 ~ 122 ~ *see also* Vol I execution of Phétéganne ~ 32 and ivory hunting ~ 99–100 ~ *see also* Vol I power and authority ~ 9, 11, 109, 123 ~ *see also* Vol I powers of deception ~ 113

Paraguay ~ A country in central South America. ~ 273

Paris ~ The capital of France, situated on the River Seine. ~ 157, 254, 271

Parker, Edward ~ English adventurer in Natal and Zululand. ~ 73 ~ *see also* Vol I

Pas de Calais ~ The narrowest part of the English Channel, known in English as the Straits of Dover. ~ 284

Peasants ~ *see* Boers

Pelissier, *Col.* ~ A contentious figure involved in the French colonization of North Africa. ~ 50

Phétéganne ~ His name was possibly Phathekani. ~ 31, 32, 33

Philip, *Dr* J. (1777–1851) ~ Appointed superintendent of the London Missionary Society stations in South Africa in 1819. His *Researches in South Africa* was published in 1828. ~ 76, 178, 179, 180 ~ *see also* Vol I

Philipolis ~ A London Missionary Society mission in what became the southern Orange Free State. It was named in honour of Dr John Philip (q.v.), superintendent for the LMS in South Africa, 1819–51. He encouraged the

Griqua to settle down and promoted the extension of British authority over them through a system of treaties which, he hoped, would protect their possession of land while *also* stabilizing the Cape frontier. ~ 178, 179 ~ *see also* Griqua

Phongolo ~ *see* Om-Pongola

Pickman, C. ~ Charles J.Pickman arrived in Natal in 1832 and worked as a trader and farmer on the Mlazi river. He signed the letter requesting Captain A.F. Gardiner to establish a mission at Port Natal and became his clerk of the peace. He escaped from the Zulu attack on Port Natal with his family on the *Comet* in 1838 and subsequently died of fever at Delagoa Bay. ~ 58

Pieters Mauritz Burg ~ 43, 46, 47, 48, 49, 73, 155, 156, 173, 174, 208, 235 ~ *see also* Vol I

Pilanne ~ Pilanne or Pilane was leader of the Kgafela branch of the Kgatla chiefdom at the time of A.D.'s visit to the region beyond the Magaliesberg. ~207, 209, 210, 211, 220, 221, 271

Pilanne, mountains of ~ Now known as the Pilansberg, so named after Pilanne or Pilane, head of the Kgafela branch of the Kgatla chiefdom, who settled in the vicinity of the Laroma-berg or Pilansberg in South Africa's present-day North-West Province. ~ 207, 209, 210, 220, 221, 271

Pillage mouzi ~ So-named by A.D. and situated somewhere north of the Waterberg mountains and north-east of the Mokolo River. ~ 249

Pit-traps ~ These game traps, according to nineteenth century travellers, were used in several parts of the southern African interior including in the vicinity of the Crocodile River, as described by A.D.. They were constructed in various ways, usually along game paths, in valley passes or near rivers and water holes. The Bakwena of Mokpolole in the south-east of present-day Botswana settled near salt-licks which attracted game and used *gopo* or pit-traps averaging 20 metres in length, 6 metres in width and 7 metres in depth which were camouflaged with twigs and grass and had sharpened stakes placed upright in the bottom. Game was forced into the *gopo* by means of communal hunting drives and two bush fences con-

structed 750 metres apart and sometimes as much as 1.5 kilometres long. The Babolaongwe and later also the Bashaga, who were more recent arrivals in the Kgalagadi desert region (present-day Botswana), used more elaborate traps, as described here by A.D. The smaller *shilekeri* comprised four thornbush fences of up to 1.5 kilometres in length which had the effect of channeling game into the pit from all four directions. These and the *gopo* of the Bakwena involved considerable labour in their construction and maintenance. The larger traps used by the Babolaongwa and Bashaga required the labour of an entire settlement. These *biruku* comprised an elaborate combination of fences, several pits with embankments, game chasers and hunters. As indicated by A.D., they offered potentially large returns for the effort expended, providing an important source of food as well as skins for domestic use, trade and tribute payment. ~ 184, 194, 228, 230, 231

Poes-kop ~ 21 ~ *see also* Vol I

Poff-adder ~ Puff adder ~ 247, 268

Point ~ The Point is the promontory of land on the north side of the entrance to Port Natal Bay, now Durban harbour, where cargo and passengers were brought ashore during the early years of the settlement there. ~ 42, 45

Polygyny ~ 118, 120 ~ *see also* Vol I

Pondock also Haart-Beest-Huis ~ 28 ~ *see also* Vol I

Pongola ~ *see* Om-Pongola

Pontin Marshes ~ The Pontine Marshes were situated in the coastal region of the Italian peninsula south-east of Rome. These highly malerial marshes were subsequently drained and settled during the 1930s. ~ 149

Poort ~ meaning 'gate' or narrow pass. A.D. is referring to Olifantspoort/Olifantsnek, a pass through the Magaliesberg south-east of present-day Rustenburg through which the Hex River courses. ~ 174

Poortman *also* Portmann ~ 155 ~ *see also* Vol I

Port Elizabeth ~ Seaport on Algoa Bay, Eastern Cape. ~ 52, 54 ~ *see also* Vol I

Port Natal ~ The natural harbour and the white settlement established on its shores in 1824. ~ 37, 58, 149, 153, 253, 282 ~ *see also* Vol I

British occupation, 1842 ~ 36–52

Portuguese ~ 177, 210, 211 ~ *see* Angola and Mozambique

Potchefstroom ~ A town in the south-western Transvaal that was laid out in 1839 by the trekker leader Hendrik Potgieter and its first magistrate, van der Chef. Contrary to A.D.'s explanation for the town's name, it is now widely held that it derived from 'Pot' (for Potgieter), 'Chief' (his status as leader) and 'Stroom' (denoting the Mooi River on which it is built). It was initially known as Mooi Rivier Dorp and served as the Boer seat of government north of the Vaal until 1863 when this was transferred to Pretoria. ~ 168 ~ *see also* Mooi River

Potgieter, E.F. ~ Evert Fredrik Potgieter (1799–1864), a lesser known member of the Volksraad of the Republic of Natalia. ~ 48

Potgieter, Henderick ~ Andries Hendrik Potgieter (1792–1852) was a prominent trekker leader who led the Boer forces in their victories over Mzilikazi's Ndebele at Vegkop and Mosega. He subsequently helped to establish the towns of Potchefstroom, Andries-Origstad and Schoemansdal. ~ 55, 66, 67,168, 173–4, 176, 228, 244, 271 ~ *see also* Massilicatzi, Mosega, Ndebele, Potchefstroom and Vegkop

Potgieter, J. ~ Possibly Pieter Johannes Potgieter (though he would have been very young at the time), second son of the trekker leader A.H. Potgieter who, like his father, became Commandant-General in the South African Republic in 1853. He accompanied his father on trek to Natal and later to the Transvaal where he farmed in the Waterberg district. He was killed in 1853 leading Boer forces against chief Makapan (Mokopane) in the northern Transvaal. ~ 67

Pretorius, Commandant-general (1798–1853) ~ Leader of the Boers in the campaign against King Dingane. ~ 48, 49, 55, 70, 78, 173–4 ~ *see also* Vol I relations with A.D. ~ 78–9, 87 ~ *see also* Vol I

relations with Captain Smith and Col. Cloete at Port Natal ~ 37, 38, 39–43, 49–50

Pretorius, Baart ~ Hercules Albertus (Bart) Pretorius (1803–89) visited Natal with his brothers Andries and Piet in 1837 before all three sold their farms in the Graaff-Reinet district and settled there. He was a member of the 'Wenkommando' which defeated the Zulu in December 1838 at Blood (Ncome) River under the leadership of his brother Andries. He established a farm 'Zee-koegat' north of Pietermaritzburg but eventually left the Colony in 1847, settling near the present Hartebeespoortdam and serving in the Transvaal Volksraad from 1852 until 1860. ~ 39, 78

Prinsloo, Joachim ~ He was chairman of the Natal Volksraad but later left Natal and died in 1844 at Delagoa Bay. ~ 49, 51

Prisoner's base ~ A very old game in which the players are tagged as they attempt to run between bases. ~ 217

Provençal ~ A native of Provence, a maritime province in south-eastern France. ~ 103

Quathlambène ~ *see* Draaken's Berg

Quai Voltaire ~ One of the many quaysides along the Seine River in Paris, it was named after the eighteenth century French scholar and philosopher Voltaire. ~ 278

Quiffua ~ A reference to one of the great lakes of east-central Africa. It is not clear whether A.D. is referring to Lake Tanganyika or Lake Victoria. ~ 264

Quilimane ~ In 1498 Vasco da Gama landed at Quilimane on the Mozambique coast. A Portuguese settlement was established there in 1544 and became a major outlet for the exportation of slaves to Brazil and the French-occupied islands of the Indian Ocean during the eighteenth and nineteenth centuries. The place was named after the 'Keliman' (in coast Arabic) or interpreter who assisted the Portuguese. ~ 211

Quimos ~ A hunter-gatherer people whom the eighteenth century French naturalist Comte de G-L.L. Buffon identified on the island of Madagascar, now known as Malagasy. ~ 275

Rabianne ~ A.D.'s description of his approach to Rabianne's homestead suggests that this chief lived east of the Crocodile and north of its confluence with the Moretele (Ourityle) River, probably at the foot of the Renosterberg. ~ 197, 198, 199, 200, 201

Retief, P. ~ A leader of the Boers in Natal. ~ 53–65, 72–3 ~ see also Vol I dealings with Mzilikazi ~ 55–6 visits Port Natal ~ 57–8

Retief emigration ~ see Emigration of Boers

Rhemkoka ~ Mafodi Ramokoka of the baPhalane (an offshoot of the baKwena) lived on the Mokoha (Sand) River, just north of its confluence with the Crocodile River. ~ 228, 230, 236–7, 241–5 passim, 270

Rhinoceros ~ 182, 195, 197, 205, 208, 212–19, 227, 228, 252, 264–5, 267–8, 269

Rixdollars ~ The currency imposed upon the Dutch Cape Colony before it was replaced by English currency following the second British occupation of the Colony in 1806. ~ 82, 98, 197, 198, 199, 200, 201, 208

Rocher, Monsieur ~ A prominent member of the settler community in Cape Town, who was of French Huguenot extraction. ~ 282

Roggeveld ~ Named after the wild rye or Wilde Rog (Secale africanum). ~ 82

Rome ~ Centre of the Roman Catholic Church, containing the Vatican City, former capital of the classical Roman Empire and, from 1871, capital of a United Italy. ~ 148

Rooye-baatjes ~ Meaning literally, 'red coats', a reference to the red jackets worn at that time by British troops. ~ 37

Rooye-Poort ~ Possibly a reference to Rooikloof, which is situated north of the source of the Mooi River near Boons and south of the Olifantsnek pass through the Magaliesberg mountains to the south-east of present-day Rustenburg. A.D. could be referring to Roodewal, situated further south between the source of the Mooi River and Olifantsnek pass. ~ 172

Saint Helena ~ A British-held island in the south Atlantic, off the west coast of Africa. Napoleon Bonaparte was imprisoned there in 1815 following his defeat at Waterloo, and died on the island in 1821. ~ 283–4

Saint Lucia Bay, hunting in vicinity of ~ 134 ~ see also Vol I

Saint-Paul de Loanda ~ see Loanda

San ~ see Boschjemanes

Sango ~ The Zulu word for hemp or dagga is insangu. ~ 124, 221

Sani-Gouschleg ~ A.D.'s rendering of Sala kahle meaning 'stay well' or 'goodbye'. ~ 34

Sapoussa ~ King Sobhuza I of the Swazi (or Dlamini Ngwane) lived in the region west of the Lebombo mountains and north of the Pongola/Phongolo River. ~ 274–5

Scheppers ~ A.D. could have been referring to Jacobus Johannes Scheppers, who was involved in the Slagter's Nek Rebellion of 1815, went on the Trek to Natal, and eventually settled in the Transvaal. ~ 168

Schlabonka ~ Ukuhlobonga means external sexual intercourse. ~ 118 ~ see also Vol I

Schlala ~ Probably Ndlela, one of Dingane's principal izinduna. ~ 65 ~ see also Vol I

Schlanvokane ~ A young servant of A.D.'s. His name was probably 'Mhlakuvana' in Zulu. ~ 134, 135, 138,152

Schloschlomé ~ A local chief who lived at the foot of the western end of the Waterberg range, just east of the Crocodile River. ~ 229, 232, 233, 234, 245

Scylla and Charybdis ~ According to classical mythology mariners trying to avoid Scylla – a dangerous rock inhabited by a sea monster – were drawn into Charybdis, a whirlpool on the coast of Sicily. ~ 6

Seine ~ A river which rises in the Côte d'Or in France, and flows past Paris and Rouen to Havre on the English Channel. ~ 271

Senegal ~ A west African region subsequently colonized by France. ~ 113, 115, 124, 184, 199, 254

Shaka ~ see Djacka

Shields, hunting ~ 63 ~ see also Vol I

Sibidely ~ A chief whom A.D. did not encounter personally and who apparently lived somewhere north of the Magaliesberg range at that time. ~ 207

Sibilo/Sibylo ~ A.D.'s version of the Zulu word isibilo, meaning magic spell or 'preparation'. ~ 166, 279

Sinkonyella ~ see Synkoyala

Si(t)sikamma ~ The Tsitikamma region in the Humansdorp district of the eastern Cape Colony, west of Port Elizabeth. ~ 214

Sissoutou ~ Meaning the language spoken by the southern Sotho speaking peoples who inhabit present-day Lesotho, Qwa Qwa and the Orange Free State. ~ 166, 277 ~ see also Bazoutous

Siswana ~ see Souzounna

Sjambok ~ see Chambock

Sképèle ~ 28, 97 ~ see also Vol I

Slave traders ~ There is evidence to suggest that slave traders/raiders had been active in south-east Africa during the eighteenth century. They emanated from the Cape Colony to the south-west, and from Delagoa Bay and possibly Port Natal on the eastern seaboard. ~ 116, 175

Sloane River ~ A.D.'s account of his journey suggests that he travelled northwards up and then down the Hex River (known to the Tswana-speaking people as the Matsukubyane River), mistaking it for the better-known Selons (Ngwaritse) River to the west. Both are situated in South Africa's North-West Province. ~ 176, 177, 206, 207

Smause/smouses ~ Hawkers, pedlars and itinerant traders who journeyed deep into the interior of southern Africa from the Cape Colony and from coastal bases like Port Natal offering manufactured articles and processed foodstuffs in exchange for the ivory, livestock, hides, skins and other natural products of the subcontinent. ~ 168,179, 229

Smith ~ Captain Thomas Charlton Smith (1797–1883) served in the British Navy and in the Army with the 27th Regiment of Foot at Waterloo prior to being posted to South Africa with the rank of major. He successfully commanded the British force which survived the Boer siege before assuming control of Durban in 1842. He subsequently attained the rank of general. ~ 29, 36, 37, 38, 39, 40, 41, 42, 46, 109

Sogoupana mountains ~ The direction taken by A.D. suggests that 'Sogoupana' refers to the Mokopoaniberg or Witfontein Rand, north of the Pilansberg and west of the Waterberg mountains and Crocodile River. ~ 211, 220, 223, 227, 254, 266

Souquaba ~ He was an Ndwandwe chief who lived on the confluence of the Black and White Mfolozis. ~ 2

Southampton ~ A British frigate which, together with the schooner H.M.S.

Congh, brought reinforcements to the relief of the British garrison at Port Natal in June 1842 and was fired upon by Boer forces. ~ 45

Souzouana ~ Possibly Msushwana or Somsushwana, a chief living on the White Mfolozi. ~ 9, 10, 11, 29, 31, 33, 34, 96, 100 ~ see also Vol I

Spartans ~ The classical Greek city-state of Sparta was renowned for its hardy soldiers who were said to wear their battle-scars with pride and never to turn their backs on the enemy. ~ 121

Stanley, Lord ~ Secretary of State (1841–45) for the War and Colonial Departments. ~ 77 ~ see also Vol I

Stellar, David ~ A Port Natal hunter-trader. ~ 58 ~ see also Vol I

St Elmo ~ The patron saint of sailors, whose protection manifests itself in a luminous glow around its object. ~ 103

Stockholm, capital of Sweden ~ 95, 276

Stroop ~ meaning syrup. ~ 170

Swazi ~ see Ama-Souasis

Swellendam ~ The western Cape town named after the Dutch Governor of the Cape Colony Swellengrebel and the maiden name of his wife, ten Damme. ~ 196

Symba ~ The Zulu word insimba means genet; the kilt or skirt to which A.D. refers being made from genet skins. ~ 116

Synkoyala ~ A.D.'s rendering of Sekonyela (Sigonyela) ka Mokotsho (1804–56), the Bathlokwa chief, who lived in the Wilge River area, in the present-day Harrismith-Vrede district before settling in 1824 in the mountainous region near present-day Ficksburg. The Bathlokwa's theft of 500 head of Zulu cattle on the eve of the Boer advance into Natal was allegedly undertaken in Boer-style clothing and on horseback, which may explain the allegation of theft levelled at Retief by Dingane. Sekonyela was indeed captured as A.D. suggests but the Boers released him after he surrendered an appropriate number of cattle and they had also confiscated a number of guns and horses from him. ~ 59, 73

Synsakona ~ A.D.'s rendering of Senzangakona (c.1757–1816), who was chief of the then relatively insignificant Zulu clan, the son of Jama who was a descendent of Zulu. Nandi became his third wife, but only after the birth of their son, Shaka in 1787. The Zulu still lived under the benign dominance of Dingiswayo, the Mthethwa chief, in whose service Shaka rose to military prominence. This promoted his claim to head the Zulu chiefdom following Senzangakona's death, despite his illegitimate birth. ~ 122, 131

Taboos ~ see Amazoulous (avoidances and taboos)

Tamboussa ~ 65 ~ see also Vol I

Tantalus ~ In classical mythology Tantalus was a son of Jupiter, the king of heaven. As punishment for revealing his father's secrets Tantalus was tortured with a raging thirst and the sight of water and fruit close to hand that always receded from his clutches. ~ 8, 203

Tchouala ~ see Beer

Thaba-Bossiou ~ Thaba Bosiu is a flat-topped hill 18 kilometres east of Maseru, which was originally chosen by King Moshoeshoe as a defensible position in 1824 and became recognised as the site where the Basotho nation was founded. ~ 273

Thaba-Uncha ~ Thaba Nchu is situated 60 kilometres west of Ladybrand and 64 kilometres east of Bloemfontein. ~ 273

umThakathi ~ see Om-Tagaty

Thames Estuary ~ The lower part of the Thames River which rises in the Cotswold Hills, Gloucester and flows past Oxford, Reading, Windsor and London on its way into the English Channel. ~ 285

Theopolis ~ Meaning 'City of God'. It was so named in 1814 by the Governor of the Cape Colony, Sir George Cathcart (1811–14). He identified the site near the mouth of the Casouga River in the eastern Cape for a mission station and awarded it to the London Missionary Society. It was burnt down during the frontier war of 1851. ~ 178, 179 ~ see also Philipolis, Philip, Dr J.

Thermopyle ~ An allusion to the narrow pass between Thessaly and central Greece where in 480 B.C. the Spartans offered heroic resistance to an invading Persian army. ~ 192

Thukela ~ see Touguela

amaTigulu ~ see Om-Matagoulou

Titan ~ In classical mythology the Titans were a race of giants who waged and lost a ten-year war with Jupiter. By conquering the Titans, Jupiter became master of the world and lord of heaven, imprisoning them in a cave near Tartarus. ~ 234

Tobacco also Gouaye, uGwayi ~ 124 ~ see also Vol I

Togela ~ see Touguela

Tom ~ A young servant and companion whom A.D. acquired from his friend the Swedish naturalist J.G. Wahlberg ~ 209, 211, 212, 213, 221, 222, 224, 225, 226, 229, 236, 237, 238, 239, 241, 242, 243, 244, 245, 248, 250, 251, 252, 255, 260, 264, 265, 266, 267, 268, 270, 272

Tongas ~ 34, 65, 114, 260 ~ see also Vol I

Toohey, D.C. ~ Daniel Charles Toohey (c.1800–68) arrived in Natal in 1835 and established himself on the Amanzimtoti River. He successfully negotiated hunting and trading concessions from King Dingane and acquired an extensive knowledge of Zulu customs and politics. This was demonstrated in his evidence to the 1852 Natal Native Commission and he may have been a significant source of information to Theophilus Shepstone. ~ 58

Torbette, Madame ~ Presumably the curator of Napoleon Bonaparte's original gravesite on the island of Saint Helena. In 1840 his body was returned to France and in 1861 was buried in the Dôme des Invalides in Paris. ~ 285

Touguela River ~ 27, 35, 36, 57, 59, 63, 66, 68, 71, 73, 92, 96, 99, 107, 108, 112, 150, 152, 156, 158 ~ see also Vol I

Toulouse ~ A.D. refers to a military engagement which took place during the Napoleonic Wars at Toulouse in southern France. ~ 50

Triechard ~ Louis Treghart/Trichardt was a Boer leader. ~ 54 ~ see also Vol I

umuTsha ~ see Motgeas

uTshwala ~ see Beer

Tugela ~ see Touguela

Tulbach ~ The village in the Tulbagh Valley of the western Cape which was previously known as Roodezand but was renamed in honour of the popular Dutch Governor of the Cape Colony, Ryk Tulbagh (1751–71). ~ 178

Umfolozi ~ see Omphilos

Umgeni ~ see Om-Guinée

Umhlatuze ~ see Om-Schlatousse

umKhonto ~ see Omkondo

Umkomaas ~ *see* Om-Komas
Umlaas ~ *see* Om-Las
Umlalazi ~ *see* Om-Lalas
Umlazi ~ *see* Om-Las
Unkunglove *also* UngunKuncklove ~ 59, 60, 63–4, 65, 67, 72, 73 ~ *see also* Vol I
Unungongo ~ One of the many lesser-known fugitives from Zulu rule. ~ 105–9, 111
Upi na ~ The Zulu words *uphi na* mean, in this context, 'where is he?'. ~ 6, 135
Uys, J. ~ Jacobus Johannes Uys (1800–71) was a brother of Comdt. Petrus Lafras Uys and member of the Volksraad of the Republic of Natalia in 1840. ~ 70
Uys, Pieter ~ Petrus (Pieter) Lafras Uys (1797–1838) farmed on the Cape's eastern frontier before joining a large family party on the Great Trek in 1837. He was killed in April 1838 in a Zulu ambush at Italeni. His young son, Dirk, died in an effort to rescue him. ~ 55, 66, 67–8

Vaal River ~ So named for the yellowish brown appearance of its waters. It is a tributary of the Orange River and a large stretch of it formed the official boundary between the Orange Free State and the Transvaal. ~ 54, 55, 92, 158, 161, 163, 164, 165, 167, 181, 184, 190, 193, 271, 272
Vaaterval-Drift ~ Possibly a reference to what subsequently became known as Skaninawiedrif, south-east of Potchefstroom. ~ 167
Valley of the Tomb ~ A.D.'s reference to the site of Napoleon Bonaparte's initial burial on the island of Saint Helena, where he died. ~ 285
Van Breda, Michiel ~ He was a member of the Boer party which in October 1839 installed Mpande as Zulu King in succession to Dingane. He was a ringleader in the looting of the ships *Pilot* and *Mazeppa* in Durban Bay, for which offence he was proclaimed a rebel but escaped and died in 1847 at Delagoa Bay. ~ 49, 51, 269
Van Breda, Mr ~ Servaas Van Breda (1813–81) arrived in Natal in 1838 and was appointed as heemraad in Port Natal. He established a farm at Congella and served the ·Natal Volksraad in various official capacities. He and his father were declared rebels after they engaged in the plun-

dering of the ships *Pilot* and *Mazeppa* in Port Natal harbour in 1842 but he was subsequently allowed to re-establish himself in the Umlaas River district and in 1875 was appointed to the Natal Parliament as a nominated member. In 1881, disillusioned with 'native' policy in the Colony, he moved to the Transvaal. ~ 49, 51, 79, 80, 81
Van Heerden, C.J. ~ A lesser known member of the Natal Boer community. ~ 48
Van Niekerk ~ *see* Niewkerk
Vegkop ~ *see* Gevecht-kop
Veld cornet ~ Veld kornet, meaning field cornet or local military-cum-police official. ~ 168
Vermaes, Mr ~ Possibly Hendrik Cornelius Wilhelmus Vermaes later of 'Hartebeesfontein' in the present-day Klerksdorp district. ~ 92, 171, 172, 271
Victoria ~ In June 1835 a meeting of fifteen Port Natal residents resolved to establish a town named D'Urban in honour of the current Governor of the Cape Colony, Sir Benjamin D'Urban, and to name the settlement as a whole Victoria, in honour of the royal princess Victoria. One of the coastal districts of Natal came to be known as Victoria County. ~ 52
Victoria, *Queen* ~ Born in 1819 she came to the throne in 1837 in succession to her uncle William IV and ruled as Queen of Great Britain and Ireland and Empress of India until her death in 1901. ~ 37
Vouma ~ The Zulu word *vuma* means agree(d). ~ 31, 108

Waayen-Poort ~ On the lower reaches of the Crocodile River north of its confluence with the Elands River in the present-day North-West Province. ~ 207
White Mfolozi ~ *see* Omphilos-om-Schlopu
Wilhelm ~ A hunter in A.D.'s employ. ~ 134, 141 ~ *see also* Vol I
William IV ~ The British monarch who reigned from 1830 to 1837. ~ 75
Wood, William ~ He arrived at Port Natal at the age of six in 1830 to join his father and was quick to learn Zulu. This greatly assisted him in his subsequent career as a hunter-trader, and as a temporary interpreter to the Revd Francis Owen who had estab-

lished a mission at Dingane's capital, Mgungundlovu in 1837. He was an eye-witness to the deaths of Pieter Retief and his men, narrowly escaping a similar fate. He and his mother left for Cape Town after his father was killed on the Thukela River in an unsuccessful attack on the Zulu kingdom and their home at Port Natal was destroyed in the Zulu raid that followed. He recorded his experiences in a valuable first-hand account published in 1840. ~ 64

Xhosa people ~ *see* Cafres

Zand Rivier ~ 56 ~ *see also* Vol I
Zee-koe-spek ~ Meaning hippopotamus (*zee-koe*) fat (*spek*). ~ 150
umuZi ~ *see Mouzi*
Zimpy ~ An iron-forging site between the Mkouzane and Mkuze Rivers in northern Zululand. ~ 16, 17, 21, 25, 26
Zitten Myn-Heer ~ Meaning 'sit' or 'be seated sir'. ~ 173
Zoulou ~ *see* Amazoulou
Zoulouland ~ *see* Amazoulou country
Zout pan ~ Salt pan ~ 252
Zulu kingdom ~ *see* Amazoulou country
Zulu people ~ *see* Amazoulous
Zuyker-Bosch-Rand ~ Suikerbosrand comprises three ranges of hills, extending north-east and south-west in the Heidelberg and Balfour region approximately 25 kilometres south of the Witwatersrand. ~ 54